THE WORLD'S
MOST AMAZING
PLACES

THE WORLD'S MOST AMAZING PLACES

Collins
An imprint of HarperCollins Publishers
Westerhill Road
Bishopbriggs
Glasgow G64 2QT

First Edition 2011

The contents of this edition of The World's Most Amazing Places are believed correct
at the time of printing. Nevertheless the publisher can accept no
responsibility for errors or omissions, changes in the detail
given or for any expense or loss thereby caused.

Printed in Thailand

British Library Cataloguing in Publication Data
A catalogue record for this book is available from the British Library

ISBN 978 0 00 789915 9
Imp 001

All mapping in this book is generated from Collins Bartholomew digital databases.
Collins Bartholomew, the UK's leading independent geographical information supplier,
can provide a digital, custom, and premium mapping service to a variety of markets.
For further information:
Tel: +44 (0) 141 306 3752
e-mail: collinsbartholomew@harpercollins.co.uk

or visit our website at: www.collinsbartholomew.com

Cover image: Taj Mahal, India
© Shutterstock / Luciano Mortula

CONTENTS

UNESCO

The United Nations Educational, Scientific and Cultural Organization (UNESCO) seeks to encourage the identification, protection and preservation of cultural and natural heritage around the world considered to be of outstanding universal value to humanity. This is embodied in a unique international treaty, called the *Convention Concerning the Protection of the World Cultural and Natural Heritage* adopted by UNESCO in 1972 (*see* http://whc.unesco.org/en/conventiontext).

UNESCO's World Heritage mission is to:

- encourage countries to sign the World Heritage Convention and to ensure the protection of their natural and cultural heritage;
- encourage States Parties to the Convention to nominate sites within their national territory for inclusion on the World Heritage List;
- encourage States Parties to establish management plans and set up reporting systems on the state of conservation of their World Heritage sites;
- help States Parties safeguard World Heritage properties by providing technical assistance and professional training;
- provide emergency assistance for World Heritage sites in immediate danger;
- support States Parties' public awareness-building activities for World Heritage conservation;
- encourage participation of the local population in the preservation of their cultural and natural heritage;
- encourage international cooperation in the conservation of our world's cultural and natural heritage.

HOW TO USE THIS BOOK

Sites are arranged chronologically by the year in which they were first inscribed on the World Heritage List and introduced by a colour coded bullet point to distinguish whether a site is classified as natural (green), cultural (red) or mixed (blue). The site title gives the official UNESCO World Heritage title for each entry and is followed by the country where the site can be found. Territories are listed under the countries to which they are affiliated. The criteria by which they were selected is given at the end of the entry along with the year the site was inscribed. See example below:

• SITE OF CARTHAGE Tunisia

Carthage was founded in the ninth century BC by Phoenician traders from Tyre, in modern Lebanon. By the sixth century BC it had conquered and controlled much of the southern Mediterranean. It became the home to a brilliant civilization and one of the largest cities in the pre-industrial world. Carthage came into conflict with the empires of Greece and then of Rome. The wars against Rome, known as the Punic Wars, were divided into three periods between 264 BC and 146 BC, when the Romans finally triumphed. They razed Carthage and much of the evidence and artefacts of the ancient city was destroyed.
Criteria: ii, iii, vi Inscribed 1979

THE CRITERIA FOR SELECTION

To be included, sites must be of outstanding universal value and meet at least one of the following ten selection criteria:

i   **Human creative genius**

to represent a masterpiece of human creative genius;

ii   **Interchange of values**

to exhibit an important interchange of human values, over a span of time or within a cultural area of the world, on developments in architecture or technology, monumental arts, town-planning or landscape design;

iii   **Testimony to cultural tradition**

to bear a unique or at least exceptional testimony to a cultural tradition or to a civilization which is living or which has disappeared;

iv   **Significance in human history**

to be an outstanding example of a type of building, architectural or technological ensemble or landscape which illustrates (a) significant stage(s) in human history;

v   **Traditional human settlement**

to be an outstanding example of a traditional human settlement, land-use, or sea-use which is representative of a culture (or cultures), or human interaction with the environment especially when it has become vulnerable under the impact of irreversible change;

vi   **Heritage associated with events of universal significance**

to be directly or tangibly associated with events or living traditions, with ideas, or with beliefs, with artistic and literary works of outstanding universal significance. (The Committee considers that this criterion should preferably be used in conjunction with other criteria);

vii   **Natural phenomena or beauty**

to contain superlative natural phenomena or areas of exceptional beauty and aesthetic importance;

viii   **Major stages of Earth's history**

to be outstanding examples representing major stages of Earth's history, including the record of life, significant on-going geological processes in the development of landforms, or significant geomorphic or physiographic features;

ix   **Significant ecological and biological processes**

to be outstanding examples representing significant on-going ecological and biological processes in the evolution and development of terrestrial, fresh water, coastal and marine ecosystems and communities of plants and animals;

x   **Significant natural habitat for biodiversity**

to contain the most important and significant natural habitats for in-situ conservation of biological diversity, including those containing threatened species of outstanding universal value from the point of view of science or conservation.

▪ GALÁPAGOS ISLANDS Ecuador

Situated in the Pacific Ocean approximately 1,000 km from the South American mainland, the Galápagos Archipelago and its marine reserve have been called a unique 'living museum and showcase of evolution'.

Volcanic processes formed the islands, most of which are volcanic summits, some rising over 3,000 m from the Pacific floor. They vary greatly in altitude, area and orientation and these differences, combined with their physical separation, contributed towards the species diversity and endemism on particular islands. Ongoing seismic and volcanic activity reflects the processes that formed the islands and it was these processes, together with the islands' extreme isolation, that led to the development of unusual animal life – such as the marine iguana, the giant tortoise and the flightless cormorant – that inspired Charles Darwin's theory of evolution following his visit in 1835. The endemic fauna includes invertebrate, reptile, marine and bird species. There are a few indigenous mammals. All the reptiles, except for two marine turtles, are endemic.

Criteria: vii, viii, ix x Inscribed 1978

▪ MESA VERDE NATIONAL PARK USA

Standing on the Mesa Verde plateau in southwest Colorado at a height of more than 2,600 m is this concentration of ancestral Pueblo Indian dwellings. Their originality derives in part from the unique local topography of mesas, or tablelands, intersected by deep canyons, that dictated their construction. The dwellings were also designed to cope with the challenging local climate: a semi-arid environment with irregular rainfall and extremes of temperature between day and night.

The dwellings were built by the Anasazi Indians, ancestors of the Pueblos, between the sixth and twelfth centuries, and the earliest habitations are found largely on the plateau.

Criteria: iii Inscribed 1978

▪ ISLAND OF GORÉE Senegal

The island of Gorée, which lies off the coast of Senegal opposite Dakar, is a memorial to the African diaspora. From the fifteenth to the nineteenth century, it was the largest slave-trading centre on the African coast. Ruled in succession by the Portuguese, Dutch, English and French, its architecture is characterised by the contrast between the grim slave-quarters and the elegant houses of the slave traders. An estimated 20 million Africans passed through the island between the mid-1500s and the mid-1800s. Today it continues to serve as a reminder of human exploitation and as a sanctuary for reconciliation.

Criteria: vi Inscribed 1978

▪ ROCK-HEWN CHURCHES, LALIBELA Ethiopia

The eleven medieval monolithic churches of this thirteenth-century 'New Jerusalem' are situated in a mountainous region in the heart of Ethiopia near a traditional village with circular-shaped dwellings. The rock-hewn churches are recessed below ground level and connected by maze-like tunnels, with a small river running between them called the Jordan, with churches on one side representing the earthly Jerusalem and those on the other the heavenly Jerusalem. Lalibela is a high place of Ethiopian Christianity, tended by Coptic priests and still today a place of pilgrimage and devotion.

Criteria: i, ii, iii Inscribed 1978

▪ CITY OF QUITO Ecuador

Quito, the capital of Ecuador, was founded in the sixteenth century on the ruins of an Inca city and stands at an altitude of 2,850 m. Quito is built on uneven land traversed by two deep ravines (*quebradas*). One of the ravines is arched over partly to preserve the alignment of the streets. Despite the 1917 earthquake, the city has the best-preserved, least altered historic centre in Latin America.

Criteria: ii, iv Inscribed 1978

▪ CRACOW'S HISTORIC CENTRE Poland

The historic centre of Cracow (Kraków), the former capital of Poland, is an outstanding example of medieval architecture. The 13th-century

An endemic Galápagos giant tortoise. Adults in the wild can grow up to 1.2 m in length and live for 150 years.

An endemic Galápagos Sally Lightfoot (*Graspus graspus*) crab lives on the rocky shore, feeding on algae and dead fish, birds and seals.

Villages in the Mesa Verde grew in and around the cave-studded sides of the cuestas where erosion had left protective cliffs. Some of these imposing stone-built cliff dwellings comprise more than 100 rooms.

merchants' town has Europe's largest medieval market square and numerous historical houses, palaces and churches with magnificent interiors. Remnants of the 14th-century fortifications, the medieval Kazimierz with its ancient synagogues, Jagellonian University, one of Europe's oldest, and the Gothic Wawel Cathedral all testify to the town's fascinating history. The layout of Cracow is based on four core areas: Stare Miasto, or old town, around the market square; the Wawel, site of the imperial palace and the cathedral; the urban district of Kazimierz; and the Stradom quarter. Kazimierz, which was an island until 1880, was the Jewish quarter of Cracow until its 64,000 residents were deported, many to Auschwitz in the Second World War.
Criteria: iv Inscribed 1978

• YELLOWSTONE NATIONAL PARK USA

Yellowstone National Park covers 9,000 km² of a vast natural forest of the southern Rocky Mountains in the North American west. The park holds half of the world's known geothermal features, and is equally renowned for its wildlife which includes grizzly bears, wolves, bison and wapitis. Established as America's first national park in 1872, Yellowstone contains geysers, lava formations, fumaroles, hot springs, mud pots and waterfalls, lakes and canyons. There are more than 580 geysers – the world's largest concentration, and two-thirds of all those on the planet. The source of these phenomena lies under the ground for Yellowstone is part of the most seismically active region of the Rocky Mountains, a volcanic 'hot spot'. The most recent period of volcanism began in the region about 2 million years ago, when thousands of cubic kilometres of magma filled immense chambers under the plateau and then erupted to the surface. Three cycles of eruption produced huge explosive outbursts of ash. The latest cycle formed a caldera 45 km wide and 75 km long when the active magma chambers erupted and collapsed. Great differences in altitude give a range of plant communities, from semi-arid steppe to alpine tundra. Thermal areas have unique assemblages of thermal algae and bacteria.
Criteria: vii, viii, ix, x Inscribed 1978

• L'ANSE AUX MEADOWS NATIONAL HISTORIC SITE Canada

Located at the tip of the Great Northern Peninsula on the Island of Newfoundland, L'Anse aux Meadows is the only authenticated Viking site on the American continent. Here, archaeologists have uncovered the remnants of eight wood-framed, peat-turf buildings similar to those found in Greenland and Iceland, dating back around 1000 years, well before Columbus or Cabot. It was from here that exploration around the Gulf of St Lawrence and into Vinland by the Vikings led to the first encounters between Europeans and North American Aboriginal peoples.
Criteria: vi Inscribed 1978

• NAHANNI NATIONAL PARK Canada

Located in the southwest corner of the Northwest Territories, along the course of the South Nahanni and Flat rivers, the park lies in a mountainous area comprising mountain ranges, rolling hills, rugged plateaus, deep canyons and spectacular waterfalls, as well as a globally significant limestone cave system. The park has many unique geological features including tufa mounds known as the Rabbitkettle Hotsprings, which rise in a succession of terraces to a height of 27 m. There are also wind-eroded sandstone landforms known as the Sand Blowouts.
Criteria: vii, viii Inscribed 1978

• AACHEN CATHEDRAL Germany

With its columns of Greek and Italian marble, bronze doors, octagonal basilica and cupola, the Palatine Chapel of Aachen was from its inception regarded as an exceptional architectural achievement. Construction began around 790–800 under the Emperor Charlemagne, who was buried there. German emperors continued to be crowned there until 1531. Two parts of Charlemagne's palace have survived: the Coronation Hall, which is currently located in the Town Hall, built in the fourteenth century, and the Palatine Chapel, around which the cathedral was later built.
Criteria: i, ii, iv, vi Inscribed 1978

Wawel Cathedral was for centuries the scene of the main events of the Polish royal families – coronations, weddings, funerals and burials. *Cracow's Historic Centre*

Castle Geyser is located in the Upper Geyser Basin in Yellowstone National Park. The geyser is thought to be approximately 5,000 years old, and will erupt hot water for 20 minutes up to a height of 27 m, once every 12 hours.

• WIELICZKA SALT MINE Poland

The Wieliczka Salt Mine, near Cracow (Kraków), has been worked as a source of rock salt since the late thirteenth century. Spread over nine levels, it has 300 km of galleries, connecting more than 2,000 excavation chambers. Over the centuries, miners have carved sculptures out of the native rock salt. As a result, it contains underground churches, altars, and sculptures. The subterranean lake, open to tourists since the 15th century, completes this curious complex.
Criteria: iv Inscribed 1978

• SIMIEN NATIONAL PARK Ethiopia

Massive erosion over many years on the Ethiopian plateau has created one of the most spectacular landscapes in the world, with jagged mountain peaks, deep valleys and sharp precipices dropping some 1,500 m. The park is home to some extremely rare animals such as the Gelada baboon, the Simien fox and the Walia ibex, a goat found nowhere else in the world.
Criteria: vii, x Inscribed 1978

• MEIDAN EMAM, ESFAHAN Islamic Republic of Iran

The Royal Square (Meidan Emam) of the Safawid capital, Esfahan, was built by Shah Abbas the Great at the beginning of the seventeenth century. It is bordered on each side by four monumental buildings linked by a series of two-storey arcades: the Portico of Qeyssariyeh, the Royal Mosque, the Mosque of Sheyx Loffollah, and the pavilion of Ali Qapu, a small fifteenth-century Timurid palace, enlarged and decorated by the shah and his successors. The Royal Square, with its vast sandy esplanade, was used for promenades, assembling troops, playing polo, celebrations and public executions. On all sides, the arcades house shops.
Criteria: i, v, vi Inscribed 1979

• ANCIENT CITY OF DAMASCUS
Syrian Arab Republic

Founded in the third millennium BC, Damascus is considered to be the oldest city in the world. It had many rulers, including King David of Israel and Alexander the Great, before it became part of the Arab world as the capital of Umayyad caliphate in 636. Damascus preserves a few traces of its long history prior to the Arabic conquest, including some from the Roman period. Over the centuries guilds of craftsmen and merchants established themselves around the Great Mosque, while the important Christian minority settled in the northeast quarters, around churches and sites associated with the conversion of St Paul.
Criteria: i, ii, iii, iv, vi Inscribed 1979

• NGORONGORO CONSERVATION AREA
Tanzania

The diverse landforms, altitude range and variable climate of the Ngorongoro crater have produced several distinct habitats: scrub heath and the remains of dense montane forests on its steep slopes, with grassy plains, lakes, swamps and woodland on the crater floor. At nearby Olduvai Gorge, excavations uncovered the existence of one of our more distant ancestors, *Homo habilis*. Laitoli is one of the main sites for early hominid footprints, dating back 3.6 million years. Leopard, African elephant, mountain reedbuck, flamingo, wildebeest and buffalo are among the species that live on the crater rim.
Criteria: vii, viii, ix, x Inscribed 1979

• AUSCHWITZ BIRKENAU, GERMAN NAZI CONCENTRATION AND EXTERMINATION CAMP (1940-1945) Poland

Auschwitz-Birkenau was the principal and most notorious of the six concentration and mass extermination camps established by Nazi Germany to implement its 'Final Solution', the mass murder of the Jewish people in Europe. It was built in Poland under Nazi German occupation initially as a concentration camp for prisoners of war. In the years 1942–4 over a million Jewish men, women and children were tortured and killed there. In addition tens of thousands of Polish victims, and thousands of Roma and Sinti were also murdered. The site has a key place in our collective memory of this dark chapter

The largest of the underground chapels at Wieliczka Salt Mine, the Chapel of the Blessed Kinga, is located 101 m below the surface; it is over 50 m long, 15 m wide and 12 m high.

One of the most spectacular monuments in Damascus is the eighth-century Great Mosque of the Umayyads, built on the site of an Assyrian sanctuary.

The perfect crater of Ngorongoro is, on average, 16–19 km wide, its floor is 264 km² and its rim soars to a height of 400–610 m. Around 25,000 large animals live in the crater.

in the history of humanity and is warning sign of the many threats and tragic consequences of extreme ideologies and denial of human dignity.
Criteria: vi Inscribed 1979

▪ PREHISTORIC SITES AND DECORATED CAVES OF THE VÉZÈRE VALLEY France

The Vézère Valley contains 147 prehistoric sites dating from the Palaeolithic period, including twenty-five decorated caves. It is particularly significant because of the cave paintings, especially those of the Lascaux Cave, whose discovery in 1940 was of great importance for the history of prehistoric art. The hunting scenes show some 100 animal figures, which are remarkable for their detail, rich colours and lifelike quality. The Lascaux Cave is closed to the public, but replicas of the Great Hall of the Bulls and the Painted Gallery have been created nearby.
Criteria: i, iii Inscribed 1979

▪ BRYGGEN Norway

Bryggen is the old wharf of the city of Bergen. With its traditional wooden buildings, Bryggen is a relic of an ancient urban street plan once common in Northern Europe and is a reminder of the town's importance as part of the trading empire of the powerful Hanseatic League from the fourteenth to the mid-sixteenth century. Over the centuries several devastating fires, the most recent in 1955, have ravaged the traditional wooden houses. However, rebuilding has traditionally followed old patterns and methods, so retaining the medieval appearance.
Criteria: iii Inscribed 1979

▪ FORTS AND CASTLES, VOLTA, GREATER ACCRA, CENTRAL AND WESTERN REGIONS Ghana

The remains of fortified trading-posts, established between 1482 and 1786, can still be seen along the coast of Ghana between Keta and Beyin. They were links in the trade routes established by the Portuguese in many areas of the world during their era of great maritime exploration. During the slave trade Accra took on greater importance owing to these nearby forts, many of which were by then owned and controlled by the Dutch, a prominence that lasted until the abolition of the slave trade in 1807.
Criteria: vi Inscribed 1979

▪ VIRUNGA NATIONAL PARK Dem. Rep. of the Congo

The range of altitudes in Virunga National Park provides great variety in habitats, from swamps and savannas to the Rwenzori snowfields at a height of over 5,000 m; and from lava plains to forests on the slopes of volcanoes. There are hot springs in the Rwindi plains, and some of the Virunga Massif volcanoes are still active. The rivers of Virunga have one of the largest hippopotamus concentrations in Africa. The Rwindi savanna is home to elephant, buffalo, antelope, warthog, lion and various monkeys. The park also includes wetlands, which are important transit and wintering areas for some bird species.
Criteria: vii, viii, x Inscribed 1979

▪ SITE OF CARTHAGE Tunisia

Carthage was founded in the ninth century BC by Phoenician traders from Tyre, in modern Lebanon. By the sixth century BC it had conquered and controlled much of the southern Mediterranean. It became the home to a brilliant civilisation and one of the largest cities in the pre-industrial world. Carthage came into conflict with the empires of Greece and then of Rome. The wars against Rome, known as the Punic Wars, were divided into three periods between 264 BC and 146 BC, when the Romans finally triumphed. They razed Carthage and much of the evidence and artefacts of the ancient city was destroyed.
Criteria: ii, iii, vi Inscribed 1979

▪ DINOSAUR PROVINCIAL PARK Canada

Dinosaur Provincial Park contains some of the most important fossils from the 'Age of Reptiles' – including about thirty-nine species of dinosaur, dating back some 75 million years. The park stands at the

The fortified walls, barbed wire, railway sidings, platforms, barracks, gallows, gas chambers and crematoria at Auschwitz-Birkenau provide irrefutable evidence of how the Holocaust was undertaken.

The sixty-two surviving buildings of Bryggen are constructed along narrow streets running parallel to the dock. A courtyard (*gård*) is common to several three-storey wooden houses whose gabled façades, walls and roofs are covered with shingles.

Part of the Antonine Baths at Carthage. In the first century AD the Roman Emperor Augustus refounded the city and it prospered quickly, becoming second only to Rome in splendour and wealth.

heart of Alberta's badlands, a beautiful, barren and deeply eroded area of sparse vegetation. During the late Cretaceous period 75 million years ago, the landscape of the area was very different, with lush forests and rivers flowing into a warm inland sea. Its low swamps were home to a variety of animals, including dinosaurs. The conditions were also perfect for the preservation of their bones as fossils.
Criteria: vii, viii Inscribed 1979

• ABU MENA Egypt
The church, baptistry, basilicas, public buildings, streets, monasteries, houses and workshops in this early Christian holy city were built over the tomb of the martyr Menas of Alexandria, who died in AD 296. The Thermal Basilica, built in the fifth century to accommodate the increasing number of Christian pilgrims, was used to store the curative waters for the surrounding heated baths and pools. The city exhibits an important fusion of Eastern and Western religious influences.
Criteria: iv Inscribed 1979

• THRACIAN TOMB OF KAZANLAK Bulgaria
Discovered in 1944, this Hellenistic tomb is located in Bulgaria's romantic Valley of Roses. Part of a large necropolis with more than 500 burial mounds, it lies near Seuthopolis, the capital city of the Thracian king Seutes III. The art and archaeological discoveries of the site reflect a rich culture that was at its peak in the fifth to third centuries BC. The murals of the Kazanlak Tomb are particularly important because they are the only entirely preserved work of Hellenistic art that has been found in exactly the state in which it was originally designed and executed.
Criteria: i, iii, iv Inscribed 1979

• KATHMANDU VALLEY Nepal
The Kathmandu Valley is the principal centre of settlement in Nepal and is a prime cultural focus of the Himalayas. It contains seven groups of monuments and buildings: the Durbar Square of Hanuman Dhoka (or Hanuman Gate) in Kathmandu, the Durbar Square of Patan and the Durbar Square of Bhaktapur; the Buddhist stupas of Swayambhu and of Bauddhanath; and the Hindu temples of Pashupati and Changu Narayan. Most of Kathmandu's principal monuments are in Durbar Square, built between the twelfth and the eighteenth centuries by the ancient Malla kings of Nepal. Pashupati Temple is a sprawling collection of temples, ashrams, images and inscriptions, and is one of the most important Hindu temples in Nepal.
Criteria: iii, iv, vi Inscribed 1979

• KLUANE / WRANGELL-ST ELIAS / GLACIER BAY / TATSHENSHINI-ALSEK Canada and USA
Mountain peaks, foothills, glacial systems, lakes, valleys and coastal landscapes make up these spectacular parks stretching from British Columbia and Yukon Territory in Canada across the border to Alaska in the USA. The Wrangell–St Elias region has the largest array of glaciers and ice fields outside the polar region, including the 130 km-long Bagley ice field. There are three major biomes or ecological areas: coastal coniferous; northern coniferous; and alpine tundra. The great variety of birds and wildlife, including grizzly bears, caribou and Dall's sheep, reflects this habitat diversity.
Criteria: vii, viii, ix, x Inscribed 1979

• EVERGLADES NATIONAL PARK USA
The Everglades National Park lies at the interface between temperate and subtropical America, between fresh and brackish water and between shallow bays and deeper coastal waters. Consequently it hosts a complex of habitats supporting a high diversity of flora and fauna including many endemic to this area. Its exceptional variety of water habitats has made it a sanctuary for large numbers of birds and reptiles, including threatened species such as the manatee. Hammocks or tree islands are dominated by tropical and temperate hardwood species. The most important trees are mangroves, taxa, slash pine and cypress. Prairies can be dominated by sawgrass, muhley grass, or cordgrass in coastal areas.
Criteria: viii, ix, x Inscribed 1979

The Durbar Square of Patan, which is just across the holy Bagmati River about 14 km east of Kathmandu.

The Everglades National Park, on the southern tip of the Florida Peninsula, has been called 'a river of grass flowing imperceptibly from the hinterland into the sea'.

• GRAND CANYON NATIONAL PARK USA

The Grand Canyon, carved nearly 1,500 m deep into the rock by the Colorado River, is the most spectacular gorge in the world. It also contains prehistoric traces of human adaptation to a particularly harsh environment. The Grand Canyon is a steep, twisting gorge, 1.5 km deep and 445.8 km long, and was formed during some 6 million years of geological activity and erosion by the Colorado River on the raised Earth's crust (2.5 km above sea level). The gorge, which ranges from 200 m–30 km wide, divides the park into the North Rim and South Rim: the buttes, spires, mesas and temples in the canyon are in fact mountains, looked down upon from the rims. The canyon is also a vast biological museum in which there are five different life and vegetation zones.

Criteria: vii, viii, ix, x Inscribed 1979

• NUBIAN MONUMENTS FROM ABU SIMBEL
  TO PHILAE Egypt

This part of southern Egypt is an area of outstanding archaeological importance containing magnificent ancient monuments, including the temples at Abu Simbel and the Sanctuary of Isis at Philae. The Great Temple at Abu Simbel has four colossal statues of the pharaoh carved into the rocky cliff wall. Nearby is the Little Temple, dedicated to the Goddess Hathor in memory of the pharaoh's wife Queen Nefertari. Built by Ramses II, the Abu Simbel temples reaffirmed Egyptian domination of Nubia. In the 1960s the sites faced inundation by the river Nile as a consequence of the construction of the Aswan High Dam. UNESCO launched a successful campaign to save the temples, which led to their removal to higher ground.

Criteria: i, iii, vi Inscribed 1979

• PLITVICE LAKES NATIONAL PARK Croatia

Plitvice Lakes National Park contains a series of outstandingly beautiful lakes, caves and waterfalls. There are approximately twenty interlinked lakes between Mala Kapela Mountain and Pljesevica Mountain. The park's features were formed over thousands of years by the waters flowing over the limestone and chalk and depositing barriers of travertine rock, in the process creating natural dams; these in turn created the lakes, caves and waterfalls. The dense forests of the park are rich in wildlife and are home to brown bears, wolves and many rare bird species.

Criteria: vii, viii, ix Inscribed 1979

• FASIL GHEBBI, GONDAR REGION Ethiopia

The fortress-city of Fasil Ghebbi, on the northern plateau of Tana, was, in the sixteenth and seventeenth centuries, the residence of the Ethiopian emperor Fasilides and his successors. Surrounded by a 900-m-long wall, the city contains palaces, churches, monasteries and private buildings marked by Hindu and Arab influences, subsequently transformed by the Baroque style brought to Gondar by the Jesuit missionaries. Beyond the confines of the city is a fine bathing palace, a two-stored battlemented structure situated beside a rectangular pool of water which was supplied by a canal from the nearby river.

Criteria: ii, iii Inscribed 1979

• MONT-SAINT-MICHEL AND ITS BAY France

Mont-Saint-Michel is one of the most important sites of medieval Christian civilisation. The Gothic Benedictine abbey dedicated to the archangel Saint Michael and the village that grew up in the shadow of its great walls are together known as the 'Wonder of the West'. Built between the eleventh and sixteenth centuries, the abbey is a technical and artistic tour de force, having adapted to the problems posed by its unique position and site: perched on a rocky islet in the midst of vast sandbanks exposed to powerful tides between Normandy and Brittany. Mont-Saint-Michel forms an architectural complex of great originality, built by successive restructurings and additions throughout the Middle Ages.

Criteria: i, iii, vi Inscribed 1979

Low sunlight helps to reveal the Grand canyon's horizontal strata that span some 2,000 million years of geological history, providing evidence of four major geological eras: early and late Precambrian, Palaeozoic, Mesozoic and Cenozoic.

The upper Plitvice Lakes lie in a dolomite valley surrounded by thick forests and linked by numerous waterfalls. The lower Plitvice Lakes, smaller and shallower, lie on limestone bedrock and are surrounded by sparse underbrush.

The architectural advances of the later medieval Gothic period allowed Mont-Saint-Michel's restricted area to be used to best advantage, in the high walls, soaring masses and airy pinnacles which crown the rock and provide a unique silhouette.

• BOYANA CHURCH Bulgaria

Located on the outskirts of Sofia, Boyana Church consists of three buildings. The eastern church was built in the tenth century, then enlarged at the beginning of the thirteenth century by Sebastocrator Kaloyan, who ordered a second two-storey building to be erected next to it. The frescoes in this second church, painted in 1259, make it one of the most important collections of medieval icon-style paintings. The ensemble is completed by a third church, built at the beginning of the nineteenth century. This site is one of the most complete monuments of east European medieval art.
Criteria: ii, iii Inscribed 1979

• BELOVEZHSKAYA PUSHCHA / BIAŁOWIEŻA FOREST Belarus and Poland

The Białowieża Forest dates back to 8000 BC and is the only remaining example of the original forests that once covered much of Europe. Located on the watershed of the Baltic and Black seas, this immense forest of evergreens and broadleaved trees is the home of some remarkable animal life, including rare mammals such as the wolf, the lynx and the otter, as well as some 300 European Bison, a species which was reintroduced in 1929. Białowieża National Park comprises about one-tenth of the entire forest.
Criteria: vii Inscribed 1979

• PALACE AND PARK OF VERSAILLES France

The Palace of Versailles, built and embellished by several generations of the foremost French architects, sculptors, decorators and landscape architects, was one of the largest royal palaces in the world. Versailles, some 20 km southwest of Paris, was chosen by Louis XIII as his personal hunting ground and he built a modest château in 1623. Under the direction of Louis Le Vau, Louis XIV's architect, a programme of expansion began in the 1660s. The decoration of the palace interior was supervised by the painter Charles Le Brun who, with teams of painters, decorators and craftsmen, created a remarkable complex of frescoes, marble, stucco, gilded bronzes, fabrics and furniture. The gardens were designed by André Le Nôtre, with paths extending as far as the eye can see, punctuated geometrically by parterres of flowers and low hedges, little streams, large ponds and fountains.
Criteria: i, ii, vi Inscribed 1979

• VÉZELAY, CHURCH AND HILL France

Established in the ninth century as a Benedictine abbey on the hill at Vézelay, the church came to prominence in the mid-eleventh century when the belief spread that it held the relics of St Mary Magdalene. On Easter Sunday in 1146 St Bernard preached at the assembly celebrating the departure of the Second Crusade. In 1190 the kings of France and England, Philippe II and Richard I, the Lionheart, united their armies at Vézelay and left together for the Third Crusade. In 1217 Francis of Assisi chose the hill of Vézelay to found the first Franciscan establishment on French soil.
Criteria: i, vi Inscribed 1979

• CHARTRES CATHEDRAL France

Partly built, starting in 1145, and then reconstructed over a 26-year period after a fire in 1194, Chartres Cathedral marks the high point of French Gothic art. It is a place of pilgrimage, attracting throngs from all over the Christianised West. The cathedral, with its vast nave, its porches adorned with fine sculptures from the mid-twelfth century, and the magnificent twelfth and thirteenth-century stained-glass windows, all in remarkable condition, combine to make it a masterpiece. Chartres Cathedral has exerted a considerable influence on the development of Gothic art both within and outside France.
Criteria: i, ii, iv Inscribed 1979

• PERSEPOLIS Islamic Republic of Iran

The magnificent ruins of Persepolis lie at the foot of Kuh-i-Rahmat (Mountain of Mercy), about 650 km south of Teheran. Founded by Darius I in 518 BC, Persepolis was the capital of the Achaemenid Empire. It was built on an immense half-artificial, half-natural stone terrace (530 m by 330 m), where an impressive palace complex was

Almost 90 per cent of the Białowieża Forest is covered with 'old growth' virgin stands of mixed broadleaved and conifer forests.

After 1678 the Palace of Versailles was considerably enlarged by Jules Hardouin Mansart, who introduced a sober and majestic architecture, that is inseparable, even today, from the memory of the 'Sun King', Louis XIV.

Chartres Cathedral has retained nearly all its original stained-glass windows. In total there are 1,359 images from biblical stories or of saints contained within over 146 windows.

constructed, inspired by Mesopotamian models. It seems that Darius planned Persepolis not only as the seat of government but also, and primarily, as a show place and a spectacular centre for the receptions and festivals of the Achaemenid kings and their empire.
Criteria: i, iii, vi Inscribed 1979

• INDEPENDENCE HALL USA
Independence Hall in Philadelphia may be considered the birthplace of the USA: it was here that the Declaration of Independence was signed in 1776, the Articles of Confederation uniting the thirteen colonies were ratified in 1781, and the Constitution setting out the nation's basic laws was adopted in 1787, after George Washington had presided over the debate, which ran from May to September. The universal principles of freedom and democracy set forth in these documents are of fundamental importance to American history and have also had a profound impact on law-makers around the world.
Criteria: vi Inscribed 1979

• MADARA RIDER Bulgaria
The Madara Rider is a majestic horseman carved 23 m above ground level in an almost vertical 100-m high cliff. The horseman is thrusting a spear into a lion lying at his horse's feet, while a dog runs after the horseman. Madara was the principal sacred place of the first Bulgarian Empire. The Madara Horseman was carved at the very beginning of the eighth century, about three decades after the foundation of the Bulgarian state in AD 681. The sculpture thus marks a triumph: the Byzantine Empire had recognised the new state.
Criteria: i, iii Inscribed 1979

• ROCK-HEWN CHURCHES OF IVANOVO
  Bulgaria
This rock-hewn complex lies in the valley of the Roussenski Lom River. The first hermits dug out small cells and churches here during the twelfth century. Then, in the thirteenth century, Bulgaria once again embraced Orthodox Christianity. The first Patriarch was the monk Gioacchino, who had lived as a hermit in one of the Ivanovo caves, and the Tsar commissioned him to construct a larger monastery. After 1396, the monastery was abandoned. The limestone out of which it was carved enabled it to resist the weather, saving its remarkable labyrinth of cells, rooms, churches and frescoes to this day.
Criteria: ii, iii Inscribed 1979

• MEMPHIS AND ITS NECROPOLIS – THE PYRAMID FIELDS FROM GIZA TO DAHSHUR
  Egypt
The capital of the Old Kingdom of Egypt in the third millennium BC, Memphis was one of the Seven Wonders of the Ancient World. The ruins of the temple of Ptah are all that survive today. At nearby Saqqara, the necropolis of Memphis, is the first great stone pyramid, built as a mausoleum for the pharaoh Djoser, founder of the Third Dynasty, who ruled from around 2668 BC. Designed by his architect and vizier, Imhotep, it is the oldest step pyramid in the world. To the south lies the necropolis of Dahshur, where the founder of the Fourth Dynasty, Snefru, who reigned from around 2613 BC, transformed the structure of Egyptian royal tombs by choosing the now familiar pyramid shape with a square base. He built both the Red Pyramid, named after its reddish-coloured limestone, and the Rhomboid (or Bent) Pyramid, with its double-angled slope on each of the four faces. To the north, the great pyramids of Giza were built by Snefru's son Khufu or Cheops, and his successors Khafre (Chephren) and Menkaure (Mycerinus). The 'Horizon of Cheops' was the name given to the Pharaoh's tomb, the oldest and largest. The other two pyramids were known in antiquity as 'Great is Chepren' and 'Divine is Mycerinus' respectively.
Criteria: i, iii, vi Inscribed 1979

• ANCIENT THEBES WITH ITS NECROPOLIS
  Egypt
Thebes was the capital of Egypt at the height of its power in the Middle and New Kingdoms, around 2134–1070 BC. Thebes of the Living is on the right bank of the Nile. From the Middle Kingdom

Persepolis was the example *par excellence* of the dynastic city, the symbol of the Achaemenid dynasty, which is why it was burned by the Greeks of Alexander the Great in 330 BC.

The Great Sphinx of Giza and the Pyramid of Khafre (Chephren). The pyramid is a symbol of the Sun, the great god Ra, whose cult became pre-eminent from the Fourth Dynasty.

to the first century AD the city was sacred to the god Amon, the supreme Sun God, and temples of incomparable splendour and size were dedicated to him. The temple of Luxor, built by Amenophis III and Ramses II, was connected to the sanctuary of Karnak by a long processional avenue lined by sphinxes. The monumental Karnak complex is composed of three temples: one consecrated to Mut, mother goddess of Egypt and wife of Amon; one to the warrior god Montu; and one to Amon. On the opposite bank of the river is Thebes of the Dead, including the Valley of the Kings and the Valley of the Queens. Great funerary temples were built at the foot of the hills, entirely separate from their corresponding tombs which were dug into the mountains to keep them safe from violation and tomb robbers. The colossi of Memnon, massive twin statues of Amenhotep III, face eastwards over the river Nile.

Criteria: i, iii, vi Inscribed 1979

• MEDINA OF TUNIS Tunisia

The Medina of Tunis is a rare survivor as most other historic Islamic centres have suffered serious destruction and reconstruction over the centuries. It extends over 2.7 km² and includes most of the 700 historic monuments in the city, including palaces, mosques, mausoleums and fountains. It is divided between the central core, which still bears traces from the period of its foundation (the eighth century), and two quarters dating back to the thirteenth century.

Criteria: ii, iii, v Inscribed 1979

• ROCK DRAWINGS IN VALCAMONICA Italy

Valcamonica, situated in the Lombardy plain, has one of the world's greatest collections of prehistoric petroglyphs – more than 140,000 symbols and figures carved in the rock over a period of 8,000 years, depicting themes connected with agriculture, navigation, war and magic. Several periods of carving can be identified: Upper Palaeolithic (c. 8000 BC), with scenes depicting hunting and early civilisation; Neolithic (4000–3000 BC), in which the first depictions of a religious nature appear; and Eneolithic (3000–2000 BC), with rural scenes and scenes depicting female initiation rituals. After 1000 BC battle scenes appear as well as drawings showing huts, wagons, harvests and weapons.

Criteria: iii, vi Inscribed 1979

• STARI RAS AND SOPÓCANI Serbia

On the outskirts of Stari Ras, the first capital of Serbia, there is an impressive group of medieval monuments consisting of fortresses, churches and monasteries. Situated on a hill at the border between the small kingdom of Raska and the Byzantine Empire, its many monuments date from the city's architectural and cultural prime, which lasted until the early fourteenth century. The Church of St Peter, built in the ninth century on the foundations of an Illyrian cemetery and an early Christian basilica, is an example of early Christian architecture, and was the religious centre of Serbia for several centuries.

Criteria: i, iii Inscribed 1979

• ANTIGUA GUATEMALA Guatemala

Antigua Guatemala is an outstanding example of Spanish colonial architecture. Built 1,500 m above sea level in an earthquake-prone region, Antigua, the capital of the Captaincy-General of Guatemala, was founded in the early sixteenth century as Santiago de Guatemala. It was the cultural, economic, religious and educational centre for the entire region until the capital was moved to Guatemala City after damaging earthquakes in 1773. The city, which was built on a grid pattern inspired by the Italian Renaissance, contains a number of superb monuments, many of which are preserved today as ruins.

Criteria: ii, iii, iv Inscribed 1979

• NATURAL AND CULTURAL HERITAGE OF THE OHRID REGION
The Former Yugoslav Republic of Macedonia

Ohrid is one of Europe's most ancient settlements, and writing, education and Slavic culture all spread out from here. More than 250 archaeological sites dating from between the Neolithic period

The Great Hypostyle Hall in the Temple of Amon at Karnak, in ancient Thebes. There are 134 columns, resembling papyrus stalks, in 16 rows. Each column is covered in hieroglyphics or battle scenes.

The Church of our Lady of Mercy in Antigua Guatemala. Much of Antigua's architecture today dates from the seventeenth and eighteenth centuries.

and the late Middle Ages have been excavated. The city is on the shores of the beautiful Lake Ohrid and has the best preserved and most complete ensemble of ancient urban buildings in the Slavic lands. It also has the oldest Slav monastery, St Pantelejmon, and more than 800 Byzantine-style icons dating from the eleventh to the fourteenth century, one of the world's most important icon collections.
Criteria: i, iii Inscribed 1979

• HISTORIC CAIRO Egypt

Cairo, founded in the tenth century, became the new capital and centre of the Islamic world, and its wealth of architectural treasures – mosques, *madrasas*, palaces and caravanserais, *hammams* and fountains – reflect its importance at that time. The al-Azhar quarter includes the three large gates and the huge, square towers of the city's walls and five mosques. Among these, the Mosque of al-Hakim, compact and severe, is the last example of a military mosque. The Mosque of al-Azhar, built 970-72 also housed a university which became the most important centre for Islamic studies. In the 12th century Saladin constructed the Citadel which remained the heart of Egyptian government until the nineteenth century. Cairo thrived under the dynasty of the Mamelukes, rulers from 1250–1517. In addition to religious buildings the sultans created splendid mausoleums in the City of the Dead, the huge cemetery to the east of the city.
Criteria: i, v, vi Inscribed 1979

• AMPHITHEATRE OF EL JEM Tunisia

The impressive ruins of the largest colosseum in North Africa are found in the small village of El Jem, known in classical times as Thysdrus, located 60 km south of Sousse. Built during the first half of the third century, it may have accommodated up to 60,000 spectators. Elliptical in form, it is constructed from large stone blocks and probably comprised four floors. The theatre was never completed, because of political rivalries and lack of funds within the Empire. Later it served as a stronghold: it was the last Berber bastion against Arab invaders.
Criteria: iv, vi Inscribed 1979

• URNES STAVE CHURCH Norway

The stave church of Urnes, built in the twelfth and thirteenth centuries, is an outstanding example of traditional Scandinavian wooden architecture. It brings together traces of Celtic art, Viking traditions and Romanesque architectural design. A stave church is constructed just from wood: the columns, capitals and arches replicate in wood the style of stone Romanesque architecture – and even the roof is covered with wooden shingles. On the outside, there are outstanding panels of eleventh-century carved strapwork taken from an earlier church. Inside is an amazing series of twelfth-century figurative capitals and a wealth of medieval liturgical objects.
Criteria: i, ii, iii Inscribed 1979

• HISTORICAL COMPLEX OF SPLIT WITH THE PALACE OF DIOCLETIAN Croatia

The ancient city of Split is renowned for the massive palace built at the turn of the fourth century AD by the Roman Emperor Diocletian near his Dalmatian birthplace. Unique in terms of its massive scale and completeness, it is integrated into an array of important medieval buildings including the cathedral, twelfth- and thirteenth-century Gothic palaces, and other palaces in Renaissance and Baroque style. In the early Middle Ages the town was built within the palace until commercial prosperity inspired its growth and spread outside in the thirteenth and the fourteenth centuries. Much of the Roman and medieval town exists today.
Criteria: ii, iii, iv Inscribed 1979

• NATURAL AND CULTURO-HISTORICAL REGION OF KOTOR Montenegro

The region of Kotor has played an exceptionally important role in the diffusion of Mediterranean culture in the Balkans. Founded by the Romans, Kotor developed in the Middle Ages into an important commercial and artistic centre, under Byzantine, Serbian and then,

The Mosque and Madrasa of Sultan Hassan in Cairo is a masterpiece of Mameluke architecture, built between 1356 and 1363.

Split, with tower of the cathedral of St Dominus in the foreground. Originally the mausoleum of Diocletian, its octagonal form is complete and a dome, once covered by mosaics, forms the roof.

from 1420, Venetian control. Its most impressive building is
St Tryphon Cathedral, built in 1166, damaged during the 1667
earthquake and then restored. Most of Kotor's palaces and houses,
many Romanesque churches and all of neighbouring Dobrota's
palaces and Perast's main buildings have suffered from earthquakes.
Criteria: i, ii, iii, iv Inscribed 1979

• SAGARMATHA NATIONAL PARK Nepal

This is an exceptional area with dramatic mountains, glaciers
and deep valleys, dominated by Mount Everest (Sagarmatha),
the highest peak in the world (8,848 m), and is the homeland of
the Sherpa, with their unique culture. The park is fan-shaped and
enclosed on all sides by high, geologically young mountain ranges.
The deep valleys drain southwards into the Dudh Kosi and its
tributaries, which form part of the Ganges River system. Most
of the park (69 per cent) comprises barren land above 5,000 m.
Several rare species, such as the snow leopard and the lesser
panda, are found here.
Criteria: vii Inscribed 1979

• OLD CITY OF DUBROVNIK Croatia

The 'Pearl of the Adriatic', Dubrovnik was an important
Mediterranean power from the thirteenth century. The city's
self-confidence, wealth and culture are reflected in its beautiful
Gothic, Renaissance and Baroque churches, monasteries, palaces and
fountains, many of which are survivors of a massive earthquake in
1667. UNESCO is currently coordinating a major programme to
restore Dubrovnik's architecture, damaged in armed conflict in the
1990s after the break-up of the communist state of Yugoslavia, of
which it had been part. Dubrovnik is a remarkably well-preserved
example of a late-medieval walled city, with a regular street layout
within its magnificent fortifications and the monumental gates.
Criteria: i, iii, iv Inscribed 1979

• TCHOGHA ZANBIL Islamic Republic of Iran

The ruins of the holy city of the Kingdom of Elam, surrounded by
three huge concentric walls, are found at Tchogha Zanbil. Founded
c. 1250 BC, the city remained unfinished after it was invaded by
Ashurbanipal, as shown by the thousands of unused bricks left at
the site. The site contains the best preserved and the largest of all
the ziggurats of Mesopotamia.
Criteria: iii, iv Inscribed 1979

• TIKAL NATIONAL PARK Guatemala

Tikal National Park contains the largest area of tropical rainforest in
Central America, well-known for its great wealth of animal life. At its
heart is one of the major sites of Mayan civilisation, inhabited from
the sixth century BC to the tenth century AD. The ceremonial centre
contains superb temples and palaces, and public squares. Remains
of dwellings are scattered throughout the surrounding countryside.
There are over 3,000 separate buildings, including religious
monuments decorated with hieroglyphic inscriptions, and tombs.
The ruined city reflects the cultural evolution of Mayan society from
hunter-gathering to farming, with an elaborate religious, artistic and
scientific culture.
Criteria: i, iii, iv, ix, x Inscribed 1979

• HISTORIC CENTRE OF ROME, THE PROPERTIES OF THE HOLY SEE IN THAT CITY ENJOYING EXTRATERRITORIAL RIGHTS AND SAN PAOLO FUORI LE MURA Holy See and Italy

Founded, according to legend, by Romulus and Remus in 753 BC,
Rome was first the centre of the Roman Republic, then of the
Roman Empire, and from the fourth century the capital of the
Christian world. This site comprises outstanding buildings and
monuments from ancient and medieval Roman history. These
include the forums, the Mausoleum of Augustus, the Mausoleum of
Hadrian, the Pantheon, Trajan's Column and the Column of Marcus
Aurelius; and the religious and public buildings of papal Rome,
including Santa Maria Maggiore, St John Lateran and St Paul Outside
the Walls that were all architecturally and artistically influential in

The distinctive rooftops of Dubrovnik, many of which were reconstructed after the 1990s' armed conflict.

Namche Bazar village in Sagarmatha National Park.

The Pantheon in Rome is one of the best preserved ancient Roman buildings. The current building dates from c. AD 125 during Emperor Hadrian's reign.

the Christian world for centuries. In 1990 the site was extended out to the seventeenth-century city walls built by Pope Urban VIII.
Criteria: i, ii, iii, iv, vi Inscribed 1980

• MAYA SITE OF CÓPAN Honduras

The ruins of Cópan are among the most important sites of the indigenous American Mayan civilisation, with temples, plazas and terraces that are among the most characteristic of any Mayan complex. There is evidence that Cópan was inhabited from 2000 BC onwards, but its full flourishing, along with other Mayan cities, came in the period AD 250–900, with important advances in mathematics, astronomy and hieroglyphic writing, as well as major cultural developments. Cópan's ruined citadel and imposing public squares reveal the three main stages of city development, during which the temples, plazas, altar complexes and ball courts that can be seen today, evolved. For unknown reasons the site was abandoned shortly after AD 900.
Criteria: iv, vi Inscribed 1980

• ASANTE TRADITIONAL BUILDINGS Ghana

To the northeast of Kumasi, these buildings are the last of the great Asante civilisation, which reached its high point in the eighteenth century. Since they are made of earth, wood and straw, they are vulnerable to the onslaught of time and weather and only a few traditional homes and temples survive, of which the majority are less than 100 years old. These are constructed with a framework of poles linked by bamboo slats which support the thatched roof. The main façade is built of earth over a core of wood and has a balustrade and sometimes windows. The decoration consists of geometric, floral, animal or anthropomorphic motifs.
Criteria v Inscribed 1980

• GARAMBA NATIONAL PARK
Dem. Rep. of the Congo

The park's immense savannas, grasslands and woodlands, interspersed with forests along the river banks and the swampy depressions, are home to species such as the Northern white rhinoceros and the Congo giraffe, which are found nowhere else. High concentrations of elephants are also found here. Lying on the watershed between the river Nile and the river Congo the park is a vast undulating plateau broken up by inselbergs (generally of granitic formation) and sizeable marshland depressions.
Criteria vii, x Inscribed 1980

• HAL SAFLIENI HYPOGEUM Malta

The Hypogeum is the only known subterranean Bronze Age structure, excavated c. 2500 BC. The walls are constructed of large irregular blocks of chalky coralline stone without mortar. The workmanship is all the more impressive when it is considered that the chambers were meticulously carved using only flint and stone tools. The principal rooms are distinguished by their domed vaulting and by elaborate bays inspired by the doorways and windows of contemporary terrestrial buildings. Curvilinear and spiral paintings in red ochre are still visible in some areas. The carved façade is magnificent and is in a remarkable state of preservation. Perhaps originally a sanctuary, the Hypogeum became a necropolis in prehistoric times.
Criteria: iii Inscribed 1980

• CITY OF VALLETTA Malta

Valletta is inextricably linked to the military, charitable and religious Order of St John of Jerusalem, the Knights Hospitaller, who were based in Malta from 1530 to 1798. The city's design is late Renaissance with a grid-based street layout, fortified and bastioned walls modelled around its peninsular site, and the planned building of great monuments in well-chosen locations. Churches and palaces, museums and theatres, gardens and piazzas retain their original features almost completely. Remarkably, the city has undergone no important modifications since 1798, when the Knights left.
Criteria i, vi Inscribed 1980

A carved stone pillar in the ruins of the great Mayan complex of Cópan.

Valletta, Malta.

• HISTORIC CENTRE OF WARSAW Poland

The historic centre of the Polish capital Warsaw was almost completely rebuilt after fighting during the Second World War destroyed 85 per cent of the Old Town. The city is an outstanding example of a near-total reconstruction of a span of history covering the thirteenth to the twentieth centuries. Almost every building in Warsaw Old Town is of a unique architectural style, from Gothic to Baroque. All have been restored: among the more famous are the market square, city walls and Barbican as well as the Royal Castle and numerous churches.
Criteria: ii, vi Inscribed 1980

• MEGALITHIC TEMPLES OF MALTA Malta

These seven megalithic temples have been described as the oldest free-standing monuments in the world. All date from the third millennium BC and each is the result of an individual development, differing from the others in plan, execution and construction techniques. The two temples of Ggantija on the island of Gozo are gigantic Bronze Age structures. On Malta, the temples of Hagar Qim, Mnajdra and Tarxien are unique architectural masterpieces, given the limited resources available to their builders. The Ta'Hagrat and Skorba complexes show how the tradition of temple-building was handed down in Malta. Each one is remarkable for diversity of form and decoration.
Criteria iv Inscribed 1980

• KAHUZI-BIEGA NATIONAL PARK
Dem. Rep. of the Congo

A vast area of primary tropical forest dominated by two spectacular mountains, Kahuzi (3,308 m) and Biega (2,790 m), the park has a diverse and abundant fauna. It consists of a smaller eastern sector, covering part of the Mitumba Mountains, and a larger western sector in the central Congo basin. The park was established to protect 200–300 eastern lowland (Grauer's) gorilla occurring mainly in the forests at 2,100–2,400 m, but also in the lower rainforest. The park is also home to other primates including eastern chimpanzee, and numerous Cercopithecinae and Colobinae. Other mammals include elephant, forest hog and many antelope and duiker.
Criteria x Inscribed 1980

• ICHKEUL NATIONAL PARK Tunisia

The Ichkeul lake and wetland are a major stopover point for hundreds of thousands of migrating birds, such as ducks, geese, storks and pink flamingos, who come to feed and nest there. Ichkeul is the last remaining lake in a chain that once extended across North Africa. Due to increased salinity in the lake and marshes, conservation efforts, including a high-quality scientific monitoring programme, have resulted in improved water quality, leading towards the restoration of vegetation critical to the functioning of the ecosystem, the gradual return of wintering and breeding birds, and the recovery of fish populations.
Criteria x Inscribed 1980

• CHURCH AND DOMINICAN CONVENT OF SANTA MARIA DELLE GRAZIE WITH 'THE LAST SUPPER' BY LEONARDO DA VINCI Italy

Leonardo da Vinci was commissioned in 1495 to paint a mural on the north wall of the refectory in the convent Santa Maria delle Grazie in Milan and finished work in 1497. 'The Last Supper' depicts the moment in John's Gospel (chapter 13, verse 21) immediately after Jesus says, 'One of you will betray me'. In composition, perspective and execution the painting broke with tradition and heralded a new era in art. It was not technically a fresco in that Leonardo worked on dry plaster, sealing the wall and painting in tempera. Within years the painting began to deteriorate and repeated conservation has been carried out.
Criteria i, ii Inscribed 1980

• AKSUM Ethiopia

The ruins of the ancient city of Aksum are close to Ethiopia's northern border. They mark the location of the heart of ancient

The triangular-shaped Kanonia Square contains Warsaw's narrowest house (the yellow house in the corner), built to reduce payment of property tax, which depended on the number of windows and width of the street-facing wall.

A section of the Temple of Hagar Qim, a megalithic temple on the island of Malta.

Renaissance Church and Convent of Santa Maria delle Grazie in Milan is a striking monument, made all the more remarkable by containing da Vinci's masterpiece, 'The Last Supper'.

Ethiopia, when the Kingdom of Aksum was the most powerful state between the Eastern Roman Empire and Persia. The massive ruins, dating from between the first and the thirteenth centuries AD, include giant stone stelae, royal tombs and the ruins of ancient castles. Long after its political decline in the tenth century, Ethiopian emperors continued to be crowned in Aksum.
Criteria: i, iv Inscribed 1980

• FORTIFICATIONS ON THE CARIBBEAN SIDE OF PANAMA: PORTOBELO – SAN LORENZO
Panama

The group of seventeenth- and eighteenth-century fortifications of the Caribbean coast of Panama are magnificent examples of contemporary Spanish colonial military architecture. The forts of Portobelo and San Lorenzo formed part of the defence system of the Spanish Crown to guard the access to the Isthmus of Panama that was crucial to Europe's trade with its colonies. Portobelo's forts, castles, barracks and batteries created a defensive line around its bay and protected the harbour, while the works at San Lorenzo guarded the mouth of the Chagres River. The forts are now in a poor state of preservation.
Criteria: i, iv Inscribed 1980

• SITE OF PALMYRA Syrian Arab Republic

An oasis in the Syrian desert, northeast of Damascus, Palmyra contains the monumental ruins of a great city that was one of the most important cultural centres of the ancient world. In the first and the second centuries, the art and architecture of Palmyra, standing at the crossroads of several civilisations, married Graeco-Roman techniques with local traditions and Persian influences. The city offers the consummate example of an ancient urbanised complex, with its large public monuments such as the Agora, theatre and temples. Alongside these, the residential quarters are preserved, and there are immense cemeteries outside the fortified centre.
Criteria: i, ii, iv Inscribed 1980

• ARCHAEOLOGICAL RUINS AT MOENJODARO
Pakistan

The ruins of the huge city of Moenjodaro – built entirely of unbaked brick in the third millennium BC – lie in the Indus valley. The acropolis, set on high embankments, the ramparts, and the lower town, which is laid out according to strict rules, provide evidence of an early system of town planning. Moenjodaro is the most ancient and best-preserved urban ruin on the Indian subcontinent. It has exercised a considerable influence on the subsequent development of urbanisation on the Indian peninsula.
Criteria: ii, iii Inscribed 1980

• LOWER VALLEY OF THE AWASH Ethiopia

The Awash valley contains one of the most important groupings of palaeontological sites in Africa. The remains found here, the oldest of which date back at least four million years, provide evidence of human evolution which has modified our conception of human history. The most spectacular discovery came in 1974, when fifty-two fragments of a skeleton enabled the famous Lucy to be reconstructed. In life, Lucy would have stood about 1 m tall and weighed 27–30 kg. By dating the deposits in which her fossilised remains were found, she is estimated to have lived 3.18 million years ago.
Criteria: ii, iii, iv Inscribed 1980

• PAPHOS Cyprus

Paphos was a centre of the cult of Aphrodite and of pre-Hellenic fertility deities. According to legend, Aphrodite's birthplace was on this island, and her temple was erected here by the Mycenaeans in the twelfth century BC. The remains of villas, palaces, theatres, fortresses and tombs mean that the site is of exceptional architectural and historic value. The mosaics of Nea Paphos are among the most beautiful in the world. Excavations have also unearthed the spectacular third- to fifth-century mosaics of the Houses of Dionysus, Orpheus and Aion, and the Villa of Theseus.
Criteria: iii, vi Inscribed 1980

Fort Geronimo, Portobelo, one of the Spanish forts built on the Caribbean coast of Panama.

Part of the ruined city of Palmyra which exerted a decisive influence on the evolution of neoclassical architecture and modern urbanisation.

Mosaic floor from the Villa of Theseus at Paphos, depicting Theseus' fight with the minotaur in the labyrinth. The villa dates from the second half of the second century AD and contained 100 rooms.

• REDWOOD NATIONAL PARK USA

Redwood National Park comprises a region of coastal mountains north of San Francisco. It is covered with a forest of coastal redwood trees, the tallest and most impressive trees in the world. The park was established specifically to protect these trees, because it is only here and in Oregon that they now survive. Descendants of the giant evergreens that grew during the age of the dinosaurs, redwoods thrived in moist temperate regions. The park's marine and land life are equally remarkable, in particular the sea lions, the bald eagle and the endangered California brown pelican.

Criteria: vii, ix Inscribed 1980

• RØROS MINING TOWN Norway

Røros is an extensive mining settlement dating from 1644, when copper mining began. Completely rebuilt after its destruction by Swedish troops in 1679, the town has some eighty wooden houses, most of them standing around courtyards. Many retain their dark pitch-log façades, giving the town a medieval appearance. The buildings reflect the dual occupations of the inhabitants – mining and farming – the domestic groups being arranged as compact farmyards. These groups are disposed on a regular urban pattern adapted to the mountain terrain, reflecting the industrial planning introduced by the Danish kings of Norway in the sixteenth and seventeenth centuries.

Criteria: iii, iv, v Inscribed 1980

• TIYA Ethiopia

Tiya is among the most important of approximately 160 archaeological sites discovered so far in the Soddo region, south of Addis Ababa. The site contains thirty-six monuments, including thirty-two carved stelae covered with symbols, most of which are difficult to decipher. The stelae could have had a funerary significance, as there are tombs scattered around the carvings. They are the remains of an ancient Ethiopian culture whose age has not yet been precisely determined.

Criteria: i, iv Inscribed 1980

• LOWER VALLEY OF THE OMO Ethiopia

The lower valley of the Omo is a renowned prehistoric site near Lake Turkana, where *Australopithecine* fossils that have been fundamental in the study of human evolution were discovered. The area is unlike any other place on Earth in that so many different types of people have inhabited such a small area of land over many millennia. It is believed that it was the crossroads where early humans of many different ethnicities passed through. Evidence of the oldest-known humanoid technological activity has been found, as well as stone objects attesting to an encampment of prehistoric human beings that is among the oldest known today.

Criteria: iii, iv Inscribed 1980

• ANCIENT CITY OF BOSRA
Syrian Arab Republic

Bosra, once the capital of the Roman province of Arabia, was an important stopover on the ancient caravan route to Mecca. A Roman theatre, early Christian ruins and several mosques and *madrasas* are found within its great walls. The Roman theatre is enclosed by the walls and square towers of a citadel fortified between 481 and 1231. From outside it could be an Arab fortress, but right at its heart lies this ancient theatre. The cathedral of Bosra, completed in 513, has influenced Christian and, to a lesser extent, Islamic architectural forms. The Mosque of Omar is one of the rare buildings of the first century of the Hegira in Syria.

Criteria: i, iii, vi Inscribed 1980

• AL QAL'A OF BENI HAMMAD Algeria

Al Qal'a of Beni Hammad is situated on the southern flank of the Jebel Maâdid 1,000 m above sea level. It is one of the most precisely dated Islamic complexes and provides an authentic picture of a fortified Muslim city. The Great Mosque is one of the largest in Algeria: its minaret is 25 m high and its prayer room has thirteen aisles with eight bays. The first capital of the Hammadid emirs,

Redwood trees can grow to around 100 m in only a few hundred years. They take 400 years to mature and some are more than 2,000 years old.

The magnificent second-century Roman theatre of Bosra, probably built under Trajan, with room for 15,000 spectators.

it was established in 1007. The city was abandoned in 1090 when it was menaced by a Hilalian invasion, and finally destroyed in 1152 by the Almohads.
Criteria: iii Inscribed 1980

DURMITOR NATIONAL PARK Montenegro

This breathtaking national park was formed by glaciers and is traversed by rivers and underground streams. Along the Tara River canyon, which has the deepest gorges in Europe (1,300 m), the dense pine forests are interspersed with clear lakes. The park comprises the Mount Durmitor plateau and the valley formed by the canyon of the Tara River. Because of its range in altitude, the park is influenced by both Mediterranean and alpine microclimates, resulting in an exceptional range of flora and fauna. Forest fauna includes the brown bear, wolf, wild boar, wild cat, chamois, various species of eagle, capercaillie, black grouse and rock partridge.
Criteria: vii, viii, x Inscribed 1980

HISTORIC TOWN OF OURO PRETO Brazil

Ouro Preto (Black Gold) played a leading role in Brazil's Golden Age in the eighteenth century. It was created by soldiers of fortune eager to exploit local gold deposits; they were followed by many artists who produced works of outstanding quality, such as the Church of São Francisco de Assis. A 'Mining Baroque' style developed which successfully fused Brazilian influences with European Baroque and Rococo. At its centre is Tiradentes Square containing imposing public and private buildings, such as the old Parliament House (1784) and the Palace of the Governors. It became a centre of the movement campaigning against colonial rule known as Inconfidência Mineira.
Criteria: i, iii Inscribed 1980

TAXILA Pakistan

From the ancient Neolithic tumulus of Saraikala to the ramparts of Sirkap (second century BC) and the city of Sirsukh (first century AD), Taxila illustrates the development of a city on the Indus that was influenced by Persia, Greece and Central Asia and which, from the fifth century BC to the second century AD, was an important Buddhist centre of learning that became destinations for pilgrims from as far afield as Central Asia and China. Situated strategically on a branch of the Silk Road that linked China to the West, Taxila flourished economically and culturally.
Criteria: iii, vi Inscribed 1980

BUDDHIST RUINS AT TAKHT-I-BAHI AND NEIGHBOURING CITY REMAINS AT SAHR-I-BAHLOL Pakistan

The Buddhist monastic complex of Takht-i-Bahi (Throne of Origins) was founded in the early first century. Owing to its location on the crest of a high hill, it the best preserved Buddhist monastery in Pakistan. Nearby are the ruins of Sahr-i-Bahlol, a small fortified city dating from the same period. The complex consists of four main groups: the Court of Stupas; the early monastic complex with residential cells around an open court; the temple complex; and the tantric monastic complex with an open courtyard in front of a series of dark cells for mystical meditation, in keeping with tantric practice.
Criteria: iv Inscribed 1980

LOS GLACIARES Argentina

Los Glaciares is the best place in South America to see glaciers in action. Glacial activity is concentrated around two main lakes, Argentino and Viedma. Lake Argentino, 160 km long, is particularly spectacular, with three glaciers dumping their massive blue icebergs into the lake. This vast alpine area includes the Patagonian ice field: at over 14,000 km² it is the largest ice mantle outside Antarctica. It has a total of forty-seven glaciers while a further 200 smaller glaciers are independent of the main ice field. The most impressive wildlife are the birds including swans, ducks, geese and flamingos, while overhead glides the huge Andean condor.
Criteria: vii, viii Inscribed 1981

Black Lake, below the slopes of Mount Durmitor, is the largest and deepest lake in the Durmitor National Park.

Ouro Preto was shaped by grouping together small settlements (arriais), forming an irregular urban layout that follows the contours of the landscape. With the exhaustion of the gold mines in the nineteenth century, the city's influence declined.

In Los Glaciares, the Perito Mereno glacier often advances so far that its snout dams the normal escape stream of Lake Rico. When the glacier retreats in summer a wall of water roars down the valley.

• SERENGETI NATIONAL PARK Tanzania

The vast plains of the Serengeti comprise 15,000 km² of savanna and open woodland. They contain the largest herds of grazing animals in the world and the carnivores that prey on them, providing a wildlife spectacle that is second to none. The annual migration is dominated by wildebeest, gazelles and zebras. The herds are followed by prides of lion numbering up to 3,000 individuals, hyenas and jackals. The great herds are continuously moving but the sight is most impressive in May and June, when millions of animals travel en masse from the central plains to the permanent water holes on the western side of the park.
Criteria: vii, x Inscribed 1981

• PALACE AND PARK OF FONTAINEBLEAU France

Surrounded by an immense and beautiful park, Fontainebleau combines Renaissance and French artistic influences. Fontainebleau was first enlarged and embellished by François I who commissioned artists from Renaissance Italy to begin work in 1528. The painting, stucco work, sculpture and statuary at Fontainebleau gave its name to a style that became influential throughout Europe in the sixteenth and seventeenth centuries. Successive modifications continued until in the nineteenth century the palace complex reached its present layout with five courtyards, arranged irregularly and surrounded by wings of buildings and gardens.
Criteria: ii, vi Inscribed 1981

• RUINS OF KILWA KISIWANI AND RUINS OF SONGO MNARA Tanzania

The remains of two great East African ports are situated on two small islands near the coast. From the thirteenth to the sixteenth century, the merchants of Kilwa dealt in gold, silver, pearls, perfumes, Arabian crockery, Persian earthenware and Chinese porcelain; much of the trade in the Indian Ocean thus passed through their hands. These sites are of prime importance to the understanding of the Swahili culture and the Islamisation of the east coast of Africa. They include the remarkable Great Mosque, constructed in the twelfth century of coral tiles imbedded in a core of puddled clay.
Criteria: iii Inscribed 1981

• OLD CITY OF JERUSALEM AND ITS WALLS Jerusalem (Site proposed by Jordan)

As a holy city for Judaism, Christianity and Islam, Jerusalem has always been of enormous symbolic importance. The First Temple was built on Mount Moriah, or Temple Mount, by King Solomon and was completed in 957 BC. It was destroyed in 586 BC by Nebuchadnezzar II of Babylon. In 515 BC the Second Temple was completed and during the Roman rule, Herod the Great (73–4 BC) enlarged it, the famous Western Wall being part of the supporting structure for the levelled platform on which the temple stood. The Romans destroyed the Second Temple in AD 70. Jerusalem's period of Christian rule, from the fourth century, was one of its most peaceful. Among the Christian shrines was the Church of the Holy Sepulchre, completed in 335, marking the site of the crucifixion, tomb and resurrection of Jesus and the most sacred place in the Christian world. The Arabs captured Jerusalem in 638 and the new rulers commissioned the Dome of the Rock. Close by, the Al-Aqsa Mosque was built between the late seventh and early eighth centuries. Temple Mount became known as the Haram ash-Sharif. In 969 control of the city passed to the Egyptian Arab Fatimids who systematically destroyed all synagogues and churches. Their prohibition on Christian pilgrimage became a contributing cause of the Crusades that culminated in the Christians' capture of Jerusalem in 1099. During the Christian Kingdom, the Church of the Holy Sepulchre was rebuilt, and hospices and monasteries were founded.
Criteria: ii, iii, vi Inscribed 1981

• NIOKOLO-KOBA NATIONAL PARK Senegal

Niokolo-Koba National Park covers almost 10,000 km² of the Guinea savanna of Senegal, with significant areas of bush land and gallery forest along both banks of the upper Gambia River. This varied landscape is home to an incredible range of wildlife, including Derby's eland, an endangered species and the world's largest

Larger mammals of the Serengeti include giraffe, leopard, cheetah, African elephant, black rhino and hippopotamus. Smaller mammals include, bushbaby, monkey, baboon, aardvark, hare, porcupine, fox and mongoose.

Standing at the heart of a vast forest in the Île-de-France, Fontainebleau was transformed from a medieval royal hunting lodge into a dazzling Italianate palace that became one of the most important sites of the French court.

The golden-domed building is the Dome of the Rock. Intended as a shrine rather than a mosque, it was completed around 691 and is one of the most ancient Islamic buildings in existence. *Old city of Jerusalem*

antelope. Other important species include chimpanzee, leopard, dwarf crocodile and hippopotamus. The park is the last refuge in Senegal for giraffe and elephant, of which there is a large population. Niokolo-Koba demonstrates the key aspects of the Guinea savanna ecosystem.
Criteria: x Inscribed 1981

•AMIENS CATHEDRAL France
The building of Amiens Cathedral, in the heart of Picardy, began in 1220, two years after its Romanesque predecessor was destroyed by fire. Its builders used the technical knowledge of other church builders to construct their cathedral quickly, resulting in a uniform style that is very rare: the nave, the largest part of the church, was completed in 1245. The great height of the cathedral and its design allow in an exceptional amount of light. From 1292 to 1375 the cathedral was enhanced by a series of chapels built between the buttresses of the side aisles. This style of the seven radiating chapels became a model for other cathedrals.
Criteria: i, ii Inscribed 1981

•HEAD-SMASHED-IN BUFFALO JUMP Canada
Among the many buffalo hunting techniques of the Plains Peoples, the Buffalo Jump was perhaps the most effective. A bison herd was enticed towards the cliff edge by 'buffalo runners', dressed in the skins of calves and imitating the sound of a calf separated from its mother. The lead buffalo were forced over the precipice by the pressure of the herd racing behind. In a typical hunt, dozens of animals were killed in the fall from the cliff or by the weapons of the hunters waiting below. It was first used around 3600 BC and was still being used as late as 1850.
Criteria: vi Inscribed 1981

•HISTORIC MONUMENTS AT MAKLI, THATTA
Pakistan
The capital of three successive dynasties and later ruled by the Mughal emperors of Delhi, Thatta was constantly embellished from the fourteenth to the eighteenth century. It provides a unique view of civilisation in Sind. The site preserves an imposing monumental complex, with the remains of the city itself in the valley and those of the necropolis at the edge of the Makli plateau. The Grand Mosque of Shah Jahan, with its complex of blue and white buildings capped by ninety-three domes, is outstanding.
Criteria: iii Inscribed 1981

•MEDINA OF FEZ Morocco
The Medina of Fez, a jewel of Spanish-Arabic civilisation, is densely packed with monuments – madrasas, fondouks (shops), palaces, residences, mosques and fountains. Founded in the ninth century and home to the oldest university in the world, Fez el Bali (the name of the old city) has two distinct centres on the right and left banks of the river Fez, settled by Arab refugees from Córdoba in Spain and from Kairouan (in modern-day Tunisia). In the fourteenth century a Jewish quarter, the Mellah, was joined to the newly founded city. The principal monuments in the Medina date from this period.
Criteria: ii, v Inscribed 1981

•ROMAN THEATRE AND ITS SURROUNDINGS AND THE 'TRIUMPHAL ARCH' OF ORANGE
France
Situated in the Rhône valley, the ancient theatre of Orange, with its 103 m-long façade, is one of the best preserved of all the great Roman theatres. The theatre was closed by imperial command in 391 and it was abandoned and later sacked and pillaged by barbarians. It was only in the nineteenth century that it slowly recovered its original splendour, thanks to the restoration work begun in 1825. The Roman Triumphal Arch is located to the north of the town.
Criteria: iii, vi Inscribed 1981

•CISTERCIAN ABBEY OF FONTENAY France
Fontenay Abbey is located in northern Burgundy. It was founded by St Bernard in 1119 and built from 1130 onwards, making it one of the

The western façade of Amiens Cathedral, which is flanked by two square towers without spires, has three portals decorated with the elaborate statuary for which the cathedral is famous (the central portal is shown here).

The Triumphal Arch of Orange is one of the most beautiful examples of a provincial 'triumphal arch' from the reign of Augustus. It is decorated with low reliefs commemorating the establishment of the Pax Romana.

oldest Cistercian monasteries in Europe. With its church, cloister, refectory, sleeping quarters, bakery, and ironworks, it is an excellent illustration of the ideal of self-sufficiency practised by the earliest communities of Cistercian monks. The forge, dated to the end of the twelfth century, is one of the oldest industrial buildings in France. Despite changes in the thirteenth, fifteenth and sixteenth centuries, the abbey has the appearance of a generally authentic and well-preserved whole.

Criteria: iv Inscribed 1981

● DJOUDJ NATIONAL BIRD SANCTUARY Senegal

Situated in the Senegal River delta, the Djoudj Sanctuary is a wetland of 160 km², comprising a large lake surrounded by streams, ponds and backwaters. It forms a fragile sanctuary for some 1.5 million birds, such as the white pelican, the purple heron, the African spoonbill, the great egret and the cormorant. The park is also one of the first sources of fresh water for more than three million migrant birds after crossing 2,000 km of the Sahara. The waters also hold populations of crocodile and African manatee.

Criteria: vii, x Inscribed 1981

● GREAT BARRIER REEF Australia

The Great Barrier Reef is the world's most extensive stretch of coral reefs. The great diversity of its fauna reflects the maturity of an ecosystem that has evolved over millions of years on the northeast continental shelf of Australia. Extending to Papua New Guinea, the reef system comprises some 2,900 individual reefs covering more than 20,000 km², including 760 fringing reefs. The reefs range in size from under 0.01 km² to over 100 km² and vary in shape to provide the most spectacular marine scenery on Earth. There are approximately 600 continental islands including many with towering forests and freshwater streams, and some 300 coral cays and unvegetated sand cays. The site contains a huge range of species including over 1,500 species of fish, about 360 species of hard coral and 5,000 species of mollusc, plus a great diversity of sponges, sea anemones, marine worms and crustaceans. About 215 species of birds are found in its islands and cays. The site includes major feeding grounds for the endangered dugong and nesting grounds for four species of marine turtle including the endangered loggerhead turtle.

Criteria: vii, viii, ix, x Inscribed 1981

● FORT AND SHALAMAR GARDENS IN LAHORE Pakistan

The Fort and Shalamar Gardens in Lahore bear exceptional testimony to the Mughal civilisation and have exercised a considerable influence throughout the Indian subcontinent. The first references to Lahore Fort date from before the eleventh century. Destroyed and rebuilt several times by the Mughals, the current fort was rebuilt from the reign of Emperor Akbar (1542–1605) onwards for more than two centuries. The complex of fairytale-like buildings surrounding the Court of Shah Jahan, and especially the Shah Burj or Shish Mahal, built in 1631–2, sparkle with mosaics of glass, gilt, semi-precious stones and marble screening.

Criteria: i, ii, iii Inscribed 1981

● WILLANDRA LAKES REGION Australia

The Willandra Lakes Region is a unique landmark in the study of human evolution in Australia. The fossil remains from a series of lakes and sand formations that date from the Pleistocene (2.5 million to 5,000 years ago) can be found in this region, together with archaeological evidence of human occupation dating from 45–60,000 years ago. Fossils of giant marsupials and other animals, some of which are now extinct, have also been found here. The site includes the entire lake and river system from Lake Mulurulu, the latest to hold water, to the Prungle Lakes, dry for more than 15,000 years.

Criteria: iii, viii Inscribed 1981

● MAMMOTH CAVE NATIONAL PARK USA

Mammoth Cave National Park, located in Kentucky, has the world's largest network of natural limestone caves and underground

The Great Barrier Reef viewed from above. The form and structure of the individual reefs show great variety. There are two main classes: radial platform or patch reefs and elongated wall reefs.

A clown fish, one of over 1,500 species of fish found in the Great Barrier Reef.

Lake Mungo Lunette in the Willandra Lakes Region. Erosion of this dune has exposed extensive evidence of Aboriginal occupation over the millennia.

passageways, carved out by the Green River and its tributaries. The park and its underground network of more than 560 km of surveyed passageways is the most extensive and diverse cave ecosystem in the world, with over 200 species indigenous to the network of caves, and forty-two species adapted to life in total darkness. Surface features are also important and Big Woods, a temperate deciduous oak-hickory dominated forest, is one of the largest and best remaining examples of the ancient forests of eastern North America.
Criteria: vii, viii, x Inscribed 1981

▪ MOUNT NIMBA STRICT NATURE RESERVE
Côte d'Ivoire and Guinea
Located on the borders of Guinea, Liberia and Côte d'Ivoire, Mount Nimba rises above the surrounding savanna. Its slopes are covered by dense forest at the foot of grassy mountain pastures. They harbour an especially rich flora and fauna, with more than 200 endemic species such as the viviparous toad, chimpanzees that use stones as tools, multiple types of duikers, big cats and civets.
Criteria: ix, x Inscribed 1981

▪ KAKADU NATIONAL PARK Australia
This spectacular cultural landscape has been cared for continuously by Aboriginal Bininj/Mungguy for more than 50,000 years. They believe that during the creation time, their ancestors or *Nayahunggi*, created the landforms, plants, and animals and left language, ceremonies, kinship, and rules to live by. The park encompasses soaring sandstone escarpment, floodplains, monsoon forests, savanna woodlands and tidal flats. These habitats support a wide range of rare plant and animal species, some of which are found nowhere else in the world. Wet season rains create a vast shallow sea, where ducks, geese and wading birds abound. As the floodplains start to dry, these waterbirds congregate around the permanent rivers and billabongs.
Criteria: i, vi, vii, ix, x Inscribed 1981

▪ OLYMPIC NATIONAL PARK USA
Renowned for the diversity of its ecosystems, Olympic National Park contains glacier-clad peaks interspersed with alpine meadows surrounded by temperate rainforest. The park is divided into two segments: a mountainous core and a separate coastal strip. The mountains contain about sixty active glaciers; the area is unique because it is the lowest latitude in the world at which glaciers begin, at an elevation lower than 2,000 m. The 80-km coastal strip of wilderness beach is characterised by rocky headlands and a wealth of intertidal life, and the arches, caves and buttresses are evidence of the continuous battering of the waves.
Criteria: vii, ix Inscribed 1981

▪ SPEYER CATHEDRAL Germany
Speyer Cathedral exerted a considerable influence on the development of Romanesque architecture in the eleventh and twelfth centuries, and also on the evolution of the principles of building restoration in Europe and in the world from the eighteenth century to the present. A basilica with four towers and two domes, it was founded by Conrad II in 1030 and remodelled at the end of the eleventh century. It is one of the most important Romanesque monuments from the time of the Holy Roman Empire. The cathedral was the burial place of the German emperors for almost 300 years.
Criteria: ii Inscribed 1981

▪ DARIEN NATIONAL PARK Panama
Forming a land-bridge between the Central and South American continents, Darien National Park contains an exceptional variety of habitats – sandy beaches, rocky coasts, mangroves, swamps, and lowland and upland tropical forests – containing remarkable wildlife. The area is both anthropologically and historically rich, with two major indigenous groups – Chocó and Kuna Indians – and a number of smaller groups still living by traditional practices. The park's remarkably varied fauna is largely unstudied and includes bush dog, giant anteater, jaguar, ocelot, capybara and howler monkey. Harpy eagles are also found, as are cayman and American crocodile.
Criteria: vii, ix, x Inscribed 1981

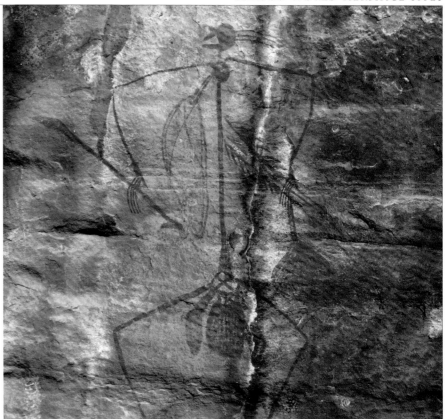

Kakadu's rock art and archaeological sites record the way of life of the region's inhabitants, from the hunter-gatherers of prehistoric times to the Aboriginal people living there today.

The temperate rainforest of the Olympic National Park is dominated by conifers. The coniferous forest of Pacific northwest is of prime commercial interest and practically all the original forest outside the park has been harvested.

• WÜRZBURG RESIDENCE WITH THE COURT GARDENS AND RESIDENCE SQUARE Germany

This magnificent Baroque palace – one of the largest and most beautiful in Germany – was created under the patronage of the Prince-Bishops of Schönborn and was home to one of the most brilliant courts of Europe during the eighteenth century. The main part of the Residence was built between 1720 and 1744 and decorated internally between 1740 and 1770. The plans were supervised by the official architect of the Prince Bishop, Balthasar Neumann. Sculptors and stucco-workers came from Italy, Flanders and Munich. The Venetian painter Giovanni Battista Tiepolo decorated the staircase and the walls of the Imperial Hall with frescoes.
Criteria: i, iv Inscribed 1981

• ARCHAEOLOGICAL PARK AND RUINS OF QUIRIGUA Guatemala

Quirigua's monumental Mayan complexes are remarkable for their elaborate system of pyramids, terraces, and staircases. The ruins contain some outstanding eighth-century monuments and an impressive series of carved stelae that were the principal written chronicles of this lost civilisation, as well as the key to their highly advanced calendar system. Quirigua's huge stone monolithic sculptures were carved without the benefit of metal tools as stone chisels were the only tools available. Inhabited since the second century AD, by the reign of Cauac Sky (723–84), Quirigua was the capital of a prosperous state, built on the extraction of jade and obsidian in the upper valley of the Rio Motagua.
Criteria: i, ii, iv Inscribed 1981

• ARLES, ROMAN AND ROMANESQUE MONUMENTS France

Arles has some impressive Roman monuments, of which the earliest – the arena, the theatre and the *cryptoporticus* (subterranean galleries) – date back to the first century BC. The Roman theatre could hold 10,000 people, and the arena 20,000 spectators. Gladiator fights and animal hunts took place here until the end of the fifth century. During the fourth century Arles experienced a second golden age, as attested by the Baths of Constantine and the necropolis of Les Alyscamps. In the eleventh and twelfth centuries, Arles once again became one of the most attractive cities in the Mediterranean.
Criteria: ii, iv Inscribed 1981

• SGANG GWAAY Canada

The village of Nan Sdins is on SGang Gwaay (Anthony Island) in the Queen Charlotte Islands (Haida Gwaii) of British Columbia. The Haida people lived here for thousands of years, until disease forced its abandonment in the 1880s. Most of the village has returned to the forest. What is left is unique: remains of a nineteenth-century Haida village where the remnants of twenty-three houses and thirty-two memorial or mortuary poles depict a rich and flamboyant society. The protected area epitomises the rugged beauty of the Pacific coast, and commemorates the culture of the Haida people and their relationship to the land and sea.
Criteria: iii Inscribed 1981

• ALDABRA ATOLL Seychelles

The Aldabra Atoll comprises four large coral islands which enclose a shallow lagoon; the group of islands is itself surrounded by a coral reef. Due to difficulties of access and the atoll's isolation, Aldabra has been protected from human influence and thus retains the world's largest population of giant tortoises. Aldabra is the least-disturbed large island in the Indian Ocean and the only place in the world where a reptile is the dominant herbivore. The only endemic mammal is a flying fox.
Criteria: vii, ix, x Inscribed 1982

• HISTORIC CENTRE OF FLORENCE Italy

Florence is the symbol and cradle of the Renaissance and its 600 years of extraordinary artistic activity can be seen in a wealth of buildings and artefacts, especially the cathedral Santa Maria del Fiore (the Duomo), the church of Santa Croce, the Uffizi Gallery and the

Tiepolo painted the staircase vault of the Würzburg Residence with a fresco that included the portraits of those responsible for the design.

The Duomo dominates the Florence skyline. The dome was designed by Filippo Brunelleschi and completed in 1436, while the campanile was designed by Giotto in 1334 and completed in 1359.

Medicis' Pitti Palace, now a gallery with paintings by great masters such as Giotto, Brunelleschi, Botticelli and Michelangelo. Founded in 59 BC as a Roman colony known as Florentia, the free commune of Florence gained supremacy over rival towns in Tuscany until, under the powerful Medici family, its rulers in the fifteenth and sixteenth centuries, Florence exerted a major influence on the development of architecture and the monumental arts throughout Europe.
Criteria: i, ii, iii, iv, vi Inscribed 1982

▪ SELOUS GAME RESERVE Tanzania
The Selous Game Reserve is one of the largest wildlife reserves in the world (50,000 km²). It is noted for the range of its wildlife – large numbers of elephant, black rhinoceros, cheetah, giraffe, impala, hippopotamus and crocodile – and for its remoteness. The reserve has a variety of vegetation zones, ranging from dense thickets to open wooded grasslands. The deciduous miombo woodland is dominant and has a higher density and species diversity than any other miombo woodland, thanks to its size, the diversity of its habitats, the availability of food and water, and the lack of human settlement.
Criteria: ix, x Inscribed 1982

▪ LORD HOWE ISLAND GROUP Australia
A remarkable example of isolated oceanic islands, born of volcanic activity more than 2,000 m under the sea, the Lord Howe Island Group boasts exceptional variety of landscapes within a small area. The sheer slopes of its volcanic mountains and the dramatic rock formation, Ball's Pyramid, rise out of an underwater world that is one of the most beautiful in the world. Its isolation at the junction of tropical and temperate latitudes has led to tremendous biodiversity. This islands are one of the major breeding sites for seabirds in the southwest Pacific and contain numerous endemic species of flora and fauna.
Criteria: vii, x Inscribed 1982

▪ ARCHAEOLOGICAL SITE OF CYRENE
Libyan Arab Jamahiriya
A colony of the Greeks of Thera, Cyrene was one of the principal cities in the Hellenic world. It was Romanised and remained a great capital until the earthquake of AD 365. The site contains three monumental complexes, the sanctuary of Apollo, the Acropolis and the Agora, and also has a necropolis complex which is among the most extensive and varied of the ancient world. Once given by Mark Anthony to Cleopatra, myths, legends and stories about Cyrene have been woven over more than 1,000 years.
Criteria: ii, iii, vi Inscribed 1982

▪ SACRED CITY OF ANURADHAPURA
Sri Lanka
Anuradhapura, a political and religious capital that flourished for 1,300 years, is a principal shrine of Buddhism. Founded in the fourth century BC, Anuradhapura has remarkable monuments, particularly the huge dagabas (relic chambers), palaces and monasteries. A cutting from the 'tree of enlightenment', under which the Buddha gained enlightenment, was brought here in the third century BC. This bodhi tree now spreads out over the centre of the site from a sanctuary near the Brazen Palace. The city was attacked by waves of invaders from southern India and, in 933, was abandoned to the jungle.
Criteria: ii, iii, vi Inscribed 1982

▪ TAÏ NATIONAL PARK Côte d'Ivoire
The park is one of the last remaining portions of the vast forest that once stretched across Ghana, Côte d'Ivoire, Liberia and Sierra Leone, and is the largest island of forest remaining in West Africa. Its rich natural flora, and threatened mammal species, such as the pygmy hippopotamus and eleven species of monkeys, are of great scientific interest. There is a gradation from north to south, with the southern third of the park being the moistest area. Vegetation is predominantly dense evergreen forest characterised by tall trees (40–60 m) with massive trunks. Plants thought to be extinct, such as *Amorphophallus staudtii*, have been discovered in the area.
Criteria: vii, x Inscribed 1982

Impalas in the Selous Game Reserve in Tanzania.

The Temple of Zeus at Cyrene, one of the most impressive complexes of ruins in the world.

Jetavanaramaya dagaba at Anuradhapura. A dagaba is a relic chamber, typically set on circular foundations and surrounded by a ring of monolithic columns, much like Sinhalese stupas.

• NATIONAL HISTORY PARK – CITADEL, SANS SOUCI, RAMIERS Haiti

These Haitian monuments date from the beginning of the nineteenth century, when Haiti proclaimed its independence. The Palace of Sans Souci, the buildings at Ramiers and, especially, the Citadelle Henry serve as universal symbols of liberty, as they were the first to be built by black slaves who had gained their freedom. The Citadelle, constructed at an altitude of 970 m, is one of the best examples of early nineteenth-century military engineering. It was designed specifically to allow an integrated use of artillery; an elaborate system of cisterns supplied water; and colossal defensive walls rendered it impregnable. It can shelter a garrison of up to 5,000 men.
Criteria: iv, vi Inscribed 1982

• ANCIENT CITY OF POLONNARUWA Sri Lanka

Polonnaruwa was the immense new capital of the megalomaniac sovereign, Parakramabahu I, in the twelfth century. He created within the boundary walls a garden city, where palaces and sanctuaries prolonged the enchantment of the countryside. This required the construction of a series of sophisticated irrigation systems that are still used today. In addition, he built the Lankatilaka, an enormous brick structure which has preserved a colossal image of Buddha; and the Gal Vihara, with its gigantic rock sculptures which is among the masterpieces of Sinhalese art. Polonnaruwa also contains the Brahmanic monuments built in the eleventh century by the Chola invaders from southern India.
Criteria: i, iii, vi Inscribed 1982

• TIPASA Algeria

Tipasa was an ancient Punic trading port conquered by Rome and turned into a strategic base for the conquest of the kingdoms of Mauritania. It comprises Phoenician, Roman and Christian ruins alongside indigenous monuments such as the Kbor er Roumia, the great royal mausoleum of Mauritania. The oldest Roman settlement is in the centre of the city on a steep slope. The impressive ruins of the civic buildings are set within a dense network of houses (many decorated with paintings and mosaics), warehouses, and industrial establishments of the second and third centuries. Of the numerous Christian religious buildings, the immense fourth-century, seven-aisled basilica is particularly striking.
Criteria: iii, iv Inscribed 1982

• RÍO PLÁTANO BIOSPHERE RESERVE Honduras

Situated in the Mosquita region of northeast Honduras, the reserve protects virtually the entire watershed of the 100 km-long Plátano River, as well as major portions of the Paulaya, Guampu and Sicre rivers. These three waterways, together with the Caribbean, form the boundaries of the reserve, which is the largest surviving area of virgin tropical rainforest in Honduras. Its varied topography ranges from mountains and waterfalls to placid coastal lagoons. The site includes both Ciudad Blanca (White City), one of the most important Mayan archaeological sites, and the place where Christopher Columbus first landed in the Americas in 1492.
Criteria: vii, viii, ix, x Inscribed 1982

• OLD HAVANA AND ITS FORTIFICATIONS Cuba

Havana was the last city the Spanish conquistadors founded in Cuba and is the finest surviving Spanish complex in the Americas. Established in 1519, by 1550 it was the most important city on the island. It became one of the Caribbean's main shipbuilding centres and has been Cuba's capital since 1607. The modern-day city is a large metropolis but its old centre retains an interesting mix of Baroque and neoclassical monuments, and a homogeneous ensemble of private houses with arcades, balconies, wrought-iron gates and internal courtyards. Spain fortified the city in the 1760s when Europe's Seven Years' War spilled over into the Americas.
Criteria: iv, v Inscribed 1982

• TASSILI N'AJJER Algeria

Tassili, a mountainous region in the centre of the Sahara, is a strange landscape of deep gorges, dry river beds and 'stone forests'.

A carving of Buddha at Polonnaruwa. After its golden age in the twelfth century, the city declined until government finally moved to Kurunegala at the end of the thirteenth century.

The Castillo de la Real Fuerza in Havana is the oldest extant colonial fortress in the Americas: its west tower is crowned by a bronze weathervane dating back to 1632.

During the prehistoric period Tassili had a very different climate, with abundant game, regular rainfall and fertile land. The plants and animals found here bear witness to former wetter periods, including, until the 1940s, the dwarf Saharan crocodile. In 1933 one of the most important groupings of prehistoric cave art in the world was discovered here. More than 15,000 drawings and engravings record the climatic changes, the animal migrations and the evolution of human life on the edge of the Sahara from 6000 BC to the first centuries AD.
Criteria: i, iii, vii, viii Inscribed 1982

• TASMANIAN WILDERNESS Australia

Covering 13,800 km², the Tasmanian Wilderness contains some of the last expanses of temperate rainforest in the southern hemisphere. It comprises a vest network of reserved lands that extends over much of southwestern Tasmania, including several coastal islands. Glacial erosion and other geomorphological processes have contributed to spectacular landforms and the area contains rocks from almost every geological period. The isolation of the Tasmanian Wilderness has contributed to the uniqueness of its flora and fauna, which includes some of the world's longest-lived trees and largest carnivorous marsupials. Remains found in limestone caves attest to human occupation for at least 35,000 years through periods of great climatic variation.
Criteria: iii, iv, vi, vii, viii, ix, x Inscribed 1982

• M'ZAB VALLEY Algeria

The five *ksour* (fortified cities) in the M'Zab valley are miniature citadels encircled by walls and dominated by a mosque, whose minaret functioned as a watchtower. The mosque, with its arsenal and grain stores, was conceived as a fortress, the last bastion of resistance in the event of a siege. Simple and functional, they date from the tenth century. The pattern of the life in the M'Zab Valley included a seasonal migration of the population to the palm groves, where the 'summer cities' were marked by a looser organization. The settlement of the M'Zab Valley has exerted considerable influence on modern architects and city planners.
Criteria: ii, iii, v Inscribed 1982

• DJÉMILA Algeria

Situated 900 m above sea level, Djémila, or Cuicul, is one of the world's most beautiful Roman ruins. The classic Roman urban plan was adapted to the physical constraints of the site: at both ends of the *cardo maximus*, the backbone of the city, are two gates. In the centre is the forum, an enclosed square surrounded by public buildings. Aristocratic dwellings set with rich mosaics multiplied here in the second century AD. At the same time the city expanded to the south, where a new quarter, rich in public buildings (including two Christian basilicas and a baptistery) and private dwellings, was established.
Criteria: iii, iv Inscribed 1982

• ARCHAEOLOGICAL SITE OF LEPTIS MAGNA
Libyan Arab Jamahiriya (Libya)

Leptis Magna was one of the most beautiful cities of the Roman Empire, with its imposing public monuments, harbour, marketplace and residential districts. It was enlarged and embellished by Septimius Severus, who was born there and later became emperor. The forum, basilica and Severan arch rank among the foremost examples of a new Roman art, strongly influenced by African and Eastern traditions. Pillaged from the fourth century and reconquered by the Byzantines, it succumbed to the second wave of Arab invasion, that of the Hilians, in the eleventh century, and became buried under drifting sands.
Criteria: i, ii, iii Inscribed 1982

• TIMGAD Algeria

Timgad, which lies on the northern slopes of the Aurès mountains, is a consummate example of a Roman military colony created by Emperor Trajan in AD 100. With its square enclosure measuring 355 m on each side and its precise design based on the *cardo* and

The Liffey Falls in the Tasmanian Wilderness. Tasmania was cut off from mainland Australia by the flooding of the Bass Strait approximately 8,000 years ago, thereby isolating Tasmanian Aborigines for some 500 generations.

The theatre at Leptis Magna with the ruins of the market, the forum and the harbour in the background.

decumanus (the two perpendicular routes running through the city), it is an excellent example of Roman town planning at its height. Large public buildings in the south of the city include the forum, temples, a theatre with a seating capacity of 3,500, a market and baths. In the northeast, there are other baths and a public library.
Criteria: ii, iii, iv Inscribed 1982

• ARCHAEOLOGICAL SITE OF SABRATHA
Libyan Arab Jamahiriya (Libya)

A Phoenician trading post that served as an outlet for the products of the African hinterland, Sabratha was part of the short-lived Numidian kingdom of Massinissa before being Romanised and rebuilt in the second and third centuries AD. The spectacular ruins highlight its wealth in Roman times, which saw the construction of grandiose monuments, of which the most renowned is the theatre, probably built during the reign of the Emperor Commodus (AD 161–192), with a capacity of 5,000 seats. Near the theatre stands the amphitheatre, and other monuments include the temples of Liber Pater, Serapis, Hercules and Isis, the Basilica of Justinian and the Capitolium.
Criteria: iii Inscribed 1982

• HISTORIC CENTRE OF THE TOWN OF OLINDA
Brazil

Founded in 1537 by the Portuguese, the town's history is linked to the sugar cane industry. Rebuilt after being looted by the Dutch, its basic urban fabric dates from the eighteenth century. The balance between the buildings, gardens, Baroque churches, convents and numerous small *passos* (chapels) all contribute to Olinda's particular charm. Among the more important of the eighteenth-century buildings are the Episcopal Church, the Jesuit College and Church (now the Church of Graça), and the Franciscan, Carmelite, Benedictine monasteries. The refined décor of these Baroque buildings contrasts with the simplicity of the houses, which are painted in vivid colours or faced with ceramic tiles.
Criteria: ii, iv Inscribed 1982

• CAHOKIA MOUNDS STATE HISTORIC SITE
USA

Cahokia Mounds, northeast of St Louis, Missouri, is the largest pre-Columbian settlement north of Mexico. It was occupied primarily during the Mississippian period 800–1400, when it covered nearly 16 km² and included some 120 earthwork mounds. It is a striking example of a complex chiefdom society, with satellite mound centres and numerous outlying hamlets and villages. This agricultural society may have had a population of up to 20,000 at its peak between 1050 and 1150. The site includes Monks Mound, the largest prehistoric earthwork in the Americas, standing 30 m high.
Criteria: iii, iv Inscribed 1982

• ANCIENT CITY OF SIGIRIYA Sri Lanka

The ruins of Sigiriya, the capital built by the parricidal King Kassapa I (477–95), lie on the steep slopes and at the summit of a granite peak, the 'Lion's Rock'. A series of galleries and staircases emerging from the mouth of a gigantic lion constructed of bricks and plaster provide access to the site. The 'Sigiriya graffiti' are poems inscribed on the rock, and are among the most ancient texts in the Sinhalese language. They show the considerable influence exerted by the city on the literature and thought of ancient Ceylon.
Criteria: ii, iii, iv Inscribed 1982

• OLD WALLED CITY OF SHIBAM Yemen

Shibam is built on a hillock, which has allowed it to escape the devastating floods of Wadi Hadramaut. Its plan is almost rectangular; and it is enclosed by earthen walls within which blocks of dwellings, built from *unfired clay blocks*, have been laid out on a grid. The tallest house is eight storeys and the average is five. The buildings for the most part date from the sixteenth century. However, some older houses and large buildings still remain from the first centuries of Islam, such as the Friday Mosque, built in 904, and the castle, built in 1220.
Criteria: iii, iv, v Inscribed 1982

The Roman theatre at Sabratha. The best conserved part is the *frons scena*, at the back of the stage, which has been reconstructed with original fragments and is divided into three levels with overlapping marble columns.

The Convent do Carmo is one of many outstanding buildings in Olinda – a city much appreciated by artists – that has been restored in recent years.

The sixteenth-century city of Shibam is one of the oldest and best examples of urban planning based on the principle of vertical construction, giving the city the nickname of 'the Manhattan of the desert'.

The Ajanta Caves, dating from the second century BC, are cut into hillside rock. They were abandoned in AD 650 and were forgotten until their rediscovery by a British tiger-hunting party in 1819.

• FROM THE GREAT SALTWORKS OF SALINS-LES-BAINS TO THE ROYAL SALTWORKS OF ARC-ET-SENANS, THE PRODUCTION OF OPEN-PAN SALT France

The Great Saltworks of Salins-les-Bains, where brine has been extracted since the Middle Ages, has three buildings above ground: salt stores, the Amont well building and a former dwelling. It is linked to the Royal Saltworks of Arc-et-Senans, a factory designed with the same sense of architectural quality as a palace. Located near Besançon, the Royal Saltworks was designed by Claude-Nicolas Ledoux. This vast semicircular complex was designed to permit a rational and hierarchical organisation of work, but the building of an ideal city, the city of Choux, was never realised.

Criteria: i, ii, iv Inscribed 1982

• AJANTA CAVES India

The Ajanta Caves, situated 100 km northeast of Ellora, are cut into the volcanic lava of the Deccan in the forest ravines of the Sahyadri Hills and are set in beautiful wooded surroundings. They contain carvings that depict the life of Buddha, and these carvings and sculptures are considered to mark the beginning of classical Indian art. The twenty-nine caves were first excavated around 200 BC and work went on for several hundred years until they were abandoned in AD 650 in favour of another site of cave monuments, at Ellora. Five of the Ajanta caves were temples, and twenty-four were monasteries.

Criteria: i, ii, iii, vi Inscribed 1983

• COMOÉ NATIONAL PARK Côte d'Ivoire

One of the largest protected areas in West Africa, the park comprises the land between the Comoé and Volta rivers, with a mean altitude of 250–300 m and a series of ridges rising to 600 m. The Comoé and its tributaries form the principal drainage; the river runs through the park for 230 km. Due to the presence of the Comoé, the park contains plants which are normally found only much farther south, such as shrub savannas and patches of thick rainforest. Its remarkable variety of habitats supports many mammal species, including eleven species of monkey.

Criteria: ix, x Inscribed 1983

• TAJ MAHAL India

An immense mausoleum of white marble, the Taj Mahal was built in Agra between 1631 and 1648 by order of the Mughal emperor Shah Jahan in memory of his third and favourite wife, Mumtaz Mahal, who died in 1631. The Taj Mahal stands at the northern end of the garden on a square platform in a chequerboard design topped by a huge white marble terrace. At the corners are four minarets. The *rauza*, the mausoleum itself, is square with bevelled corners. Each corner has a small dome while in the centre the main double dome is topped by a brass finial. The main chamber inside is octagonal with a high domed ceiling. This chamber contains false tombs of Mumtaz and Shah Jahan, both inlaid with precious stones. The architectural precision is balanced by the delicate white marble decoration of floral arabesques, decorative bands and calligraphic inscriptions.

Criteria: i Inscribed 1983

• BENEDICTINE CONVENT OF ST JOHN AT MÜSTAIR Switzerland

In the church of the Convent of Müstair, which stands in a valley in the Grisons, there are frescoes from the Carolingian period (c. 800), now recognised as the most important cycle of painting from this time, and from the Romanesque period (c. 1150–70). These figurative paintings (scenes from the Old and New Testaments) are of a fine aesthetic quality and are particularly important in understanding the evolution of certain Christian iconographic themes, such as the Last Judgement. Other precious artworks include stucco statues and reliefs from the eleventh century.

Criteria: iii Inscribed 1983

• CITY OF CUZCO Peru

Set in a fertile valley high in the Peruvian Andes, Cuzco was the capital of the Incas, the largest civilisation in the Americas before the

Situated on the right bank of the Yamuna River, the Taj Mahal stands in a vast Mughal garden. The unique Mughal style combines elements and styles of Persian, Central Asian and Islamic architecture.

arrival of Europeans. The city developed under its ruler Pachacutec (1438–71) into a complex urban centre with distinct religious and administrative functions. Its sixteenth-century Spanish conquerors preserved its structure while building over its monuments. Of the Inca capital, it preserves impressive vestiges, especially its plan with rectilinear streets within its walls, and the ruins of the Sun Temple. Of the colonial city, there are whitewashed squat houses, the palace and churches with their fusion of Spanish Baroque and Inca influences.
Criteria: iii, iv Inscribed 1983

• OLD CITY OF BERNE Switzerland

The buildings in the walled Old City of Berne, dating from a variety of periods, include fifteenth-century arcades and sixteenth-century fountains. The cathedral (the Münster) was mainly constructed between 1421 and 1575, with the tower added in the nineteenth century. In the seventeenth century, many patrician houses were built from sandy limestone. Like many European capitals, Berne preserves in localised areas, traditional old streets with arcades, the majority of which are pedestrianised. One of Berne's most recognisable symbols is the Zytglogge, the ornately decorated thirteenth-century clocktower with its moving gilded figure striking the hour.
Criteria: iii Inscribed 1983

• JESUIT MISSIONS OF THE GUARANIS: SAN IGNACIO MINÍ, SANTA ANA, NUESTRA SEÑORA DE LORETO AND SANTA MARÍA MAYOR (ARGENTINA), RUINS OF SAÕ MIGUEL DAS MISSÕES (BRAZIL) Argentina and Brazil

These five Jesuit missions were built in the land of the Guaranis during the seventeenth and eighteenth centuries. The ruins of Saõ Miguel das Missões in Brazil and those of San Ignacio Miní, Santa Ana, Nuestra Señora de Loreto and Santa María la Mayor in Argentina lie in the heart of a tropical forest. All these *reducciones* (settlements) are laid out on the same basic model: the church, the residence of the Fathers, and the regularly spaced houses of the Indians are arranged around a large square. However, each has a specific layout and is in a different state of conservation.
Criteria: iv Inscribed 1983

• ELLORA CAVES India

The Ellora Caves not only bear witness to the three great religions of ancient India (Buddhism, Brahminism and Jainism), they also illustrate the spirit of tolerance which permitted these three religions to establish their sanctuaries in a single place. The thirty-four monasteries and temples of Ellora were dug side by side in the wall of a high basalt cliff, not far from Aurangabad, in Maharashtra. The caves, with their uninterrupted sequence of remarkable reliefs, sculptures and architecture, date from AD 600–1000. The Brahmin group are the best known, with the 'Cavern of the Ten Avatars' and especially the Kailasha Temple.
Criteria: i, iii, vi Inscribed 1983

• AGRA FORT India

Near the gardens of the Taj Mahal stands this exquisite sixteenth-century Mughal monument. With its walls of red sandstone rising above a moat, the Agra Fort encloses within its walls the imperial city of the Mughal rulers. It comprises many fairy-tale palaces, such as the Jahangir Palace and the Khas Mahal; audience halls, such as the Diwan-i-Khas; and two very beautiful mosques. Several of the buildings are made from pure marble with beautiful carvings; all of these monuments mark the high point of an Indo-Muslim art strongly marked by influences from Persia.
Criteria: iii Inscribed 1983

• TALAMANCA RANGE-LA AMISTAD RESERVES / LA AMISTAD NATIONAL PARK Costa Rica and Panama

The Cordillera de Talamanca is the highest and wildest non-volcanic mountain range in Central America. The park includes lowland tropical rainforest and cloudforest, and four communities unique in Central America: subalpine paramo forests, pure oak stands, glacial

Founded in the twelfth century on a hill site looped by the Aare River, the historic centre of Berne is dominated by the bell tower of the Münster.

Rock-carved images of Buddha in meditation in cave number twelve at Ellora. From south to north along the cliff are the twelve caves of the Buddhist group then the Brahmin group and finally the Jain group.

Part of the walls of red sandstone at the Agra Fort, one of the most obvious symbols of the Mughal grandeur under Akbar, Jahangir and Shah Jahan.

lakes and high-altitude bogs. There is great species diversity. Signs of tapir are abundant on the Panama side of the border. All Central American wild cats are found including puma, ocelot, jaguarundi, tiger cat and jaguar, as well as the Central American squirrel monkey. The rarely seen green and black high-altitude viper is present. Four different Indian tribes inhabit this property.
Criteria: vii, viii, ix, x Inscribed 1983

• CENTRAL ZONE OF THE TOWN OF ANGRA DO HEROISMO IN THE AZORES Portugal

Angra do Heroismo played a highly significant role in maritime exploration from the fifteenth to the nineteenth century. Situated on the island of Terceira in the Azores archipelago, the site was protected from the prevailing winds by a series of hills and had two natural basins: the Beacon and the Anchorage (Angra) from which the village took its name. The port was an obligatory port of call for fleets from Africa and the Indies. The 400-year-old San Sebastião and San João Baptista fortifications are unique examples of military architecture. Damaged by an earthquake in 1980, Angra is now being restored.
Criteria: iv, vi Inscribed 1983

• MONASTERY OF THE HIERONYMITES AND TOWER OF BELÉM IN LISBON Portugal

Standing at the entrance to Lisbon harbour, the Monastery of the Hieronymites, construction of which began in 1502, exemplifies Portuguese art at its best, with very rich carvings of animals, vegetables, and twining ropes. The nearby Tower of Belém was built around 1514 to commemorate Vasco da Gama's expedition. The cross of the Knights of Christ is repeated on the parapets of this fortress, while the watchtowers that flank it are capped with ribbed cupolas inspired by Islamic architecture. The complex of Belém is one of the most representative monuments to Portuguese power during the time of the Great Discoveries.
Criteria: iii, vi Inscribed 1983

• GREAT SMOKY MOUNTAINS NATIONAL PARK USA

Great Smoky Mountains National Park is of world importance as an example of temperate deciduous hardwood forest. Stretching over more than 2,000 km², the park is home to more than 3,500 plant species, including almost as many species of tree, 130, as in all of Europe. Many endangered animal species are also found there, including probably the greatest variety of salamanders in the world. The dominant topographic feature are the Great Smoky Mountains with sixteen peaks over 1,800 m. The park contains evidence of four pre-Columbian Indian cultures and the first example of primitive agriculture in North America.
Criteria: vii, viii, ix, x Inscribed 1983

• ANCIENT CITY OF NESSEBAR Bulgaria

Situated on a rocky peninsula on the Black Sea, Nessebar has been occupied for over 3,000 years. Originally a Thracian settlement, at the beginning of the sixth century BC, it became a Greek colony. Hellenistic remains include the acropolis, a temple of Apollo, an agora and a wall from the Thracian fortifications. Until its capture by the Turks in 1453, Nessebar was an important Byzantine town. From this period come churches of exceptional quality: for example, the Stara Mitropolia basilica. Its cobbled streets, well-kept medieval churches, and timbered houses from the nineteenth century illustrate its chequered past.
Criteria: iii, iv Inscribed 1983

• LA FORTALEZA AND SAN JUAN NATIONAL HISTORIC SITE IN PUERTO RICO USA

Founded in 1521, San Juan was the second city established by the Spanish in the Americas, and between the fifteenth and nineteenth centuries a series of defensive structures was built to protect the city and the Bay of San Juan. La Fortaleza, completed in 1540, was the first fortification to be built. It served as an arsenal, prison, and residence for the Governor-General of the island. El Morro, from the sixteenth century, and San Cristóbal, from the eighteenth century, are other

The two-storey cloisters of the Monastery of the Hieronymites in Lisbon, showing the ornate carving for which the monastery is renowned.

The walls of Fort San Felipe del Morro (El Morro) in San Juan. This triangular fort has stout walls, carefully planned steps, ramps for moving men and artillery and was defended by more than 400 cannons.

major fortifications. San Juan National Historic Site includes forts, bastions, powder houses, walls and El Cañuelo Fort, located on the Isla de Cabras at the western end of San Juan Bay.

Criteria: vi Inscribed 1983

▪ SREBARNA NATURE RESERVE Bulgaria

The Srebarna Nature Reserve is a freshwater lake adjacent to the Danube and extending over 6 km². The reserve was set up primarily to protect the rich diversity of wildfowl, which represent half of all Bulgarian bird species. It is the breeding ground of almost a hundred species of bird, many of which are rare or endangered. Some eighty other bird species migrate and seek refuge there every winter. Reeds occupy two-thirds of the reserve and form a thick barrier around the lake. They form reed-mace islands which birds use for nesting.

Criteria: x Inscribed 1983

▪ ABBEY CHURCH OF SAINT-SAVIN SUR GARTEMPE France

Known as the 'Romanesque Sistine Chapel', the Abbey Church of Saint-Savin contains many beautiful eleventh- and twelfth-century murals which are in a remarkable state of preservation. During the reign of Charlemagne the bodies of two martyrs, Savin and Cyprian, were discovered by Baidilius, Abbot of Marmoutier, who ordered a church built to shelter the holy remains. By coincidence, Charlemagne decided to have a castle erected next to the sanctuary. Because the abbey was sheltered by the castle it escaped pillage from the Viking raids. The beautifully proportioned building primarily dates to the end of the eleventh century.

Criteria: i, iii Inscribed 1983

▪ PLACE STANISLAS, PLACE DE LA CARRIÈRE AND PLACE D'ALLIANCE IN NANCY France

These three squares in Nancy formed a carefully conceived project that succeeded in creating a capital that not only enhanced the sovereign's prestige but was also functional. The foundation stone of the first building in the square was officially laid in March 1752 and the royal square solemnly inaugurated in November 1755. In addition to some prestigious architecture conceived to exalt a sovereign with triumphal arches, statues, and fountains, the project provided the public with three squares that gave access to the town hall, the courts of law, and the Palais des Fermes as well as to other public buildings.

Criteria: i, iv Inscribed 1983

▪ SANGAY NATIONAL PARK Ecuador

Sangay National Park is in the Cordillera Oriental region of the Andes in central Ecuador and includes two active volcanoes, Tungurahua (5,016 m) and Sangay (5,230 m). The park's ecosystems range from tropical rainforests to glaciers, with striking contrasts between the snowcapped peaks and the forests of the plains. Major rivers drain eastwards into the Amazon Basin and there are numerous waterfalls, especially in the hanging valleys of the glaciated zone and along the eastern edge of the Cordillera. The area's isolation has encouraged the survival of indigenous species such as the mountain tapir and the Andean condor.

Criteria: vii, viii, ix, x Inscribed 1983

▪ WOOD BUFFALO NATIONAL PARK Canada

Situated in a vast wilderness area, Wood Buffalo was created specifically to protect North American bison, one of the largest free-roaming, self-regulating herds in existence. The park is also the natural nesting place of the whooping crane and contains the world's largest inland delta, located at the mouth of the Peace and Athabasca rivers. The park has four main landscape features: a glacially eroded plateau; glaciated plains; a major freshwater delta; and alluvial river lowlands. The upper surface of the plateau is about 1,500 m above the rest of the park. The park contains the largest undisturbed grass and sedge meadows in North America.

Criteria: vii, ix, x Inscribed 1983

Fountain of Amphitrite in Place Stanislas, named after the patron of the project, Stanislas Leszczynski, Duke of Lorraine (and father-in-law of Louis XV) who 'reigned' (peacefully) in Nancy from 1737 to 1766.

Wood Buffalo National Park is home to herds of North American bison and forty-six other mammal species, including black bear, woodland caribou, Arctic fox, moose, grey wolf and lynx.

•VALLÉE DE MAI NATURE RESERVE Seychelles

Vallée de Mai is a valley in the heart of Praslin National Park, an area which was untouched until the 1930s. It still retains primaeval palm forest in a near-natural state, including the endemic palm, coco de mer, the bearer of the largest nut in the world, and five other endemic palms. Notable bird species include the black parrot, which is totally dependent on the palm forest. In a densely populated island, the survival of the Vallée de Mai in itself is a remarkable achievement; too small to be self-sustaining, it survives through some replanting of coco de mer.

Criteria: vii, viii, ix, x Inscribed 1983

•HISTORIC SANCTUARY OF MACHU PICCHU
Peru

Set on a granite mountain and dominating a meander in the Rio Urubamba, Machu Picchu is one of the most spectacular creations of the Incas, the largest civilisation in the Americas before the arrival of Europeans. It appears to date from the period of the two great Inca rulers, Pachacutec Inca Yupanqui (1438–71) and Tupac Inca Yupanqui (1472–93). The function of this city, which is over 100 km from the Inca capital, Cuzco, is still unknown. The surrounding valleys have been cultivated continuously for well over 1,000 years, and those living around Machu Picchu continue a way of life closely resembling that of their Inca ancestors, being based on potatoes, maize and llamas. Machu Picchu also provides a secure habitat for several endangered species, notably the spectacled bear.

Criteria: i, iii, vii, ix Inscribed 1983

•GULF OF PORTO: CALANCHE OF PIANA, GULF OF GIROLATA, SCANDOLA RESERVE France

This reserve, on the central western coast of Corsica, includes a coastline of astonishing beauty studded with offshore islets, sea pillars rising out of translucent waters, hidden coves and long beaches of fine sand, sea grottoes and high cliffs of blood-red porphyry. The clear waters host a rich marine life. The vegetation is an outstanding example of typical Mediterranean maquis (shrubland). This is replaced by arborescent plants at an altitude of 200 m and oaks replace this in certain areas. This area conserves traditional agriculture and grazing activities, and contains architecturally interesting fortifications.

Criteria: vii, viii, x Inscribed 1983

•CONVENT OF CHRIST IN TOMAR Portugal

During the second half of the twelfth century, the Knights Templar came to Tomar to assist in the Reconquista, the retaking of Portuguese territory from Islamic rule. Their original church, built by the first great Master of the Templars, Gualdim Pais, was based on a polygonal ground plan of sixteen bays with a central octagonal choir and an ambulatory, typical of Templar architecture. It was under Manuel I that the choir was lavishly decorated and Diego de Arruda created the enormous nave built above the chapter room. The prodigious exterior decoration combines with stupefying ease Gothic and Moorish influences.

Criteria: i, vi Inscribed 1983

•CONVENT OF ST GALL Switzerland

The Convent of St Gall is a perfect example of a great Carolingian monastery and was, from the eighth century to its secularization in 1805, one of the most important in Europe. Its library is one of the richest and oldest in the world with more than 160,000 books and many precious manuscripts. An abbey has existed on this site since 719 and successive restructurings of its buildings attest to ever-changing religious requirements. In 1755–68, the convent area was rebuilt in Baroque style. The cathedral and the library are the main features of this remarkable architectural complex.

Criteria: ii, iv Inscribed 1983

•PILGRIMAGE CHURCH OF WIES Germany

The sanctuary of Wies, a pilgrimage church in an Alpine valley, is a masterpiece of Rococo art. Wies, in Bavaria, was the setting of a miracle in 1738 and pilgrims became so numerous that the Abbot of

Machu Picchu stands 2,430 m above sea level in the middle of a tropical mountain forest. The city's giant walls, terraces and ramps seem to have been cut out of the continuous rock escarpments.

The Convent of Christ in Tomar, originally conceived as a monument to the Reconquista, became the most spectacular example of highly decorated Manueline architecture.

Steingaden decided to construct a splendid sanctuary. Accordingly, work began in 1745 under the direction of Dominikus Zimmermann. The choir was consecrated in 1749 and the remainder of the church finished by 1754. Its frescoes and stuccowork interpenetrate to produce a décor of unprecedented richness. The ceilings, painted as *trompe-l'œil*, appear to open on to an iridescent sky, across which angels fly.
Criteria: i, iii Inscribed 1983

• RILA MONASTERY Bulgaria
Rila Monastery was founded in the tenth century by St John of Rila, a hermit whose ascetic dwelling and tomb became a holy site. It was transformed into a monastic complex that played an important role in the spiritual and social life of Bulgaria. Destroyed by fire at the beginning of the nineteenth century, the monastery was rebuilt between 1834 and 1862. Only the Hrelyu Tower, built in 1355, survives from an earlier period. The buildings occupy a vast irregular square, with two entrances, both decorated with frescoes. In the centre is the Cathedral of Our Lady of the Assumption.
Criteria: vi Inscribed 1983

• MONASTERY OF BATALHA Portugal
The Monastery of Batalha was built to commemorate the Portuguese victory over the Castilians at the battle of Aljubarrota in 1385. It was to be the Portuguese monarchy's main building project for the next two centuries, out of which a highly original, national Gothic style evolved. Much dates from the reign of João I, when the church (finished in 1416), the royal cloister, the chapterhouse, and the funeral chapel of the founder were constructed. A century later Manuel I built the monumental vestibule and the portal of the unfinished chapels, and restored the royal cloister, creating a masterpiece of Manueline art.
Criteria: i, ii Inscribed 1983

• PIRIN NATIONAL PARK Bulgaria
Pirin National Park, in southwest Bulgaria, has a limestone landscape, with lakes, waterfalls, caves and pine forests. There are many rivers and waterfalls. The presence of limestone rocks, its southerly position and close proximity to the Aegean, coupled with its relative isolation, have made the park an important refuge for many species. Winter in the upper parts is cold and long with snow cover remaining for five to eight months. Summer is cool and short. In the subalpine zone there are thickets of dwarf mountain pine. Above 2,400–2,600 m are alpine meadows, stony slopes, screes and rocks.
Criteria: vii, viii, ix Inscribed 1983

• VATICAN CITY Holy See
Vatican City, one of the most sacred places in Christendom, is a tiny enclave within Rome. It has been the centre of Christianity since the time of Constantine in the fourth century and the seat of papal power. At its heart is the Basilica of St Peter, with its double colonnade and circular piazza in front and bordered by palaces and gardens. The basilica was first built in 315 over the tomb of St Peter the Apostle but its present-day appearance dates from the sixteenth century, when Pope Julius II inaugurated a massive artistic project for the refoundation of the entire basilica, along with the decoration of the Stanze Vaticane (the papal apartments) and the Sistine Chapel, and the construction of his own tomb. The result is the fruit of the combined genius of Bramante, Raphael, Michelangelo, Bernini and Maderno. The Apostolic Palace or Vatican Palace arose out of a long series of construction campaigns in which successive popes, from the Middle Ages onwards, rivalled each other in their munificence. It is the official residence of the Pope and houses the Vatican Museum, the Vatican Library and various chapels including the Sistine Chapel.
Criteria: i, ii, iv, vi Inscribed 1984

• WORKS OF ANTONI GAUDÍ Spain
The works of the architect Antoni Gaudí (1852–1926) in and around Barcelona represent outstanding and highly creative examples of early twentieth century residential and public architecture. The seven buildings in the World Heritage Site are Casa Vicens, Gaudí's work on the Nativity façade and Crypt of La Sagrada Familia, Casa Batlló, Casa

A fresco at Rila Monastery. The reconstruction of the monastery in the nineteenth century symbolised an awakening of a Slavic cultural identity.

Part of Bernini's colonnade in the foreground and the Basilica of St Peter in Vatican City. The dome was designed by Michelangelo and the great façade by Maderno.

Milà, Park Güell, Palacio Güell and the crypt in Colonia Güell. These monuments represent an eclectic and very personal style which was given free rein in the design of gardens, sculpture and all decorative arts, as well as architecture.
Criteria: i, ii, iv Inscribed 1984

• SUN TEMPLE, KONÂRAK India
On the shores of the Bay of Bengal, the temple at Konârak was an early centre of sun worship. Built around 1250, the entire temple was conceived as a representation of the Sun God Surya's chariot. Its twenty-four wheels are decorated with symbolic designs referring to the cycle of the seasons and the months, and it is led by a team of seven horses, six of which still exist. The temple is carefully oriented so as to permit the first rays of the sun to strike its principal entry. It is one of the most famous Brahmin sanctuaries of Asia.
Criteria: i, iii, vi Inscribed 1984

• PORT, FORTRESSES AND GROUP OF MONUMENTS, CARTAGENA Colombia
Cartagena is an outstanding example of colonial Spanish military architecture, the most extensive in the New World. The fortifications, finally completed in the seventeenth century, made Cartagena an impregnable stronghold, which successfully resisted attack until 1697. Within the shelter of the formidable defences, the city continued to grow. The plan, characteristic of colonial foundations of the sixteenth century, illustrates a rigorous zoning system, divided into three quarters corresponding to the major social categories: San Pedro, with the cathedral and many Andalusian-style palaces; San Diego, where merchants and the middle class lived; and Gethsemani, the 'popular quarter'.
Criteria: iv, vi Inscribed 1984

• YOSEMITE NATIONAL PARK USA
Yosemite National Park on the western slope of the central Sierra Nevada Mountains in the heart of California is an area of outstanding wilderness. With its hanging valleys, many waterfalls, cirque lakes, polished domes, moraines and U-shaped valleys, it provides excellent evidence of landscape fashioned by glaciation. The variety of flora in the park is reflected in six distinct vegetation zones which are governed by altitude. There are 1,200 species of flowering plant along with various other ferns, bryophytes and lichens. Yosemite's natural beauty was the impetus for the concept of the national park. The evidence of Indian habitation adds to its importance.
Criteria: vii, viii Inscribed 1984

• SALONGA NATIONAL PARK Dem. Rep. of the Congo
Salonga is the largest tropical forest national park in the world. Situated at the heart of the central basin of the Congo river, the park is very isolated and accessible mainly by water. Equatorial forest covers most of the area, varying in composition according to the landscape: there are three types, low plateaus, river terraces and high plateaus. The total area of grassland is under 0.5 per cent of the park area. The park is the habitat of many endangered species, the most important of which is the endemic dwarf chimpanzee, or bonobo. Other species include colobus monkeys, hippopotamus and leopard.
Criteria: vii, ix Inscribed 1984

• MANA POOLS NATIONAL PARK, SAPI AND CHEWORE SAFARI AREAS Zimbabwe
On the banks of the Zambezi, great cliffs overhang the river and the floodplains. The Mana Pools are former channels of the Zambezi. The area contains the last remaining natural stretch of the Middle Zambezi and there is virtually no permanent human habitation. It is home to a remarkable concentration of wild animals, including elephants, buffalo, leopards and cheetahs. Nile crocodiles are also found there. Much of the Chewore is heavily dissected and the Mupata Gorge (some 30 km long) is on the northern border of this area. Above the Mupata Gorge the river is broad and sandy, flowing through numerous channels, sandbanks and islands.
Criteria: vii, ix, x Inscribed 1984

One of the twenty-four ornately carved stone wheels on the Sun Temple at Konârak.

El Capitan, in the Yosemite National Park, is a 910 m rock formation predominantly carved out during the Sherwin Glaciation around one million years ago.

• STATUE OF LIBERTY USA

The Statue of Liberty was a gift from France in 1886 to celebrate the centenary of American independence – ten years late. It welcomed immigrants at the entrance to New York harbour. That the statue was paid for by international subscription and built in Paris by Bartholdi, a French sculptor, only strengthens its symbolic significance. It was dedicated on 28 October 1886 and features a woman holding a book and a torch. It stands on Liberty Island and was designated a National Monument in 1924. Ellis Island, the immigrants' former landing place, became part of the Statue of Liberty National Monument in 1965.
Criteria: i, vi Inscribed 1984

• LAKE MALAWI NATIONAL PARK Malawi

Located at the southern end of the great expanse of Lake Malawi, with its deep, clear waters and mountain backdrop, the national park is home to many hundreds of fish species, nearly all endemic. The park is rich in birdlife, including fish eagle, along the shoreline. Mammals include hippo, baboon, warthog and occasional elephant. The islands, especially Mumbo and Boadzulu, are important nesting areas for white-throated cormorant which number several thousand. Reptiles include crocodiles and abundant monitor lizards. The area's importance for the study of evolution is comparable to that of the Galápagos Islands.
Criteria: vii, ix, x Inscribed 1984

• BAALBEK Lebanon

Originally a Phoenician city, the arrival of the Romans in Phoenicia in 64 BC saw the beginning of monumental buildings at the place they called Heliopolis. The first was the Temple of Jupiter, begun in the late first century BC and completed soon after AD 60. The immense sanctuary of Jupiter Heliopolitanus, which attracted thousands of pilgrims, was lined by 104 massive granite columns imported from Aswan and held a temple. Construction of the Great Court began during the reign of Trajan (98–117). It contained religious buildings and altars and was surrounded by a colonnade of 128 rose granite columns.
Criteria: i, iv Inscribed 1984

• CASTLES OF AUGUSTUSBURG AND FALKENLUST AT BRÜHL Germany

The castle of Augustusburg and the hunting lodge of Falkenlust represent the first masterpieces of the Rococo style in eighteenth-century Germany and, for more than a century, they served as models for most of the princely courts. The castle was the sumptuous residence of the prince-archbishops of Cologne and is home to a true piece of creative genius, the staircase of Balthasar Neumann. The beautiful decoration of the new grand summer apartments, with its delicate faïence tiles, is also striking. Falkenlust, a small rural folly, is a dazzling creation which, with the castle, is set in an idyllic garden landscape.
Criteria: ii, iv Inscribed 1984

• IGUAZU NATIONAL PARK Argentina

One of the world's most spectacular waterfalls, the Iguazu Falls, lies at the heart of this vast, rich and diverse national park. The waterfall is semicircular, some 80 m high and 2,700 m in diameter. The site is in Misiones Province, northeastern Argentina and borders the Iguaçu National Park World Heritage site in Brazil. The vegetation is mostly subtropical wet forest rich in lianas and epiphytes and is particularly luxuriant near the falls due to the constant spray. Almost half of Argentina's bird species is found here. The fauna are typical of the region and include tapir, coatimundi, and tamandua.
Criteria: vii, x Inscribed 1984

• MONASTERY AND SITE OF THE ESCURIAL, MADRID Spain

This royal monastery dedicated to St Lawrence was built on a remote and impressive site in Castile in the sixteenth century. It is said to resemble an inverted grid-iron, the instrument of the martyrdom of St Lawrence. The handle is represented by the Royal Palace, while four angle towers, 55 m high, represent the feet. Its outwardly austere

The towering Statue of Liberty (46 m tall) symbolises the ideals of Washington and Lincoln and was extensively restored for its centenary and the annual celebration of American independence on 4 July 1986.

The Iguazu Falls on the Argentina–Brazil border. The Tupi-Guarani tribe coined the name Iguazu (Big Water). The first European to reach the falls was the Spanish explorer Don Alvar Nuñes Cabeza de Vaca in 1541.

architecture, a break with previous styles, had a considerable influence on Spanish architecture for more than half a century. In the last years of Philip II's reign it became the centre of the greatest political power of the time.
Criteria: i, ii, vi Inscribed 1984

▪CANADIAN ROCKY MOUNTAIN PARKS Canada

Studded with mountain peaks, glaciers, lakes, waterfalls, canyons and limestone caves, the Canadian Rocky Mountain Parks form a spectacular mountain landscape. The Burgess Shale fossil site, well known for its fossil remains of soft-bodied marine animals, is also found there. Active glaciers and ice fields still exist throughout the region. The most significant is the Columbia Ice Field, the largest in North America's subarctic interior. The Rockies have been divided into three ecoregions. Montane vegetation occurs in major valley bottoms and on the foothills and lower sun-exposed mountain slopes. The subalpine ecoregion occupies mountainsides between 1,800 m and 2,100 m, and valley bottoms of high elevations and is the most extensive ecoregion in the Rockies. The alpine ecoregion occurs above the timberline and is characterised by diminutive and hardy vegetation. Fifty-six mammal species have been recorded.
Criteria: vii, viii Inscribed 1984

▪BYBLOS Lebanon

Byblos, one of the oldest Phoenician cities, has been inhabited since Neolithic times. It developed into a highly structured city, enclosed by a massive fortified wall, which was burned around 2150 BC by the invading Amorites. Approximately two centuries later, the city was rebuilt with new temples. Byblos was able to accommodate successive rulers, whether Assyrian, Babylonian, Achaemenid or Greek. During the Roman period, its commercial role declined, but the city assumed a religious function: pilgrims crowded its temples, which were constantly reconstructed and embellished. Its decline began during the Byzantine period and continued during the Arab occupation after AD 636.
Criteria: iii, iv, vi Inscribed 1984

▪TYRE Lebanon

The great Phoenician city of Tyre ruled the seas and founded prosperous colonies such as Cadiz and Carthage. Constructed on an impregnable island, it succumbed eventually in 332 BC to the attack of Alexander of Macedonia. The original Greek city was followed in 64 BC by a Roman city. Following the Crusades, the historic role of the city declined. Almost totally destroyed by the Mamelukes at the end of the thirteenth century, it was only modestly reconstructed in the eighteenth century. In the present souk (market), archaeological remains include the Roman city and the medieval constructions of the Crusades.
Criteria: iii, vi Inscribed 1984

▪ROYAL CHITWAN NATIONAL PARK Nepal

At the foot of the Himalaya, Chitwan is one of the few remaining undisturbed vestiges of the 'Terai' region, which formerly extended over the foothills of India and Nepal. The park's subtropical lowland has a particularly rich flora and fauna. One of the last populations (estimated at 400) of single-horned Asiatic rhinoceros lives in the park, which is also one of the last refuges of the Bengal tiger. Prior to its re-introduction to Royal Bardia National Park in 1986, the park also contained the last Nepalese population of the Indian rhinoceros. Other endangered mammals include leopard, wild dog and sloth bear.
Criteria: vii, ix, x Inscribed 1984

▪ANJAR Lebanon

The ruins of Anjar reveal a very regular layout, reminiscent of ancient palace-cities, and are a unique example of Umayyad city planning. On a site that had long been occupied, Anjar was founded at the beginning of the eighth century by Caliph Walid I (705–715). Re-used parts of earlier Greek, Roman and early Christian buildings are frequently found in the masonry of its walls. It flourished for only 20–30 years before the Abbasids overran the city and it fell into disuse. At its peak, it housed more than 600 shops, Roman-style baths, two palaces and a mosque.
Criteria: iii, iv Inscribed 1984

Emerald Lake in Yoho National Park, one of the seven parks that make up the Canadian Rocky Mountain Parks.

The Castle of the Crusaders, Byblos.

Royal Chitwan National Park is situated in a river valley basin along the flood plains of the Rapti, Reu and Narayani rivers. The Narayani originates in the high Himalaya and drains into the Bay of Bengal.

• HISTORIC CENTRE OF CÓRDOBA Spain

Córdoba's period of greatest glory began in the eighth century after the Moorish conquest, when some 300 mosques and innumerable palaces and public buildings were built to rival the splendours of Constantinople, Damascus and Baghdad. In the thirteenth century, under Ferdinand III, Córdoba's Great Mosque was turned into a cathedral and new defensive structures, particularly the Alcázar de los Reyes Cristianos and the Torre Fortaleza de la Calahorra, were erected. Córdoba's historic centre, clustering round the mosque-cathedral, the Mezquita, preserves much of its medieval urban fabric with narrow, winding streets. The city's Roman past can be seen in the sixteen-span bridge that crosses the river Guadalquivir.

Criteria: i, ii, iii, iv Inscribed 1984

• BURGOS CATHEDRAL Spain

Begun in 1221 and completed in 1567, the plan of the great Gothic cathedral of Santa María de Burgos is based on a Latin cross. Initial work on the cathedral was completed in 1293. After a hiatus of nearly 200 years, work was resumed in the mid-fifteenth century and continued for more than 100 years. These embellishments were of great splendour – including paintings, choir stalls, reredos, tombs, and stained-glass windows. The three-storey elevation, the vaulting, and the tracery of the windows and the two-storeyed cloister that was completed towards 1280 are closely related to contemporary Gothic buildings in northern France.

Criteria: ii, iv, vi Inscribed 1984

• ALHAMBRA, GENERALIFE AND ALBAYZÍN, GRANADA Spain

Granada became an important centre of Muslim Spain in 1238, when Muhammad ibn al Ahmar founded the present Alhambra (in Arabic 'the Red'). It incorporates a palace, guard rooms, patios and gardens as well as workshops, shops, baths and mosque, all enclosed by a massive fortified wall with towers. The palace was completed in the fourteenth century. Organised around two rectangular courts, the Patio de los Arrayanes and the Patio de los Leones, it has many, highly decorated rooms with marble columns, stucco work, *azulejos* (ceramic tiles), precious wood, and paintings on leather. At a short distance to the east of the Alhambra, are the gardens of the Generalife, rural residence of the emirs who ruled this part of Spain in the thirteenth and fourteenth centuries. Standing on an adjacent hill is the residential district of the Albayzín, a rich repository of Moorish vernacular architecture into which traditional Andalusian architecture blends harmoniously.

Criteria: i, iii, iv Inscribed 1984

• GROUP OF MONUMENTS AT MAHABALIPURAM India

These exceptional sanctuaries on the Coromandel coast, founded by the Pallava kings, date from the seventh and eighth centuries. There are five types of monument: ratha temples in the form of processional chariots, cut into the rocks which emerge from the sand; mandapa, or rock sanctuaries, modelled as rooms covered with bas-reliefs; rock reliefs in the open air that illustrate episodes in the story of Siva; temples built from cut stone; and monolithic rathas, of one to three storeys. In addition the Shore Temple represents the peak of Pallava architecture, although it has been eroded and the sculptures are indistinct.

Criteria: i, ii, iii, vi Inscribed 1984

• HISTORIC CENTRE OF SALVADOR DE BAHIA Brazil

Founded by the Portuguese, Salvador de Bahia was the first colonial capital of Brazil from 1549 until the administration was transferred to Rio de Janeiro in 1763. An eminent example of Renaissance town planning, the city has many outstanding monuments and Renaissance buildings. It was the first slave market in the New World and became a major point of convergence of European, African and American Indian cultures from the sixteenth to the eighteenth century. Its situation on a ridge parallel to the Atlantic coast made it defensible against attack in the sixteenth and seventeenth centuries.

Criteria: iv, vi Inscribed 1985

The building of the Great Mosque (the Mezquita of Córdoba) began in 736 on the site of a church that was originally a Roman temple. In 1236 the mosque became the cathedral and Christian chapels were added.

A view across the basin in the Patio de los Arrayanes (Myrtle Courtyard) looking towards the Hall of the Ambassadors, Alhambra Palace.

• HISTORIC DISTRICT OF OLD QUÉBEC Canada

Québec, the most complete fortified colonial town in North America, was founded as the capital of New France in 1608 by Samuel de Champlain, on a steep promontory, Cap-aux-Diamants, overlooking the St Laurent River. The old heart of the city was protected by Fort St Louis and the Upper City remains the religious and administrative centre. The Upper City, with the Lower City and its harbour and old quarters, forms a coherent urban ensemble.

The oldest quarters are found in the Lower City around the Place Royale which, along with the Rue Notre Dame, is lined with old seventeenth- and eighteenth-century houses.

Criteria: iv, vi Inscribed 1985

• CHAVÍN (ARCHAEOLOGICAL SITE) Peru

The archaeological site of Chavín gave its name to the culture that developed between 1500 and 300 BC in this high valley of the Peruvian Andes. This former place of worship, located at an altitude of 3,177 m, is one of the earliest and best-known pre-Columbian sites. Its appearance is striking, with the complex of terraces and squares, surrounded by structures of dressed stone, and the mainly zoomorphic ornamentation. Chavín's architects and artists produced some remarkable structures including immense sculpted megaliths, one of which is more than 4 m in height.

Criteria: iii Inscribed 1985

• PAINTED CHURCHES IN THE TROODOS REGION Cyprus

The complex of ten monuments, all richly decorated with murals, provides an overview of Byzantine and post-Byzantine painting in Cyprus. They range from small churches, whose rural architectural style is in stark contrast to their highly refined decoration, to monasteries such as that of St John Lampadistis. Among the most significant are Panagia Phorbiotissa of Nikitari, painted in 1105–6, and Panagia tou Arakou in Lagoudera, painted in 1192. The Church of Ayia Sotira in Palaichori has a steep-pitched wooden roof with flat hooked tiles. This type of roofing over a Byzantine church is not found elsewhere.

Criteria: ii, iii, iv Inscribed 1985

• SANTIAGO DE COMPOSTELA (OLD TOWN) Spain

Santiago became a symbol in the Spanish Christians' struggle against the Islamic Moors after its destruction by the Muslims at the end of the tenth century. During the Romanesque and Baroque periods the city exerted a decisive influence on the development of architecture and art across the northern Iberian peninsula. The Old Town of Santiago, with Romanesque, Gothic and Baroque buildings, is one of the world's most beautiful urban areas. Santiago is one of the most famous pilgrimage sites in the Christian world. Thousands carrying the pilgrims' scallop shell and staff walk to the tomb of St James the Great.

Criteria: i, ii, vi Inscribed 1985

• OLD TOWN OF SEGOVIA AND ITS AQUEDUCT Spain

Roman hydraulic engineers brought water from the Río Frío in the Sierra de Guadarrama 18 km to Segovia. The biggest natural obstacle they encountered was the valley of the Río Clamores, across which they built an enormous stone aqueduct 813 m long, with four straight segments and two superimposed arcades borne by 128 pillars. Other important monuments in the old town of Segovia, one of the world's most beautiful historic cities, include the Alcázar, the castle begun around the eleventh century, and the stunning sixteenth-century Gothic cathedral, one of the last in Europe in that style.

Criteria: i, iii, iv Inscribed 1985

• HUASCARÁN NATIONAL PARK Peru

The park has twenty-seven snow-capped peaks 6,000 m above sea level. Deep ravines watered by numerous torrents, glacial lakes and the variety of the vegetation make it a site of spectacular beauty. It is home to such species as the spectacled bear and the Andean condor. The national park is uninhabited, although there is some grazing in

Château Frontenac (shown at the top) is part of the Upper City, built on a cliff and defended by walls with bastions, which overlooks Québec's Lower City.

Roman Aqueduct of Segovia – the best known of Spain's remaining Roman aqueducts owing to its monumentality, excellent state of conservation and location. At the valley's lowest point, the aqueduct stands 28.5 m above the ground.

the lowlands by native livestock (llama and alpaca) under an agreement with the local people. The Cordillera region has for centuries been a site for the settlement of ethnic groups, as witnessed by ruins at Gekosh, Chuchumpunta and elsewhere.
Criteria: vii, viii Inscribed 1985

• PETRA Jordan
Half-built, half-carved in the rock and approached by a narrow gorge, Petra was first established around the sixth century BC by the Nabataean Arabs. Three large structures (Royal Tombs) are carved into the rock face, which is known as the King's Wall: the Urn Tomb, the Corinthian Tomb and the Palace Tomb (Silk Tomb), named for the extraordinary chromatic effect of the rock. In AD 106 the Roman Emperor Trajan annexed the Nabataean Kingdom. Petra has notable Roman relics, including its first century AD theatre: carved almost entirely in the rock, it could hold more than 8,000 spectators.
Criteria: i, iii, iv Inscribed 1985

• HATRA Iraq
Hatra was a large fortified city under the influence of the Parthian Empire and capital of the first Arab Kingdom. It is circular, almost 2 km in diameter, with four fortified gates set in immense double walls consisting of an earthen bank and a stone wall separated by a wide ditch. Hatra withstood invasions by the Romans in AD 116 and 198 thanks to its defences. The city's remains, especially the temples where Hellenistic and Roman architecture blend with Eastern decorative features, attest to the greatness of an entire facet of Assyro–Babylonian civilisation influenced by Greeks, Parthians, Romans and Arabs.
Criteria: ii, iii, iv, vi Inscribed 1985

• MANAS WILDLIFE SANCTUARY India
On a gentle slope in the foothills of the Himalaya, where wooded hills give way to alluvial grasslands and tropical forests, the Manas sanctuary is home to a great variety of wildlife. Named after the Goddess Manasa, the site is noted for its spectacular scenery, with a variety of habitat types that support a diverse fauna, making it the richest of all Indian wildlife areas. The park represents the core of an extensive tiger reserve that protects an important migratory wildlife resource along the West Bengal to Arunachal Pradesh and Bhutan borders. Its wetlands are of international importance.
Criteria: vii, ix, x Inscribed 1985

• KEOLADEO NATIONAL PARK India
The park's location in the Gangetic Plain makes it an unrivalled breeding site for herons, storks and cormorants and an important wintering ground for large numbers of aquatic birds from Afghanistan, Turkmenistan, China and Siberia. Some 364 species of bird, including the rare Siberian crane, have been recorded in the park. An estimated sixty-five million fish fry are carried into the park's water impoundments by river flooding every year during the monsoon season, providing the food base for large numbers of wading and fish-eating birds. Large predators are absent, leopard having been deliberately exterminated. There are many birds of prey.
Criteria: x Inscribed 1985

• MONUMENTS OF OVIEDO AND THE KINGDOM OF THE ASTURIAS Spain
In the ninth century Christianity was kept alive in the Iberian peninsula in the tiny Kingdom of the Asturias. The pre-Romanesque architectural style created here influenced the peninsula's religious architecture. Its highest achievements are seen in the churches of Santa María del Naranco, San Miguel de Lillo, Santa Cristina de Lena, the Cámara Santa and San Julián de los Prados, in and around Oviedo. These churches, basilical in layout and entirely vaulted, have columns instead of piers and very rich decor combining influences from many sources. Associated with them is the remarkable contemporary hydraulic engineering structure known as La Foncalada.
Criteria: i, ii, iv Inscribed 1985

The Khazneh, or Treasury, is the only rock-cut building in Petra with no Nabataean element and links exclusively with the Alexandrian world and Hellenistic artistic traditions.

Keoladeo National Park, former duck hunting reserve of the Maharajas, consists of a flat patchwork of marshes, artificially created in the 1850s and maintained by a system of canals, sluices and dykes.

• MEDINA OF MARRAKESH Morocco

Marrakesh was founded in 1070–72 by the Almoravids, and its medina walls were built in 1126–7. The Almohads took the city in 1147, destroyed many of their predecessors' buildings, but built new quarters, extended the city wall and fortified the Kasbah. Marrakesh declined after the Almohads lost power in 1269. The arts blossomed under Saadian rule (1510–1669) – seen in the ruins of the El Badi Palace and the magnificent elaborately decorated tombs. Marrakesh's Alawite rulers, from the seventeenth century onwards, built a new mosque, *madrasas*, palaces and residences, all harmoniously integrated into the town.
Criteria: i, ii, iv, v Inscribed 1985

• CAVE OF ALTAMIRA AND PALAEOLITHIC CAVE ART OF NORTHERN SPAIN Spain

Altamira, a unique artistic achievement was discovered by chance in 1869. The first figurative representations on its walls date from the Aurignacian period, around 18,500 years ago. The largest room in the cavern was decorated at the start of the Magdalenian period, around 15,500 years ago. There are superb paintings of bison, horses, deer and boars using a palette of colours consisting of only a small number of shades (ochre, reds and blacks). In 2008, seventeen decorated caves, from the Urals to the Iberian Peninsula, from 35,000 to 11,000 BC, were inscribed as an extension to the Altamira Cave site.
Criteria: i, iii Inscribed 1985

• PUNIC TOWN OF KERKUANE AND ITS NECROPOLIS Tunisia

This Phoenician city was active for over 400 years and then abandoned during the First Punic War *c.* 250 BC. It is the only surviving example of a Phoenicio–Punic city. Its port, ramparts, residential districts, shops, workshops, streets, squares, temples and necropolis remain as they were when the city was abandoned. The city was carefully laid out, with advanced use of hydraulics and high standards of hygiene. Houses were built to a standard plan: a single entrance and a corridor gave access to an interior courtyard with a well, washbasin and bath.
Criteria: iii Inscribed 1985

• QUSEIR AMRA Jordan

Quseir Amra was probably built under either Walid I (705–15) or Walid II (743–4). The most outstanding features of this small pleasure palace are the reception hall and the *hammam* (steam bath), whose walls and vaults are both richly decorated with figurative murals that reflect the secular art of the time. The murals consist of historical themes (royal figures defeated by the Umayyad caliphs), mythological representations (the muses of Poetry, Philosophy and History), a zodiac, hunting scenes and *hammam* scenes as well as some imaginary themes. The bath complex is fed by an aqueduct.
Criteria: i, iii, iv Inscribed 1985

• RUINS OF THE BUDDHIST VIHARA AT PAHARPUR Bangladesh

Somapura Mahavira (Great Monastery) was a renowned intellectual centre until the twelfth century, epitomising the rise of Mahayana Buddhism in Bengal from the seventh century onwards. The simple, harmonious lines and carved decoration of this monastery–city represent both an artistic and a religious achievement. The monastery had cells for 177 monks around its central quadrangle. Its layout influenced Buddhist architecture as far away as Cambodia. Terracotta plaques, images of gods and goddesses, pottery, coins, inscriptions and ornamental bricks have been excavated from the site – the most important and largest known monastery south of the Himalaya to have been excavated.
Criteria: i, ii, vi Inscribed 1985

• GREAT MOSQUE AND HOSPITAL OF DIVRIĞI Turkey

The Divriği mosque, founded in 1228–9 by Emir Ahmet Shah, and the *marestan* (hospital for the insane) endowed by his wife, were built simultaneously by the same architect. Divriği is an outstanding

The minaret of the Koutoubia Mosque, built by the Almohads on Almoravid foundations. Its incomparable minaret is one of the major features of the cityscape and the symbol of the city. *Medina of Marrakesh*

The exceptionally well-preserved early eighth-century desert castle of Quseir Amra was both a fortress with a garrison and a residence of the Umayyad caliphs.

example of Selçuk mosques in Anatolia. The mosque has a single prayer room and is crowned by two cupolas. The highly sophisticated technique of vault construction, and a creative, exuberant type of decorative sculpture – particularly on the three doorways, in contrast to the unadorned walls of the interior – are the unique features of this masterpiece of Islamic architecture.
Criteria: i, iv Inscribed 1985

• SANCTUARY OF BOM JESUS DO CONGONHAS
Brazil

Buried in the luxuriant Brazilian highlands, the Church of Bom Jesus, completed in the 1770s, is a simple construction in the tradition of the area. However, after the death of its founder, Feliciano Mendes, in 1765 it was given a sumptuous Rococo interior. Externally, the flight of steps, begun in 1770, was later decorated with twelve soapstone statues of the Prophets by Antônio Francisco Lisboa (Aleijadinho). In seven small chapels in the grounds are housed 'The Passos', seven Stations of the Cross, sculpted in wood by Aleijadinho. Christian art in Latin America reached its unquestioned zenith with these multicoloured groups.
Criteria: i, iv Inscribed 1985

• GÖREME NATIONAL PARK AND THE ROCK SITES OF CAPPADOCIA Turkey

On the Cappadocia plateau, natural erosion has sculpted rocks into shapes eerily reminiscent of towers, spires, domes and pyramids, among which men have made cells, churches and veritable subterranean cities, forming one of the world's largest cave-dwelling complexes. Monastic activity probably dates from the fourth century, when hermit communities began inhabiting cells dug into the rock. They then formed troglodyte villages or subterranean towns (Kaymakli, Derinkuyu) as refuges from Arab forays. Cappadocian monasticism was well established in the iconoclast period (725–842), and between the tenth and thirteenth centuries many richly decorated churches were dug in the Göreme valley.
Criteria: i, iii, v, vii Inscribed 1985

• KAZIRANGA NATIONAL PARK India

In the heart of Assam, this park is one of the last areas in eastern India undisturbed by human activity. The site, home to about fifteen species of India's threatened mammals, is in the flood plains on the southern bank of the Brahmaputra River at the foot of the Mikir Hills. It consists primarily of tall, dense grasslands interspersed with open forests, streams and numerous small lakes (*bheels*). Over three-quarters of the area is submerged annually by the flood waters of the Brahmaputra. The numerous areas of water provide food for thousands of migratory birds, representing over 100 species.
Criteria: ix, x Inscribed 1985

• ST MARY'S CATHEDRAL AND ST MICHAEL'S CHURCH AT HILDESHEIM Germany

The ancient Benedictine abbey church of St Michael built (1010–22) by Bernward, Bishop of Hildesheim, has a symmetrical plan with two apses – characteristic of Ottonian Romanesque art in Old Saxony. In the nave, square impost pillars alternate with cubic-capital columns. St Mary's Cathedral, rebuilt after the fire of 1046, retains its original crypt. Notable treasures of the churches include a corona of light and baptismal fonts of gold-plated bronze. St Michael's bronze doors (c. 1015) depict stories from Genesis and the life of Christ, and the Bernward bronze column (c. 1020) illustrates scenes from the New Testament.
Criteria: i, ii, iii Inscribed 1985

• HISTORIC MOSQUE CITY OF BAGERHAT
Bangladesh

Formerly known as Khalifatabad this historic city, situated in the suburbs of Bagerhat at the meeting point of the Ganges and Brahmaputra rivers, was founded by the Turkish general Ulugh Khan Jahan in the fifteenth century. The city had 360 mosques, public buildings, mausoleums, bridges, roads, water tanks and other public buildings, all built from baked brick. The infrastructure – water

The Sanctuary of Bom Jesus do Congonhas.

The Göreme Valley is a spectacular example of the effects of wind and water erosion on soft volcanic tuff. Pillars, columns, towers, obelisks and needles reaching heights of 40 m are typical features of the landscape.

supply, roads and bridges – reveals perfect mastery of planning techniques. This remarkable city had no sooner been created than it was swallowed up by the jungle, after its founder died in 1459.
Criteria: iv Inscribed 1985

• PONT DU GARD (ROMAN AQUEDUCT) France
The Pont du Gard was probably built on the initiative of Agrippa around 20 BC. It carries an aqueduct – which brought water from springs near Uzès to the colony of Nemausus (Nîmes) – across the Gardon River. The first level of the aqueduct, used as a bridge in the Middle Ages, consists of six semi-circular arches, the second level eleven, and the third level, at the top of which runs the water channel, has thirty-five. On the two lower levels large stone blocks, which weigh up to 6 tonnes, were used while the upper level was constructed of small stone rubble.
Criteria: i, iii, iv Inscribed 1985

• HISTORIC AREAS OF ISTANBUL Turkey
First as Byzantium then as Constantinople and currently as Istanbul, the city was successively the capital of three empires. The ancient city and the Eastern Roman Empire are represented, by the Hippodrome of Constantine (324), the aqueduct of Valens (378), and the ramparts (begun in 413). The Byzantine Empire is represented by several major monuments – the churches of St Sophia (Hagia Sophia) and St Irene, built in the reign of Justinian (527–65), the ancient Pantocrator Monastery, founded under John II Comnenus (1118–43) and the old church of the Holy Saviour in Chora (now the Kariye Camii). The Ottoman Empire is represented by Topkapı Saray, the Blue Mosque, the Sehzade and Süleymaniye mosques and traces of vernacular settlement in the Süleymaniye quarter.
Criteria: i, ii, iii, iv Inscribed 1985

• ROYAL PALACES OF ABOMEY Benin
Under the twelve kings who succeeded one another from 1695 to 1900, the kingdom of Abomey (later Dahomey), founded in 1625 by the Fon people, became one of the most powerful on the west coast of Africa – its wealth largely derived from the slave trade. Each of the twelve kings built a lavish palace on the royal grounds in Abomey, the capital city, all within the same cob-walled area. Bas-relief decorations provide a unique history of this society that had no written records. The palace buildings are still used regularly for rituals and royal ceremonies.
Criteria: iii, iv Inscribed 1985

• ROCK ART OF ALTA Norway
Close to the Arctic Circle, the petroglyphs of the Alta fjord are a valuable illustration of human activity between 4200 and 500 BC in the far North. The thousands of paintings and engravings are located at forty-five sites scattered over seven localities and show a definite chronological sequence. The position of the paintings and engravings with respect to sea level at different postglacial periods constitutes a relative dating element, corroborated by objective iconography data. There are depictions of hunting, trapping and fishing, dancing and ceremonial acts then, as time passed, the climate warmed and the latest drawings show agricultural activities.
Criteria: iii Inscribed 1985

• OLD TOWN OF ÁVILA WITH ITS EXTRA-MUROS CHURCHES Spain
Ávila, founded in the eleventh century to protect Spanish territories from the Moors, is an outstanding example of a fortified city – its walls are intact. There are many religious and secular monuments, inside (*intra*) and outside (*extra*) the city walls (*muros*). The cathedral, with its crenellated Romanesque choir linked to the curtain wall, is part of the fortifications. This 'City of Saints and Stones', the birthplace of St Teresa and the burial place of the Grand Inquisitor Torquemada, has kept its medieval austerity. The church of San Pedro Extra-Muros, begun in 1100, held Royal receptions in its beautiful open atrium.
Criteria: iii, iv Inscribed 1985

The Blue Mosque, Istanbul.

The walls of Ávila, dating back to 1090 (but mostly rebuilt during the twelfth century), have an average thickness of 3 m and are flanked by eighty-two semicircular towers, with nine gates of different periods.

•THRACIAN TOMB OF SVESHTARI Bulgaria

This third-century BC tomb, discovered in 1982, illustrates the basic structural principles of Thracian cult buildings, and is testimony to the culture of the Getae, a Thracian people living in the north of Hemus. It consists of a corridor (dromos) and three square chambers: antechamber, lateral chamber, and main burial chamber covered by a semi-cylindrical vault. It is decorated with polychrome half-human, half-plant caryatids and painted murals. The ten female figures carved in high relief on the walls of the central chamber and the decoration of the lunette in its vault are unique in this area.
Criteria: i, iii Inscribed 1985

•ROCK-ART SITES OF TADRART ACACUS
Libyan Arab Jamahiriya

This rocky massif has thousands of cave paintings reflecting marked changes in this region of the Sahara. The oldest images (12,000 BC) show large savanna mammals such as elephant and rhinoceros. Paintings from around 8000 BC depict a humid landscape, while those from about 1500 BC show the domesticated horse in a semi-arid climate. The first centuries BC saw the intensification of a desert environment. The dromedary settled in the region at this time and became the main subject of the last rock art paintings. Tadrart Acacus also boasts extraordinary rock shapes and canyons eroded by wind and ancient rivers.
Criteria: iii Inscribed 1985

•IGUAÇU NATIONAL PARK Brazil

The park shares with Iguazú National Park in Argentina the Iguaçu Falls, which span the border between Argentina and Brazil. At 80 m high and 2,700 m wide, the falls produce vast clouds of spray that encourage the growth of lush vegetation of which around 90 per cent is subtropical rainforest. The park is home to many rare and endangered species of flora and fauna, among them the giant otter and the giant anteater. The lower park has subtropical rainforest, while the upper is mainly humid subtropical deciduous forest.
Criteria: vii, x Inscribed 1986

•ANCIENT CITY OF ALEPPO Syrian Arab Republic

The ancient city of Aleppo is one of the world's oldest continuously inhabited cities. Located at the crossroads of trade routes between the Mediterranean and the East, it prospered from the third millennium BC. Successive occupiers have left their mark in the architecture and the city plan. Aleppo is dominated by its huge medieval castle, the Citadel, which stands on a partly artificial mound towering 50 m above the city. The old city was surrounded by a defensive wall, parts of which still exist. The souks or bazaars of Aleppo's old town are among the most famous in the Middle East.
Criteria: iii, iv Inscribed 1986

•CHURCHES AND CONVENTS OF GOA India

The churches and convents of Goa, the former capital of the Portuguese Indies – particularly the Church of Bom Jesus, which contains the tomb of St Francis Xavier – illustrate the evangelisation of Asia. These monuments were influential in spreading forms of Manueline, Mannerist and Baroque art in all the countries of Asia where missions were established. The Sé Cathedral is a fine example of Renaissance architecture, with a Tuscan exterior, Corinthian columns, a raised platform with steps leading to the entrance, and barrel vaulting.
Criteria: ii, iv, vi Inscribed 1986

•CHAN CHAN ARCHAEOLOGICAL ZONE Peru

Chan Chan, largest city of pre-Hispanic America and a unique testimony to the disappeared Chimú kingdom, was the capital of the kingdom of Chimor which reached its zenith in the fifteenth century, shortly before its fall to the Incas. This huge city is divided into nine 'palaces' – autonomous units delineated by high, earthen walls. Each 'palace' was grouped around one or more squares and their buildings include temples, dwellings, storehouses, kitchens, orchards, gardens and funeral platforms. Nearby lie four industrial sectors, whose main activities appear to have been woodworking, weaving and precious-metal working. Remains of an irrigation system suggest some farming activity.
Criteria: i, iii Inscribed 1986

Iguaçu Falls.

The Citadel of Aleppo.

Walls around one of the 'palaces' in the Chan Chan archaeological zone.

• IRONBRIDGE GORGE United Kingdom

Ironbridge Gorge – a concentration of mining areas, foundries, factories, warehouses and other infrastructure of the eighteenth and nineteenth centuries – provides a fascinating summary of the progress of the Industrial Revolution. In particular, the towns of Coalbrookdale and Ironbridge influenced the development of industrial techniques and architecture. There are five major areas of interest: Coalbrookdale, with Abraham Darby's coke-fired blast furnace, where important iron production techniques were developed; Ironbridge; Hay Brook valley with its open-air museum featuring extraction galleries and preserved blast furnaces; Jackfield, a former mining town; and Coalport with a porcelain museum in its former porcelain-production factory.

Criteria: i, ii, iv, vi Inscribed 1986

• HATTUSHA: THE HITTITE CAPITAL Turkey

In the thirteenth century BC, Hattusha exerted a dominating influence upon the civilisations in Anatolia and northern Syria. Its palaces, temples, trading quarters and necropolis provide a comprehensive picture of a capital city and bear unique testimony to the vanished Hittite civilisation. Inside the walls, the city is built on two levels. To the northwest is the lower town with its great temple, dedicated to the god of storms and the goddess of the Sun, Arinna. Thousands of cuneiform tablets were found in this area. To the south is the upper city with the royal residence of Büyükkale.

Criteria: i, ii, iii, iv Inscribed 1986

• ST KILDA United Kingdom

St Kilda is a remote archipelago – comprising the islands of Hirta, Dun, Soay and Boreray – lying in the Atlantic 66 km west of Benbecula. It is unique in the very high bird densities occurring in a relatively small area. Its cliffs, home to large colonies of endangered birds, especially puffins and gannets, are among the highest in Europe. Humans lived on St Kilda for over 2,000 years in extreme conditions. Relics of their subsistence economy – based on the products of birds, agriculture and sheep farming – remain, reflecting age-old traditions. The islanders of St Kilda were evacuated by the British government in 1930.

Criteria: iii, v, vii, ix, x Inscribed 1986

• GREAT ZIMBABWE NATIONAL MONUMENT
Zimbabwe

The ruins of Great Zimbabwe – legendary capital of the Queen of Sheba – are a unique testimony to the civilisation of the Shona people of the eleventh to fifteenth centuries. In the fourteenth century, it was the principal city of a major state extending over the gold-rich plateaus, with a population of more than 10,000, and it was an important trading centre with both European and Asian cultures. There are three main areas of interest: the Hill Ruins, the remains of a royal city; the Great Enclosure, a series of brick-built living quarters; and the Valley Ruins.

Criteria: i, iii, vi Inscribed 1986

• HISTORIC CITY OF TOLEDO Spain

A centre of power for centuries, Toledo was successively a self-governing Roman *municipium*, the capital of the Visigothic Kingdom, a fortress of the Emirate of Córdoba, an outpost of the Christian kingdoms fighting the Moors and, in the sixteenth century, the temporary seat of supreme power under Holy Roman Emperor and King of Spain Charles V, who endowed it with the status of imperial and crowned city. Each set of inhabitants left their mark: Rome, with vestiges of the circus, aqueduct and sewer; the remains of Visigoth walls; the Islamic monuments of the Emirate of Córdoba; and remarkable churches and synagogues built after the Reconquista of 1085.

Criteria: i, ii, iii, iv Inscribed 1986

• TEMPLE OF APOLLO EPICURIUS AT BASSAE
Greece

This temple, dedicated by the inhabitants of Phigalia to the god of healing and the sun, was built towards the middle of the fifth century

Ironbridge, built in 1779 and known throughout the world as the symbol of the Industrial Revolution, was the world's first cast iron bridge and gave its name to the town.

Traces of human habitation on St Kilda include built structures and field systems – cleits (dry-stone huts) and traditional Highland stone houses.

The Alcázar of Toledo.

BC in the lonely heights of the Arcadian mountains. It has the oldest Corinthian capital yet found, and combines the Archaic style and the serenity of the Doric style with some daring architectural features. The decoration is notable: the walls and the bases of the columns are limestone, and the Ionic capitals and the Corinthian capital are in Doliana marble. The temple's marble frieze of twenty-two sculptured plates was transferred to the British Museum along with the Corinthian capital.
Criteria: i, ii, iii Inscribed 1986

The Giant's Causeway, which has inspired legends of giants striding over the sea to Scotland.

▪ GIANT'S CAUSEWAY AND CAUSEWAY COAST
United Kingdom

The Causeway Coast is a 6 km stretch of extraordinary geological formations representing volcanic activity during the early Tertiary period some 50–60 million years ago. The Giant's Causeway is a sea-level promontory of around 40,000 polygonal columns of basalt in perfect horizontal sections forming a pavement. It featured in the eighteenth-century geological controversies on the origins of basalts, and geological studies of these formations over the last 300 years have greatly contributed to the development of the earth sciences. Other features of the Causeway Coast include the Giant's Organ, the Chimney Tops, and Hamilton's Seat (a viewpoint).
Criteria: vii, viii Inscribed 1986

▪ OLD CITY OF SANA'A Yemen

Situated in a mountain valley at an altitude of 2,200 m, Sana'a (Arabic for 'fortified place') has been inhabited for more than 2,500 years and has been the capital of the Yemen since 1962. The Great Mosque is said to have been constructed while the Prophet Muhammad was still living, and in the seventh and eighth centuries the city became a major centre for the propagation of Islam. This religious and political heritage can be seen in the 103 mosques, fourteen hammams (steam baths) and over 6,000 houses, all built before the eleventh century.
Criteria: iv, v, vi Inscribed 1986

Sana'a's many-storeyed tower-houses, built of rammed earth, add to the beauty of the site.

▪ DURHAM CASTLE AND CATHEDRAL
United Kingdom

Located on a rocky promontory overlooking a bend in the river Wear, the monumental array of the cathedral to the south and the castle to the north constitutes one of the best-known cityscapes of medieval Europe. Durham Cathedral was built in the late-eleventh and early twelfth centuries to house the relics of St Cuthbert, evangeliser of Northumbria, and the Venerable Bede. The innovative audacity of its vaulting foreshadowed Gothic architecture. Behind the cathedral stands the castle, an ancient Norman fortress. It later became the residence of the Prince Bishops of Durham and in the nineteenth century was incorporated into Durham University.
Criteria: ii, iv, vi Inscribed 1986

▪ FATEHPUR SIKRI India

Constructed between 1571 and 1573 by the Emperor Akbar, Fatehpur Sikri – the City of Victory – was the capital of the Mughal Empire for a mere fourteen years. Described by the English traveller Ralph Fitch in 1585 as 'considerably larger than London and more populous', it comprised a series of palaces, public buildings and mosques. The site was largely abandoned until its archaeological exploration in 1892. The complex of monuments and temples in the city, all in a uniform architectural style, includes one of the largest mosques in India, the Jama Masjid.
Criteria: ii, iii, iv Inscribed 1986

▪ ROMAN MONUMENTS, CATHEDRAL OF ST PETER AND CHURCH OF OUR LADY IN TRIER Germany

Trier, a Roman colony from the first century AD, was one of the capitals of the Tetrarchy at the end of the third century. The number and quality of the surviving monuments are an outstanding testimony to Roman civilisation. The centre of the colonial town, mainly built during the reign of Claudius (41–54), had extended so much by the mid-second century that a wall was built and a bridge constructed over the Moselle. The restored amphitheatre and thermae,

Walls of the fort at Fatehpur Sikri.

the Circus maximus, and what remains of an immense imperial palace date from the time of Constantine the Great, after 306.
Criteria: i, iii, iv, vi Inscribed 1986

• KHAJURAHO GROUP OF MONUMENTS India

The temples at Khajuraho were built during the Chandela dynasty, which reached its apogee between 950 and 1050. Of the eighty-five temples built, only about twenty remain; and they belong to two different religions – Hinduism and Jainism. Yasovarman (AD 954) built the temple of Vishnu, now famous as Lakshmana temple. The largest and grandest temple is the Kandariya Mahadeva, attributed to Ganda (1017–29). Greatly influenced by the Tantric school of thought, the Chandela kings promoted various Tantric doctrines through royal monuments, including temples. The sculptors of Khajuraho depicted all aspects of life, secular, spiritual and sexual.
Criteria: i, iii Inscribed 1986

• STUDLEY ROYAL PARK INCLUDING THE RUINS OF FOUNTAINS ABBEY United Kingdom

Fountains Abbey was founded in 1132 by thirteen Cistercian monks from York in search of a devout and simple life. However, by the time the monastic community was abolished by Henry VIII in 1530 it had become the richest abbey in the kingdom. This prosperity is reflected in the magnificence of the ruins – the largest medieval ruins of the United Kingdom – although the nave of the abbey church is close to the pristine ideal of Cistercian austerity. In the eighteenth century, a strikingly beautiful landscape garden, with a geometric water garden, was created between Fountains Abbey and Studley Royal Church.
Criteria: i, iv Inscribed 1986

• GROUP OF MONUMENTS AT HAMPI India

The city of Hampi bears exceptional testimony to the vanished civilisation of the Hindu kingdom of Vijayanagar, which reached its peak under Krishna Deva Raya (1509–30). Enriched by the cotton and the spice trade, Hampi was one of the most beautiful cities of the medieval world. Conquered by the Deccan Muslim confederacy in 1565, the city was pillaged over a period of six months before being abandoned. The temples of Ramachandra (1513) and Hazara Rama (1520) are among the most extraordinary buildings in India. The impressive complex of civil, princely and public buildings are enclosed in massive fortifications.
Criteria: i, iii, iv Inscribed 1986

• GARAJONAY NATIONAL PARK Spain

Garajonay National Park, situated in the middle of the island of La Gomera in the Canary Islands archipelago, consists of an eroded plateau and gently sloping central terrain with steep escarpments running to the park edges. Some 70 per cent of the park is covered by one of the world's largest continuous areas of laurisilva (laurel) forest, a habitat which has almost disappeared from southern Europe and North Africa due to long-term climatic changes. Over 450 floral species have been recorded, of which eighty-one are endemic to the archipelago, thirty-four to the island, and eight to the national park.
Criteria: vii, ix Inscribed 1986

• STUDENICA MONASTERY Serbia

The Studenica Monastery, established in the late twelfth century, is the largest and richest of Serbia's Orthodox monasteries. It was the necropolis of the ruling dynasty and the founding-place of the Serbian Orthodox church. Its two principal monuments, the Church of the Virgin and the Church of the King, both built of white marble, enshrine priceless collections of thirteenth- and fourteenth-century Byzantine painting. The Church of the King houses a cycle of the Life of the Virgin Mary, and the murals in the Church of the Virgin are an essential milestone in the history both of Byzantine and Western art.
Criteria: i, ii, iv, vi Inscribed 1986

• OLD TOWN OF CÁCERES Spain

Cáceres is a feudal city that developed following conflicts between Christians and Moors. Its architecture is a blend of Roman, Islamic, Northern Gothic and Italian Renaissance styles. Originally a

Vishwanath Temple at Khajuraho.

Ancient water pool and temple (background) at Krishna market, Hampi.

The old Town of Cáceres.

Roman city, the Islamic Almohads built fortifications which completely changed the appearance of the Roman walls. The street pattern, with winding backstreets and tiny squares, dates from the Muslim period. After the Reconquista, the city became the stage for power struggles between clans and fortified houses dotted the landscape. In the fifteenth and sixteenth centuries, noble pride was demonstrated by adding richly decorated coats of arms to the front of houses.

Criteria: iii, iv Inscribed 1986

• STONEHENGE, AVEBURY AND ASSOCIATED SITES United Kingdom

Together with their associated sites, Stonehenge and Avebury represent a masterpiece of human creative genius of the Neolithic age. They consist of circles of menhirs arranged in a pattern of obvious astronomical significance which is still being explored. Stonehenge was built in several distinct phases from 3100–1100 BC and the menhirs used are huge: large lintels were placed upon the vertical blocks, thereby creating a type of bonded entablature. The Avenue, an earthwork cut into the chalk soil, runs straight into the northeast corner of Stonehenge. Avebury, about 30 km to the north, is Europe's largest circular megalithic ensemble. There are four avenues at Avebury, but only West Kennet Avenue is still lined with megaliths. There are several other Neolithic satellite sites around Avebury, including Silbury Hill, Windmill Hill, The Sanctuary and West Kennet chambered long barrow.

Criteria: i, ii, iii Inscribed 1986

• MUDÉJAR ARCHITECTURE OF ARAGON Spain

Mudéjar art represents the fusion of Islamic and Christian artistic traditions in Aragon following the twelfth century Reconquista. It is characterised by an extremely refined and inventive use of brick and glazed tiles, especially in belfries, the most visible element of Mudéjar architecture. Teruel's painted and decorated wooden ceilings (e.g. Santa María de Mediavilla) are another typical Mudéjar feature. The Mudéjars were forced to convert to Christianity in the sixteenth and seventeenth centuries, becoming 'new Christians' (Moriscos). This was followed by a period of intolerance, resulting in their expulsion in 1609–10, and the extinction of Mudéjar art.

Criteria: iv Inscribed 1986

• KHAMI RUINS NATIONAL MONUMENT Zimbabwe

Khami, located in an area where human presence can be traced back roughly 100,000 years, grew between 1450 and 1650 and is scattered over more than 2 km. The chief's residence (*mambo*) is towards the north on a hill created largely of earth used to level the terraces which are supported by walls. Some highly significant imported goods have been found here. Khami's people lived in huts made from cob (a mixture of earth, sand and straw) surrounded by granite walls. There are many decorative friezes, with chevron and chequered patterns, and narrow passageways and galleries.

Criteria: iii, iv Inscribed 1986

• HISTORIC CENTRE OF ÉVORA Portugal

Évora has Roman roots, and the cathedral, begun in 1186, is its best known medieval building. The city's golden age began in the fifteenth century when the Portuguese kings began living there. Splendid convents and royal palaces were built in the Manueline style, and the Palace of the Counts of Basto and the Church of the Knights of Calatrava are major sixteenth century creations. The Agua da Prata aqueduct was built in 1537 and many fountains remain from that time. Évora's character derives from the coherence of the myriad low, whitewashed, tile-roofed houses, and in the terraces which line the narrow medieval streets.

Criteria: ii, iv Inscribed 1986

• CASTLES AND TOWN WALLS OF KING EDWARD IN GWYNEDD United Kingdom

The castles of Beaumaris and Harlech, largely the work of the greatest military engineer of the time, James of St George, and the

Two different materials were used for the Stonehenge constructions: irregular sandstone blocks, known as sarsens, which were quarried in a plain near Salisbury; and bluestones, quarried about 200 km away in Pembrokeshire in Wales.

University of the Holy Spirit in Évora. The Jesuits taught at the University of the Holy Spirit from 1553 until their expulsion in 1759, when the city's rapid decline began.

fortified complexes of Caernarfon and Conwy are located in the former principality of Gwynedd, in north Wales. These extremely well-preserved monuments are examples of the colonisation and defence works carried out throughout the reign of Edward I (1272–1307). From 1283, Edward I undertook a castle-building programme of unprecedented scale. In twenty years, ten fortresses were built, not to mention those restored after being wrested from the enemy, creating a strategic and symbolic expression of English power.
Criteria: i, iii, iv Inscribed 1986

▪ GONDWANA RAINFORESTS OF AUSTRALIA
Australia

This site, comprising approximately forty separate reserves, is situated predominantly along the Great Escarpment on Australia's east coast. The outstanding geological features displayed around shield volcanic craters and the 200 rare and threatened rainforest species are of international significance for science and conservation. The site includes the most extensive areas of subtropical rainforest in the world and large areas of warm temperate rainforest. There is a concentration of primitive plant families that shows a direct link with the origin of flowering plants over 100 million years ago, and some of the oldest of the world's ferns and conifers.
Criteria: viii, ix, x Inscribed 1986

▪ ŠKOCJAN CAVES Slovenia

The site, located in the Kras region (literally meaning 'karst'), is one of the most famous in the world for the study of karstic phenomena. An underground system of passages runs from the source of the Reka river to Timavo on the Gulf of Trieste in Italy. The river enters the Škocjan grotto through an underground passage, reappearing at the bottom of a deep chasm. A gallery of stalactites and stalagmites leads to the surface. The protected area includes four deep and picturesque chasms, Sokolak in the south, Globocak in the west, and Lisicina and Sapen dol in the north.
Criteria: vii, viii Inscribed 1986

▪ OLD TOWN OF GHADAMÈS
Libyan Arab Jamahiriya

The historic city of Ghadamès, known as 'the pearl of the desert', is a small oasis city situated next to a palm grove. It is one of the oldest pre-Saharan cities and an outstanding example of a traditional settlement. Reinforced outer walls of houses on the city's edge form a fortified wall. The houses are characterised by a vertical division of functions: storage on the ground floor; an upper floor for the family, connecting to overhanging covered alleys forming a network of passageways, principally reserved for men; and at the top, connected open-air terraces reserved for women.
Criteria: v Inscribed 1986

▪ ARCHAEOLOGICAL SITE OF DELPHI Greece

The sanctuary of Delphi, on Mount Parnassus, was the site of the Delphic Oracle through which the god Apollo spoke. By the sixth century BC Delphi was both the religious centre and symbol of unity in the ancient Greek world. Among the monuments are the Temple of Apollo, erected in the fourth century BC on the remains of an earlier temple and within which was the seat of the Pythia, the priestess who presided over the Oracle and delivered the prophesies inspired by Apollo; the Theatre, originally built in the fourth century BC, the visible ruins date from the Roman imperial period; and the Stadium, constructed in the fifth century BC and remodelled in the second century AD.
Criteria: i, ii, iii, iv, vi Inscribed 1987

▪ HAWAII VOLCANOES NATIONAL PARK USA

The park extends from the volcanic headlands of the southern coast of Hawaii to the summit calderas of Kilauea, the world's most active volcano, and Mauna Loa. The latter is a massive, flat-domed shield volcano, extending from 5,581 m below sea level to 4,170 m above. Volcanic eruptions have created a constantly changing landscape. Climate varies with altitude from tropical humid to alpine desert and the park contains twenty-three distinct vegetation types, grouped

Rainforest near Protestors Falls, Nightcap National Park, New South Wales – one of the reserves in Gondwana Rainforests of Australia.

The Tholos at Delphi. This circular building with columns of the Doric order, was built around 380 BC. Although its function is unknown, it must have been important, judging from the fine workmanship.

into five major ecosystems. Except for a single species of Hawaiian hoary bat, the park has no native mammals and most endemic birds are rare or endangered.
Criteria: viii Inscribed 1987

• PIAZZA DEL DUOMO, PISA Italy
The monuments of the Piazza del Duomo are medieval masterpieces. The cathedral, its baptistry, its campanile – the Leaning Tower – and its walled cemetery are of great architectural significance. Work on the cathedral began in 1064 and was completed in the twelfth century. The cathedral is in the shape of a Latin cross, with five nave aisles. Its Romanesque baptistry, with a pulpit by the sculptor Nicola Pisano, commenced in 1152 and was completed in 1363. The cathedral's famous leaning bell tower began subsiding soon after construction began in 1173. War meant it remained unfinished until almost 200 years later.
Criteria: i, ii, iv, vi Inscribed 1987

• CATHEDRAL, ALCÁZAR AND ARCHIVO DE INDIAS IN SEVILLE Spain
The cathedral and Alcázar date from the Reconquista, and reflect elements of the civilisations of the Berber Almohads and of Christian Andalusia. Begun in the late sixteenth century, the Casa Lonja was intended as a Trades Hall but by the 1790s it had become the Archivo General de Indias, housing documents about the Spanish overseas empire. The cathedral, the largest Gothic cathedral in the world, houses the tomb of Christopher Columbus. The Alcázar is a palatial fortress first built in 712 by the conquering Arabs. After the Spanish retook Seville in 1248 it became a Spanish royal residence.
Criteria: i, ii, iii, vi Inscribed 1987

• SIAN KA'AN Mexico
This biosphere reserve on a coastal limestone plain on the east coast of the Yucatán peninsula contains tropical forests, mangroves, marshes and a large marine section intersected by a barrier reef. The complex hydrological system provides a habitat for a rich flora and a fauna comprising more than 300 species of birds and a large number of the region's characteristic terrestrial vertebrates. There are an estimated 1,200 plant species. In the medium and low semi-deciduous forest, abundance of palm is a characteristic feature. Coastal dunes stretch along 64 km of the coast.
Criteria: vii, x Inscribed 1987

• SUNDARBANS NATIONAL PARK India
The Sundarbans cover 10,000 km² of land and water in the Ganges delta, more than half of it in India, the rest in Bangladesh. The area contains the world's largest area of mangrove forests. A number of rare or endangered species live in the park, including tigers, aquatic mammals, birds and reptiles. The Sundarban waterways now carry little freshwater as the outflow of the Ganges has shifted progressively eastwards since the seventeenth century. Waterways in the tiger reserve are maintained largely by the diurnal tidal flow.
Criteria: ix, x Inscribed 1987

• BLENHEIM PALACE United Kingdom
Blenheim Palace, near Oxford, was presented by the English nation to John Churchill, first Duke of Marlborough, in recognition of his victory in 1704 over French and Bavarian troops at the Battle of Blenheim. Designed by Sir John Vanbrugh and Nicholas Hawksmoor between 1705 and 1722, it is a perfect example of an eighteenth-century Baroque palace. Between 1764 and 1774 'Capability' Brown, one of the most famous English landscape gardeners, turned the classical park laid out by Vanbrugh into a wonderful Romantic landscape by the creation of two lakes. Sir Winston Churchill was born in the palace in 1874.
Criteria: ii, iv Inscribed 1987

• ELEPHANTA CAVES India
The 'City of Caves' consists of seven caves on an island in the Arabian Sea close to Mumbai. With their decorated temples and images from Hindu mythology, they contain one of the most striking collections

The cathedral and its campanile (the Leaning Tower) in the Piazza del Duomo at Pisa.

Part of the west front of Blenheim Palace.

of rock art in India. There are two groups of caves, from the sixth to eighth century AD. To the east, Stupa Hill contains two caves, one of which is unfinished. To the west, the larger group consists of five rock-cut Hindu shrines. The main cave is famous for its huge reliefs to the glory of Shiva, who is exalted in various forms and actions.
Criteria: i, iii Inscribed 1987

• VENICE AND ITS LAGOON Italy
Standing in the Venetian Lagoon on a tiny archipelago, Venice was one of the greatest capitals in the medieval world. Venetian power grew steadily from the twelfth to the fifteenth century and the independent city-state dominated trade between Europe and the Byzantine Empire and the Near East. The fabulous wealth that its trading empire brought is reflected in the scale, grandeur and architectural influence of its beautiful buildings and monuments. The city has been inspiration to some of the world's greatest artists, including Canaletto, Giorgione, Titian, Tintoretto and Veronese. Transport in this necessarily car-free area is by water. Canals – such as the Grand Canal – and the network of *rii*, or rivers, are the arteries of the city.
Criteria: i, ii, iii, iv, v, vi Inscribed 1987

• WESTMINSTER PALACE, WESTMINSTER ABBEY AND SAINT MARGARET'S CHURCH
United Kingdom
After a fire destroyed Westminster Palace in 1834, the neo-Gothic Houses of Parliament was designed by Barry and Pugin. The seat of Parliament, which includes the House of Lords to the south of a central tower and the House of Commons to the north is a vivid symbol of one of the oldest parliamentary institutions in the world. The site also includes the medieval church of Saint Margaret and Westminster Abbey, where all England's sovereigns have been crowned since the eleventh century. The Abbey represents successive phases of English Gothic architecture, ending with the Henry VII Lady Chapel, completed in 1519.
Criteria: i, ii, iv Inscribed 1987

• FRONTIERS OF THE ROMAN EMPIRE
United Kingdom and Germany
The Roman Limes or frontier mark the greatest extent of the Roman Empire in the second century AD. The two sections in Germany cover 550 km from the northwest to the Danube in the southeast. The 118 km-long Hadrian's Wall in northern England was built on the orders of the Emperor Hadrian around AD 122 at what were then the northernmost limits of the Roman province of Britannia. The 60 km-long Antonine Wall, across central Scotland, was started by Emperor Antoninus Pius in AD 142 as a defence against the 'barbarians' of the north and was the most northerly Roman frontier.
Criteria: ii, iii, iv Inscribed 1987

• GREAT LIVING CHOLA TEMPLES India
The Great Living Chola Temples were built by kings of the Chola Empire in south India. The site includes three great eleventh- and twelfth-century temples: the Brihadisvara Temple at Thanjavur (Tanjore), the Brihadisvara Temple at Gangaikondacholisvaram and the Airavatesvara Temple at Darasuram. The great temple of Thanjavur was built in a few years, from 1003–10, during the reign of the great king Rajaraja and was richly endowed by the sovereign. The Airavatesvara temple complex, built by Rajaraja II, at Darasuram, features a 24-m vimana and a stone image of Shiva.
Criteria: ii, iii Inscribed 1987

• IMPERIAL PALACES OF THE MING AND QING DYNASTIES IN BEIJING AND SHENYANG China
The Imperial Palaces illustrate the grandeur of the imperial institution in China. Seat of supreme power for five centuries (1416–1911) under the Ming and Qing dynasties, the Forbidden City in Beijing contains landscaped gardens and many magnificent buildings containing nearly 10,000 rooms. Lying to the north of Tiananmen Square, it is now known as the Palace Museum and it is the world's largest palace complex. The Imperial Palace of the Qing

Part of the Grand Canal that winds through the centre of Venice and which is lined with medieval and renaissance palazzi.

The façade of Westminster Palace by the river Thames, is 266 m long; the Victoria Tower is to the south, and the Clock Tower (Big Ben) to the north.

The Imperial Palace in Beijing (the Forbidden City) has a very formal structure: it is almost symmetrical and hierarchically arranged so that all the important buildings run down the centre, north to south.

Dynasty in Shenyang consists of 114 buildings built in 1625–36. It contains an important library and offers insight into the Qing Dynasty and their Manchu cultural traditions.
Criteria: i, ii, iii, iv Inscribed 1987

• BUDAPEST, INCLUDING THE BANKS OF THE DANUBE, THE BUDA CASTLE QUARTER AND ANDRÁSSY AVENUE Hungary

The Danube divides Buda on the spur on the right bank and Pest in the plain on the left bank. The city's historic importance dates from the Roman period. After the Hungarian invasion in the ninth century, Pest became the first medieval urban centre, only to be devastated by Mongol raids in 1241–2. A few years later Bela IV built the castle of Buda where the inhabitants of Pest found shelter. Buda's importance ended when the Turks ransacked the city in 1526, precipitating its final fall in 1541. In the nineteenth century Buda and Pest were formally reunified in 1873 and the city's role as capital was enhanced by the construction of the Parliament building (1884–1904). After reunion Andrássy Avenue was built straight through a suburban area, radically transforming the city's structure.
Criteria: ii, iv Inscribed 1987

• BRASILIA Brazil

Brasilia is a capital that was created *ex nihilo* in the centre of Brazil in 1956. Urban planner Lucio Costa and architect Oscar Niemeyer intended that every element – from the layout of the residential and administrative districts to the symmetry of the buildings themselves – should be in harmony with the city's overall design. Along the curving north–south axis of the city are the residential zones, each with its own commercial and leisure centres, green spaces, schools, churches, etc. The perpendicular east–west axis, known as the Monumental Axis, links the administrative sections of the new city and contains Niemeyer's most renowned buildings.
Criteria: i, iv Inscribed 1987

• HANSEATIC CITY OF LÜBECK Germany

Lübeck – the former capital of the Hanseatic League – was founded in the twelfth century and prospered until the sixteeenth century as the major trading centre for northern Europe. Despite the damage it suffered during the Second World War, the basic structure of the old city, consisting mainly of fifteenth- and sixteenth-century patrician residences, public monuments, churches and salt storehouses, remains unaltered. The plan of Lübeck, with its blade-like outline, dates to the beginnings of the site. To the west lay the richest quarters with the trading houses and the homes of the merchants and to the east were small traders and artisans.
Criteria: iv Inscribed 1987

• KILIMANJARO NATIONAL PARK Tanzania

At 5,895 m, the volcanic massif of Mount Kilimanjaro is the highest point in Africa. It stands in splendid isolation above the surrounding plains, encircled by mountain forest, its snowy peak looming over the savanna. Numerous mammals, many of them endangered, live in the park. The national park and forest reserve occupy the upper part of Kilimanjaro. It comprises all the mountain above the timberline and six forest corridors stretching down through the montane forest belt. Kilimanjaro has five main vegetation zones: savanna bushland and densely populated submontane agroforest; the montane forest belt; subalpine moorland; alpine bogs; and alpine desert.
Criteria: vii Inscribed 1987

• HISTORIC CENTRE OF MEXICO CITY AND XOCHIMILCO Mexico

Mexico City was built in the sixteenth century by the Spanish on the ruins of Tenochtitlan, the old Aztec capital. It has the largest cathedral in the Americas and fine nineteenth- and twentieth-century buildings. Templo Mayor was one of the main Aztec temples in Tenochtitlan. Construction started in 1390 and it may have been rebuilt up to six times on top of the original until destroyed by the Spanish in 1521. The lakeside area of Xochimilco, 28 km south of Mexico City, still features some *chinampas*, the Aztec floating gardens

The Danube River at dusk with W.T. Clark's suspension bridge of 1849 (foreground) and the imposing neo-Gothic Houses of Parliament on the far riverbank.

Kilimanjaro, one of the world's largest volcanoes, last showed signs of major activity in the Pleistocene period (between 1.8 million and 10,000 years ago). It has three main volcanic peaks of varying ages.

that the Spanish so admired. Buildings from the colonial period have also been preserved.
Criteria: ii, iii, iv, v Inscribed 1987

• ACROPOLIS, ATHENS Greece

In the fifth century BC an exceptional group of artists put into effect the ambitious plans of Athenian statesman Pericles and, under the inspired guidance of the sculptor Pheidias, transformed the rocky hill of the Acropolis. The years from 447–406 BC saw the successive building of the Parthenon, the main temple dedicated to Athena; the Propylaea, the monumental entrance to the Acropolis; the temple of Athena Nike; and the Erechtheion – the four masterpieces of classical Greek art. The sacred hill of Athens was protected throughout the period of Roman domination until the Herulian raid in AD 267. Since then, and despite long periods of relative calm, the monuments have been damaged many times. The Byzantines converted the temples into churches and removed their art treasures to Constantinople. When the Turks took the city in 1456, it became a mosque and the Erechtheion was the occasional harem of the Turkish governor. In 1687 the siege of the Acropolis by Venetian armies resulted in the explosion of the Parthenon, used as the Turks' powder magazine. Finally in the nineteenth century, the British ambassador Lord Elgin pillaged the marble carvings, which, since 1815, have been in the British Museum.
Criteria: i, ii, iii, iv, vi Inscribed 1987

• HISTORIC CENTRE OF PUEBLA Mexico

Puebla, which was founded *ex nihilo* in 1531, is situated about 100 km east of Mexico City, at the foot of the Popocatepetl volcano. It was the first city in central Mexico founded by the Spanish conquerors that was not built upon the ruins of a conquered Amerindian settlement. The Historic Centre of Puebla comprises major religious buildings such as the Cathedral of Santo Domingo and the Jesuit Church, as well as superb palaces and many houses with walls covered in tiles (*azulejos*). The new aesthetic concepts resulting from the fusion of European and American styles were adopted locally.
Criteria: ii, iv Inscribed 1987

• CHACO CULTURE USA

For over 2,000 years, Pueblo peoples occupied a vast region of the southwestern USA. Chaco Canyon is the area with the highest concentration of archaeological sites. The Chaco people combined architectural designs, astronomical alignments, geometry, landscaping and engineering to create an ancient urban centre of spectacular public architecture. It became a major centre of ancestral Pueblo culture between 850 and 1250 (when the Chaco population died out), and was a focus for ceremonials, trade and political activity. In addition to the Chaco Culture National Historical Park, this site includes the Aztec Ruins National Monument and several smaller Chaco sites.
Criteria: iii Inscribed 1987

• HISTORIC CENTRE OF OAXACA AND ARCHAEOLOGICAL SITE OF MONTE ALBÁN Mexico

This site covers the historic centre of Oaxaca, founded by the Spanish; the pre-Hispanic site of Monte Albán; and the village of Cuilapan, where the Dominicans built a vast monastery in the mid-sixteenth century. Monte Albán is an outstanding example of a pre-Columbian ceremonial centre. With its pelota court, magnificent temples, tombs and bas-reliefs with hieroglyphic inscriptions, Monte Albán was created during the pre-Classic and Classic periods (1800 BC to AD 900). A short time before the arrival of the Spanish conquistadores, the Aztecs took control of the valley and founded the stronghold of Huaxyacac. This place name survived, when in 1521 the Spanish erected the fort of Antequera de Oaxaca on the same site. Oaxaca is built on a grid pattern and is a good example of Spanish colonial town planning, with major religious monuments and superb patrician town houses.
Criteria: i, ii, iii, iv Inscribed 1987

The Acropolis of Athens and its monuments form the greatest architectural and artistic complex of Greek antiquity. It stands on a rocky promontory 156 m above the Ilissos valley.

Monte Albán was carved out from a solid mountain. Man-made terraces and esplanades replaced the natural unevenness of the site with a whole new sacred topography of pyramids, and artificial knolls and mounds.

• OLD VILLAGE OF HOLLÓKŐ AND ITS SURROUNDINGS Hungary

Hollókő, which developed mainly during the seventeenth and eighteenth centuries, is a living example of rural life, using traditional farming and forestry techniques. Located about 100 km northeast of Budapest, Hollókő is a small community of 126 houses and farm buildings, strip-field farming, orchards, vineyards, meadows and woods. As was customary, the first generation of inhabitants settled on either side of the main street, while subsequent generations built their houses at the back of the narrow family plots, thus progressively enlarging the built-up area. The barns were built apart from the village, on the edges of the fields.
Criteria: v Inscribed 1987

• PRE-HISPANIC CITY OF TEOTIHUACAN Mexico

Located 48 km northeast of Mexico City, the holy city of Teotihuacan ('the place where the gods were created') is one of the oldest known archaeological sites in Mexico. Built between the first and seventh centuries AD, it is characterised by the vast size of its sacred monuments, which were laid out on geometric and symbolic principles. Lining the immense Avenue of the Dead, this unique group of monuments and places of worship (Pyramids of the Sun, the Moon and Quetzalcoatl, and Palaces of Quetzalmariposa, Jaguars, Yayahuala and others) constitutes an outstanding example of a pre-Columbian ceremonial centre.
Criteria: i, ii, iii, iv, vi Inscribed 1987

• CITY OF POTOSÍ Bolivia

Potosí owes its importance to the discovery (1542–5) of the New World's biggest silver lodes in the Cerro de Potosí, the mountain south of the city and which overlooks it. It quickly became the world's largest industrial complex, with the extraction of silver ore relying on a series of hydraulic mills. The site consists of the industrial monuments of the Cerro Rico, where water is provided by an intricate system of aqueducts and artificial lakes; the colonial town; the Church of San Lorenzo; several patrician houses; and the *barrios mitayos*, the areas where the workers lived.
Criteria: ii, iv, vi Inscribed 1987

• CITY OF BATH United Kingdom

Bath grew around a temple the Romans built between AD 60 and 70 on the site of a geothermal spring. Between the first and fourth centuries the Romans built a bath complex whose remains have been incorporated into later buildings. In the eighteenth century Bath developed into an elegant and fashionable spa town. The neoclassical style, scale and grandeur of its public buildings (the Rooms, the Pump Room, the Circus, and especially, Royal Crescent) reflect the city's confidence and ambitions during the reign of George III. John Wood was architect of many buildings, including the Circus; his son John oversaw the building and also planned the Assembly Rooms and Royal Crescent. As Master of Ceremonies, dandy and gambler Beau Nash masterminded Bath's metamorphosis into the most fashionable resort in England.
Criteria: i, ii, iv Inscribed 1987

• NEMRUT DAĞ Turkey

The rulers of Commagene, a kingdom founded north of Syria and the Euphrates, left behind several beautiful funerary sanctuaries. The most impressive is at Nemrut Dağ, of Antiochos I of Commagene (69–34 BC). Dominating the summit of Nemrut Dağ is a conical tumulus of stone chips. This funerary mound, whose interior layout remains unknown, is surrounded by artificial terraces. On the east terrace are five colossal seated figures (7 m high) representing deities, with a lion and an eagle at either end. On the north side, relief sculptures represent the Persian ancestors of Antiochos. On the south side are his Macedonian ancestors.
Criteria: i, iii, iv Inscribed 1987

• MANÚ NATIONAL PARK Peru

The biological diversity found in the Manú National Park exceeds that of any other place on Earth. The park is located on the eastern

A house in Hollókő built in the traditional style: half-timbered on a stone base with roughcast white-washed walls, enhanced by high wooden pillared galleries with balconies on the street side protected by overhanging porch roofs.

Pulteney Bridge which crosses the river Avon in Bath. Constructed in the eighteenth century, it is one of the few bridges in the world with shops built into it on both sides.

slopes of the Andes and within the Amazon river basin. It has successive tiers of vegetation rising from 150 m to 4,200 m. The flora of Manú is still poorly known; in the last ten years, 1,147 plant species have been identified, and it is likely many more species will be found. Some 850 species of birds have been identified and rare mammals, such as the giant otter and the giant armadillo, also find refuge there.
Criteria: ix, x Inscribed 1987

• THE GREAT WALL China

The building of defensive walls was a common strategy against potential invasion and several were built in China from the eighth century BC onwards. From 220 BC Qin Shi Huangdi, the first emperor of a unified China, restored and linked the separate sections of the Great Wall which stretched from the region of the Ordos to Manchuria. These were to form the first cohesive defence system against invasions from the north, and by the first century BC, extensions meant the wall spanned approximately 6,000 km between Dunhuang in the west and the Bohai Sea in the east. After the downfall of the Han dynasty in AD 220, construction and maintenance works on the Great Wall were halted. It was the Ming emperors (1368–1644) who revived the principles of Qin Shi Huangdi's defence policy and during these centuries 5,650 km of wall were built.
Criteria: i, ii, iii, iv, vi Inscribed 1987

• MOGAO CAVES China

Situated at a strategic point along the Silk Route, at the crossroads of trade as well as religious, cultural and intellectual influences, the 492 cells and cave sanctuaries in Mogao (also known as Dunhuang) are famous for their statues and wall paintings, spanning 1,000 years of Buddhist art. The group of caves at Mogao were still occupied by Buddhist monks until 1930, making this a fine example of a traditional monastic settlement as well as a unique artistic achievement.
Criteria: i, ii, iii, iv, v, vi Inscribed 1987

• PEKING MAN SITE AT ZHOUKOUDIAN China

The discovery of hominid remains in the sediment of a cave in 1926 by the Chinese archaeologist Pei Wenzhong excited universal interest and overthrew the then-accepted chronology of the beginnings of human history. Scientific work at the site, which lies 42 km southwest of Beijing, is still underway. So far, it has led to the discovery of the remains of *Sinanthropus pekinensis*, who lived in the Middle Pleistocene, along with various objects, and remains of *Homo sapiens* dating as far back as 18,000–11,000 BC.
Criteria: iii, vi Inscribed 1987

• MOUNT TAISHAN China

On Mount Taishan evidence of human activity dates back 400,000 years to the Palaeolithic Yiyuan Man. For over 3,000 years, Chinese emperors have made pilgrimages to Mount Taishan for sacrificial and other ceremonial purposes. Rock inscriptions, stone tablets and temples bear testimony to such visits. Renowned scholars, including Confucius whose home town, Qufu, is only 70 km away, composed poetry and prose and left their calligraphy on the mountain. Mount Taishan was also an important religious centre for both Buddhism and Taoism. The way in which this rich cultural heritage has been integrated with the natural landscape is one of China's most precious legacies.
Criteria: i, ii, iii, iv, v, vi, vii Inscribed 1987

• PRE-HISPANIC CITY AND NATIONAL PARK OF PALENQUE Mexico

A prime example of a Mayan sanctuary of the classical period, Palenque was at its height between AD 500 and 700, when its influence extended throughout the basin of the Usumacinta river. The dominant element in the central cleared area is the Palacio. Erected at different periods on an immense artificial knoll shaped like a truncated pyramid, the various buildings include a four-storey watchtower or astronomical observatory, unique in Mayan architecture. Even larger is the Temple of Inscriptions. Towards the end of the tenth century, coastal peoples from the Gulf of Mexico region invaded and caused its downfall and abandonment.
Criteria: i, ii, iii, iv Inscribed 1987

A section of the Great Wall of China near Beijing, dating from the Ming dynasty. Walkways along the top of the wall made it possible to move troops rapidly and for imperial couriers to travel.

A Temple on Mount Taishan.

• MAUSOLEUM OF THE FIRST QIN EMPEROR
China

Qin Shi Huangdi, the first Emperor of China, arranged for his burial long before his accession. As king of Qin in 247 BC he selected a site at the foot of Mount Li. However, after his accession as emperor in 221 BC, work at his mausoleum took on extraordinary dimensions. About 700,000 workers from every Chinese province worked to construct a subterranean city within a gigantic mound. The resulting necropolis complex was a scale model of the emperor's palace, the empire and the Earth. Its treasures were safeguarded by automatically triggered weapons designed to kill tomb robbers and its principal craftsmen were walled up alive within the complex to prevent their betraying its secrets. Qin Shi Huangdi died in 210 BC and is buried, surrounded by the famous terracotta warriors, at the centre of a complex designed to mirror the urban plan of the capital Xianyang. According to current estimates, the statue army must have represented the exact number of the imperial guards. The emperor's tomb and much of the site, discovered in 1974, remain unexcavated.
Criteria: i, iii, iv, vi Inscribed 1987

• GROS MORNE NATIONAL PARK Canada

With spectacular scenery, outstanding geology and diverse ecology, Gros Morne, located on the western shore of Newfoundland, provided the evidence that helped define the theory of plate tectonics. These geological formations are the remnants of an ancient continent and ocean from hundreds of millions of years ago. More recent glacial action has resulted in fjords, glacial valleys, and waterfalls from the alpine plateau of the Long Range Mountains to the Gulf of St Lawrence coastal lowlands with its estuaries, beaches, cliffs and dunes. These distinctly different landscapes provide a range of habitats for a wide variety of flora and fauna.
Criteria: vii, viii Inscribed 1987

• BAHLA FORT Oman

Bahla Fort is an outstanding example of the military architecture of the Sultanate of Oman. The oasis of Bahla owed its prosperity to the Banu Nabhan who, from the mid-twelfth century to the end of the fifteenth century, imposed their rule on other tribes. Built on a stone base, the adobe walls and towers of the immense fort probably include some structural elements of the pre-Islamic period, but the major part dates from the time of the Banu Nabhan. At its foot lies the Friday Mosque with its beautiful sculpted *mihrab* (prayer niche) probably dating back to the fourteenth century.
Criteria: iv Inscribed 1987

• GROUP OF MONUMENTS AT PATTADAKAL
India

Pattadakal, in Karnataka, achieved, in the seventh and eighth centuries under the Chalukya dynasty, a harmonious blend of architectural forms from northern and southern India. Nine Hindu temples, as well as a Jain sanctuary, can be seen there. One masterpiece stands out – the Temple of Virupaksha, built *c.* 740 by Queen Lokamahadevi to commemorate her husband's victory over southern kings. The evocative sanctuary ruins in the enclosure may be reached through monumental gates on the west and east sides. In the axis of the courtyard, before the temple, is a pavilion housing a black stone statue of Siva's sacred bull.
Criteria: iii, iv Inscribed 1987

• KSAR OF AIT-BEN-HADDOU Morocco

Ait-Ben-Haddou is a striking example of a southern Moroccan *ksar*, a group of earthen buildings surrounded by high walls, that is a traditional pre-Saharan village community. Inside the defensive walls, which are reinforced by angle towers, each with a zigzag-shaped gate, houses crowd together. Some are modest, others resemble small urban castles with their high angle towers whose upper portion includes decorative motifs in clay brick. There are also public buildings and community areas: collective sheep pens and stables, lofts and silos, a market place, a meeting room for the assembly of family chiefs, a mosque and *madrasas*.
Criteria: iv, v Inscribed 1987

The life-size terracotta figures at the Mausoleum of the First Qin Emperor are all different; with their horses, chariots and weapons, they are masterpieces of realism and of great historical interest.

The ksar of Ait-Ben-Haddou is an extraordinary ensemble of buildings offering a complete panorama of pre-Saharan construction techniques using rammed and moulded earth, clay and brick.

• ULURU-KATA TJUTA NATIONAL PARK
Australia

Formerly called Ayers Rock – Mount Olga National Park, Uluru-Kata Tjuta National Park is in the traditional lands of the Western Desert Aboriginal people, locally known as Anangu. Anangu are part of one of the oldest human societies in the world. For Anangu the huge rock formations of Uluru and Kata Tjuta are physical evidence of the actions, artefacts and bodies of the ancestral beings (*tjukuritja*) who travelled the Earth in the creation time. These ancestors, who combined the attributes of humans and animals, journeyed across the landscape creating not only its features, but also *Tjukurpa* (the law) – the code of behaviour followed by Anangu today. Uluru and the rock domes of Kata Tjuta dominate the vast red plain, dwarfing the desert oak and spinifex grass of central Australia. The thirty-six steep-sided rock domes of Kata Tjuta, lying about 32 km west of Uluru, are interspersed with moisture-rich gullies and rocky valleys that are home to rare plants and desert animals.
Criteria: v, vi, vii, viii Inscribed 1987

• MONTICELLO AND THE UNIVERSITY OF VIRGINIA IN CHARLOTTESVILLE USA

Thomas Jefferson designed Monticello (1769–1809), his plantation home, and his 'academical village' (1817–26), which remains the heart of the University of Virginia. The originality of design, the refined proportions and décor, and its integration into the landscape make Monticello an outstanding neoclassical *villa rustica*. The University of Virginia is an ideal Enlightenment institution. A half-scale copy of the Pantheon in Rome, which houses the library, dominates the academic village. The ten pavilions housing the professors of the ten schools that made up the university are connected by colonnades that give a feeling of unity to this space.
Criteria: i, iv, vi Inscribed 1987

• DJA FAUNAL RESERVE Cameroon

This is one of the largest and best-protected rainforests in Africa, with 90 per cent of its area left undisturbed. Almost completely surrounded by the Dja river, which forms a natural boundary, the relief of the reserve mainly consists of a succession of round-topped hills. Cliffs in the south are associated with a section of the river broken up by rapids and waterfalls. Although the area is poorly studied, it is known to have many primates. Other mammals include elephant, buffalo, leopard, warthog and pangolin. Reptiles include python, lizard and two species of crocodile, both of which are threatened.
Criteria: ix, x Inscribed 1987

• MOUNT ATHOS Greece

Mount Athos (the 'Holy Mountain') is a self-governing monastic republic within Greece, which is forbidden to women and children. There are twenty monasteries, twelve sketes (convents), and about 700 houses, cells or hermitages. The monasteries of Mount Athos house a wealth of artistic masterpieces, including wall paintings, portable icons, gold objects, embroideries and illuminated manuscripts which each monastery carefully preserves. Mount Athos is the spiritual centre of the Orthodox world, and has exerted a lasting influence both on it and on the development of religious architecture and monumental painting.
Criteria: i, ii, iv, v, vi, vii Inscribed 1988

• OLD TOWNS OF DJENNÉ Mali

Inhabited since 250 BC, Djenné became a market centre and was an important link in the trans-Saharan gold trade. In the fifteenth and sixteenth centuries it was one of the centres for the propagation of Islam. Its traditional houses, of which nearly 2,000 have survived, are built on hillocks called *toguère*, as protection from the seasonal Niger floods. Djenné spreads over several *toguère* and is bisected by a wide avenue. Traditional houses extend from both sides of this thoroughfare, over approximately 2km². The main feature of the domestic architecture, influenced by that of Morocco, is its verticality.
Criteria: iii, iv Inscribed 1988

Uluru, composed of hard red sandstone, is 9.4 km in circumference and rises to a relatively flat top that is more than 340 m above the shallow, red sandy dunes around it.

Monticello, Thomas Jefferson's plantation home.

Over 1,000 monks live on Mount Athos, either in communities or alone, as well as in the 'desert' of Karoulia where cells cling to the cliff face rising steeply above the sea.

• WET TROPICS OF QUEENSLAND Australia

The Wet Tropics of Queensland provides an unparalleled living record of the ecological and evolutionary processes shaping the flora and fauna of Australia: first when it was part of the Pangaean landmass; then as the ancient continent Gondwana; and for the past 50 million years an island continent. The rainforests, which make up about 80 per cent of the site, have more plant families with primitive characteristics than any other area on Earth. Australia's unique marsupials and many of its other animals originated in rainforest ecosystems, and the Wet Tropics of Queensland still contains many of their closest surviving members.
Criteria: vii, viii, ix, x Inscribed 1988

• TOWER OF LONDON United Kingdom

The Tower of London is an imposing fortress with a long history. Built by William the Conqueror to protect his London base and to assert his power over the newly conquered English, it became a symbol of royalty. The Tower is a complex of fortifications, courtyards and buildings extending over 73,000 m². The Water Gate entrance was nicknamed Traitors' Gate because prisoners were brought through it to the Tower. Although a royal residence for centuries, the White Tower was regarded as a stronghold rather than the main royal palace. The Crown Jewels are displayed in the Tower of London.
Criteria: ii, iv Inscribed 1988

• MANOVO-GOUNDA ST FLORIS NATIONAL PARK Central African Republic

The importance of this park derives from its wealth of flora and fauna. Its vast savannas are home to a wide variety of species: black rhinoceroses, elephants, cheetahs, leopards, wild dogs, red-fronted gazelles and buffalo, while various types of waterfowl are to be found in the northern floodplains. Some 320 species of bird have been identified in the park, with at least twenty-five species of raptor including bateleur and African fish eagle. There are large seasonal populations of pelican and marabou stork, and many waterbirds and shorebirds.
Criteria: ix, x Inscribed 1988

• PALAEOCHRISTIAN AND BYZANTINE MONUMENTS OF THESSALONIKA Greece

Founded in 315 BC, the provincial capital and sea port of Thessalonika was one of the first bases for the spread of Christianity. St Paul visited twice, in AD 50 and 56, and founded a church. Some of Thessalonika's churches were built on the Greek cross plan and others on the three-nave basilica plan. They were constructed over a long period, from the fourth to the fifteenth century and had considerable influence in the Byzantine world. The mosaics of the rotunda, St Demetrius and St David are among the great masterpieces of early Christian art.
Criteria: i, ii, iv Inscribed 1988

• SANCTUARY OF ASKLEPIOS AT EPIDAURUS Greece

The shrine of Asklepios, the god of medicine, developed in the sixth century BC from an earlier cult of Apollo Maleatas. There are several exceptional examples of Hellenic architecture of the fourth century BC and Epidaurus flourished during the Hellenistic period. Despite pillaging by Sulla in 87 BC and by Cilician pirates, the sanctuary prospered during the Roman period, and the group of temples and hospital facilities comprising the Sanctuary of Epidaurus testify to the healing cults of both the Hellenic and Roman worlds.
Criteria: i, ii, iii, iv, vi Inscribed 1988

• SINHARAJA FOREST RESERVE Sri Lanka

Sinharaja, a narrow strip of land consisting of a series of ridges and valleys, is Sri Lanka's last viable area of primary tropical rainforest. There are two main types of forest: Dipterocarpus forest in valleys and lower slopes; and secondary forest and scrub where original forest cover has been removed. Some of the forest has been

The White Tower, begun around 1078 and completed around nine years later, is the centrepiece of the Tower of London. It stands more than 27 m high with walls over 4.5 m thick at their base.

The theatre at Epidaurus, famed for its setting and the perfection of its proportions and acoustics, is an architectural masterpiece by Polycletes the Younger of Argos.

replaced by rubber and tea plantations. Mesua-Doona forest is the climax vegetation in most of the reserve. The reserve is home to over 50 per cent of Sri Lanka's endemic species of mammals and butterflies, and to many kinds of insects, reptiles and rare amphibians.
Criteria: ix, x Inscribed 1988

• SACRED CITY OF KANDY Sri Lanka

The sacred Buddhist city of Kandy, founded in the fourteenth century and popularly known as the city of Senkadagalapura, was the last capital of the Sinhala kings, whose patronage enabled the Dinahala culture to flourish for more than 2,500 years. It is the site of the Temple of the Tooth Relic (Dalada Maligawa), where the sacred tooth of the Buddha is enshrined. Each year, on the feast of Esala Perahera, one of the inner caskets used for covering the tooth relic is taken in a grand procession through the streets of the city.
Criteria: iv, vi Inscribed 1988

• MEDINA OF SOUSSE Tunisia

Sousse was an important commercial and military port during the ninth century Aghlabid period. Among the earliest buildings is the *ribat*, a combined fort and religious building which had a tower serving both as a watchtower and a minaret. Under the Aghlabids, Sousse rapidly flourished: significant monuments constructed in this golden century included the mosque of Bu Ftata, the first *kasbah*, and the Great Mosque. By 859, the town walls neared completion, and the limits of the medina were broadly drawn. The surrounding fortifications made the military function of the *ribat* less vital and it reverted to its religious function.
Criteria: iii, iv, v Inscribed 1988

• OLD TOWN OF GALLE AND ITS FORTIFICATIONS Sri Lanka

Founded in the sixteenth century by the Portuguese, Galle reached the height of its development in the eighteenth century. It is the best example of a European fortified city in south and southeast Asia, showing the interaction between European architecture and south Asian traditions. Protected by a sea wall, Galle was laid out on a regular grid pattern adapted to the configuration of the terrain, and the Commandant's residence, the arsenal and the powder house were prominent features of the original plan. Coral is frequently used along with granite in the structure of the ramparts.
Criteria: iv Inscribed 1988

• HISTORIC TOWN OF GUANAJUATO AND ADJACENT MINES Mexico

Founded by the Spanish in the early sixteenth century, Guanajuato became the world's leading silver-extraction centre in the eighteenth century. Spanish conquistadores discovered rich outcrops of silver at Guanaxhuata in 1548. Fortified structures were erected at Marfil, Tepetapa, Santa Ana and Cerro del Cuarto and these formed the nuclei of the later town of Guanajuato. The past can be seen in its 'subterranean streets' and beautiful Baroque and neoclassical buildings, built with the prosperity from the mines. The churches of La Compañía (1745–65) and above all La Valenciana (1765–88) are masterpieces of the Mexican Churrigueresque style.
Criteria: i, ii, iv, vi Inscribed 1988

• TIMBUKTU Mali

Home of the prestigious Koranic Sankore University and other *madrasas*, Timbuktu was an important centre for the dissemination of Islam throughout Africa in the fifteenth and sixteenth centuries. Its three great mosques, Djingareyber, Sankore and Sidi Yahia, recall Timbuktu's golden age. Although continuously restored, these monuments are today under threat from desertification. Apart from the mosques, the World Heritage site comprises sixteen cemeteries and mausoleums, essential elements in a religious system as, according to popular belief, they constitute a rampart that shields the city from all misfortune.
Criteria: ii, iv, v Inscribed 1988

A Buddhist temple in Kandy.

One of Guanajuato's subterranean streets.

• MEDIEVAL CITY OF RHODES Greece

The Order of St John of Jerusalem occupied Rhodes from 1309 to 1523 and transformed the city into a stronghold. With the Palace of the Grand Masters, the Great Hospital and the Street of the Knights, the Upper Town (Collachium) is a beautiful example of an urban area from the Gothic period. At the eastern end of the Street of the Knights, built against the wall, is St Mary's Church which the Knights transformed into a cathedral. Rhodes subsequently came under Turkish and Italian rule. In the Lower Town, Gothic architecture coexists with mosques, public baths and other buildings from the Ottoman period.

Criteria: ii, iv, v Inscribed 1988

• HENDERSON ISLAND United Kingdom

Henderson Island, a raised coral atoll forming part of the Pitcairn Island group in the South Pacific, is one of the few atolls in the world whose ecology has been practically untouched by human presence. Its isolated location provides the ideal context for studying the dynamics of insular evolution and natural selection. The island is arid with only one freshwater spring and has a rugged topography beneath the dense tangled vegetation. It is particularly notable for the ten plant species and four land bird species native to the island.

Criteria: vii, x Inscribed 1988

• ARCHAEOLOGICAL SITES OF BAT, AL-KHUTM AND AL-AYN Oman

The settlement and necropolises of Bat, dating from the third millennium BC, illustrate the evolution of funeral practices during the first Bronze Age in the Oman peninsula. In the settlement, there are five stone 'towers', one of which has been entirely excavated. From the tower, a series of rectangular houses with central courts can be seen to the east and, to the north a vast necropolis. There are two neighbouring contemporary archaeological sites: the tower of Al-Khutm, 2 km west of Bat, and the group of beehive tombs of Qubur Juhhal at Al-Ayn, 22 km east-southeast of Bat.

Criteria: iii, iv Inscribed 1988

• TRINIDAD AND THE VALLEY DE LOS INGENIOS Cuba

Towards the end of the eighteenth century, the sugar industry was firmly established in the Valle de Los Ingenios near Trinidad (founded by the Spanish in the early sixteenth century); by 1796 it was the third-largest city in Cuba. Trinidad owes its charm to its eighteenth- and nineteenth-century buildings, such as the Palacio Brunet and the Palacio Cantero. Valle de Los Ingenios features seventy-five ruined sugar mills, summer mansions, barracks, and other related facilities. The Manaca-Iznaga Tower, built in 1816, is 45 m high, and the tolling of its bells once marked the working day on the sugar plantations.

Criteria: iv, v Inscribed 1988

• HISTORIC CENTRE OF LIMA Peru

Although severely damaged by earthquakes Lima – 'City of the Kings' – founded in 1535 was, until the mid-eighteenth century, the capital and most important city of the Spanish dominions in South America. Historic buildings such as the Torre Tagle Palace date from the seventeenth and eighteenth centuries and are typical examples of Hispano-American Baroque. There are other buildings of the same period and style, with the result that, despite certain nineteenth-century constructions such as the Art Nouveau Casa Courret, the town's historic centre recalls Lima at the time of the Spanish Kingdom of Peru.

Criteria: iv Inscribed 1988

• CANTERBURY CATHEDRAL, ST AUGUSTINE'S ABBEY AND ST MARTIN'S CHURCH
United Kingdom

Canterbury has been the seat of the Archbishop of Canterbury since 597 when Augustine was sent from Rome to bring Christianity to Kent. Three distinct cultural properties are listed: the oldest church in England, St Martin's, which already existed when Augustine

The Knights built the fortifications of Rhodes over two centuries. The ramparts, partially erected on the foundations of the Byzantine enclosure, were constantly maintained and remodelled between the fourteenth and sixteenth centuries.

The San Francisco Convent in Lima.

arrived; the ruins of St Augustine's Abbey, which fell into disuse following the dissolution of the community by Henry VIII in 1538; and the superb Christ Church Cathedral, a breathtaking mixture of Romanesque and Perpendicular Gothic. The cathedral's beauty is enhanced by exceptional stained glass windows which constitute the richest collection in the United Kingdom.
Criteria: i, ii, vi Inscribed 1988

• OLD CITY OF SALAMANCA Spain
From the fifteenth to the eighteenth centuries buildings in many styles grew up around Salamanca's university. The oldest university building, now the Rectorate, is the former Hospital del Estudio, built in 1413. The main university buildings, Las Escuelas Mayores, are grouped around a central patio and were built between 1415 and 1433. Many of Salamanca's other old buildings remain: a Roman bridge; the Old Cathedral and San Marcos (twelfth century); the Salina and the Monterrey palaces (sixteenth century). Salamanca was a key centre of the Churriguera, a group of architects, decorators and sculptors – influential in eighteenth-century Latin America.
Criteria: i, ii, iv Inscribed 1988

• HIERAPOLIS-PAMUKKALE Turkey
The thermal spa of Hierapolis was established at the end of the second century BC by the dynasty of the Attalids, the kings of Pergamon. The Romans took control in 129 BC and the site prospered as a cosmopolitan city where Anatolians, Graeco-Macedonians, Romans and Jews intermingled. The therapeutic virtues of the waters were exploited with immense hot basins and pools for swimming. Hydrotherapy was accompanied by religious practices. Ruins of baths, temples and other Greek monuments can be seen at the site, and also Christian remains, including the cathedral, baptistery, churches and the martyrium of St Philip the Apostle.
Criteria: iii, iv, vii Inscribed 1988

• PRE-HISPANIC CITY OF CHICHEN-ITZA Mexico
The town was established around the early or mid-fifth century AD close to two sources of water in natural cavities (*cenotes* or *chenes*). Following the tenth century conquest of Yucatán by Toltec warriors from the Mexican plateau, a new style (now known as Maya–Yucatec) blending Mayan and Toltec traditions developed. Chichen-Itza clearly illustrates this fusion; examples are the Caracol, a circular observatory, and the Pyramid of Kukulcán (El Castillo) which is surrounded by terraces and major monumental complexes. After the thirteenth century no major monuments appear to have been constructed at Chichen-Itza. The city rapidly declined in the fifteenth century.
Criteria: i, ii, iii Inscribed 1988

• METEORA Greece
The Meteora, or rock pinnacles, are enormous masses of sandstone and conglomerate. Hermits and ascetics probably began settling here in the eleventh century. In the late-twelfth century a small church – the Panaghia Doupiani or 'Skete' – was built at the foot of one such 'heavenly column'. During political instability in fourteenth-century Thessaly, monasteries were systematically built on top of these inaccessible peaks and there were twenty-four by the end of the fifteenth century. They continued to flourish until the seventeenth century. Only four monasteries – the Aghios Stephanos, the Aghia Trias, Varlaam and the Meteoron – now house religious communities.
Criteria: i, ii, iv, v, vii Inscribed 1988

• NANDA DEVI AND VALLEY OF FLOWERS NATIONAL PARKS India
India's richly diverse Valley of Flowers National Park is home to meadows of alpine flowers and to rare and endangered animals. The area is a vast glacial basin, divided by a series of parallel, north–south oriented ridges which rise up to the encircling mountain rim. Nanda Devi West, India's second-highest mountain, lies on a short ridge projecting into the basin. The gentle landscape of the Valley of Flowers National Park complements the rugged

Plaza Mayor, Salamanca, the most sumptuous Baroque square in Spain.

Pyramid of Kukulcán, Chichen-Itza, around which are the Great Ball Court, Skull Wall, Jaguar Temple, House of Eagles, Temple of the Warriors, Group of the Thousand Columns, Tomb of the High Priest, market and ball courts.

mountain wilderness of Nanda Devi National Park. Together they encompass a unique transition zone between the mountain ranges of the Zanskar and Great Himalaya.
Criteria: vii, x Inscribed 1988

• KAIROUAN Tunisia

Founded in 670 Kairouan, one of Islam's holy cities, flourished under the ninth century Aghlabid dynasty. Its rich architectural heritage includes the Great Mosque, with marble and porphyry columns, the ninth century Mosque of the Three Gates and the Basin of the Aghlabids, filled by water brought by an aqueduct. The medina is surrounded by more than 3 km of walls with three gates: its skyline is punctuated by the minarets and cupolas of its mosques and *zawiyas* (monasteries), and it has preserved its network of winding streets and courtyard houses.
Criteria: i, ii, iii, v, vi Inscribed 1988

• XANTHOS-LETOON Turkey

This site, which was the capital of Lycia, illustrates the blending of Lycian traditions and Hellenic influence, especially in its funerary art. The epigraphic inscriptions are crucial for our understanding of the history of the Lycian people and their Indo-European language. The Lycians were one of the 'Sea Peoples' who invaded the Hittite Empire around 1200 BC. The Greek historian Herodotus, who lived in the fifth century BC, related that they came from Crete to take part in the Trojan War.
Criteria: ii, iii Inscribed 1988

• STRASBOURG – GRANDE ÎLE France

Surrounded by two arms of the river Ill, the Grande Île (Large Island) of Strasbourg is the historic centre of the Alsatian capital. Rising above the high-pitched roofs with multi-storeyed dormer windows, the cathedral and four ancient churches stand out on the skyline. Facing the south transept of the cathedral is the Palais Rohan, built by the Rohan family in 1732–42 as a residence for the cardinals, princes and bishops of the family. The tight network of streets contain public buildings such as the Hôtel de Ville and also inns, shops, workshops and elegant town mansions.
Criteria: i, ii, iv Inscribed 1988

• ARCHAEOLOGICAL SITE OF OLYMPIA Greece

Olympia has been inhabited since prehistoric times. Religious centres of worship succeeded one another during the Hellenic period until, in the tenth century BC, Olympia became a centre for the worship of Zeus. Consecrated to Zeus, the Altis is a major sanctuary that includes the ruins of the two principal temples: the Temple of Hera (sixth century BC) and the Temple of Zeus (fifth century BC). In addition, the site includes the remains of the sports stadia and other structures erected for the Olympic Games, which were held in Olympia every four years beginning in 776 BC.
Criteria: i, ii, iii, iv, vi Inscribed 1989

• MOSI-OA-TUNYA / VICTORIA FALLS
Zambia and Zimbabwe

When the Zambezi is in full flood (usually February or March) the Victoria Falls form the largest curtain of falling water in the world. During these months over 500 million litres of water per minute go over the falls, which are 1,708 m wide, and drop 99 m at Rainbow Falls in Zambia. At low water in November flow can be reduced to around 10 million litres per minute, and the river is divided into a series of braided channels that descend in many separate falls. The riverine 'rainforest' within the waterfall splash zone is of particular interest: a fragile ecosystem of discontinuous forest on sandy alluvium, dependent upon maintenance of abundant water and high humidity resulting from the spray plume. There are many tree species within this forest and also some herbaceous species. Several herds of elephant live in Zambezi National Park, occasionally crossing to the islands and Zambian mainland during the dry season when water levels are low.
Criteria: vii, viii Inscribed 1989

The Zawiya of Sidi Sahab at Kairouan, where the remains of Abu Djama, one of Muhammad's companions, are kept, is the first Islamic place of worship, founded only thirty-eight years after the Prophet Muhammad's death.

The Victoria Falls: the Zambezi River, which is more than 2 km wide at this point, plunges down a series of basalt gorges and raises an iridescent mist that can be seen more than 20 km away.

▪ MONASTERY OF ALCOBAÇA Portugal

This Cistercian monastery contains the Gothic church of Santa Maria d'Alcobaça and a significant grouping of medieval monastic buildings (cloister and lavabo, chapter room, parlour, dormitory, the monks' room and the refectory). The monastery was given by King Alfonso I to the Cistercians after 1152 on the understanding that they would colonise and work the surrounding lands. The ultimate symbol of its privileged relationship with the Portuguese monarchy is found in the tombs of Dom Pedro and Doña Inés de Castro, dating from 1360, among the most beautiful of Gothic funerary sculptures.
Criteria: i, iv Inscribed 1989

▪ CLIFF OF BANDIAGARA (LAND OF THE DOGONS) Mali

Bandiagara is an outstanding landscape of cliffs and sandy plateaus and one of the main centres for the Dogon culture. The Dogon subsistence farmers did not arrive until the fifteenth and sixteenth centuries, yet the region is rich in unique architecture, from flat-roofed huts to tapering granaries capped with thatch, cliff cemeteries and communal meeting-places. Several age-old social traditions live on in the region, through masks, feasts, rituals, and ceremonies involving ancestor worship. The Dogon people also maintain a strong relationship with the environment with their use of curative and medicinal wild plants and the sacred associations with pale fox, jackal and crocodile.
Criteria: v, vii Inscribed 1989

▪ BANC D'ARGUIN NATIONAL PARK Mauritania

Banc d'Arguin is located on the Atlantic desert-coast of Mauritania, and is a transition zone between the Sahara and the Atlantic, with dunes of windblown Saharan sand, shallow coastal pools, mudflats and mangrove swamps. The contrast between the harsh desert environment and the biodiversity of the marine zone has resulted in area of outstanding natural significance. Shallow water vegetation comprises extensive seagrass beds and various seaweeds, offering a favourable habitat for fish. This attracts huge numbers of birds, hosting the largest concentration of wintering waders in the world and an extremely diversified community of nesting fish-eating birds.
Criteria: ix, x Inscribed 1989

▪ BUDDHIST MONUMENTS AT SANCHI India

On a hill, about 40 km from Bhopal, Sanchi comprises a group of Buddhist monuments, monolithic pillars, palaces, temples and monasteries, mainly dating back to the second and first centuries BC. It is the oldest Buddhist sanctuary in existence and was a major centre of Buddhism in India until the twelfth century AD. The principal monument at Sanchi, known as Stupa 1, consists of a gigantic mound of sandstone surrounded by sumptuous porticoes with stone railings. When it was discovered in 1818, Sanchi had lain abandoned for 600 years. Gradually the hill was cleared, uncovering the ruins of about fifty monuments.
Criteria: i, ii, iii, iv, vi Inscribed 1989

▪ ARCHAEOLOGICAL SITE OF MYSTRAS Greece

Mystras was built around the fortress erected in 1249 on a hill overlooking Sparta by William of Villehardouin. For almost six centuries, Mystras had a troubled existence and was abandoned in 1832, leaving only the breathtaking medieval ruins. The bishopric of Sparta was transferred to the new city: the Metropolis, dedicated to St Demetrios, was built in 1264, and convents were built and richly decorated. Mystras was a cosmopolitan city and capital of the Despotate of Morea (1348–1460). Its fall to the Turks on 30 May 1460 was seen as almost equal in importance to the fall of Constantinople in 1453.
Criteria: ii, iii, iv Inscribed 1989

▪ MONASTERIES OF DAPHNI, HOSIOS LOUKAS AND NEA MONI OF CHIOS Greece

The monasteries at Daphni, in Attica, near Athens, Hosios Loukas, in Phocida near Delphi, and Nea Moni, on the island of Chios in the Aegean Sea all belong to the same typological series and share the

Front entrance of the Monastery of Alcobaça. In the thirteenth century, the abbey's intellectual and political influence spread throughout the western part of the Iberian Peninsula.

The ruined churches of Mystras, which, during the fourteenth century had been covered with frescoes; the renown of its libraries and the glory of its writers gave substance to the legend of the 'Wonder of Morea'.

same characteristics. The churches are built on a cross-in-square plan with a large dome supported by squinches defining an octagonal space. In the eleventh and twelfth centuries they were decorated with superb marble works as well as mosaics on a gold background, all characteristic of the 'second golden age of Byzantine art'.
Criteria: i, iv Inscribed 1990

• HISTORIC CENTRE OF SAINT PETERSBURG AND RELATED GROUPS OF MONUMENTS
Russian Federation

The city of St Petersburg on Russia's Baltic coast is the result of a vast urban project begun in 1703 under Peter the Great. Known as the 'Venice of the North', a network of canals, streets and quays was gradually constructed, giving the urban landscape of St Petersburg its monumental splendour. Foreign architects rivalled one another in their designs of huge palaces and convents, and in imperial and princely suburban residences. The city's architectural heritage reconciles the very different Baroque and pure neoclassical styles, as can be seen in the Admiralty, the Winter Palace, the Marble Palace and the Hermitage.
Criteria: i, ii, iv, vi Inscribed 1990

• PALACES AND PARKS OF POTSDAM AND BERLIN Germany

King Frederick the Great of Prussia (1712–1786) transformed Potsdam into the 'Prussian Versailles'. With 5 km² of parks and 150 buildings constructed between 1730 and 1916, Potsdam's complex of palaces and parks forms an artistic whole. The area extends into the district of Berlin-Zehlendorf, with palaces and parks lining the banks of the river Havel and Lake Glienicke. The Marble Palace, the king's summer residence, stands in the middle of the New Garden, and at this park's northern end is the Chateau of Cecilienhof – the site of the Potsdam Conference that decided the fate of postwar Germany.
Criteria: i, ii, iv Inscribed 1990

• COLONIAL CITY OF SANTO DOMINGO
Dominican Republic

The Colonial City (Ciudad Colonial) of Santo Domingo, founded in 1498, became the site of the first cathedral (constructed between 1514 and 1542), hospital, customs house and university in the Americas. The town was laid out on a grid pattern that became the model for almost all town planners in the New World. The Ozama Fortress and Tower of Homage were built in 1503: this stone group is said to be the oldest formal military outpost still standing in the Americas. The Tower of Homage in the centre of the grounds is an impressive architectural structure.
Criteria: ii, iv, vi Inscribed 1990

• KIEV: SAINT-SOPHIA CATHEDRAL AND RELATED MONASTIC BUILDINGS, KIEV-PECHERSK LAVRA Ukraine

Kiev's Saint-Sophia Cathedral symbolises the 'new Constantinople', capital of the Christian principality of Kiev, created in the eleventh century. Devastated by the Mongols and the Tatars, Kiev-Pechersk Lavra was almost entirely rebuilt from the seventeenth century onwards. The Clock Tower and the Refectory Church are two of the main landmarks. Other important monuments include Trinity Church, whose twelfth-century structure is hidden by extremely rich Baroque decor, and the catacombs, which include the Near Caves and the Far Caves, whose entrances are respectively at All Saints' Church and at the Church of the Conception of St Anna.
Criteria: i, ii, iii, iv Inscribed 1990

• JESUIT MISSIONS OF THE CHIQUITOS Bolivia

Jesuit fathers arrived in Peru in 1567, and between 1696 and 1760, six groupings of *reducciones* (settlements of Christianised Indians inspired by the 'ideal cities' of the sixteenth-century philosophers) were founded by the Jesuits in a style combining Catholic architecture with local traditions. The *reducciones* defined the urban model: houses were spaced along three sides of a rectangular space, with the fourth reserved for the church, workshops and schools,

The Winter Palace in St Petersburg.

Chinese Tea House in Sanssouci Park, Potsdam.

Saint-Sophia Cathedral in Kiev, designed to rival Hagia Sophia in Constantinople.

and sometimes for the Casa de la Misericordia (almshouse), for widows and abandoned women. Six *reducciones* remain – San Francisco Javier, Concepción, Santa Ana, San Miguel, San Rafael and San José.
Criteria: iv, v Inscribed 1990

▪TONGARIRO NATIONAL PARK New Zealand

Tongariro National Park is situated on the central North Island volcanic plateau. The mountains at the heart of the park have cultural and religious significance for the Maori people, symbolising the spiritual links between this community and its environment. Glaciers are currently restricted to Mount Ruapehu, although all are now less than 1 km in length. Habitats range from remnants of rainforest to practically barren ice fields. The vertebrate fauna is restricted mainly to birds, although native mammals are represented by short-tailed bat and long-tailed bat. More than fifty-six bird species have been recorded in the park.
Criteria: vi, vii, viii Inscribed 1990

▪ITCHAN KALA Uzbekistan

Itchan Kala is the inner town, protected by brick walls some 10 m high, of the old Khiva oasis, which was the last resting-place of caravans before crossing the desert to Iran. Although few very old buildings still remain, it is a coherent and well-preserved example of the Muslim architecture of Central Asia. There are several outstanding structures such as the Djuma Mosque, the mausoleums and the *madrasas*, and the two magnificent palaces built at the beginning of the nineteenth century by Alla-Kulli-Khan.
Criteria: iii, iv, v Inscribed 1990

▪KREMLIN AND RED SQUARE, MOSCOW
Russian Federation

The citadel of the Kremlin was built between the fourteenth and seventeenth centuries. It contains a unique series of architectural and artistic masterpieces. These include religious monuments of exceptional beauty such as the Church of the Annunciation, Cathedral of the Dormition, Church of the Archangel and the bell tower of Ivan Veliki; and palaces such as the Great Palace of the Kremlin, the yellow-and-white palace of the tsars which contains the Church of the Nativity of the Virgin, and the Teremnoi Palace. Red Square lies next to the Kremlin, and is closely associated with it.
Criteria: i, ii, iv, vi Inscribed 1990

▪TSINGY DE BEMARAHA STRICT NATURE RESERVE Madagascar

This reserve contains spectacular karstic landscapes and limestone uplands cut into impressive *tsingy* peaks (sharp-edged tall towers of limestone). To the east of this karsitic area, abrupt cliffs rising some 300–400 m above the Manambolo river form an impressive canyon. The western part of the reserve forms a plateau with rounded hillocks. To the north undulating hills alternate with limestone extrusions, whereas in the south extensive pinnacle formations make access extremely restricted. Vegetation is characteristic of the calcareous karst regions of western Madagascar, with dense, dry, deciduous forest, and extensive savannas and some mangrove swamps.
Criteria: vii, x Inscribed 1990

▪DELOS Greece

Delos – the birthplace of Apollo according to Greek mythology – illustrates Aegean civilisations from the third millennium BC to the early Christian era. The island's landscape now consists solely of exceptionally extensive and rich ruins unearthed systematically since 1872. The principal zones are the northeast coastal plain (Sanctuary of Apollo, Agora of the Compitaliasts, Agora of the Delians); the Sacred Lake region (Agora of Theophrastos, Agora of the Italians, the renowned Terrace of the Lions); the Mount Kynthos area (Terrace of the Sanctuaries of the Foreign Gods, Heraion); and the theatre quarter, whose poignant ruins have been overrun by vegetation.
Criteria: ii, iii, iv, vi Inscribed 1990

Emerald Lake in Tongariro National Park.

St Basil's Cathedral, at the south end of Red Square, is one of the most beautiful monuments of Orthodox art.

•TE WAHIPOUNAMU – SOUTH WEST NEW ZEALAND New Zealand

Te Wahipounamu has some 20,000 km² of temperate rainforest, 450 km² of alpine communities, and a distinctive fauna. The park contains the best modern representation of the ancient flora and fauna of the original southern supercontinent of Gondwanaland. The area is overwhelming mountainous and glaciers are an important feature, especially in the vicinity of Westland and Aoraki/Mount Cook national parks. There are luxuriant rainforest and wetlands in the west; more open forest, shrublands and tussock grasslands in the drier, more continental east. The most extensive and least modified natural freshwater wetlands in New Zealand are found in this area.
Criteria: vii, viii, ix, x Inscribed 1990

•KIZHI POGOST Russian Federation

The *pogost* of Kizhi (the Kizhi enclosure) is on an island in Lake Onega, in Karelia. Kizhi Pogost represents the adaptation of the Orthodox Church parish organisation to the challenges posed by the immense distances and far-flung communities of northern Russia. Here, all the buildings needed in the parish's religious life were grouped in one place. There are two eighteenth-century wooden churches, and an octagonal wooden clock tower built in 1862. These unusual constructions, in which carpenters created a bold visionary architecture, perpetuate an ancient model of parish space.
Criteria: i, iv, v Inscribed 1990

•RÍO ABISEO NATIONAL PARK Peru

Río Abiseo National Park, renowned for pristine primary cloud forest and highland grasslands (*paramo*), is mountainous, often with very steep slopes. Its soils are generally acidic and have never been disturbed by agriculture or timber extraction. The park was created in 1983 to protect the fauna and flora of the rainforests, which includes many rare and important species. Thirty-six archaeological sites which give a good picture of pre-Inca society have been found at altitudes of between 2,500 and 4,000 m. Evidence suggests that humans settled in the area from as early as 6000 BC.
Criteria: iii, vii, ix, x Inscribed 1990

•MOUNT HUANGSHAN China

Huangshan has been acclaimed in art and literature for much of Chinese history. It is renowned for its magnificent scenery of granite peaks and strangely shaped rocks emerging out of a sea of clouds, and it has many beautiful ridges, gorges, forests, lakes and waterfalls. Many of the lakes have clear blue, turquoise or green waters, and in autumn many of the leaves turn a range of rich colours. A number of trees are celebrated for their age, grotesque shape or precipitously perched position, including 1,000-year-old specimens of Huangshan pine, ginkgo and alpine juniper.
Criteria: ii, vii, x Inscribed 1990

•HISTORIC CENTRE OF SAN GIMIGNANO Italy

San Gimignano demonstrates life in the Italian Middle Ages, grouping together squares and streets, houses and palaces, wells and fountains in a small area. Frescoes commissioned by the township in 1303 to decorate the chambers of the podestà in the Palazzo del Popolo illustrate early fourteenth century daily life. Seventy-two tower houses, some as high as 50 m, were built by members of two rival families as symbols of wealth and power. Fourteen such tower houses have survived. The historic centre of San Gimignano contains a series of masterpieces of fourteenth- and fifteenth-century Italian art in their original settings.
Criteria: i, iii, iv Inscribed 1990

•HISTORIC CITY OF AYUTTHAYA Thailand

Founded around 1350, Ayutthaya was the second Siamese capital after Sukhothai and became one of the largest and wealthiest cities in the East. Initially, Ayutthayan art was characterised by a mixture of local traditions with strong influences from Sukhothai. It was only from the fifteenth century that a true national Thai art was born, the product of diverse cultural influences. The city's characteristic architectural feature was the *prang*, a reliquary tower. The kings of

Aoraki (Mount Cook) in Te Wahipounamu.

One of the few undamaged buddhas remaining at Ayutthaya. The city was destroyed by the Burmese in 1765 but its remains give an idea of its past splendour.

Ayutthaya richly endowed the city with monasteries, such as Wat Mahathat, as well as the Royal Palace, Wang Luang, and gigantic Buddha statues.
Criteria: iii Inscribed 1991

•PARIS, BANKS OF THE SEINE France

From the Louvre to the Eiffel Tower, from the Place de la Concorde to the Grand and Petit Palais, the evolution of Paris and its history can be seen from the river Seine. The Cathedral of Notre Dame and the Sainte Chapelle are architectural masterpieces while Baron Haussmann's wide squares and boulevards of the nineteenth century influenced town planning the world over. The present historic city, which developed between the sixteenth and the twentieth century, shows the evolution of the relationship between the river and the people: for defence, for trading, for promenades, and so on. Haussmann's urban plan, which marks the western part of the city, inspired the construction of the great cities of the New World, particularly in Latin America. The Eiffel Tower and the Palais de Chaillot are living testimony of the great universal exhibitions which were of such great importance in the nineteenth and twentieth centuries.
Criteria: i, ii, iv Inscribed 1991

•DANUBE DELTA Romania

As it flows into the Black Sea, the Danube forms Europe's second largest delta. The area has numerous freshwater lakes interconnected by narrow channels with huge expanses of aquatic vegetation. It has been classified into twelve habitat types: aquatic, lakes covered with flooded reedbeds; '*plaur*', or flooded islets; flooded reeds and willows; riverine forest of willows and poplars; cane fields; sandy and muddy beaches; wet meadows; dry meadows; human settlements; sandy and rocky areas; steep banks; and forests on high ground. Over 300 bird species have been recorded, of which over 176 breed, the most important being cormorant, pygmy cormorant, white pelican and Dalmatian pelican.
Criteria: vii, x Inscribed 1991

•THUNGYAI-HUAI KHA KHAENG WILDLIFE SANCTUARIES Thailand

The site comprises two wildlife sanctuaries: Thung Yai and Huai Kha Khaeng, which cover more than 6,000 km² along Thailand's western border with Myanmar (Burma). The sanctuaries contain examples of almost all the forest types of continental southeast Asia and are among the few areas in Asia large enough to support viable populations of large herbivores (300 elephants) and predators (e.g. tigers). They are home to a very diverse array of animals. The reason for such exceptional diversity is partly due to its status as one of only two evergreen forest refuges during the driest periods of the Pleistocene glaciations.
Criteria: vii, ix, x Inscribed 1991

•GOLDEN TEMPLE OF DAMBULLA Sri Lanka

A sacred pilgrimage site for twenty-two centuries, this cave monastery, with its five sanctuaries, is the largest and best-preserved cave-temple complex in Sri Lanka. The site was originally occupied by a Buddhist monastic establishment; remains of eighty rock-shelter residences established at that time have been identified. Most probably in the first century BC, the uppermost shelters on Dambulla's south face were transformed into shrines. Cave-temples were extended into the sheltering rock, and brick walls constructed to screen the caves. By the end of the twelfth century, with the introduction of sculpture on the upper terrace, the caves assumed their present form.
Criteria: i, vi Inscribed 1991

•ISLAND OF MOZAMBIQUE Mozambique

The Island of Mozambique saw the development of the Portuguese trade routes to India and Asia, starting with Vasco da Gama's first visit in 1498. Its towns and the fortifications, and those on the smaller island of St Laurent, are an outstanding example of an architecture in which local traditions, Portuguese influences, and to a lesser extent

The river Seine in Paris, with the Eiffel Tower on the left.

The Danube delta is a remarkable alluvial feature that provides the major remaining wetland for migratory birds on the flyway between central and Eastern Europe and the Mediterranean, Middle East and Africa.

The Buddhist mural paintings at the Golden Temple of Dambulla cover an area of 2,100 m² and are of particular importance, as are the 157 statues.

Indian and Arab influences, are all interwoven. Its architectural unity derives from the uninterrupted use of the same building techniques, materials and decorative principles, as seen in its oldest fortress – St Sebastian (1558–1620) – other defensive buildings and numerous religious buildings, many from the sixteenth century.
Criteria: iv, vi Inscribed 1991

•POBLET MONASTERY Spain

Santa María of Poblet is a majestic and austere Cistercian abbey. North of the church is the great cloister with its fountain, chapter room, monks' dormitory, closed cloister, calefactory, refectory and kitchens. The former lay brothers' buildings are on the west and the infirmary to the north. As a fortress, its walls are an excellent example of fourteenth-century military architecture. Poblet is directly associated with the history of the royal houses of Barcelona, Aragon and Castile. Shortly after 1349 Peter IV had a dynastic burial place built in the abbey church and part of the monastery was used as a royal residence.
Criteria: i, iv Inscribed 1991

•HISTORIC CITY OF SUCRE Bolivia

Sucre was founded as the city of La Plata in 1538. The city's buildings blend local architectural traditions with styles imported from Europe. There are many well-preserved sixteenth-century religious buildings, such as San Lázaro, San Francisco and Santo Domingo. The impressive Metropolitan Cathedral was begun in 1559 but not finished until 250 years later. In August 1825, the republic of Bolivia declared its independence and the city's name was changed in honour of Mariscal António José de Sucre, who fought against Spanish rule. Many key events that led to independence took place at the House of Freedom in Sucre.
Criteria: iv Inscribed 1991

•AÏR AND TÉNÉRÉ NATURAL RESERVES Niger

This is the second-largest protected area in Africa, covering some 77,000 km². It includes the volcanic rock mass of the Aïr, a small Sahelian pocket, isolated as regards its climate and flora and fauna, and situated in the Saharan desert of Ténéré. The reserves boast an outstanding variety of landscapes, plant species and wild animals. The reserves harbour significant populations of the wild relatives of several important crop species: olive, millet and sorghum. Both Sudanese and Mediterranean flora are found above 1,000 m in the sheltered wetter localities in the massifs.
Criteria: vii, ix, x Inscribed 1991

•SHARK BAY, WESTERN AUSTRALIA Australia

At the most westerly point of the Australian continent, Shark Bay, with its islands, is an area of major zoological importance, primarily due to its isolation. The region has three exceptional natural features: its vast seagrass beds, which are the largest and richest in the world; its population of around 10,000 dugongs or 'sea cows'; and its stromatolites, colonies of algae which form hard, dome-shaped deposits and are among the oldest forms of life on Earth. Shark Bay is home to five species of endangered mammals and has a rich birdlife, with over 230 species, or 35 per cent of Australia's bird species, having been recorded.
Criteria: vii, viii, ix, x Inscribed 1991

•OLD RAUMA Finland

Situated on the Gulf of Bothnia, Rauma is one of the oldest harbours in Finland. Built around a Franciscan monastery, where the mid-fifteenth-century Holy Cross Church still stands, it is an outstanding example of an old Nordic city constructed in wood. Although ravaged by fire in the late seventeenth century, it has preserved its ancient vernacular architectural heritage.
Criteria: iv, v Inscribed 1991

•HISTORIC CENTRE OF MORELIA Mexico

Built in the sixteenth century, Morelia combines the ideas of the Spanish Renaissance with the Mesoamerican experience. In 1537 a Franciscan monastery was established near the Indian village of

Lying midway between Tarragona and Lérida, at the foot of the Sierra de Montsant, the Cistercian monastery of Poblet was founded in 1150 by the monks of Fontfroide.

Part of the landscape of the Aïr and Ténéré Natural Reserves, in the Sahara desert.

A courtyard with a fountain in the historic centre of Morelia. In 1828 Valladolid was renamed Morelia in honour of José Maria Morelos, a priest born in the town, who helped lead Mexico to independence.

Guayangareo. In 1541, it became the new provincial capital, renamed Valladolid. Although fifty noble families settled here, as did many Europeans over the next few centuries, the population remained predominantly of Indian origin. Well-adapted to its hilly site, streets still follow the original grid layout. More than 200 historic buildings, including twenty public buildings and twenty-one churches, all in the region's characteristic pink stone, reflect the town's architectural history.
Criteria: ii, iv, vi Inscribed 1991

•KOMODO NATIONAL PARK Indonesia

These volcanic islands in southern Indonesia, of which Komodo is the largest, are best known for the Komodo monitors, giant lizards that exist nowhere else in the world and are of great interest in the study of evolution. Mammals include primates such as crab-eating macaque. Introduced species, such as wild boar, as well as feral domestic animals, form important prey species for the Komodo monitor. The rugged hillsides of dry savanna and pockets of thorny green vegetation contrast starkly with the brilliant white sandy beaches and the blue waters surging over coral.
Criteria: vii, x Inscribed 1991

•ROYAL DOMAIN OF DROTTNINGHOLM
Sweden

With its castle, its perfectly preserved theatre, its Chinese pavilion and gardens, Drottningholm is the finest example of an eighteenth-century north European royal residence inspired by the Palace of Versailles. The royal domain of Drottningholm (meaning 'Queen's Island') is located on Lake Mälaren, outside Stockholm, and the island's name acknowledges the closely interwoven history of the castle with the queens of Sweden. The castle was begun in the seventeenth century but work on it continued throughout the eighteenth century. The Chinese pavilion, built in 1769, is a most important European example of this type of structure.
Criteria: iv Inscribed 1991

•SERRA DA CAPIVARA NATIONAL PARK Brazil

Many of the numerous rock shelters in the Serra da Capivara National Park are decorated with cave paintings, some more than 25,000 years old. Those in the Pedra Furada shelter appear to be the oldest traces of rock art in South America. The paintings' iconography reveals major aspects of the religious beliefs and practices of the area's ancient inhabitants. In total, over 300 archaeological sites have been found within the park. Certain geological formations and palaeofauna that included giant sloths, horses, camelids and early llamas indicate that the Ice Age environment was quite different from today's semi-arid conditions.
Criteria: iii Inscribed 1991

•CATHEDRAL OF NOTRE-DAME, FORMER ABBEY OF SAINT-RÉMI AND PALACE OF TAU, REIMS France

The outstanding Gothic architecture and sculpture of Reims cathedral influenced numerous buildings, particularly in regions of Germany. Its thirteenth-century builders, perhaps conscious of erecting the cathedral for the coronation of the kings of France, gave its structure great lightness and made more windows to allow more light to filter through the stained glass and illuminate the sacred space within. The former abbey of Saint Rémi still has its beautiful ninth-century nave in which lie the remains of Archbishop Saint Rémi (440–533). The former archepiscopal palace, known as the Tau Palace was almost entirely rebuilt in the seventeenth century.
Criteria: i, ii, vi Inscribed 1991

•UJUNG KULON NATIONAL PARK Indonesia

This national park, located in the extreme southwest tip of Java on the Sunda shelf, includes the Ujung Kulon peninsula and several offshore islands and encompasses the nature reserve of Krakatoa. In addition to its natural beauty and geological interest – particularly for the study of inland volcanoes – it contains the largest remaining

A Komodo monitor, the world's largest living lizard. Their appearance and aggressive behaviour have led to them being called 'Komodo dragons'.

Drottningholm Castle.

The east end of the towering Gothic Cathedral of Notre-Dame, Reims.

area of lowland rainforests in the Java plain. Several species of endangered plants and animals can be found there, the Javan rhinoceros being the most under threat.
Criteria: vii, x Inscribed 1991

•PRAMBANAN TEMPLE COMPOUNDS Indonesia

Prambanan is a magnificent Hindu temple complex in Java, built in the ninth century and designed as three concentric squares. In all there are 224 temples in the entire complex. The inner square contains sixteen temples, the most significant being the imposing 47-m high Siva temple flanked to the north by the Brahma temple and to the south by the Vishnu temple. There are also three smaller temples for the animals who serve them (Bull for Siva, Eagle for Brahma and Swan for Vishnu). The compound was deserted soon after it was completed, possibly owing to the eruption of nearby volcano, Mount Merapi.
Criteria: i, iv Inscribed 1991

•HISTORIC TOWN OF SUKHOTHAI AND ASSOCIATED HISTORIC TOWNS Thailand

Sukhothai was the capital of the first Kingdom of Siam in the thirteenth and fourteenth centuries. The great civilisation of Sukhothai absorbed numerous influences and local traditions to create the 'Sukhothai style'. It has a number of fine monuments illustrating the beginnings of Thai architecture, including the monastery (*wat*) Mahathat, with its royal temple and its cemetery; Sra Si Wat, with two stupas, their graceful lines reflected in the water of the town's biggest reservoir; and a large part of its fortifications. The associated towns of Si Satchanm, famous for its ceramics, and Kamohena Pet are also included in the site.
Criteria: i, iii Inscribed 1991

•BOROBUDUR TEMPLE COMPOUNDS Indonesia

Borobudur is one of the greatest Buddhist monuments in the world. Founded by a king of the Saliendra dynasty, it was built between AD 750 and 842. It was built on several levels around a hill which forms a natural centre. The first level comprises five square terraces, graduated in size and forming the base of a pyramid. Above this level are three concentric circular platforms crowned by the main *stupa* (relic mound) to which stairways provide access. The base and balustrades enclosing the square terraces are decorated in reliefs sculpted in the stone. They illustrate the different phases of the soul's progression towards redemption and episodes from the life of Buddha. The circular terraces are decorated with seventy-two openwork *stupas*, each containing a statue of Buddha. At the beginning of the eleventh century AD, because of the political situation in Central Java, the Borobudur Temple became completely neglected and it was not rediscovered until the nineteenth century.
Criteria: i, ii, vi Inscribed 1991

•FORTRESS OF SUOMENLINNA Finland

Located on islands off Helsinki, Suomenlinna is one of the largest maritime fortresses in the world. Built in the second half of the eighteenth century by Sweden, when Finland was part of the Swedish realm, the purpose was to link and fortify several islands so that entry into the city's harbour could be controlled. The work began in 1748 under the supervision of the Swedish Admiral Augustin Ehrensvärd, who adapted Vauban's theories to the very special geographical features of Helsinki. By the time of his death in 1772, Ehrensvärd had produced the chain of forts to protect the approaches to Helsinki.
Criteria: iv Inscribed 1991

•ABBEY AND ALTENMÜNSTER OF LORSCH Germany

The religious complex of the ruined Lorsch Abbey with its 1,200-year-old Torhalle (gatehouse) comprises a rare architectural survivor from the Carolingian era with impressively preserved sculptures and paintings. The abbey was founded around 760–4 and its zenith was probably in 876 when, on the death of Louis II the German,

Dedicated to the three great Hindu divinities, Siva, Brahma and Vishnu, Prambanan Temple or Lorojonggrang (Slender Maiden) Temple, as it is known locally, is an outstanding example of Siva art in Indonesia.

One of the statues of Buddha and openwork *stupas* on the circular terraces at Borobudur, whose name is believed to have been derived from the Sanskrit words *vihara Buddha uhr*, meaning 'the Buddhist monastery on the hill'.

it became the burial place for the Carolingian kings of Germany. The monastery flourished throughout the tenth century, but in 1090 was ravaged by fire. Only the Torhalle, part of the Romanesque church, insignificant vestiges of the medieval monastery, and later classical buildings still survive.
Criteria: iii, iv Inscribed 1991

•BOURGES CATHEDRAL France
The Cathedral of St Etienne of Bourges, built between the late twelfth and late thirteenth centuries, is one of the great masterpieces of Gothic art. Its sculptures, including the tympanum of the central portal of the west façade, with its representation of the Last Judgement, and stained-glass windows are particularly striking. The cathedral was built to a simple but harmonious plan: it is basilical in form, with chapels surrounding the nave. The cathedral is still surrounded by the half-timbered houses of the medieval town and is essentially as it was when it was completed, both in form and materials.
Criteria: i, iv Inscribed 1992

•KASBAH OF ALGIERS Algeria
The Kasbah of Algiers preserves traditional houses in which the ancestral Arab lifestyle and Muslim customs have blended with other architectural traditions. It also contains the remains of the citadel, old mosques and Ottoman-style palaces. It stands in one of the finest coastal sites on the Mediterranean, overlooking the islands where a Phoenician trading-post was established in the fourth century BC. This unique natural site has helped define the city's characteristic winding streets and ancient alleys, while the wealth that its position helped create is reflected in the extreme richness of the interior decoration of the houses.
Criteria: ii, v Inscribed 1992

•PUEBLO DE TAOS USA
Situated in the valley of a tributary of the Rio Grande, this adobe pueblo represents the culture of the Pueblo Indians of Arizona and New Mexico. It consists of two clusters of houses built from adobe (sun-dried mud brick). Rooms are stepped back so the roofs of lower units form terraces for those above. Access to upper units is by ladders through holes in the roof. The living quarters are on the top and outside, while the rooms deep within were used for grain storage. The roofs are made from cedar logs, their ends protruding through the walls.
Criteria: iv Inscribed 1992

•JIUZHAIGOU VALLEY SCENIC AND HISTORIC INTEREST AREA China
Stretching over 720 km² in the northern part of Sichuan Province, the jagged Jiuzhaigou valley reaches a height of more than 4,800 m, and comprises a series of diverse forest ecosystems. Its superb landscapes are particularly interesting for their series of narrow conic karst landforms, ribbon lakes and spectacular waterfalls. Some 140 bird species also inhabit the valley, as well as a number of endangered plant and animal species, including the giant panda and the Sichuan takin.
Criteria: vii Inscribed 1992

• HISTORIC CENTRE OF PRAGUE Czech Republic
Prague was founded on the banks of the Vltava in the ninth century. Under Charles IV, the Holy Roman Emperor (1316–78), the city enjoyed a golden age as the imperial capital and became a major centre of culture, attracting artists and architects from across Europe. The historic city of Prague comprises three separate cities: the Old Town (Stare Město), the Lesser Town (Malá Strana) and the New Town (Nove Město). Buildings of particular importance are Prague Castle, the Cathedral of St Vitus, Hradčany Square, the Charles Bridge, the Rotunda of the Holy Rood, the arcaded houses round the Old Town Square, the Church of St James in the Stare Město, and the late-nineteenth-century buildings and town plan of the Nove Město.
Criteria: ii, iv, vi Inscribed 1992

Stained glass window in the choir of the Bourges cathedral.

The Charles Bridge and bridge tower in Prague on the Stare Město side of the river Vltava. Construction started in 1357 and finished in the early fifteenth century.

OLD CITY OF ZAMOŚĆ Poland

Zamość was the personal creation of the Hetman (head of the army) Jan Zamysky, on his own lands. Located on the trade route linking western and northern Europe with the Black Sea, the town was modelled on Italian theories of the 'ideal city' and built by the Paduan architect Bernando Morando. Zamość is a perfect example of a late-sixteenth-century Renaissance town. To populate the city, Zamysky brought in merchants of various nationalities and displayed great religious tolerance to encourage people to settle there.
Criteria: iv Inscribed 1992

WULINGYUAN SCENIC AND HISTORIC INTEREST AREA China

Wulingyuan in China's Hunan Province, is dominated by more than 3,000 narrow sandstone pillars and peaks, many over 200 m high. Between the peaks lie ravines and gorges with streams, pools and waterfalls. Karst features include some forty caves, many of them with spectacular calcite deposits. There are two natural bridges: Xianrenqiao (Bridge of the Immortals) and Tianqiashengkong (Bridge Across the Sky), which at 357 m above the valley floor may be the highest natural bridge in the world. In addition, the region is also notable for being home to a number of endangered plant and animal species.
Criteria: vii Inscribed 1992

ANGKOR Cambodia

Angkor Archaeological Park contains the remains of the different capitals of the Khmer Empire, from the ninth to the fifteenth century. In total, there are over a hundred temples throughout the site. The first city had the fundamental elements of a Khmer capital: a defensive bank and ditch; a brick- or stone-built state temple at the centre; and a wooden palace. In the 960s, Rajendravarman built a second capital at Angkor; the state temple was situated at Pre Rup. He also built the exquisite temple of Banteay Srei. Rajendravarman's son Jayavarman V built his state temple at Ta Kev. Shortly afterwards he was overthrown by Suryavarman I, who erected formidable fortifications around his Royal Palace and state temple, the Phimeanakas. In 1050 his successor created a new state temple, the Baphuon. The accession of Suryavarman II in 1113 brought the next great phase of building. He was responsible for Angkor Wat. Instability after Suryavarman's death was ended in the 1180s by Jayavarman VII who created yet another capital at Angkor Thom and built the towering state temple of Bayon, dedicated to Buddha.
Criteria: i, ii, iii, iv Inscribed 1992

HISTORIC CENTRE OF ČESKÝ KRUMLOV Czech Republic

Situated on the banks of the river Vltava, Český Krumlov was built around a thirteenth-century castle with Gothic, Renaissance and Baroque elements. The wealth of the town is reflected in the high quality of many of the burgher houses; as the seat of government Český Krumlov became an important craft and trade centre. There was also considerable ecclesiastical development, illustrated by the major fifteenth-century church of St Vitus and monasteries of various preaching and itinerant orders. There are two main historic areas: the Latrán area below the castle and the town proper on the opposite bank of the Vltava.
Criteria: iv Inscribed 1992

BUTRINT Albania

Inhabited since prehistoric times, Butrint has been a Greek colony, a Roman city and an early Christian bishopric. It became an important trading city, reaching its height in the fourth century BC. The fortifications date from the sixth century BC. The amphitheatre, from the third century BC, has stone banks of seating, while the theatre is situated at the foot of the acropolis, close by two temples. Under Roman rule the city fell slowly into decay and was abandoned in the late Middle Ages.
Criteria: iii Inscribed 1992

MINES OF RAMMELSBERG AND HISTORIC TOWN OF GOSLAR Germany

Goslar held an important place in the Hanseatic League because of the rich Rammelsberg metallic ore deposits. It was the site of mining and metal production (silver, copper, lead, zinc and gold) from as early as the third century BC. From the tenth to the twelfth century it was one of the seats of the Holy Roman Empire and the town grew up around the imperial residence. The revenues from mining, metal production, and trade financed the building of late medieval fortifications, churches, public buildings, and richly decorated mine-owners' residences. Mining and metallurgical operations continued until the last mine closed in 1988.
Criteria: i, iv Inscribed 1992

HISTORIC MONUMENTS OF NOVGOROD AND SURROUNDINGS Russian Federation

On the trade route between Central Asia and northern Europe, Novgorod was Russia's first capital in the ninth century, an outstanding cultural and spiritual centre, birthplace of the national style of stone architecture and one of the oldest national schools of painting. Novgorod is a veritable 'conservatory' of Russian architecture of the Middle Ages and later periods. Foremost amongst these are the Kremlin with its fifteenth-century fortifications, the church of St Sophia from the mid-eleventh century and the Church of the Transfiguration, decorated with frescoes at the end of the fourteenth century.
Criteria: ii, iv, vi Inscribed 1992

BAN CHIANG ARCHAEOLOGICAL SITE Thailand

Ban Chiang, dating from the fifth millennium BC, is without question the most important prehistoric settlement so far discovered in southeast Asia. It presents the earliest evidence for true farming in the region and for the manufacture and use of metals: its long cultural sequence, size and economic status has no parallel in any other contemporary site in the region. Although occupation ended at Ban Chiang in the third century AD, it was the principal settlement in this area of the Khorat plateau and has given its name to a distinctive archaeological culture.
Criteria: iii Inscribed 1992

PYTHAGOREION AND HERAION OF SAMOS Greece

Many civilisations have inhabited the small Aegean island of Samos since the third millennium BC. The remains of Pythagoreion, an ancient fortified port, can still be seen, as well as the Heraion or Temple of Hera, fundamental to an understanding of classical architecture. The fortifications date back to the classical period, with Hellenistic additions. Excavations have revealed much of the street plan of the city, together with its aqueduct, sewage system, public buildings, sanctuaries and temples, *agora*, public baths, stadium and town houses. The complex around the Heraion includes altars, smaller temples and statue bases.
Criteria: ii, iii Inscribed 1992

HISTORIC CENTRE OF TELČ Czech Republic

After a fire in the late fourteenth century, Telč was rebuilt in stone, surrounded by walls and further strengthened by a network of artificial ponds. It is an outstanding example of Renaissance town planning and architecture. Baroque elements were introduced by the Jesuits, who built a college (1651–65) and the Church of the Name of Jesus (1666–7). Baroque gables were added to the façades of some of the houses in the triangular marketplace; Rococo and classical elements also followed in later remodelling. The result is a public place of great beauty as well as great cultural importance.
Criteria: i, ii, iii, iv Inscribed 1992

CULTURAL AND HISTORIC ENSEMBLE OF THE SOLOVETSKY ISLANDS Russian Federation

The Solovetsky archipelago comprises six islands in the western part of the White Sea. Inhabited since the fifth century BC, traces of a human presence go back as far back as the fifth millennium BC. The archipelago has been the site of fervent monastic activity since the fifteenth century, and there are several churches dating from the sixteenth to the nineteenth century. There are four monasteries on Solovetsky Island; the early-seventeenth-century Trinity monastery on Anzer Island; a sixteenth-century complex on Big Zayatsky Island; and St Sergius Monastery, founded in the sixteenth century on Big Muksalma Island.
Criteria: iv Inscribed 1992

EL TAJIN, PRE-HISPANIC CITY Mexico

El Tajin, occupied from 800–1200, became the most important centre in northeast Mesoamerica after the fall of the Teotihuacan Empire. Its architecture, which is unique in Mesoamerica, is characterised by elaborate columns of carved reliefs and key-pattern friezes. The 'Pyramid of the Niches' rises in six steps to a temple at the top, with each storey having rows of square niches. It is a masterpiece of ancient Mesoamerican architecture, which reveals the astronomical and symbolic significance of the building. The site was abandoned when the region came under the rule of the powerful Mexico-Tenochtitlan kingdom.
Criteria: iii, iv Inscribed 1992

WHITE MONUMENTS OF VLADIMIR AND SUZDAL Russian Federation

The towns of Vladimir and Suzdal hold an important place in Russia's architectural history. In Vladimir the single-domed Cathedral of the Assumption (1158) contains frescoes by the master painters Andrei Rublev and Daniil Chernii (1408). The Golden Gate (1164) formed part of the twelfth-century defences. The exterior of the Cathedral of St Demetrius (1194–7) is noteworthy for over 1,000 stone carvings on the general theme of King David. Suzdal is dominated by the Cathedral of the Nativity, built in the thirteenth century and reconstructed in the sixteenth century, with its five-domed top and thirteenth-century Golden Doors.
Criteria: i, ii, iv Inscribed 1992

FRASER ISLAND Australia

Stretching over 120 km along the eastern coast of Queensland, Fraser Island is the largest sand island in the world. It is a place of exceptional beauty, with long white beaches flanked by strikingly coloured sand cliffs, tall rainforests and numerous freshwater lakes. Its highest dunes reach up to 260 m above sea level. A surprising variety of vegetation types grow here, ranging from coastal heath to subtropical rainforests. Birds are the most abundant form of animal life with over 230 species being recorded. It is a particularly important site for migratory wading birds.
Criteria: vii, ix Inscribed 1992

• HUANGLONG SCENIC AND HISTORIC INTEREST AREA China

Situated in the northwest of Sichaun Province, the Huanglong valley boasts extensive areas of precipitous mountain scenery, snow-covered for much of the year. Xuebaoding, or Snow Mountain Peak, is permanently snow-covered and bears the easternmost glacier in China. A diverse forest ecosystems can also be found, as well as spectacular limestone formations, waterfalls and hot springs. The area has a large number of endangered mammals including giant panda, golden snub-nosed monkey, brown bear, Asiatic black bear, leopard, Pallas' cat, Asiatic wild dog, Szechwan takin, mainland serow, common goral, argali and three species of deer.
Criteria: vii Inscribed 1992

• ROUTE OF SANTIAGO DE COMPOSTELA Spain

This route from the border between France and Spain was – and still is – taken by pilgrims to Santiago de Compostela in Galicia. Some 1,800 buildings along the route, both religious and secular, are of great historic interest. Pilgrimages were an essential part of western European spiritual and cultural life in the Middle Ages. The Route of St James of Compostela has preserved the most complete material record in its ecclesiastical and secular buildings, settlements and civil-engineering structures. Two access routes into Spain from France enter at Roncesvalles (Valcarlos Pass) and Canfranc (Somport Pass) and merge west of Pamplona.
Criteria: ii, iv, vi Inscribed 1993

• WHALE SANCTUARY OF EL VIZCAINO Mexico

Located in the central part of Baja California peninsula, the coastal lagoons of Ojo de Liebre and San Ignacio are an exceptional reproduction and wintering site for grey whales as well as other mammals such as harbour seal, California sea lion, northern elephant seal and blue whale. The lagoons have a series of shallow, sandy bays and saltwater inlets as well as extensive mangroves, with dune communities, bushes and halophytic vegetation surrounding them, which are important refuges for wintering wildfowl. The coastal zone is a vital habitat for approximately twenty threatened animal species, including four species of marine turtle.
Criteria: x Inscribed 1993

• HISTORIC TOWN OF ZABID Yemen

Zabid's domestic and military architecture and its urban plan make it an outstanding archaeological and historical site. Besides being the capital of Yemen from the thirteenth to the fifteenth century, the city played an important role in the Arab and Muslim world for many centuries because of its Islamic university. Zabid has a remarkable network of streets and alleys, some as little as 2 m wide, which spreads over the town. Occasionally this labyrinth opens out into small squares, but the only large open space is that in front of the citadel.
Criteria: ii, iv, vi Inscribed 1993

• BIRKA AND HOVGÅRDEN Sweden

Birka-Hovgården is a Viking trading settlement of the eighth–tenth centuries AD. It is also the site of the first Christian congregation in Sweden, founded in 831 by St Ansgar. Birka occupies much of the western part of the island of Björkö. The surface evidence is confined mostly to the ramparts of the hill fort, the long ramparts of the town wall, traces of harbours and stone jetties along the shore, and some 3,000 burial mounds and stone settings surrounding the main settlement. Its location on a small island has preserved the entire site. Hovgården is situated on the neighbouring island of Adelsö.
Criteria: iii, iv Inscribed 1993

• JESUIT MISSIONS OF LA SANTÍSIMA TRINIDAD DE PARANÁ AND JESÚS DE TAVARANGUE Paraguay

The Spanish Crown granted the frontier zone of Paraguay to the Jesuits in 1609, and they created thirty *reducciones* (settlements) in the Rio de la Plata basin, each with its own mission. One of the Jesuits' objectives became the protection of the Indians against the abuses of the colonial *encomienda* system of tribute or labour, which reduced

The greatest Khmer monument, Angkor Wat, is set within an extensive enclosure and is dedicated to Vishnu.

Český Krumlov is an outstanding example of a small central European medieval town whose architectural heritage has remained intact thanks to its peaceful evolution over more than five centuries.

View from Indian Head, Fraser Island.

them to virtual slavery. La Santísima Trinidad was the most ambitious of these missions and the capital of the Guayrá area. Designed by noted Jesuit architect Juan Bautista Primoli, it was constructed in stone in 1706; its church had a fine dome and elaborate decoration.
Criteria: iv Inscribed 1993

•VILLAGES WITH FORTIFIED CHURCHES IN TRANSYLVANIA Romania

These villages with their fortified churches provide a vivid picture of the cultural landscape of southern Transylvania. The seven villages in the site were founded by the Transylvanian Saxons and are characterised by a specific land-use system, settlement pattern and organisation of the family farmstead that have been preserved since the late Middle Ages. They are dominated by their fortified churches, which illustrate building styles from the thirteenth to the sixteenth century.
Criteria: iv Inscribed 1993

•YAKUSHIMA Japan

Located in the interior of Yaku Island, at the northern end of the Ryukyu archipelago, Yakushima exhibits a rich flora, with some 1,900 species and subspecies. Of these, ninety-four are endemic, mostly concentrated in the central high mountains. Yakushima is almost 2,000 m high and is the highest mountain in southern Japan. Several other peaks are over 1,800 m with mountain ridges over 1,000 m surrounding these central high peaks. Of great significance to the area is the presence of indigenous Japanese cedar. The fauna of the island is diverse, with sixteen mammal species.
Criteria: vii, ix Inscribed 1993

•THE SASSI AND THE PARK OF THE RUPESTRIAN CHURCHES OF MATERA Italy

The Sassi of Matera is the most outstanding example of a rock-cut settlement in the Mediterranean region. The Matera region, in southern Italy, has been inhabited since the Palaeolithic period and resisted invaders after the Byzantine period. The earliest house form was a simple cave in the tufa with a closing wall formed from the excavated blocks. This developed into a vaulted room built out into the open space. Groups of dwellings around a common courtyard evolved into a *vicinato* (neighbourhood), with shared facilities such as a cistern. The area was also very attractive to monastic and utopian communities.
Criteria: iii, iv, v Inscribed 1993

•CORO AND ITS PORT Venezuela

With its earthen constructions unique to the Caribbean, Coro is the only surviving example of a rich fusion of local traditions with Spanish Mudéjar and Dutch architectural techniques. One of the first colonial towns founded in 1527, it has some 602 historic buildings. It has conserved its original layout and early urban landscape, presenting a remarkable record of the earliest years of Spanish colonisation.
Criteria: iv, v Inscribed 1993

•ARCHAEOLOGICAL ENSEMBLE OF THE BEND OF THE BOYNE Ireland

The three main prehistoric sites of the Brú na Bóinne (Bend of the Boyne) Complex – Newgrange, Knowth and Dowth – are situated on the north bank of the river Boyne 50 km north of Dublin. These three great burial mounds are surrounded by about forty satellite passage-graves, creating a great prehistoric funerary landscape. The passage tomb complex in particular represents a spectacular survival of outstanding historical significance unequalled in its European counterparts. The site's ritual significance attracted later monuments, both in protohistory and in the Christian period.
Criteria: i, iii, iv Inscribed 1993

•HUMAYUN'S TOMB, DELHI India

This tomb is of particular cultural significance as it is the earliest surviving example of the Mughal garden-tomb on the Indian subcontinent. The tomb of Humayun, second Mughal Emperor of India, was built by his widow in 1569–70, fourteen years after his death. It was later used for the burial of various members of the

The Fortified Church in Viscri, Transylvania.

Matera's development was due to its geological setting. A belt of soft tufa is located between 350 m and 400 m above the valley bed, and the settlement grew here in two natural depressions.

Humayun had travelled widely in the Islamic world, and brought back ideas that were applied by the architect of his tomb. Humayun's tomb and its surrounding structures are substantially in their original state.

ruling family and contains some 150 graves. The tomb itself is in the centre of a large garden, laid out in *char baah* (four-fold) style, with pools joined by channels. It inspired major architectural innovations, culminating in the Taj Mahal a century later.
Criteria: ii, iv Inscribed 1993

▪ HISTORIC CENTRE OF BUKHARA Uzbekistan

Bukhara, situated on the Silk Route, is the most complete example of a medieval city in Central Asia, with an urban fabric that has remained largely intact. Monuments of particular interest include the famous tomb of Ismail Samani, a masterpiece of tenth-century Muslim architecture, the decorated brick minaret of Poi-Kalyan from the eleventh century, the Magoki Mosque and the Chasma Ayub Shrine, along with a large number of seventeenth-century *madrasas*. *Bukhara* became a major cultural centre of the Caliphate of Baghdad in 709, and in 892 the capital of the independent Samanid Kingdom. The city was sacked in 1220 by the Mongol horde of Genghis Khan.
Criteria: ii, iv, vi Inscribed 1993

▪ ROYAL MONASTERY OF SANTA MARÍA DE GUADALUPE Spain

The monastery is an outstanding repository of four centuries of Spanish religious architecture. It symbolises two significant events in world history that occurred in 1492: the Christian reconquest of the Iberian peninsula and Christopher Columbus' arrival in the Americas. Its famous statue of the Virgin became a powerful symbol of the Christianisation of much of the New World. The monastery was, and still is, a centre of pilgrimage. Its hospitals and medical school were renowned, as was its scriptorium and library. Many famous artists were attracted here, including, Francisco de Zurbarán and Luca Giordano.
Criteria: iv, vi Inscribed 1993

▪ TOWN OF BAMBERG Germany

Bamberg is an outstanding example of an early medieval town in central Europe, both in its plan and in its many surviving ecclesiastical and secular buildings. The town was laid out according to medieval planning rules as a cross, with the churches of St Michael, St Stephen, St Gangolf, and St Jacob at the four cardinal points. Its period of greatest prosperity was from the twelfth century to the later Middle Ages. In the late eighteenth century it was the centre of the Enlightenment in southern Germany, with eminent philosophers and writers such as Hegel and Hoffmann living there.
Criteria: ii, iv Inscribed 1993

▪ ENGELSBERG IRONWORKS Sweden

Engelsberg is the most complete example of a self-contained iron-working estate in Sweden. Local peasants had been mining ore and smelting since the thirteenth century, but it was not until the introduction of the waterwheel to power the furnace and hammer bellows in the later Middle Ages that the iron industry began to develop significantly. The first forge was operating at Engelsberg in the closing years of the sixteenth century, and by the mid-seventeenth century the scale of operations there was substantial. The estate also included administrative and residential buildings for management and workers, including those who worked on the associated farm.
Criteria: iv Inscribed 1993

▪ ARCHAEOLOGICAL ENSEMBLE OF MÉRIDA Spain

The Roman colony of Augusta Emerita, in Mérida, Estremadura, was founded in 25 BC at the end of the Spanish Campaign and was the capital of Lusitania. Its main monuments are the Guadiana bridge; the amphitheatre, for 15,000 spectators; the Vitruvian theatre; the Temple of Diana, probably from the first century AD; the alleged 'Arch of Trajan', which may have been an entrance gate to the original town or, more likely, to the Temple of Diana; and the Circus, one of the largest in the Roman world. The aqueducts and other elements of Roman water management are especially well preserved.
Criteria: iii, iv Inscribed 1993

The historic centre of Bukhara, which is, in effect, an open-air museum, combines the city's long history with its importance in the development of urban planning and architecture.

Altes Rathaus (Old Town Hall) in Bamberg.

The Roman Vitruvian Theatre, set into a low hill and inaugurated under M. Agrippa, in Mérida.

• MONASTERY OF HOREZU Romania

Founded in 1690 by the Cantacuzene Prince Constantine Brancovan, the monastery of Horezu in Wallachia is a masterpiece of the Brancovan style. It is laid out according to the precepts of the Athonite Order around the catholicon, which is enclosed by a wall and surrounded by a series of skites (daughter houses of the main monastery). The overall layout is symmetrical on an east–west axis, the skites forming a cruciform plan. The monastery is renowned for its architectural purity and the richness of its sculptural detail. Its school of mural and icon painting was famous throughout the Balkan region.
Criteria: ii Inscribed 1993

• HIMEJI-JO Japan

Himeji-jo is the finest surviving example of early seventeenth-century Japanese hill-top castle, comprising eighty-three buildings with highly developed systems of defence and ingenious protection devices dating from the beginning of the Shogun period. The centre of the complex is the Tenshu-gun, consisting of a main keep and three subsidiary keeps. This is surrounded by a system of watchtowers, gates and plastered earthen walls. The main keep has six storeys and a basement. The striking appearance of this great wooden structure with its white plastered walls is the source of its common name, the Castle of the White Heron (Shirasagi-jo).
Criteria: i, iv Inscribed 1993

• CHURCHES OF MOLDAVIA Romania

With their painted exterior walls, decorated with fifteenth- and sixteenth-century frescoes that are considered masterpieces of Byzantine art, seven churches around Suceava in northern Moldavia are unique in Europe. Far from being merely wall decorations, the paintings are complete cycles of religious murals on all façades. The Church of St George of the former Voronet Monastery, was painted between 1488 and 1552. The walls and the vault of the exonarthex are covered by the 365 scenes of the Calendar of Saints. The exterior murals depict traditional scenes; the Last Judgement is on the western wall.
Criteria: i, iv Inscribed 1993

• MAULBRONN MONASTERY COMPLEX Germany

Founded in 1147, the Cistercian Maulbronn Monastery is considered the most complete and best-preserved medieval monastic complex north of the Alps. Only the monks' refectory and the lay brethren's dormitories have undergone transformations since the Reformation, in order to adapt them for use as a Protestant seminary. Surrounded by fortified walls, the main buildings were constructed between the twelfth and sixteenth centuries. The monastery's church, mainly in Transitional Gothic style, had a major influence in the spread of Gothic architecture over much of northern and central Europe. Its original wooden beams were replaced by Gothic vaulting in 1424.
Criteria: ii, iv Inscribed 1993

• COMPLEX OF HUÉ MONUMENTS Vietnam

Established as the capital of unified Vietnam in 1802, Hué was the political, cultural and religious centre under the Nguyen dynasty until 1945. Four citadels or defended enclosures made up the city: Kinh Thanh (Capital City), for official administrative buildings; Hoang Thanh (Imperial City), for royal palaces and shrines; Tu Cam Thanh (Forbidden Purple City), for the royal residences; and Dai Noi (Inner City), defended by brick walls and a moat. A fifth fortress, Tran Hai Thanh, was constructed a little later to protect the capital against assault from the sea. The Perfume River divides the capital in two.
Criteria: iii, iv Inscribed 1993

• QUTB MINAR AND ITS MONUMENTS, DELHI India

These important Islamic buildings are dominated by the 72.5 m tall, tapering red sandstone tower of Qutb Minar, begun around 1202. In its present form it consists of five storeys, with each storey separated by balconies. The surrounding area contains funerary buildings, notably the magnificent Alai-Darwaza Gate, the masterpiece of Indo-Muslim art built in 1311, and two mosques, including the Quwwatu'l-Islam. The Iron Pillar in the mosque compound is 7 m

Many castles were built in Japan in the early years of the Shogun period in the seventeenth century, and, of the handful that survive, Himeji-jo is the most complete and unaltered.

Wall and gate of Tu Duc Tomb, Hué.

tall, 0.93 m of which is below ground. It bears a Sanskrit inscription from the fourth century AD and is the largest known composite iron object from so early a period.
Criteria: iv Inscribed 1993

• HISTORIC TOWN OF BANSKÁ ŠTIAVNICA AND THE TECHNICAL MONUMENTS IN ITS VICINITY Slovakia

Banská Štiavnica, on the steep slopes of the Glanzenberg and Paradajz mountains, is the oldest mining town in Slovakia. Its ore deposits have been exploited since the late Bronze Age. The fifteenth century was a time of immense prosperity: defences were built round the town, the parish church was rebuilt and fortified, and many new houses were built. In 1627 Banská Štiavnica saw the first use of gunpowder in mining, an important breakthrough, and much work on the application of water power in deep mining and on ancillary processes was carried out, particularly in the eighteenth century.
Criteria: iv, v Inscribed 1993

• TUBBATAHA REEFS NATURAL PARK Philippines

The Tubbataha Reefs Natural Park comprises two uninhabited coral atolls, North and South Reef, separated by an 8 km channel, and the Jessie Beazley Reef, an emergent coral cay. The North Reef is an oblong-shaped platform 2 km wide completely enclosing a sandy lagoon. North Islet serves as a nesting site for birds and marine turtles. Steep walls extending to a depth of 100 m characterise the seaward face of the reef. The South Reef is a small triangular-shaped reef 1–2 km wide. Like the North Reef, it consists of a shallow platform enclosing a sandy lagoon and is used by birds and marine turtles.
Criteria: vii, ix, x Inscribed 1993

• ARCHITECTURAL ENSEMBLE OF THE TRINITY SERGIUS LAVRA IN SERGIEV POSAD Russian Federation

The Trinity Sergius Lavra is an outstanding Orthodox monastery (*lavra*) of the fourteenth–eighteenth centuries and has exerted a profound influence on architecture in Russia. It was founded in the 1330s by St Sergius and fortified in 1540–60. Among its most important buildings are the Trinity Cathedral, completed in 1425, containing the Rublev's icon of 'The Trinity'; the Church of the Holy Spirit (Dukhovskaya); the Cathedral of the Assumption; and the Belfry, which is the tallest building in the complex, begun in 1740 at the instigation of Catherine the Great. The monks' cells were built up against the fortress walls.
Criteria: ii, iv Inscribed 1993

• BUDDHIST MONUMENTS IN THE HORYU-JI AREA Japan

There are around forty-eight Buddhist monuments in the Horyu-ji area, in Nara Prefecture. Several date from the late seventh or early eighth century, making them some of the oldest surviving wooden buildings in the world. These masterpieces of wooden architecture are important not only for the history of art, since they illustrate the adaptation of Chinese Buddhist architecture and layout to Japanese culture, but also for the history of religion, since their construction coincided with the introduction of Buddhism to Japan from China by way of the Korean peninsula.
Criteria: i, ii, iv, vi Inscribed 1993

• BAROQUE CHURCHES OF THE PHILIPPINES Philippines

The churches are outstanding examples of the Philippine interpretation of the Baroque style and had an important influence on later church architecture in the region. They represent the fusion of European church design and construction with local materials and decorative motifs. The four churches, are in Manila (San Agustín in Intramuros), Santa Maria (Nuestra Señora de la Asuncion), Paoay (San Agustín) and Miag-ao (Santo Tomas de Villanueva). The façade of Santo Tomas de Villanueva exemplifies this Filipino adaptation, with the figure of St Christopher dressed in native clothes, carrying the Christ Child and holding on to a coconut palm for support.
Criteria: ii, iv Inscribed 1993

The stone cloisters of the Quwwatu'l-Islam (Might of Islam), the oldest mosque in northern India, built of materials reused from some twenty Brahman temples. This mosque is part of the Qutb Minar complex.

Cathedral of the Assumption, a towering structure echoing the Cathedral of the Assumption in the Moscow Kremlin, at the Trinity Sergius Lavra.

• HISTORIC CENTRE OF ZACATECAS
Mexico

Founded in 1546 after the discovery of a rich silver lode, Zacatecas reached the height of its prosperity in the sixteenth and seventeenth centuries. Built on the steep slopes of a narrow valley, the town became the economic centre for the region, with a system of forts (*presidios*), villages and agricultural estates (*haciendas*) for defence and supply. The cathedral, built between 1730 and 1760, dominates the centre of the town and is a highly decorated Baroque structure. The Jesuit church of Santo Domingo has a quiet beauty which contrasts with the Baroque flamboyance of the college alongside it.
Criteria: ii, iv Inscribed 1993

• SHIRAKAMI-SANCHI Japan

Situated in the mountains of northern Honshu, the area includes the last remaining virgin stand of Siebold's beech forest, which once covered the hills of northern Japan. The protected area covers about one-third of the Shirakami Mountains which rise to just over 1,200 m and comprise a maze of steep-sided hills and deep valleys. It is a refuge for many typical Honshu flora and fauna. The eighty-seven bird species include golden eagle, which has a limited breeding record and is endangered in Japan. Japanese black bear is common. The area is a wilderness with no access trails or man-made facilities.
Criteria: ix Inscribed 1993

• LEVOČA, SPIŠSKÝ HRAD AND THE ASSOCIATED CULTURAL MONUMENTS
Slovakia

The town of Levoča was founded in the thirteenth century, and includes the church of St James. Spišský Hrad (castle) and its three related sites contains a major grouping of thirteenth- and fourteenth-century military, political and religious buildings. The castle stands on a dramatic hill rising out of the plain of western Slovakia. The town of Spišské Podhradie was founded at its base. Its street pattern was laid out formally in the fourteenth century and extended in the fifteenth century. Spišskà Kapitula is a fortified ecclesiastical complex of buildings by the Cathedral of St Martin, begun in 1285. Zehra is an early Slovak settlement.
Criteria: iv Inscribed 1993

• JOYA DE CERÉN ARCHAEOLOGICAL SITE El Salvador

Joya de Cerén was a pre-Hispanic farming community that was buried under an eruption of the Laguna Caldera volcano c. AD 600. Because of the exceptional condition of the remains, they provide an insight into the daily lives of the Central American populations who worked the land at that time. Twelve structures have been excavated, including living quarters, storehouses, workshops, kitchens and a communal sauna. Cerén is thought to have been home to about 200 people, although no human remains have been found. The buildings are grouped into compounds that include structures for sleeping, storage, cooking and handicrafts.
Criteria: iii, iv Inscribed 1993

• ROCK PAINTINGS OF THE SIERRA DE SAN FRANCISCO Mexico

From c. 100 BC to AD 1300, the Sierra de San Francisco in Baja California was home to a people who have left one of the most outstanding collections of rock paintings in the world that are remarkably well-preserved because of the dry climate and their inaccessibility. Showing human figures and many animal species, and illustrating the relationship between humans and their environment,

they reveal a highly sophisticated culture. Their composition, size, precision, variety of colours, and especially the number of sites (over 400), make them an impressive testimony to a unique artistic tradition.
Criteria: i, iii Inscribed 1993

• VLKOLÍNEC Slovakia

Vlkolínec, situated in central Slovakia, is a remarkably intact settlement of forty-five vernacular buildings. Although most buildings date from the nineteenth century, Vlkolínec has retained its medieval layout. The characteristic houses of Vlkolínec are situated on the street frontages of narrow holdings, with stables, smaller outbuildings, and barns ranged behind them. The houses are of a traditional timber construction with log walls on stone footings, the walls being coated with clay and whitewashed or painted blue. The parcels of land that surround Vlkolínec retain the elongated strip-shape characteristic of medieval land allotment over most of feudal Europe.
Criteria: iv, v Inscribed 1993

• ANCIENT BUILDING COMPLEX IN THE WUDANG MOUNTAINS China

The palaces and temples which form the nucleus of this group of secular and religious buildings exemplify the architectural and artistic achievements of China's Yuan, Ming and Qing dynasties. Situated in the scenic valleys and on the slopes of the Wudang mountains in Hubei Province, the site, which was built as an organised complex during the Ming dynasty (fourteenth–seventeenth centuries), contains Taoist buildings from as early as the seventh century. It represents the highest standards of Chinese art and architecture over a period of nearly 1,000 years.
Criteria: i, ii, vi Inscribed 1994

• BWINDI IMPENETRABLE NATIONAL PARK Uganda

Bwindi Park covers 320 km² and is known for its exceptional diversity of flora and fauna. Its forest gets the name 'impenetrable' from the dense cover of herbs, vines and shrubs inhabiting the valley floors. The forest is the most diverse in East Africa for tree species and ferns. It also has one of the richest fauna communities, including over 214 species of forest bird, 120 species of mammals and 202 species of butterfly. Highly significant is the presence of almost half of the world's population of mountain gorillas and many other endangered species. The earliest evidence of forest clearance dates back 4,800 years, most likely due to the presence of the Batwa hunter-gatherer people manipulating vegetation with fire.
Criteria: vii, x Inscribed 1994

• LOS KATÍOS NATIONAL PARK Colombia

Extending over 720 km² in northwestern Colombia, the park comprises two main regions: the mountains of the Serranía del Darién in the west, and in the east the floodplain of the Atrato River, the fastest-flowing river in the world. Lowland swamp forests cover approximately half of the park, while the remainder is lowland through to montane tropical rainforest. The wetlands of the Atrato floodplain are of special interest. An exceptional biological diversity is found in the park, which is home to many threatened animal species and endemic plants.
Criteria: ix, x Inscribed 1994

• CHURCH OF THE ASCENSION, KOLOMENSKOYE Russian Federation

The Church of the Ascension was built in 1532 on the imperial estate of Kolomenskoye, near Moscow, to

celebrate the birth of the prince who became Tsar Ivan IV (the Terrible). As the first example of a traditional wooden tent-roofed church in stone and brick, it represents an imaginative and innovative advance in Russian Orthodox church design. Its ground plan is an equal-armed cross and it is unusual in that it has no apse. The interior of the church is small, as the walls are 3–4 m thick, but it is open to the roof, 41 m above.
Criteria: ii Inscribed 1994

• JELLING MOUNDS, RUNIC STONES AND CHURCH Denmark

The Jelling complex is an outstanding example of pagan Nordic culture. Jelling was a royal manor in the tenth century, during the reign of King Gorm and Queen Thyre. Following Thyre's death, her husband raised a stone in her memory and laid out a joint funerary monument of two large mounds. After introducing Christianity into Denmark, their son Harald Bluetooth set up a stone proclaiming his achievements and built an impressive wooden church. The present church was preceded by at least three others that were destroyed by fire. There are mural paintings dating from around 1100 on the chancel walls.
Criteria: iii Inscribed 1994

• AUSTRALIAN FOSSIL MAMMAL SITES (RIVERSLEIGH / NARACOORTE) Australia

These two sites are representative of the development of Australia's mammal fauna during the Cenozoic era (65 million years ago to the present). Fossils from Riversleigh have profoundly altered understanding about Australia's Middle Cenozoic vertebrate diversity. They record mammalian evolution over twenty million years, providing the first records for many distinctive groups of living mammals, as well as many other unique and now extinct Australian mammals such as 'marsupial lions'. Naracoorte also spans the probable time of arrival of humans in Australia and thus is of additional value in helping to unravel the complex relationships between humans and their environment.
Criteria: viii, ix Inscribed 1994

• DOÑANA NATIONAL PARK Spain

In the context of a crowded and long-inhabited continent Doñana National Park in Andalusia is one of the few national parks in Europe that can match the international significance met by parks in other parts of the world. The park is notable for the great diversity of its habitats, especially lagoons, marshlands, fixed and mobile dunes, scrub woodland and maquis. It is home to five threatened bird species. It has one of the largest heronries in the Mediterranean region and is the wintering site for more than 500,000 water fowl each year.
Criteria: vii, ix, x Inscribed 1994

• RWENZORI MOUNTAINS NATIONAL PARK Uganda

Covering nearly 1,000 km² in western Uganda, the park comprises the main part of the Rwenzori mountain chain which includes Africa's third highest peak, Mount Margherita (5,109 m). The region's glaciers, waterfalls and lakes make it one of Africa's most beautiful alpine areas. The park has many natural habitats for endangered species and a rich and unusual flora including the giant heather. Its four major vegetation zones are: broken montane forest below 2,400 m; bamboo forest up to 3,000 m; a tree-heath zone of giant heathers up to 3,800 m; and Afro-alpine moorland up to 4,400 m.
Criteria: vii, x Inscribed 1994

• CANAIMA NATIONAL PARK Venezuela

Canaima National Park extends over 30,000 km² in southeastern Venezuela along the border with Guyana and Brazil. Roughly 65 per cent of the park is covered by table mountain (*tepui*) formations, resulting in a landscape of great geological interest. The sheer cliffs and waterfalls, including the world's highest waterfall (Angel Falls), make this a spectacular place. The fauna is diverse: 118 mammal species, 550 birds, 72 reptiles and 55 amphibians have been recorded. The forests and savanna of Canaima have been occupied for 10,000 years by various groups of Amerindians of the Carib family, collectively known as the Pemon.

Criteria: vii, viii, ix, x Inscribed 1994

• EARLIEST 16TH-CENTURY MONASTERIES ON THE SLOPES OF POPOCATEPETL Mexico

These fourteen monasteries stand on the slopes of Popocatepetl, an active volcano, to the southeast of Mexico City. They were built to a similar plan, with an atrium, church, and monastic buildings set around a small courtyard. They are in an excellent state of conservation and are good examples of the architectural style adopted by the first missionaries – Franciscans, Dominicans and Augustinians – who converted the indigenous populations to Christianity in the early sixteenth century. Between 1525 and 1570 more than100 monasteries were built in this region. By the end of the century over 300 had been established.

Criteria: ii, iv Inscribed 1994

• CITY OF LUXEMBOURG: ITS OLD QUARTERS AND FORTIFICATIONS Luxembourg

Luxembourg was one of Europe's greatest fortified sites from the sixteenth century. Until their partial demolition after 1867, the fortifications were a fine example of military architecture spanning several centuries. The old quarter extends westwards from the Bock promontory with its honeycomb of seventeenth- and eighteenth-century casemates (fortified gun emplacements). The Marché-aux-Poissons was the first open space in the town and the Church of Saint Michel, located there, originates from the tenth century. Notre Dame Cathedral is an outstanding example of Netherlands late-Gothic architecture, and the sixteenth-century Grand Ducal Palace stands at the heart of the old town.

Criteria: iv Inscribed 1994

• HISTORIC ENSEMBLE OF THE POTALA PALACE, LHASA China

The Potala Palace, winter palace of the Dalai Lama since the seventh century, symbolises Tibetan Buddhism and its central role in the traditional administration of Tibet. Comprising the White and Red Palaces with their ancillary buildings, it stands on Red Mountain in the Lhasa Valley at an altitude of 3,700 m. Also founded in the seventh century, the Jokhang Temple Monastery is an exceptional Buddhist religious complex. Norbulingka, the Dalai Lama's former summer palace, is from the eighteenth century. The architectural beauty and originality of these sites in a striking landscape add to their historic and religious interest.

Criteria: i, iv, vi Inscribed 1994

• ROCK CARVINGS IN TANUM Sweden

Tanum, in northern Bohuslän is an area of granite bedrock, parts of which were scraped clean as the ice cap slowly moved northwards, leaving gently curved rock faces exposed. Sited just above the shoreline of the period, these rocks were selected by the Bronze Age artists. There are at least 1,500 known rock-carving sites. The elaborate motifs illustrate everyday life, warfare, cults and religion. Some of the panels were obviously planned in advance. The carvings vary from 1 mm deep to as much as 30 or 40 mm. It is suggested that the more deeply engraved figures were of greater symbolic significance.

Criteria: i, iii, iv Inscribed 1994

• SKOGSKYRKOGÅRDEN Sweden

In 1912 a competition was held to create a new cemetery on the site of former gravel pits overgrown with pine trees. It was won by two

A typical Vlkolínec building. The first recorded settlement here was in the fourteenth century. A decree of 1630 suggests that its name derives from the requirement that villagers maintain wolf-pits in good order.

The Stiechen Bridge. Luxembourg's defences earned it the nickname 'Gibraltar of the North'. However, the agreement of the European powers to the Grand Duchy's perpetual neutrality in 1867, led to their demolition.

The Potala Palace contains the White Palace, which holds the throne of the Dalai Lama and his personal apartments, and the Red Palace, which contains chapels and the stupa tombs of previous Dalai Lamas.

young architects, Asplund and Lewerentz, whose design stands out for its intense romantic naturalism, turning the untouched Nordic forest into the dominant experience. The evocation of raw Nordic wilderness constituted a radical departure in landscape architecture as well as cemetery layout. Nonetheless, skilful use was made of elements from Mediterranean antiquity. The impact of footpaths, meandering freely through the woodland, is minimal. Graves are laid out without excessive regimentation in the natural forest.
Criteria: ii, iv Inscribed 1994

• CITY OF VICENZA AND THE PALLADIAN VILLAS OF THE VENETO Italy

Founded in the second century BC in northern Italy, Vicenza prospered under Venetian rule from the early fifteenth to the end of the eighteenth century. It was Andrea Palladio (1508–80) that gave Vicenza its enduring form. Palladio was profoundly influenced by the surviving monuments of classical Rome. For Vicenza, he created both public (Basilica, Loggia del Capitaniato, Teatro Olimpico) and private buildings. A total of twenty-six individual buildings or parts of buildings known to have been designed or reconstructed by Palladio make up the World Heritage site – twenty-three in the city and three villas in the surrounding Veneto.
Criteria: i, ii Inscribed 1994

• VILNIUS HISTORIC CENTRE Lithuania

Despite invasions and partial destruction, the Lithuanian capital Vilnius has preserved an impressive complex of Gothic, Renaissance, Baroque and classical buildings, as well as its medieval layout. The town grew against the background of a series of major fires from the fifteenth to the eighteenth centuries. The notable churches that exist today date from the seventeenth century, but it was the successive reconstructions that gave the town many of its buildings of special character, including the cathedral, town hall and palaces. Many of the surviving earlier buildings were rebuilt or refurbished in the Baroque style.
Criteria: ii, iv Inscribed 1994

• LINES AND GEOGLYPHS OF NASCA AND PAMPAS DE JUMANA Peru

The geoglyphs of Nasca and the pampas of Jumana, which were scratched on the ground between 500 BC and AD 500, are among archaeology's greatest enigmas because of their quantity, nature, size and cultural continuity. The geoglyphs fall generally into two categories. The first group is representational, depicting animals, birds, insects, plants, fantastic figures and even everyday objects. The second group comprises lines, generally straight and criss-crossing in all directions; some stretch several kilometres and depict geometrical shapes. Their concentration and juxtaposition demonstrate that this was an important and long-lasting activity. They are believed to have had ritual astronomical functions.
Criteria: i, iii, iv Inscribed 1994

• TEMPLE AND CEMETERY OF CONFUCIUS AND THE KONG FAMILY MANSION IN QUFU China

The temple, cemetery and family mansion of Confucius, the great philosopher, politician and educator of the sixth–fifth centuries BC, are located at Qufu in Shandong Province. Two years after his death, Confucius's house in Qufu was consecrated as a temple, within which were preserved his clothing, musical instruments, carriage and books. The temple was rebuilt in AD 153 and today comprises more than 100 buildings. The cemetery contains Confucius's tomb and the remains of more than 100,000 of his descendants. The small house of the Kong family developed into a gigantic aristocratic residence, of which 152 buildings with 480 rooms remain.
Criteria: i, iv, vi Inscribed 1994

• BAGRATI CATHEDRAL AND GELATI MONASTERY Georgia

The construction of Bagrati Cathedral, named after Bagrat III, the first king of united Georgia, started at the end of the tenth century and was completed in the early years of the eleventh century. Although partly destroyed by the Turks in 1691, its ruins still lie in

The Villa Rotunda (1566–71), in the Veneto near Vicenza was designed in by Andrea Palladio, who had a decisive influence on the development of architecture and inspired a distinct style known as Palladian.

The Nasca geoglyphs are located in the arid Peruvian coastal plain 400 km south of Lima, and cover 450 km², both in the desert and in the Andean foothills

The Qufu complex of Confucian monuments has retained its outstanding artistic and historic character due to the devotion of successive Chinese emperors over more than 2,000 years.

the centre of Kutaisi. Richly ornamented capitals and fragments of piers and vaulting are scattered around. The Gelati Monastery, whose main buildings were erected between the twelfth and seventeenth centuries, is well-preserved, with wonderful mosaics and wall paintings. The cathedral and monastery epitomise the flowering of medieval architecture in Georgia.
Criteria: iv Inscribed 1994

▪ HA LONG BAY Vietnam

Ha Long Bay in the Gulf of Tonkin includes some 1,600 islands and islets that form a spectacular seascape of limestone pillars. Because of their precipitous nature, most of the islands are uninhabited. The site's outstanding scenic beauty is complemented by its great biological interest. Ha Long Bay is known as a drowned karst landscape. The limestones of Ha Long Bay have been eroded into a mature landscape of *fengcong* (clusters of conical peaks) and *fenglin* (isolated towers) karst features, modified by sea invasion at a later stage.
Criteria: vii, viii Inscribed 1994

▪ MOUNTAIN RESORT AND ITS OUTLYING TEMPLES, CHENGDE China

The Mountain Resort, the Qing dynasty's summer palace, in Hebei Province, was built between 1703 and 1792. It is a vast complex of palaces and administrative and ceremonial buildings. Temples of various architectural styles and imperial gardens blend harmoniously into a landscape of lakes, pastureland and forests. Each year the Emperor would bring his ministers, royal troops, family and concubines to hunt at Mulan. To accommodate this entourage of several thousand people, twenty-one temporary palaces were built, among them the Mountain Resort. The Mountain Resort is also a rare historic reminder of the final development of feudal society in China.
Criteria: ii, iv Inscribed 1994

▪ HISTORICAL MONUMENTS OF MTSKHETA Georgia

The historic churches of Mtskheta, former capital of Georgia, are outstanding examples of medieval religious architecture in the Caucasus, and include the eleventh-century Svetitskhoveli Cathedral; the Mtskhetis Jvari (Church of the Holy Rood), the most sacred place in Georgia; and Samtavro (the Place of the Ruler), also built in the eleventh century, which contains the graves of Mirian, the first Georgian Christian king, and his wife. The Armaztsikhe (citadel and royal residence) was at the heart of the city and fortified quarters allocated to specialised trades clustered around it, making up 'Great Mtskheta'.
Criteria: iii, iv Inscribed 1994

▪ HISTORIC MONUMENTS OF ANCIENT KYOTO (KYOTO, UJI AND OTSU CITIES) Japan

Kyoto was the imperial capital of Japan from its foundation until the mid-nineteenth century. As the centre of Japanese culture for more than 1,000 years, it illustrates the development of Japanese wooden architecture, particularly religious architecture, and the art of Japanese gardens, which has influenced landscape gardening the world over. Both Chinese culture and Buddhism were having a profound influence on Japan when the capital moved to Kyoto, then named Heian-kyo, in AD 794. Aristocratic society clustered around the imperial court for the four centuries of the Heian period (794–1192). The Sekisui-in at Kozan-ji is the best example of the residential architecture of this period, which ended in 1332 with the establishment of the Muromachi Shogunate. This period saw the building of large temples of the Rinzai Zen sect, such as Temyu-ji, and the creation of Zen gardens, of which that at Saiho-ji is a representative example. The political stability of the late sixteenth century was reflected in the opulence and boldness of the architecture; the Sanpo-in residential complex and garden at Daigo-jo are examples of this.
Criteria: ii, iv Inscribed 1994

The smaller islands in Ha long Bay are *fenglin* towers 50–100 m high, many with sheer faces. There is the abundance of lakes and limestone caves within the larger limestone islands.

Kinkaku-ji, the 'Golden Pavilion', Kyoto.

• CITY OF SAFRANBOLU Turkey

From the thirteenth century to the early twentieth century, Safranbolu was an important caravan station on the main east–west trade route. The Old Mosque, Old Bath and Süleyman Pasha *madrasa* were built in 1322. During its apogee in the seventeenth century, Safranbolu's architecture influenced urban development throughout much of the Ottoman Empire. Many buildings survive from this period, including the Cinci Inn with its sixty guest rooms (1640–8), Köprülü Mosque (1661) and Let Pasha Mosque (1796), as well as many stores, stables and baths.

Criteria: ii, iv, v Inscribed 1994

• PETÄJÄVESI OLD CHURCH Finland

The Petäjävesi Evangelical Lutheran Old Church is a unique log church built between 1763 and 1765 on a peninsula where lakes Jamsa and Petäjävesi meet. The location was specifically chosen so that the congregation could reach it by boat or over the ice in the winter. The church combines the layout of a Renaissance central church with older Gothic forms. The church suffered a period of neglect between 1879 and the 1920s. When restoration began the historical importance of the building was recognised and only traditional techniques and materials were used.

Criteria: iv Inscribed 1994

• COLLEGIATE CHURCH, CASTLE, AND OLD TOWN OF QUEDLINBURG Germany

The importance of Quedlinburg, in Saxony-Anhalt, rests on three main elements: the preservation of the medieval street pattern; the wealth of urban vernacular buildings, especially timber-framed houses of the sixteenth and seventeenth centuries; and the important Romanesque collegiate church of St Servatius. The area comprises the historic town enclosed within the city walls, consisting of the old (tenth century) and new (twelfth century) towns, the Westendorf district with the collegiate church and the buildings of the imperial foundation, St Wipert's Church and the Münzenberg, the hill on which a Benedictine monastery was founded in 946.

Criteria: iv Inscribed 1994

• VÖLKLINGEN IRONWORKS Germany

The ironworks dominate the city of Völklingen and are the only intact example of an integrated works that was built and equipped in the nineteenth and twentieth centuries. Völklingen was the first ironworks in the world to use blast-furnace gas on a large scale to drive blowers providing blast to the furnaces. By the end of the nineteenth century it was one of Europe's most productive works and Germany's largest producer of steel beams. From the end of the Second World War until pig-iron production ceased in 1986, only minor modernisation took place, giving the site the appearance of an ironworks of the 1930s.

Criteria: ii, iv Inscribed 1994

• PILGRIMAGE CHURCH OF ST JOHN OF NEPOMUK AT ZELENÁ HORA Czech Republic

Constructed on a star-shaped plan, this church is the most unusual work by the great architect Jan Blazej Santini, whose highly original Baroque and Neo-Gothic style displays great imagination and inventiveness. Work began in 1719, three years before the formal canonisation of John of Nepomuk. The construction of the main building was completed by 1721. The main impression given by the interior is its loftiness. The central space opens into five niches; of these, four are partitioned horizontally and the fifth, on the east, is filled by the main altar. The church retains many of its original furnishings.

Criteria: iv Inscribed 1994

• HISTORIC CENTRE OF AVIGNON: PAPAL PALACE, EPISCOPAL ENSEMBLE AND AVIGNON BRIDGE France

Avignon was the seat of the papacy in the fourteenth century and an exceptional group of monuments testify to the city's importance. The austere Gothic palace-fortress of the Palais des Papes dominates the

Part of the city of Safranbolu, a typical Ottoman city that has survived to the present day.

The historic centre of Avignon, with the Palais des Papes on the right and Notre-Dame-des-Domes on the left. Part of the city walls can be seen at the bottom.

historic centre and comprises two parts: the Palais Vieux (Old Palace) and the Palais Neuf (New Palace). The main courtyard is between the two palace buildings which also house the pontiffs' chapel and private rooms. The Romanesque Cathedral of Notre-Dame-des-Doms lies to the north of the Palais des Papes. The Petit Palais on the western side of the Place du Palais, built as a cardinal's residence, was expanded in the fourteenth and fifteenth centuries. Saint Bénézet Bridge, the Pont d'Avignon, is one of the most important medieval bridges in Europe. Originally built in the twelfth century, it spanned 900 m across the Rhône but suffered several collapses in the following centuries. It was not rebuilt after a flood in 1668 swept much of it away, and only four of its original twenty-two arches remain.
Criteria: i, ii, iv Inscribed 1995

Pena Palace on its hill above Sintra influenced mid-nineteenth century Romantic architecture and landscape design across Europe.

• CULTURAL LANDSCAPE OF SINTRA Portugal

The Serra de Sintra, Ptolemy's 'Mountains of the Moon', rise up above the town of Sintra. Almost all the historic buildings there were destroyed in the 1755 earthquake, but in the 1840s Ferdinand II transformed a ruined monastery into a Romantic royal summer palace, the Pena Palace, employing Gothic, Egyptian, Moorish and Renaissance elements, and created a park blending local and exotic species of trees. Other fine dwellings were built along the same lines in the surrounding mountains. The Royal Palace in the town of Sintra is faced with tiles (*azulejos*), the finest example of this Mudejar technique on the Iberian Peninsula.
Criteria: ii, iv, v Inscribed 1995

• HISTORIC CENTRE OF NAPLES Italy

Naples is one of Europe's most ancient cities. Its street pattern, its wealth of historic buildings from many periods, and its setting on the Bay of Naples has had a profound influence in Europe and beyond. Above ground, little survives of the Greek town founded in 470 BC beyond three sections of the original town walls. The surviving Roman remains, notably the large theatre, cemeteries and catacombs, are more substantial. Naples has retained the imprint of the successive European and Mediterranean cultures, with many outstanding churches, such as Santa Chiara and San Lorenzo Maggiore, and monuments such as the Castel Nuovo.
Criteria: ii, iv Inscribed 1995

Castel Nuovo, Naples, dates from the late thirteenth century. The cylindrical towers and the triumphal arch were added in the fifteenth century.

• CARLSBAD CAVERNS NATIONAL PARK USA

This karst landscape in New Mexico comprises eighty-one recognised caves that are outstanding not only for their size but also for the profusion, diversity and beauty of their mineral formations. An extensive cave system has developed here as a result of sulphuric acid dissolution. Of the known caves, Carlsbad Cavern is the largest, and Lechuguilla Cave is the most extensive and decorated in the world. The caves are noted for their migratory bat species. Various species of fungi and bacteria growing inside are of particular scientific and medical interest.
Criteria: vii, viii Inscribed 1995

• SCHOKLAND AND SURROUNDINGS Netherlands

Schokland was a peninsula that by the fifteenth century had become an island. Occupied and then abandoned as the sea encroached, it had to be evacuated in 1859. But following the draining of the Zuider Zee, it has, since the 1940s, formed part of the land reclaimed from the sea. Schokland has vestiges of human habitation going back to prehistoric times. It symbolises the heroic, age-old struggle of the people of the Netherlands against the encroachment of the sea.
Criteria: iii, v Inscribed 1995

• RAPA NUI NATIONAL PARK Chile

Rapa Nui, the indigenous name of Easter Island, was settled around AD 300 by Polynesians, probably from the Marquesas. It is best known by its monumental sculptures (*moai*) and ceremonial shrines (*ahu*); it is also noteworthy for a form of pictographic writing (*rongo rongo*), so far undeciphered. The *moai*, believed to represent sacred ancestors who watch over the villages and ceremonial areas, range in height from 2 m to 20 m and are for the most part carved from scoria or

Ahu Tongariki, the largest *ahu* on Rapa Nui. The *ahu* are generally located on the coast and orientated parallel to it.

solidified lava, and lowered down the slopes into previously dug holes. The *ahu* vary considerably in size and form. There are certain constant features: notably a raised rectangular platform of large worked stones filled with rubble; a ramp often paved with rounded beach pebbles; and a levelled area in front of the platform. Some have *moai* on them, and there are tombs in a number of the *ahu* in which skeletal remains have been discovered.
Criteria: i, iii, v Inscribed 1995

▪ WATERTON GLACIER INTERNATIONAL PEACE PARK Canada and USA

In 1932 Waterton Lakes National Park in Alberta, Canada joined with Glacier National Park in Montana, USA, to form the world's first International Peace Park. Situated on the border between the two countries and offering outstanding scenery, the combined park is exceptionally rich in plant and mammal species, and in prairie, forest, alpine and glacial features. Both parks feature long, narrow, glacial lakes and colourful, ancient rocks. Local topography is dominated by the 2,500 m peaks of the Rocky Mountains, and the park is roughly split lengthwise by the Continental Divide. The mountains were largely shaped by glacial erosion, whereas the rolling grasslands are a result of glacial deposition.
Criteria: vii, ix Inscribed 1995

▪ VIRGIN KOMI FORESTS Russian Federation

The Virgin Komi Forests is one of Europe's most extensive virgin boreal forest. It is dominated by lowlands in the west that rise to form the glaciated northern Ural mountains in the east. The lowland vegetation comprises marshes and flood plain islands. Boreal forest extends from the marshes to the foothills of the Urals and is superseded by subalpine scrub woodlands, meadows, tundra and bedrock. This vast area of conifers, aspens, birches, peat bogs, rivers and natural lakes has been monitored and studied for over fifty years. The forests form a haven for many threatened mammal species.
Criteria: vii, ix Inscribed 1995

▪ ROSKILDE CATHEDRAL Denmark

Built in the twelfth and thirteenth centuries, Roskilde was Scandinavia's first Gothic cathedral built of brick and its influence was felt throughout northern Europe. The original structure was Romanesque; however, when only the eastern half had been built, the plan was changed to Gothic. The transept was located further back and the towers planned for the choir were moved to the west end. Work was virtually complete by around 1275, apart from the north tower, which was finished at the end of the fourteenth century. It has been the mausoleum of the Danish royal family since the fifteenth century.
Criteria: ii, iv Inscribed 1995

▪ MESSEL PIT FOSSIL SITE Germany

Messel Pit gives the most complete view of the living environment of the Eocene, between 57 and 36 million years ago. During this period, North America, Europe and Asia were in continuous land contact and the partial explanation of current distribution patterns is provided by the Eocene fossil record. Messel provides particularly rich information about the early stages of the evolution of mammals and includes exceptionally well-preserved mammal fossils, ranging from fully articulated skeletons to the contents of stomachs of animals of this period. Large quantities of bird, reptile, fish, insects and plant remains all contribute to this extraordinarily significant fossil site.
Criteria: viii Inscribed 1995

▪ SEOKGURAM GROTTO AND BULGUKSA TEMPLE Korea, Republic of

Established in the eighth century on the slopes of Mount T'oham, the Seokguram Grotto consists of an antechamber, a corridor and a main rotunda. It is built from granite and features thirty-nine Buddhist engravings on the main wall and the principal sculpture of the Buddha in the centre. This monumental statue is posed in the *bhumisparsha mudra* position, the gesture with which Buddha summoned the Earth as witness to his realisation of Enlightenment.

Waterton Lake in Canada, part of the Waterton Glacier International Peace Park, which celebrates the peace and goodwill existing along the world's longest undefended border.

Multi-coloured lanterns decorate the Dabotap Pagoda, which is located in the Bulguksa Temple. The lanterns are to celebrate Buddha's birthday.

It is surrounded by portrayals of gods, bodhisattvas and disciples. The Temple of Bulguksa, built in 774, and the Seokguram Grotto form a religious and architectural complex of exceptional significance.
Criteria: i, iv Inscribed 1995

• FERRARA, CITY OF THE RENAISSANCE, AND ITS PO DELTA Italy

Ferrara is an outstanding example of a planned Renaissance city which has retained its urban fabric virtually intact. Among the great Italian cities its plan alone is not derived from a Roman layout but on a linear axis, along the banks of the Po River, with longitudinal streets and many cross streets, around which the medieval city was organised. In the fifteenth and sixteenth centuries the city became an intellectual and artistic centre that attracted the greatest minds of the Italian Renaissance, and the humanist concept of the 'ideal city' came to life in the neighbourhoods built by Biagio Rossetti.
Criteria: ii, iii, iv, v, vi Inscribed 1995

• HISTORIC CENTRE OF SIENA Italy

Siena is the embodiment of a medieval city, and its influence on art, architecture and town planning in the Middle Ages, both in Italy and elsewhere in Europe, was immense. At its centre is the Piazza del Campo, at the junction of three hills on which the city stands, one of the most remarkable urban open spaces in Italy. At the end of the twelfth century, the communal government decided to create a unique semicircular open space, and promulgated a series of ordinances that regulated not only commercial activities, but also the dimensions of the houses, in order to make the façades around the piazza uniform. It became the setting for spectacular festivals and the Palio, the famous horse race between teams from the different quarters of the city. The highest point of the town is crowned by the Cathedral of Santa Maria.
Criteria: i, ii, iv Inscribed 1995

• CAVES OF AGGTELEK KARST AND SLOVAK KARST Hungary and Slovakia

The variety of formations and the fact that they are concentrated in a restricted area means that the 712 caves currently identified make up a typical temperate-zone karstic system. These caves are remarkable for having the world's highest stalagmite and an ice-filled abyss, which considering their height above sea level, is a unique phenomenon for Central Europe. Because the caves display an extremely rare combination of tropical and glacial climatic effects, they make it possible to study geological history over tens of millions of years.
Criteria: viii Inscribed 1995

• SAN AGUSTÍN ARCHEOLOGICAL PARK Colombia

The megalithic statuary in this park in northern Andes date from the first to the eighth centuries. Altogether some 300 enormous sculptures of gods, warriors and mythical beasts were created, in styles ranging from abstract to realist. The huge monumental platforms, terraces and mounds, and the temple-like architecture reflect a complex system of religious and magical beliefs. The principal archaeological monuments are Las Mesitas, containing artificial mounds, terraces, funerary structures and stone statues; the Fuente de Lavapatas, a religious monument carved in the stone bed of a stream; and the Bosque de Las Estatuas, with stone statues from the whole region.
Criteria: iii Inscribed 1995

• OLD TOWN LUNENBURG Canada

Lunenburg is the best surviving example of a planned British colonial settlement in North America. The Lunenburg plan (1753) incorporated all the principles of the 'model town': geometrically regular streets and blocks; the allocation of public spaces; an allowance for fortifications; and a distinction between urban and non-urban areas. Of these, all but the fortifications survive. The plan consisted of six divisions of eight blocks each, each block being in turn subdivided into fourteen lots. Each settler was given a town lot and a larger 'garden lot' outside the town limits.
Criteria: iv, v Inscribed 1995

Castello Estense at Ferrara. Court painters to the Este family included Piero della Francesca, Jacopo Bellini and Andrea Mantegna.

The fourteenth-century Palazzo Pubblico, or town hall, is the focal point of the Piazza del Campo in Siena. Its campanile, the Torre del Mangia, was completed in 1344 and is one of the tallest towers is Italy.

The waterfront buildings at Lunenburg. The layout of the town has changed little since 1753. Wood remains the principal construction material and traditional techniques have been maintained.

• TOWN OF LUANG PRABANG Lao People's Democratic Republic

Luang Prabang fuses traditional Lao architecture and urban structures with European colonial building of the nineteenth and twentieth centuries. The political and religious centre of the town is on a peninsula formed by the Mekong River and its tributaries, and contains royal and noble residences, religious foundations and commercial buildings. The majority are built from wood (parts of the temples are in stone). The traditional Lao houses are divided into two basic spaces: the private rooms and the public terraces and are usually raised on wooden piles. The colonial buildings are typically one- or two-storey terraced brick houses.

Criteria: ii, iv, v Inscribed 1995

• HANSEATIC TOWN OF VISBY Sweden

A former Viking site on the island of Gotland, Visby was the main centre of the Hanseatic League in the Baltic in the twelfth to fourteenth centuries. Guild houses and churches were built, and the earlier small wooden buildings were replaced by large stone houses, built in parallel rows eastwards from the harbour. Visby became an impressive international town, enclosed by a strong defensive wall, and increasingly divorced from its rural hinterland. Its thirteenth-century ramparts and more than 200 buildings (warehouses and wealthy merchants' dwellings) from the same period make it the best-preserved fortified commercial city in northern Europe.

Criteria: iv, v Inscribed 1995

• HISTORIC VILLAGES OF SHIRAKAWA-GO AND GOKAYAMA Japan

Located in an isolated mountainous region, these villages subsisted on the cultivation of mulberry trees and the rearing of silkworms. The need for large, enclosed spaces to store mulberry leaves and for silkworm beds was important in the development of the characteristic *gassho*-style houses. Their steeply pitched roofs are also ideally designed to withstand the area's heavy snowfalls and are the only examples of their kind in Japan. Despite economic upheavals, the villages of Ogimachi, Ainokura and Suganuma are outstanding examples of a traditional way of life adapted to the environment and people's social and economic circumstances.

Criteria: iv, v Inscribed 1995

• RICE TERRACES OF THE PHILIPPINE CORDILLERAS Philippines

Terracing began in the Philippine Cordilleras some 2,000 years ago. Complex knowledge of structural and hydraulic engineering was needed by the terrace builders. The groups of terraces blanket the mountainsides, following their contours. Above them, rising to the mountain tops, is a ring of private woods (*muyong*), intensively managed to ensure an adequate water supply to keep the terraces flooded. A system of communally maintained dams, sluices, channels and bamboo pipes, which drain into a stream at the bottom of the valley, provide an equitable supply of water. Villages are associated with groups of terraces, and consist of single-family tribal dwellings.

Criteria: iii, iv, v Inscribed 1995

• HAEINSA TEMPLE JANGGYEONG PANJEON, THE DEPOSITORIES FOR THE TRIPITAKA KOREANA WOODBLOCKS Korea, Republic of

The Temple of Haeinsa, on Mount Kaya, is home to the Tripitaka Koreana, the most complete collection of Buddhist texts, engraved on 80,000 woodblocks between 1237 and 1248 in an appeal to the authority of the Buddha in the defence of Korea against Mongol invasions. The buildings of Janggyeong Panjeon date from the fifteenth century and were constructed to house the woodblocks which are also revered as exceptional works of art. As the oldest depository of the Tripitaka, they reveal an astonishing mastery of the invention and implementation of the conservation techniques used to preserve these woodblocks.

Criteria: iv, vi Inscribed 1995

Wat Xieng Thong, a temple in Luang Prabang.

The main differences between the rice terraces of the Philippines and those elsewhere are their higher altitudes (700–1,500 m) and their slopes that are too steep to permit the use of animals or machinery.

CRESPI D'ADDA Italy

Crespi d'Adda is an outstanding example of a late nineteenth-century 'company town' that survives remarkably intact. In 1878 Cristoforo Crespi, an enlightened Lombardy textile manufacturer, built three-storey multi-family houses for his workers around his mill. When his son, Silvio Crespi, took over the management in 1889, he completed the project with single-family houses with their own gardens, which he saw as conducive to harmony, and a defence against industrial strife. In addition to small houses, he provided workers with free electricity and many social and community facilities.
Criteria: iv, v Inscribed 1995

JONGMYO SHRINE Korea, Republic of

Dedicated to the forefathers of the Choson dynasty (1392–1910), the Jongmyo shrine has existed in its present form since the sixteenth century and houses tablets bearing the teachings of members of the former royal family. Ritual ceremonies linking music, song and dance still take place there, perpetuating a tradition that goes back to the fourteenth century. Jongmyo is surrounded by low hills, with artificial additions created to reinforce the balance of natural elements as laid out in traditional geomancy. The complex is composed of three sets of buildings, each centred around an important shrine or other religious building.
Criteria: iv Inscribed 1995

OLD AND NEW TOWNS OF EDINBURGH
United Kingdom

The Scottish capital since 1437, Edinburgh has two distinct areas: the Old Town, dominated by the medieval fortress of Edinburgh Castle; and the neoclassical New Town, whose development from the eighteenth century onwards had a far-reaching influence on European urban planning. In the Old Town the pressure on space and the steep slopes on either side of the High Street led to the development of multi-storey dwellings from the late medieval period onwards, with some streets effectively being built underground. By the eighteenth century the town had become so crowded that the city authorities held a competition to design a new area north of the Old Town, won in 1766 by a 26-year-old local architect, James Craig. His design for a formally organised grid of streets, was considered to reflect the rational ideas of the Scottish Enlightenment in its order and in its neoclassical styling. The linking of the Old and New Towns by road and bridge, and the construction of neoclassical buildings in both helped to unite the two areas.
Criteria: ii, iv Inscribed 1995

GOUGH AND INACCESSIBLE ISLANDS
United Kingdom

The spectacular cliffs of Gough Island in the South Atlantic make it one of the most important seabird colonies in the world. At least fifty-four bird species occur here, including nearly half the world's population of the northern rockhopper penguin. Gough is also a major breeding site of the great shearwater with up to three million breeding pairs. The endangered wandering albatross is virtually restricted to Gough. The last survivors of the southern giant petrel also breed here. Inaccessible Island is almost as rich in wildlife, with two bird, eight plant and at least ten invertebrate species endemic to the island.
Criteria: vii, x Inscribed 1995

HISTORIC QUARTER OF THE CITY OF
COLONIA DEL SACRAMENTO Uruguay

Founded by the Portuguese in 1680, Colonia del Sacramento was built on the extreme west side of a peninsula by the Río de la Plata. It illustrates the successful fusion of Portuguese, Spanish and Uruguayan styles. Sacramento became the commercial and cultural centre of the Portuguese colony but a siege in 1777 saw it incorporated into the Spanish Empire. There are excellent examples of seventeenth- to nineteenth-century buildings, ranging from elegant town houses to artisans dwellings, and the town has preserved its wide main streets, large squares, cobbled lanes and intimate open spaces.
Criteria: iv Inscribed 1995

The entrance to the factory at Crespi d'Adda, shown here, is on one side of the main road. The houses, constructed within a rectangular grid of roads in three lines, are on the opposite side.

Edinburgh Castle in the Old Town was built in the twelfth century on top of Castle Rock, a crag-and-tail formation, and the main medieval High Street runs downhill from the Castle to the Palace of Holyroodhouse.

A cobbled lane in the city of Colonia del Sacramento.

NATIONAL ARCHEOLOGICAL PARK OF TIERRADENTRO Colombia

The *hypogea* (underground tombs) of Tierradentro are a unique testimony to the everyday life, ritual and burial customs of a stable but now vanished northern Andean pre-Hispanic society. In particular their anthropomorphic carvings and polychrome paintings are unique in America. Dating from the sixth to the tenth centuries, these huge burial chambers are up to 12 m wide. There is a symbolic symmetry between the houses of the living above ground and the underground *hypogea* for the dead. Tierradentro is also remarkable for its stone statues of standing human figures. Masculine figures have banded head-dresses, loincloths and various adornments whereas female figures wear turbans, sleeveless blouses and skirts.

Criteria: iii Inscribed 1995

KUTNÁ HORA: HISTORICAL TOWN CENTRE WITH THE CHURCH OF ST BARBARA AND THE CATHEDRAL OF OUR LADY AT SEDLEC Czech Republic

Kutná Hora, as a result of its silver mines, was one of the most important political and economic centres of Bohemia. In the fourteenth century it became a royal city and one of the richest in Europe. It is endowed with monuments that symbolised its prosperity and influenced the architecture of central Europe: the Church of St Barbara, the Church of St James, the Stone House and the Gothic fountain. The Cistercian Cathedral of Our Lady at Sedlec was restored in line with the Baroque taste of the early eighteenth century. These masterpieces today form part of a well-preserved medieval urban fabric, with some particularly fine private dwellings.

Criteria: ii, iv Inscribed 1995

HISTORIC CENTRE OF SANTA CRUZ DE MOMPOX Colombia

Founded in 1540 on the banks of the river Magdalena, Mompox played a key role in the Spanish colonisation of northern South America. The town initially grew along the river banks. Walls were built to protect it during periods of high water and, instead of a central square, it had three plazas, each corresponding to a former Indian settlement and each with its own church, which initially also served as a fort. Most of its historic buildings are still used for their original purposes, providing an exceptional picture of what a Spanish colonial city was like.

Criteria: iv, v Inscribed 1995

LAKE BAIKAL Russian Federation

More than twenty-five million years old and 1,700 m deep, Lake Baikal in southeast Siberia is the oldest and deepest lake in the world. It contains 20 per cent of the world's total unfrozen freshwater reserves. Its age and isolation have produced some of the richest and most unusual endemic freshwater flora and fauna, including the freshwater Baikal seal. The formation of the lake took place during the Palaeozoic, Mesozoic and Cenozoic eras (from 540 million years ago to the present). Various tectonic forces are still ongoing, shown by recent thermal vents in the depths of the lake.

Criteria: vii, viii, ix, x Inscribed 1996

MOUNT EMEI SCENIC AREA, INCLUDING LESHAN GIANT BUDDHA SCENIC AREA China

The first Buddhist temple in China was built here in Sichuan Province in the first century AD in very beautiful surroundings atop Mount Emei. The addition of other temples turned the site into one of Buddhism's main holy places. Over the centuries, the cultural treasures grew in number. Mount Emei is also a vital sanctuary for a many threatened animal species, including lesser (red) panda, Asiatic black bear, and Asiatic golden cat, and is notable for its very diverse vegetation, ranging from subtropical to sub-alpine pine forests. Some of the trees are more than 1,000 years old.

Criteria: iv, vi, x Inscribed 1996

ANCIENT KSOUR OF OUADANE, CHINGUETTI, TICHITT AND OUALATA Mauritania

Founded in the eleventh and twelfth centuries to serve the caravans crossing the Sahara, these trading and religious centres became focal points of Islamic culture. Sited on the outskirts of a fertile valley or oasis, they originally provided religious instruction, and grew around mosques, accompanied by houses for teachers and students. Warehouses were built by traders to safeguard their goods, while inns were provided for those passing through on business. From these elements grew the characteristic settlement known as the *ksar* or *ksour*, with houses crowded along narrow streets around a mosque with a square minaret.

Criteria: iii, iv, v Inscribed 1996

OKAPI WILDLIFE RESERVE Dem. Rep. of the Congo

The Okapi Wildlife Reserve occupies about one-fifth of the Ituri forest in the northeast of the Democratic Republic of the Congo. The Congo River basin, of which the reserve and forest are a part, is one of the largest drainage systems in Africa. The reserve contains threatened species of primates and birds and about 5,000 of the estimated 30,000 okapi surviving in the wild. It also has some dramatic scenery, including waterfalls on the Ituri and Epulu rivers. The reserve is inhabited by traditional nomadic pygmy Mbuti and Efe hunters.

Criteria: x Inscribed 1996

MILLENARY BENEDICTINE ABBEY OF PANNONHALMA AND ITS NATURAL ENVIRONMENT Hungary

Benedictine monks came in 996 to this sacred mountain and established the monastery as the eastern bridgehead of medieval European culture. The present church, of 1224, is the third on the site; it contains fragments of its predecessors. In 1472 the king took over the monastery and undertook extensive renovations. The cloister and other buildings were built, and the monastery was fortified. However, the monastery was badly damaged by fire and largely abandoned in 1575. The Benedictine community returned in 1638, and the Baroque elements of the monastery, such as the refectory, were added.

Criteria: iv, vi Inscribed 1996

CANAL DU MIDI France

This 360-km network of navigable waterways linking the Mediterranean and the Atlantic through locks, aqueducts, bridges and tunnels is a remarkable feat of civil engineering. Built between 1667 and 1694, it paved the way for the Industrial Revolution. It was designed by Pierre-Paul Riquet, who was conscious that he was creating a symbol of the power of seventeenth-century France, as well as a functional waterway. He made sure, therefore, that the quality of the architecture on the Canal was worthy of this role. The bridges, locks and associated structures were designed with monumental dignity and simplicity.

Criteria: i, ii, iv, vi Inscribed 1996

UPPER SVANETI Georgia

Preserved by its long isolation, the Upper Svaneti region of the Caucasus has a characteristic landscape of small villages dominated by their church towers, set in a natural environment of gorges, alpine valleys and with a backdrop of snow-covered mountains. The unique tower-houses of the area served as dwellings, storehouses and defence posts against the invaders who plagued the region. The village of Chazhashi still has more than 200 of these unusual buildings. The excellent natural conditions and the unity of architecture and landscape give this region an original quality of its own. The wealth of monumental and minor art (metal work, manuscript illustrations, textiles and embroidery, wood-carving, icon painting, vernacular architecture) is of great importance in the study of Georgia and the Caucasus.

Criteria: iv, v Inscribed 1996

LUSHAN NATIONAL PARK China

Mount Lushan, in Jiangxi, is one of the spiritual centres of Chinese civilisation. Buddhist and Taoist temples, along with landmarks of Confucianism, where the most eminent masters taught, blend effortlessly into a strikingly beautiful landscape. It is an area that has inspired philosophy and art, and into which high-quality cultural properties have been selectively and sensitively integrated up to recent times. Some 200 historic buildings are scattered over Lushan National Park. The most celebrated is the East Grove Temple complex at the foot of Xianglu Peak. Begun in AD 386, it has been added to progressively over the centuries.

Criteria: ii, iii, iv, vi Inscribed 1996

BELIZE BARRIER REEF RESERVE SYSTEM Belize

The coastal area of Belize is an outstanding natural system consisting of the largest barrier reef in the northern hemisphere, offshore atolls, several hundred sand cays, mangrove forests, coastal lagoons and estuaries. The system's seven sites illustrate the evolutionary history of reef development and are a significant habitat for threatened species, including marine turtles, manatees and the American marine crocodile. The approximately 450 sand and mangrove cays confined within the barrier and atolls range in size from small, ephemeral sand spits to larger, permanent islands capable of sustaining human settlements. There are over 500 species of fish plus a great diversity of corals, molluscs, sponges, marine worms and crustaceans.

Criteria: vii, ix, x Inscribed 1996

BAUHAUS AND ITS SITES IN WEIMAR AND DESSAU Germany

Between 1919 and 1933 the Bauhaus School, based first in Weimar and then in Dessau, revolutionised architectural and aesthetic concepts and practices. The buildings constructed and decorated by the school's professors, Walter Gropius, Hannes Meyer, Laszlo Moholy-Nagy and Wassily Kandinsky, launched the Modern Movement, which shaped much of the architecture of the twentieth century. The Weimar Bauhaus was obliged to close in 1925 for political reasons, after which Gropius found support for his cultural and political stance in Dessau, along with the opportunity to create a number of large-scale new buildings. These were situated on the outskirts of the town, and comprise the Bauhaus itself and the Masters' Houses (Meisterhäuser), which served as the residences of the Bauhaus directors and some of its distinguished teachers.

Criteria: ii, iv, vi Inscribed 1996

• HIROSHIMA PEACE MEMORIAL (GENBAKU DOME) Japan

The Hiroshima Peace Memorial is a stark symbol of the most destructive force ever created by humankind; it also expresses the hope for world peace and the ultimate elimination of nuclear weapons. The Hiroshima Prefectural Industrial Promotion Hall was the only structure left standing, albeit in skeletal form, in the area where the first atomic bomb exploded on the morning of 6 August 1945. It was preserved in that state when reconstruction of the city began, and became known as the Genbaku (Atomic Bomb) Dome. In 1966 Hiroshima City Council adopted a resolution that the dome should be preserved in perpetuity.
Criteria: vi Inscribed 1996

• LA LONJA DE LA SEDA DE VALENCIA Spain

La Lonja de la Seda de Valencia is an exceptional late Gothic secular building, which illustrates the wealth of one of the great Mediterranean mercantile cities. Built between 1482 and 1533, this group of buildings was originally used for trading in silk – hence its name, the Silk Exchange – and it has always been a centre for commerce, now dealing primarily in agricultural products. The land occupied by the Lonja is rectangular in plan. About half of the total area is covered by the main Sala de Contratación; the Tower (including the Chapel), the Consulado, and the large garden complete the ensemble.
Criteria: i, iv Inscribed 1996

• COLOGNE CATHEDRAL Germany

Cologne Cathedral, constructed over six centuries from 1248, is a masterpiece of High Gothic architecture. The cathedral is a five-aisled basilica with a projecting transept and two-tower façade. The western section changes in style but this is not perceptible in the overall building. Nineteenth-century work followed medieval forms and techniques faithfully. The original liturgical appointments of the choir include the high altar on a slab of black marble, carved-oak choir stalls (1308–11), painted choir screens (1332–40), fourteen statues on the pillars in the choir (1270–90) and the stained-glass windows, the largest extant cycle of fourteenth-century windows in Europe.
Criteria: i, ii, iv Inscribed 1996

• W NATIONAL PARK OF NIGER Niger

The 'W' National Park, named after the local configuration of the Niger river, is located in a transition zone between savanna and forest landscapes. W hosts important ecosystems that represent the interaction between natural resources and humans since Neolithic times, and a rich biodiversity. The park is known for its large mammals, including aardvarks, baboons, buffalo, cheetahs, elephants, hippopotamuses, leopards, lions and warthogs. The wetland area of the park is of international importance for the conservation of birds. A total of 454 plant species has been recorded. More than seventy mammal and 350 bird species are found in the area.
Criteria: ix, x Inscribed 1996

• ITSUKUSHIMA SHINTO SHRINE Japan

The island of Itsukushima, in the Seto inland sea, has been a holy place of Shintoism since the earliest times. The first shrine buildings here were probably erected in the sixth century. The present shrine dates from the twelfth century. The design of the buildings plays on the contrasts in colour and form between mountains and sea, and illustrates the Japanese concept of scenic beauty, which combines nature and human creativity. The Honsha and Sessha Marodo-jinja buildings were influenced by the aristocratic dwelling-house style of the Heian period.
Criteria: i, ii, iv, vi Inscribed 1996

• VERLA GROUNDWOOD AND BOARD MILL Finland

The Verla Groundwood and Board Mill and its associated residential area is an outstanding example of a small-scale rural industrial settlement. The Industrial Revolution reached the Kymi river valley in the first half of the 1870s. Soon dozens of steam sawmills, groundwood mills and board mills were established. Output at Verla

The Hiroshima Peace Memorial, all that remained of the Hiroshima Prefectural Industrial Promotion Hall, that was only 150 m from the hypocentre of the explosion of the first atomic bomb.

Cologne Cathedral, started in 1248 to replace a smaller building that could not accommodate pilgrims wishing to see relics of the Three Kings, was finally completed in 1880.

gradually diminished throughout the twentieth century, until it was closed down in 1964 and preserved intact as an industrial heritage museum, just as it had been when the last worker left.
Criteria: iv Inscribed 1996

• HISTORIC CENTRE OF OPORTO Portugal

The Romans named the town Portus, or port, and its growth, linked to the sea, can be seen in its rich and varied architecture, from the cathedral with its Romanesque choir to the neoclassical Stock Exchange and the typically Portuguese Manueline-style Church of Santa Clara. Oporto supported the expeditions of Henry the Navigator, born here in the fifteenth century. In the eighteenth century English entrepreneurs invested in the vineyards of the Douro valley to supply port to the huge English market. Oporto benefited greatly as the shipping port for these wines, as the town's many Baroque buildings demonstrate.
Criteria: iv Inscribed 1996

• DEFENCE LINE OF AMSTERDAM Netherlands

Extending 135 km around the city of Amsterdam, this defence line, the Stelling, was built between 1883 and 1920. Since the sixteenth century, the Dutch have used their knowledge of hydraulic engineering for defence purposes. Earlier defensive lines were strengthened and linked so that the centre of the country was protected by a network of forty-five armed forts, acting in concert with temporary flooding of polders and an intricate system of canals and locks. The sites of the forts are connected to the existing infrastructure of roads, waterways, dykes and settlements.
Criteria: ii, iv, v Inscribed 1996

• PRE-HISPANIC TOWN OF UXMAL Mexico

The ruins of the ceremonial structures at Uxmal, in Yucatán, represent the pinnacle of late-Mayan art and architecture in their design, layout and ornamentation. The layout of the buildings, dating between 700 and 1000, reveals a detailed knowledge of astronomy. The Pirámide del Adivino, as the Spaniards called it – or Pyramid of the Soothsayer – dominates the ceremonial centre, which has well-designed buildings decorated with a profusion of symbolic motifs and sculptures depicting Chaac, the god of rain.
Criteria: i, ii, iii Inscribed 1996

• VOLCANOES OF KAMCHATKA
Russian Federation

Kamchatka is one of the world's most volcanic regions, with over 300 volcanoes, twenty-nine of which are currently active. In addition, there are thermal and mineral springs, geysers and other phenomena of active volcanism. The interplay of active volcanoes and glaciers forms a dynamic landscape of great beauty, and the area contains great species diversity, including the world's largest-known variety of salmonid fish, and large populations of sea otter, brown bear and Steller's sea eagle. The diverse vegetation cover embraces conifer and deciduous forests, peat and coastal wetlands, subalpine shrub and mountain tundra.
Criteria: vii, viii, ix, x Inscribed 1996

• SKELLIG MICHAEL Ireland

This monastery, perched on the rocky island of Skellig Michael, some 12 km off the coast of southwest Ireland, illustrates the extremes of early Christian monasticism. The principal monastic remains are situated on a sloping shelf on the ridge running north–south on the northeastern side of the island; the hermitage is on the steeper South Peak. The monastery comprises a church, oratories, cells and many crosses and cross-slabs. It was occupied from the seventh to the late twelfth century, when increased storms forced the community to move to the mainland.
Criteria: iii, iv Inscribed 1996

• HISTORIC CITY OF MEKNES Morocco

Meknes was founded in the eleventh century by the Almoravids as a military settlement. Later, the founder of the Alawite dynasty, Moulay Ismail (1672–1727), made Meknes his capital city and reconstructed

The beautiful city of Oporto, built along the hillsides overlooking the Douro river, is an exceptional urban landscape with a 2,000-year history.

The Pirámide del Adivino dominates Uxmal and is from the Late Classic period, bringing together several artistic traditions, including that of the Toltec of Central Mexico.

An active crater on Mutnovsky volcano. The six designated parks within this site group together the majority of volcanic features of the Kamchatka Peninsula.

many mosques, mausoleums and gardens. He also created an impressive new imperial city, built in the Hispano-Moorish style. Enclosed by high walls pierced by monumental gates, the blending of the Islamic and European styles of seventeenth-century Maghreb are still evident today. Within the walls are: the palace, with its enormous stables; a military academy; vast granaries; and water storage cisterns.
Criteria: iv Inscribed 1996

• LEDNICE-VALTICE CULTURAL LANDSCAPE
Czech Republic
Between the seventeenth and twentieth centuries, the dukes of Liechtenstein transformed their domains in southern Moravia into a striking landscape that married Baroque architecture with romantic English landscape design. Work on this grandiose scheme began in the seventeenth century with the creation of avenues connecting Valtice with other parts of the estate, and continued in the eighteenth and nineteenth centuries, making designed parks with the deliberate planting of local and exotic tree species. The Chateau of Valtice has medieval foundations, but it underwent successive reconstructions in Renaissance, Mannerist and, most significantly, Baroque style.
Criteria: i, ii, iv Inscribed 1996

• HISTORIC CENTRE OF THE CITY OF PIENZA
Italy
It was in this Tuscan town that Renaissance town-planning concepts were first put into practice after Pope Pius II decided, in 1459, to transform the look of his birthplace. This new vision was realised in the superb square known as Piazza Pio II and the buildings around it: the Piccolomini Palace, the Borgia Palace and the cathedral. Pius II's project also required the building of large houses for the cardinals in his retinue, while the hospital and the inn in front of the Church of St Francis, were built on his orders.
Criteria: i, ii, iv Inscribed 1996

• HISTORIC MONUMENTS ZONE OF
QUERÉTARO Mexico
The old colonial town of Querétaro is unusual in having retained the geometric street plan of the Spanish conquerors side by side with the twisting alleys of the Indian quarters. The town has many ornate civil and religious Baroque monuments from its golden age in the seventeenth and eighteenth centuries. The Plaza de Armas, the seat of government, was surrounded by government buildings and residences of leading citizens. Many monastic orders established themselves and left behind outstanding Baroque buildings. The old buildings are enhanced by the pink stone of Querétaro.
Criteria: ii, iv Inscribed 1996

• CASTEL DEL MONTE Italy
When the Emperor Frederick II built this castle near Bari in the thirteenth century, he imbued it with symbolic significance, reflected in the precision of its design. Castel del Monte blends elements from classical antiquity, the Islamic Orient and north European Cistercian Gothic. It is sited on a rocky peak that dominates the surrounding countryside and consists of a regular octagon surrounding a courtyard, with a tower, also octagonal, at each angle and eight rooms on each floor. Unlike most castles, there is no outer bailey, moat, drawbridge or ancillary buildings.
Criteria: i, ii, iii Inscribed 1996

• HISTORIC CENTRE OF THE CITY OF
SALZBURG Austria
Salzburg preserves its dramatic townscape and a large number of outstanding ecclesiastical and secular buildings from the Middle Ages to the nineteenth century, when it was a city-state ruled by prince-archbishops. Its flamboyant Gothic art attracted many craftsmen and artists before the city became even better known through the work of the Italian architects Vincenzo Scamozzi and Santini Solari, to whom Salzburg owes much of its Baroque appearance. This meeting point of northern and southern Europe perhaps sparked the genius of Salzburg's most famous son, Wolfgang Amadeus Mozart.
Criteria: ii, iv, vi Inscribed 1996

Lednice Chateau began as a Renaissance villa in around 1570, and then was progressively changed and reconstructed to take account of Baroque, Classical and Neo-Gothic fashions.

Pope Pius II was born in Corsignano, situated on a hill southeast of Siena. When he returned there he was inspired to improve the town with new buildings and a new name, Pienza, and to make it his summer court.

The skyline of Salzburg with its profusion of spires and domes, is dominated by the fortress of Hohensalzburg, originally a Roman fort and enlarged many times up to the late seventeenth century.

• THE TRULLI OF ALBEROBELLO Italy

The extraordinary drystone dwellings of Alberobello, the *trulli*, mostly date from before the end of the eighteenth century. Constructed using roughly worked limestone boulders, they were built directly on the underlying natural rock. The walls that form the rectangular rooms are pierced by small windows. Fireplaces, ovens and alcoves are recessed into the thickness of the walls. The stone roofs, which are circular or oval, develop a patina of mosses and lichens; they sometimes bear mythological or religious symbols in white ash. The walls of the *trulli* are whitewashed at regular intervals.
Criteria: iii, iv, v Inscribed 1996

• LAPONIAN AREA Sweden

This area, close to the Arctic Circle in northern Sweden, has been occupied by the Saami people since prehistoric times. It is the largest area in the world with an ancestral way of life based on the seasonal movement of livestock (transhumance), the Saami spending the summer in the mountains in the west and the winters in the coniferous forests to the east. There are no permanent settlements occupied throughout the year anywhere in this area. The nomadic life based on herding of tame reindeer did not develop until the seventeenth and eighteenth centuries.
Criteria: iii, v, vii, viii, ix Inscribed 1996

• MONASTERIES OF HAGHPAT AND SANAHIN
Armenia

These two Byzantine monasteries represent the highest flowering of Armenian religious architecture, which blends Byzantine ecclesiastical architecture with vernacular architecture of the Caucasian region. Sanahin consists of a large group of buildings on the plateau above the Debet gorge. The main church, built in the tenth century, is the Cathedral of the Redeemer. It was renowned for its school of illuminators and calligraphers. Construction of the main church of the large fortified monastic complex of Haghpat, dedicated to the Holy Cross, began in 966–7 and was completed in 991.
Criteria: ii, iv Inscribed 1996

• LUTHER MEMORIALS IN EISLEBEN AND
WITTENBERG Germany

These places in Saxony-Anhalt are all associated with the lives of Martin Luther and his fellow-reformer Melanchthon. They include Melanchthon's house in Wittenberg, the houses in Eisleben where Luther was born in 1483 and died in 1546, his room in Wittenberg, the local church and the castle church where, on 31 October 1517, Luther posted his famous '95 Theses' on its bronze door, thereby launching the Reformation and a new era in the religious and political history of the Western world. This church now houses the tombs of Luther and Melanchthon.
Criteria: iv, vi Inscribed 1996

• PALACE AND GARDENS OF SCHÖNBRUNN
Austria

The Baroque palace of Schönbrunn illustrates the tastes, interests and aspirations of successive Habsburg monarchs. Apart from some minor additions, the palace and its gardens were built in the eighteenth century. The Great Gallery is elaborately decorated with ceiling frescoes symbolising the Habsburg Empire, while the Ceremonial Hall contains paintings depicting events in Empress Maria Theresa's reign. The courtyard provides access to the Palace Chapel and the Palace Theatre. The orangery was used to cultivate exotic plants, and the Schönbrunn zoo, founded in 1752, is the oldest in the world.
Criteria: i, iv Inscribed 1996

• SANGIRAN EARLY MAN SITE Indonesia

Sangiran is a key site for understanding of human evolution. Excavations from 1936 to 1941 led to the discovery of the first hominid fossil. Later, fifty early human fossils (*Pithecanthropus erectus/Homo erectus*) were found – half of all the world's known hominid fossils – together with numerous animal and floral fossils.

The trulli of Alberobello are an exceptional example of vernacular architecture.

The palace of Schönbrunn. Initially designed from 1693 by Johann Bernhard Fischer von Erlach for Leopold I, it was greatly expanded from 1743 by Nicolaus Pacassi for Empress Maria Theresa.

Palaeolithic stone tools found at Ngebung include flakes, choppers and cleavers in chalcedony and jasper and, more recently, bone tools indicating that hominids have inhabited the area for at least 1.5 million years.

Criteria: iii, vi Inscribed 1996

• HISTORIC WALLED TOWN OF CUENCA Spain

Built by the Moors at the heart of the Caliphate of Cordoba, Cuenca is an unusually well-preserved medieval fortified town. Conquered by the Castilians in the twelfth century, it became a royal town and bishopric. In the upper town some remains of the Moorish fortress still survive among the large aristocratic houses, monasteries, and churches from the medieval, Renaissance and Baroque periods. The twelfth-century cathedral, built on the site of the former Great Mosque, was the first Gothic cathedral in Spain.

Criteria: ii, vi Inscribed 1996

• ARCHAEOLOGICAL SITE OF AIGAI (MODERN NAME VERGINA) Greece

Aigai, the ancient capital of Macedonia, was discovered in the nineteenth century near Vergina, in northern Greece. The most important building found so far is the sumptuously decorated royal palace, directly below the acropolis. The site also has a necropolis which contains over 300 grave-mounds, some as early as the eleventh century BC. One of the royal tombs in the Great Tumulus contained a solid gold casket with remains identified as those of Philip II. His conquest of Greek cities paved the way for his son Alexander and the expansion of the Hellenistic world.

Criteria: i, iii Inscribed 1996

• EARLY CHRISTIAN MONUMENTS OF RAVENNA Italy

Ravenna was the seat of the Roman Empire in the fifth century and then of Byzantine Italy until the eighth century. It has a unique collection of early Christian mosaics and monuments. All eight buildings – the Mausoleum of Galla Placidia, the Neonian Baptistery, the Basilica of Sant'Apollinare Nuovo, the Arian Baptistery, the Archiepiscopal Chapel, the Mausoleum of Theodoric, the Church of San Vitale and the Basilica of Sant'Apollinare in Classe – were constructed in the fifth and sixth centuries. They show great artistic skill, including a wonderful blend of Graeco-Roman tradition, Christian iconography and oriental and Western styles.

Criteria: i, ii, iii, iv Inscribed 1996

• CHURCH VILLAGE OF GAMMELSTAD, LULEÅ Sweden

Gammelstad, ('Old Town') at the head of the Gulf of Bothnia, is the best-preserved example of a 'church village', a unique kind of village formerly found throughout northern Scandinavia. The 424 wooden houses, huddled round the early fifteenth-century stone church, were used only on Sundays and at religious festivals to house worshippers from the surrounding countryside who could not return home the same day because of the distance and difficult travelling conditions. Gammelstad's church is the largest of its type in northern Scandinavia.

Criteria: ii, iv, v Inscribed 1996

• PORTOVENERE, CINQUE TERRE, AND THE ISLANDS (PALMARIA, TINO AND TINETTO) Italy

The jagged, steep eastern Ligurian coastline between Cinque Terre and Portovenere has, over the centuries, been transformed into an intensively terraced landscape, to give small areas of land suitable for agriculture, such as growing vines and olive trees. Most of these cultivation terraces were built in the twelfth century. People have adapted to this inhospitable terrain by building compact settlements directly on the rock, giving these settlements their characteristic appearance. They are generally grouped round religious buildings or medieval castles.

Criteria: ii, iv, v Inscribed 1997

The famous *casas colgadas* ('hanging houses') of Cuenca were built in the sixteenth century on the spectacular steep bluffs overlooking the bend of the Huécar river.

The mausoleum of Galla Placidia at Ravenna.

One of the five medieval villages of the Cinque Terre, Riomaggiore. Off the coast at Portovenere are the three islands of Palmaria, Tino and Tinetto, with many remains of early monastic establishments.

• OLD TOWN OF LIJIANG China

The Old Town of Lijiang, in Yunnan Province, is built on a mountain slope, facing a deep river. The northern part was a commercial district and the main streets there radiate from the broad thoroughfare known as Sifangjie.. Lijiang possesses an ancient water-supply system of great complexity and ingenuity that still functions effectively today. The system of channels, culverts and watercourses requires over 350 bridges, from which it derives its name, the 'City of Bridges'. The great number and style of wooden houses are typical of the local Naxi people.
Criteria: ii, iv, v Inscribed 1997

• MARITIME GREENWICH United Kingdom

The oldest building at Greenwich is the Queen's House, designed by Inigo Jones in 1616, and the first true Palladian building in Britain. The Queen's House and its associated buildings have housed the National Maritime Museum since 1937. The Baroque splendour of the former Royal Naval College was designed by Sir Christopher Wren and Nicholas Hawksmoor. Greenwich Royal Park contains the Old Royal Observatory, the work of Wren and the scientist Robert Hooke. Greenwich was central to England's scientific and maritime endeavours in the seventeenth and eighteenth centuries.
Criteria: i, ii, iv, vi Inscribed 1997

• HISTORIC CENTRE (OLD TOWN) OF TALLINN Estonia

Tallinn is a well-preserved northern European medieval trading city. Its origins date back to the thirteenth century, when a castle was built by the knights of the Teutonic Order. It developed into a major centre of the Hanseatic League, and its wealth is demonstrated by the opulence of the public buildings and merchants' houses. The lower town preserves the medieval pattern of narrow winding streets and fine public and burgher buildings. There are several medieval churches within the city walls including the restored Church of St Nicholas (Niguliste) and the Church of St Olaf (Oleviste).
Criteria: ii, iv Inscribed 1997

• MACQUARIE ISLAND Australia

Macquarie Island lies in the Southern Ocean, approximately halfway between Australia and the Antarctic continent. It is the exposed crest of the undersea Macquarie Ridge and is of major geoconservation significance, being the only island in the world composed entirely of rocks from the Earth's mantle 6 km below the ocean floor that are being actively exposed above sea-level. Macquarie Island's beauty lies in its remote and windswept landscape of steep escarpments, lakes, dramatic changes in vegetation, and the vast congregations of royal penguins, albatrosses and elephant seals around its dark, dramatic shores.
Criteria: vii, viii Inscribed 1997

• HISTORIC FORTIFIED CITY OF CARCASSONNE France

Carcassonne is an outstanding example of a medieval fortified town, with its massive defences encircling the castle and its fine Gothic cathedral. During the turbulent years of the late third and early fourth centuries, the town was protected by a defensive wall some 1,200 m long. The twelfth-century count's castle was built over the western part of this Roman wall, and by the end of the thirteenth century the town's defences were complete. The second half of the nineteenth century saw a lengthy restoration and rebuilding scheme undertaken by the architect Viollet-le-Duc.
Criteria: ii, iv Inscribed 1997

• LUMBINI, THE BIRTHPLACE OF THE LORD BUDDHA Nepal

Siddhartha Gautama, the Lord Buddha, was born in 623 BC in the famous gardens of Lumbini, which soon became a place of pilgrimage. Archaeological remains associated with the birth of the Lord Buddha form a central feature of a new pilgrimage centre. Lumbini is situated at the foothills of the Himalaya in modern Nepal. In the Buddha's time, Lumbini was a beautiful garden full of green and shady sal trees, and the site still retains its legendary charm and serenity.
Criteria: iii, vi Inscribed 1997

A view over the roof tops of the traditional wooden houses of Lijiang: wooden frames are walled with adobe on the ground floor and planks on the upper floors and decorated with elaborate wooden carvings.

The tower of St Olaf's church overlooks the Old Town of Tallinn. Its basilical design, with lofty vaulting, is typical of the Tallinn School of design.

The walls of Carcassonne, as restored by the architect Viollet-le-Duc in the nineteenth century.

• MORNE TROIS PITONS NATIONAL PARK
Dominica

Luxuriant tropical forest blends with scenic volcanic features of great scientific interest in this national park, centred on the 1,342 m-high volcano known as Morne Trois Pitons. The landscape is characterised by volcanic piles with precipitous slopes and deeply incised valleys. The so-called Valley of Desolation (Grand Soufriere) contains fumaroles, hot springs, mud pots, sulphur vents and the Boiling Lake, which is the world's second largest of its kind. The valley is a large amphitheatre surrounded by mountains and consists of at least three separate craters.

Criteria: viii, x Inscribed 1997

• HEARD AND MCDONALD ISLANDS Australia

Heard and McDonald Islands lie in the Southern Ocean, approximately 1,700 km from the Antarctic continent and over 4,100 km southwest of Perth. As the only volcanically active subantarctic islands they provide the opportunity to observe ongoing geomorphic processes. Permanent snow and ice cover about 70 per cent of Heard Island and its relatively fast-flowing glaciers respond quickly to changes in climate. Heard and McDonald Islands are two of the world's rare pristine island ecosystems, with no introduced plants and animals.

Criteria: viii, ix Inscribed 1997

• LAKE TURKANA NATIONAL PARKS Kenya

The area around Lake Turkana is mostly semi-desert, with open plains flanked by volcanic formations including Mount Sibiloi, the site of a petrified forest. The most saline of Africa's large lakes, Turkana is an outstanding laboratory for the study of plant and animal communities. The three National Parks are major breeding grounds for the Nile crocodile, hippopotamus and a variety of venomous snakes. More than 350 bird species of bird have been recorded in Lake Turkana, and it serves as a stopover for migrant birds. Fossil evidence supports the existence here of a relatively intelligent hominid two million years ago.

Criteria: viii, x Inscribed 1997

• PYRÉNÉES – MONT PERDU France and Spain

This outstanding mountain landscape, which spans the borders of France and Spain, is centred around the peak of Mont Perdu, a calcareous massif that rises to 3,352 m. The site includes two of Europe's largest and deepest canyons on the Spanish side and three major cirque walls on the more abrupt northern slopes within France. The site is also a pastoral landscape reflecting an agricultural way of life that was once widespread in the upland regions of Europe but now survives only in this part of the Pyrenees.

Criteria: iii, iv, v, vii, viii Inscribed 1997

• THE SUNDARBANS Bangladesh

The large Sundarbans mangrove forest lies on the delta of the Ganges, Brahmaputra and Meghna rivers on the Bay of Bengal. It is adjacent to India's Sundarbans World Heritage site inscribed in 1987. The site is intersected by a complex network of tidal waterways, mudflats and small islands of salt-tolerant mangrove forests. The area is known for its wide range of fauna, including 260 bird species, the Bengal tiger and other threatened species such as the estuarine crocodile and the Indian python.

Criteria: ix, x Inscribed 1997

• HALLSTATT-DACHSTEIN / SALZKAMMERGUT CULTURAL LANDSCAPE Austria

Human activity in the magnificent natural landscape of the Salzkammergut began in prehistoric times, with the salt deposits being exploited as early as the second millennium BC. This resource formed the basis of the area's prosperity, reflected in the fine architecture in Hallstatt, whose name is derived from *hal* (salt) and *stat* (settlement). The site also includes the limestone Dachstein Mountains, rising to some 3,000 m, which contain a large number of caves, the longest being the Hirlatzhöhle (96 km).

Criteria: iii, iv Inscribed 1997

Middleham Falls which feeds the Emerald Pool, in the Morne Trois Pitons National Park.

Arid land around Lake Turkana.

A traditional lakeside settlement in the Salzkammergut that makes maximum use of the restricted space and the steep topography.

• CLASSICAL GARDENS OF SUZHOU China

Located on the lower Yangtze river, Suzhou is crossed by numerous waterways and Marco Polo called it 'Venice of the Orient' when he visited in the thirteenth century. Classical Chinese garden design, which seeks to recreate natural landscapes in miniature, is nowhere better illustrated than in the nine Suzhou gardens included in this site, which are acknowledged as masterpieces. Dating from the eleventh to the nineteenth centuries, they reflect in their meticulous design the profound importance of natural beauty in Chinese culture. The earliest, the Humble Administrator's Garden, has been the residence of Suzhou notables since the second century AD and is one of China's most famous gardens.

Criteria: i, ii, iii, iv, v Inscribed 1997

• COCOS ISLAND NATIONAL PARK Costa Rica

Cocos Island National Park, 550 km off the Pacific coast of Costa Rica, is the only island in the tropical eastern Pacific with a tropical rainforest. The underwater world of the National Park is one of the best places in the world to view large pelagic species such as sharks, rays, tuna and dolphins. Cocos Island has an impoverished flora compared to that of the continent, but has a high number of endemic species (at least seventy species of vascular plant). The vegetation owes its lushness to the heavy rainfall and rugged relief.

Criteria: ix, x Inscribed 1997

• EPISCOPAL COMPLEX OF THE EUPHRASIAN BASILICA IN THE HISTORIC CENTRE OF POREČ Croatia

Christianity was established in Pore as early as the fourth century. In the sixth century, Bishop Euphrasia erected the basilica, atrium, baptistery and episcopal palace, now the most complete such grouping to survive from that time. The basilica combines classical and Byzantine elements and all these buildings were richly ornamented with mosaics, alabaster, marble, mother-of-pearl and stucco. Later additions to the Episcopal complex were the Kanonika (Canon's House) of 1257, the sixteenth-century bell tower, and some minor buildings.

Criteria: ii, iii, iv Inscribed 1997

• CATHEDRAL, TORRE CIVICA AND PIAZZA GRANDE, MODENA Italy

The magnificent twelfth-century cathedral at Modena, the work of two great artists Lanfranco and Wiligelmo, is a supreme example of Romanesque art. The Torre Civica, its soaring bell tower, and the Piazza Grande complete this architectural complex. Wiligelmo provided much of the cathedral's sculpture, particularly in the façade. The Maestri Campionesi – architects and sculptors commissioned to maintain the building from the second half of the twelfth century onwards – made various alterations and improvements to the building. Only minor changes have been made to the Piazza Grande: its quadrangular shape has been preserved.

Criteria: i, ii, iii, iv Inscribed 1997

• ARCHAEOLOGICAL AREAS OF POMPEI, HERCULANEUM AND TORRE ANNUNZIATA Italy

When Vesuvius erupted on 24 August AD 79 it engulfed the two flourishing Roman towns and many villas in the area. Since the mid-eighteenth century these have been progressively excavated. The vast expanse of the commercial town of Pompei contrasts with the smaller but better-preserved remains of the holiday resort of Herculaneum, while the superb wall paintings of the Villa Oplontis at Torre Annunziata show the opulent lifestyle of wealth Roman citizens. The main forum of Pompei is flanked by the foundations of several imposing public buildings including the Capitolium (temple), Basilica (courthouse) and public baths. Pompei is renowned for its domestic buildings, ranged along well-paved streets. At Herculaneum, there are several impressive public buildings and many large houses. Those facing the sea have large courtyards and rich decoration. Its shops still contain fittings such as enormous wine jars. In both towns there is a wealth of sculptures, mosaics and wall paintings.

Criteria: iii, iv, v Inscribed 1997

Chinese gardens, as exemplified by this garden in Suzhou, have certain elements in common governing their positioning, layout, scenery, planting, contents and philosophy in order to create great beauty and harmony.

Part of Pompei. The remains of Pompei and Herculaneum provide a complete and vivid picture of society and daily life at a specific moment in the past that is without parallel anywhere in the world.

• MILL NETWORK AT KINDERDIJK-ELSHOUT
Netherlands

The Kinderdijk-Elshout mill network illustrates the typical features associated with handling water – dykes, reservoirs, pumping stations, administrative buildings and a series of beautifully preserved windmills. At one time, there were more than 150 such mills in the Alblasserwaard and Vijfheerenlanden area, but today there are only 28. The World Heritage Site contains nineteen of these mills, mostly dating from the mid-eighteenth century. Although they went out of use in the late 1940s, all nineteen are still in operating condition.
Criteria: i, ii, iv Inscribed 1997

• CHANGDEOKGUNG PALACE COMPLEX
Korea, Republic of

In the early fifteenth century, the Emperor T'aejong ordered the construction of a new palace, which he named Changdeokgung (Palace of Illustrious Virtue). A Bureau of Palace Construction created the complex in accordance with traditional design principles. These included the palace in front, the market behind, three gates and three courts (administrative court, royal residence court and official audience court). The compound was divided into two parts: the main palace buildings and the Piwon (royal secret garden). The result is an exceptional Far Eastern palace, which influenced Korean architecture and garden design for many centuries.
Criteria: ii, iii, iv Inscribed 1997

• HISTORIC CITY OF TROGIR Croatia

The ancient town of Tragurion (island of goats) was founded as a trading settlement by Greek colonists in the third century BC and its street plan dates back to the Hellenistic period. From the thirteenth century new building took place, including the cathedral and the Camerlengo fortress while Renaissance and Baroque buildings were added during the Venetian rule after 1420. Throughout the town, particularly round the ramparts, are the palaces of leading families, many built on the foundations of late Classical or Romanesque buildings.
Criteria: ii, iv Inscribed 1997

• MEDINA OF TÉTOUAN (FORMERLY KNOWN AS TITAWIN) Morocco

From the eighth century onwards Tétouan was the main point of contact between Morocco and Islamic Andalusia. After the Reconquista, the town was rebuilt by Andalusian refugees who had been expelled by the Spanish, and its design and architecture reveal clear Andalusian influence. Although one of the smallest of the Moroccan medinas, Tétouan is unquestionably the most complete and it has been largely untouched by subsequent outside influences.
Criteria: ii, iv, v Inscribed 1997

• ARCHAEOLOGICAL SITE OF PANAMÁ VIEJO AND HISTORIC DISTRICT OF PANAMÁ Panama

Panamá Viejo is the oldest European town on the American mainland, founded in 1519 by the conquistador Pedrarías Dávila. It soon became a commercial and administrative centre, but its unhealthy climate restricted its development. The old town was destroyed by fire in 1672, and a new town (the 'Historic District' of Panamá), 8 km to the southwest, replaced it; the ruins of its cathedral, churches, and other buildings are now preserved. The architecture of the 'Historic District' of Panamá is an unusual mixture of Spanish, French and early American styles.
Criteria: ii, iv, vi Inscribed 1997

• MEDIEVAL TOWN OF TORUŃ Poland

Toruń, on the Vistula, has its origins in a Teutonic Order castle built in the mid-thirteenth century as a base for its colonisation of Prussia. It soon developed a commercial role as part of the Hanseatic League. In the Old and New Towns, there are many imposing public and private buildings from the fourteenth and fifteenth centuries, among them the birthplace of Copernicus. Most of the southern sector of the Old Town walls with gates and towers survives. The New Town developed from 1264 as a centre for crafts and industry.
Criteria: ii, iv Inscribed 1997

Most of the mills in the Kinderdijk-Elshout mill network are bonnet mills; only the top section revolves with the wind. Their large sails come within 30 cm of the ground, hence their name 'ground sailers'.

The ruins of the cathedral at Panamá Viejo.

• PALAU DE LA MÚSICA CATALANA AND HOSPITAL DE SANT PAU, BARCELONA Spain

These two monuments are by the Catalan art nouveau architect Lluís Doménech i Montaner. The Palau de la Música Catalana is an exuberant steel-framed structure, full of light and space and decorated by many of the leading designers of the day. Construction began in 1905 and was completed three years later. The Hospital de Sant Pau is equally bold in its design and decoration, Montaner believing that beauty has therapeutic value. Work began in 1901 and was completed in 1930.
Criteria: i, ii, iv Inscribed 1997

• HISTORIC AREA OF WILLEMSTAD, INNER CITY AND HARBOUR, NETHERLANDS ANTILLES Netherlands

The people of the Netherlands established a trading settlement at a fine natural harbour on the Caribbean island of Curaçao in 1634. The town developed continuously over the following centuries. The modern town consists of four distinct historic districts whose architecture reflects not only European urban-planning concepts but also styles from the Netherlands and from the Spanish and Portuguese colonial towns with which Willemstad engaged in trade.
Criteria: ii, iv, v Inscribed 1997

• DOUGGA / THUGGA Tunisia

Before the Roman annexation of Numidia in 46 BC, Thugga was the capital of an important Libyco-Punic state. It flourished under Roman and Byzantine rule, but declined in the Islamic period. Its ruins include temples and sanctuaries, a forum, public baths, a theatre, an amphitheatre, a circus, a market, fountains, private houses, shops and mausoleums. The small rectangular forum, is crossed by part of the later Byzantine fortifications. One of the most significant monuments is the Libyco-Punic mausoleum, the only major monument of Punic architecture in Tunisia.
Criteria: ii, iii Inscribed 1997

• EIGHTEENTH-CENTURY ROYAL PALACE AT CASERTA WITH THE PARK, THE AQUEDUCT OF VANVITELLI, AND THE SAN LEUCIO COMPLEX Italy

In 1750, the King of Naples decided to build a new palace to rival the Palace of Versailles. Designed by Luigi Vanvitelli, the Royal Palace is rectangular in plan, with four large interior courtyards, and contains 1,200 rooms and thirty-four staircases. The main axis of the park is punctuated by a series of Baroque fountains and stretches of water and terminates in the Great Waterfall, where water cascades down from a height of 150 m. In 1778 the king established and managed his silk factory at San Leucio on idealistic principles.
Criteria: i, ii, iii, iv Inscribed 1997

• BOTANICAL GARDEN (ORTO BOTANICO), PADUA Italy

The world's first botanical garden is at Padua. It was created in 1545 and still preserves its original layout: a circular central plot, symbolising the world, surrounded by a ring of water, representing the ocean. Various additions have been made – a pumping installation to supply ten fountains, four monumental entrances, greenhouses, an arboretum, an English garden and a belvedere. The garden has traditionally collected and grown particularly rare plants, which have then been introduced into the rest of Europe.
Criteria: ii, iii Inscribed 1997

• ROHTAS FORT Pakistan

Following his defeat of the Mughal emperor Humayun in 1541, Sher Shah Suri built a strong fortified complex in northern Pakistan at Rohtas, surrounding a small hill alongside the Kahan river. Its stone walls vary according to the terrain, with heights of 10-18 m, a thickness of up to 12.5 m and an extent of more than 4 km; they are lined with bastions and pierced by monumental gateways. Rohtas Fort, also called Qila Rohtas, is an exceptional example of Muslim military architecture that was never taken by force.
Criteria: ii, iv Inscribed 1997

• HOSPICIO CABAÑAS, GUADALAJARA Mexico

The Hospicio Cabañas, designed by Manuel Tolsá, was built at the beginning of the nineteenth century by the Bishop of Guadalajara, Juan Ruiz de Cabañas, to provide care and shelter for the disadvantaged. It is laid out on a rectangular plan: all the buildings, which are single storey, except the chapel and the kitchen, are ranged round twenty-three courtyards. In the 1930s, the chapel was decorated with a superb series of murals by José Clemente Orozco, one of the greatest Mexican muralists of the period.
Criteria: i, ii, iii, iv Inscribed 1997

• MOUNT KENYA NATIONAL PARK / NATURAL FOREST Kenya

At 5,199 m, Mount Kenya, an ancient extinct volcano, is the second-highest peak in Africa. There are twelve remnant glaciers on the mountain, all receding rapidly, and four secondary peaks that sit at the head of the U-shaped glacial valleys. With its rugged glacier-clad summits and forested middle slopes, Mount Kenya is one of the most impressive landscapes in East Africa. The evolution of its afro-alpine flora provide an outstanding example of ecological processes. Mount Kenya is regarded as a holy mountain by all the communities (Kikuyu and Meru) living adjacent to it.
Criteria: vii, ix Inscribed 1997

• LAS MÉDULAS Spain

Las Médulas gold-mining area is an outstanding example of innovative Roman technology, based on hydraulic power. The Archaeological Zone of Las Médulas (ZAM) comprises the mines themselves and also large areas where the tailings were deposited. There are dams used to collect the vast amounts of water needed for the mining process and the intricate canals to covey water to the mines. Human settlement is represented by villages, of both the indigenous workers and the imperial administrative and support personnel (including army units).
Criteria: i, ii, iii, iv Inscribed 1997

• ARCHAEOLOGICAL AREA OF AGRIGENTO Italy

Agrigento, in Sicily, was one of the greatest cities of the ancient world. Founded as a Greek colony in the sixth century BC, it reached its height during the rule of the tyrant Thero (488–473). The most substantial remains are from this time and include the foundations of the Temple of Olympian Zeus, one of the largest of all Greek temples, and the Temple of Concord, one of the most impressive Doric temples. In addition, there are excavated areas of residential Hellenistic and Roman Agrigento, and extensive ancient cemeteries with tombs and monuments from the pagan and Christian periods.
Criteria: i, ii, iii, iv Inscribed 1997

• SAN MILLÁN YUSO AND SUSO MONASTERIES Spain

The monastic community founded by St Millán at Suso in the mid-sixth century became a place of pilgrimage. The monastery consists of a series of hermits' caves and a Romanesque church. The caves, originally used by the monks, are cut into the southern slope of the mountain. It was here that the first literature was produced in Castilian, from which Spanish is derived. In the early sixteenth century the community moved to a fine new monastery of Yuso, in the valley below the older complex; it is still a thriving community today.
Criteria: ii, iv, vi Inscribed 1997

• HWASEONG FORTRESS Korea, Republic of

When the Choson emperor Chongjo moved his father's tomb to Suwon at the end of the eighteenth century, he had it surrounded by Hwaseong Fortress, planned by a military architect who incorporated the latest developments from both East and West. It was completed by 1796. The massive walls, extending for nearly 6 km, still survive. There were originally forty-eight defensive features along the length of the walls – four gates, floodgates, observation towers, command posts, multiple-arrow launcher towers, firearms bastions, angle towers, secret gates, beacon towers, bastions and bunkers – and most are still intact.
Criteria: ii, iii Inscribed 1997

• HISTORIC CENTRE OF SÃO LUÍS Brazil

The late seventeenth-century core of São Luís, founded by the French in 1612, and occupied by the Dutch before coming under Portuguese rule, has preserved the original rectangular street plan. Private houses were built round courtyards, and the most outstanding examples have tiled roofs; façades adorned with Portuguese *azulejos* (painted ceramic tiles) or painted, ornamented cornices; tall, narrow window bays with decorated surrounds; balconies with forged or cast-iron railings; and floors of dressed stone. There are some 4,000 buildings within the Historic Centre.
Criteria: iii, iv, v Inscribed 1997

• RESIDENCES OF THE ROYAL HOUSE OF SAVOY Italy

When Emmanuel-Philibert, Duke of Savoy, moved his capital to the small fortified medieval town of Turin in 1562, he began a vast series of building projects, continued in Baroque style by his successors, to demonstrate the power of the ruling house. The Palazzo Reale (Royal Palace) in the centre of Turin, late seventeenth century in its present form, was built around a courtyard and opens onto landscaped gardens. Other buildings were designed and embellished by the leading architects and artists, including further palaces in Turin and many country residences and hunting lodges.
Criteria: i, ii, iv, v Inscribed 1997

• ARCHAEOLOGICAL SITE OF VOLUBILIS Morocco

The Mauritanian capital, founded in the third century BC, became a colonial town on the fringes of the Roman Empire after AD 40. During the Roman period, a town wall, with eight monumental gates, and a new centre including a capitol, basilica and baths, were constructed. Many buildings contain mosaic floors still in situ. At the beginning of the reign of Diocletian, in 285, the Romans abruptly abandoned the region, for reasons that remain obscure. It was later briefly the capital of Idris I, founder of the Idrisid dynasty.
Criteria: ii, iii, iv, vi Inscribed 1997

•COSTIERA AMALFITANA Italy

Costiera Amalfitana (Amalfi Coast) has been intensively settled since the early Middle Ages. Towns, such as Amalfi and Ravello, contain significant buildings such as Romanesque Amalfi cathedral and its 'Cloister of Paradise' and Ravello's cathedral and superb Villa Rufolo. Rural areas show the versatility of farmers in adapting to the diverse terrain, ranging from terraced vineyards and orchards on lower slopes to wide upland pastures. Further inland, the natural landscape survives intact, supporting the traditional Mediterranean flora, with little, if any, human intervention.

Criteria: ii, iv, v Inscribed 1997

•SAN PEDRO DE LA ROCA CASTLE, SANTIAGO DE CUBA Cuba

The Castle of San Pedro de la Roca and its associated defensive works are the most comprehensive example of Renaissance military engineering in the Caribbean. Commercial and political rivalries in the Caribbean region in the seventeenth century resulted in the construction of this massive series of fortifications on a rocky promontory, to protect the important port of Santiago. This intricate complex of forts, magazines, bastions and batteries underwent little change from the late nineteenth century, when it went out of use, until the 1960s, when restoration work began.

Criteria: iv, v Inscribed 1997

•VILLA ROMANA DEL CASALE Italy

Villa del Casale in Sicily is the supreme example of a luxury Roman villa. The excavated area, which only covers part of the villa, may be divided into four groups of rooms, all decorated with floor mosaics of superlative quality. The first is the entrance, which opens into a courtyard, onto which faces the elaborate baths complex. Next comes the main peristyle with its fountain in the centre. To the south is the third group, around the elliptical peristyle. The fourth group lies to the east of the main peristyle, linked by the Corridor of the Great Hunting Scene.

Criteria: i, ii, iii Inscribed 1997

•SU NURAXI DI BARUMINI Italy

During the late second millennium BC, a unique prehistoric defensive structure known as a *nuraghe* developed on the island of Sardinia. A nuraghe consists of a circular defensive tower in the form of a truncated cone built of dressed stone, with vaulted internal chambers. Su Nuraxi at Barumini, which was extended and reinforced in the first half of the first millennium under Carthaginian pressure, is the finest and most complete example. In the seventh century BC, Su Nuraxi was sacked by the Carthaginians and the defensive works neglected.

Criteria: i, iii, iv Inscribed 1997

•HISTORIC CENTRE OF RIGA Latvia

Riga was a major centre of the Hanseatic League of Baltic traders, and its medieval centre reflects this prosperity, though most of the earliest buildings were destroyed by fire or war. Riga became an important economic centre in the nineteenth century, when the suburbs surrounding the medieval town were laid out, first with imposing wooden buildings in the classical Russian style and then in Jugendstil or German Art Nouveau architecture, of a quality and quantity unparalleled anywhere in the world. The boulevards are lined with many important public buildings.

Criteria: i, ii Inscribed 1997

•ANCIENT CITY OF PINGYAO China

Pingyao in Shanxi Province offers a picture of the cultural, economic and religious development of a Chinese city of the Ming and Qing dynasties (fourteenth–twentieth centuries). In 1370, during the reign of the Ming emperor Hongwu, the city was fortified with monumental defensive walls and the internal layout was greatly altered. The circuit of walls measures 6 km and there are six fortified gates and seventy-two massive bastions. Prosperity derived from trade and banking meant that, in addition to public buildings and temples, it had many high-quality, traditional private houses, many of which have survived.

Criteria: ii, iii, iv Inscribed 1997

The layout of the settlements on the Costiera Amalfitana shows an eastern influence, with closely spaced houses climbing steep hillsides; a distinctive Arab-Sicilian architecture originated and developed in Amalfi.

A traditional courtyard house in the Ancient City of Pingyao.

• CASTLE OF THE TEUTONIC ORDER IN MALBORK Poland

The immense brick castle at Malbork was started by the Teutonic Order after 1270. The importance of Malbork increased greatly after 1309, when the seat of the Grand Master of the Order was moved here from Venice. The original Fore Castle was adapted as his residence and administrative headquarters, the impressive Palace of the Grand Masters being built in its southwest corner. The Great Refectory was built to the north of the palace. The whole complex is surrounded by an intricate system of defensive works, including massive walls and bastions, wet and dry moats and ditches, earthen ramparts and ponds.
Criteria: ii, iii, iv Inscribed 1997

• HISTORIC MONUMENTS ZONE OF TLACOTALPAN Mexico

Tlacotalpan, on the Gulf coast of Mexico, was founded by the Spanish in the mid-sixteenth century but economic expansion only came in 1821. It became the port for the products of Oaxaca and Puebla destined for Veracruz and beyond to New Orleans and Bordeaux. By 1855 its fleet had eighteen steamers. Tlacotalpan has preserved its 'chequerboard' town plan, with wide streets, colonnaded houses in a profusion of styles and colours, and many mature trees in the public open spaces and private gardens, bringing together Spanish and Caribbean traditions.
Criteria: ii, iv Inscribed 1998

• FUERTE DE SAMAIPATA Bolivia

The archaeological site of Samaipata has two parts: the hill with its many rock carvings, believed to have been the ceremonial centre of the old town in the fourteenth–sixteenth centuries, and the administrative and residential area to the south of the hill. The huge sculpted rock, dominating the town below, is a testimony to pre-Hispanic traditions. Occupied by people from the Mojocoyas culture as early as AD 300, this was when work on shaping the rock began.
Criteria: ii, iii Inscribed 1998

• ARCHAEOLOGICAL AREA AND THE PATRIARCHAL BASILICA OF AQUILEIA Italy

Excavations at Aquileia, one of the largest and wealthiest cities of the early Roman Empire, have revealed part of the forum and its basilica, the Republican *macellum*, one of the sets of baths, and two luxurious residential complexes. Outside the city walls, a cemetery with some impressive funerary monuments, the amphitheatre and the circus have been revealed. The most striking remains of the Roman city are those of the port installations, a row of warehouses and quays stretching along the bank of the river.
Criteria: iii, iv, vi Inscribed 1998

• CLASSICAL WEIMAR Germany

In the late-eighteenth and early nineteenth centuries Weimar became the cultural centre of Europe. Enlightened ducal patronage attracted many leading German writers and artists , including Johann Sebastian Bach, Johann Wolfgang Goethe, Friedrich Schiller and Franz Liszt. The World Heritage site comprises twelve areas including Goethe's House, Schiller's House, Belvedere Palace, and the Dowager's Palace, which was the centre of intellectual life at the height of classical Weimar. The site also includes the Princes' Tomb and the Historic Cemetery, constructed in 1823, where Schiller and Goethe are both buried.
Criteria: iii, vi Inscribed 1998

• HOLAŠOVICE HISTORICAL VILLAGE RESERVATION Czech Republic

Situated in the heart of South Bohemia, Holašovice is a fine example of a traditional central European village. It has many eighteenth- and nineteenth-century vernacular buildings in a style known as South Bohemian Folk Baroque, and preserves a ground plan dating from the Middle Ages. The village now consists of 120 buildings arranged round an elongated village square, with a small chapel and cross on it, and some more recent buildings on the outskirts. There are twenty-three protected farmsteads along with their attached farm buildings and gardens.
Criteria: ii, iv Inscribed 1998

The Castle of the Teutonic Order in Malbork, which has been twice restored, once in the nineteenth century and once in the twentieth century after being severely damaged in the Second World War.

The Belvedere Palace, Weimar.

•SUMMER PALACE AND IMPERIAL GARDEN IN BEIJING China

The Imperial Garden and Summer Palace in Beijing – first built in 1750, largely destroyed in the Second Opium War of 1860, and restored in 1886 – is a masterpiece of Chinese garden design, on a grandiose scale. The natural landscape of hills and open water is combined with artificial features such as pavilions, halls, palaces, temples and bridges. The site covers an area of almost 3km², three-quarters of which is covered by water. It is divided into three areas, each with its particular function: political and administrative activities, residence, and recreation and sightseeing.

Criteria: i, ii, iii Inscribed 1998

•THE FOUR LIFTS ON THE CANAL DU CENTRE AND THEIR ENVIRONS, LA LOUVIÈRE AND LE ROEULX (HAINAULT) Belgium

The four hydraulic boat-lifts on this short stretch of the Canal du Centre represent the apogee of canal engineering. They are the only such boat-lifts still in their original working condition. They consist of two compartments, each supported by a single hydraulic press. When one is at the level of the upper bay, the other is at the lower level; as the first descends, the other rises. Lift No. 1 at Houdeng-Gœgnies was completed in 1888. The others were built thirteen years later and incorporate a number of modifications to the basic design.

Criteria: iii, iv Inscribed 1998

• ARCHAEOLOGICAL SITE OF TROY Turkey

Troy, with its 4,000 years of history, is one of the world's most famous archaeological sites. Heinrich Schliemann carried out major excavations between 1868 and 1890. He uncovered evidence of the first contact between the civilisations of Anatolia and the Mediterranean world. There are several levels of archaeological significance – Troy II and Troy VI in particular are characteristic examples of the ancient city, with a fortified citadel enclosing palaces and administrative buildings, surrounded by an extensive lower town, also fortified. The Greek and Roman cities at Troy are represented by the sanctuary complex.

Criteria: ii, iii, vi Inscribed 1998

•NEW ZEALAND SUB-ANTARCTIC ISLANDS New Zealand

The New Zealand Sub-Antarctic Islands consist of five island groups – the Snares, Bounty Islands, Antipodes Islands, Auckland Islands and Campbell Island. With the exception of the Bounty Islands, the islands together with neighbouring Macquarie Island constitute a Centre of Plant Diversity. Many types of pelagic seabirds and penguins nest there, and the islands support major populations of ten albatross species. In total there are 126 bird species, of which five breed nowhere else. It is a critical breeding site for the southern right whale and 95 per cent of the world's population of New Zealand sea lion breed here.

Criteria: ix, x Inscribed 1998

•SEMMERING RAILWAY Austria

The Semmering Railway, built over 41 km of high mountains between 1848 and 1854, is one of the greatest feats of civil engineering from this pioneering phase of railway building. The high standard of the tunnels, viaducts and other works has ensured the continuous use of the line up to the present day. It runs through a spectacular mountain landscape. There are many fine buildings designed for leisure activities along the way, built when the area was opened up by the advent of the railway.

Criteria: ii, iv Inscribed 1998

•GOLDEN MOUNTAINS OF ALTAI Russian Federation

The Altai mountains form the major mountain range in western Siberia and provide the source of its greatest rivers – the Ob and the Irtysh. There are three separate areas: Altaisky Zapovednik and a buffer zone around Lake Teletskoye; Katunsky Zapovednik and a

The Seventeen-Arch Bridge at the Summer Palace and Imperial Garden in Beijing.

Troy's Roman *odeion* (concert hall) has the traditional horseshoe-shaped plan and tiers of seats made from limestone blocks. The nearby *bouleuterion* (council house) is smaller but similar in plan.

Kalte Rinne viaduct on the Semmering Railway.

buffer zone around Mount Belukha; and the Ukok Quiet Zone on the Ukok plateau. The sequence of altitudinal vegetation zones goes from steppe, forest-steppe, mixed forest, subalpine vegetation to alpine vegetation. The site is also an important habitat for endangered animal species such as the snow leopard.
Criteria: x Inscribed 1998

• NAVAL PORT OF KARLSKRONA Sweden

Karlskrona, founded in 1680, is a late-seventeenth-century planned naval city. The centre of the town is Stortorget (Great Square), at the highest point of the island of Trossö. Here are the two main churches of the town, both dating from the first half of the eighteenth century, Rådhuset (the City Hall) from the same period, and later public buildings. The naval harbour is to the south of the town, from which it was originally separated by a wall. To the south of the Parade Ground is Gamle Varvet (the Old Shipyard).
Criteria: ii, iv Inscribed 1998

• ROUTES OF SANTIAGO DE COMPOSTELA IN FRANCE France

Santiago de Compostela was the goal for pilgrims, who converged there from all over Europe throughout the Middle Ages. To reach Spain, pilgrims had to pass through France, and the historic monuments included in this site mark out the four routes by which they did so. Many bridges on the routes are known as 'pilgrims' bridges', and that over the Borade at Saint-Chély-d'Aubrac even has the figure of a pilgrim carved on it. The Pont du Diable over the Hérault at Aniane is one of the oldest medieval bridges in France.
Criteria: ii, iv, vi Inscribed 1998

• CILENTO AND VALLO DI DIANO NATIONAL PARK WITH THE ARCHEOLOGICAL SITES OF PAESTUM AND VELIA, AND THE CERTOSA DI PADULA Italy

The sanctuaries and settlements along three mountain ridges vividly represent the area's historical evolution: it was a major route for trade and for cultural and political interaction during the prehistoric and medieval periods. The sites of two major cities from classical times, Paestum – at which a number of public buildings have been revealed – and Velia, are there. Of the monasteries, the most impressive is the Certosa di San Lorenzo at Padula in the Vallo di Diano. Construction began in 1306, but in its present form it is essentially Baroque, built in the seventeenth and eighteenth centuries.
Criteria: iii, iv Inscribed 1998

• LA GRAND-PLACE, BRUSSELS Belgium

La Grand-Place in Brussels is a mainly late-seventeenth century group of public and private buildings. The earliest written reference to the Nedermarckt (Lower Market), as it was originally known, dates from 1174; the present name came into use in the last quarter of the eighteenth century. The rectangular outline of today's Grand-Place has developed over the centuries, and did not take on its definitive form until after 1695, when it was restored to its original layout and appearance following bombardment by the French. It has, however, always had seven streets running into it.
Criteria: ii, iv Inscribed 1998

• IR. D.F. WOUDA-GEMAAL (D.F. WOUDA STEAM PUMPING STATION) Netherlands

For centuries, windmills were used to discharge excess water in the Netherlands. The first steam pump was built in 1825 and the construction of steam-driven pumping stations reached its peak between 1870 and 1885. Extreme flooding in 1894 led to a decision to reclaim the Lauwerszee and drain the southwestern part of Friesland province. The Wouda Pumping Station at Lemmer, opened in 1920, was the key to this operation. It is the largest steam-pumping station ever built and is still in operation.
Criteria: i, ii, iv Inscribed 1998

Karlskrona

The façade of Hôtel de Ville (City Hall) in Brussels that faces La Grand-Place dates from the fifteenth century and is decorated with nineteenth century statues.

• TEMPLE OF HEAVEN: AN IMPERIAL SACRIFICIAL ALTAR IN BEIJING China

The Altar of Heaven and Earth was completed in 1420. The central structure was a large hall where sacrifices were offered to Heaven and Earth. In the ninth year of the reign of Emperor Jiajing (1530) it was decided to offer separate sacrifices to Heaven and to Earth, so the Circular Mound Altar was built for sacrifices to Heaven, and the Altar of Heaven and Earth was renamed the Temple of Heaven. The Circular Mound represents the ancient Chinese belief that Heaven is round and the Earth square – the central round feature (Heaven) is within a square enclosure (Earth).
Criteria: i, ii, iii Inscribed 1998

• EAST RENNELL Solomon Islands

East Rennell is the southern third of Rennell Island, the southernmost island in the Solomon Island group. Rennell, 86 km long by 15 km wide, is the largest raised coral atoll in the world. A major feature of the island is Lake Tegano, the largest lake (155 km²) in the insular Pacific. It is brackish, contains many rugged limestone islands and was the former lagoon on the atoll. Rennell is mostly covered with dense forest, with a canopy averaging 20 m in height.
Criteria: ix Inscribed 1998

• HISTORIC MONUMENTS OF ANCIENT NARA Japan

Nara, Japan's capital (710–84), was laid out with palaces, Buddhist temples, Shinto shrines and public buildings. The palace comprised the official buildings, notably the Daigokuden (imperial audience hall) and Chōdō-in (state halls) and the imperial residence (Dairi). The main Buddhist temples were the Tōdai-ji, the Kōfuku-ji, the Gangō-ji (the first Buddhist temple in Japan) and the Tōshōdai-ji, which still retains two buildings from the Nara period, the Kondō and the Kōdō. After 784, Nara was abandoned and the palace became paddy fields (now being excavated and reconstructed), while most of the temples and shrines survived intact.
Criteria: ii, iii, iv, vi Inscribed 1998

• PREHISTORIC ROCK-ART SITES IN THE CÔA VALLEY Portugal

These rock carvings, mostly from the Upper Palaeolithic (22,000–10,000 BC) are at three sites: at Faia; on either side of the Côa at Quinta da Barca and Penascosa; and starting at Ribeira de Piscos, continuing down the Côa to the Douro. Some of the Côa material dates from the Neolithic to the early modern period. The species represented in over 214 panels include aurochs, horses, red deer, ibex and fish, but there are no domestic animals. Single bodies appear with two or three heads, conveying a sense of movement.
Criteria: i, iii Inscribed 1998

• CHOIROKOITIA Cyprus

The Neolithic settlement of Choirokoitia, occupied from the seventh to the fourth millennia BC, is an important prehistoric site in the eastern Mediterranean. The earliest occupation, consisting of circular houses built from mud-brick and stone with flat roofs, was protected by natural slopes on three sides and a massive wall barring access from the west. A second defensive wall was erected to protect a later extension of the village. The finds from the site have thrown much light on the evolution of human society in this key region.
Criteria: ii, iii, iv Inscribed 1998

• HISTORIC SITE OF LYONS France

Lyons was founded by the Romans in the first century BC. Notable ruins, including a first century AD theatre, capable of seating some 10,000 spectators, remain on the Fourvière Hill. By the mid-fifteenth century it was one of the mostly heavily populated cities in Europe: overpopulation and the risk of epidemics led to a planned expansion. The resulting urban fabric contains areas of medieval streets and of eighteenth- and nineteenth-century town planning. The city has a rich stock of houses from the thirteenth century onwards and many fine public buildings.
Criteria: ii, iv Inscribed 1998

The Hall of Prayer for Good Harvests, one of the structures of the Temple of Heaven.

Tōdai-ji Temple, with its monumental wooden Kondō (Great Buddha Hall), is one of the main Buddhist temples in ancient Nara, Japan.

Bellecour Square with a statue of Louis XIV in the foreground and Fourvière Hill in the background. *Historic site of Lyons*

• FLEMISH BÉGUINAGES Belgium

The Béguines were women who dedicated their lives to God without retiring from the world. In the thirteenth century they founded the béguinages, enclosed communities designed to meet their spiritual and material needs. The Flemish *béguinages* are architectural ensembles composed of houses, churches, ancillary buildings and green spaces, with an urban or rural layout and built in styles specific to the Flemish cultural region. They are a fascinating reminder of the tradition of the Béguines that developed in northwestern Europe in the Middle Ages.

Criteria: ii, iii, iv Inscribed 1998

• L'VIV – THE ENSEMBLE OF THE HISTORIC CENTRE Ukraine

The city of L'viv, founded in the late-Middle Ages, was a flourishing administrative, religious and commercial centre for several centuries. In its urban fabric and its architecture, it is an outstanding example of the fusion of the architectural and artistic traditions of Eastern Europe with those of Italy and Germany. The medieval plan of L'viv has been preserved virtually intact; in particular, there is evidence of the different communities who lived there – Ukrainian, Armenian, Jewish, German, Polish, Italian, Hungarian – along with many fine Baroque and later buildings. Notable is Rynok Square with a tower at its centre, and around it fine houses in Renaissance, Baroque, and Empire style, many of them retaining their original medieval layout. There are fountains with figures from classical mythology at each corner of the square, dating from 1793.

Criteria: ii, v Inscribed 1998

• ARCHAEOLOGICAL ZONE OF PAQUIMÉ, CASAS GRANDES Mexico

The archaeological site of Paquimé, Casas Grandes is estimated to contain remains of some 2,000 rooms, in clusters of living rooms, workshops, stores and patios. Only part of the extensive remains have been excavated. Around 10,000 people are thought to have lived here at the height of its prosperity in the fourteenth–fifteenth centuries. The predominant building material is unfired clay (adobe). The presence of platform mounds, ball courts, a sophisticated water-distribution system, and storage buildings for exotic products such as macaws and turkeys, , indicates influence from Mesoamerica.

Criteria: iii, iv Inscribed 1998

• GARDENS AND CASTLE AT KROMĚŘÍŽ Czech Republic

Kroměříž stands at the foot of the Chriby mountain range which dominates the central part of Moravia. The Gardens and Castle at Kroměříž are a fine example of a princely residence and its associated landscape from the seventeenth and eighteenth centuries. The site, particularly the pleasure garden in the southwestern part of the historic centre of Kroměříž, played a significant role in the development of Baroque garden and palace design in central Europe. The pleasure garden is a formal garden in the Italian style, entered by an arcaded gallery which contains many statues and busts.

Criteria: ii, iv Inscribed 1998

• HISTORIC CENTRE OF URBINO Italy

During its short cultural pre-eminence in the fifteenth century, the hill-town of Urbino attracted some of the most outstanding humanist scholars and artists of the Renaissance. In the mid-fifteenth century Federico II da Montefeltro, ruler of the city and duchy of Urbino, undertook a radical rebuilding campaign. The city walls

were rebuilt according to the designs of Leonardo da Vinci. The new Ducal Palace, by Luciano Laurana and Francesco di Giorgio Martini, incorporated existing medieval structures and, along with the adjacent cathedral, became the model for new buildings in the Renaissance style. Owing to Urbino's economic and cultural stagnation from the sixteenth century onwards, it has preserved much of its Renaissance appearance.

Criteria: ii, iv Inscribed 1998

• UNIVERSITY AND HISTORIC PRECINCT OF ALCALÁ DE HENARES Spain

Founded by Cardinal Jiménez de Cisneros in the early sixteenth century from a partly abandoned medieval town, Alcalá de Henares was the world's first planned university city. This included the creation of houses to lodge professors and students. The little Chapel of St Justus was rebuilt as a church and given the title 'Magistral'. Centres of learning were added progressively: there were eventually twenty-five Colegios Menores, while eight large monasteries were also colleges of the university. Its primary objective was to provide administrators for the Church and for the Spanish Empire, training over 12,000 students in the sixteenth century. From the mid-seventeenth century, the number of students declined, and in 1836 the university was transferred to Madrid.

Criteria: ii, iv, vi Inscribed 1998

• ROCK ART OF THE MEDITERRANEAN BASIN ON THE IBERIAN PENINSULA Spain

There are more than 700 sites of late prehistoric rock art on the Mediterranean seaboard of the Iberian Peninsula, making this the largest such collection in Europe. Many scenes of domestic daily life and of hunting are depicted. Representations of the human figure provide information on clothing and personal ornament, such as different hairstyles, bracelets, arm-rings and necklaces, and mark the beginnings of social inequality. Funerary rites are shown in the form of recumbent corpses and ritual scenes. Scenes illustrate the mythologies of these prehistoric societies: sorcerers in strange costumes are common, as are figures combining human characteristics with those of fauna (deer, bulls, birds).

Criteria: iii Inscribed 1998

• OUADI QADISHA (THE HOLY VALLEY) AND THE FOREST OF THE CEDARS OF GOD (HORSH ARZ EL-RAB) Lebanon

The deep Qadisha Valley, one of the most important early Christian monastic settlements in the world, is located at the foot of Mount al-Makmal. Its slopes form natural ramparts and their steep cliffs contain rock-cut chapels and hermitages, often surrounded by terraces made by hermits for growing grain, grapes and olives. The monasteries, many of which are ancient, stand in dramatic positions in a rugged landscape. Remains of the great forest of cedars of Lebanon, highly prized in antiquity for the construction of great religious buildings, are nearby.

Criteria: iii, iv Inscribed 1998

• ROBBEN ISLAND South Africa

Robben Island, 7 km off the coast from Cape Town, was used at various times between the seventeenth and twentieth centuries as a prison, a hospital for socially unacceptable groups and a military base. Its buildings, particularly those of the late twentieth century such as the maximum security prison for political prisoners,

witnessed the triumph of democracy and freedom over oppression and racism. Nelson Mandela was imprisoned on Robben Island for twenty years. The last political prisoners left in 1991 and the prison closed in 1996; it is now a museum.

Criteria: iii, vi Inscribed 1999

• IBIZA, BIODIVERSITY AND CULTURE Spain

Ibiza provides an excellent example of the interaction between marine and coastal ecosystems. The dense prairies of oceanic *Posidonia* (seagrass), an important endemic species found only in the Mediterranean basin, contain and support a diversity of marine life. The archaeological sites at Sa Caleta settlement and Puig des Molins necropolis show the role played by the island in the Mediterranean economy, particularly during the Phoenician–Carthaginian period. In 1235, Ibiza town was dominated by Christians, who built the Catalan castle, the medieval fortifications, and the Gothic cathedral. The Upper Town, Alta Vila, is an example of Renaissance military architecture.

Criteria: ii, iii, iv, ix, x Inscribed 1999

• HISTORIC CENTRE OF SANTA ANA DE LOS RÍOS DE CUENCA Ecuador

Santa Ana de los Ríos de Cuenca is set in a valley surrounded by the Andean mountains in the south of Ecuador. This inland colonial town (entroterra), now the country's third city, was founded in 1557 on the rigorous planning guidelines issued thirty years earlier by the Spanish king Charles V. Cuenca's architecture, much of which dates from the eighteenth century, was 'modernised' in the economic prosperity of the nineteenth century, but the Andean mountain chains have allowed Cuenca to maintain close contact with its natural environment.

Criteria: ii, iv, v Inscribed 1999

• STATE HISTORICAL AND CULTURAL PARK 'ANCIENT MERV' Turkmenistan

The cities of the vast Merv oasis exerted considerable influence over the cultures of Central Asia and Iran for four millennia. The oasis formed part of the Great Seljuk Empire, which had its capital here. This was one of the principal cities of its time, and its famous libraries attracted scholars from all over the Islamic world. It also had a pronounced influence in the development of architecture, science and culture. Merv is the oldest and best-preserved of the oasis-cities along the Silk Route in Central Asia. A number of monuments are still visible, particularly from the last two millennia. These include the central Beni Makhan mosque and its cistern, the Buddhist stupa and monastery, and the 'Oval Building' in the northwest quarter.

Criteria: ii, iii Inscribed 1999

• ARCHAEOLOGICAL SITES OF MYCENAE AND TIRYNS Greece

Mycenae and Tiryns were the two greatest cities of the Mycenaean civilisation, dominating the eastern Mediterranean from the fifteenth to the twelfth centuries BC. The Palace at Mycenae was constructed on the summit of the hill and surrounded by massive walls in three stages (c. 1350, 1250 and 1225 BC). A series of tholos (beehive-shaped tombs) were also built on the slopes of the hill. The oldest architectural remains at Tiryns are from the early Bronze Age (c. 3000 BC). A new fortified palace complex was constructed in the fourteenth century BC.

Criteria: i, ii, iii, iv, vi Inscribed 1999

• HEART OF NEOLITHIC ORKNEY
United Kingdom

The Neolithic monuments of Orkney demonstrate the cultural achievements of the Neolithic peoples of northern Europe during the period 3000–2000 BC. The monuments consist of Maes Howe, a large chambered tomb; the Stones of Stenness and the Ring of Brodgar, two ceremonial stone circles; and Skara Brae, a settlement which has particularly rich surviving remains. The group constitutes a major prehistoric cultural landscape which demonstrates the domestic, ritual and burial practices of a now-vanished culture, giving a graphic depiction of life in this remote archipelago in the far north of Scotland some 5,000 years ago.
Criteria: i, ii, iii, iv Inscribed 1999

• BELFRIES OF BELGIUM AND FRANCE Belgium
and France

Built between the eleventh and seventeenth centuries, invariably in an urban setting, these belfries are potent symbols of the transition from feudalism to mercantile urban society. They illustrate the transition in style from Norman Gothic to late Gothic, which then mingles with Renaissance and Baroque forms. In the fourteenth and fifteenth centuries, the belfries abandoned the model of the keep in favour of finer, taller towers, such as those of Dendermonde, Lier and Aalst.
Criteria: ii, iv Inscribed 1999

• ISIMANGALISO WETLAND PARK South Africa

Wind, rivers and sea have all played a part in producing a variety of landforms – including coral reefs, long sandy beaches, coastal dunes, lake systems, swamps, and extensive reed and papyrus wetlands. The effects of major floods and coastal storms on the park's diverse range of habitats, together with its location between subtropical and tropical Africa, have resulted in exceptional species diversity. The site contains critical habitats for a range of species from Africa's marine, wetland and savanna environments.
Criteria: vii, ix, x Inscribed 1999

• DESEMBARCO DEL GRANMA NATIONAL PARK
Cuba

The park includes the world's largest and best-preserved systems of marine terraces (both above and below sea level), and impressive, pristine coastal cliffs. It contains examples of many ecosystems, including the coral reef of Cabo Cruz, seagrass beds and mangroves and old submarine terraces up to 30 m deep. It is an important centre for plant diversity in Cuba. It has a remarkable archaeological value as it was the original settlement of groups belonging to the Taina Culture. Many events related to the Cuban Revolution took place in the area.
Criteria: vii, viii Inscribed 1999

• MUSEUMSINSEL (MUSEUM ISLAND), BERLIN
Germany

The five museums were built between 1824 and 1930 on the Museumsinsel, a small island in the river Spree. The Altes Museum was built to the designs of Karl Friedrich Schinkel in 1824–8. A plan to develop the part of the island behind this museum was drawn up by the court architect, Friedrich August Stüler in 1841, followed by the building of the Neues Museum (1843–7). In 1866 the Nationalgalerie was built and in 1897–1904 the Kaiser-Friedrich-Museum (now the Bode Museum). Stüler's plan was completed in 1909–30 with the construction of Alfred Messel's Pergamonmuseum.
Criteria: ii, iv Inscribed 1999

• MY SON SANCTUARY Vietnam

Between the fourth and thirteenth centuries a unique culture, which owed its spiritual origins to Indian Hinduism, developed on the coast of what is now Vietnam. This is illustrated by the remains of a series of impressive tower-temples located in a dramatic site that was the religious and political capital of the Champa Kingdom for most of its existence. The site marks the introduction of Hindu architecture from the Indian subcontinent to the area.
Criteria: ii, iii Inscribed 1999

Part of the Ring of Brodgar in Orkney at sunset – the Ring of Brodgar is the finest known truly circular late-Neolithic or early Bronze Age stone ring.

Bode Museum on Museuminsel, Berlin.

• HISTORIC FORTIFIED TOWN OF CAMPECHE
Mexico

The historic centre of Campeche has kept its outer walls and system of fortifications, designed to defend this Caribbean port against attacks from the sea. It has a chequerboard plan, with a Plaza facing the sea. Among almost 1,000 buildings of historic value are the Cathedral of the Immaculate Conception, several churches, the Toro theatre and the municipal archives. The system of fortifications includes the redoubts of San José and San Miguel, and the batteries of San Lucas, San Matiás and San Luís.
Criteria: ii, iv Inscribed 1999

• DISCOVERY COAST ATLANTIC FOREST RESERVES Brazil

The Discovery Coast Atlantic Forest Reserves, in the states of Bahia and Espírito Santo, consist of eight separate protected areas containing 1,120 km² of Atlantic forest and associated shrub (restingas). The rainforests of Brazil's Atlantic coast are the world's richest in terms of biodiversity. The site contains a distinct range of species which reveals a pattern of evolution that is not only of great scientific interest but is also of importance for conservation.
Criteria: ix, x Inscribed 1999

• MOUNTAIN RAILWAYS OF INDIA India

This site includes three railways, all still fully operational. The Darjeeling Himalayan Railway, opened in 1881, applied bold and ingenious engineering solutions to establish an effective rail link across mountainous terrain. The Nilgiri Mountain Railway, a 46-km metre-gauge single-track railway in Tamil Nadu State, scaling an elevation of 326 m to 2,203 m, was completed in 1908. The Kalka Shimla Railway, a 96-km, single track working rail link was built in the mid-19th century to provide a service to the highland town of Shimla.
Criteria: ii, iv Inscribed 1999

• HORTOBÁGY NATIONAL PARK – THE PUSZTA
Hungary

The Hortobágy Puszta is a vast area of plains and wetlands. Traditional patterns of land use, such as the grazing of domestic animals, have been present here for more than two millennia. The oldest surviving structures on the plains are thirteenth-century stone bridges (including Nine Arch Bridge at Hortobágy, the longest stone bridge in Hungary), and *csárdas*, built in the eighteenth and nineteenth centuries. The typical *csárda* consists of two buildings facing one another, both single-storeyed and thatched or, occasionally, roofed with shingles or tiles. These contained a tavern, guest rooms and provision for horses and carriages.
Criteria: iv, v Inscribed 1999

• HISTORIC TOWN OF VIGAN Philippines

Established in the sixteenth century, Vigan's layout conforms closely to the traditional Spanish chequerboard plan and it is the best-preserved example of a planned Spanish colonial town in Asia. However, the blending of the Latin tradition with strong Chinese, Ilocano and Filipino influences makes it unique. As the major commercial centre for the region, Vigan traded directly with China. It is located in the delta of the Abra River, close to the north-east tip of the island of Luzon. Large sea-going vessels could berth in the delta.
Criteria: ii, iv Inscribed 1999

• WOODEN CHURCHES OF MARAMUREŞ
Romania

The eight narrow, high, wooden churches of Maramure stand on bases of stone blocks and pebble fillings, and are characterised by tall, slim clock towers. They are: the Church of the Presentation of the Virgin to the Temple (Bârsana); the Church of Saint Nicholas (Budeşti); the Church of the Pious Paraskeva (Deseşti); the Church of the Nativity of the Mother of God (Ieud-Deal); the Church of the Holy Archangels (Plopiş); the Church of the Holy Paraskeva (Poienile Izei); the Church of the Holy Archangels (Rogoz); and the Church of the Holy Archangels (Şurdeşti).
Criteria: iv Inscribed 1999

A colourful street in Campeche.

Typical wooden church of the Maramureş region. The churches date from the seventeenth and eighteenth centuries.

• DROOGMAKERIJ DE BEEMSTER (BEEMSTER POLDER) Netherlands

The seventeenth-century Beemster Polder is the oldest area of reclaimed land in the Netherlands. It has preserved intact its well-ordered landscape of fields, roads, canals, dykes and settlements, laid out in accordance with classical planning principles. Draining large areas like Beemster was made possible by the dramatic improvement in pumping technology using windmills driving waterwheels. Pumps were later converted to steam power, then diesel in the twentieth century. Now drainage is carried out by a fully automated electric pumping station.
Criteria: i, ii, iv Inscribed 1999

• DAZU ROCK CARVINGS China

Carvings in the steep hillsides of Dazu County date back to AD 650, but the main period began in the late ninth century continuing for over 400 years. There are seventy-five sites containing some 50,000 statues. Tantric Buddhism from India and the Chinese Taoist and Confucian beliefs came together here to create a highly original and influential manifestation of spiritual harmony. The carvings are remarkable for their subject matter, both secular and religious, and the light that they shed on everyday life in China during this period.
Criteria: i, ii, iii Inscribed 1999

• CITY OF GRAZ – HISTORIC CENTRE Austria

Graz displays styles of art and architecture from the Balkans, the Mediterranean and the Germanic region. Frederick III built the present cathedral in late-Gothic style (1438–64). The façade of the Mausoleum of Emperor Ferdinand II, started in 1614, reflects the transition from Renaissance to Baroque style, and the Seminary (former Jesuit College), started in 1572, illustrates the severe Renaissance architecture adopted by that order. All that remains of the castle where Emperor Frederick III lived, is a hall, a chapel, and a double spiral staircase dating back to 1499.
Criteria: ii, iv Inscribed 1999

• SUKUR CULTURAL LANDSCAPE Nigeria

The Sukur Cultural Landscape, with the Palace of the Hidi Chief on a hill dominating the villages below, is a remarkably intact expression of a society and its spiritual and material culture. There are many shrines and altars, particularly in and around the Hidi Palace. The remains of disused iron-smelting furnaces illustrate an elaborate pattern of production and distribution. There are also subterranean wells, surmounted by conical stone structures and surrounded by an enclosure wall. The landscape of the Sukur plateau is characterised by extensive terracing which has a spiritual significance, in addition to providing agricultural land.
Criteria: iii, v, vi Inscribed 1999

• SAN CRISTÓBAL DE LA LAGUNA Spain

Founded in 1497, San Cristóbal de La Laguna, in the Canary Islands, has two nuclei: the original, unplanned Upper Town; and the Lower Town, the first ideal unfortified 'city-territory'. In 1502, a regular town plan based on Leonardo da Vinci's model for Imola was drawn up. Wide streets linked public open spaces, forming the grid on which smaller streets were superimposed. A piped water supply was installed in 1521, and public buildings were constructed. Many fine churches and public and private buildings dating from the sixteenth to the eighteenth centuries remain.
Criteria: ii, iv Inscribed 1999

• HOI AN ANCIENT TOWN Vietnam

Hoi An Ancient Town was a thriving trading port between the fifteenth and nineteenth centuries. Most of the buildings are aligned along narrow lanes and include many religious establishments, such as pagodas, temples, meeting houses, etc. The rise of other ports on the coast of Vietnam, in particular Da Nang, and the silting of Hoi An's harbour, led to its final eclipse. As a result of this economic stagnation, it has preserved its early appearance in a remarkably intact state, the only town in the country to have done so.
Criteria: ii, v Inscribed 1999

The village of De Rijp, Beemster Polder.

Dazu rock carvings.

The harbour of Hoi An.

• WARTBURG CASTLE Germany

Wartburg Castle was, most notably the place of exile of Martin Luther, who composed his German translation of the New Testament here. The castle is reached from the northern end of the spur on which it stands by a tower with a drawbridge, followed by an outer courtyard. Next follows the lower courtyard, the main features of which are the keep and the palace, onto which the Knights' Baths back. The South Tower marks the farther end of the spur. The centre of the lower courtyard is occupied by a cistern.
Criteria: iii, vi Inscribed 1999

• LITOMYŠL CASTLE Czech Republic

Litomyšl Castle is an arcade castle, a type of building first developed in Italy and modified in the Czech lands. Its design and decoration are particularly fine, including the later High Baroque features added in the eighteenth century. It preserves intact the range of ancillary buildings associated with an aristocratic residence: the Brewery stylishly blends elements of High Baroque and neoclassicism. A most striking interior features is its late-eighteenth-century neoclassical theatre. Constructed entirely of wood, it seats 150 in nine loggias and a lower floor.
Criteria: ii, iv Inscribed 1999

• HISTORIC CENTRE OF THE TOWN OF DIAMANTINA Brazil

Portuguese colonisers of Diamantina, a village set in inhospitable rocky mountains, transposed some of the features of their home towns to their adopted land, while respecting the original settlement. The architecture is of Baroque inspiration, its streets are paved in a uniquely picturesque style and the *casario*, a regular alignment of eighteenth- and nineteenth-century semi-detached houses, has brightly coloured façades , displaying some affiliations with Portuguese Mannerist architecture. Other features include the Passadiço, a covered footbridge in blue and white wood, and the *chafariz*, a sculpted fountain.
Criteria: ii, iv Inscribed 1999

• PENÍNSULA VALDÉS Argentina

Península Valdés is a promontory, protruding 100 km eastwards into the South Atlantic. The 400-km shoreline includes a series of gulfs, rocky cliffs, shallow bays and lagoons with extensive mudflats, beaches, coastal sand dunes and small islands. It is a site of global significance for the conservation of marine mammals such as southern right whales, orcas and the southern elephant seal. Península Valdés has a high diversity of birds, and terrestrial mammals are also abundant. The peninsula's intertidal mudflats and coastal lagoons are important staging sites for migratory shorebirds.
Criteria: x Inscribed 1999

• HISTORIC CENTRE OF SIGHIŞOARA Romania

Founded in the thirteenth century by German craftsmen and merchants, Sighişoara is composed of a fortified citadel on a steeply sloping plateau, and the lower town with its woody slopes below. It has kept its medieval urban character and network of narrow streets. Many of the houses still have a barrel-vaulted basement, workshops on the ground floor, and living rooms on the upper floors. The imposing Clock Tower dominates the three squares of the historic centre and protects the stairway connecting the upper town and the lower town.
Criteria: iii, v Inscribed 1999

• FOSSIL HOMINID SITES OF STERKFONTEIN, SWARTKRANS, KROMDRAAI, AND ENVIRONS South Africa

The Sterkfontein area contains a significant group of sites that throw light on the origin and evolution of humanity. They constitute a vast reserve of scientific data linked to the history of the most ancient periods of humanity. Fossils found there have enabled the identification of several specimens of early hominids, more particularly of *Paranthropus*, dating back between 4.5 million and 2.5 million years, as well as evidence of the domestication of fire 1.8 million to 1 million years ago.
Criteria: iii, vi Inscribed 1999

In the midst of the forest, Wartburg Castle occupies a rocky spur that looks down over the city of Eisenach.

The tail (fluke) of a submerging right whale just off the coast of Península Valdés.

▪ VILLA ADRIANA (TIVOLI) Italy

The complex of classical buildings at the Villa Adriana at Tivoli, near Rome, was created in the second century AD by the Roman emperor Hadrian who wished to distance himself and his power from the capital. After Hadrian's death in 138, his successors preferred Rome as their permanent residence, but the villa continued to be enlarged and further embellished. Study of the villa's monuments played a crucial role in the rediscovery of the elements of classical architecture by the architects of the Renaissance and the Baroque period.

Criteria: i, ii, iii Inscribed 1999

▪ VIÑALES VALLEY Cuba

The Viñales Valley is encircled by mountains and its landscape is interspersed with dramatic rocky outcrops. Traditional techniques are still in use for agricultural production, particularly of tobacco for cigars. The quality of this cultural landscape is enhanced by the vernacular architecture of its farms and villages, where a rich multi-ethnic society survives, illustrating the cultural development of the islands of the Caribbean, and of Cuba.

Criteria: iv Inscribed 1999

▪ KALWARIA ZEBRZYDOWSKA: THE MANNERIST ARCHITECTURAL AND PARK LANDSCAPE COMPLEX AND PILGRIMAGE PARK Poland

The Counter-Reformation in the late-sixteenth century led to the creation of many calvaries in Europe. Mikolaj Zebrzydowski, the Voivod of Cracow, had completed a private hermitage on this site when he was persuaded by Bernardine (Cistercian) monks to enlarge his original design. Building work on the new calvary started in 1600, eventually covering an extensive landscape complex with many chapels, linked in form and theme to those in Jerusalem at the time of Christ. Its layout has remained virtually unchanged and it is a sacred place of pilgrimage.

Criteria: ii, iv Inscribed 1999

▪ BRIMSTONE HILL FORTRESS NATIONAL PARK Saint Kitts and Nevis

Brimstone Hill Fortress is an example of seventeenth- and eighteenth-century military architecture in the Caribbean. Designed by the British and built by African slave labour, it is testimony to European colonialism and the African slave trade. The heart of the fortress is Fort George, the massive masonry structure on one of the twin peaks that dominate the complex. The fortress is the earliest surviving British example of the type of fortification known as the 'polygonal system', and one of the finest in the world. It was abandoned in 1853.

Criteria: iii, iv Inscribed 1999

▪ AREA DE CONSERVACIÓN GUANACASTE Costa Rica

Guanacaste is in northwestern Costa Rica. It includes the Guanacaste Cordillera and surrounding flatlands and coastal areas, and contains important natural habitats for the conservation of biological diversity, including the best dry-forest habitats from Central America to northern Mexico and key habitats for endangered or rare plant and animal species. The marine area includes various near-shore islands and islets, open ocean marine zones, beaches, rocky coasts, and approximately 20 km of sea turtle nesting beaches and a high diversity of wetland ecosystems.

Criteria: ix, x Inscribed 1999

▪ DACIAN FORTRESSES OF THE ORASTIE MOUNTAINS Romania

Built in the first centuries BC and AD, these Dacian fortresses bring together military and religious architecture from the classical world and the late-European Iron Age. The Dacians inhabited the central and western regions between the Carpathians and the Danube. These six fortresses, which formed the nucleus of the Dacian Kingdom, were conquered by the Romans at the beginning of the second century AD. The system developed by the Dacians to defend their capital, Sarmizegetusa Regia, had three distinct elements: sites on dominant physical features, fortresses, and linear defences.

Criteria: ii, iii, iv Inscribed 1999

The Maritime Theatre at Villa Adriana.

The Monastery of Kalwaria Zebrzydowska.

The circular sanctuary at Sarmizegetusa Regia, capital of the Dacian Kingdom.

▪ MOUNT WUYI China

Mount Wuyi is an important area for biodiversity in southeast China, containing what is probably the largest and best preserved areas of humid subtropical forest in the world. It is a refuge for a large number of ancient, relict species, many of them endemic. The landscape of the Nine Bend River (lower gorge) is very beautiful in its juxtaposition of smooth rock cliffs with clear, deep water, complemented by numerous temples and monasteries. Mount Wuyi has received international recognition for its high diversity and large numbers of rare and unusual fauna.

Criteria: iii, vi, vii, x Inscribed 1999

▪ BRONZE AGE BURIAL SITE OF SAMMALLAHDENMÄKI Finland

The Sammallahdenmäki cemetery includes thirty-three burial cairns and provides a unique insight into the funerary practices and social and religious structures of northern Europe more than three millennia ago. The cairns lie along the crest and upper slopes of a 700 m ridge, and are disposed in several distinct clusters. The structures were built using granite boulders quarried from the cliff face or collected from the site itself. They can be classified according to their shapes and sizes: small low round cairns, large mound-like cairns, and round walled cairns.

Criteria: iii, iv Inscribed 1999

▪ MIGUASHA NATIONAL PARK Canada

Miguasha Park, in southeastern Quebec on the southern coast of the Gaspé peninsula, is the world's most outstanding illustration of the Devonian Period known as the 'Age of Fishes'. Dating from 380 million years ago, the Upper Devonian Escuminac Formation represented here contains five of the six fossil fish groups associated with this period. Its importance is due to it having the greatest number and best-preserved fossil specimens of the lobe-finned fishes that gave rise to the first four-legged, air-breathing terrestrial vertebrates – the tetrapods.

Criteria: viii Inscribed 1999

▪ WESTERN CAUCASUS Russian Federation

The Western Caucasus is one of the few large mountain areas of Europe that has not experienced significant human impact. Its subalpine and alpine pastures have only been grazed by wild animals, and its extensive tracts of undisturbed mountain forests, extending from the lowlands to the subalpine zone, are unique in Europe. The site has a great diversity of ecosystems, with important endemic plants and wildlife, and is the place of origin and reintroduction of the mountain subspecies of the European bison.

Criteria: ix, x Inscribed 1999

▪ JURISDICTION OF SAINT-EMILION France

The Jurisdiction of Saint-Emilion has a historic vineyard landscape that has survived intact to the present day. Viticulture was introduced by the Roman emperor Augustus. He created the province of Aquitania in 27 BC and established the first vineyards by grafting new varieties of grape on the *Vitis biturica* that grew naturally in the region. This industry prospered in the Middle Ages when the Saint-Emilion area benefited from being on the pilgrimage route to Santiago de Compostela. Many churches, monasteries and hospices date from the eleventh century onwards.

Criteria: iii, iv Inscribed 1999

▪ PUERTO-PRINCESA SUBTERRANEAN RIVER NATIONAL PARK Philippines

This park features spectacular limestone karst landscape with an extensive 8.km underground river system – one of the most unique of its type in the world, with chambers up to 120 m wide and 60 m high. One of the river's distinguishing features is that it emerges directly into the sea, and its lower portion is subject to tidal influences. Its habitats are important for biodiversity conservation. The site contains a full 'mountain-to-sea' ecosystem and has some of the most important forests in Asia.

Criteria: vii, x Inscribed 1999

Yunu Peak, the symbol of Mount Wuyi.

Vineyards at Saint-Emilion – the special status of a 'jurisdiction' was granted during the period of English rule in the twelfth century.

LAURISILVA OF MADEIRA Portugal

Fossil evidence shows that laurisilva flora once covered much of southern Europe in the Tertiary era, 15–40 million years ago, but this vegetation is now confined to the Azores, Madeira and the Canary Islands. The laurisilva on Madeira is the largest area surviving, with approximately 150 km² within the 270 km² Madeira Nature Reserve. It is in very good condition, with around 90 per cent believed to be primary forest. The laurisilva of Madeira is notable for its biological diversity with at least sixty-six vascular plant species endemic to the island.
Criteria: ix, x Inscribed 1999

LORENTZ NATIONAL PARK Indonesia

Lorentz National Park is the only protected area in the world to incorporate a continuous transect from snowcap to tropical marine environment, including extensive lowland wetlands, and is one of only three equatorial regions of sufficiently high altitude to retain permanent ice. Located at the meeting-point of two colliding continental plates, the area has ongoing mountain formation as well as major sculpting by glaciation. It also contains fossil sites which provide evidence of the evolution of life on New Guinea, a high level of endemism and the highest level of biodiversity in the region.
Criteria: viii, ix, x Inscribed 1999

HISTORIC CENTRE (CHORÁ) WITH THE MONASTERY OF SAINT JOHN 'THE THEOLOGIAN' AND THE CAVE OF THE APOCALYPSE ON THE ISLAND OF PÁTMOS Greece

The Monastery of Saint John 'the Theologian' and the Cave of the Apocalypse was founded in the late-tenth century on the island of Pátmos. Together with the medieval settlement of Chorá, it is a traditional Greek Orthodox pilgrimage centre of outstanding architectural interest. There are few other places where religious ceremonies dating back to early Christian times are still being practised unchanged. St John is reputed to have written both his Gospel and the Revelation, two books of the New Testament of the Bible on Pátmos.
Criteria: iii, iv, vi Inscribed 1999

SHRINES AND TEMPLES OF NIKKO Japan

The shrines and temples of Nikko, together with their natural surroundings, have for centuries been a sacred site, known for its architectural and decorative masterpieces. The site is associated with the Shinto perception of the relationship of man with nature, in which mountains and forests have a sacred meaning; this religious practice is still alive today. The shrines and temples of Nikko are closely associated with the history of the Tokugawa Shoguns.
Criteria: i, iv, vi Inscribed 1999

ATLANTIC FOREST SOUTH-EAST RESERVES Brazil

From mountains covered by dense forests down to wetlands, and to coastal islands with isolated mountains and dunes this area, made up of twenty-five reserves, comprises a rich natural environment of great scenic beauty. Partially isolated since the Ice Age, the Atlantic forests have evolved into a complex ecosystem with exceptionally high endemism. More than 450 tree species per hectare can be found in some areas, indicating that the diversity of woody plants in the region is larger than in the Amazon rainforest.
Criteria: vii, ix, x Inscribed 1999

ARCHAEOLOGICAL MONUMENTS ZONE OF XOCHICALCO Mexico

The architecture and art of Xochicalco represent the fusion of cultural elements from different parts of Mesoamerica from the troubled period of 650–900 that followed the break-up of the great Mesoamerican states such as Teotihuacan, Monte Albán, Palenque and Tikal. The resulting cultural regrouping fuelled the city's growth. The city was built on a series of natural hills. The highest of these was the core of the settlement, with many public buildings, but evidence of occupation has been found on six of the lower hills surrounding it.
Criteria: iii, iv Inscribed 1999

Laurisilva of Madeira. The ancient trees have great ecological value. By collecting and retaining moisture they help protect the micro-climate and maintain water supplies.

The Monastery of Saint John 'the Theologian' (Hagios Ioannis Theologos) on Pátmos.

There are some 120 species of mammals in the Atlantic Forest South-East Reserve, including *jaguar* (pictured here), ocelot, bush dog, La Plata otter, twenty species of bat and various species of endangered primate.

• CUEVA DE LAS MANOS, RÍO PINTURAS Argentina

The Cueva de las Manos on the Río Pinturas takes its name from the stencilled outlines of human hands in the cave. There are also many depictions of animals, such as guanaco as well as hunting scenes which depict animals and human figures interacting in a dynamic and naturalistic manner. This cave art was executed between 13,000 and 9,500 years ago, and the people who were responsible may have been the ancestors of the historic hunter-gatherer communities of Patagonia found by European settlers in the nineteenth century.
Criteria: iii Inscribed 1999

• LAND OF FRANKINCENSE Oman

This group of archaeological sites relate to the production and distribution of frankincense, one of the most important luxury items of trade in antiquity, from the Mediterranean and Red Sea regions to Mesopotamia, India and China. The Oasis of Shishr and the entrepôts of Khor Rori and Al-Baleed are medieval fortified settlements and were important sites on the frankincense trade routes. There were sources of frankincense in the Dhofar region where the frankincense tree is still found, represented by the Frankincense Park of Wadi Dawkah.
Criteria: iii, iv Inscribed 2000

• WALLED CITY OF BAKU WITH THE SHIRVANSHAH'S PALACE AND MAIDEN TOWER Azerbaijan

Built on a site inhabited since the Palaeolithic period, the Walled City of Baku reveals evidence of Zoroastrian, Sasanian, Arabic, Persian, Shirvani, Ottoman and Russian presence. The Inner City (Icheri Sheher) has preserved much of its twelfth-century defensive walls. The twelfth-century Maiden Tower (Giz Galasy) is built over earlier structures dating from the seventh to sixth centuries BC, and the fifteenth-century Shirvanshahs' Palace is one of the pearls of Azerbaijan's architecture.
Criteria: iv Inscribed 2000

• KRONBORG CASTLE Denmark

Located on a strategically important site commanding the Sund – the stretch of water between Denmark and Sweden – work began on this outstanding Renaissance castle in 1574. In 1629 Kronborg was devastated by fire. Christian IV immediately commissioned the restoration of the castle, largely returning it to its original appearance. Thereafter large fortifications were built, the outer defensive works were considerably enlarged and the castle itself underwent substantial restoration and alteration. In 1785 it passed to the military and has remained intact to the present day.
Criteria: iv Inscribed 2000

• GARDEN KINGDOM OF DESSAU-WÖRLITZ Germany

In the Garden Kingdom of Dessau-Wörlitz the philosophical principles of the Age of the Enlightenment were applied to landscape design. The first work began in 1683 with the plan for Oranienbaum, which unified town, palace and park. The Baroque design, with obvious Dutch influence from its designer, Cornelis Ryckwaert, survives. Further developments took place around 1700 with the reclamation of marshy areas along the river Elbe and the creation of planned villages and farmsteads. By the time Prince Leopold III Friedrich Franz died in 1817 virtually the entire principality had become a unified garden whose characteristic features have been preserved.
Criteria: ii, iv Inscribed 2000

• GREATER BLUE MOUNTAINS AREA Australia

The Greater Blue Mountains consists of a mostly forested sandstone plateau that commences about 60 km west of central Sydney. It contains eight protected areas: the Blue Mountains, Wollemi, Yengo, Nattai, Kanangra-Boyd, Gardens of Stone and Thirlmere Lakes National Parks, and the Jenolan Caves Karst Conservation Reserve. The plateau has enabled the survival of a rich diversity of plant and animal life by providing a refuge from climatic changes during recent geological history. It is particularly noted for its wide representation of eucalypt communities ranging from wet and dry sclerophyll forests to mallee heathlands and for the diversity of species of eucalypts. It also contains ancient, relict species of global significance, the most famous being the recently discovered Wollemi pine, a 'living fossil' from the age of the dinosaurs.
Criteria: ix, x Inscribed 2000

• THREE CASTLES, DEFENSIVE WALL AND RAMPARTS OF THE MARKET-TOWN OF BELLINZONE Switzerland

The Bellinzone site consists of a group of fortifications grouped around the castle of Castelgrande, which stands on a rocky peak looking out over the Ticino valley. Running from the castle, a series of fortified walls protect the ancient town and block the passage through the valley. A second castle, Montebello, forms an integral part of the fortifications; a third but separate castle, Sasso Corbaro, was built on an isolated rocky promontory southeast of the other fortifications.
Criteria: iv Inscribed 2000

• UKHAHLAMBA / DRAKENSBERG PARK South Africa

Drakensberg Park, or uKhahlamba Park, is the largest protected area on the Great Escarpment of the southern African subcontinent. It comprises a nothern and a significantly larger southern section. There is considerable variation in topography, including vast basalt and sandstone cliffs, deep valleys, intervening spurs and extensive plateau areas. Among a total of 2,153 species of plant, there are a large number of threatened species. The fauna includes 48 mammal, 296 bird, 48 reptile, 26 amphibian and 8 fish species. This spectacular natural site also contains many caves and rock-shelters with the largest and most concentrated group of paintings in Africa south of the Sahara, made by the San people over a period of 4,000 years.
Criteria: i, iii, vii, x Inscribed 2000

• RUINS OF LEÓN VIEJO Nicaragua

León Viejo is one of the oldest Spanish colonial settlements in the Americas, founded in 1524 It developed round a central plaza, on the extreme northeast shore of what was to be called the Lake of León. The town reached its peak of development around 1545. An eruption of the nearby volcano, Momotombo, in 1578, combined with raging inflation drove the richer inhabitants away and a severe earthquake destroyed what was left in 1610. Excavations have uncovered remains of the Cathedral, the Convent of La Merced and the Royal Foundry.
Criteria: iii, iv Inscribed 2000

• EARLY CHRISTIAN NECROPOLIS OF PÉCS (SOPIANAE) Hungary

In the fourth century, a remarkable series of decorated tombs were constructed in the cemetery of the Roman provincial town of Sopianae, modern Pécs. The funerary monuments were built as underground burial chambers with memorial chapels above the ground. The tombs are important in artistic terms, since they are richly decorated with Christian-themed murals of outstanding quality. One of the most exceptional chambers has a niche carved above the sarcophagus with a painting of a wine pitcher and glass, symbolising the thirst of the soul journeying to the netherworld.
Criteria: iii, iv Inscribed 2000

• CURONIAN SPIT Lithuania and Russian Federation

Human habitation on this elongated sand dune peninsula, 98 km long and 0.4–4 km wide, dates back to prehistoric times. It survives only by ceaseless efforts to combat the natural erosion of the Spit, dramatically illustrated by continuing stabilisation and reforestation projects. The most significant element of the Spit's cultural heritage is represented by the old fishing settlements. The earliest of these were buried in sand. The surviving homesteads consisted of two or three buildings: a dwelling house, a cattle shed, and a smokehouse for curing fish.
Criteria: v Inscribed 2000

• CITY OF VERONA Italy

The historic city of Verona was founded in the first century BC. It prospered under the rule of the Scaliger family in the thirteenth and fourteenth centuries and then as part of the Republic of Venice. Verona has preserved a remarkable number of monuments from antiquity, and from the medieval and Renaissance periods. Its core is the Roman town in the loop of the Adige river, where the remains include city gates, the theatre and the Amphitheatre Arena, the second-largest after the Colosseum in Rome. The heart of the medieval and Renaissance Verona is around the Piazza delle Erbe and the Piazza dei Signori with their historic buildings, including the Palazzo del Comune.
Criteria: ii, iv Inscribed 2000

• CHURCHES OF CHILOÉ Chile

The mestizo culture, resulting from Jesuit missionary activities in the seventeenth and eighteenth centuries, has survived in the Chiloé archipelago in its wooden churches. Traditionally Chiloé churches are located near the shore. The tower façade, facing the sea, is made up of an entrance portico, the gable wall or pediment, and the tower, usually of two or three storeys, with hexagonal or octagonal drums to reduce wind resistance. There were over 100 churches by the end of the nineteenth century; over fifty survive and fourteen constitute the World Heritage site.
Criteria: ii, iii Inscribed 2000

• THE LOIRE VALLEY BETWEEN SULLY-SUR-LOIRE AND CHALONNES France

The Loire Valley is an outstanding cultural landscape of great beauty, containing historic towns and villages, the great architectural monuments of the chateaux and cultivated lands formed by two millennia of interaction between their population and the physical environment, primarily the river Loire itself. Roman impact on the landscape was massive and still strongly influences settlement location and roads; the Loire was one of the most important arteries for communications and trade in Gaul. Around 372, St Martin, Bishop of Tours, founded an abbey at Marmoutier, a model for many others. The valley has a rich architectural heritage in its historic towns such as Blois, Chinon, Orléans, Saumur and Tours, and in its world-famous castles, such as the Château de Chambord.
Criteria: i, ii, iv Inscribed 2000

• STONE TOWN OF ZANZIBAR Tanzania

The Stone Town of Zanzibar is a Swahili coastal trading town. It retains its street pattern of narrow, winding streets virtually intact with many fine buildings that reflect its culture, which has brought together elements from Africa, Arabia (particularly Oman), India and Europe over more than a millennium. There was intense trading activity between Asia and Africa, reflected in the palaces, fine mansions and mosques built by the Omanis. Zanzibar also has great symbolic significance in the history of slavery as one of the main slave-trading ports in east Africa and a key location in the Arab slave trade.

Criteria: ii, iii, vi Inscribed 2000

• BLAENAVON INDUSTRIAL LANDSCAPE
United Kingdom

The area around Blaenavon is evidence of the pre-eminence of south Wales as the world's major producer of iron and coal in the nineteenth century. All the necessary elements can still be seen – coal and ore mines, quarries, a primitive railway system, furnaces, workers' homes, and the social infrastructure of the community. During the 1840s and 1850s, as population numbers increased with the influx of migrant workers, the scattered housing of the workers and the associated school, church and chapels were complemented by the evolution of the town of Blaenavon.

Criteria: iii, iv Inscribed 2000

• HISTORIC TOWN OF ST GEORGE AND RELATED FORTIFICATIONS, BERMUDA
United Kingdom

St George is the oldest English town (1612) in the New World. The first of many barracks were built on Barrack Hill in 1780, followed by other buildings such as hospitals and a chapel. These were constructed in standard British military style but using local materials. The town's fortifications illustrate the development of English military engineering from the seventeenth to the twentieth centuries. The civic architecture of Bermuda has changed little. The simple, well-proportioned houses, of one or two storeys, have roofs of stone slabs painted white.

Criteria: iv Inscribed 2000

• ARCHAEOLOGICAL ENSEMBLE OF TÁRRACO
Spain

Tárraco, modern-day Tarragona, was a major administrative and mercantile city in Roman Spain and the centre of the Imperial cult for all the Iberian provinces. It was endowed with many fine buildings, and parts of these have been revealed in a series of exceptional excavations. Although most of the remains are fragmentary, with many preserved beneath more recent buildings, they present a vivid picture of the grandeur of this Roman provincial capital.

Criteria: ii, iii Inscribed 2000

• IMPERIAL TOMBS OF THE MING AND QING DYNASTIES China

The Imperial Tombs of the Ming and Qing Dynasties are seven groups of tombs in five provinces of eastern China dating from the fourteenth century onwards. The sites were selected in keeping with the Chinese principles of geomancy. A plain or broad valley was chosen, with the perspective of a mountain range to the north, against which the tombs would be built, with a lower elevation to the south. The site had to be framed on the east and west by chains of hills, and feature at least one waterway. A road several kilometres long, known as the Way of the Spirits, led to the tomb.

Criteria: i, ii, iii, iv, vi Inscribed 2000

• THE CATHEDRAL OF ST JAMES IN ŠIBENIK
Croatia

The three successive architects of the Cathedral of St James in Šibenik (built 1431–1535) came from northern Italy, Dalmatia and Tuscany They developed a structure built entirely from stone, using unique construction methods for the vaulting and the dome of the cathedral. There is a close correspondence between the interior and

The restored old dispensary, now the Stone Town Cultural Centre. It was constructed between 1885 and 1894, originally to be the 'Tharia Topan Jubilee Hospital'.

A pavilion at the Western Qing tombs, which contains fourteen imperial tombs, the Yongfu Tibetan Buddhist temple and the temporary palace where the imperial family resided when it came to honour its ancestors.

exterior forms of the building. The decorative elements of the cathedral, such as a remarkable frieze containing seventy-one sculptured faces of men, women, and children, also illustrate the successful fusion of Gothic and Renaissance art.
Criteria: i, ii, iv Inscribed 2000

▪ CENTRAL AMAZON CONSERVATION COMPLEX Brazil

The Central Amazon Conservation Complex makes up the largest protected area in the Amazon Basin (over 60,000 km²) and is one of the planet's richest regions in terms of biodiversity. It includes an important sample of annually flooded (*várzea*) ecosystems, *igapó* forests, lakes and channels, which take the form of a constantly evolving aquatic mosaic that is home to the largest array of electric fish in the world. Numerous species of conservation concern live within the park, including jaguar, giant otter, Amazonian manatee, South American river turtle and black cayman.
Criteria: ix, x Inscribed 2000

▪ ISLAND OF SAINT-LOUIS Senegal

Founded as a French colonial settlement in the seventeenth century, Saint-Louis was urbanised in the mid-nineteenth century. It was the capital of Senegal from 1872 to 1957. It is situated in a magnificent lagoon formed by the two arms of the Senegal river. The regular town plan, the system of quays, and the characteristic colonial architecture give Saint-Louis its distinctive appearance. The main historic buildings include the ancient fort, now the Governor's Palace and next to it is the cathedral, completed in 1828.
Criteria: ii, iv Inscribed 2000

▪ HISTORICAL CENTRE OF THE CITY OF AREQUIPA Peru

The Historical Centre of Arequipa, built in a form of soft volcanic rock called sillar, combines European and native building styles as seen in the city's robust walls, archways and vaults, courtyards and open spaces, and the intricate Baroque decoration of its façades. The historic core is the Plaza de Armas (Plaza Mayor) with its mid-nineteenth-century cathedral. At one corner are the church and cloisters of La Compañia, from the Baroque mestizo period. The city contains many *casonas*, well-proportioned vernacular houses enhanced with ornamental designs around windows and doors or by flat carvings.
Criteria: i, iv, Inscribed 2000

▪ GOCHANG, HWASUN AND GANGHWA DOLMEN SITES Korea, Republic of

Dolmens arrived in the Korean Peninsula in the Bronze Age and usually consist of two or more undressed stone slabs supporting a huge capstone. They were simple burial chambers, erected over the bodies or bones of Neolithic and Bronze Age worthies. The cemeteries at Gochang, Hwasun and Ganghwa contain many hundreds of excellent examples, preserving important evidence of how the stones were quarried, transported and raised and of how dolmen types changed during the second and first millennia BC in northeast Asia.
Criteria: iii Inscribed 2000

▪ ISCHIGUALASTO / TALAMPAYA NATURAL PARKS Argentina

The Talampaya and Ischigualasto Parks cover most the Ischigualasto-Villa Union Triassic sedimentary basin in northwestern Argentina. It was formed by layers of continental sediments deposited by rivers, lakes and swamps over the entire Triassic period (245–208 million years ago). The sediments have provided the world's most complete continental fossil record known from the Triassic, revealing the evolution of vertebrates as well as the environments they lived in during this period. Some fifty-six genera of fossil vertebrates have been recorded, including fish, amphibians, and a great variety of reptiles.
Criteria: viii Inscribed 2000

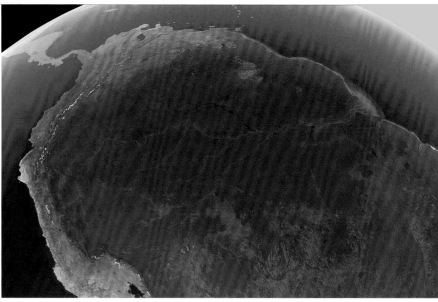

The Amazon Basin from space.

A detail of the façade of La Compañia de Jesús (the Church of the Jesuits) in Arequipa, built in the seventeenth century.

ISOLE EOLIE (AEOLIAN ISLANDS) Italy

The Isole Eolie (Aeolian Islands) are located off the northern coast of Sicily and provide an outstanding record of volcanic island-building and volcanic phenomena. The group consists of seven islands (Lipari, Vulcano, Salina, Stromboli, Filicudi, Alicudi and Panarea) and five small islets near Panarea. Studied since at least the eighteenth century, the islands have provided the science of vulcanology with examples of two types of eruption (Vulcanian and Strombolian). A total of 900 plant species have been recorded in the Aeolian Islands, including four endemic species.

Criteria: viii Inscribed 2000

HIGH COAST / KVARKEN ARCHIPELAGO
Finland and Sweden

The High Coast, Sweden, and the Kvarken Archipelago, Finland, are situated in the Gulf of Bothnia. The Archipelago is rising from the sea as the land is no longer pressed down under the weight of a glacier. As a consequence islands appear and unite, peninsulas expand, and lakes evolve from bays and develop into marshes and peat fens. The High Coast has been largely shaped by the processes of glaciation, glacial retreat and the emergence of new land from the sea. Since the last retreat of the ice 9,600 years ago, the uplift has been in the order of 285 m.

Criteria: viii Inscribed 2000

MONASTERY OF GEGHARD AND THE UPPER AZAT VALLEY Armenia

The monastery of Geghard contains a number of churches and tombs, most of them cut into the rock, which illustrate the very peak of Armenian medieval architecture. The monastery, founded in the fourth century and later rebuilt, was famous for its relics. The complex of medieval buildings is set into a landscape of great natural beauty, surrounded by towering cliffs at the entrance to the Azat Valley.

Criteria: ii Inscribed 2000

HISTORIC CENTRE OF SHAKHRISYABZ
Uzbekistan

Shakhrisyabz was the birthplace of Timur and was at its greatest during the period of Timurid rule in the fifteenth and sixteenth centuries. The site consists of a number of monuments, including Timur's summer palace, the grandiose Ak-Sarai Palace, begun in 1380; the Dorus Saodat complex, housing the royal mausoleum, including the white marble tomb intended for Timur, a masterpiece of the architecture of this period, and religious areas including a mosque, a prayer hall and accommodation for pilgrims; and the eighteenth-century Chor-su bazaar and baths.

Criteria: iii, iv Inscribed 2000

WACHAU CULTURAL LANDSCAPE Austria

The Wachau is a stretch of the Danube valley between Melk and Krems. The architecture, the human settlements, and the agricultural use of the land in the Wachau present a basically medieval landscape which has evolved organically over time. Radical changes in the landscape did not take place until around 800, when the Bavarian and Salzburg monasteries began to cultivate the slopes of the Wachau, creating the landscape of vine terraces. There are several impressive castles and many architecturally and artistically significant ecclesiastical buildings in the area.

Criteria: ii, iv Inscribed 2000

RIETVELD SCHRÖDERHUIS (RIETVELD SCHRÖDER HOUSE) Netherlands

The Rietveld Schröder House in Utrecht was commissioned by Ms Truus Schröder-Schräder, designed by the architect Gerrit Thomas Rietveld, and built in 1924. This small family house, with its flexible spatial arrangement and visual and formal qualities, was a manifesto for the ideals of the De Stijl group of artists and architects in the Netherlands in the 1920s, and has since become one of the icons of the Modern Movement in architecture.

Criteria: i, ii Inscribed 2000

Stromboli is the only island in the Aeolian archipelago that has permanent volcanic activity.

At Shakhrisyabz, the dimensions of the magnificent Ak-Sarai Palace, known as the 'White Palace', can be deduced from the original size of these gate-towers: two towers each 50 m in height, once joined by an arch with a span of 22 m.

• KINABALU PARK Malaysia

Kinabalu Park is dominated by Mount Kinabalu. It has a wide range of habitats, from rich tropical lowland and hill rainforest to tropical mountain forest, sub-alpine forest and scrub on the higher elevations. It is exceptionally rich in plant species, with examples of flora from the Himalaya, China, Australia and Malaysia. *Rafflesia*, a rare parasitic plant, is found here as are 'living fossils' such as the celery pine and the trig-oak, the evolutionary link between oaks and beeches. Four species of primate have been recorded.
Criteria: ix, x Inscribed 2000

• ASSISI, THE BASILICA OF SAN FRANCESCO AND OTHER FRANCISCAN SITES Italy

The medieval hill town of Assisi became famous through the life and work of Francis of Assisi (1182–1226), who initiated the Franciscan Order. His companion Clare, also later canonised, founded the sister order to the Franciscans, the Order of St Clare. After the canonisation of Francis in 1228 it was decided to build a monumental church in his honour. Its construction was followed in 1257 by the Basilica of Santa Chiara to honour St Clare. The Cathedral of San Rufino probably dates from the eighth century; it was rebuilt around 1036 as a cathedral. The west front is a masterpiece of Umbrian Romanesque architecture.
Criteria: i, ii, iii, iv, vi Inscribed 2000

• TIWANAKU: SPIRITUAL AND POLITICAL CENTRE OF THE TIWANAKU CULTURE Bolivia

The ruins of Tiwanaku bear witness to an empire that dominated a large area of the southern Andes and beyond between 500 and 900. Tiwanaku began as a small settlement around 1200 BC. Its self-sufficient form of farming was based on frost-resistant crops, essential at this high altitude. In more sheltered locations near Lake Titicaca, maize and peaches were also cultivated. The inhabitants lived in rectangular adobe houses that were linked by paved streets. Its buildings are exceptional examples of the ceremonial and public architecture.
Criteria: iii, iv Inscribed 2000

• NOEL KEMPFF MERCADO NATIONAL PARK Bolivia

This National Park is one of the largest (15,230 km²) in the Amazon Basin and includes a large section of the Huanchaca Plateau. With an altitude range from 200 m to nearly 1,000 m, it has a rich mosaic of habitat types from Cerrado savanna and forest to upland evergreen Amazonian forest. This diversity favours a wide range of wildlife. More than 130 species of animals live in the park including many rare mammals as river otters and jaguars. Several rivers have their sources on the plateau and form spectacular waterfalls.
Criteria: ix, x Inscribed 2000

• GUNUNG MULU NATIONAL PARK Malaysia

Gunung Mulu National Park on the island of Borneo contains seventeen vegetation zones, exhibiting some 3,500 species of vascular plants, 80 species of mammal and 270 species of bird. It is one of the world's richest sites for palms with 109 species identified. The park is dominated by Gunung Mulu, a 2,377-m sandstone pinnacle. Another outstanding karst feature is the 'pinnacles', 50-m high blades of rock that project through the rainforest canopy. The site also has large cave passages which provide a major spectacle of cave swiftlets and bats.
Criteria: vii, viii, ix, x Inscribed 2000

• PALMERAL OF ELCHE Spain

The Palmeral (a landscape of date palm groves) of Elche was laid out towards the end of the tenth century AD, when the Muslim city of Elche was also erected. Much of the Iberian peninsula was Arab at this time and the Palmeral represents a unique transference of Arab agricultural practices to the European continent. Cultivation of date palms in Elche is known at least since Iberian times, dating from around the fifth century BC, but the Arabs introduced more systematic practices, including an elaborate irrigation system which is still functioning.
Criteria: ii, v Inscribed 2000

The summit of Mount Kinabalu (4,095 m) in the Malaysian state of Sabah on Borneo. It is the highest mountain between the Himalaya and New Guinea.

Basilica of San Francesco, showing the entrance to the upper basilica. The Basilica contains magnificent frescos by Giotto and Cimabue and others relating to the faith and life of the saint.

King's Chamber in Wind Cave in Gunung Mulu National Park. There are at least 295 km of explored caves. Sarawak Chamber, 600 m by 415 m and 80 m high, is the largest known cave chamber in the world.

• AGRICULTURAL LANDSCAPE OF SOUTHERN ÖLAND Sweden

The interaction between man and the natural environment in the south of Öland, an island in the Baltic sea, has evolved over five thousand years. There is abundant evidence of continuous human settlement from prehistoric times to the present day and of adaptations to the way of life in response to the physical constraints of the island. Land use has not changed significantly, with arable farming and animal husbandry still remaining the principal economic activity. The southern part of the island is dominated by Stora Alvaret, one of the largest limestone pavements in Europe.
Criteria: iv, v Inscribed 2000

• HOLY TRINITY COLUMN IN OLOMOUC Czech Republic

Following the Thirty Years' War (1618–48) the city of Olomouc took on a new appearance. Many impressive public and private buildings were constructed in 'Olomouc Baroque', a local variant of the prevailing style. The crowning glory of this style is the Holy Trinity Column. Erected in the early years of the eighteenth century and rising to a height of 35 m, it is decorated with many fine religious sculptures, including the work of the distinguished Moravian artist Ondrej Zahner.
Criteria: i, iv Inscribed 2000

• MONASTIC ISLAND OF REICHENAU Germany

The island of Reichenau on Lake Constance preserves the traces of the Benedictine monastery, founded in 724, It was a significant artistic centre in tenth- and eleventh-century Europe, as illustrated by its wall paintings and illuminations, and it became a famous centre for teaching literature, science, and the arts. The churches of St Mary and St Marcus, St Peter and St Paul, and St George, mainly built between the ninth and eleventh centuries, provide a panorama of early medieval monastic architecture.
Criteria: iii, iv, vi Inscribed 2000

• MIR CASTLE COMPLEX Belarus

Mir Castle, a national symbol of Belarus, lies in a fertile region in the centre of Europe, at the crossroads of trade routes and different religious and cultural traditions. Its construction, in the Gothic style, began at the end of the fifteenth century. It was subsequently extended and reconstructed, first in the Renaissance and then in the Baroque style. After being abandoned and suffering severe damage during the Napoleonic period, the castle was restored at the end of the nineteenth century. Its present form is graphic testimony to its often turbulent history.
Criteria: ii, iv Inscribed 2000

• GYEONGJU HISTORIC AREAS Korea, Republic of

The Gyeongju Historic Areas contain a remarkable concentration of Korean Buddhist art, in the form of sculptures, reliefs, pagodas, and the remains of temples and palaces from the seventh and tenth centuries. There are three major areas ('belts') at Gyeongju. Mount Namsan Belt has a large number of prehistoric and historic remains. Wolsong Belt is home to the ruined palace of Wolsong, the Kyerim woodland and the Ch'omsongdae Observatory. Tumuli Park Belt consists of three groups of royal tombs. Excavations have produced rich grave-goods of gold, glass and fine ceramics.
Criteria: ii, iii Inscribed 2000

• GUSUKU SITES AND RELATED PROPERTIES OF THE KINGDOM OF RYUKYU Japan

For several centuries the Ryukyu Islands served as a centre of economic and cultural interchange between southeast Asia, China, Korea and Japan. In the tenth to twelfth centuries, Ryukyuan farming communities began to enclose their villages with simple stone walls for protection. From the twelfth century onwards powerful groups known as *aji* began to emerge. They enlarged the defences, converting them into fortresses (*gusuku*). Ryukyu stone architecture is represented by the erection in 1519 of the Stone Gate of the Sonohyan Shrine, guardian shrine of the Ryukyu Kingdom.
Criteria: ii, iii, vi Inscribed 2000

The Olomouc Holy Trinity Column forms a triumphal stone statement of the creeds of both Christianity and of citizenship. Faith and religious tradition are combined with the idea of the city.

Mir Castle is situated on the bank of a small lake by the Miryanka river. Its fortified walls feature four exterior corner towers rising to five storeys and a six-storey external gate tower.

• ENSEMBLE OF THE FERRAPONTOV MONASTERY Russian Federation

The Ferrapontov Monastery, in the Vologda region of northern Russia, is an exceptionally well-preserved Russian Orthodox monastic complex of the fifteenth to seventeenth centuries. There are six major elements in the complex. The Cathedral of the Nativity of the Virgin (1490) is the earliest; it contains the magnificent wall paintings of Dionisy, the greatest Russian artist at that time. This was followed by the Church of the Annunciation, the Treasury Chamber and ancillary buildings. In the seventeenth century the Gate Church, the Church of St Martinian and the bell tower were added.
Criteria: i, iv Inscribed 2000

• HISTORIC AND ARCHITECTURAL COMPLEX OF THE KAZAN KREMLIN Russian Federation

The Kazan Kremlin consists of an outstanding group of historic buildings dating from the sixteenth to nineteenth centuries. It is the only surviving Tatar fortress of the Kazan Khanate and is an excellent example of a synthesis of Tatar and Russian influences in architecture. Kazan was conquered by Ivan the Terrible in 1552 and became the Christian See of the Volga Land. The oldest building within the Kazan Kremlin complex is the sixteenth-century Annunciation Cathedral, constructed of local light sandstone, an important place of pilgrimage.
Criteria: ii, iii, iv Inscribed 2000

• CIUDAD UNIVERSITARIA DE CARACAS Venezuela

The Ciudad Universitaria de Caracas, built to the design of Carlos Raúl Villanueva between 1940 and 1960, is an outstanding example of the Modern Movement in architecture. The university campus integrates the large number of buildings and functions in a clearly articulated ensemble, including such masterpieces as the auditorium (Aula Magna) that incorporates 'Clouds' by the sculptor Alexander Calder, the Olympic Stadium and the Covered Plaza. The design uses elements from Venezuelan colonial architecture, such as bright colours, latticed windows for ventilation and internal gardens of tropical vegetation.
Criteria: i, iv Inscribed 2000

• CATALAN ROMANESQUE CHURCHES OF THE VALL DE BOÍ Spain

The narrow Vall de Boí is in the high Pyrenees. Its picturesque villages are set amid woodland and meadows. Each village has a Romanesque church, and is surrounded by a pattern of enclosed fields. The churches of the Vall de Boí are an especially pure and consistent example of Romanesque art in a virtually untouched rural setting. Most were built at the instigation of a single family, at the same time as historical Catalonia was being created.
Criteria: iii, iv Inscribed 2000

• ANCIENT VILLAGES IN SOUTHERN ANHUI – XIDI AND HONGCUN China

The traditional villages of China, which have largely disappeared during the twentieth century, are exceptionally well preserved in the villages of Xidi and Hongcun. The two villages are typical of settlements created during a feudal period and based on a prosperous trading economy. In their buildings and their street patterns, they reflect the socio-economic structure of a long-lived, settled period of Chinese history. The streets are all paved with granite and the buildings, which are widely spaced, are timber-framed with brick walls and elegantly carved decoration.
Criteria: ii, iv, v Inscribed 2000

• BARDEJOV TOWN CONSERVATION RESERVE Slovakia

Bardejov is a well-preserved fortified trading town typical of the major trade routes in medieval central Europe. It is on a floodplain of the Topl'a River, in northeastern Slovakia in the Beskyd Mountains. From the first quarter of the eighteenth century, Slovaks and Hassidic Jews came into Bardejov in large numbers. The town's small Jewish quarter was centred around the Great Synagogue, a fine

The tower of the Kazan Kremlin.

Hongcun, in southern Anhui, retains many fine buildings and its exceptional water system. The open watercourse runs through the village and forms two ponds, one in the centre and one to the south of the village.

building of 1725–47, which also contains ritual baths, a kosher slaughterhouse and a meeting building, now a school.
Criteria: iii, iv Inscribed 2000

• HISTORIC CENTRE OF BRUGGE Belgium

Brugge (Bruges) was one of medieval Europe's major trading centres. The city's prosperity was reflected in the construction of public buildings such as the imposing belfry in the Grand Place. Under Philippe le Bon (1419–67), the Duke of Burgundy, who set up his court in Brugge, the city became a centre of court life, of Flemish art, of miniature painting and printing. Owing to the presence of Italians it soon became a centre of humanism and the Renaissance. The architecture of Brugge has been characterised by brick Gothic, particularly the style of construction known as *travée brugeoise*.
Criteria: ii, iv, vi Inscribed 2000

• ARCHAEOLOGICAL SITE OF ATAPUERCA Spain

The evolutionary line or lines from the African ancestors of modern man are documented in the rich fossil record found in the caves of the Sierra de Atapuerca. The earliest human fossil remains in Europe, dating from around 800,000 years ago, were found in the Gran Dolina site here. The Galería del Sílex site contains more than fifty painted and engraved panels with geometrical motifs, hunting scenes, and human and animal figures. Excavation has revealed human remains (largely young adults and children) and ceramic fragments, identified as being related to sacrificial activities.
Criteria: iii, v Inscribed 2000

• MOUNT QINGCHENG AND THE DUJIANGYAN IRRIGATION SYSTEM China

Construction of the Dujiangyan irrigation system began in the third century BC. This system still controls the waters of the Minjiang river and distributes it to the fertile farmland of the Chengdu plains. In AD 142 the philosopher Zhang Daoling founded the doctrine of Taoism on Mount Qingcheng. During the Jin dynasty (265–420) several Taoist temples were built on the mountain and the teachings of Taoism were disseminated widely from here throughout China.
Criteria: ii, iv, vi Inscribed 2000

• MAJOR TOWN HOUSES OF THE ARCHITECT VICTOR HORTA (BRUSSELS) Belgium

Victor Horta, one of the earliest initiators of Art Nouveau, designed four major town houses in Brussels – Hôtel Tassel, Hôtel Solvay, Hôtel van Eetvelde, and Maison and Atelier Horta. The stylistic revolution represented by these works is characterised by their open plan, the diffusion of light within the building and the integration of the fluid lines of the Art Nouveau decoration with the structure of the building. They are some of the most remarkable pioneering works of architecture at the end of the nineteenth century.
Criteria: i, ii, iv Inscribed 2000

• LONGMEN GROTTOES China

The grottoes and niches of Longmen contain the largest and most impressive collection of Chinese art of the late Northern Wei and Tang dynasties. These works, entirely devoted to the Buddhist religion, represent the high point of Chinese stone carving. Work began on the Longmen Grottoes in 493, when Emperor Xiaowen of the Northern Wei dynasty moved his capital to Luoyang, and was to continue for the next four centuries. The group of giant statues in Fengxiansi Cave is most fully representative of this phase of Chinese art at Longmen.
Criteria: i, ii, iii Inscribed 2000

• ROMAN WALLS OF LUGO Spain

The walls of Lugo were built in the later part of the third century. The entire circuit survives and is the finest example of late Roman fortifications in western Europe. Of the original interval towers, forty-six have survived intact, and a further thirty-nine are wholly or partly dismantled. There are ten gates: five ancient and five recent. One of the best preserved is the Miñá Gate, which still has its original vaulted arch set between two towers, in characteristic Roman form.
Criteria: iv Inscribed 2000

The Belfry on Grand Place in Brugge. This confident Gothic brick structure, 83 m high, was built in two stages in the thirteenth and fifteenth centuries.

Boddhisatvas in the main grotto at Longmen. In total 2,345 niches or grottoes have been recorded at Longmen. They house more than 100,000 Buddhist statues.

• PANTANAL CONSERVATION AREA Brazil

The Pantanal Conservation Area in western central Brazil consists of a cluster of four protected reserves in part of the Pantanal region, one of the world's largest freshwater wetland ecosystems. The headwaters of the region's two major river systems, the Cuiabá and the Paraguay rivers, are located here, and the abundance and diversity of its vegetation and animal life are spectacular. The Pantanal is a sanctuary for birds. It is one of the most important breeding grounds for wetland birds such as Jabiru stork, as well as heron, ibis and duck.
Criteria: vii, ix, x Inscribed 2000

• ARCHAEOLOGICAL LANDSCAPE OF THE FIRST COFFEE PLANTATIONS IN THE SOUTH-EAST OF CUBA Cuba

The site consists of the remains of nineteenth-century coffee plantations on the rugged slopes of the Sierra Maestra in southeastern Cuba. The traditional plantation had, at its centre, the owner's house, surrounded by much more modest accommodation for slaves, both domestic and agricultural. The main industrial element was the terraced drying floor (*secadero*), on which the coffee beans were steeped in water in preparation for processing. The *secaderos* are recognisable as large sunken areas surrounded by low walls and linked with cisterns or water channels.
Criteria: iii, iv Inscribed 2000

• JESUIT BLOCK AND ESTANCIAS OF CÓRDOBA Argentina

Córdoba, established in 1573, was laid out on the standard Spanish colonial chequerboard pattern and the Jesuits were allocated one of the seventy blocks. The Jesuit Block, heart of the former Jesuit Province of Paraguay, contained the school, university, church and residence of the Society of Jesus. The Jesuits also held five *estancias*, or farming estates, outside the city, each with its own church. The Block and the *estancias* illustrate the unique religious, social, and economic experiment carried out by the Jesuits for over 150 years in the seventeenth and eighteenth centuries.
Criteria: ii, iv Inscribed 2000

• NOTRE-DAME CATHEDRAL IN TOURNAI Belgium

The Cathedral of Notre-Dame in Tournai was built in the first half of the twelfth century. The cathedral lies at the heart of the old town, not far from the left bank of the river Escaut. It is the product of three design periods: the Romanesque nave is of extraordinary dimensions with a wealth of sculpture on its capitals; the choir, rebuilt in the thirteenth century, is in the pure Gothic style; these are linked by a transept in a transitional style featuring an impressive group of five bell towers.
Criteria: ii, iv Inscribed 2000

• NEOLITHIC FLINT MINES AT SPIENNES (MONS) Belgium

The Neolithic flint mines at Spiennes, covering more than 1 km², are the largest and earliest concentration of ancient mines in Europe. They are also remarkable for the diversity of technological solutions used to extract flint and that they are directly linked to a contemporary settlement. On the surface there are meadows and fields strewn with millions of scraps of worked flint. Underground the site is an immense network of galleries linked to the surface by vertical shafts dug by Neolithic man.
Criteria: i, iii, iv Inscribed 2000

• CENTRAL SURINAME NATURE RESERVE Suriname

The Central Suriname Nature Reserve comprises 16,000 km² of primary tropical forest of western central Suriname. Its montane and lowland forests contain a high diversity of plant life with more than 5,000 vascular plant species collected to date. The Reserve's animals are typical of the region and include the jaguar, giant armadillo, giant river otter, tapir, sloths, eight species of primates and 400 bird species such as harpy eagle, Guianan cock-of-the-rock, and scarlet macaw. The reserve remains inaccessible, and so is largely unaffected and unthreatened by human activity.
Criteria: ix, x Inscribed 2000

The Panatal Conservation Area is home to the hyacinth macaw, the world's largest parrot, now endangered as a result of habitat destruction and capture for the pet trade.

Inside a Neolithic flint mine at Spiennes. The remains of the mines show the gradual development of technology by prehistoric man to extract a material essential for the production of tools and implements.

• CATHEDRAL AND CHURCHES OF ECHMIATSIN AND THE ARCHAEOLOGICAL SITE OF ZVARTNOTS Armenia

The cathedral and churches of Echmiatsin and the archaeological remains at Zvartnots graphically illustrate the evolution and development of the Armenian central-domed cross-hall type of church, which exerted a profound influence on architectural and artistic development in the region. The Cathedral of Holy Echmiatsin, built in 301–3, is Armenia's most ancient Christian place of worship. Together with the other religious buildings and archaeological remains in Echmiatsin and Zvartnots, it bears witness to the founding of Christianity in the country.

Criteria: ii, iii Inscribed 2000

• NEW LANARK United Kingdom

The first cotton mill at New Lanark, south of Glasgow, went into production in 1786 and the philanthropist and idealist Robert Owen began to remodel the village around 1809 into an ideal industrial community. The imposing mill buildings, the spacious and well-designed workers' housing, and the dignified educational institute and school all testify to Owen's humanism. The success of New Lanark had a profound influence on developments in progressive education, factory reform, humane working practices, international cooperation, and the concept of the garden city.

Criteria: ii, iv, vi Inscribed 2001

• LAMU OLD TOWN Kenya

Lamu Old Town is the oldest and best-preserved Swahili settlement in east Africa. Built in coral stone and mangrove timber, the town is characterised by the simplicity of structural forms enriched by such features as inner courtyards, verandas, and elaborately carved wooden doors. Lamu has hosted major Muslim religious festivals since the nineteenth century, and has become a significant centre for the study of Islamic and Swahili cultures.

Criteria: ii, iv, vi Inscribed 2001

• SWISS ALPS JUNGFRAU-ALETSCH Switzerland

The Jungfrau-Aletsch region is the most glaciated part of the Alps, containing Europe's largest glacier and a range of classic glacial features including U-shaped valleys, cirques, horn peaks and moraines. The diversity of flora and wildlife is represented in a range of Alpine and sub-Alpine habitats, and plant colonisation in the wake of retreating glaciers provides an outstanding example of plant succession. The area's scenic and aesthetic appeal is one of the most dramatic in the Alps. The impressive northern wall of the site with the panorama of the Eiger, Mönch and Jungfrau mountains provides a classic view that has played an important role in European art and literature.

Criteria: vii, viii, ix Inscribed 2001

• TOMBS OF BUGANDA KINGS AT KASUBI Uganda

The Tombs of Buganda Kings site at Kasubi is on a hillside within Kampala district. At its core on the hilltop is the former palace of the Kabakas of Buganda, built in 1882 and converted into the royal burial ground in 1884. Four royal tombs now lie within the Muzibu Azaala Mpanga, the main building, which is circular and surmounted by a dome. It has been built using organic materials, principally wood, thatch, reed, wattle and daub. The site's main significance lies, however, in its intangible values of belief, spirituality, continuity and identity.

Criteria: i, iii, iv, vi Inscribed 2001

• ALTO DOURO WINE REGION Portugal

The Alto Douro Region has been producing wine for some 2,000 years and, since the eighteenth century, its main product has been port wine. The landscape in the Demarcated Region of the Douro is formed by steep hills and boxed-in valleys that flatten out into plateaux above 400 m. The most dominant feature of the landscape is the terraced vineyards that blanket the countryside. The earliest were narrow, irregular terraces buttressed by walls of stone that were regularly taken down and rebuilt. The long lines of continuous, regularly shaped terraces date mainly from the end of the nineteenth century.

Criteria: iii, iv, v Inscribed 2001

One of the mill buildings at New Lanark. All the buildings show good proportion, good masonry and simplicity of detail.

The Aletsch Glacier in the Swiss Alps is the largest and longest glacier in western Eurasia in terms of area (128 km²), length (23 km) and depth (900 m).

Vineyard by the river Douro. This long tradition of viticulture has produced a cultural landscape of outstanding beauty.

THE ROYAL HILL OF AMBOHIMANGA
Madagascar

The Royal Hill of Ambohimanga is a significant symbol of the cultural identity of the people of Madagascar. Its traditional design, materials and layout are representative of the social and political structure of Malagasy society from at least the sixteenth century. The site consists of a royal city and burial site and an ensemble of sacred places (wood, spring, lake, public meeting place). Fortifications protected the royal city in an arrangement of banks, ditches, and fourteen stone gateways. It remains a place of worship for pilgrims from Madagascar and elsewhere.
Criteria: iii, iv, vi Inscribed 2001

CENTRAL SIKHOTE-ALIN Russian Federation

The Sikhote-Alin mountain range in the Russian Far East contains one of the richest temperate forests in the world. The combination of severe climate, physical isolation and traditional uses by the indigenous peoples has meant that 80–90 per cent of its vegetation still remains as dense temperate forest and taiga. Alpine tundra, coastal shrub-lands, meadows and bogs account for the rest of the area. In this mixed zone between taiga and subtropics, southern species such as the tiger and Himalayan bear cohabit with northern species such as the brown bear and lynx.
Criteria: x Inscribed 2001

SALTAIRE United Kingdom

Saltaire in West Yorkshire is a well-preserved industrial village, established by the wealthy and paternalistic businessman, Titus Salt. Work on his mill at Saltaire began in 1851 and it was opened in 1853. Salt's new village eventually had over 800 dwellings in wide streets, with a large dining hall and kitchens, baths and wash houses, almshouse for retired workers, hospital and dispensary, educational institute and church, and ample recreational land and allotments. Saltaire represents an important stage in the development of modern town planning.
Criteria: ii, iv Inscribed 2001

FERTÖ / NEUSIEDLERSEE CULTURAL LANDSCAPE Austria and Hungary

The Fertö / Neusiedler Lake area lies between the Alps and the lowlands in Austria and Hungary. It has been the meeting place of different cultures for eight millennia, and the landscape is the result of ancient land-use forms based on stockraising and viticulture. The remarkable rural architecture of the villages surrounding the lake is typified by the historic centre of the medieval free town of Rust. There are several eighteenth- and nineteenth-century palaces including the Fertöd Esterházy Palace, the most important eighteenth-century palace in Hungary, built on the model of Versailles.
Criteria: v Inscribed 2001

MEDINA OF ESSAOUIRA (FORMERLY MOGADOR) Morocco

Since its foundation, Essaouira has been a major seaport, linking Morocco with Europe. As Morocco increasingly opened up to the rest of the world in the later seventeenth century, the old town needed to expand and a new plan was laid out by a French architect. The result was to take a late-eighteenth-century European fortified seaport and translated it to North Africa. The joining of European and Moroccan techniques produced some unique buildings: the Sqalas (fortifications) of the port and medina, the Bab Marrakesh bastion, mosques, synagogues and churches.
Criteria: ii, iv Inscribed 2001

PROVINS, TOWN OF MEDIEVAL FAIRS
France

Of the four towns where great medieval trade fairs were held in the territory of the Counts of Champagne, Provins is the only one to retain its original medieval fabric. There are two large buildings: the so-called 'Tour de César' or the Big Tower, dating initially from the twelfth-century and the Romanesque-Gothic church of Saint-Quiriace. A characteristic of medieval buildings in Provins is their system of vaulted cellars which open out to the street through a large door to which access is gained by a wide stone staircase.
Criteria: ii, iv Inscribed 2001

ZOLLVEREIN COAL MINE INDUSTRIAL COMPLEX IN ESSEN Germany

Zollverein in Essen on the Ruhr is an exceptional industrial monument consisting of the complete infrastructure of a major coal-mining site, with some twentieth-century buildings of outstanding architectural merit. Mining began in the mid-nineteenth century at a depth of some 120 m and finished at 1,200 m. By the end of mining the underground roadways extended over 120 km; they were accessed by twelve shafts, opened up progressively between 1847 and 1932. Elements of the original pits, the central coking plant, railway lines, associated buildings and housing all survive today.
Criteria: ii, iii Inscribed 2001

BRAZILIAN ATLANTIC ISLANDS: FERNANDO DE NORONHA AND ATOL DAS ROCAS RESERVES Brazil

Peaks of the Southern Atlantic submarine ridge form the Fernando de Noronha Archipelago and Rocas Atoll off the coast of Brazil. The islands are home to the largest concentration of tropical seabirds in the western Atlantic. Baia de Golfinhos has an exceptional population of resident dolphin and at low tide the Rocas Atoll provides a seascape of lagoons and tidal pools teeming with fish. The rich waters are extremely important for the breeding and feeding of tuna, shark, turtle and marine mammals.
Criteria: vii, ix, x Inscribed 2001

TSODILO Botswana

With one of the highest concentrations of rock art in the world, Tsodilo has been called the 'Louvre of the Desert'. For thousands of years these rocky outcrops in the hostile landscape of the Kalahari Desert have been visited and venerated by humans, who have left rich traces in the form of outstanding rock art. Over 4,500 paintings are preserved, some thought to be more than 2,000 years old, while geometric art is regarded as about 1,000 years old. The outcrops had immense symbolic and religious significance to those who survived here.
Criteria: i, iii, vi Inscribed 2001

MINING AREA OF THE GREAT COPPER MOUNTAIN IN FALUN Sweden

The Great Copper Mountain (Stora Kopparberget) is the oldest and most important mine in Sweden. Mining began as early as the ninth century and came to an end in the closing years of the twentieth century. By the seventeenth century, Falun was producing 70 per cent of the world's copper, enabling Sweden to become a leading European power. The seventeenth-century planned town, with its many fine historic buildings, together with settlements in the Dalarna region, provide a vivid picture of what was for centuries one of the world's most important mining areas.
Criteria: ii, iii, v Inscribed 2001

DERWENT VALLEY MILLS
United Kingdom

The Derwent Valley, between Matlock Bath and Derby in central England, contains a series of eighteenth- and nineteenth-century cotton mills and an industrial landscape of high historical and technological interest. The modern factory system was effectively born here, when new types of building were erected to house the latest technology for spinning cotton developed by Richard Arkwright. This was large-scale industrial production in a hitherto rural landscape, and the need to provide housing and other facilities for workers and managers resulted in the creation of the first industrial towns.
Criteria: ii, iv Inscribed 2001

ALEJANDRO DE HUMBOLDT NATIONAL PARK Cuba

The park, in southeastern Cuba, includes a complex system of mountains, tablelands, coastal plains, bays and coral reefs. It is the least explored natural area on the island and has locations where the plant life has not yet been assessed. Many of the underlying rocks are toxic to plants so species have had to adapt to survive, resulting in the evolution of many new species. The park is one of the most important sites in the Western Hemisphere for the conservation of endemic flora. Endemism of vertebrates and invertebrates is also very high.
Criteria: ix, x Inscribed 2001

YUNGANG GROTTOES China

The Yungang Grottoes in Shanxi Province, comprise 252 caves and 51,000 statues, the outstanding achievement of Buddhist cave art in China in the fifth and sixth centuries. The grottoes of the early period (AD 460–65) are composed of five main caves. They have a U-shaped plan with an arched roof, a door and a window. The central images occupy the major part of the caves, while on the outer walls 1,000 Buddhist statues are carved. The site also includes four groups of twin caves and one group of triple caves.
Criteria: i, ii, iii, iv Inscribed 2001

HISTORIC CENTRE OF THE TOWN OF GOIÁS Brazil

In its layout and architecture the historic town of Goiás is an outstanding example of a European town admirably adapted to the climatic, geographical and cultural constraints of central South America. In 1748, Goiás' gold wealth meant it was chosen as the headquarters of a new subdistrict, and its first governor transformed the village into a small capital. Although modest, both public and private architecture form a harmonious whole, thanks to the coherent use of local materials and vernacular techniques.
Criteria: ii, iv Inscribed 2001

CHURCHES OF PEACE IN JAWOR AND SWIDNICA Poland

The Churches of Peace in Jawor and Swidnica, the largest timber-framed religious buildings in Europe, were built in former Silesia in the mid-seventeenth century, following the Peace of Westphalia (1648). In most of the Catholic Hapsburg empire Protestants were persecuted but, through the agency of the Lutheran king of Sweden, in Silesia the Emperor allowed three Lutheran churches, of which two survive. As a result of conditions imposed by the Emperor, the builders had to employ pioneering constructional techniques of a scale and complexity unknown in wooden architecture.
Criteria: iii, iv, vi Inscribed 2001

• DORSET AND EAST DEVON COAST
United Kingdom

This 155 km stretch of coast in southern England contains textbook examples of common coastal features such as sea stacks and sea caves. The site includes a near-continuous sequence of Triassic, Jurassic and Cretaceous rocks representing approximately 185 million years of the Earth's history. A large number of vertebrate, invertebrate and plant fossils have been discovered. Among the finds are fossil dinosaur footprints, flying reptiles and marine reptiles. Chesil Beach is famous for the volume, type and grading of its pebbles. The Fleet Lagoon is one of the most important saline lagoons in Europe.

Criteria: viii Inscribed 2001

• VAT PHOU AND ASSOCIATED ANCIENT SETTLEMENTS WITHIN THE CHAMPASAK CULTURAL LANDSCAPE
Lao People's Dem. Republic

The Temple Complex of Vat Phou bears exceptional testimony to the culture of the Khmer Empire, which dominated the region in the tenth to fourteenth centuries. Vat Phou was shaped to express the Hindu vision of the relationship between nature and humanity, using an axis from mountain top to river bank to lay out a geometric pattern of temples, shrines and waterworks extending over some 10 km. Two planned cities on the banks of the Mekong River are also part of the site, as well as Phou Kao mountain.

Criteria: iii, iv, vi Inscribed 2001

• SAMARKAND – CROSSROADS OF CULTURES
Uzbekistan

Located on the crossroads of the great trade routes that traversed central Asia, the historic town of Samarkand emerged as a major centre through the efforts of Timur the Lame (Tamerlane, c. 1336–1405). It became the capital of Timur's powerful state and the repository of the material riches from conquered territories that extended from central Asia to Persia, Afghanistan, and India. The major monuments include the Registan and its *madrasas*, Bibi-Khanum Mosque, the Shakhi-Zinda necropolis and the Gur-Emir (Timur's mausoleum), as well as Ulugh-Beg's Observatory.

Criteria: i, ii, iv Inscribed 2001

• CERRADO PROTECTED AREAS: CHAPADA DOS VEADEIROS AND EMAS NATIONAL PARKS Brazil

Comprising the Chapada dos Veadeiros and the Emas National Parks, the area contains flora and fauna and key habitats that characterise the Cerrado – one of the world's oldest and most diverse tropical ecosystems. For millennia, it has served as refuge for several species during periods of climate change and will be vital for maintaining the biodiversity of the Cerrado region during future climate fluctuations. The area is home to many threatened and endemic species, while mammals include giant anteater, giant armadillo, maned wolf, jaguar and pampas deer.

Criteria: ix, x Inscribed 2001

• MASADA Israel

Masada is a rugged natural fortress of majestic beauty set in the Judaean Desert overlooking the Dead Sea. It is a symbol of the ancient kingdom of Israel. Its violent destruction and the last stand of Jewish patriots against the Roman army came at the end of the First Jewish–Roman War in AD 73. The camps, fortifications and attack ramp are the most complete surviving Roman siege works. Masada was built as a palace complex in the classic style of the early Roman Empire by Herod the Great of Judaea, who ruled from 37–4 BC.

Criteria: iii, iv, vi Inscribed 2001

• TUGENDHAT VILLA IN BRNO Czech Republic

The Tugendhat Villa in Brno is a masterpiece of the Modern Movement in architecture. Completed in 1930, it designer, Mies van der Rohe (1886–1969), applied the radical new concepts of the Modern Movement to the design of residential buildings and made extensive use of modern industrial techniques. He designed

Man o' War Beach on the Dorset coast.

The Registan (literally 'place of sand') in the centre of Samarkand, the site of three magnificent *madrasas*, the oldest dating from the early fifteenth century.

Aerial view of Masada, with one of the Roman camps in the foreground. The great ramp used for the final assault was built from soil and stones braced by timber beams.

furniture specifically for this house, such as the steel and leather Tugendhat chair. The mechanical equipment designed and built for the house was also exceptional, including electrically operated large steel-frame windows, central heating and an air-conditioning system.
Criteria: ii, iv Inscribed 2001

•OLD CITY OF ACRE Israel

The port of Acre preserves the substantial remains of the medieval Crusader buildings beneath the existing Ottoman fortified town which dates from the eighteenth and nineteenth centuries. The remains of the Crusader town, dating from 1104–1291, lie almost intact, both above and below today's street level, providing an exceptional picture of the layout and structure of the capital of the medieval Crusader kingdom of Jerusalem. During the two centuries of Crusader rule, Acre symbolised, better than any other city, the interchange between eastern and western cultures.
Criteria: ii, iii, v Inscribed 2001

•HISTORIC CENTRE OF VIENNA Austria

Vienna developed from early Celtic and Roman settlements into a Medieval and Baroque city, the capital of the Austro-Hungarian Empire. The historic centre of Vienna is rich in architectural treasures, including Baroque castles and gardens, as well as the late-nineteenth-century Ringstrasse lined with grand buildings, monuments and parks. The inner city contains a number of medieval historic buildings, including the Schottenkloster, the oldest monastery in Austria, and the church of Maria am Gestade from the thirteenth century. St Stephen's Cathedral dates from the fourteenth and fifteenth centuries.
Criteria: ii, iv, vi Inscribed 2001

•HISTORIC CENTRE OF GUIMARÃES Portugal

Guimarães is associated with the emergence of Portuguese national identity in the twelfth century. It is an exceptionally well-preserved town illustrating the evolution of particular building types from the medieval settlement onwards. The residential buildings use two construction techniques, a half-timbered one (*taipa de rodízio*) dating from before the sixteenth century, and another from the nineteenth century (*taipa de fasquio*) that uses timber alone. Guimarães is of particular significance because these specialised building techniques were transmitted to Portuguese colonies in Africa and the New World, becoming their characteristic feature.
Criteria: ii, iii, iv Inscribed 2001

•ARANJUEZ CULTURAL LANDSCAPE Spain

Aranjuez, to the south of Madrid, appears as a green oasis in a landscape of sierra type, dry, brown and fairly barren of vegetation. In the sixteenth century, Philip II built a new royal palace and large ornamental and vegetable gardens were laid out according to geometric principles. It became a place of pageantry and hunting, and a source of inspiration for the greatest Spanish poets of the Golden Age. The eighteenth century culminated with the building of a new planned town close to the palace.
Criteria: ii, iv Inscribed 2001

•VILLA D'ESTE, TIVOLI Italy

The gardens of the Villa d'Este had a profound influence on garden design throughout Europe. They are among the earliest and finest of Renaissance gardens. One of many outstanding features is the Alley of the Hundred Fountains, the waters from which cross the entire garden, which also features its own artificial mountain, with three alcoves holding statues, and a water organ. The plan of the villa is irregular because the architect used parts of the previous monastic building. The main rooms of the villa open on to the magnificent garden.
Criteria: i, ii, iii, iv, vi Inscribed 2001

•TOKAJ WINE REGION HISTORIC CULTURAL LANDSCAPE Hungary

The pattern of vineyards, farms, villages, and small towns demonstrates the long tradition of Tokaj wine production. The most characteristic structures are the wine cellars, the most famous being

Destroyed in the sixteenth century, Acre was a deserted ghost town until reconstruction began in the mid-eighteenth century, under Daher El Amar and later El Jazar, who rebuilt the port and fortifications.

The Rathaus (City Hall) of Vienna. Several historic buildings are associated with Mozart, Beethoven, Schubert and others, when the city played an essential role as a leading European musical centre.

The Neptune Fountain (foreground) and the Organ Fountain (background) in the gardens of the Villa D'Este, Tivoli.

the multi-level network in the Ungvari district of Satoraljaujhely. Tokaji Aszu, for which the region became famous, was first produced during the Ottoman period. Legend has it that fears of Turkish raiders delayed the harvest until the grapes had shrivelled and botrytis infection had set in, thereby creating the 'noble rot' (*pourriture noble*) for which the wine is renowned.
Criteria: iii, v Inscribed 2002

▪ MINARET AND ARCHAEOLOGICAL REMAINS OF JAM Afghanistan

The Minaret of Jam is a graceful, soaring structure, dating back to the twelfth century, believed to have been built to commemorate a major victory of the sultans of the Ghurid dynasty. Rising to 65 m from a 9-m-diameter octagonal base, its four tapering cylindrical shafts are constructed of fired brick. The exterior of the minaret is completely covered with geometric decoration in relief laid over the plain structural bricks. The first cylinder is the most decorated: it is divided into eight vertical segments, matching those of the base.
Criteria: ii, iii, iv Inscribed 2002

▪ ANCIENT MAYA CITY OF CALAKMUL, CAMPECHE Mexico

The site is deep in the tropical forest of the Tierras Bajas of southern Mexico, within the Calakmul Biosphere Reserve. Calakmul has a very well-preserved series of imposing monuments representative of Maya architectural, artistic and urban development which create a vivid picture of life in an ancient Maya capital. The site is one of the most ancient in the region: buildings in the site's central zone indicate continuous occupation over some twelve centuries, and analysis of the complex iconography of a frieze shows that this antedates similar structures from Uaxactún and El Mirador.
Criteria: i, ii, iii, iv Inscribed 2002

▪ HISTORIC INNER CITY OF PARAMARIBO Suriname

Paramaribo is a former Dutch colonial town from the seventeenth and eighteenth centuries on the northern coast of tropical South America. The original street plan remains intact. Its buildings illustrate the gradual fusion of Dutch architectural influence with traditional local techniques and materials. The layout of the Inner City consists of a main axis stretching northwest behind Fort Zeelandia, with streets crossing at right angles. To the north of Fort Zeelandia is a large public park, the Garden of Palms. The wide streets and public open spaces are tree-lined.
Criteria: ii, iv Inscribed 2002

▪ UPPER MIDDLE RHINE VALLEY Germany

As one of the most important transport routes in Europe, the 65-km-stretch of the Middle Rhine Valley has facilitated the exchange of culture between the Mediterranean region and the north for two millennia. With its castles, historic towns, and vineyards, it illustrates the long history of human involvement with a dramatic and varied natural landscape. The terracing of its steep slopes in particular has shaped the landscape. It is intimately associated with history and legend, and for centuries has exercised a powerful influence on writers, artists and composers.
Criteria: ii, iv, v Inscribed 2002

▪ HISTORIC CENTRES OF STRALSUND AND WISMAR Germany

The medieval towns of Stralsund and Wismar, on Germany's Baltic coast, were major trading centres of the Hanseatic League in the fourteenth and fifteenth centuries. In the seventeenth and eighteenth centuries they became Swedish administrative and defensive centres for its German territories. Stralsund developed an architectural style known as Sundische Gothik, seen in its fourteenth-century town hall. Several buildings reflect the architectural forms of the Renaissance, Baroque and neoclassical periods, while respecting the original medieval pattern. Wismar's most sumptuous building is the Fürstenhof and its medieval port has been largely preserved.
Criteria: ii, iv Inscribed 2002

The Minaret of Jam, an outstanding example of Islamic architecture and ornamentation. Remains of the Ghurid settlement's castles and towers are on the opposite bank of the Hari River, high on the cliff.

The Rhine Valley at Oberwesel, where the valley landscape begins to change from soft clay-slates to hard sandstone. The result is a series of narrows, the most famous of which is the Lorelei.

• ST CATHERINE AREA Egypt

The area is sacred to three world religions: Christianity, Islam, and Judaism. Ascetic monasticism in remote areas prevailed in the early Christian church and resulted in the establishment of monastic communities. St Catherine's Monastery is the oldest to have survived intact, having been used without interruption since the sixth century. Its walls and buildings are very significant in the study of Byzantine architecture and the monastery houses outstanding collections of early Christian manuscripts and icons. The Christian communities of St Catherine's Monastery have always maintained close relations with Islam.

Criteria: i, iii, iv, vi Inscribed 2002

• MAHABODHI TEMPLE COMPLEX AT BODH GAYA India

The Mahabodhi Temple Complex is one of the four holy sites related to the life of the Lord Buddha as the place where, in 531 BC, he attained the supreme and perfect insight while seated under the Bodhi Tree. Emperor Asoka made a pilgrimage to this spot around 260 BC and built the first temple at the site of the Bodhi Tree. The present temple dates from the fifth or sixth centuries and is one of the earliest Buddhist temples built entirely in brick still standing in India.

Criteria: i, ii, iii, iv, vi Inscribed 2002

• LATE BAROQUE TOWNS OF THE VAL DI NOTO (SOUTH-EASTERN SICILY) Italy

This group of eight Sicilian towns – Caltagirone, Militello Val di Catania, Catania, Modica, Noto, Palazzolo, Ragusa and Scicli – represents the culmination and final flowering of Baroque art in Europe and depicts distinctive innovations in town planning and urban building. The homogeneity of the art and architecture in the Val di Noto towns is a direct result of rebuilding on or beside existing towns after an earthquake in 1693. The towns represent a considerable collective undertaking, successfully carried out at a high level of architectural and artistic achievement.

Criteria: i, ii, iv, v Inscribed 2002

• TAKHT-E SOLEYMAN Islamic Republic of Iran

The archaeological site of Takht-e Soleyman, in northwestern Iran, is in a valley set in a volcanic mountain region. The site includes the principal Zoroastrian sanctuary partly rebuilt in the Ilkhanid Mongol period (thirteenth century) as well as a temple of the Sassanian period (sixth and seventh centuries) dedicated to Anahita. Sassanian temple architecture has influenced the development of religious architecture. The site is an outstanding example of a Zoroastrian sanctuary integrated with Sassanian palatial architecture, illustrating the Zoroastrian fire and water cult that lasted for more than two-and-a-half millennia.

Criteria: i, ii, iii, iv, vi Inscribed 2003

• ROYAL BOTANIC GARDENS, KEW United Kingdom

Created in 1759, the Royal Botanic Gardens of Kew have made a significant contribution to the study of plant diversity, and this is reflected in the richness of its collections. The first botanic garden at Kew was originally for medicinal plants. Later, architects such as William Chambers and 'Capability' Brown not only created many new edifices, but also remodelled the earlier Baroque gardens to make a pastoral landscape in the English style. As visitor numbers increased, the scientific collections were enriched and glasshouses and spaces were altered to house living plant collections.

Criteria: ii, iii, iv Inscribed 2003

• MAPUNGUBWE CULTURAL LANDSCAPE South Africa

Mapungubwe lies on the northern edge of South Africa in open savanna landscape at the confluence of the Limpopo and Shashe rivers. At its height, Mapungubwe was the largest and wealthiest kingdom in southern Africa through its trade of rich natural resources with Arabia, India and China. It was abandoned in the

The Orthodox Monastery of St Catherine stands at the foot of Mount Horeb, of the Old Testament, where Moses received the Tablets of the Law.

Azar Goshnab Fire Temple at Takht-e Soleyman.

The Palm House at Kew, the iron and glass structure designed by Decimus Burton and Richard Turner and built 1844–48, is at the centre of the landscape garden designed by William Nesfield.

fourteenth century following drastic climatic cooling. The almost untouched remains of the palace sites, the settlement area and the remains of two earlier capital sites show the development of social and political structures over some 400 years.
Criteria: ii, iii, iv, v Inscribed 2003

• PURNULULU NATIONAL PARK Australia

The park, in the Kimberley region in the far north of Western Australia, comprises four major ecosystems: the Bungle Bungle Mountain Range; wide sand plains surrounding the Bungle Bungles; the Ord River valley; and limestone ridges and ranges to the west and north of the park. Devonian-age quartz sandstone has been eroded over a period of twenty million years into a series of beehive-shaped towers or cones amid sheer-sided gorges 100–200 m deep. The towers' surfaces are distinctly marked by regular horizontal bands of dark-grey, single-celled cyanobacterial crust.
Criteria: vii, viii Inscribed 2003

• UVS NUUR BASIN Mongolia and Russian Federation

The Uvs Nuur Basin is the northernmost of the enclosed basins of central Asia. It takes its name from Uvs Nuur, a large, shallow and very saline lake, important for migrating birds, waterfowl and seabirds. The site is made up of twelve protected areas representing the major biomes of eastern Eurasia. The steppe ecosystem supports a rich diversity of birds and the desert is home to the rare gerbil, jerboa and marbled polecat. The mountains are an important refuge for the globally endangered snow leopard, mountain sheep (argali) and the Asiatic ibex.
Criteria: ix, x Inscribed 2003

• THE WHITE CITY OF TEL-AVIV – THE MODERN MOVEMENT Israel

Tel Aviv was founded in 1909 and developed as a metropolitan city under the British Mandate in Palestine. The White City was constructed from the early 1930s until the 1950s, based on a 'garden city' plan by Sir Patrick Geddes. The buildings reflect influences from the Bauhaus, Le Corbusier and Erich Mendelsohn adapted for local conditions. The large glazed surfaces of European buildings, for example, are reduced to relatively small, strip window openings, more suitable for the hot climate. The result is an outstanding example of the Modern Movement in a new cultural context.
Criteria: ii, iv Inscribed 2003

• CULTURAL LANDSCAPE AND ARCHAEOLOGICAL REMAINS OF THE BAMIYAN VALLEY Afghanistan

The Bamiyan Valley is a high pass (2,500 m) that formed one of the branches of the Silk Road. The artistic and religious developments here, from the first to the thirteenth centuries, characterized ancient Bakhtria, integrating various cultural influences into the Gandhara school of Buddhist art. The area contains numerous Buddhist monastic ensembles and sanctuaries, as well as fortified edifices from the Islamic period. The site is also testimony to the tragic destruction by the Taliban of the two standing Buddha statues in March 2001.
Criteria: i, ii, iii, iv, vi Inscribed 2003

• THREE PARALLEL RIVERS OF YUNNAN PROTECTED AREAS China

This area covers sections of the upper reaches of three rivers: the Yangtze (Jinsha), the Mekong and the Salween. The rivers run roughly parallel, north to south for over 300 km, through steep gorges which, in places, are 3,000 m deep and bordered by glaciated peaks more than 6,000 m high. It includes the equivalents of seven climatic zones: southern, central and northern subtropical zones, with dry hot valleys; warm, cool and cold temperate zones; and cold zones. This is one of the world's least-disturbed temperate ecological areas, a natural gene pool of great richness.
Criteria: vii, viii, ix, x Inscribed 2003

Sandstone tower karst in the Bungle Bungle Range, Purnululu National Park. The Bungle Bungle Range is one of the most extensive and impressive occurrences of sandstone tower karst in the world.

Snow-capped Baimang Snow Mountain between the Yangtze and Mekong rivers, in the Three Parallel Rivers of Yunnan Protected Areas.

• MATOBO HILLS Zimbabwe

The Matobo Hills rise above the granite shield covering much of Zimbabwe. The boulders, cliff faces and natural caves feature an outstanding collection of rock paintings which, together with archaeological evidence, provide a detailed picture of foraging societies in the Stone Age and the agricultural societies replacing them. The earlier paintings, dating back at least 13,000 years, are naturalistic interpretations of people, animals and trees associated with hunting and gathering, and are mostly executed using a red ochre pigment. The later paintings, associated with farming communities, used white pigment from kaolin or quartz.
Criteria: iii, v, vi Inscribed 2003

• SACRI MONTI OF PIEDMONT AND LOMBARDY Italy

Sacri Monti (Sacred Mountains) were conceived as places of prayer and devotion, intended to be alternatives to the Holy Places in Jerusalem and the Holy Land. The nine Sacri Monti of northern Italy are groups of chapels and other architectural features created mostly in the late sixteenth and seventeenth centuries and dedicated to different aspects of the Christian faith. In addition to their symbolic spiritual value, they house much important artistic material in the form of wall paintings and statuary. The earliest Sacro Monte is the 'New Jerusalem' of Varallo.
Criteria: ii, iv Inscribed 2003

• GEBEL BARKAL AND THE SITES OF THE NAPATAN REGION Sudan

Gebel Barkal and the other sites are a reminder of the Napatan, Meroïtic and Kushite civilizations that existed along the Nile between 900 BC and AD 600. The Amun temple at Gebel Barkal is a centre of what was once an almost universal religion. Tombs, with and without pyramids, temples, living complexes and palaces, are spread throughout the 60 km site. Many of the temples, still considered sacred, are beautifully decorated and have carved hieroglyphic inscriptions. There are thirty explored tombs, accessible by stairs, but vast areas still await excavation.
Criteria: i, ii, iii, iv, vi Inscribed 2003

• ASHUR (QAL'AT SHERQAT) Iraq

The ancient city of Ashur is located on the Tigris River in northern Mesopotamia, at the borderline between rain-fed and irrigation agriculture. The city dates back to the third millennium BC. From the fourteenth to the ninth centuries BC it was the first capital of the Assyrian Empire, a city-state and trading centre of international importance. It also served as the religious capital of the Assyrians, associated with the god Ashur. The city was destroyed by the Babylonians, but revived during the Parthian period in the first and second centuries AD.
Criteria: iii, iv Inscribed 2003

• QUEBRADA DE HUMAHUACA Argentina

Quebrada de Humahuaca follows a major cultural route, the Camino Inca, along the valley of the Rio Grande, from its source in the cold High Andean desert plateau to its confluence with the Rio Leone some 150 km to the south. The valley shows signs of its use as a trade route over the past 10,000 years, with the scattered remains of successive settlements featuring visible traces of prehistoric hunter-gatherer communities, of the Inca Empire (fifteenth–sixteenth centuries) and of the fight for independence in the sixteenth and twentieth centuries.
Criteria: ii, iv, v Inscribed 2003

• RENAISSANCE MONUMENTAL ENSEMBLES OF ÚBEDA AND BAEZA Spain

The contrasting character of these two small towns, located 10 km apart between the regions of Castile and Andalusia, is reflected in the urban fabric, Arabic and Andalusian in origin, along with more northern influences. Both towns prospered for a time in the sixteenth century and have survived until the present day. The urban functions of the towns are distributed so that Baeza's public, ecclesiastic and educational buildings complement Úbeda's aristocratic and palace buildings to form a Renaissance urban scheme of high architectural quality.
Criteria: ii, iv Inscribed 2003

• ROCK SHELTERS OF BHIMBETKA India

The Rock Shelters of Bhimbetka are in the foothills of the Vindhyan Mountains on the southern edge of the central Indian plateau. Within massive sandstone outcrops, above comparatively dense forest, are five clusters of natural rock shelters, displaying paintings that appear to date from the Mesolithic Period right through to the historical period. The cultural traditions of the inhabitants of the twenty-one villages adjacent to the site bear a strong resemblance to those represented in the rock paintings.
Criteria: iii, v Inscribed 2003

• CITADEL, ANCIENT CITY AND FORTRESS BUILDINGS OF DERBENT Russian Federation

The location of the ancient city of Derbent forms a natural pass – the Caspian Gates. The city was crucial for the control of this north–south passage on the western side of the Caspian Sea from the first millennium BC until the nineteenth century. The fifth century AD Sassanian defences were used by the Persian, Arabic, Mongol and Timurid governments for some fifteen centuries. The Defence Walls extend some 3.6 km from the Caspian Sea up to the citadel on the mountain, with two parallel walls 300–400 m apart. The city was built between them.
Criteria: iii, iv Inscribed 2003

• JAMES ISLAND AND RELATED SITES The Gambia

There are seven separate sites, all of which were directly associated with the slave trade: James Island, including the fort and slave house, the remains of a Portuguese chapel and a colonial warehouse in the village of Albreda, the Maurel Frères Building in the village of Juffureh, the remains of the small Portuguese settlement of San Domingo, as well as Fort Bullen and the Six-Gun Battery. The river formed the first trade route into the interior of Africa and became an early corridor for the slave trade.
Criteria: iii, vi Inscribed 2003

• FRANCISCAN MISSIONS IN THE SIERRA GORDA OF QUERÉTARO Mexico

The five Franciscan missions of Sierra Gorda were built during the last phase of the conversion to Christianity of the interior of Mexico in the mid-eighteenth century and became an important reference for the continuation of the evangelisation of California, Arizona and Texas. The architecture of the missions follows a similar pattern and generally includes an atrium, sacramental doorway, church with processional chapels and a cloister. The richly decorated church façades were the joint creative efforts of the missionaries and the native Indios. The settlements around the missions retain their vernacular character.
Criteria: ii, iii Inscribed 2003

• HISTORIC QUARTER OF THE SEAPORT CITY OF VALPARAÍSO Chile

Valparaíso consists of a bay, a narrow coastal plain and a series of hills. To ease movement up and down these hillsides, there used to be around thirty elevators. In this natural amphitheatre-like setting, the city is characterized by a vernacular urban fabric adapted to the hillsides that are dotted with a great variety of church spires. The architecture of La Matríz Church (1842), Valparaíso's founding church, although rebuilt four times after destruction by pirates and earthquakes, is typical of the transition between colonial and republican styles.
Criteria: iii Inscribed 2003

• MONTE SAN GIORGIO Switzerland

The pyramid-shaped, wooded mountain 1,096 m above sea level, to the south of Lake Lugano in Canton Ticino, has given the best and richest fossil record of marine life from the Triassic Period, 245–230 million years ago. The sequence records life in a tropical lagoon environment, sheltered and partially separated from the open sea by an offshore reef. Diverse marine life flourished within this lagoon, including reptiles, fish, bivalves, ammonites, echinoderms and crustaceans. As the lagoon was near land, some land-based fossils including reptiles, insects and plants have also been found.
Criteria: viii Inscribed 2003

• JEWISH QUARTER AND ST PROCOPIUS' BASILICA IN TŘEBÍČ Czech Republic

The grouping of the Jewish Quarter, old Jewish cemetery and Basilica of St Procopius in Třebíč, is a reminder of the co-existence of Jewish and Christian cultures from the Middle Ages until all the Jewish residents were deported during the Second World War. The area has synagogues and schools and a leather factory. St Procopius' Basilica, built in the thirteenth century as a monastic church, is a mixture of Romanesque and early Gothic styles and is an example of the influence of western European architectural heritage in this region.
Criteria: ii, iii Inscribed 2003

• MAUSOLEUM OF KHOJA AHMED YASAWI Kazakhstan

The Mausoleum of Khoja Ahmed Yasawi, a distinguished twelfth century Sufi master, is situated in the city of Turkestan (Yasi) in southern Kazakhstan. It was built at the time of Timur (Tamerlane), from 1389 to 1405. Persian master builders experimented with techniques later used in the construction of Samarkand. Today it is one of the largest and best-preserved constructions of the Timurid period. The Mausoleum's Main Hall has a conic-spherical dome, the largest in central Asia) and a mosque, where fragments of the original wall paintings are preserved.
Criteria: i, iii, iv Inscribed 2003

• WOODEN CHURCHES OF SOUTHERN LITTLE POLAND Poland

The wooden churches of southern Little Poland were built using the horizontal log technique common in eastern and northern Europe since the Middle Ages, making them different from stone churches. Churches have been particularly significant in Polish wooden architecture, and an essential element of settlement structures, both as landmarks and as ideological symbols. They were an outward sign of the cultural identity of communities, reflecting the artistic and social aspirations of their patrons and creators. The six sites in southern Little Poland represent different aspects of these developments.
Criteria: iii, iv Inscribed 2003

▪ PHONG NHA-KE BANG NATIONAL PARK
Vietnam

The karst formation of the park has evolved since the Palaeozoic era, some 400 million years ago. This vast area has 65 km of caves and underground rivers. The Phong Nha Cave, the most famous, has a currently surveyed length of 44.5 km. Its entrance is part of an underground river and tour boats can venture 1,500 m inside. Other extensive caves include the Vom cave and the Hang Khe Rhy cave. Most of the park is covered by tropical forest and is home to a rich variety of fauna.

Criteria: viii Inscribed 2003

▪ ILULISSAT ICEFJORD Greenland (Denmark)
Located on the west coast of Greenland, 250 km north of the Arctic Circle, Ilulissat Icefjord is the sea mouth of Sermeq Kujalleq, one of the few glaciers through which the Greenland icecap reaches the sea. Sermeq Kujalleq is one of the fastest moving (19 m per day) and most active glaciers in the world. Studied for over 250 years, it has helped to develop our understanding of climate change and icecap glaciology. The dramatic sight and sounds of a fast-moving glacial ice-stream calving into a fjord makes an awe-inspiring natural phenomenon.

Criteria: vii, viii Inscribed 2004

▪ LIVERPOOL – MARITIME MERCANTILE CITY
United Kingdom

Liverpool developed as of one of the world's major trading centres in the eighteenth and nineteenth centuries, assisted by its involvement in the slave trade. It played an important role in the growth of the British Empire and became the major port for the mass movement of people, e.g. emigrants from northern Europe to America, and for the import of raw materials and the export of manufactured goods around the world. The site stretches along the waterfront from Albert Dock to Pier Head and Stanley Dock and includes the city centre.

Criteria: ii, iii, iv Inscribed 2004

▪ ÞINGVELLIR NATIONAL PARK Iceland
Þingvellir (Thingvellir) is the National Park where the Althing, an open-air assembly which represented the whole of Iceland, was established in 930 and continued to meet until 1798. Over two weeks a year, the assembly set laws – seen as a covenant between free men – and settled disputes. The Althing has deep historical and symbolic associations for the people of Iceland and fragments of around fifty booths built from turf and stone remain here. The park also shows how the landscape has been husbanded over the last 1,000 years.

Criteria: iii, vi Inscribed 2004

▪ BAM AND ITS CULTURAL LANDSCAPE
Islamic Republic of Iran

Bam is situated in a desert environment on the southern edge of the Iranian high plateau. Its heyday was from the seventh to eleventh centuries, being at the crossroads of important trade routes and known for the production of silk and cotton garments. The existence of life in the oasis was based on the underground irrigation canals, the *qanāts*. Arg-e Bam is the most representative example of a fortified medieval town built in a vernacular technique using mud layers (*Chineh*).

Criteria: ii, iii, iv, v Inscribed 2004

▪ TROPICAL RAINFOREST HERITAGE OF SUMATRA Indonesia
The 25,000 km² Tropical Rainforest Heritage of Sumatra comprises three widely-separated national parks along the Bukit Barisan mountain range: Gunung Leuser National Park, Kerinci Seblat National Park and Bukit Barisan Selatan National Park. The site holds great potential for long-term conservation of the distinctive biodiversity of Sumatra, including many endangered species. The protected area is home to an estimated 10,000 plant species; more than 200 mammal species including the endemic Sumatran orang-utan; and some 580 bird species. The site also provides biogeographic evidence of the evolution of the island.

Criteria: vii, ix, x Inscribed 2004

The Church of St Philip and St James the Apostles (Sekowa), one of the Wooden Churches of Southern Little Poland.

Stalactites and pillar formations in Phong Nha-Ke Bang National Park.

• PITONS MANAGEMENT AREA Saint Lucia

Dominating the mountainous landscape of St Lucia are the Pitons, two steep-sided volcanic spires rising side by side from the sea. Gros Piton (770 m) is 3 km in diameter at its base, and Petit Piton (743 m) is 1 km in diameter and linked to the former by the Piton Mitan ridge. The coral reefs, which cover almost 60 per cent of the area, are healthy and diverse. Agriculture, artisan fishing, human settlement (1,500 residents) and tourism (four large hotel developments) share the coastal strip.
Criteria: vii, viii Inscribed 2004

• COMPLEX OF KOGURYO TOMBS Korea, Democratic People's Republic of

This site includes several group and individual tombs – totalling about thirty – from the later period of the Koguryo Kingdom, one of the strongest kingdoms in northeast China and the northern half of the Korean peninsula between the third century BC and seventh century AD. The tombs, many with beautiful wall paintings, are almost the only remains of this culture. They are thought to have been made for the burial of kings, members of the royal family and the aristocracy. These paintings offer a unique testimony to daily life of this period.
Criteria: i, ii, iii, iv Inscribed 2004

• UM ER-RASAS (KASTROM MEFA'A) Jordan

Um er-Rasas started as a Roman military camp and grew to become a town from the fifth century onwards. It contains remains from the Roman, Byzantine and early Muslim periods, the end of the third to ninth centuries AD. The site also has sixteen churches. The mosaic floor of the church of St Stephen shows an incredible representation of towns in Palestine, Jordan and Egypt. Two square towers are probably remains of the practice of the stylites (ascetic monks who spent time in isolation atop a column or tower).
Criteria: i, iv, vi Inscribed 2004

• KERNAVĖ ARCHAEOLOGICAL SITE (CULTURAL RESERVE OF KERNAVĖ) Lithuania

This site, about 35 km northwest of Vilnius, includes the town of Kernavė, hill forts, some unfortified settlements and burial sites from the late Palaeolithic Period to the Middle Ages. The site has preserved the traces of ancient land-use, as well as remains of five impressive hill forts. Kernavė was an important feudal town in the Middle Ages until it was destroyed by the Teutonic Order in the late fourteenth century. Its burial ground was situated in the Kriveikiókis hill fort. Funeral customs reflect the traditions of the last pagan state in Europe.
Criteria: iii, iv Inscribed 2004

• VEGAØYAN – THE VEGA ARCHIPELAGO Norway

A cluster of dozens of islands centred on Vega, just south of the Arctic Circle, bear testimony to a distinctive frugal way of life based on fishing and the harvesting of the down of eider ducks, in an inhospitable environment. There are fishing villages, quays, warehouses, eider houses built for eider ducks to nest in, farms, lighthouses and beacons. There is evidence of human settlement from the Stone Age onwards. By the ninth century, the islands had become an important centre for the supply of down.
Criteria: v Inscribed 2004

• PASARGADAE Islamic Republic of Iran

Pasargadae was the first dynastic capital of the Achaemenid Empire, founded by Cyrus the Great in the sixth century BC. Its palaces, gardens and the mausoleum of Cyrus are outstanding examples of the first phase of royal Achaemenid art and architecture. Particularly noteworthy remains include: the Mausoleum of Cyrus the Great; Tall-e Takht, a fortified terrace; and a gatehouse, audience hall and royal palace, originally located within a formal garden (the so-called 'Four Gardens'). Pasargadae was the capital of the first great multicultural empire in western Asia.
Criteria: i, ii, iii, iv Inscribed 2004

Petit Piton, St Lucia. At least 148 plant species have been recorded on Gros Piton and 97 on Petit Piton. Among these are several endemic or rare plants, including eight rare species of tree.

The southern area of Um er-Rasas.

The Mausoleum of Cyrus the Great at Pasargadae was built from white limestone around 540–530 BC. In the medieval period, it was thought to be the tomb of Solomon's mother, and a mosque was built around it.

• ROYAL EXHIBITION BUILDING AND CARLTON GARDENS Australia

The Royal Exhibition Building, in its original setting of the Carlton Gardens, is the only substantially intact example of a Great Hall from a major international exhibition. The building and gardens were designed for the great exhibitions of 1880 and 1888 in Melbourne. The building is constructed of brick and timber, steel and slate. It is typical of these buildings, which showcased technological innovation, and boasts many features that made the expositions so dramatic, including a dome, a great hall, giant entry portals and formal gardens.
Criteria: ii Inscribed 2004

• NATURAL SYSTEM OF WRANGEL ISLAND RESERVE Russian Federation

Located well above the Arctic Circle, the site includes the mountainous Rangel Island, Herald Island and surrounding waters. Wrangel was not glaciated during the Quaternary Ice Age, resulting in exceptionally high levels of biodiversity for this region. The island boasts the world's largest population of Pacific walrus and the highest density of ancestral polar bear dens. It is a major feeding ground for the grey whale migrating from Mexico and the northernmost nesting ground for 100 migratory bird species, many endangered.
Criteria: ix, x Inscribed 2004

• PORTUGUESE CITY OF MAZAGAN (EL JADIDA) Morocco

Mazagan was an early settlements of Portuguese explorers on the route to India. Now part of the city of El Jadida, 90 km southwest of Casablanca, Mazagan was built as a fortified colony in the early sixteenth century. It was taken over by the Moroccans in 1769. The fortification, with its bastions and ramparts, is an early example of Renaissance military design. The surviving Portuguese buildings include the cistern and the Church of the Assumption. The minaret of the nineteenth-century mosque is an adaptation of the old Torre de Rebate.
Criteria: ii, iv Inscribed 2004

• MEDIEVAL MONUMENTS IN KOSOVO Serbia

These four churches represent the appearance of the new so-called Palaiologian Renaissance style, combining eastern Orthodox Byzantine and the western Romanesque traditions, which influenced subsequent Balkan art. The Dečani Monastery built in the mid-fourteenth century for the Serbian king Stefan Dečanski is also his mausoleum. The Patriarchate of Peč Monastery is a group of four domed churches. The thirteenth-century frescoes of the Church of Holy Apostles at Gračanica are painted in a unique, monumental style, while there are early fourteenth-century frescoes in the Church of the Holy Virgin of Ljevisa.
Criteria: ii, iii, iv Inscribed 2004

• CAPE FLORAL REGION PROTECTED AREAS South Africa

Eight protected areas make up the Cape Floral Region, one of the richest areas for plants in the world. It represents less than 0.5 per cent of the area of Africa but is home to nearly 20 per cent of the continent's flora. The site displays ecological and biological processes associated with the *fynbos* (fine bush) vegetation which is unique to the Cape Floral Region. The diversity, density and endemism of the flora are among the highest anywhere in the world. Unique plant-reproductive strategies adaptive to fire, patterns of seed dispersal by insects and patterns of endemism and adaptive radiation found in the flora, are of great value to science.
Criteria: ix, x Inscribed 2004

• ORKHON VALLEY CULTURAL LANDSCAPE Mongolia

The Orkhon Valley Cultural Landscape encompasses an extensive area of pastureland on both banks of the Orkhon River and includes numerous archaeological remains dating back to the sixth century. The site also includes Kharkhorum, the thirteenth- and fourteenth-century capital of Chingis (Genghis) Khan's vast empire. Collectively the remains in the site reflect the links between nomadic, pastoral

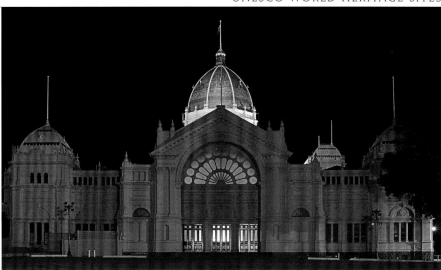

Unlike the structures at many international exhibitions, the Royal Exhibition Building was conceived as a permanent construction that would have a future role in the cultural activities of Melbourne.

Fynbos, Afrikaans for 'fine bush' is the natural, primarily evergreen, shrubland vegetation of the Cape Floral region, a great part of which is rugged mountain passes, rivers, rapids, cascades and pools.

societies and their administrative and religious centres, and the importance of the Orkhon valley in the history of central Asia. The grassland is still grazed by Mongolian nomadic pastoralists.
Criteria: ii, iii, iv Inscribed 2004

• CHHATRAPATI SHIVAJI TERMINUS (FORMERLY VICTORIA TERMINUS) India

The Chhatrapati Shivaji Terminus, formerly known as Victoria Terminus Station, in Mumbai (Bombay), is an outstanding example of Victorian Gothic Revival architecture in India. British architects worked closely with Indian craftsmen on the building to include local architectural traditions. The resulting structure, with its remarkable stone dome, turrets, pointed arches and eccentric ground plan is close to traditional Indian palace architecture, making it an outstanding example of the meeting of two cultures. The building soon came to symbolise Bombay as the 'Gothic City' and major international mercantile port of India.
Criteria: ii, iv Inscribed 2004

• MUSKAUER PARK / PARK MUZAKOWSKI Germany and Poland

A landscaped park astride the Neisse River and the border between Poland and Germany, Muskauer Park was created by Prince Hermann von Pückler-Muskau from 1815 to 1844. The park pioneered new and influential approaches to landscape design. It did not seek to evoke classical landscapes, paradise, or some lost perfection, instead it used local plants to enhance the inherent qualities of the existing landscape. This integrated landscape extends into the town of Muskau with green passages that formed urban parks framing areas for development. The site also features a reconstructed castle, bridges and an arboretum.
Criteria: i, iv Inscribed 2004

• LUIS BARRAGÁN HOUSE AND STUDIO Mexico

Built in 1948, the House and Studio of architect Luis Barragán in the suburbs of Mexico City represents an outstanding example of the architect's creative work in the post-Second World War period. The concrete building, consists of three storeys, as well as a small private garden. Barragán's work integrated modern and traditional artistic and vernacular elements into a new synthesis, which has been greatly influential, especially in the contemporary design of gardens, plazas and landscapes.
Criteria: i, ii Inscribed 2004

• CAPITAL CITIES AND TOMBS OF THE ANCIENT KOGURYO KINGDOM China

The site bears testimony to the vanished Koguryo civilisation that ruled over parts of northern China and the northern half of the Korean Peninsula from the third century BC to the seventh century AD. Wunu Mountain City, Guonei City and Wandu Mountain City are early examples of mountain capital cities and were later imitated by neighbouring cultures. Wandu Mountain City contains many remains including a large palace and thirty-seven tombs. Some of the tombs have elaborate ceilings, which roof wide spaces without columns and support a heavy covering.
Criteria: i, ii, iii, iv, v Inscribed 2004

• VAL D'ORCIA Italy

Val d'Orcia is 25 km from Siena's centre and was, in effect, colonised by the city's merchants in the fourteenth and fifteenth centuries in the Renaissance. They aimed to create an area of efficient agricultural units that was also pleasing to the eye. The carefully planned landscape that resulted led to the beginning of the concept of 'landscape' as a man-made creation. The images of fortified settlements on conical hills rising out of flat chalk plains or of farmhouses and avenues of trees bordering roads have inspired artists.
Criteria: iv, vi Inscribed 2004

• VARBERG RADIO STATION Sweden

The Varberg Radio Station at Grimeton in southern Sweden built 1922–24 is an exceptionally well-preserved monument to early

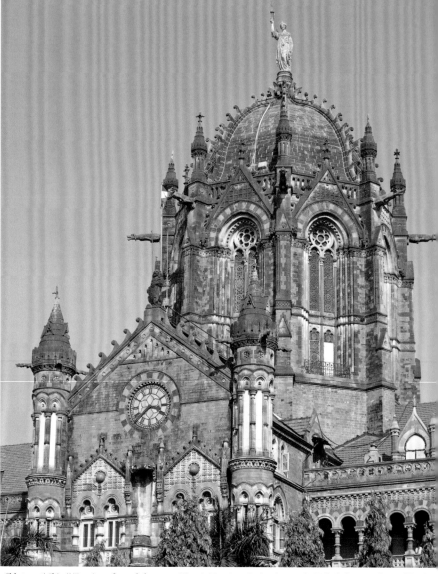

Chhatrapati Shivaji Terminus, formerly known as Victoria Terminus Station, in Mumbai is built from a judicious blend of Indian sandstone and limestone, while Italian marble was used for the key decorative elements.

Val d'Orcia is an exceptional reflection of the way the landscape was rewritten in Renaissance times.

wireless transatlantic communication. It consists of the transmitter equipment, including the aerial system of six 127-m-high steel towers. The architect Carl Åkerblad designed the main buildings in neoclassical style and the structural engineer Henrik Kreüger was responsible for the antenna towers, the tallest built structures in Sweden at that time. The site is the only surviving example of a major transmitting station based on pre-electronic technology.
Criteria: ii, iv Inscribed 2004

• TOWN HALL AND ROLAND ON THE MARKETPLACE OF BREMEN Germany

The medieval town of Bremen was oblong, limited by the river Weser on the south side and by the moat of the ancient defence system on the north side. The Town Hall and Roland statue represent civic autonomy and market freedom, as developed in the Holy Roman Empire. The old Town Hall was built in the Gothic style in the early fifteenth century, after Bremen joined the Hanseatic League. The building was expertly renovated in the Weser Renaissance style in the early seventeenth century.
Criteria: iii, iv, vi Inscribed 2004

• TOMB OF ASKIA Mali

The dramatic 17-m pyramidal structure of the Tomb of Askia was built by Askia Mohamed, the Emperor of Songhai, in 1495 in his capital Gao. It bears testimony to the power and wealth of the empire that flourished in the fifteenth and sixteenth centuries through its control of the trans-Saharan trade, notably in salt and gold. It is also a fine example of the monumental mud-building traditions of the Sahel.
Criteria: ii, iii, iv Inscribed 2004

• ENSEMBLE OF THE NOVODEVICHY CONVENT Russian Federation

The Novodevichy Convent is an exceptionally well-preserved monastic complex in southwest Moscow, built in seventeenth-century Moscow Baroque style, with rich interiors and an important collection of paintings and artefacts. Enclosed by a high masonry wall with twelve towers and surrounded by a park, the convent formed part of a chain of monastic ensembles that were integrated into the defence system of the city. It was used by women of the Tsar's family and the aristocracy, and members of the Tsar's family and entourage were buried in its cemetery.
Criteria: i, iv, vi Inscribed 2004

• KOUTAMMAKOU, THE LAND OF THE BATAMMARIBA Togo

The Koutammakou landscape in northeastern Togo, which extends into neighbouring Benin, is home to the Batammariba whose remarkable mud tower-houses, *Takienta*, have become a symbol of Togo. They are a reflection of social structure; its farmland and forest; and the associations between people and landscape. Many are two-storeys high and those with granaries feature an almost spherical form above a cylindrical base. Some have flat roofs, others have conical thatched roofs. They are grouped in villages, which also include ceremonial spaces, springs and sites reserved for initiation ceremonies.
Criteria: v, vi Inscribed 2004

• CHAMPANER-PAVAGADH ARCHAEOLOGICAL PARK India

The Champaner-Pavagadh Archaeological Park represents a blend of Hindu and Muslim architecture, and is the only complete and unchanged Islamic pre-Mughal city. The Great Mosque (Jami Masjid) was a model for later mosque architecture in India, and the site also includes fortifications, palaces, religious buildings, residential areas and water installations, from the eighth to the fourteenth centuries. Some houses had running water and many of the gardens and pavilions were decorated with water channels. The Kalikamata Temple on top of Pavagadh Hill is an important shrine, attracting large numbers of pilgrims.
Criteria: iii, iv, v, vi Inscribed 2004

The stone statue of Roland (a legendary figure in medieval Europe) is about 5.5 m tall, and was initially erected in 1404. It symbolises the rights and privileges of the free and imperial city of Bremen.

The Novodevichy Convent was founded by Grand Duke Vasily III in 1524 to mark the liberation of Smolensk in 1514. These buildings date from the late seventeenth century.

Ruins of one of the mosques at Champaner-Pavagadh Archaeological Park.

• LANDSCAPE OF THE PICO ISLAND VINEYARD CULTURE Portugal

The landscape of Pico in the Azores reflects a unique response to viticulture on a small volcanic island. The extraordinarily beautiful man-made landscape of small, stone-walled fields is testimony to generations of farmers who, in a hostile environment, created a sustainable living and a much-prized wine. The walls were built to protect thousands of small, rectangular plots (*currais*) from wind and seawater. The resourcefulness and artistry of the inhabitants is also evident in the island's manor houses, wine-cellars, wells, churches and ports.
Criteria: iii, v Inscribed 2004

• MADRIU-PERAFITA-CLAROR VALLEY Andorra

The cultural landscape of Madriu-Perafita-Claror Valley illustrates the way people have harvested the resources of the high Pyrenees over millennia. Its glacial landscapes of craggy cliffs and glaciers, with high open pastures and steep wooded valleys is dramatic. It reflects changes in climate, economic fortune and social systems, as well as the persistence of pastoralism and a strong mountain culture, including the survival of a communal land-ownership system dating back to the thirteenth century. The site features houses, notably summer settlements, terraced fields, stone tracks and evidence of iron smelting.
Criteria: v Inscribed 2004

• SACRED SITES AND PILGRIMAGE ROUTES IN THE KII MOUNTAIN RANGE Japan

Set in the dense forests of the Kii Mountains, south of Osaka and overlooking the Pacific Ocean, these three sacred sites – Yoshino and Omine, Kumano Sanzan, Koyasan – linked by pilgrimage routes to the ancient capital cities of Nara and Kyoto, reflect the fusion of Shinto, rooted in the ancient tradition of nature worship in Japan, and Buddhism. The area, abundant with streams, rivers and waterfalls, is still part of the living culture of Japan and is much visited for ritual purposes. Some shrines were founded in the ninth century.
Criteria: ii, iii, iv, vi Inscribed 2004

• PETROGLYPHS WITHIN THE ARCHAEOLOGICAL LANDSCAPE OF TAMGALY Kazakhstan

Set around the lush Tamgaly Gorge, amidst the vast, arid Chu-Ili mountains, are some 5,000 petroglyphs (rock carvings) dating from the second millennium BC to the beginning of the twentieth century. The most exceptional engravings are the earliest and include solar deities and zoomorphic beings. There are many ancient tombs including stone enclosures and mounds (*kurgans*) of stone and earth. The central canyon contains the densest concentration of engravings and what are believed to be altars, suggesting that these places were used for sacrificial offerings.
Criteria: iii Inscribed 2004

• ETRUSCAN NECROPOLISES OF CERVETERI AND TARQUINIA Italy

The Etruscans developed the earliest urban civilisation in the northern Mediterranean. These two cemeteries date from the ninth to first centuries BC. Some tombs are monumental, cut in rock, many feature wall carvings and others have wall paintings of outstanding quality. The necropolis near Cerveteri contains thousands of tombs organised in a city-like plan, with streets and small squares, the only surviving evidence of Etruscan residential architecture. The necropolis of Tarquinia contains 6,000 graves cut in the rock, including 200 painted tombs, the earliest of which date from the seventh century BC.
Criteria: i, iii, iv Inscribed 2004

• ISLANDS AND PROTECTED AREAS OF THE GULF OF CALIFORNIA Mexico

The site comprises 244 islands, islets and coastal areas located in the Gulf of California in northwestern Mexico. Its striking natural beauty is characterized by rugged islands with high cliffs and sandy beaches. The diversity and abundance of the marine life and the high water

The stone-walled plots of vineyards (in the foreground) on Pico Island. Pico is the second largest of the nine islands of the Azores and was uninhabited until the mid-fifteenth century.

A rock formation near Cabo San Lucas at the southern tip of the Baja California peninsula on the Gulf of California.

transparency make it a diver's paradise. It is home to 695 vascular plant species; 891 fish species, of which 90 are endemic; and 39 per cent of the world's total number of marine mammals species and a third of the world's marine cetacean species.

Criteria: vii, ix, x Inscribed 2005

▪ OLD BRIDGE AREA OF THE OLD CITY OF MOSTAR Bosnia-Herzegovina

The Old Bridge area of Mostar, with its medieval, Ottoman, Mediterranean and Western European architectural features, is an outstanding example of a multicultural urban settlement. Mostar has long been known for its old Turkish houses and Old Bridge, Stari Most. In the conflict of the 1990s, however, most of the historic town and the Old Bridge, designed by the renowned architect Sinan (1489–1588), was destroyed. The Old Bridge was recently rebuilt and many buildings in the Old Town have been restored or rebuilt with the contribution of an international scientific committee established by UNESCO.

Criteria: vi Inscribed 2005

▪ HISTORIC CENTRES OF BERAT AND GJIROKASTRA Albania

The historic towns of Gjirokastra and Berat, in the Drinos River valley in southern Albania, are towns typical of the Ottoman period. The thirteenth-century citadel of Gjirokastra provides the focal point of the town with its typical tower houses (*kule*). The *kule* has a tall basement, a first floor for use in the cold season, and a second floor for the warm season. The town also retains a bazaar. Berat has a thirteenth-century castle, and its citadel area contains many thirteenth-century Byzantine churches and several mosques of the Ottoman era.

Criteria: iii, iv Inscribed 2005

▪ ARCHITECTURAL, RESIDENTIAL AND CULTURAL COMPLEX OF THE RADZIWILL FAMILY AT NESVIZH Belarus

The Radziwill family came to Nesvizh in central Belarus in the sixteenth century. The ten interconnected buildings of their castle include the palace, the galleries, the residence and the arsenal, all of which are set within the remains of medieval fortifications. The castle is connected via a dam to the Church of Corpus Christi, completed in 1603 as their mausoleum. It was the first Baroque building in Eastern Europe. Due to the efforts of the Radziwills, the town of Nesvizh came to exercise great influence in the sciences, arts, crafts and architecture.

Criteria: ii, iv, vi Inscribed 2005

▪ HISTORIC CENTRE OF MACAO China

Macao, a historic trading port on the Pearl river estuary was under Portuguese administration from the mid-sixteenth century until 1999, when it came under Chinese sovereignty. The central area of the historic settlement of Macao includes a series of urban spaces and buildings that reflect the integration of Portuguese and Chinese elements. The Rua Direita leads from the ancient Chinese harbour in the south to the old Christian city in the north. The Guia Fortress, located on the Guia Hill incorporates Guia Chapel (1622) and Guia Lighthouse (1885).

Criteria: ii, iii, iv, vi Inscribed 2005

▪ LE HAVRE, THE CITY REBUILT BY AUGUSTE PERRET France

The city of Le Havre, on the English Channel in Normandy, was severely bombed during the Second World War. The destroyed area was rebuilt from 1945 to 1964, according to the plan of a team headed by Auguste Perret. Le Havre's reconstruction combines the earlier pattern of the town and its extant historic structures with the new ideas of town planning and construction technology. It is an outstanding post-war example of urban planning and architecture based on the unity of methodology and the use of prefabrication, the systematic utilization of a modular grid, and the innovative exploitation of the potential of concrete.

Criteria: ii, iv Inscribed 2005

The Old Bridge and Old City of Mostar, reconstructed after conflict in 1990, is a symbol of reconciliation, international co-operation and of the coexistence of diverse cultural, ethnic and religious communities.

Leal Senado Square is the main public square in Macao. Further north is St Dominic's Square with St Dominic's Church (founded in 1587), the old Chinese bazaar area and the Sam Kai Vui Kun Temple.

• BIBLICAL TELS – MEGIDDO, HAZOR, BEER SHEBA Israel

Tels (prehistoric settlement mounds) are characteristic of the flatter lands of the eastern Mediterranean. Of more than 200 tels in Israel, Megiddo, Hazor and Beer Sheba are representative of those that contain substantial remains of cities with biblical connections. The three tels also preserve the remains of their impressive underground water catchment systems, which reflect sophisticated engineering solutions to water storage. Beer Sheba was a planned city, rather than one that evolved, divided into three blocks, encircled by a wall and gate to the south.
Criteria: ii, iii, iv, vi Inscribed 2005

• WADI AL-HITAN (WHALE VALLEY) Egypt

Wadi Al-Hitan, Whale Valley, in the Western Desert of Egypt, contains invaluable fossil remains of the earliest, and now extinct, suborder of whales, *archaeoceti*. These fossils represent one of the major stories of evolution: the emergence of the whale as an ocean-going mammal from a previous life as a land-based animal. The fossils of Al-Hitan show the youngest *archaeocetes*, in the last stages of losing their hind limbs. Other fossil material in the site makes it possible to reconstruct the surrounding environmental and ecological conditions of the time.
Criteria: viii Inscribed 2005

• COIBA NATIONAL PARK AND ITS SPECIAL ZONE OF MARINE PROTECTION Panama

Coiba National Park, off the southwest coast of Panama, contains Coiba Island, thirty-eight smaller islands and marine areas within the Gulf of Chiriqui. Protected from the cold winds of El Niño, Coiba's Pacific tropical forest maintains exceptionally high levels of endemism of mammals, birds and plants due to the ongoing evolution of new species. It is also the last refuge for a number of threatened species such as the crested eagle. The site provides a key ecological link to the tropical eastern Pacific for the transit and survival of fish and marine mammals.
Criteria: ix, x Inscribed 2005

• DONG PHAYAYEN–KHAO YAI FOREST COMPLEX Thailand

The Dong Phayayen–Khao Yai Forest Complex spans 230 km between Ta Phraya National Park on the Cambodian border in the east, and Khao Yai National Park in the west. The forest is a rugged mountainous area that is home to globally endangered species including tiger, elephant, leopard cat, banteng and two species of gibbon. The area contains important tropical forest ecosystems, which provide a viable habitat for the long-term survival of these species. It also plays an important role in the conservation of migratory birds, including the spot-billed pelican and greater adjutant.
Criteria: x Inscribed 2005

• OSUN-OSOGBO SACRED GROVE Nigeria

The dense forest of the Osun Sacred Grove is one of the last remnants of primary high forest in southern Nigeria. Regarded as the abode of the goddess of fertility Osun, one of the pantheon of Yoruba gods, the landscape of the grove and its meandering river is dotted with sanctuaries and shrines, sculptures and art works in honour of Osun and other deities. The sacred grove, a symbol of identity for all Yoruba people, is probably the last in Yoruba culture. It testifies to the once widespread practice of establishing sacred groves outside all settlements.
Criteria: ii, iii, vi Inscribed 2005

• HUMBERSTONE AND SANTA LAURA SALTPETRE WORKS Chile

Humberstone and Santa Laura contain over 200 former saltpetre works where workers from Chile, Peru and Bolivia lived in company towns and forged a distinctive communal *pampinos* culture. That culture is manifest in their rich language, creativity and, above all, in their pioneering struggle for social justice, which had a profound impact on social history. Situated in the remote Chilean Altiplano (high plains), near one of the driest deserts on Earth, the Atacama, thousands of *pampinos* lived and worked in this hostile environment for over sixty years, from 1880, to process the largest deposit of saltpetre in the world.
Criteria: ii, iii, iv Inscribed 2005

• PLANTIN-MORETUS HOUSE-WORKSHOPS-MUSEUM COMPLEX Belgium

The Plantin-Moretus Museum is a printing plant and publishing house dating from the Renaissance and Baroque periods. Situated in Antwerp, it is associated with the history of the invention and spread of typography. Its name refers to the greatest printer-publisher of the second half of the sixteenth century: Christophe Plantin *c.* 1520–89. It contains exhaustive evidence of the life and work of what was the most prolific printing and publishing house in Europe in the late sixteenth century. The company remained active until 1867.
Criteria: ii, iii, iv, vi Inscribed 2005

• SOLTANIYEH Islamic Republic of Iran

The mausoleum of Oljaytu was constructed in 1302–12 in the city of Soltaniyeh, the capital of the Ilkhanid dynasty, which was founded by the Mongols. Situated in the province of Zanjān, Soltaniyeh is one of the outstanding examples of the achievements of Persian architecture and a key monument in the development of its Islamic architecture. The octagonal building is crowned with a 50-m tall dome covered in turquoise-blue faïence and surrounded by eight slender minarets. The mausoleum's interior decoration is also outstanding and has been described as 'anticipating the Taj Mahal'.
Criteria: ii, iii, iv Inscribed 2005

• INCENSE ROUTE – DESERT CITIES IN THE NEGEV Israel

The four Nabatean towns of Haluza, Mamshit, Avdat and Shivta are on routes linking them to the Mediterranean end of the incense and spice routes. The trade in frankincense and myrrh from south Arabia to the Mediterranean flourished from the third century BC until the second century AD. The Romans used frankincense in enormous quantities as incense, medicine and cosmetics. The Nabateans grew rich on the profits of the spice trade, and the remains of their towns, forts, caravanserai and sophisticated agricultural systems demonstrate an outstanding response to a hostile environment.
Criteria: iii, v Inscribed 2005

• QAL'AT AL-BAHRAIN – ANCIENT HARBOUR AND CAPITAL OF DILMUN Bahrain

Qal'at al-Bahrain is a typical tel – an artificial mound created by many successive layers of human occupation. The strata of the 300–600 m tel testify to continuous human presence from about 2300 BC to the sixteenth century AD. About 25 per cent of the site has been excavated, revealing structures of different types: residential, public, commercial, religious and military. They testify to the importance of the site, a trading port, over the centuries. On the top of the 12 m mound there is the impressive Portuguese fort, which gave the whole site its name, *qal'a* (fort). The site was the capital of the Dilmun, one of the most important ancient civilizations of the region. It contains the richest remains inventoried of this civilization, which was hitherto only known from written Sumerian references.
Criteria: ii, iii, iv Inscribed 2005

• STRUVE GEODETIC ARC Belarus, Estonia, Finland, Latvia, Lithuania, Norway, Moldova, Russian Fed., Sweden and Ukraine

The Struve Arc is a chain of survey triangulations stretching from Hammerfest in Norway to the Black Sea over 2,820 km away. Thirty-four of the original station points, in ten countries, exist today. They are commemorated by different marks: a drilled hole in rock, an iron cross, cairns, or built obelisks. The survey, carried out between 1816 and 1855 by the astronomer Friedrich Georg Wilhelm Struve, was the first accurate measurement of a long segment of a meridian, helping to establish the exact size and shape of the world.
Criteria: ii, iii, vi Inscribed 2005

• VREDEFORT DOME South Africa

Vredefort Dome, 120 km southwest of Johannesburg, is part of a larger meteorite impact structure, or astrobleme. Dating back 2,023 million years, it is the oldest astrobleme yet found on Earth. With a radius of 190 km, it is also the largest and the most deeply eroded. Vredefort Dome bears witness to the world's greatest known single energy release event, which had devastating global effects including, according to some scientists, major evolutionary changes. It provides critical evidence for our understanding of the geological history and evolution of the Earth.
Criteria: viii Inscribed 2005

• SHIRETOKO Japan

Shiretoko Peninsula, on the northern island of Hokkaido, has a central spine of volcanoes and is one of Japan's most unspoiled areas. There is much interaction of marine and terrestrial ecosystems, influenced by the formation of seasonal sea ice at the lowest latitude in the northern hemisphere. The site is globally important for threatened seabirds and migratory birds, a number of salmonid species, for marine mammals including Steller's sea lion and some cetacean species, and for endemic species such as Blackiston's fish owl and the *Viola kitamiana* plant.
Criteria: ix, x Inscribed 2005

• URBAN HISTORIC CENTRE OF CIENFUEGOS Cuba

Cienfuegos was founded in 1819 on the Caribbean coast of southern-central Cuba, at the heart of the country's sugar cane, mango, tobacco and coffee region. Trading powered the city's growth, with wax production, as well as timber and sugar, becoming increasingly important in the nineteenth century. This historic town exhibits cultural and social influences based on the Spanish Enlightenment. It is also the first and finest example of the new ideas of modernity, hygiene and order in urban planning as developed in Latin America from the nineteenth century.
Criteria: ii, iv Inscribed 2005

• WEST NORWEGIAN FJORDS – GEIRANGERFJORD AND NÆRØYFJORD Norway

Geirangerfjord and Nærøyfjord, 120 km from one another, are part of the west Norwegian fjord landscape that stretches from Stavanger to Andalsnes, 500 km to the northeast. They are archetypical fjords and among the most scenically outstanding anywhere in the world. Their exceptional natural beauty is derived from their narrow and steep-sided crystalline rock walls that rise up to 1,400 m from the Norwegian Sea and extend 500 m below sea level. The sheer walls of the fjords have numerous waterfalls, while free-flowing rivers cross their deciduous and coniferous forests from glacial lakes, glaciers and rugged mountains.

Criteria: vii, viii Inscribed 2005

• HISTORICAL CENTRE OF THE CITY OF YAROSLAVL Russian Federation

Yaroslavl is renowned for its numerous seventeenth-century churches and is an outstanding example of urban planning reform. Situated at the confluence of the Volga and Kotorosl rivers some 250 km northeast of Moscow, the city developed into a major commercial centre from the eleventh century. The Spassky Monastery, one of the oldest in the Upper Volga region, was built on the site of a pagan temple in the late twelfth century but has been reconstructed over time. The city was renovated in neoclassical style in 1763 when Catherine the Great ordered town planning reform across Russia.

Criteria: ii, iv Inscribed 2005

• KUNYA-URGENCH Turkmenistan

Situated at the crossing of trade routes, Kunya-Urgench was the capital of Khorezm from the twelfth century and the second city after Bukhara in central Asia. The influence of the architecturally outstanding monuments of Kunya-Urgench extended as far as Mughal India. The site's three sections include a mosque, the gates of a caravanserai, fortresses, mausoleums and a 60-m high minaret; a large Muslim graveyard with a group of three mausoleums at its centre; part of the old town containing the monument of Ibn Khajib.

Criteria: ii, iii Inscribed 2005

• SYRACUSE AND THE ROCKY NECROPOLIS OF PANTALICA Italy

The site in southeastern Sicily consists of two parts. The Necropolis of Pantalica contains over 5,000 tombs cut into the rock, most of them dating from the thirteenth to seventh centuries BC, and the Byzantine foundations of the Anaktoron Prince's Palace. Ancient Syracuse, which Cicero described as 'the greatest Greek city and the most beautiful of all', includes the Temple of Athena, fifth century BC, later used as a cathedral, a Greek theatre, a Roman amphitheatre and a fort. Many remains bear witness to the troubled history of Sicily, from the Byzantines to the Bourbons.

Criteria: ii, iii, iv, vi Inscribed 2005

• SICHUAN GIANT PANDA SANCTUARIES – WOLONG, MT SIGUNIANG AND JIAJIN MOUNTAINS China

Sichuan Giant Panda Sanctuaries, home to more than 30 per cent of the world's pandas which are classed as highly endangered, covers 9,245 km² with seven nature reserves and nine scenic parks in the Qionglai and Jiajin Mountains. The sanctuaries constitute the largest remaining contiguous habitat of the giant panda. They are also home to other globally endangered animals such as the red panda, the snow leopard and clouded leopard. The sanctuaries are among the botanically richest sites of any region in the world outside the tropical rainforests, with between 5,000 and 6,000 species.

Criteria: x Inscribed 2006

• CENTENNIAL HALL IN WROCLAW Poland

The Centennial Hall in Wroclaw is a landmark in the history of reinforced-concrete architecture. It was erected in 1911–13 by the architect Max Berg as a multi-purpose recreational building with a vast circular central space that can seat some 6,000 persons. The dome is topped with a lantern in steel and glass. With a diameter of 65 m, it was at the time twice as large as any other dome: this stunning achievement was made possible by the new material (ferroconcrete) and Berg's innovative approach to structural design.

Criteria: i, ii, iv Inscribed 2006

Geirangerfjord. 'Fjord' is a word of Norwegian origin, meaning a glacially over-deepened valley, usually narrow and steep-sided and extending below sea level. Norway's fjords are among the most extensive on Earth.

Yaroslavl Kremlin Tower.

A young panda cub in the Sichuan Giant Panda Sanctuaries. In the wild the panda feeds almost exclusively on bamboo, and its preferred habitat is between altitudes of 2,200 m and 3,200 m.

• OLD TOWN OF REGENSBURG WITH STADTAMHOF Germany

Located on the Danube in Bavaria, this medieval trading centre contains many buildings of exceptional quality. Regensburg's eleventh- to thirteenth-century architecture – including the market, city hall and cathedral – defines the character of the town marked by tall buildings, narrow lanes and strong fortifications. The buildings include patrician houses, a large number of churches and monasteries as well as the twelfth-century Old Bridge. A particular feature are the towers built by patrician families. Similar to north Italian towers, they were built more for display than protection. The Goldene Turm (twelfth-century) is nearly 50 m high.
Criteria: ii, iii, iv Inscribed 2006

• HARAR JUGOL, THE FORTIFIED HISTORIC TOWN Ethiopia

The fortified historic town of Harar is located in eastern Ethiopia on a plateau with deep gorges surrounded by desert and savanna. The walls surrounding this sacred Muslim city were built between the thirteenth and sixteenth centuries. Harar Jugol, said to be the fourth holiest city of Islam, has eighty-two mosques, three of which date from the tenth century, and 102 shrines. The townhouses with their exceptional interior design constitute the most spectacular part of Harar's cultural heritage. Harar Jugol is the centre of an Islamic region within otherwise Christian Ethiopia.
Criteria: ii, iii, iv, v Inscribed 2006

• KONDOA ROCK-ART SITES Tanzania

On the eastern slopes of the Masai escarpment bordering the Great Rift Valley are natural rock shelters, whose vertical planes have been used for rock paintings for at least two millennia. The spectacular collection of images from over 150 shelters, many with high artistic value, displays images that show the changes from hunter-gatherer to agro-pastoralist, and the beliefs and ideas associated with the different societies. Some of the shelters have ritual associations for the people who live nearby, reflecting their beliefs, rituals and cosmological traditions.
Criteria: iii, vi Inscribed 2006

• GENOA: LE STRADE NUOVE AND THE SYSTEM OF THE PALAZZI DEI ROLLI Italy

The Strade Nuove and the system of the Palazzi dei Rolli in Genoa's historic centre date from the late sixteenth and early seventeenth centuries when the Republic of Genoa was at the height of its financial and seafaring power. The site represents the first example in Europe of an urban development project parcelled out by a public authority. The Palazzi dei Rolli are generally three- or four-storeys high with spectacular open staircases, courtyards and loggias overlooking gardens. Their owners' obligation to host state visits led to a widespread knowledge of this architectural model.
Criteria: ii, iv Inscribed 2006

• AGAVE LANDSCAPE AND ANCIENT INDUSTRIAL FACILITIES OF TEQUILA Mexico

Stretching between the Tequila Volcano foothills and the deep Rio Grande valley is a 347-km² landscape of blue agave. Cultivation of the plant, a staple since prehistoric times, has shaped the area, and the agave landscape and local architecture of *haciendas*, distilleries, factories and *tabernas* have stimulated Mexican national cultural identity. The area includes the settlements of Tequila, Arenal, and Amatitan together with working distilleries where the agave 'pineapple' is fermented and distilled into tequila. The Teuchitlan cultures (AD 200–900) grew rich on the monopoly of agave, which they used for many basic necessities.
Criteria: ii, iv, v, vi Inscribed 2006

• CORNWALL AND WEST DEVON MINING LANDSCAPE United Kingdom

The substantial remains of the copper- and tin-mining industries are a testimony to the contribution of Cornwall and West Devon to the Industrial Revolution in Britain. Much of the local landscape was

The Gothic west front of Regensburg Cathedral. The town has a rich history as one of the centres of the Holy Roman Empire that turned to Protestantism.

The Tequila area's poor soils and rough terrain are the ideal environment for growing the agave plant, used in numerous manufactures since prehistoric times. Agave culture is now seen as part of Mexican national identity.

transformed in the eighteenth and early nineteenth centuries as a result of the rapid growth of mining. The deep underground mines, engine houses, foundries, new towns and harbours, together with ancillary industries such as smelting, canals and railways, reflect the prolific innovation which led to the region producing two-thirds of the world's copper supply in the early nineteenth century.
Criteria: ii, iii, iv Inscribed 2006

▪ CHONGONI ROCK-ART AREA Malawi

Situated within forested granite hills, high up the plateau of central Malawi, the 127 sites of this area are the richest concentration of rock art in central Africa. They reflect the comparatively scarce tradition of farmer rock art, as well as paintings by BaTwa hunter-gatherers who inhabited the area from the late Stone Age. The Chewa agriculturalists practised rock painting until well into the twentieth century. The symbols in the rock art, which are strongly associated with women, have cultural relevance amongst the Chewa, and the sites are associated with ceremonies and rituals.
Criteria: iii, vi Inscribed 2006

▪ VIZCAYA BRIDGE Spain

Vizcaya Bridge (Bizkaiko Zubia in Basque) which straddles the mouth of the Ibaizabal estuary in the Basque Country, was the first 'transporter' bridge in the world, carrying people and traffic over the river on a suspended gondola without disrupting shipping on the river. It is among the outstanding architectural iron constructions of the Industrial Revolution. Its construction combined nineteenth-century ironworking traditions with then-innovative technology using lightweight twisted steel ropes. The bridge suffered bomb damage during the Spanish Civil War but has otherwise been in continuous operation since it opened in 1893.
Criteria: i, ii Inscribed 2006

▪ SEWELL MINING TOWN Chile

Situated 2,000 m up in the Andes, Sewell Mining Town was built in 1905 to house workers for a large underground copper mine, El Teniente. It is an outstanding example of a remote company town. It was built on land too steep for wheeled vehicles around a large central staircase rising from the railway station. Along its route were formal squares of irregular shape with ornamental trees and plants. The buildings lining the paths are of timber, often painted in vivid green, yellow, red and blue. At its peak, Sewell numbered 15,000 inhabitants, but was largely abandoned in the 1970s.
Criteria: ii Inscribed 2006

▪ CRAC DES CHEVALIERS AND QAL'AT SALAH EL-DIN Syrian Arab Republic

Still towering over the surrounding landscape, the magnificent Crac des Chevaliers (Fortress of the Knights) or Qala'at al-Hosn was built on the site of an existing fortification by the Order of St John of Jerusalem, who held it from 1142, turning it into the largest Crusader fortress in the Holy Land. It finally fell to a Mameluke siege in 1271. The Qal'at Salah El-Din (Fortress of Saladin) is partly in ruins but retains features from its tenth-century Byzantine construction, its reinforcement by the Crusaders in the twelfth century, and modifications after Saladin captured it in 1188.
Criteria: ii, iv Inscribed 2006

▪ AFLAJ IRRIGATION SYSTEMS OF OMAN Oman

The property includes five representative *aflaj* irrigation systems still in use in Oman. The origins of this system of irrigation may date back to AD 500, but archaeological evidence suggests that irrigation systems existed as early as 2500 BC. Using gravity, water is channelled from underground sources or springs to support agriculture and domestic use. Numerous watchtowers were built to defend the water systems, reflecting the dependence of communities on the *aflaj* system. Equitable sharing of a scarce resource to ensure sustainability remains the hallmark of this ancient irrigation system.
Criteria: v Inscribed 2006

Tonwanroath pumping engine house at Wheal Coates mine, St Agnes in Cornwall. The area was the heartland from which mining expertise and technology was exported around the world.

Vizcaya Bridge was designed by the noted Basque architect Alberto de Palacio, a student of Gustave Eiffel. The bridge structure is 45 m high and spans 160 m across the river.

Crac des Chevaliers, one of the greatest medieval castles in the world, guarded the route from Syria to the Holy Land and was one of a chain of Crusader castles commanding the eastern Mediterranean.

•STONE CIRCLES OF SENEGAMBIA
Gambia and Senegal

The site consists of four large groups of stone circles that represent an extraordinary concentration of over 1,000 monuments in a band 100 km wide along some 350 km of the river Gambia. The four groups, Sine Ngayène, Wanar, Wassu and Kerbatch, cover ninety-three stone circles and numerous tumuli, (burial mounds). The stones have been shaped into almost identical pillars, either cylindrical or polygonal in section, on average around 2 m in height and weighing up to 7 tonnes. Each circle contains between eight and fourteen pillars and has a diameter of 4 to 6 m.
Criteria: i, iii Inscribed 2006

•YIN XU China

The archaeological site of Yin Xu, close to the city of Anyang, 500 km south of Beijing, is an ancient capital of the late Shang Dynasty 1300–1046 BC. A number of royal tombs and palaces have been unearthed, more than eighty house foundations, and the Tomb of Fu Hao, the only intact tomb of a member of the Shang royal family. The superb craftsmanship of the burial accessories testify to the advanced level of Shang crafts industry. Inscriptions on oracle bones provide evidence for the development of one of the world's oldest writing systems.
Criteria: ii, iii, iv, vi Inscribed 2006

•AAPRAVASI GHAT Mauritius

In the Port Louis, is Aapravasi Ghat (the Immigration Depot) where the modern indentured labour diaspora began. In 1834, the British Government selected Mauritius to be the first site for what it called 'the great experiment' in the use of 'free' labour to replace slaves. Between 1834 and 1920, almost half a million indentured labourers arrived from India to work in the sugar plantations of Mauritius, or to be transferred elsewhere. The buildings of Aapravasi Ghat are among the earliest explicit manifestations of what was to become one of the greatest migrations in history.
Criteria: vi Inscribed 2006

•BISOTUN Islamic Republic of Iran

Bisotun is located along the ancient trade route linking the Iranian high plateau with Mesopotamia and features remains from prehistoric times onwards. The principal monument is the bas-relief on Mount Bisotun ordered by Darius I, The Great, when he rose to the throne of the Persian Empire in 521 BC. Roughly 15 m high and 25 m long it depicts Darius triumphant over a rival. Below and around are cuneiform inscriptions, in three languages – Elamite, Babylonian and Old Persian – detailing the king's battles.
Criteria: ii, iii Inscribed 2006

•MALPELO FAUNA AND FLORA SANCTUARY
Colombia

Located some 506 km off the coast of Colombia, the site includes Malpelo Island, whose rocky surface supports a sparse vegetation of ferns, lichen, mosses and algae, and the surrounding marine park. The largest no-fishing zone in the eastern tropical Pacific, it provides a habitat for internationally threatened marine species, and is a major source of nutrients. It is in particular a 'reservoir' for sharks, giant grouper and billfish. One of the top diving sites in the world, these deep waters support important populations of large predators and pelagic species in an undisturbed environment.
Criteria: vii, ix Inscribed 2006

•SYDNEY OPERA HOUSE Australia

Inaugurated in 1973, the Sydney Opera House is an amazing architectural work. In 1957, when the project of the Sydney Opera House was awarded by an international jury to Danish architect Jørn Utzon, it marked a radically new approach, given his original design concept and his unique approach to building. Ove Arup's engineering achievements helped make Utzon's vision a reality. It has three groups of interlocking vaulted 'shells' which roof two main performance halls and a restaurant. These shell-structures are set upon a vast platform and are surrounded by terrace areas.
Criteria: i Inscribed 2007

A stone circle at Wassu. Excavations of some tumuli in the site have revealed material that suggest dates between the third century BC and sixteenth century AD. *Stone Circles of Senegambia*

Sydney Opera House is a great urban sculpture set in a remarkable waterscape, at the tip of a peninsula projecting into Sydney Harbour. The building has had an enduring influence on architecture.

• RED FORT COMPLEX India

The Red Fort, completed in 1648, represents the zenith of Mughal creativity. The palace plan is based on standard Islamic designs but each pavilion displays architectural elements typical of Mughal building – a fusion of Persian, Timurid, Hindu and Islamic traditions. Emperor Shah Jahan established his capital at Shahjahanabad (now Old Delhi) and built the Red Fort Complex as his palace fort, enclosing it in ornate red sandstone walls that stretch for 2.5 km. The innovative planning, gardens and architectural style of the fort complex strongly influenced later work in Rajasthan, Delhi and Agra.
Criteria: ii, iii, vi Inscribed 2007

• IWAMI GINZAN SILVER MINE AND ITS CULTURAL LANDSCAPE Japan

A cluster of mountains in the southwest of Honshu Island, interspersed with deep river valleys contain the remains of silver mines, smelting and refining sites and mining settlements worked between the sixteenth and twentieth centuries. By the first half of the seventeenth century, when production at Iwami Ginzan was at its peak, Japan's output accounted for almost a third of the world's silver production. The mining area is now heavily wooded. Included in the site are fortresses, shrines, parts of Kaidô transport routes to the coast, and three port towns.
Criteria: ii, iii, v Inscribed 2007

• RICHTERSVELD CULTURAL AND BOTANICAL LANDSCAPE South Africa

This area of dramatic mountainous desert in northwestern South Africa sustains the semi-nomadic pastoral livelihood of the Nama people, reflecting seasonal patterns that may have persisted for as much as two millennia. Their seasonal pastoral grazing regimes sustain the extensive biodiversity of the area. The extensive communal grazed lands have ensured the protection of the succulent Karoo vegetation. The pastoralists collect medicinal and other plants and have a strong oral tradition associated with different places. It is the only area where the Nama still construct portable rush-mat houses (*haru om*).
Criteria: iv, v Inscribed 2007

• SAMARRA ARCHAEOLOGICAL CITY Iraq

Samarra Archaeological City, on the river Tigris, is the large site of a powerful Islamic capital city that ruled for a century over the provinces of the Abbasid Empire. The ninth-century Great Mosque and its spiral minaret are among the numerous remarkable architectural monuments of the site, 80 per cent of which remains to be excavated. Carved stucco, known as the Samarra style, was developed there and spread to other parts of the region, as was a new type of ceramic, known as lustre ware, imitating utensils made of precious metals.
Criteria: ii, iii, iv Inscribed 2007

• TEIDE NATIONAL PARK Spain

Situated on the island of Tenerife, Teide National Park features the Teide-Pico Viejo stratovolcano – at 3,718 m, the highest peak on Spanish soil. The visual impact of the site is all the greater due to atmospheric conditions that create constantly changing textures and tones in the landscape and a 'sea of clouds' that forms a visually impressive backdrop to the mountain. Teide is of global importance in providing evidence of the geological processes that underpin the evolution of oceanic islands.
Criteria: vii, viii Inscribed 2007

• GOBUSTAN ROCK ART CULTURAL LANDSCAPE Azerbaijan

Gobustan Rock Art Cultural Landscape covers three areas of a plateau of rocky boulders rising out of the semi-desert of east-central Azerbaijan, with an outstanding collection of more than 6,000 rock engravings bearing testimony to 40,000 years of rock art. It also has remains of inhabited caves, settlements and burials, all reflecting an intensive human use of the area during the wet period that followed the last Ice Age up to the Middle Ages. Nearby are inscriptions left by troops of Alexander the Great and Roman soldiers of the Emperor Trajan.
Criteria: iii Inscribed 2007

The Red Fort in Delhi has been a powerful symbol for the Indian nation since its construction.

Rising 7,500 m above the ocean floor, Teide, on the island of Tenerife, is regarded as the world's third-tallest volcanic structure and stands in a spectacular environment.

141

• SOUTH CHINA KARST China

The South China Karst region extends over 500,000 km² lying mainly in Yunnan, Guizhou and Guangxi provinces. The region contains a series of karst landforms in three clusters: Shilin Karst, Libo Karst and Wulong Karst. Shilin, in Yunnan province, contains classic examples of stone-forest landscapes, noted for high limestone pinnacles and towers decorated with deep, sharp karren. Libo contains carbonate outcrops of different ages that erosive processes shaped over millions of years into impressive cone and tower karsts. Wulong includes giant collapse depressions and high natural bridges between stretches of deep, unroofed caves.

Criteria: vii, viii Inscribed 2007

• LAVAUX, VINEYARD TERRACES Switzerland

The Lavaux Vineyard Terraces stretch for about 30 km along the south-facing northern shores of Lake Geneva from the Chateau de Chillon to the eastern outskirts of Lausanne, covering the lower slopes of the mountainside between the villages and the lake. The present vine terraces can be traced back to the eleventh century when monks from Benedictine and Cistercian monasteries cultivated the area. There are more than 10,000 terraces together with buildings – churches, castles, cellars and houses – that reflect local history from monastic times to the twentieth century.

Criteria: iv Inscribed 2007

• KAIPING DIAOLOU AND VILLAGES China

Kaiping Diaolou and Villages feature the *diaolou*, multi-storeyed defensive village houses, which display a complex and elaborate fusion of Chinese and Western structural and decorative forms. The building of defensive towers was a local tradition in the Kaiping area since Ming times. The conspicuous wealth of the returning Chinese émigrés in the late nineteenth century onwards contributed to the spread of banditry in the area and the *diaolou* were an extreme response to the threat.

Criteria: ii, iii, iv Inscribed 2007

• TWYFELFONTEIN OR /UI-//AES Namibia

Twyfelfontein or /Ui-//aes has one of the largest concentrations of rock petroglyphs (engravings) in Africa. Most of these are well-preserved and represent rhinoceros, elephant, ostrich and giraffe, as well as drawings of human and animal footprints. The site also includes six painted rock-shelters with motifs of human figures in red ochre. The objects excavated from two sections, date from the Late Stone Age. The site forms a high-quality record of ritual practices relating to hunter-gatherer communities in this part of southern Africa over at least 2,000 years.

Criteria: iii, v Inscribed 2007

• PRIMEVAL BEECH FORESTS OF THE CARPATHIANS Slovakia and Ukraine

The Primeval Beech Forests of the Carpathians provide the largest area of virgin forests of European beech (*Fagus sylvatica*) in existence. They represent all stages of beech forest in age and development, and they contain the largest and tallest beech specimens in the world. The forests are an invaluable genetic reservoir of beech and many species associated with, and dependent on, these forest habitats. Flora and fauna are rich and include rare plants and animals. Some species, such as black stork, depend on undisturbed forest habitats.

Criteria: ix Inscribed 2007

• RAINFORESTS OF THE ATSINANANA Madagascar

The Rainforests of the Atsinanana comprise six national parks on the eastern side of the island. These relict forests are critically important for maintaining the survival of Madagascar's unique biodiversity, with around 12,000 endemic plants. Having completed its separation from all other land masses more than sixty million years ago, Madagascar's plant and animal life evolved in isolation. The rainforests are important to both ecological and biological processes as well as their biodiversity and the threatened species they support.

Criteria: ix, x Inscribed 2007

Sharp karren in the Shilin stone forest in Yunnan province, part of the South China Karst area.

The Primeval Beech Forests of the Carpathians are comprised of ten separate sites at altitudes ranging from 210 m to 1700 m. Six of the sites are in the Ukraine and four in Slovakia.

• OLD TOWN OF CORFU Greece

The Old Town of Corfu, on the island of Corfu, is in a strategic position at the entrance to the Adriatic Sea. Its three forts, designed by Venetian engineers, were used for four centuries to defend the trading interests of the Republic of Venice against the Ottoman Empire. The forts were repaired and partly rebuilt several times, more recently under British rule in the nineteenth century. The mainly neoclassical houses of the Old Town are partly from the Venetian period and partly of later construction, notably the nineteenth century.
Criteria: iv Inscribed 2007

• PARTHIAN FORTRESSES OF NISA Turkmenistan

The Parthian Fortresses of Nisa consist of two tels (prehistoric settlement mounds) of Old and New Nisa, the site of one of the earliest and most important cities of the Parthian Empire, a major power from mid-third century BC to the third century AD. They conserve the unexcavated remains of a civilisation that combined its own culture with those of the Hellenistic and Roman west. Archaeological excavations have revealed richly decorated architecture, illustrative of domestic, state and religious functions. The Parthians formed a barrier to Roman expansion while trading between east and west.
Criteria: ii, iii Inscribed 2007

• RIDEAU CANAL Canada

The Rideau Canal, built by the British to defend Canada against the USA after the war of 1812, was one of the first canals designed for steam-powered vessels. The Rideau Canal was completed in 1832 and covers 202 km of the Rideau and Cataraqui rivers, from Ottawa south to Kingston on Lake Ontario. It is the only canal from the great North American canal-building era that remains operational along its original line with most of its structures intact. It has served important commercial and recreational purposes since its construction.
Criteria: i, iv Inscribed 2007

• CENTRAL UNIVERSITY CITY CAMPUS OF THE UNIVERSIDAD NACIONAL AUTÓNOMA DE MÉXICO (UNAM) Mexico

The buildings and open spaces of the Central University City Campus of the Universidad Nacional Autónoma de México (UNAM) were created from 1949 to 1952 by more than sixty architects, engineers and artists. The campus is a unique example of twentieth-century modernism integrating urbanism, architecture, engineering, landscape design and fine arts with reference to local traditions, especially to Mexico's pre-Hispanic past. Most famous is the Biblioteca Central (Central Library), covered with tiled murals, the work of Mexican artist Juan O'Gorman, representing historic and modern Mexico and the university.
Criteria: i, ii, iv Inscribed 2007

• BORDEAUX, PORT OF THE MOON France

The Port of the Moon is a popular name for Bordeaux in southwest France. From the twelfth century, its importance grew after commercial links were established with Britain and the Low Countries. However, the age of Enlightenment produced Bordeaux's best known architectural and urban features. Louis-Urbain Aubert, Marquis de Tourny, arrived in Bordeaux in 1743, staying there until 1757. He undertook major projects for the renovation and opening up the medieval city, especially to the façades of buildings on the quays along the river Garonne, and inspired an architectural style that continued into the twentieth century.
Criteria: ii, iv Inscribed 2007

• ECOSYSTEM AND RELICT CULTURAL LANDSCAPE OF LOPÉ-OKANDA Gabon

This area features an interface between dense and well-conserved tropical rainforest and relict savanna environments with great species diversity, including endangered large mammals, and habitats. There is evidence of the successive passages of different peoples. The Neolithic and Iron Age sites, together with the rock art found there, reflects a major migration route of Bantu and other peoples from west Africa along the river Ogooué valley to the north of the dense Congo forests and to central, east and southern Africa, that has

A view over the fortified Mediterranean port of the Old Town of Corfu.

Rideau Canal and The Houses of Parliament, Parliament Hill, Ottawa.

The water mirror and Place de la Bourse, Bordeaux, a place with more protected buildings than any other French city except Paris.

shaped the development of the whole of sub-Saharan Africa.
Criteria: iii, iv, ix, x Inscribed 2007

• GAMZIGRAD-ROMULIANA, PALACE OF GALERIUS Serbia

The Palace of Galerius in the east of Serbia, is one of the most
important Late Roman sites. It was built by the Tetrarch Galerius
Maximianus (c. AD 260–311), between the late third and early fourth
centuries. The site consists of fortifications, a palace, basilicas,
temples, hot baths, a memorial complex and a tetrapylon. The
buildings' intertwining of ceremonial and memorial functions is
unique, as are the spatial and visual relationships between the palace
and the memorial complex, where the mausoleums of Galerius and
his mother Romula are located.
Criteria: iii, iv Inscribed 2007

• JEJU VOLCANIC ISLAND AND LAVA TUBES
Korea, Republic of

The volcanic island of Jeju site comprises three locations:
Geomunoreum with its multicoloured carbonate roofs and floors
and dark lava walls, is the finest lava-tube system of caves in the
world; Seongsan Ilchulbong tuff cone, rising out of the ocean; and
the primary volcano of Mount Hallasan, with waterfalls, multi-
shaped rock formations and a lake-filled crater. There are around 360
subsidiary cones , many of which, on cooling, formed the lava-tube
caves. A lava tube is a conduit through which lava is expelled during a
volcanic eruption. After the rock cools, the empty lava tube remains.
Criteria: vii, viii Inscribed 2007

• MEHMED PAŠA SOKOLOVIĆ BRIDGE IN
VIŠEGRAD Bosnia-Herzegovina

The Mehmed Paša Sokolović Bridge of Višegrad crosses the Drina
River and was built between 1571 and 1577. It was commissioned by
the Grand Vizier Mehmed Paša Sokolović (1505–79), the sultan's chief
adviser, who was a Bosnian. The building of the bridge was primarily
a tribute to his native region. It is a masterpiece of the renowned
Ottoman architect Sinan and is enhanced by architectural features
typical of the classical Ottoman period. It is on the route linking the
plains of the Danube to Sarajevo and the Adriatic coast.
Criteria: ii, iv Inscribed 2007

• PROTECTIVE TOWN OF SAN MIGUEL AND
THE SANCTUARY OF JESÚS NAZARENO DE
ATOTONILCO Mexico

This fortified town, established in the sixteenth century, reached
its apogee in the eighteenth century, when many of its outstanding
religious and civic buildings were built in the Mexican Baroque style.
It was a melting pot of Spanish, Creole and Amerindian cultures.
The Jesuit sanctuary, 14 km away, is one of the finest examples of
eighteenth-century Baroque art and architecture in Latin America.
The town was the birthplace of national hero General Ignacio
Allende and was renamed San Miguel de Allende in 1926 in his
honour.
Criteria: ii, iv Inscribed 2008

• SACRED MIJIKENDA KAYA FORESTS Kenya

Spread out along the Kenyan coast are a number of forested sites,
mostly on low hills, in which are the remains of fortified villages,
kayas, of the Mijikenda people. Tradition tells how *kayas* were created
from the sixteenth century onwards as the Mijikenda migrated south
from Somalia. The kayas began to fall out of use in the early
twentieth century and are now revered as the repositories of spiritual
beliefs of the Mijikenda people. The forests around the *kayas* have
been nurtured to protect the sacred graves and groves.
Criteria: iii, v, vi Inscribed 2008

• BERLIN MODERNISM HOUSING ESTATES
Germany

The site consists of six housing estates that testify to innovative
housing policies from 1910 to 1933, especially during the Weimar
Republic, when Berlin was progressive socially, politically and

The Palace of Galerius at Gamzigrad-Romuliana is representative of Late Roman imperial and religious symbolism:
the glorification of the emperor as all-powerful ruler and as a god underlies its construction.

The sixteenth-century Mehmed Paša Sokolović Bridge of Višegrad has eleven masonry arches with spans of 10.7 m to 15 m,
and an access ramp at right angles with four arches on the left bank of the river.

culturally. The estates are an outstanding example of the building reform movement that contributed to improving housing and living conditions for people through novel approaches to town planning, architecture and garden design. Bruno Taut, Martin Wagner and Walter Gropius were among the leading architects of these projects which exercised considerable influence on the development of housing around the world.
Criteria: ii, iv Inscribed 2008

• MANTUA AND SABBIONETA Italy

Mantua and Sabbioneta in the Po valley of northern Italy, linked by the vision of the local ruling Gonzaga family, represent two aspects of Renaissance town planning. Mantua's layout is irregular with parts showing different stages of its growth since the Roman period. The participation of renowned architects and painters made it a prominent capital of the Renaissance. Sabbioneta was a new town built according to Renaissance ideals with defensive walls, grid-patterned streets, public spaces and monuments. Together they offer exceptional testimony to the urban, architectural and artistic realisations of the Renaissance.
Criteria: ii, iii Inscribed 2008

Mantua from Lago di Mezzo.

• FORTIFICATIONS OF VAUBAN France

The Fortifications of Vauban comprise twelve groups of fortified buildings and sites that together represent the peak of classic bastioned fortification typical of Western military architecture. They are the finest examples of the work of Sébastien Le Prestre de Vauban (1633–1707), the renowned military engineer of Louis XIV. The twelve properties in the site form a ring around France's borders. The fortifications include towns built from scratch by Vauban, citadels built on plains, urban bastion walls and bastion towers. There are also mountain forts, sea forts, a mountain battery and two mountain communication structures.
Criteria: i, ii, iv Inscribed 2008

• RHAETIAN RAILWAY IN THE ALBULA / BERNINA LANDSCAPES Italy and Switzerland

The Rhaetian railway brings together two mountain railway lines that cross the Swiss Alps through two passes. Opened in 1904, the Albula line is 67 km long. It features an impressive set of structures including forty-two tunnels and covered galleries and 144 viaducts and bridges and reaches a height of 1,819 m. The 61 km Bernina Pass line features thirteen tunnels and galleries and fifty-two viaducts and bridges and reaches a height of 2,253 m. They display outstanding architectural and civil engineering achievements, built in harmony with the landscapes through which they pass.
Criteria: ii, iv Inscribed 2008

Vauban's fortress at Briançon in the French Alps. Vauban's theories and models were studied and used across the world and made a major contribution to military architecture.

• SAN MARINO HISTORIC CENTRE AND MOUNT TITANO San Marino

San Marino, an enclave in the Apennine Mountains surrounded by Italy, is one of the world's oldest republics. It was the only city-state not to be brought into union with the rest of Italy by Garibaldi during the Risorgimento, and maintains its independence. The Historic Centre of San Marino is strategically sited on the top of Mount Titano and its many monuments include fortification towers, walls, gates and bastions; a neoclassical basilica; fourteenth- and sixteenth-century convents; the nineteenth-century Palazzo Publico; and the Titano Theatre, dating from the eighteenth century.
Criteria: iii Inscribed 2008

• SOCOTRA ARCHIPELAGO Yemen

Socotra is globally important for biodiversity conservation because of its exceptionally rich and distinct flora and fauna; 37 per cent of its plant species, 90 per cent of its reptile species and 95 per cent of its land snail species do not occur anywhere else in the world. One of the most distinct islands in the world, it has been termed the 'Galápagos of the Indian Ocean'. The site covers about 75 per cent of the land area, protecting all the major vegetation types, important bird areas, and areas of marine biodiversity.
Criteria: x Inscribed 2008

First tower (Guaita) on Mount Titano in San Marino.

• HISTORIC CENTRE OF CAMAGÜEY
Cuba

Camagüey is relatively isolated from main trade routes. It was one of the first villages founded by the Spaniards in Cuba and was the centre of a region dedicated to cattle breeding and the sugar industry. Settled in 1528, its irregular urban pattern developed with large and small squares, winding streets, alleys and irregular blocks of buildings. The layout reflects medieval European towns, highly unusual for Latin American colonial towns on flat land. The centre shows the influence of numerous styles including neoclassical, neocolonial, Art Nouveau and Art Deco.
Criteria: iv, v Inscribed 2008

• KUK EARLY AGRICULTURAL SITE
Papua New Guinea

Kuk, in the southern highlands of New Guinea, 1,500 m above sea level, is the site of the earliest, independent agriculture in Oceania and archaeological evidence indicates that it may have contributed to the spread of domesticated plants across the region. It demonstrates the technological leap from plant exploitation to agriculture, initially with taro and yam around 7,000 years ago, and then with domestication and cultivation of bananas on drained ground some 4,000 years ago. It shows the changes in agricultural practices over time.
Criteria: iii, iv Inscribed 2008

• SARYARKA – STEPPE AND LAKES OF NORTHERN KAZAKHSTAN
Kazakhstan

The wetlands of the site are crucial for migratory birds, including the globally threatened Siberian white crane, Dalmatian pelican and Pallas's fish eagle, that travel from Africa, Europe and south Asia to their breeding grounds in Siberia. The Korgalzhyn-Tengiz lakes provide feeding grounds for up to 15–16 million birds. They also support 350,000 nesting waterfowl, while the Naurzum lakes support 500,000. The site provides a refuge for over half the flora species of central Asian steppe, a number of threatened bird species and the critically endangered Saiga antelope.
Criteria: ix, x Inscribed 2008

• FUJIAN TULOU China

Set amongst the fields of southwest Fujian Province, this site contains forty-six extraordinary communal earthen houses (*tulou*), built between the twelfth and the twentieth centuries. They are up to five storeys high, with an inward-looking, circular or square floor plan, each housing a whole clan of up to 800 people. They were built for defensive purposes around a central open courtyard with few windows to the outside and only one entrance. In contrast with their plain exterior, the inside of the *tulou* were built for comfort and were often highly decorated.
Criteria: iii, iv, v Inscribed 2008

• TEMPLE OF PREAH VIHEAR Cambodia

Preah Vihear, a Hindu temple dedicated to the god Shiva, is an outstanding masterpiece of Khmer architecture. The temple stands on a cliff top at the edge of a plateau that dominates the plain of Cambodia. It is a unique complex comprising a series of sanctuaries linked by pavements and staircases. The temple began in ninth-century as a hermitage and developed into a royal temple in the eleventh and twelfth centuries. The temple was adapted for use by Buddhists after Hinduism declined in the region.
Criteria: i Inscribed 2008

• SURTSEY Iceland

Surtsey, a new volcanic island off the south coast of Iceland, was formed by volcanic eruptions between 1963 and 1967. Free from human interference, its colonisation by plant and animal life has been studied. The first seeds arrived in 1964, carried by ocean currents. By 2004, sixty vascular plants, together with seventy-five bryophytes, seventy-one lichens, twenty-four fungi, eighty-nine species of birds, and 335 species of invertebrates have been recorded. Coastal erosion has already halved Surtsey's area and is predicted to remove another two-thirds, leaving only the most resistant core.
Criteria: ix Inscribed 2008

• MELAKA AND GEORGE TOWN, HISTORIC CITIES OF THE STRAITS OF MALACCA Malaysia

Melaka and George Town were forged from the mercantile interaction of Malay, Chinese, and Indian cultures and of three successive European colonial powers over almost 500 years. Each has left its imprint on the local architecture and urban form. Melaka originated in the fifteenth-century Malay sultanate and, beginning in the early sixteenth century, Portuguese and Dutch rule began; its notable monuments are government buildings, churches, squares and fortifications. Residential and commercial buildings feature strongly in George Town, which represents the British era from the end of the eighteenth century until the twentieth century.
Criteria: ii, iii, iv Inscribed 2008

• STARI GRAD PLAIN Croatia

The fertile plain near the port, now known as Stari Grad, on the Adriatic island of Hvar, was colonised by Greeks from Paros in the fourth century BC. It quickly became an important Greek colony because of its flourishing agriculture, based on grapes and olives, which has been maintained since Greek times. The landscape features ancient stone walls and *trims*, or small stone shelters, and still exhibits, after twenty-four centuries, the regular geometrical system of land division used by the ancient Greeks, the *chora*. This system was completed with rainwater tanks.
Criteria: ii, iii, v Inscribed 2008

• LE MORNE CULTURAL LANDSCAPE
Mauritius

Le Morne, a rugged mountain in the southwest of Mauritius, was used as a shelter by runaway slaves, called 'maroons', through the eighteenth and early years of the nineteenth centuries. Mauritius became known as the 'Maroon republic' because of the comparatively large number of escaped slaves who hid there. Since the abolition of slavery in 1835 the 'maroons' have achieved legendary status and Le Morne has become the symbol of their suffering, their bid for freedom and their sacrifice. The mountain, together with its surrounding foothills and lagoons, is a place of great scenic beauty.
Criteria: iii, vi Inscribed 2008

• ARMENIAN MONASTIC ENSEMBLES OF IRAN Islamic Republic of Iran

The fortified Armenian monasteries of northwest Iran bear testimony, since at least the seventh century, to Armenian culture and its contact with Persian civilisations. The monasteries of St Thaddeus and St Stepanos and the Chapel of Dzordzor are outstanding examples of Armenian architectural and decorative traditions. Situated on the south-eastern fringe of Armenian influence, the monasteries were a major centre for the dissemination of that culture. The monastery of St Thaddeus, the presumed location of the tomb of St Thaddeus, the apostle of Jesus Christ, remains a living place of pilgrimage.
Criteria: ii, iii, vi Inscribed 2008

• WOODEN CHURCHES OF THE SLOVAK PART OF THE CARPATHIAN MOUNTAIN AREA Slovakia

These churches, two Roman Catholic, three Protestant and three Greek Orthodox, were built between the sixteenth and eighteenth centuries, mostly in quite isolated villages, using mainly wood and traditional construction techniques. They are good examples of a rich local tradition of religious architecture, marked by the meeting of Latin and Byzantine cultures. Their floor plans, interior spaces and external appearance vary due to their differing religious practices. They are an outstanding testimony to the inter-ethnic and inter-cultural character of this small area in the Carpathian Mountains.
Criteria: iii, iv Inscribed 2008

• CHIEF ROI MATA'S DOMAIN Vanuatu

The domain comprises three early seventeenth-century sites on the islands of Efate, Lelepa and Artok associated with the life and death of the last paramount chief, or Roi Mata, of what is now central Vanuatu. It includes Roi Mata's residence, the site of his death and his burial site. It is closely associated with the oral traditions surrounding the chief and the moral values he espoused. Roi Mata still lives for many in contemporary Vanuatu as a source of power and inspiration.
Criteria: iii, v, vi Inscribed 2008

• JOGGINS FOSSIL CLIFFS Canada

The Joggins Fossil Cliffs have been called the 'coal age Galápagos' due to their wealth of fossils from the Carboniferous (354 to 290 million years ago). These include the intact remains and tracks of the first known reptiles, and the rainforest in which they lived. The site contains remains of three ecosystems: estuarine bay, floodplain rainforest and fire-prone forested alluvial plain with freshwater pools. Joggins offers the richest assemblage known of the fossil life in these three ecosystems with 96 genera and 148 species of fossils and 20 footprint groups.
Criteria: viii Inscribed 2008

• MOUNT SANQINGSHAN NATIONAL PARK China

Mount Sanqingshan National Park contains a unique array of fantastically shaped granite pillars and peaks. The looming, intricate rock formations intermingled with delicate forest cover and combined with ever-shifting weather patterns create a landscape of arresting beauty. It is located in the west of the Huyaiyu mountain range in the northeast of Jiangxi Province. It also features numerous waterfalls, some of them 60 m in height, lakes and springs. Mount Sanqingshan has been a Taoist shrine since a priest, Ge Hong, came to the mountain 400 years ago.
Criteria: vii Inscribed 2008

• AL-HIJR ARCHAEOLOGICAL SITE (MADÂIN SÂLIH) Saudi Arabia

The remarkable archaeological site of Al-Hijr – formerly known as Hegra – is the largest conserved site of the Nabataean civilisation south of Petra. It is located at a meeting point on trade routes between the Arabian Peninsula, the Mediterranean world and Asia. The site has 111 well-preserved monumental tombs cut directly into the local sandstone, ninety-four of which have decorated façades dating from the first century BC to the first century AD. There are also fifty inscriptions of the pre-Nabataean period and some cave drawings.
Criteria: ii, iii Inscribed 2008

▪ SWISS TECTONIC ARENA SARDONA Switzerland

The Swiss Tectonic Arena Sardona northeastern Switzerland is a dramatic example of the process of mountain building through continental collision. The Glarus Alps are glaciated mountains rising dramatically above narrow river valleys. The Glarus Overthrust is where, in a break in the Earth's crust, compression forces push the upper side of two tectonic plates further upwards over the lower one. The exposures of the rocks below and above this feature are visible in three dimensions and they have made substantial contributions to the understanding of mountain-building tectonics.

Criteria: viii Inscribed 2008

▪ MONARCH BUTTERFLY BIOSPHERE RESERVE
Mexico

The Monarch Butterfly Biosphere Reserve protects key overwintering sites for the monarch butterfly. The biosphere lies within rugged forested mountains about 100 km northwest of Mexico City. In a dramatic manifestation of insect migration, up to a billion monarch butterflies return annually from northern breeding areas to land in close-packed clusters within fourteen overwintering colonies in central Mexico's oyamel fir forests. The biosphere reserve protects eight of these colonies and an estimated 70 per cent of the total overwintering population of the monarch butterfly's eastern population.

Criteria: vii Inscribed 2008

▪ LAGOONS OF NEW CALEDONIA: REEF DIVERSITY AND ASSOCIATED ECOSYSTEMS
France

The tropical lagoons and coral reefs of New Caledonia are some of the most beautiful reef systems in the world, with a great diversity of coral and fish species and a continuum of habitats from mangroves to seagrasses. The ecological condition of the reefs is remarkable, in particular the number of large fish and top predators, such as sharks and barracuda. The lagoons support a number of threatened fish, turtles and marine mammals, including a large population of dugongs. The reefs are of varying age, from living reefs to ancient fossil reefs.

Criteria: vii, ix, x Inscribed 2008

▪ BAHÁ'Í HOLY PLACES IN HAIFA AND THE WESTERN GALILEE Israel

The Bahá'í Faith is a monotheistic religion that emphasises the spiritual unity of all peoples. It was founded by Bahá'u'lláh in Persia in the nineteenth century. This site includes the two most holy places in the Bahá'í religion associated with its founders, the Shrine of Bahá'u'lláh in Acre and the Shrine of the Báb in Haifa, together with their surrounding gardens. These two shrines are part of a larger complex of sites at seven distinct locations in Haifa and the Western Galilee that draw large numbers of pilgrims from around the world.

Criteria: iii, vi Inscribed 2008

▪ CIDADE VELHA, HISTORIC CENTRE OF RIBEIRA GRANDE Cape Verde

Ribeira Grande, renamed Cidade Velha in the late eighteenth century, was the first European colonial town built in the tropics. Its position on the shipping routes between Europe, Africa and the Americas, made it central to further Portuguese colonisation and administration. It became an important centre in the West African slave trade and the large-scale mixing of European and African cultures and people led to the development in the town of the first Creole culture. Its climate led to new forms of colonial agriculture in the Ribeira Grande valley.

Criteria: ii, iii, vi Inscribed 2009

▪ ROYAL TOMBS OF THE JOSEON DYNASTY
Korea, Republic of

The Royal Tombs of the Joseon Dynasty were built between 1408 and 1966 to honour the memory of ancestors, show respect for their achievements, assert royal authority, protect ancestral spirits from evil and provide protection from vandalism. They form a collection of forty tombs in eighteen locations. Sites of natural beauty were

Klöntaler Lake and the Glarus Alps in the Swiss Tectonic Arena Sardona site.

The millions of monarch butterflies in the Biosphere Reserve colour the trees orange, bend branches with their massed weight, fill the sky when they take flight and sound like light rain with the beating of their wings.

The Shrine of the Báb and the Bahá'í Gardens, Haifa. There is a strong tradition of pilgrimage to these sites among the estimated over five million Bahá'ís around the world.

chosen: typically tombs face south toward water, protected by a hill behind and ideally have mountain ridges in the distance. Alongside the burial area, each tomb features a ceremonial area, an entrance and associated buildings.

Criteria: iii, iv, vi Inscribed 2009

• PONTCYSYLLTE AQUEDUCT AND CANAL
United Kingdom

The Pontcysyllte Aqueduct and Canal was completed in 1805, at the end of the canal-building era. Due to the difficult terrain, its construction required substantial, bold engineering solutions including tunnel construction, especially as it was built without using locks. The Pontcysyllte Aqueduct is a pioneering masterpiece of engineering and monumental metal architecture, conceived by the noted civil engineers Thomas Telford and William Jessop. Both cast and wrought iron were used in the construction of arches that were light and strong, producing an overall effect that is both monumental and elegant.

Criteria: i, ii, iv Inscribed 2009

• LA CHAUX-DE-FONDS / LE LOCLE, WATCHMAKING TOWN PLANNING Switzerland

La Chaux-de-Fonds and Le Locle owe their existence to the watch-making industry. Their location, 1,000 m up in the Jura Mountains, is remote and infertile. The local watch-making culture dates to the seventeenth century but the towns were planned in the early nineteenth century following extensive fires. Their layout – a series of parallel strips of intermingled houses and workshops – was designed for manufacturing. The planning of both towns has accommodated successfully the transition from artisanal production to the more concentrated factory production that replaced it from the late nineteenth century.

Criteria: iv Inscribed 2009

• MOUNT WUTAI China

Mount Wutai, with its five flat peaks, is one of four sacred Buddhist mountains in China. The high peaks, snow-covered for much of the year, thick forests of pines, firs, poplar and willow trees and lush grassland form a landscape of great beauty that has been celebrated by artists since at least the seventh century. Temples were built there from the first century AD and many of the country's most important monasteries and temples stand on its slopes. It is the global centre for Buddhist worship of Manjusri, the Bodhisattva of Wisdom.

Criteria: ii, iii, iv, vi Inscribed 2009

• SACRED CITY OF CARAL-SUPE Peru

The 5000-year-old site of Caral-Supe stands on a dry desert terrace overlooking the green valley of the Supe river. The city was a centre of the Norte Chico civilisation, a pre-Columbian society claimed to be the oldest in the Americas. Exceptionally well preserved, Caral is one of eighteen settlements in the same area and features complex architectural and spatial elements. Its monumental earthen platform mounds and sunken circular courts are powerful expressions of a consolidated state. These features were to influence and dominate much of the Peruvian coast for centuries.

Criteria: ii, iii, iv Inscribed 2009

• SHUSHTAR HISTORICAL HYDRAULIC SYSTEM
Iran (Islamic Republic of)

Shushtar Historical Hydraulic System is a unique example of ancient hydraulic techniques developed to allow settlement on semi-desert lands. The diversion of a mountain river by canals and other structures brought water to a vast territory for urban and domestic supply, agriculture, fish farming, mills, city defence and transport. In its present form the system dates from the third century AD, probably built on fifth-century BC foundations. It combines hydraulic engineering techniques over several centuries, from Elamites and Mesopotamians and later, Nabateans skilled in canal irrigation. Roman civil engineers also contributed.

Criteria: i, ii, v Inscribed 2009

The Pontcysyllte Aqueduct towers at heights of over 37 m above the floor of the steep-sided Dee valley bearing only a cast-iron, water-filled trough and a towpath with a handrail.

One of the many temples on Mount Wutai. Buildings in this area reflects the exchange of ideas from Nepal and Mongolia and chronicle the development of Buddhist architecture in China.

• THE WADDEN SEA Germany/Netherlands

The Wadden Sea is a large temperate coastal-wetland environment and is the world's largest unbroken system of intertidal sand and mudflats. It encompasses a multitude of transitional zones between the land, sea and freshwater environments. These coastal wetlands are unusually rich in the diversity of their fauna and are home to numerous plant and animal species, including the harbour seal, grey seal and harbour porpoise. They are also a breeding and wintering area for up to 12 million birds annually. Up to 6 million birds can be present at one time.
Criteria: viii, ix, x Inscribed 2009

• SULAIMAN-TOO SACRED MOUNTAIN
  Kyrgyzstan

Sulaiman-Too reflects both ancient religious and Islamic beliefs and particularly the cult of the horse. Its strong traditions of worship span several millennia and it presents the most complete picture of a sacred mountain in Central Asia. Its five peaks and slopes contain a large assembly of many ancient cult places and caves with petroglyphs, interconnected by a network of paths, together with later mosques. Sulaiman-Too matches iconic images from Zoroastrian and Vedic tradition: one mountain with a peak dominating four others, in the centre of a river valley and surrounded by other mountains.
Criteria: iii, vi Inscribed 2009

• STOCLET HOUSE Belgium

Stoclet House, designed and built by Austrian architect Josef Hoffmann between 1905 and 1911, was designed for banker and art-lover Adolphe Stoclet. A number of artists, including Klimt and Moser, of the Wiener Werkstätte or Vienna Workshops – the community of architects, artists and designers which grew out of the Vienna Secession movement in the early twentieth century – worked under Hoffmann to design every aspect of the house, fittings, household objects and gardens. This makes it a classic example of Gesamtkunstwerk (total artwork), a defining feature of Jugendstil or Art Nouveau.
Criteria: i, ii Inscribed 2009

• THE RUINS OF LOROPÉNI Burkina Faso

Loropéni was part of a network of settlements that flourished with the lucrative trans-Saharan gold trade which flourished between the seventh and eleventh centuries, linking the gold-hungry Mediterranean economies with sub-Saharan Africa where gold was plentiful. Loropéni, surrounded by tall, laterite stone perimeter walls, up to 6 m high, is the finest remaining example of these West African settlements. Gold was mined in the area by the Lohron or Koulango peoples who occupied Loropéni and controlled the excavation and refining processes. Loropéni was finally deserted early in the nineteenth century.
Criteria: iii Inscribed 2009

• TOWER OF HERCULES Spain

The Tower of Hercules is the only fully preserved Roman lighthouse. The sea beyond, named Finisterra as the Romans thought it the end of the world, was notoriously dangerous, and construction of the *Farum Brigantium* (Tower of Brigantium) began in the first century AD. The tower stands on a 57-m-high rock and rises a further 55 m; the Roman core is 34 m high. It is divided into three progressively smaller levels, the first corresponding to the Roman structure. The tower was restored in the late eighteenth century.
Criteria: iii Inscribed 2009

• THE DOLOMITES Italy

The Dolomites form a limestone mountain range renowned for its natural beauty. They lie over an area of 1400 km² in the northern Italian Alps and include eighteen summits over 3,000 m. The dramatic pale, vertical peaks of the limestone range have an extraordinary variety of distinctive sculptural forms, fashioned by erosion, tectonism and glaciation. Dynamic processes continue to affect the area with frequent landslides, floods and avalanches. The site also features excellent preserved carbonate platforms from the Mesozoic era (up to 251 million years ago) with fossil records.
Criteria: vii, viii Inscribed 2009

The size and diversity of the Wadden Sea is unique. It is distinctive in being almost entirely a tidal flat and barrier system with only minor river influences.

The Dolomites rise as peaks with intervening ravines, standing isolated in some places and forming sweeping panoramas in others. Talus (scree) deposits lie below, with forest- and meadow-covered foothills.

• AUSTRALIAN CONVICT SITES Australia

The property includes a selection of eleven penal sites, among the thousands established by the British Empire on Australian soil in the eighteenth and nineteenth centuries. The sites are spread across Australia, from Fremantle in Western Australia to Kingston and Arthur's Vale on Norfolk Island in the east; and from areas around Sydney in New South Wales in the north, to sites located in Tasmania in the south. Around 166,000 men, women and children were transported to Australia over 80 years between 1787 and 1868, condemned by British justice to transportation to the convict colonies. Each of the sites had a specific purpose, in terms both of punitive imprisonment and of rehabilitation through forced labour to help build the colony. The property presents the best surviving examples of large-scale convict transportation and the colonial expansion of European powers through the presence and labour of convicts.
Criteria: iv, vi Inscribed 2010

• SÃO FRANCISCO SQUARE IN THE TOWN OF SÃO CRISTÓVÃO Brazil

São Francisco Square, in the town of São Cristóvão in northeastern Brazil, is a quadrilateral open space surrounded by substantial early buildings such as São Francisco Church and convent, the Church and Santa Casa da Misericórdia, the Provincial Palace and the associated houses of different historical periods surrounding the Square. This monumental ensemble, together with the surrounding eighteenth- and nineteenth-century houses, creates an urban landscape which reflects the history of the town since its origin. The Franciscan complex is an example of the typical architecture of the religious order developed in this area. The city was the capital of Sergipe del Rey province and attracted the administrative, religious and commercial organisation and architecture attendant on its status.
Criteria: ii, iv, Inscribed 2010

• BIKINI ATOLL, NUCLEAR TEST SITE Marshall Islands

In the wake of World War II, in what would become the initial stage of the Cold War, the United States of America decided to begin testing nuclear weapons in the Pacific Ocean, on Bikini Atoll in the Marshall Islands. After the displacement of the local inhabitants, sixty-seven nuclear tests were carried out in the Marshall Islands on Bikini and Enewetak Atolls from 1946 to 1958, twenty-three of these on Bikini Atoll. The world's first deliverable hydrogen bomb, the Bravo, was detonated on Bikini Atoll in 1954. Bikini Atoll has conserved direct tangible evidence that is highly significant in conveying the power of the nuclear tests, i.e. the sunken ships sent to the bottom of the lagoon by the tests in 1946, remnants of testing facilities on various islands in the atoll, and the gigantic Bravo crater. The tests had major consequences on the geology and natural environment of Bikini Atoll and on the health of those who were exposed to radiation. Through its history, the atoll symbolises the dawn of the nuclear age, despite its paradoxical image of peace and of earthly paradise. This is the first site from the Marshall Islands to be inscribed on the World Heritage List.
Criteria: iv, vi, Inscribed 2010

• HISTORIC MONUMENTS OF DENGFENG, IN THE 'CENTRE OF HEAVEN AND EARTH' China

Mount Songshan is considered to be the central sacred mountain of China. At the foot of this 1500-m-high mountain, close to the city of Dengfeng in Henan province and spread over a 40 km² circle, stand eight clusters of buildings and sites, including three Han Que gates (remains of the oldest religious edifices in China), temples, the Zhougong Sundial Platform and the Dengfeng Observatory. Constructed over the course of nine dynasties, these buildings are reflections of different ways of perceiving the centre of heaven and earth and the power of the mountain as a centre for religious devotion. The historical monuments of Dengfeng include some of the best examples of ancient Chinese buildings devoted to ritual, science, technology and education.
Criteria: iii, vi, Inscribed 2010

• SHEIKH SAFI AL-DIN KHĀNEGĀH AND SHRINE ENSEMBLE IN ARDABIL Iran (Islamic Republic of)

Built between the beginning of the sixteenth century and the end of the eighteenth century, this place of spiritual Sufi pilgrimage uses traditional forms of Iranian architecture. Builders knew how to get the most out of a small space in order to provide multiple amenities which include among others, a library, a mosque, a school, a mausoleum, a cistern, a hospital, kitchens, a bakery and some offices.
Criteria: i, ii, iv Inscribed 2010

• CHINA DANXIA China

China Danxia is the name given in China to landscapes developed on continental red terrigenous sedimentary beds influenced by constructive forces (including uplift) and destructive forces (including weathering and erosion). The inscribed site comprises six areas found in the subtropical zone of southwest China. They are characterized by spectacular red cliffs and a range of erosional landforms, including dramatic natural pillars, towers, ravines, valleys and waterfalls. These rugged landscapes have helped to conserve subtropical broad-leaved evergreen forests, and host many species of flora and fauna, about 400 of which are considered rare or threatened.
Criteria: vii, viii Inscribed 2010

• PITONS, CIRQUES AND REMPARTS OF REUNION ISLAND France

The Pitons, cirques and remparts (ramparts) of Reunion Island site coincides with the core zone of La Réunion National Park. The property covers more than 1000 km² or 40 per cent of La Réunion, an island comprising two adjoining volcanic massifs located in the southwest of the Indian Ocean. Dominated by two towering volcanic peaks, the dormant Piton de Neiges and the highly active Piton de la Fournaise, massive walls and three cliff-rimmed cirques, the property includes a great variety of rugged terrain and impressive escarpments, forested gorges and basins creating a visually striking landscape. It is the natural habitat for a wide diversity of plants, presenting a high level of endemism. There are subtropical rainforests, cloud forests and heaths creating a remarkable and visually appealing mosaic of ecosystems and landscape features.
Criteria: vii, x Inscribed 2010

• EPISCOPAL CITY OF ALBI France

On the banks of the Tarn river in southwest France, the old city of Albi reflects the culmination of a medieval architectural and urban ensemble. Today the Old Bridge (Pont-Vieux), the Saint-Salvi quarter and its church are testimony to its initial development (tenth – eleventh centuries). Following the Albigensian Crusade against the Cathar heretics (thirteenth century) it became a powerful episcopal city. Built in a unique southern French Gothic

Kingston, Norfolk Island is one of the thousands of penal sites established in Australia.

Piton de la Fournaise, Réunion, is one of the most active volcanoes in the world.

Albi Cathedral, overlooking the River Tarn, was begun in 1282 and under construction for 200 years.

style from local brick in characteristic red and orange colours, the lofty fortified cathedral (late thirteenth century) dominates the city, demonstrating the power regained by the Roman Catholic clergy. Alongside the cathedral is the bishop's vast Palais de la Berbie, overlooking the river and surrounded by residential quarters that date back to the Middle Ages. The Episcopal City of Albi forms a coherent and homogeneous ensemble of monuments and quarters that has remained largely unchanged over the centuries.
Criteria: iv, v Inscribed 2010

▪ JANTAR MANTAR India

The Jantar Mantar, in Jaipur, is an astronomical observation site built in the early eighteenth century. It includes a set of some twenty main fixed instruments. They are monumental examples in masonry of known instruments but which in many cases have specific characteristics of their own. Designed for the observation of astronomical positions with the naked eye, they embody several architectural and instrumental innovations. This is the most significant, most comprehensive, and the best preserved of India's historic observatories. It is an expression of the astronomical skills and cosmological concepts of the court of a scholarly prince at the end of the Mughal period.
Criteria: iii, iv Inscribed 2010

▪ PAPAHĀNAUMOKUĀKEA USA

Papahānaumokuākea is a vast and isolated linear cluster of small, low-lying islands and atolls, with their surrounding ocean, roughly 250 km to the northwest of the main Hawaiian Archipelago and extending over some 1931 km. The area has deep cosmological and traditional significance for living Native Hawaiian culture, as an ancestral environment, as an embodiment of the Hawaiian concept of kinship between people and the natural world, and as the place where it is believed that life originates and to where the spirits return after death. On two of the islands, Nihoa and Makumanamana, there are archaeological remains relating to pre-European settlement and use.
Criteria: iii, vi, viii, ix, x Inscribed 2010

▪ TABRIZ HISTORIC BAZAAR COMPLEX
Iran (Islamic Republic of)

Tabriz, in the province of Eastern Azerbaijan, has been a place of cultural exchange since antiquity and its historic bazaar complex is one of the most important commercial centres on the Silk Road. Tabriz Historic Bazaar Complex consists of a series of interconnected, covered, brick structures, buildings, and enclosed spaces for different functions. The town and its bazaar were already prosperous and famous in the thirteenth century, when the town became the capital city of the Safavid kingdom. The city lost its status as capital in the sixteenth century, but remained important as a commercial hub until the end of the eighteenth century, with the expansion of Ottoman power. It is one of the most complete examples of the traditional commercial and cultural system of Iran. Tabriz Bazaar is among the oldest in the Middle East and the largest covered bazaar in the world. Italian traveller Marco Polo called the city one of the richest trading centres in the world.
Criteria: ii, iii, iv Inscribed 2010

▪ CENTRAL SECTOR OF THE IMPERIAL CITADEL
OF THANG LONG – HANOI Vietnam

The Thang Long Imperial Citadel was built in the eleventh century by the Ly Viet Dynasty, marking the independence of the Dai Viet. It was constructed on the remains of a Chinese fortress dating from the seventh century, on drained land reclaimed from the Red River Delta in Hanoi. It was the centre of regional political power for almost thirteen centuries without interruption. The Imperial Citadel buildings and the remains in the 18 Hoang Dieu Archaeological Site reflect a unique South-East Asian culture specific to the lower Red River valley, at the crossroads between influences coming from China in the north and the ancient Kingdom of Champa in the south.
Criteria: ii, iii, vi Inscribed 2010

The Jantar Mantar, said to be the world's largest stone observatory, was built between 1727 and 1734 by Maharaja Jai Singh II of Jaipur.

The historic bazaar complex in Tabriz is one of the most important commercial centres on the Silk Road

• CAMINO REAL DE TIERRA ADENTRO Mexico

Camino Real de Tierra Adentro was the Royal Inland Road, also known as the Silver Route. The inscribed property consists of fifty-five sites and five existing World Heritage sites lying along a 1400 km section of this 2600 km route, that extends north from Mexico City to Texas and New Mexico, United States of America. The route was actively used as a trade route for 300 years, from the mid-sixteenth to the nineteenth centuries, mainly for transporting silver extracted from the mines of Zacatecas, Guanajuato and San Luis Potosí, and mercury imported from Europe. Although it is a route that was motivated and consolidated by the mining industry, it also fostered the creation of social, cultural and religious links in particular between Spanish and Amerindian cultures.

Criteria: ii, iv, Inscribed 2010

• PREHISTORIC CAVES OF YAGUL AND MITLA IN THE CENTRAL VALLEY OF OAXACA Mexico

This property lies on the northern slopes of the Tlacolula valley in subtropical central Oaxaca and consists of two pre-Hispanic archaeological complexes and a series of prehistoric caves and rock shelters. Some of these shelters provide archaeological and rock-art evidence for the progress of nomadic hunter-gatherers to incipient farmers. Ten-thousand-year-old Cucurbitaceae seeds in one cave, Guilá Naquitz, are considered to be the earliest known evidence of domesticated plants in the continent, while corn cob fragments from the same cave are said to be the earliest documented evidence for the domestication of maize. The cultural landscape of the Prehistoric Caves of Yagul and Mitla demonstrates the link between man and nature that gave origin to the domestication of plants in North America, thus allowing the rise of Mesoamerican civilizations.

Criteria: iii Inscribed 2010

• PROTO-URBAN SITE OF SARAZM Tajikistan

Sarazm, which means 'where the land begins', is an archaeological site bearing testimony to the development of human settlements in Central Asia, from the fourth millennium bc to the end of the third millennium bc. The ruins demonstrate the early development of proto-urbanization in this region. This centre of settlement, one of the oldest in Central Asia, is situated between a mountainous region suitable for cattle rearing by nomadic pastoralists, and a large valley conducive to the development of agriculture and irrigation by the first settled populations in the region. Sarazm also demonstrates the existence of commercial and cultural exchanges and trade relations with peoples over an extensive geographical area, extending from the steppes of Central Asia and Turkmenistan, to the Iranian plateau, the Indus valley and as far as the Indian Ocean.

Criteria: ii, iii Inscribed 2010

• SEVENTEENTH-CENTURY CANAL RING AREA OF AMSTERDAM INSIDE THE SINGELGRACHT Netherlands

The historic urban ensemble of the canal district of Amsterdam was a project for a new 'port city' built at the end of the sixteenth and beginning of the seventeenth centuries. It comprises a network of canals to the west and south of the historic old town and the medieval port that encircled the old town, and was accompanied by the repositioning inland of the city's fortified boundaries, the Singelgracht. This was a long-term programme that involved extending the city by draining the swampland, using a system of canals in concentric arcs and filling in the intermediate spaces. These spaces allowed the development of a homogeneous urban ensemble including gabled houses and numerous monuments. This urban extension was the largest and most homogeneous of its time. It was a model of large-scale town planning, and served as a reference throughout the world until the nineteenth century.

Criteria: i, ii, iv Inscribed 2010

• PUTORANA PLATEAU Russian Federation

This site coincides with the area of the Putoransky State Nature Reserve, and is located in the central part of the Putorana Plateau in northern Central Siberia. It is situated about 100 km north of the

Canalside houses in Amsterdam. The profits from the worldwide trading networks built by the Dutch East India and West India Companies made Amsterdam not only the leading financial centre but the world's richest city.

The untouched arctic and subarctic ecosystems of the Putorana Plateau are supported by an extraordinary landscape of austere and dramatic beauty.

Arctic Circle. The part of the plateau inscribed on the World Heritage List harbours a complete set of subarctic and arctic ecosystems in an isolated mountain range, including pristine taiga, forest tundra, tundra and arctic desert systems, as well as untouched cold-water lake and river systems. A major reindeer migration route crosses the property, which represents an exceptional, large-scale and increasingly rare natural phenomenon.
Criteria: vii, ix Inscribed 2010

• AT-TURAIF DISTRICT IN AD-DIR'IYAH
Saudi Arabia
This property was the first capital of the Saudi dynasty, in the heart of the Arabian Penisula, northwest of Riyadh. Founded in the fifteenth century, it bears witness to the Najdi architectural style, which is specific to the centre of the Arabian peninsula. From the sixteenth century onwards the area around the ad-Dir'iyah oasis was the Saudi dynasty's powerbase. Ultimately they constructed a complete system of fortifications to defend it, of which at-Turaif, built in the eighteenth century, was the citadel. In the eighteenth and early nineteenth century, its political and religious role increased, and the citadel at at-Turaif became the centre of the temporal power of the House of Saud and the spread of the Wahhabi reform inside the Muslim religion.
Criteria: iv, v, vi Inscribed 2010

• PHOENIX ISLANDS PROTECTED AREA Kiribati
The Phoenix Island Protected Area (PIPA) is a 408,250 km² expanse of marine and terrestrial habitats in the Southern Pacific Ocean. The property encompasses the Phoenix Island Group, one of three island groups in Kiribati, and is the largest designated Marine Protected Area in the world. PIPA conserves one of the world's largest intact oceanic coral archipelago ecosystems, together with fourteen known underwater sea mounts (presumed to be extinct volcanoes) and other deep-sea habitats. The area contains approximately 800 known species of fauna, including about 200 coral species, 500 fish species, 18 marine mammals and 44 bird species. The structure and functioning of PIPA's ecosystems illustrate its pristine nature and importance as a migration route and reservoir.
Criteria: vii, ix Inscribed 2010

• HISTORIC VILLAGES OF KOREA: HAHOE AND YANGDONG Korea, Republic of
Founded between the fourteenth – fifteenth centuries, Hahoe and Yangdong are seen as the two most representative historic clan villages in the Republic of Korea. Their layout and location – sheltered by forested mountains and facing out onto a river and open agricultural fields – reflect the distinctive aristocratic Confucian culture of the early part of the Joseon Dynasty (1392–1910). The villages were located to provide both physical and spiritual nourishment from their surrounding landscapes. They include residences of the head families, together with substantial timber-framed houses of other clan members, also pavilions, study halls, Confucian academies for learning, and clusters of one-storey mud-walled, thatched-roofed houses, formerly for commoners. The landscapes of mountains, trees and water around the village, framed in views from pavilions and retreats, were celebrated for their beauty by seventeenth- and eighteenth-century poets.
Criteria: iii, iv Inscribed 2010

• CENTRAL HIGHLANDS OF SRI LANKA Sri Lanka
Sri Lanka's highlands are situated in the south-central part of the island. The property comprises the Peak Wilderness Protected Area, the Horton Plains National Park and the Knuckles Conservation Forest. These montane forests, where the land rises to 2,500 m above sea level, are home to an extraordinary range of flora and fauna, including several endangered species such as the western-purple-faced langur, the Horton Plains slender loris and the Sri Lankan leopard. The richness of the Central Highlands' plant and wildlife derives not just from its ecosystem but from the uplift of the land and the landforms that developed.
Criteria: ix, x Inscribed 2010

There are the remains of many palaces and an urban ensemble which were built on the edge of the ad-Dir'iyah oasis. In 1818 the town fell to the Ottoman Turks who destroyed it when they were forced out by the resurgent Saudis in 1824.

The Phoenix Island group has been only intermittently populated throughout its history. The almost complete lack of human influence on the marine environment has created an extensive and pristine ocean wilderness.

The villages of Hahoe (above) and Yangdong, in the Republic of Korea, were designed to reflect Neo-Confucian philosophy in their every aspect.

SITE INDEX

SITE INDEX

ACKNOWLEDGEMENTS

ACKNOWLEDGEMENTS

Based on official information made available by the United Nations Educational, Scientific and Cultural Organization (UNESCO) and its World Heritage Centre.

With thanks to:
The UNESCO World Heritage Centre and its staff.

IMAGE CREDITS

Images supplied by www.shutterstock.com unless noted with an asterisk. All photographers credited unless unknown.

↑ picture located at the top of the page
→ picture located in the middle of the page
↓ picture located at the bottom of the page

4↑ ©javarman; 4→ ©javarman; 4↓ ©Duncan Gilbert; 5↑ ©Wiktor Bubniak; 5↓ ©Katrina Leigh; 6↑ *©Anna Rosinska-Renaud; 6→ ©Olga Kolos; 6↓ ©Kitch Bain; 7↑ ©Wiktor Bubniak; 7→ ©PixAchi; 7↓ *©Danijela Pavlovic Markovic; 8↑ ©Om Prakash Yadav; 8↓ ©John A. Anderson; 9↑ ©Anton Foltin; 9→ ©Maugli; 9↓ ©Cristina Ciochina; 10↑ ©Aleksander Bolbot; 10→ ©Marek Slusarczyk; 10↓ ©Gautier Willaume; 11↑ ©steba; 11↓ ©Vladimir Wrangel; 12↑ ©Connors Bros.; 12↓ ©Daniel Loncarevic; 13↑ ©W H Chow; 13↓ ©Krkr; 14↑ ©paradoks_blizanaca; 14→ ©Jason Maehl; 14↓ ©lexan; 15↑ ©Grigory Kubatyan; 15↓ ©PixAchi; 16↑ ©Copestello; 16→ ©William Attard McCarthy; 16↓ ©Belle Momenti Photography; 17↑ ©Matt Ragen; 17→ ©OPIS; 17↓ ©Ioannis Ioannou; 18↑ ©Andrew Ferguson; 18↓ ©OPIS; 19↑ ©Milan Ljubisavljevic; 19→ ©David Davis; 19↓ ©David Thyberg; 20↑ ©Stephane Angue; 20→ ©Darja Vorontsova; 20↓ ©Bomshtein; 21↑ ©Claudio Giovanni Colombo; 21↓ ©Philip Lange; 22↑ ©tororo reaction; 22→ ©tororo reaction; 22↓ ©Sam DCruz; 23↑ ©Sam DCruz; 23↓ ©Natalia Bratslavsky; 24↑ ©Khirman Vladimir; 24↓ ©Sailorr; 25↑ ©faberfoto; 25→ *©UNESCO/Giovanni Boccardi; 25↓ ©Mirek Hejnicki; 26↑ ©Emma Holmwood; 26↓ ©Leonid Katsyka; 27↑ ©Ashley Whitworth; 27↓ ©WitR; 28↑ ©Clara; 28→ ©ostill; 28↓ ©Vladimir Melnik; 29↑ ©JeremyRichards; 29↓ ©Luciano Mortula; 30↑ ©Marek Slusarczyk; 30→ ©JeremyRichards; 30↓ ©Jarno Gonzalez Zarraonandia; 31↑ ©Matt Trommer; 31↓ ©Bryan Busovicki; 32↑ ©Lazar Mihai-Bogdan; 32↓ *©(CC by sa 3.0) ©Alan & Elaine Wilson; 33↑ ©Jarno Gonzalez Zarraonandia; 33↓ ©Matt Trommer; 34↑ ©sunnyfrog; 34↓ ©Slawomir Kruz; 35↑ ©JeremyRichards; 35↓ ©Susan McKenzie; 36↑ ©Marcio Jose Bastos Silva; 36↓ ©urosr; 37↑ ©Nelu Goia; 37→ ©Palis Michael; 37↓ ©Jason Maehl; 38↑ ©Brandus Dan Lucian; 38↓ ©Rafael Ramirez Lee; 39↑ ©Kenneth V. Pilon; 39↓ ©Justin Black; 40↑ ©Joseph Calev; 40↓ ©Larsek; 41↑ ©Dainis Derics;

41↓ ©Factoria singular fotografia; 42↑ *©(CC by sa 2.0) Glauco Umbelino; 42↓ ©Jaroslaw Grudzinski; 43↑ ©ImageDesign; 43↓ ©Oscar F. Chuyn; 44↑ ©Jason Maehl; 44→ ©Holger Mette; 44↓ ©Chris Howey; 45↑ ©Jean Frooms; 45→ ©Joe Gough; 45↓ ©aguilarphoto; 46↑ ©Joe Gough; 46→ ©Vladimir Melnik; 46↓ ©Nikolay Titov; 47↑ ©Asit Jain; 47→ ©Mikhail Nekrasov; 47↓ ©LianeM; 48↑ ©John Evans; 48↓ ©inacio pires; 49↑ ©Ralph Loesche; 49↓ ©dr. Le Thanh Hung; 50↑ ©edobric; 50↓ ©Rachael Russell; 51↑ *©Mark Steward; 51→ ©Vinicius Tupinamba; 51↓ ©sunxuejun; 52↑ ©Zsolt Nyulaszi; 52↓ ©enote; 53↑ ©Matt Houser; 53↓ ©Michael Levy; 54↑ ©Mary Lane; 54↓ ©Tamara Kulikova; 55↑ ©russal; 55↓ ©emily2k; 56↑ ©Jack Cronkhite; 56↓ ©Bidouze Stéphane; 57↑ ©pandeqiang; 57→ ©PRANAV VORA; 57↓ ©Koylias Ioannis; 58↑ ©Mary Lane; 58↓ ©Ivan Montero Martinez; 59↑ ©Ewen Cameron; 59↓ ©Bill Perry; 60↑ ©Jozsef Szasz-Fabian; 60↓ ©Thomas Barrat; 61↑ ©VanHart; 61↓ ©Joseph Calev; 62↑ ©Aneta Skoczewska; 62↓ ©Korobanova; 63↑ ©Pedro Pinto; 63↓ ©Ioannis Nousis; 64↑ ©Fast Snail; 64→ ©Dainis Derics; 64↓ ©Dmytro Korolov; 65↑ ©Sam DCruz; 65↓ ©Dimon; 66↑ ©Sander van Sinttruye; 66↓ ©akva; 67↑ *©Mark Steward; 67↓ ©Mircea BEZERGHEANU; 67↓ ©Magdalena Bujak; 68↑ ©Sofilou; 68→ *©Dieter Biskamp; 68↓ ©Bill Perry; 69↑ ©Specta; 69→ ©Mikael Damkier; 69↓ ©ultimathule; 70↑ ©Cristina CIOCHINA; 70↓ ©Elena Pokrovskaya; 71↑ ©POZZO DI BORGO Thomas; 71↓ ©Ferenc Cegledi; 73↑ ©Luciano Mortula; 73→ ©robert paul van beets; 73↓ ©Holger Mette; 74↑ ©PixAchi; 74→ ©Olga Zaporozhskaya; 74↓ ©paul prescott; 75↑ ©enote; 75→ ©Khirman Vladimir; 75↓ ©Jarno Gonzalez Zarraonandia; 76↑ ©Martin Mette; 76↓ ©Valery Shanin; 77↑ ©JeremyRichards; 77↓ ©krechet; 79↑ ©jpatava; 79→ ©Fedor Selivanov; 79↓ ©Pichugin Dmitry; 80↑ ©Thomas M Perkins; 80→ ©Jarno Gonzalez Zarraonandia; 80↓ ©Bill Perry; 81↑ ©Kris Vandereycken; 81↓ ©Huang Yuetao; 82↑ ©polartern; 82↓ ©carlos sanchez pereyra; 83↑ ©Ungor; 83→ ©Danilo Ascione; 83↓ ©Andrzej Gibasiewicz; 84↑ ©2009fotofriends; 84↓ ©Keith Brooks; 85↑ ©Gianluca Figliola Fantini; 85↓ ©edobric; 85↓ ©Helen & Vlad Filatov; 86↑ ©Willem Tims; 86↓ ©Jonald Morales; 87↑ ©Claudio Giovanni Colombo; 87→ ©godrick; 87↓ ©Joel Blit; 89↑ ©koi88; 89↓ ©Peter Zurek; 90↑ ©Jorge Felix Costa; 90→ ©Alex Garaev; 90↓ ©Pichugin Dmitry; 91↑ ©BESTWEB; 91→ ©L F File; 91↓ ©Tobias Guttmann; 92↑ ©Valeria73; 92↓ ©Aron Brand; 93↑ ©aguilarphoto; 93→ ©Valeria73; 93↓ ©Dan Breckwoldt; 94↑ ©szefei; 94→ ©Veronika Trofer; 94↓ ©Lagui; 95↑ ©Maksym Kalyta; 95→ *©Tito Dupret; 95↓ ©Razvan Stroie; 96↑ ©Mikhail Nekrasov; 96↓ ©Perov Stanislav; 97↑ ©Floris Slooff; 97↓ ©rj Ierich; 99↑ ©ollirg; 99↓ *©Tito Dupret; 100↑ ©Marcin-linfernum; 100↓ ©Uwe Bumann; 101↑ ©Buddhadl; 101→ ©MaxFX; 101↓ *©Austrian National Tourist Office/Diejun; 102↑ ©Joerg Hausmann; 102↓ ©Ivo Brezina; 103↑ ©sunxuejun; 103→ ©Laitr Keiows; 103↓ ©lexan; 105↑ ©David Woods; 105↓ ©Jan Schuler; 106↑ ©Alfredo Schaufelberger; 106↓ ©Tudor Stanica; 107↑ *©Tito Dupret;

107↑ *©Tito Dupret; 107↓ ©Guillermo Garcia; 108↑ ©Joerg Humpe; 108↓ ©Pablo H Caridad; 109↑ ©Valeria73; 109↓ ©Bartlomiej K. Kwieciszewski; 109↓ *©Tito Dupret; 110↑ ©Sam DCruz; 110↓ ©riekephotos; 111↑ ©Ales Liska; 111↓ ©baldovina; 111↓ ©kwest; 113↑ ©Albo; 113↓ ©zhouhui8525; 114↑ ©Joao Virissimo; 114↓ ©Jarno Gonzalez Zarraonandia; 115↑ ©slava_vn; 115↓ *©Tito Dupret; 116↑ ©Chong Wei Jin; 116→ ©Ivonne Wierink; 116↓ ©Chow Shue Ma; 117↑ ©Karel Gallas; 117↓ ©Tim Arbaev; 118↑ ©Pavel K; 118↓ ©Craig Hanson; 119↑ ©Wojciech Zbieg; 119↓ ©Buddhadl; 120↑ ©ecoventurestravel; 120↓ *©Tito Dupret; 121↑ ©rubiphoto; 121↓ ©Julia R.; 121↓ ©Sílvia Antunes; 123↑ ©Daniel Gilbey; 123↓ ©javarman; 123↓ *©Israel Ministry of Tourism www.goisrael.com; 124↑ ©Rostislav Glinsky; 124→ ©Alexander Cyliax; 124↓ ©Joseph Calev; 125↑ *©UNESCO/Claudio Margottini; 125↓ ©LianeM; 126↑ ©PavleMarjanovic; 126→ *©Tito Dupret; 126↓ ©jeff gynane; 127↑ ©urosr; 127↓ ©mastiflliu; 129↑ ©Wiktor Bubniak; 129↓ ©Andrew Barker; 130↑ ©lidian; 130→ *©Tito Dupret; 130↓ *©(CC by sa 2.0) Sorosh; 131↑ ©Joern; 131↓ *©Fleur Gayet; 132↑ ©Holger Mette; 132↓ ©Stuart Blyth; 133↑ ©Joerg Humpe; 133→ ©Eremin Sergey; 133↓ ©Plotnikoff; 134↑ ©Horácio José Lopes dos Santos; 134↓ ©alysta; 137↓ ©Ng Wei Keong; 137↑ ©GagarinART; 137↓ ©Zimins@NET; 137↓ ©newphotoservice; 138↑ ©manfredxy; 138↓ ©Jesus Cervantes; 139↑ ©Richard Griffin; 139→ ©Ruta Saulyte-Laurinaviciene; 139↓ ©Holger Mette; 140↑ *©(CC by sa 2.0) shaunamullally ; 140↓ ©Neale Cousland; 141↑ ©Holger Mette; 141↓ ©Vlad Zharoff; 142↑ ©Andy Lim; 142↓ ©Brykaylo Yuriy; 143↑ ©Petros Tsonis; 143↓ ©Vlad Ghiea; 143↓ ©Coquilleau; 144↑ ©El Choclo; 144↓ ©PavleMarjanovic; 145↑ ©RookCreations; 145→ ©Katarzyna Mazurowska; 145↓ ©Aleksandrs Jermakovichs; 147↑ ©Peter Wey; 147↓ ©Lori Skelton; 147↓ ©Tatiana Belova; 148↑ *©(CC by sa 2.5) Adrian Pingstone; 148↓ *©(CC by sa 2.0) serapio; 149↑ ©Jacques Descloitres, MODIS Rapid Response Team, NASA/GSFC; 149↓ ©Dan Breckwoldt; 150↑ ©thewhiteview; 150→ *©(CC by sa 3.0) B.navez; 150↓ ©ziggysofi; 151↑ ©Jeremy Richards; 151↓ *©(CC by sa 2.0) Ensie & Matthias; 152↑ ©Gregory James Van Raalte; 152↓ ©Dmitry Zamorin; 153↑ ©Fedor Selivanov; 153→ *©(CC 3.0) Dr. Randi Rotjan, New England Aquarium. www.neaq.org; 153↓ ©Stephan Scherhag

CC by 2.0 These works are licensed under the Creative Commons 2.0 Attribution License. To view a copy of this license, visit http://creativecommons.org/licenses/by/2.0/

CC by sa 2.0 These works are licensed under the Creative Commons Attribution Share Alike 2.0 License. To view a copy of this license, visit http://creativecommons.org/licenses/by-sa/2

CC by sa 2.5 These works are licensed under the Creative Commons Attribution Share Alike 2.5 License. To view a copy of this license, visit http://creativecommons.org/licenses/by-sa/2.5/

CC by sa 3.0 These works are licensed under the Creative Commons Attribution Share Alike 3.0 License. To view a copy of this license, visit http://creativecommons.org/licenses/by-sa/3.0/

Tito Dupret/WHTour.org (www.worldheritage-tour.org) is a non-profit organization documenting World Heritage sites in panography – 360 degree imaging – thanks to the support of the J. M. Kaplan Fund from New York, USA.

The Joy of Sex

A Cordon Bleu Guide to Lovemaking

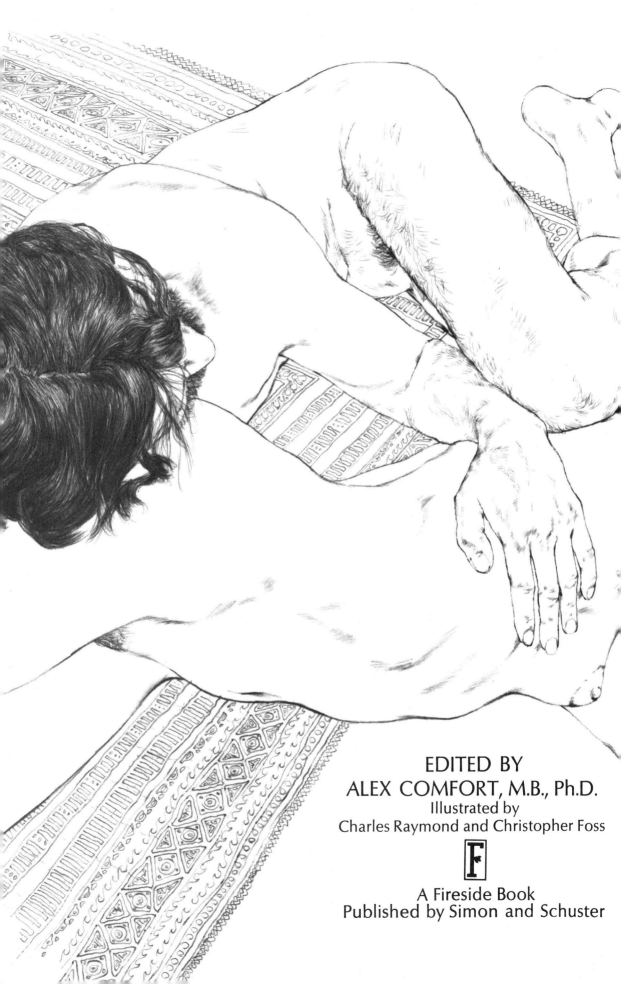

EDITED BY
ALEX COMFORT, M.B., Ph.D.
Illustrated by
Charles Raymond and Christopher Foss

A Fireside Book
Published by Simon and Schuster

The Joy of Sex
A Cordon Bleu Guide to Lovemaking

Contents

General Editor: Alex Comfort
House Editor: Max Monsarrat
Designer: Janette Palmer

Art Director: Peter Kindersley

The publishers would like to thank the artists, Charles Raymond and Christopher Foss, for the care and devotion they have lavished on their illustrations for *The Joy of Sex*. They have throughout worked closely with the Editor to reflect the style of this book – its humour, honesty and directness. The results are a magnificent tribute to their skill and dedication.

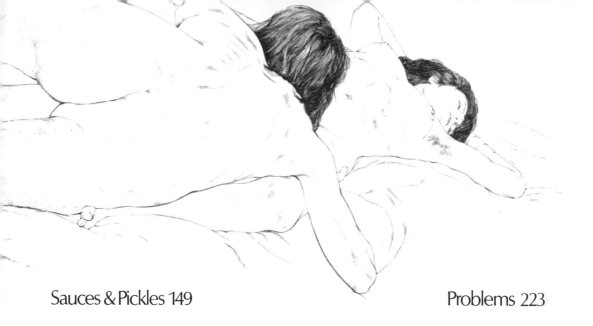

Sauces & Pickles 149

Problems 223

Index 254

Preface

A biologist-writer interested in human sexual behavior is asked to read many prospective books –
admonitary, weird, religious, naive, conventional or
just plain ignorant – all of them aiming to be helpful,
and none of them getting the key quite right.

This book is based originally on the work of
one couple. One of them is a practicing physician;
their anonymity is accordingly professional, and the
final text incorporates the suggestions of several
couples, plus a few experts. The basic idea struck
me as unique. A cookery book is a sophisticated and
unanxious account of available dishes – culinary
fantasies as well as staple diets – with the practical
details provided. This book is an equally unanxious
account of the full repertoire of human hetero-
sexuality. As such, it is long overdue. A cookbook
tells the novice how to tackle a live lobster, what to
do when the mayonnaise separates, how to fix a
chateaubriand. The authors of this book describe,
in the same unruffled detail, and with a sense of fun,
what to do about impotence or premature ejaculation, how to manage oral sex, how to play symbolically aggressive games, how to treat a partner who
is hip for 'discipline,' how not to be bothered by
fetishes, how to use kinky clothes as sex stimuli. A
good many professional counselors react to such
questions – when clients have the pluck to ask them
– if not with psychiatric and moral anxiety, at least
with a lack of detailed knowhow. Doctors can't
necessarily know your needs from their own sex

lives, and not all of them have much idea of the range and variety of human sexual behaviors: I wish I had read such a recipe book as a medical student.

I have done little to the original draft apart from expansion to cover more topics: the authors' choice of emphases and their light-hearted style have been left alone. Where explanation is needed (and explanation, in conventionally anxious matters, helps) they introduce depth-psychology in a jargonless form. This is the right approach at a moment when primatology and classical human psychodynamics look like joining hands, and for some of the explanatory biology I am to blame.

It is difficult to produce anything really new in the field of 'sex education.' The permissive society has permitted everything from worried and po-faced admonition to eccentric porn. Most book-stalls carry a rash of 'straight' books which stop short of answers, and 'counseling' magazines based on unpractical, if not pathological, fantasy. It is high time adult readers were treated to some humane and experienced sense. I hope that the book will prove as useful to professional counselors as to couples, but it is the ordinary, sexually active, reader – anxious both to enjoy sexuality and to be responsible about it – who should benefit most.

On Advanced Lovemaking

All of us who are not disabled or dumb are able to dance and sing—
after a fashion. This, if you think about it, summarizes the justification
for learning to make love. Love, like singing, is something to be taken
spontaneously. On the other hand, the difference between Pavlova and
the Palais de Danse, or opera and barber-shop singing, is much less
than the difference between sex as the last generation came to accept
it and sex as it can be.

At least we recognize this now (so that instead of worrying if sex is
sinful, most people now worry whether they are 'getting satisfaction'—
one can worry about anything, given the determination). There are
now enough books about the basics: the main use of these is to get rid
of worries over the normality, possibility, and variety of sexual experience. The people who go to Masters and Johnson are getting over
hangups so basic that in past generations the folk tradition would have
taken care of them. At least the 'permissive' scene in publishing removed some of this cover-up. Our book is slightly different, in that
there are now enough people who have the basics and really need
hard information (not simply reassurance).

Chef-grade cooking doesn't happen naturally: it starts at the point
where people know how to prepare and enjoy food, are curious about
it and willing to take trouble preparing it, read recipe hints, and find
they are helped by one or two detailed techniques. It's hard to make
mayonnaise by trial and error, for instance. Cordon Bleu sex, as we
define it, is exactly the same situation—the extra one can get from
comparing notes, using some imagination, trying way-out or new
experiences, when one already is making satisfying love and wants
to go on from there.

It is always sad when a love relationship runs aground through noncommunication (fear of rejection over some fantasy need, inability to
come to terms with aggressive needs through a misplaced idea of
tenderness, inability to accept sexuality as play). These hangups, plus
monotony, are a large part of all five- or seven-year itches, and, between loving and tolerant people, avoidable.

We shall have four sorts of readers; those who don't fancy it, find it
disturbing and would rather stay the way they are, with Reuben sand-
wiches—these should put it down, accept our apologies, and stay the
way they are: those who are with the idea, but don't like our choice
of techniques—these should remember it's a menu, not a rulebook.
We have tried to stay wide-open, but it is always difficult to write about
things one doesn't enjoy, and we have left out long discussion of the

very specialized—one-legged ladies, mackintoshes—and things like S and M, which aren't really love or even sex in quite our sense of the word. People who like these know already what they want to try. One aim of this book is to cure the notion, born of non-discussion, that common sex needs are odd or weird. As to the general repertoire, the whole joy of sex-with-love is that there are no rules, so long as you enjoy, and the choice is practically unlimited. This is the way most people will use our notes—as a personal one-couple notebook from which they might get ideas. Then there are the hardy experimentalists, bent on trying absolutely everything. They too will do best to read this exactly like a cookbook—except that sex is safer in this respect, between lovers, in that you can't get obese or atherosclerotic on it, or give yourself ulcers. The worst you can get is sore, anxious or disappointed. Sex must be physically the safest of all human activities (leaving out social repercussions). You can have infinite variety to taste. But one needs a steady basic diet of quiet, night-and-morning matrimonial intercourse to stand this experimentation on, simply because, contrary to popular ideas, the more regular sex a couple has the higher the deliberately contrived peaks—just as the more you cook routinely, the better and the more reliable banquets you can stage.

Finally, the people we are addressing are the adventurous and uninhibited lovers who want to find the limits of their ability to enjoy sex. That means we take some things for granted—having intercourse naked and spending time over it; being able and willing to make it last, up to a whole afternoon on occasion; having privacy and washing facilities; not being scared of things like genital kisses; not being obsessed with one sexual trick to the exclusion of all others, and, of course, loving each other.

This book is about love as well as sex as the title implies: you don't get high-quality sex on any other basis—either you love each other before you come to want it, or, if you happen to get it, you love each other because of it, or both. No point in arguing this, but just as you can't cook without heat you can't make love without feedback (which may be the reason we say 'make love' rather than 'make sex'). Sex is the one place where we today can learn to treat people as people. Feedback means the right mixture of stop and go, tough and tender, exertion and affection. This comes by empathy and long mutual knowledge. Anyone who *expects* to get this in a first attempt with a stranger is an optimist, or a neurotic—if he does, it is what used to be called love at first sight, and isn't expendable: 'skill', or variety, is no substitute. Also one can't teach tenderness.

This is a book about valid sexual behaviors, plus a certain amount about how and why they work. It isn't a dictionary: in particular we've avoided a lot of the name-entries attached to particular sorts of performance at the start of the century—the reason is that they are largely out of date. Rather than sticking on labels like narcissism or sadomasochism, biologists and psychiatrists now tend to start by looking at actual behaviors and seeing what use they are or what they signify. Lump names are a handy shorthand, but they tend to be offputting, especially when very general human behaviors get a label which makes them sound like an illness; and they tend to trigger pointless

collectors'-piece arguments, for example whether 'women are naturally masochistic' because they get penetrated rather than doing the penetrating.

We haven't started with a short lecture on the biology and psychology of human sex: instead we've put a little about it into the various entries. Most people now know that man's 'sexuality' starts at birth and runs continuously from mother-child to man-woman relations, that it involves some periods of programmed anxiety about the genitals ('castration fears') which probably served originally to stop young apes from falling foul of their fathers, but which, in man, are building stones for a lot of other adult behaviors; and that the wide range of human sex needs of all kinds controlled by this unique developmental background—long childhood, close mother-child contact but a taboo on mother-child or father-child sex, close pair-bonding which centers in sexual play, the way bird pair-formation centers in nest-building and display (this is the phenomenon more often described as love), and so on. Without going into details we've mentioned throughout the book how parts of this human background fit into the pattern of what humans enjoy sexually. Most human sex behaviors 'mean' a whole range of different things (the in-word is that they are 'overdetermined' —for examples of what this means in practice see what we've written about *Clothes,* for instance).

A little theory makes sex more interesting, more comprehensible, and less scarey—too much is a put-down, especially as you're likely to get it out of perspective and become a spectator of your own performance. If you have really troublesome hangups you need an expert to hold the mirror for you and go personally into what they mean— self-adhesive labels are actively unhelpful. All humans are sadistic, narcissistic, masochistic, bisexual and what have you—if you stuck on all the labels you would look like a cabin trunk. What matters is whether any of the behaviors in which you engage are bothering you or other people—if so, they are a useful pointer to what the problem is, but no more than that.

The starting point of all lovemaking is close bodily contact. Love has been defined as the harmony of two souls and the contact of two epidermes. It is also, from our infancy, the starting point of human relationships and needs. Our culture ('Anglo-Saxon'), after several centuries of intense taboos on many such contacts—between friends, between males—which are used by other cultures, has cut down 'intimacy' based on bodily contact to parent-child and lover-lover situations. We're getting over this taboo, or at least the part which has spilled over into baby-raising and explicit lovemaking, but coupled with our other cultural reservation, which says that play and fantasy are only safe for children, it has dealt us a bad hand for really full and personal sex. Our idea of sex wouldn't be recognizable to some other cultures, though our range of choice is the widest ever. For a start it's over-genital: 'sex' for our culture means putting the penis in the vagina. Man's whole skin is a genital organ. As to touching, proximity and so on, see Desmond Morris's brilliant account in *Intimate Behavior,* which catalogues our hangups. Good sex is about the only adult remedy for these.

There isn't too much point in crying over cultural spilt milk. *Our* sex repertoire has to be geared to us as we are, not to Trobriand Islanders (who have their own different hangups). We need extensive sex play which is centered in intercourse and in doing things. At the same time we might as well plan our menu so that we learn to use the rest of our equipment. That includes our whole skin surface, our feelings of identity, aggression and so on, and all of our fantasy needs. Luckily, sex behavior in humans is enormously elastic (it has had to be, or we wouldn't be here), and also nicely geared to help us express most of the needs which society or our upbringing have corked up. Elaboration in sex is something we need rather specially (though it isn't confined to our sort of society) and it has the advantage that if we really make it work it makes us more, not less, receptive to each other as people. This is the answer to anyone who thinks that conscious effort to increase our sex range is 'mechanical' or a substitute for treating each other as people—we may start that way, but it's an excellent entry to learning that we are people—probably the only one our sort of society can really use at the moment. There may be other places we can learn to express all of ourselves, and do it mutually, but there aren't many.

Those are our assumptions. Granted this feedback and mutual exploration, there are two modes of sex, the duet and the solo, and a good concert alternates between them. The duet is a cooperative effort aiming at simultaneous orgasm, or at least one orgasm each, and complete, untechnically planned let-go. This in fact needs skill, and can be built up from more calculated 'love-play' until doing the right thing for both of you becomes fully automatic. This is the basic sexual meal. The solo, by contrast, is when one partner is the player and the other the instrument; the aim of the player is to produce results on the other's pleasure experience as extensive, unexpected and generally wild as his or her skill allows—to blow them out of themselves. The player doesn't lose control, though he or she can get wildly excited by what is happening to the other. The instrument *does* lose control—in fact, with a responsive instrument and a skillful performer, this is the concerto situation—if it ends in an uncontrollable ensemble, so much the better. All the elements of music and the dance get into this scene —rhythm, mounting tension, tantalization, even actual aggression: 'I'm like the executioner,' said the lady in the Persian poem, 'but where he inflicts intolerable pain I will only make you die of pleasure.' There is indeed an element of aggression or infliction in the solo mode, which is why some lovers dislike it and others overdo it, but no major lovemaking is complete without some solo passages.

The antique idea of the woman as passive and the man as performer used to ensure that he would show off playing solos on her, and some marriage manuals perpetuate this idea. In a more liberated scene she is herself the soloist par excellence, whether in getting him excited to start with, or in controlling him and showing off all her skills. In fact there is only one really unmusical situation, and that is the reverse of a real solo, where one uses the other to obtain satisfaction, without any attempt at mutuality. True, one may say, 'Do it yourself this time,' as a quick finish, but it is no more than that.

In the old world extended solo techniques have never quite died as

a male skill: in Europe at one time calculated solo skill among women was supposed to be limited to prostitutes (most of whom conspicuously lack it, for lack of empathy). Now it is on the way back, starting half-heartedly with 'petting to climax,' but getting today to be a polite accomplishment: we shall probably have extension courses soon. This, as usual, will likely go too far, and become a substitute for full, let-go intercourse—whereas in fact it's a preparation, supplement, overture, bridging operation, tailpiece, interlude. The solo-given orgasm is unique, however—neither bigger nor smaller in either sex than in a full duet, but different. We've heard both sexes call it 'sharper but not so round,' and most people who have experienced both like to alternate them; it is also quite different from self-stimulation, which most people like occasionally too. Trying to say how they differ is a little like describing wines. Differ they do, however, and much depends on cultivating and alternating them.

Solo devices are not, of course, necessarily separate from intercourse. Apart from leading into it there are many coital solos—for the woman astride, for example—while mutual masturbation or genital kisses can be fully fledged duets. Nor is it anything to do with 'clitoral' versus 'vaginal' orgasm (this is only a crass anatomical way of trying to verbalize a real difference), since the man feels the same distinction, and you can get a roaring solo orgasm from the skin of the fingertips, the breasts, the soles of the feet, or the earlobes of a receptive woman (less commonly extra-genitally in the man). Coition which ought to be mutual but gives a solo feeling (to her) is what people who talk about 'clitoral orgasm' are trying as a rule to verbalize. Solo-response can be electrifyingly extreme in the quietest people. Skillfully handled by someone who doesn't stop for yells of murder, but does know when to stop, a woman can get orgasm after orgasm, and a man can be kept hanging just short of climax to the limit of human endurance.

Toplevel enjoyment doesn't *have* to be varied, it just often is. In fact, being stuck rigidly with one sex technique usually means anxiety. In this book we have not, for example, gone heavily on things like coital postures. The non-freak ones are now familiar to most people from writing and pictures if not from trial—the freak ones, as a rule, one could think of spontaneously, but few of them have marked advantages except as a spectator sport. Moreover, the technique of straight intercourse, which needs a suspension of self-observation, doesn't lend itself to treatment in writing, except for elementary students. This explains the apparent emphasis in our book on extras—the sauces and pickles. Most of these are psychologically and biologically geared to cover specific human needs, often left over from a 'civilized' childhood. Individuals who, through a knot in their psyche, are obliged to *live* on sauce and pickle only are unfortunate in missing the most sustaining part of the meal—kinks and exclusive obsessions in sex are very like living exclusively on horseradish sauce through allergy to beef; fear of horseradish sauce as indigestible, unnecessary and immature is another hangup, namely puritanism. As to our choice of needs and/or problems, we've based it on a good many years of listening to people.

In writing descriptively about sex it is hard not to be solemn, how-

ever unsolemnly we play in bed. In fact, one of the things still missing from the 'new sexual freedom' is the unashamed ability to use sex as play—in this, psychoanalytic ideas of maturity are nearly as much to blame as oldstyle moralisms about what is normal or perverse. We are all immature, and have anxieties and aggressions. Coital play, like dreaming, is probably man's programmed way of dealing acceptably with these, just as children express their fears and aggressions in games. If they play at Indian tortures, out of jealously of their little brother or the opposite sex, we don't call that sadism: adults are unfortunately afraid of playing games, of dressing up, of acting scenes. It makes them self-conscious: something horrid might get out.

Bed is the place to play all the games you have ever wanted to play, at the play-level—if adults could become less self-conscious about such 'immature' needs we should have fewer deeply anxious and committed fetishists creating a sense of community to enable them to do their thing without feeling isolated. We heard of a frogman who used to make his wife sleep in rubber bedsheets; he had to become a frogman for real, because dressing in a diving-suit for kicks was embarrassing and made him look odd. If we were able to transmit the sense of play which is essential to a full, enterprising and healthily immature view of sex between committed people, we would be performing a mitzvah: people who play flagellation games and are excited by them bother nobody, provided they don't turn off a partner who finds the scenario frightening. People who enact similar aggressions outside the bedroom are apt to end up at My Lai or Belsen. The aim of this book is pleasure, not psychiatry, but we suspect that the two coincide. Play is one function of sexual elaboration—playfulness is a part of love which could well be the major contribution of the Aquarian revolution to human happiness. Hence the association with pregenital and immature sauces and pickles.

But still the main dish is loving, unself-conscious intercourse—long, frequent, varied, ending with both parties satisfied but not so full they can't face another light course, and another meal in a few hours. The *pièce de résistance* is the good old face-to-face matrimonial, the finishing-off position, with mutual orgasm, and starting with a full day or night of ordinary tenderness. Other ways of making love are special in various ways, and the changes of timbre are infinitely varied—complicated ones are for special occasions, or special uses like holding off an over-quick male orgasm, or are things which, like pepper steak, are stunning once a year but not dietary.

If you don't like our repertoire or if it doesn't square with yours, never mind. The aim of *The Joy of Sex* is to stimulate your creative imagination. You can preface your own ideas with 'this is how we play it,' and play it your way. But by that time, when you have tried all your own creative sexual fantasies, you won't need books. Sex books can only suggest techniques to encourage you to experiment.

There are after all only two 'rules' in good sex, apart from the obvious one of not doing things which are silly, antisocial or dangerous. One is 'Don't do anything you don't really enjoy,' and the other is 'Find your partner's needs and don't balk them if you can help it.' In other words, a good giving and taking relationship depends on a

compromise (so does going to a show—if you both want the same thing, fine: if not, take turns and don't let one partner always dictate). This can be easier than it sounds, because unless your partner wants something you find actively off-putting, real lovers get a reward not only from their own satisfactions but from seeing the other respond and become satisfied. Most wives who don't like Chinese food will eat it occasionally for the pleasure of seeing a Sinophile husband enjoy it, and vice versa. Partners who won't do this over specific sex needs are usually balking, not because they've tried it and it's a turn-off (many experimental dishes turn out nicer than you expected), but simply through ignorance of the range of human needs, plus being scared if these include things like aggression, cultivating extragenital sensation, or play-acting, which the last half-century's social mythology pretended weren't there. Reading a full list of the unscheduled accessory sex behaviors which some normal people find helpful might be thought a necessary preliminary to any extended sex relationship, particularly marriage if you really intend to stay with it, but so far the books haven't helped much in this respect. If anything they've scared people rather than instructed them.

Couples should match up their needs and preferences (though people don't find these out at once). You won't get to some of our suggestions or understand them until you've learned to respond. It's a mistake to run so long as walking is such an enchanting and new experience, and you may be happy pedestrians who match automatically. Most people who marry rightly prefer to try themselves out and play themselves in. Where a rethink really helps is at the point where you've got used to each other socially (sex needs aren't the only ones which need matching up between people who live together) and feel that the surface needs repolishing. If you think that sexual relations are overrated, it does need repolishing, and you haven't paid enough attention to the wider use of your sexual equipment as a way of communicating totally. The traditional American expedient at the point where the surface gets dull is to trade in the relationship and start all over in an equally uninstructed attempt with someone else, on the offchance of getting a better match-up by random choice. This is emotionally wasteful and you usually repeat the same mistakes. It would be worth trying either to map each other's sex tastes before starting, or to try to learn them if you haven't done so intuitively so far. If you're planting a long term garden it's at least sensible to know a little about the biology of plants. Long-term love expressed in active sex means you have to know something about the biology of people. Don't go in for mutual do-it-yourself psychoanalysis, or you'll bring down the roof on each other. We all have pregenital needs, however we were weaned, potted or reared, just as we all have fingerprints and a navel. Finding out someone else's needs and your own, and how to express them in bed, is not only interesting and educative but rewarding, and what sexual love is about.

Read through or dip into this book together and separately. These are all techniques which some straight people need and use to fill out their sex lives, or simply enjoy as play and relaxation. Don't waste time on things which aren't for you. All the ideas in the book work as a

turn-on for some people, virtually none for everyone. Go by your own needs and your partner's. Do note anything which turns one or both of you on to the point of saying 'I'd like to try that.' If you're shy of talking about sexual needs, make a list of the page numbers you'd like your partner to read, and exchange lists (this isn't a plug to make you buy two copies—you can take turns). Then take it mutually from there. You will find out things about each other you didn't know, and all of them will be rewarding.

Colorplates Appearing in Center Insert

The Art of Making Love

'The whole joy of sex-with-love is that there are no rules, so long as you enjoy, and the choice is practically unlimited.'

'You don't get high-quality sex without love and feedback. Feedback means the right mixture of stop and go, tough and tender, exertion and affection.'

'Bed is the right place to play all the games you have ever wanted to play. This is essential to a full, enterprising and healthily immature view of sex between committed people. Take off your shell along with your clothes.'

'There are only two guidelines in good sex, "Don't do anything you don't really enjoy", and "Find out your partner's needs and don't balk them if you can help it." '

'Finding out someone else's needs and your own, and how to express them in bed, is not only interesting and educative, but rewarding, and what sexual love is all about.'

'We must learn to use the whole of our skin
surface, our feelings of identity, aggression and
so on, and all our fantasy needs.'

'A woman's greatest asset after her beauty is her natural perfume—it comes from the whole of her, hair, skin, breasts, armpits, genitals. The smell and feel of a man's skin probably have more to do with sexual attraction than any other single feature.'

'Sex ought to be a wholly satisfying link between two affectionate people from which they emerge unanxious, rewarded and ready for more.'

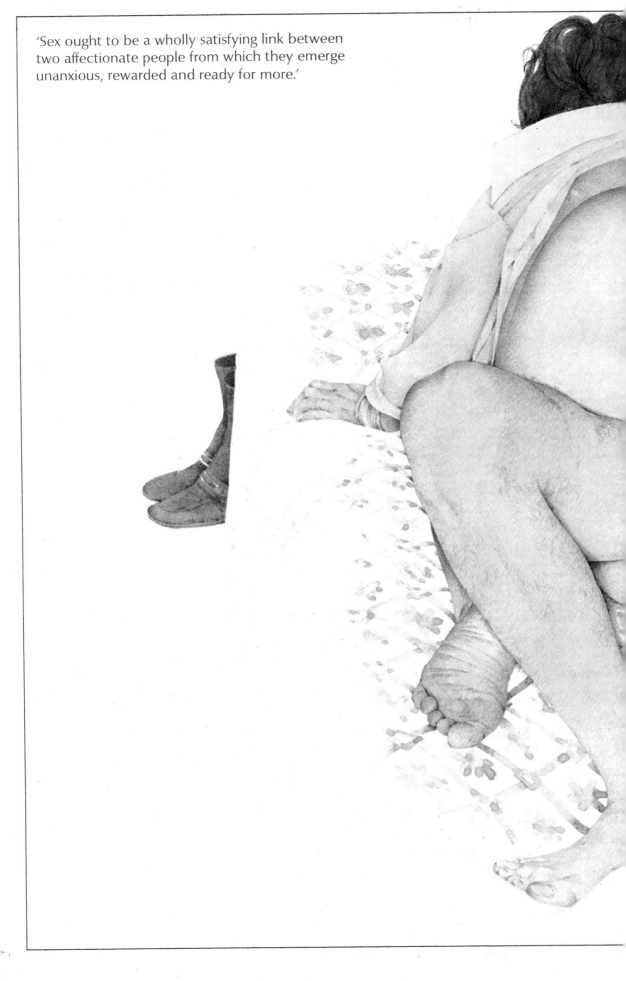

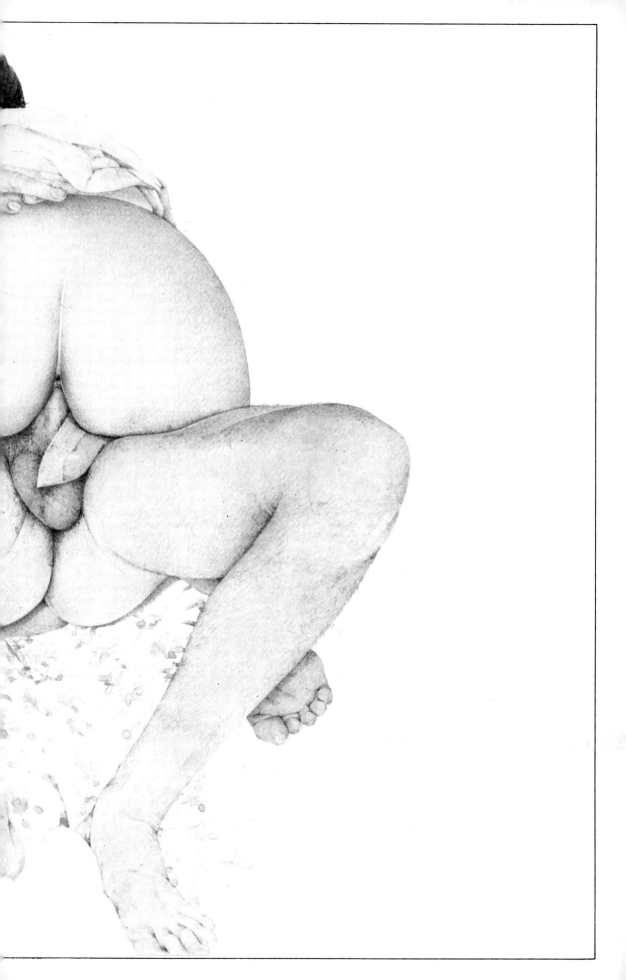

'Women who have really learned to enjoy sex are usually fascinated by their partner's penis, as men are by women's breasts, shape, odor and feel, and learn to play with it fully and skillfully. Good hand and mouth work practically guarantee a good partner.'

'Tenderness does not exclude extremely violent games (though many people neither need nor want these) but it is shown fully in the way you touch each other.'

'Women often fail to use enough pressure, especially in handwork, though the light variety is a sensation on its own. Start very gently, making full use of the skin surface and work up. Male strength, on the other hand, is a turn-on in sex, but it isn't expressed in clumsiness, bear hugs and brute force.

'Male sexual response is far brisker and more automatic than women's: it is triggered by *things*. Your clothes, breasts, odor, etc. aren't what he loves instead of you—simply the things he needs to set sex in motion to express love.'

'Uninhibited partners will tell each other about their fantasies (try free-associating just before orgasm if you are shy). Really communicating partners look for them and put them on the menu unannounced—there is no more complete communication.'

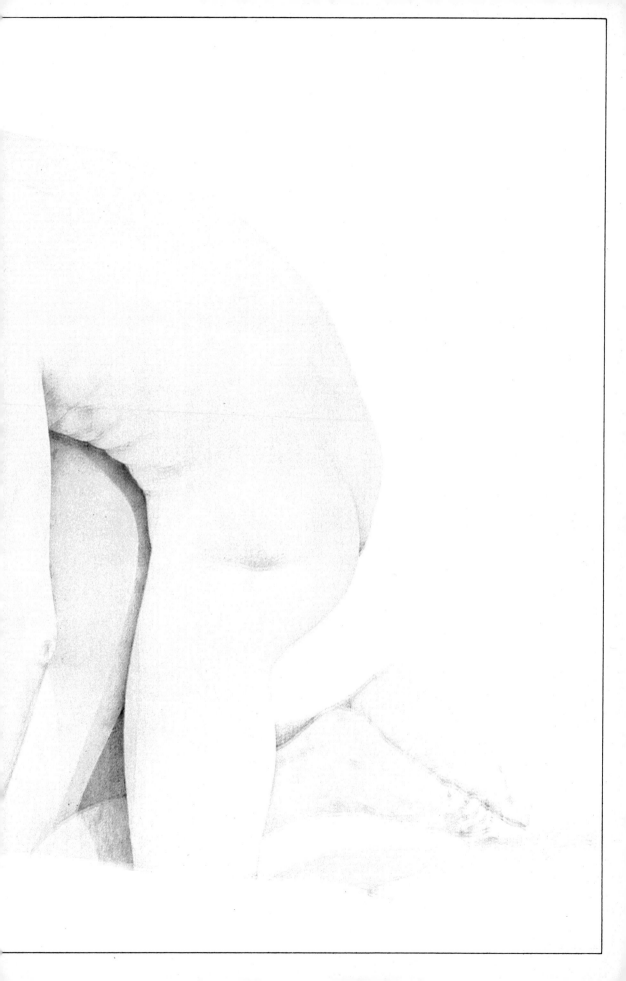

'Women probably differ sexually more than men.
Never assume that you don't need to relearn for
each person.'

'Planning and thinking about sex to come is part of
love. So is lying together in complete luxury
afterwards.'

'Cordon bleu sex is the extra one can get from comparing notes, using some imagination, trying way-out or new experiences, when one is already making satisfying love and wants to go from there.'

Starters
the basic ingredients

beds

Still the most important piece of domestic sexual equipment. Really enthusiastic sex usually involves at one time or another almost every piece of furniture in the house, at least experimentally, but the bed is its commonest venue. Most beds on the market are designed by people who think they are intended to sleep on. The problem arises from the fact that the ideal surface for most kinds of intercourse needs to be rather harder than is comfortable for a whole night's sleep. One solution is to have two beds, one for sex and the other for sleeping, but this is a counsel of luxury, and in any case the need to move disrupts the best part of the night, the total relaxation which follows complete love.

The best advice is probably to settle for a compromise and have a mattress on the floor as well. Enormous or circular beds look suggestive but have no real advantages over a full-size double bed. There are a few points we would consider before giving a seal of approval. First, since one uses the sides as well as the surface, the height needs to be right. The top of the mattress should be exactly level with the man's pubic bone – then, if you put your partner on or over it, she will be at the right height from in front or from behind. For some operations, especially bondage scenes if you like them, bedposts are essential, preferably tall ones, like those which hold up the canopy of old European beds, but not, for choice, a foot-board, as you may want to use the end edge to start with, moving directly to full-length. Massive old bed-frames have great advantages, in that they don't rattle or collapse. The mattress needs to be as hard as you can tolerate for comfortable sleep. Anything less forfeits the chief sexual joy of living and sleeping together – the fact that you can take one another at any hour of the night when both want it, and relax together immediately afterwards. If you have room, have a single bed as well, in case either partner is sick and feels more comfortable solo – twin beds have no place in a full sexual relationship.

Beside the bed itself you need four pillows – two very hard to go under the buttocks, and two soft, to sleep on. The room must be warm at all times of the year – warm enough to sleep without getting chilled and without bedclothes if you wish. Electric blankets shouldn't therefore be necessary – the sort you lie upon will in any case not stand up to sexual intercourse. Unless you are very prosperous and it excites you to set up a special 'sex room,' bedroom chairs and stools can be chosen without too much ostentation to complete the necessary equipment for all eventualities (see *Equipment*), together with a soft rug, soft enough to be really comfortable for the underneath party, and mirrors. You also need enough bedside drawers to hold extras which you may need on impulse

without having to get up and find them – lubricants, contraceptives, vibrators and so on. A well-designed bedroom can be a sexual gymnasium without it being embarrassing to let elderly relatives leave their coats there.

Water-beds are a relative innovation. They can indeed produce extraordinary sensations, and they have a natural period of resonance which tends to take over – one has to move in their rhythm, but this itself is a stimulating constraint. Expensive – best kept for the odd extramural occasion when you re-honeymoon in a hotel room that's fitted with one. With the spread of inflatables we may see a whole range of new sexual furniture-surfaces in the next few years.

birdsong at morning

What your partner says in orgasm should never be quoted at him or her – it can be played back when you are both in a suitable mood, but only then. It is the one time when people are spiritually most naked. There is a striking consistency, over ages and continents, in what women say in orgasm. Japanese, Indian, French and English all babble about dying ('Some of them,' said Abbé Brantome, 'yell out "I'm dying,"' but I think they enjoy that sort of death'), about Mother (they often call for her at the critical moment) and about religion even if they are atheists. This is natural – orgasm is the most religious moment of our lives, of which all other mystical kicks are a mere translation. Men are apt to growl like bears, or utter aggressive monosyllables like 'In, In, In!' The wife of The Leopard in the novel used to yell out 'Gesumaria!' and there are an infinite variety of sounds short of speech. Why these are so charming in both sexes it's hard to say. The Indians classified them, compared them to bird-cries, and warned how easily parrots and mynahs pick them up, with bad social vibrations when they repeat the lesson – hence no parrots in the love chamber. It is important to learn to read them while enjoying the music, and in particular to know when 'Stop' means stop and when it means 'For God's sake go on.' This is an individual language. You need simply to be a sensitive field observer.

Some of the 'words' are common – a gasp when a touch registers right, a shuddering out-breath when you follow through. Women, and some men, talk continuously in a sort of baby-whisper, or repeat four-letter words of the most unlikely kind – some you can hear several blocks away, while others still are dead silent or laugh or sob disconcertingly. Of the really noisy performers, some like to be allowed to yell, while others like to be gagged, or stuff their hair in their mouths in the style of a Japanese print (Japanese houses have paper partitions). Men can be equally noisy but are not usually so continuously vocal.

BEDS *overleaf*
Still the most important piece of sexual equipment.

The important points are these – in mutual, let-go intercourse, make as much noise as you like. It is curious that we need to write this down, but house and hotel designers haven't yet realized it – they all seem to be married to noiseless, childless partners, or they'd avoid plasterboard. Totally silent intercourse, with each partner's hand firmly over the other's mouth, can be fun if you simply can't risk being overheard. Another variation is to have two kinds of intercourse at once – straight, gentle coitus, while each partner describes some other much wilder proceeding in fantasy, perhaps for next time. The fantasy can be as wild as you like. This is the place to experience things you can't possibly act out, and to learn your partner's fantasy needs. These fantasies can be heterosexual, homosexual, incestuous, tender, wild or bloodthirsty – don't block, and don't be afraid of your partner's fantasy; this is a dream you are in. But be careful about recording such dreams, as they can be disturbing at the daylight level. Let them go with the release of orgasm.

Lovers who really know one another won't be frightened, nor take advantage. If you do find this double nakedness disturbing, set rules – practicable or happy fantasies only; never, never refer to pillow-talk in anger later on ('I always knew you were a lesbian, etc.'). This is contemptible. Fantasy apart, the only really disturbing manifestation of love-music is when the woman laughs uncontrollably – some do. Don't be up-tight about this. She isn't laughing at you.

birth control

This is the discovery which more than any other makes carefree sex possible. Before that one had to be infertile to enjoy the kind of extended sexual play which is now available to everyone who is reasonably housed (and which will eventually be available to everyone, together with control over their fertility). No other method being wholly reliable, women who have once experienced the security of the Pill and discovered the play-function of sex are not going to return to the old insecurity. The Pill is still the safest and best method, and a safer drug than aspirin. The loop, and similar indwelling appliances, which prevent implantation, don't suit everyone but work well for some. If you can't use these, it is back to the cap plus a good chemical spermicide. Some women find capping themselves before sex offputting and complain that half the sensation is lost and they get consumer resistance from their man (though if it is the only method she can use, don't make a song and dance about it; that won't change anything and will make her apprehensive); other women, given privacy and washing facilities, don't mind, though both caps and spermicides can spoil both the feel of the

BIRTH CONTROL *opposite*
The discovery which more than any other makes carefree sex possible.

vagina and the genital odor, but usually not seriously. The man should check with his finger that the cap really is over the cervix as part of loveplay. One point about the Pill is that by turning off the normal acid vaginal secretion, it makes it far easier to catch VD or thrush, even from very slight genital or oral contact.

Condoms still have their uses – for a start the very

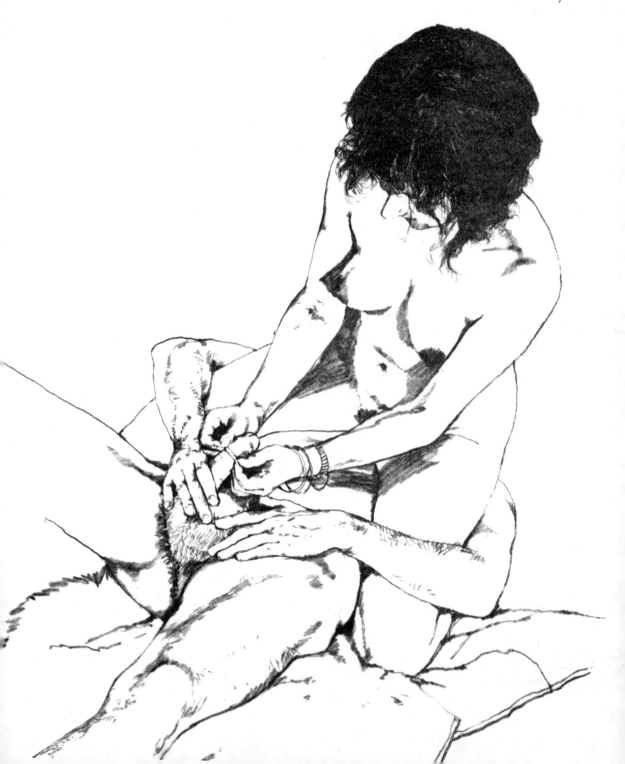

manipulation involved in letting the woman put one on her man excites some people: thin or 'gossamer' condoms can slow down some over-quick ejaculators. Uncircumcised men, and men with a pointed rather than round-ended glans, can't usually use the teat-ended kind – in this case ask for the round-ended variety. The various knobbed or otherwise decorated sheaths sold to vary vaginal sensation are not reliable or leakproof as contraceptives (see *Gadgets and Gimmicks*), so don't trust them. See *Rubber*. Many people dislike the feeling of no contact.

Finally, never take a risk. Wanted children can limit the sex play of adults by being around; this is a small price to pay if one does want them, and privacy can usually be arranged. Unwanted children are the one moral and ecological offense which nothing today can excuse. In an emergency douche thoroughly at once with soapy water, put spermicidal foam or jelly well into the vagina, rubbing it over the cervix, and see a sympathetic doctor next day – implantation can usually be prevented. But such emergencies shouldn't arise.

The so-called rhythm method ('Vatican Roulette') doesn't merit serious consideration. Not only is it highly unreliable, but it may well account for the slightly higher incidence of abnormal babies among Catholic users through stale eggs getting fertilized.

clothes

It is part of the recovery from puritanism that most people now make love naked and most lovers sleep naked. Clothes, when they are worn, are there to be taken off – making love can very well start by undressing one another, or by one partner stripping for the other. Womens' magazines and phonograph records now give what amount to courses on burlesk-type stripping as a conventional turn-on for the man, but this use of clothing *is* a conventional routine – for a start, it need not be the woman who strips. Each partner, moreover, should practice removing the clothes of the other sex without clumsiness or hold-ups, and preferably with one hand.

Clothes and their removal as a kick have, if one wants to be serious about it, a whole biology in terms of 're-leasers,' a releaser being what turns somebody on. The releasers for the male are garments which emphasize breasts and buttocks or, like tight panties, 'simplify the outline' of the female. Women are not so dependent on this sort of concrete signalling – having the right man is their chief releaser, a social and emotional one – but many of them have preferences. A well-filled jockstrap, or a man naked from the waist down, can act as part of the preliminary scenery, and habitual nudity in bed and about the house doesn't blunt these natural reactions.

Quite apart from this, some people react very strongly
to particular clothing-situations on a lock and key basis –
usually these are men, occasionally women. This is the

CLOTHES *above*
If your man has a physical turn-on
he will love you more the more
skillfully you sense and use it.

basis of kinky fashions. Exactly what works on a particular person is highly individual; in this case he often knows and will ask for it. These clothing turn-ons work exactly as a salmon-fly works for the salmon. A bunch of feathers doesn't look like anything the salmon eats (and when one fishes for them at salmon run they aren't feeding in any case) but it combines a whole range of unrelated stimuli which excite curiosity, aggression, and enough other fishy emotions to provoke a strike. Human turn-ons are equally complicated. How they become programmed in a given individual isn't known, but there is an identifiable repertoire of components, like the repertoire of feathers one can use in a lure from which most of these stimuli are made. Super-skin is one – tightness, shininess and texture: super-genitalness – firm pubis, space between the thighs, extra pubic hair; mild threat – blackness, leatheriness, sadistic-looking buckles; submission – tied-upness, slave-bangles; and the suggestion of genitals elsewhere – red lips, emphasis on the feet, which have 'some symmetry with that which thou dost crave;' shininess and tinkling – earrings, chains: woman-ness – tiny waist, big breasts and buttocks, long hair. And so on. Humans love to fool around with the body-image and alter it.

Others are textures – wetness, fur, rubber, plastic, leather. Most males, but fewer females, respond slightly to all of these, and this is another basis of sexual fashion. Some respond so strongly to a few that they don't hit full sexual function without them, but the selection is highly individual, far more so than taste in food, and to tie your fly you have to know your salmon. Every such lure has at least three layers – tight, shiny, black leather is a superskin with a womany smell – it also suggests acceptance of the aggression of sex. Tiny, tight g-strings stress but hide her pussy, hold her perfume so she can be kissed through them, and suggest wicked, sexy girls rather than chaste sister-figures. Corsets make her hourglass-shaped and suggest tightness and helplessness. And so on. A horse, seen from behind, is a male 'releaser'– it has long hair, big buttocks and a teetering walk. A cow isn't.

Prostitutes, who know all this elementary biology, use all these lures, or dress one of them and catch fish who respond to it. Women in love, unless they happen to have similar turn-ons themselves, have long tended to be a bit scared of them as kinky, and, in particular, to feel 'he's in love with gloves or black lingerie, not with me.' This is the wrong approach. If your man has a physical turn-on, it has nothing to do with his valuation of you, and he will love you more the more skillfully you sense and use it. Turn-ons are not choosable – he has them or he hasn't. If he has them, you can catch your favorite fish at every cast. If he likes long hair you'd grow it – you might even

CLOTHES *opposite and overleaf*
If he likes you to look like a cross between a snake and a seal, wear what he gives you. If you like him a particular way, see he knows it.

try to make yourself slim, or blonde, to attract him. You can't make yourself tall, or beautiful, unless you are that way already. But if he has a preference you *can* meet you are unstoppable. The 'you' part is in letting him see you sense it and meet it. If you too have turn-ons, tell him, and use them.

Accordingly, the same tactic applies here as for sexual fantasies generally. Uninhibited partners will tell each other about them (try free-associating just before orgasm if you are shy). Really communicating partners look for them and put them on the menu unannounced – there is no more complete communication. As with other fantasies, if the thing itself doesn't turn you on equally, the response will. Infantile, symbolic, fetishistic and generally wild fantasies are part of love, and only a problem if they take up too much time and start spoiling the full reciprocity of sex (see *Fetishes*). For most people they don't, and a great many people of both sexes have them. No matter how odd, they are usually rewarding – more so than ties or candy as anniversary presents. People are still rightly shy about their innermost mind-life; if your partner seems preoccupied and is blocked over this, ask him or her to give you the thing he or she would most like to see you wearing when you come to lovemaking, and wear it. If you really can't share these essential kids' games or communicate such turn-ons for fear of each other's reactions you shouldn't be in bed together at all. Noncommunication, not normal human fantasy, lands people in the divorce court for incompatibility; a fantasy which really turns you off is subject for discussion and adjustment through make-believe, and just as men tend to be programmed for concrete signals, women are programmed to pick up the kind of signal which turns their partner on – after a few big orgasms together all but the oddest fantasies get to be shared.

So, if he likes you to look like a cross between a snake and a seal, wear what he gives you. If you like him a particular way, see he knows it. Some women are bothered that a man who occasionally likes them to dress him in their clothes is unvirile (it causes less anxiety the other way round). But all of us have a person of the opposite sex inside us – Queen Omphale dressed the hero Hercules in her clothes, and he wasn't exactly unvirile. This is a common game or ceremony in other cultures. We accept sex as pleasure and are starting to accept it as play. Now we need to accept it as ceremony, plus the fact that we are all bisexual and that sex includes fantasy, self-image, psychodrama, and the other things which our society still finds worrying. Bed is the place to act these things out – that is one of the things human sex is for.

Special preferences apart, it's worth knowing at least

as much as a pro about the common turn-ons, because for most couples they have stunning surprise value as un-scheduled extras on special occasions. If a particular one doesn't work you needn't repeat it, and clothes are easy to take off.

Makers of sexy lingerie cater for honeymoon trous-seaux but don't seem to produce a sexually practicable female g-string. This should tightly cover the whole pussy and pubic hair, nothing else. It should undo from the sides with hooks, or better with ribbons, so that it can be taken off when astride without kicking your man. The traditional 'leaf' worn by Japanese prostitutes is made of silk, not nylon, because it holds your perfume better. See *G-string*. This isn't street wear – you wear it only for sex: the first direct genital kiss is given, or taken, through it. Later you can surprise him by suddenly taking the two ends and putting it hard over his nose and mouth. Men are better catered for, with what are called in Europe 'posing pouches' worn by wouldbe strong-men for near-nude photos. Use these in the same way. Two such minimum g-strings make the ideal nightwear, if you want nightwear.

come again

Not all can, but we are sure that far more could than actually do, men especially.

Multiple orgasm comes easily to many if not all women if they are responsive enough and care to go on, either with intercourse or afterplay, after one orgasm; that is, really responsive women who definitely fall in the once-and-it's-over category like men are fairly rare. Some women get one continuous series of orgasms with no single, big peak. Responsiveness is an unanalyzably subtle mixture of physiology, mood, culture, upbringing and having the man she wants. Therefore, if you can get one really intense climax you could probably get more if you went on. The chief exceptions are those who are fragile and tire easily, or who want to savor the period of intense relaxation after each orgasm rather than switch to a new kind of stimulation.

With men it is more complicated still. Some can get six or more full orgasms in a few hours provided they aren't timestressed and don't attempt it daily. Some can do it daily. Others can't get a second erection for a set time. It pays to establish this time early on – it may be shorter than you think. Whether it is alterable nobody knows – nor yet whether individual differences depend on physical or mental factors, though certainly a great many men have been hocussed by talk about sex being exhausting into a performance below what they could manage.

Since exercise and practice improve almost all per-formances it would be odd if they didn't improve this one.

In any case it's not, for the man, the number of orgasms that matter – most men can get a second by slow hand-work and a third from self-stimulation within an hour of full intercourse – it is rather the ability either to hold off your own orgasm as long as you want, or to go on after, or soon after it, even if you don't come a second time. Failing this one can't take a woman the whole way in unsupplemented intercourse. Many lovers don't try but switch their techniques to economize – yet even so it's not the same unless you manage to finish, if not together, at least fairly close together.

Ability to hold and to repeat is particularly important to the many (usually over-continent) males who have hair-trigger trouble. Don't let it become a self-aggravating worry. It matters not a jot provided you can get another erection inside half an hour – there are plenty of other things to do while you are waiting. Avoid performance anxiety: instead, find out by trial just how soon you can

COME AGAIN *below and opposite*
If he can't, doesn't or is worried, it is no use reasoning with him. You, Madam, must take over.

get a serviceable erection again – usually this will be long-lasting and won't end in a full climax, but will enable you to give her ten, twenty or more minutes of full intercourse while you concentrate on her.

If he can't, doesn't, or is worried about it, it is no use reasoning with him. You, Madam, must take over. Full technical details are given under *Hairtrigger trouble*. If you look disappointed you'll have had it for the night and possibly for keeps. Suggest some diversionary entertainment, give him half an hour, then stiffen him yourself by hand and mouth-work. Tell him out of hours what you intend doing; you want to see how soon he can get stiff again (otherwise it looks as though you were unsatisfied and he'll feel guilty and switch himself off). Bring this off neatly and you'll have added a new dimension to both your lives. Two important points – one, *immediately* after a full orgasm some men can't stand any genital stimulation – they feel it as intense pain. If he is like this, give him a half hour or more. Two, if he really is up-tight about it, quite a few women can be perfectly well penetrated with the merest half-erection if taken from behind on their side. Once started like this, full erection usually follows.

Some men when tired can't get an erection but can ejaculate on hand or mouth-work: others get an erection which lasts indefinitely but can't reach orgasm. This last sort, who are actually slow, not fast, responders, make sexual athletes. Whether it can be cultivated as a choice isn't clear, but abundant sex and a certain amount of masturbatory training in holding back a climax will help. Most over-fast responders are having sex far too rarely.

Corpse revivers: the best are skillful manual and oral work and direct suction. A woman can carefully take not only the penis but the whole scrotum as well into her mouth and hold them with her lips, then suck firmly on the penis itself while pressing with a finger at its root behind. Then, when she feels stiffening, she can switch to in and out movements. Vigorous masturbation will always produce a second ejaculation in time, even if it doesn't produce a serviceable erection Some couples, all passion spent, but still wanting one more orgasm before finishing, like to lie facing and watch one another as they bring themselves to climax. This is an added experience, not a confession of defeat, and can be immensely and unexpectedly exciting.

deodorant

Banned absolutely, the only permitted deodorant is soap and water although the unfortunates who sweat profusely may well have problems. A mouthful of aluminium chloride in a girl's armpit is one of the biggest disappointments bed can afford, and a truly deodorized woman would be

another – like a deodorized carnation. Cleanliness is another matter. Accordingly, don't give in to sales talk, unless you find that a so-called 'intimate deodorant' enhances a natural note which pleases you. Wash, and leave it at that. She says: 'Some men *should* use deodorants if they can't learn to wash.' See *Cassolette, Mouth music*.

foreskin

Cutting off this structure is possibly the oldest human sexual ritual. It still persists – on the ground, now, either that cancer of the penis and cervix is rarer when it is done (washing probably works as well) or that it slows down orgasm (for which there is no evidence). We're against it, though for some it is already too late. To cut off the uppermost skin of the secret parts,' said Dr. Bulwer, 'is directly against the honesty of nature, and an injurious insufferable trick put upon her.' The point is that if you have a foreskin, you conserve your options. It probably doesn't make very much difference, either to masturbation or to intercourse, but it makes some, and nobody wants to lose a sensitive structure. Normally one retracts it anyway for all these purposes, but if you haven't one there is a·whole range of covered-glans nuances you can't recapture. Women who have experienced both are divided – and over which looks sexier. Some find the circumcised glans 'neater' and are even turned off by an unretracted prepuce as looking 'feminine' (this can be an insight into the symbolic wilderness behind the original Stone Age custom), while others love the sense of discovery which goes with retraction. If you are uncircumcised and she prefers the other, retract it – if vice versa, you've had it. In function it's probably a scent-diffusing organ – nothing to do with sensitivity.

Holding the skin back hard with the hand (her hand) during intercourse works for both circumcised and uncircumcised as an accelerator and a sensation of its own (see *Florentine*). Much of the action of various fancy penile rings is in holding back the skin of the shaft and/or the prepuce and giving extra tightness, which is why some men get extra feeling from them. If you think your glans is over-sensitive, try keeping it constantly exposed. You can always have the exposure made permanent when you've tried it. In sum, the circumcised man isn't at any important disadvantage (or advantage), but we prefer to be able to choose our egg with or without salt and let our children do likewise.

frequency

The right frequency for sex is as often as you both enjoy it. You can no more 'have too much' sex than you can over-empty a toilet cistern (see *Excesses*) though you can

cut your fertility by having too many ejaculations, and you don't want to make intercourse such an anxious business that you have to stick to a daily schedule. Two or three times a week is a common rate. Many people have it much oftener Some people do stick to a pretty regular schedule – others like intensive weekends at intervals. Much under twice a week suggests you could be getting more out of it, unless you know by experience that the lower frequency is optimal for what you want. People who stick strictly to coital orgasm usually are opting for fewer climaxes than people who mix coitus with oral, manual and other plays, because these increase the number of climaxes most men can get. You should devise your own mix, in the light of your own responses: if one partner needs more, the accessory methods are useful to supply their needs and match them to yours. Frequency falls off normally with age, but there is no age when you won't on some special occasion, surprise yourself. Don't be compulsive about frequency (or worried if your friends say yours is lower than theirs). You aren't being scored. Realize there will be times when one of you just doesn't feel like it – through fatigue, preoccupation, etc.– and don't enforce a timetable on them or yourself.

love

We use the same word for man-woman, mother-child, child-parent, and I-mankind relations – rightly, because they are a continuous spectrum. In talking about sexual relations, it seems right to apply it to any relationship in which there is mutual tenderness, respect and consideration – from a total interdependence where the death of one maims the other for years, to an agreeable night together. The intergrades are all love, all worthy, all part of human experience. Some meet the needs of one person, some of another – or of the same person at different times. That's really the big problem of sexual ethics, and it's basically a problem of self-understanding and of communication. You can't assume that your 'conditions of love' are applicable to, or accepted by, any other party; you can't assume that these won't be changed quite unpredictably in both of you by the experience of loving; you can't necessarily know your own mind. If you are going to love, these are risks you have to take, and don't depend simply on whether or not you have sex together – though that is such a potentially overwhelming experience that tradition is right in pinpointing it. Sometimes two people know each other very well, or think they've worked things out by discussion, and they may be right. But even so if it's dignifiable by the name of love it's potentially an open-ended experience. Tradition has tried to cut the casualties by laying down all kinds of schedules of morality, but these

LOVE   *opposite and overleaf*
Sexual love can give us our best and our worst moments.

MEN *opposite*
Male sex response is triggered easily by things, like putting a quarter in a vending machine.

never work 100 per cent. Nor are they of much use in classifying the merits of different kinds of relationship. Romantic sentimentalism made a whole generation see 'love' as a kind of take-over bid by one individual for another. Some moderns in revolt from this are, like Casanova, so hung up on no hangups that they won't accept the essential open-endedness of a real relationship between people.

If sexual love can be – and it is – the supreme human experience it must be also a bit hazardous. It can give us our best and our worst moments. In this respect it's like mountain climbing – over-timid people miss the whole experience; reasonably balanced and hardy people accept the risks for the rewards, but realize that there's a difference between this and being foolhardy. Love, moreover, involves someone else's neck beside your own. At least you can make as sure as maybe that you don't exploit or injure someone – you don't take a novice climbing and abandon them halfway up when things get difficult. Getting them to sign a form of consent before they start isn't an answer either. There was a hell of a lot to be said for the English Victorian idea of not being a cad ('person devoid of finer or gentlemanly feelings'). A cad can be of either sex.

Marriage between two rival actor-managers, each trying to produce the other regardless, isn't love. The relationship between a prostitute and a casual client where, for reasons they don't quite get, real tenderness and respect occur, is.

men
(by him for her)

Prof. Higgins was right – men wish that women's sexuality was like theirs, which it isn't. Male sexual response is far brisker and more automatic: it is triggered easily by things, like putting a quarter in a vending machine. Consequently, at a certain level and for all men girls, and parts of girls, are at this stimulus level unpeople. That isn't incompatible with their being people too. Your clothes, breasts, odor, etc., aren't what he loves instead of you – simply the things he needs in order to set sex in motion to express love. Women seem to find this hard to understand.

Second, most though not all male feeling is ultimately centered in the last inch of the penis (though you can, if you start intelligently, teach him female-type sensitivity all over his skin surface). And unlike yours his sexuality depends on a positive performance – he has to be turned on to erection, and not turned off, in order to function; he can't be passively 'taken' in a neutral way. This matters intensely to men at a biological and personal level. It explains why men are emphatically penis centered and tend to start with genital play, probably before you are ready, and when you would rather wait to get in the mood.

Genital approach is how men get into the mood.

You need to understand these reactions, as he needs to understand yours. The Women's Lib bit about sex objects misses the point – sure the woman and the various parts of her are sex objects, but most men ideally would wish to be treated piecemeal in the same way. Accordingly, the most valued thing, from you, in actual love-making is intuition of these object reactions and direct initiative – *starting* the plays, taking hold of the penis, giving genital kisses ahead of being asked – being an initiator, a user of your stimulatory equipment. This is hard to put into simple terms; it is what John Wilkes meant by the divine gift of lechery – the art of sensing turn-ons and going along with them for the partner's response. It isn't the same for the two sexes because male turn-ons are concrete, while many female turn-ons are situational and atmospheric. Personal folklore apart, what the male turn-on equipment requires is the exact reverse of a virgin or a passively recipient instrument – not a demand situation, because that in itself can threaten a turn-off from inadequacy-feelings, but a skill situation; I can turn you on and turn myself on in doing so, and from that point we play it both ways and together. You can't of course control your turn-ons any more than he can, but it helps if a woman has some male-type object reactions, like being excited by the sight of a penis, or hairy skin, or by the man stripping, or by physical kinds of play (just as it helps if the man has some sense of atmosphere). It's the active woman who understands his reactions while keeping her own who is the ideal lover.

naked apes

We put a lot of biology into this book; too much exposition has been devoted to symbolisms in human sex behavior, highly important as these are, from a psychoanalytic standpoint which assumes, like old-style morality, that there is only one way of making love and only one thing it ought to express. Work on monkeys suggests that for man the possibility of prolonged and sensuous sex is something special, i.e. a 'displacement activity,' which enables all kinds of aggressions and anxieties as well as infant deprivation of skin sensation, to be worked out play-fashion in the context of mutual affection. Most people have at least one preferred sex behavior which a judge would find odd. If we saw these behaviors in fish or birds we wouldn't ask whether they were normal, but what they were for. No writer who has watched apes should say, as one did recently, that any voluntary movement in sexual intercourse is evidence of latent sadism – if it is, then 'latent sadism' means using sex to dissipate natural aggression in play. Problems only arise when the natural play-

function isn't able to dissipate deeper anxieties.

Man's chief differences from most apes are pair-formation, the extensive use of sex as social bonding and play, shift of interest from brightly-colored buttocks to breasts (one baboon has this too) and imagination. Well-known ape residues are blushing – all that is left of the mandril's red facial sex-skin (it happens all over to many women in orgasm, as a spotty-looking rash), and persisting buttock interest, which may include reddening them by smacking. Worth knowing only because sex is more fun, and preferences less alarming, if they make sense as natural history. Apes, like men, masturbate and play bi-sexual games.

nakedness

The normal state for lovers who take their work at all seriously, at least as a basic requisite – subject to the reservations under *Clothes*. They don't so much start clothed and shed what they must, as start naked and add any extras they need.

Nakedness doesn't mean lack of ornament. The oriental lady takes off all her clothes but puts on all her jewels – the only practical need, as with wrist watches, is to see they don't catch or scratch. This is for daylight; it is difficult to sleep in them. For night, probably increase in the value of lovemaking is the main reason that most people now sleep naked. The only exception may be after; warm bodies tend to stick, and a blotter worn by one or other can add to comfort. We find we spend more and more of our time together naked or wearing the en-hancing minimum. It affects our choice of clothes and of, for example, nonclammy chairs.

Nudists, incidentally, used to be a dead loss – there are no pants like invisible pants. Now, thank goodness, the swingers and, better, the uninhibited young are moving in, for whom nudity is natural not a ritual and lovemaking is included, instead of eurhythmics or basketball – or as well.

Organized 'nudism' in most countries is a family affair. This is probably a good idea. For biological reasons which we've hinted at elsewhere (see *Penis, Vulva, Children*) the nudity of one's own parents can be worrying to children, and shouldn't be overdone. Children of militant pro-gressives often develop disconcerting modesty, which should be respected even if nakedness at home comes naturally. There is accordingly a lot to be said for the op-portunity to look at men and women in general under un-forced conditions and without programmed incest and dominance anxieties: not 'father is bigger than I am' but 'all men are bigger than I am, and one day I shall be a man.' It is the discharge of residual adult anxiety of this sort about our acceptability and competitive status which

NAKEDNESS *overleaf*
The normal state for lovers who take their work at all seriously.

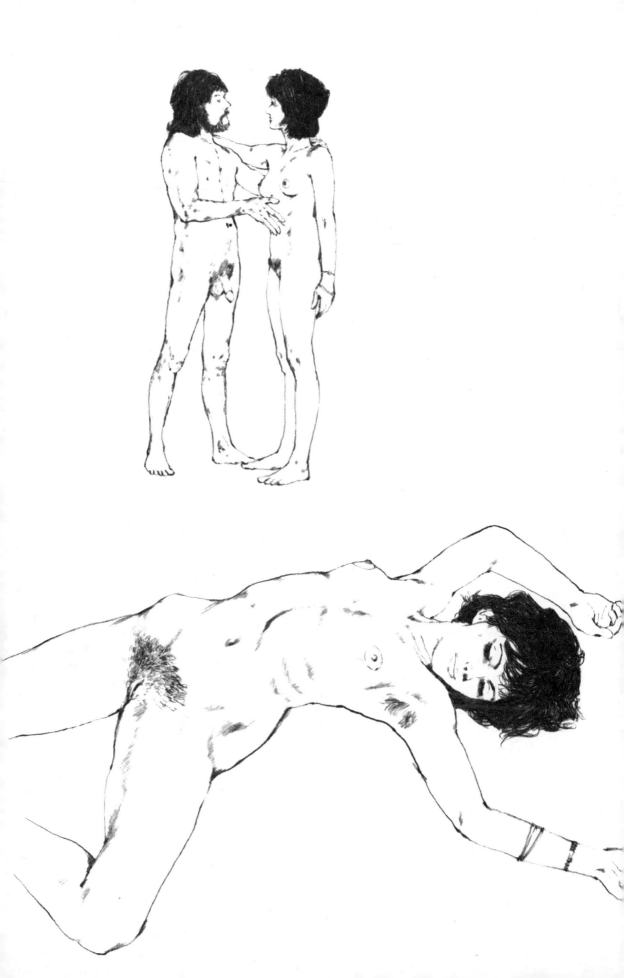

probably makes group nudity so relaxing, rather than the opportunity of getting sunburned, and explains why it acts as a lay sacrament. Career nudists at a first meeting do have the openness of hippies or Quakers, though they quarrel a fair amount over dogma. You can pick a square or a swinging club to taste – they at least give facilities for prolonged open-air nakedness which are hard to organize at home.

normal

A nineteenth-century book about sex, unless it was meant for the (then rich) underground would have started with at least a genuflection to what was and wasn't sinful. The next generation of medical books, and much counseling literature, switched to laying down rules about what is and isn't normal.

Tack 'abnormal' onto a sexual taste and it becomes worrying. 'Normal' implies that there is something which sex ought to be. There is. It ought to be a wholly satisfying link between two affectionate people, from which both emerge unanxious, rewarded and ready for more. That definition includes the awareness that people differ wildly in what they need and in their capacity to be satisfied; more, statistically, than in almost any other measurable. Since sex is cooperative you can cater to one another alternately to bridge gaps. Add to this that sex, for reasons built into the species, makes us uniquely anxious compared with other divergences of need or taste and our culture is coming out of a period of moral panic into a re-awareness that there is nothing to fear. Accordingly, a lot of people are, in their sexual assumptions, like the generation of Victorian children brought up to believe that green sweets were poisonous and rice pudding was good for you because it was unpalatable: they need reassuring.

One trouble with the last generation was that because of censorship by Auntie, many good sex techniques were simply unfamiliar, and worrying or disgusting for that reason. It is not much over a lifetime ago that Krafft-Ebing wrote a textbook in which he described every sexual routine he didn't himself enjoy as a named 'disease,' salting the narrative with examples drawn from very disturbed people. Even Freud, who recognized that all of us have not one but a whole sheaf of sexually important drives – so much so that nearly all our interests have *some* sexual overtone – regarded maturity in terms of a pretty rigid highway code. There was practically an examination in 'maturity' to take at the end.

'Abnormal' accordingly means (1) unusual for the time and place – having intercourse ten times a day on a regular basis is unusual but it happens. If you can, fine. Leonardo and Newton were statistically unusual. (2) Un-

PENIS *opposite*
Lovers treat the penis as something very like a third party.

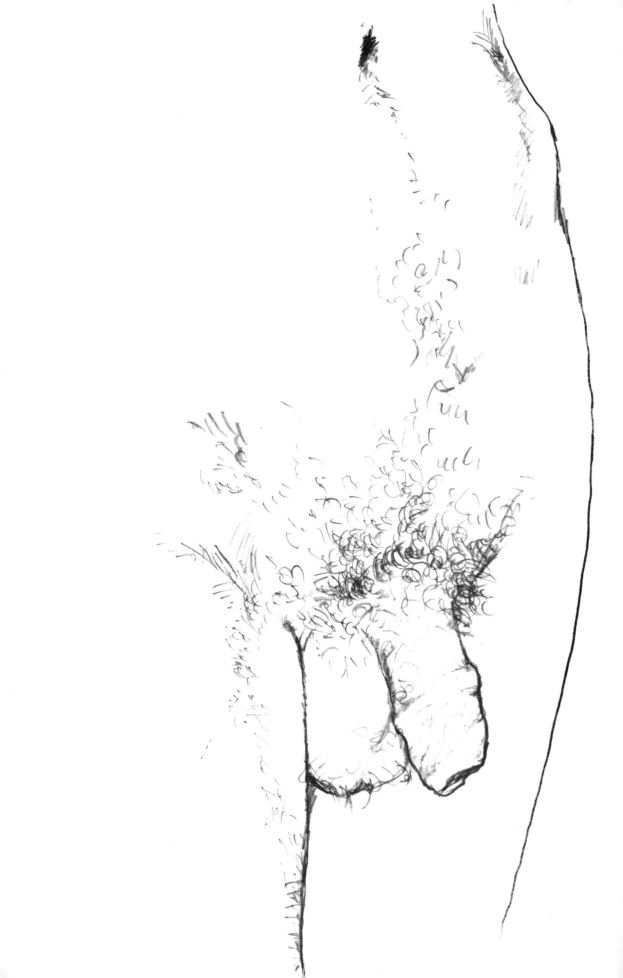

usual and disapproved. It's abnormal in Papua to bury dead relatives, and abnormal in California to eat them. Yet lovers all over the world would like 'to eat' one another, and the same idea underlies our most beautiful and moving religious rite. At the same time an Englishman or an American who actually ate a dead relative would have to be pretty sick. On a less extreme level, our society is scared of same-sex affection. In classical Greece it was a fashionable pose – everyone did it who could. In our culture the people who show exclusively this sort of response are those who must. (3) Unusual and handicapping. A slipped disk or a really worrying sexual obsession are abnormalities because they spoil life, for the owner and his or her associates.

Some sex behaviors are obviously odd, and restrict the range of enjoyment – like the man who could only get orgasm by getting into a bath of cooked spaghetti. He, however, liked it that way. Psychologists now do not usually ask 'Is this normal?' but 'Why does this particular person need this particular emphasis?' and 'Is this behavior, (a) spoiling his chances of being a full person, (b) tolerable for society?' Some, like rape or seducing children, obviously aren't tolerable.

In sum, we don't have a single 'normal' pattern of sex behavior, but a bunch of responses, like the fingers of a hand. In most people in a given culture fingers are of roughly the same lengths. Some people have one finger longer than usual – a few are unlucky enough to have one long finger and the others stunted. The difference here is that finger lengths are much more tightly programmed and vary much less than sex behaviors. Accordingly, if you must talk about 'normality,' any sex behavior is normal which (1) you both enjoy, (2) hurts nobody, (3) isn't associated with anxiety, (4) doesn't cut down your scope. Insisting on having intercourse only in the dark, in one position, and with as little pleasure as possible, which used to be the moralists' stereotype of normality, is a very anxious and limiting routine. Good, unworried lovers use all five fingers of all four hands.

penis

More than the essential piece of male equipment, even if it is often and expressively described as a 'tool,' the penis has more symbolic importance than any other human organ, as a dominance signal and, by reason of having a will of its own, generally a 'personality.' No point in reading all this symbolism back here, except to say that lovers will experience it, and find themselves treating the penis as something very like a third party. At one moment it is a weapon or a threat, at another something they share, like a child. Without going into psychoanalysis or biology it's

not a bad test of a love-relationship that while the penis is
emphatically his, it also belongs to both of them. This particular set of programmed feelings in man is in fact the
fine adjustment for all manner of experiences and feelings
connected with sex-roles, identity and development.
Freud's formulation, that the man is programmed to fear
that the woman, or a jealous parent, will confiscate his
penis, while the woman feels it is something she has lost,
is biologically true but over-simple. What is true is that in
a good sex scene it becomes their' penis. In any case its
texture, erectility and so on are fascinating to both sexes,
and its apparent autonomy a little alarming. This is programmed, and the fact that the human penis is much
bigger relatively than in other primates is probably due to
these complex psychological functions: it's an aesthetic
as well as a functional object.

For precisely the same reasons it collects anxieties and
folklore, and is a focus for all sorts of magical manipula-
tions. Male self-esteem and sense of identity tend to be
located in it, as Samson's energy was in his hair. If it won't
work, or worse, if you as a woman send it up, or down, the
results will be disastrous. This explains the irrational male
preoccupation with penile size. Size has absolutely
nothing to do with their physical serviceability in inter-

course, or – since female orgasm doesn't depend on getting deeply into the pelvis – with capacity to satisfy a partner, though many women are turned on by the idea of a large one, and a few say that they feel more. The unstretched vagina is only 4 inches long anyway. If anything, thickness matters more. Nor has flaccid size anything to do with erect size – a penis which is large when at rest simply enlarges less with erection. There is no way of 'enlarging' a penis. Size doesn't differ appreciably between 'races,' nor correlate with big muscles elsewhere. Nor, except in very rare cases, is a penis too big for a woman – the vagina will take a full-term baby. If your penis, whatever its length, hits an ovary and hurts her, don't go in so far. A woman who says she is 'too small' or 'too tight' is making a statement about her worries, exactly as the man who is obsessed with being too small. They need reassurance and a different attitude to sex, not gadgets or exercises. Shape also varies – the glans can be blunt or conical. This matters only in that the conical shape can make teat-ended condoms uncomfortable through getting jammed in the teat. As to circumcision and uncircumcision, its effects are religious rather than sexual, see *Foreskin*. If you have anxious preconceptions, get rid of them. All the preceding statements are true.

Women who have really learned to enjoy sex are usually as fascinated by their lover's penis, size included, as men are by women's breasts, shape, odor and feel, and learn to play with it fully and skillfully. Circumcised or not, it's a fascinating toy quite apart from experiencing its main use. There is a whole play scene connected with uncapping, stiffening, and handling it, making it pulsate or ejaculate, which is a major part of togetherness. This is equally important for the man – not only is it ego-boosting, but good hand and mouth work practically guarantee a good partner.

Care and maintenance: if you aren't circumcised, you need to retract the foreskin fully for cleaning purposes, and if it won't retract beyond the corona all round the glans except at the front, get it seen to (this is a trifling operation with a blunt probe and doesn't necessarily mean you need circumcising). If it won't retract properly or is over-tight and gets stuck, get that seen to also. These are about the only things that are commonly wrong with a penis. Slight asymmetry often develops with time – this does no harm. On the other hand don't bend an erect penis, or use a position in which it could get violently bent by accident. (This usually happens with the woman on top if she is careless near orgasm, or in putting him in, and he is just short of fully stiff – keep a little control here.) It is possible, though difficult, to fracture one of the two hydraulics con-

PLAYTIME *overleaf*
Sex is the most important sort of
adult play. If you can't relax here
you never will.

tained in the shaft. This is very painful and can lead to pain or kinking on subsequent erection. For the same reason avoid silly tricks with tubes, suction or 'enlarging' devices. The normal organ will stand up to extremely hard use, but not to these. Sores, discharge, etc., are illnesses and need treatment. Venereal disease apart, don't have oral intercourse with someone who has a herpes on the mouth – you can get recurrent herpes of the penis or the vulva which is a nuisance. If the foreskin is dry from masturbation or long retraction, saliva is the best lubricant unless you have a herpes yourself. Penile cosmetics are now sold – some are deodorants, others local anaesthetics to slow down response, and yet others ticklers. We don't recommend them.

playtime

We have said this before, but we repeat: sex is the most important sort of adult play. If you can't relax here you never will. Don't be scared of psychodrama. It works far better in bed than in an encounter group – be the Sultan and his favorite concubine, the burglar and the maiden, even a dog and a currant bun, anything you fancy for the hell of it. Take off your shell along with your clothes.

A few people are immensely excited by having sex with the assistance of the oldest human dramatic expedient, a mask – which suppresses you and makes you someone else (see *Masks*). Most of us can learn to do the same change without it, and when this comes the complete mental nakedness between you is the most exhilarating sort of nudism – so complete that one is healthily scared of it at first. Getting unscared is probably the most important lesson of sex. One Martini helps – more can spoil it. Real sex release when one achieves it is what alcohol, pot, etc., are substitutes *for*, however.

So let him be a Roman or a dog or a woman or a gangster, and let her be a virgin, or a slave, or a Sultana, or Lolita, or someone you're trying to rape, or indeed anything which turns either of you on. You weren't self-conscious about this when you were three – grow backwards again in an adult context. The rules are only those of childplay – if it gets nasty or spiteful or unhappy, stop the game: while it stays wild and exciting, it has a climax childrens' games lack; that is the privilege of adult play.

pubic hair

Shave it off if you prefer: we don't, but some people do. If you do once shave it, you're committed to a prickly interregnum while it regrows. Some prefer it off in the interest of total nudity or prefer the hardness of the bare pubis – most find it decorative. Most lovers regard pubic hair as a resource. Try brushing it lightly and learn to caress with it.

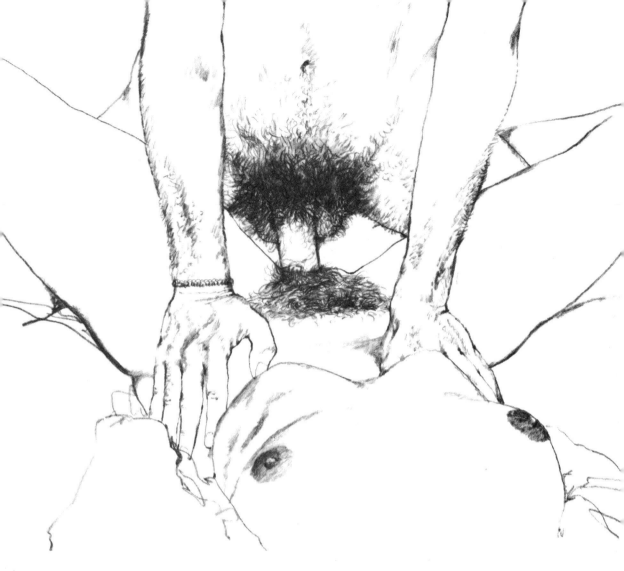

It can be combed, twirled, kissed, held, even pulled. In the woman it can move the whole pubis, skillfully handled, to the point of orgasm. For the woman, it's often best not to shave but to trim, confining the triangle to the middle of the pubis with a bare strip each side – the pattern of youth – removing hair which comes outside a g-string or bathing slip, and trimming enough to make the vulva fully visible. Better not try to dye it to match head hair – it never looks right – still less to bleach it. *M.A.S.H.* is quite wrong – you can't tell whether a blonde is natural by her pubic hair color. It is often shades darker than head hair – in black-haired women it can be nearly blue. Men can shave if they like, or their partners like, but it's difficult to shave the scrotum. Don't use depilatories around the genitals – they can burn. You may need to shave the penile shaft and root if you use a condom – otherwise the hairs can get rolled into it.

real sex   The sort our culture and most admass propaganda don't recognize: not that intercourse or masturbation or genital

kisses aren't real sex, but some other things are real sex too, which people need, but which don't excite our time and age. We can list some: being together in a situation of pleasure, or of danger, or just of rest (if we admitted these as sexual we'd run the risk of having to love other people as people, and that would be worrying or inconvenient, to us or society): touching: oldfashioned expedients like holding hands (permissiveness makes more orgasms, but we miss out on old-style restricted courtship, kisses and looks that vagina-bent, with-it males now think of as schmalz): sleeping together even without, or especially after, intercourse.

Most women don't need telling this, but are as shy about telling it to males, for fear of seeming square, as males are about object-preferences or aggressive needs. Don't get stuck with the view that only those things which Auntie calls sexual are sexual. In a book on sexual elaboration, this needs saying, if you are concerned with love rather than an Olympic pentathlon. People in our culture who are hung up on the Olympic bit don't get much from it unless it helps them to learn this.

relaxation

It is probably the general experience, and we have been assuming here, that maximum feeling in orgasm goes with maximum muscular tension. A great many techniques (postures, bondage and so on) are designed to boost this tension. On the other hand, it is by no means universally true. The orgasm of total relaxation is rather harder to manage, largely because it cannot be boosted artificially, but is both different and, when it works, overwhelming. There are also some people, chiefly women, for whom tension seems actively to interfere with full response.

We've seen ideological writings about this which infer, for example, that tension-orgasms represent fear of full release, latent sadism and so on. One writer opined that yells, grimaces and convulsions indicate fear and pain rather than love and pleasure – presumably he had never seen himself making love, or had never had a wild orgasm. In fact, the only universal generalization about sex seems to be that no one pattern fits everyone. How far these differences between people depend on physiology and how far on latent aggression and the like is probably not a practically important question – some need one and some the other. Our point is that with practice most people can widen their repertoire by learning to use both, and sense the needs of the moment so as to alternate them, thereby doubling their range of physical sensation and making sex still more communicative. Certainly some tension represents fear of letting-go, and some people prefer to be 'forced,' voluntarily, to accept orgasms – in this case,

PUBIC HAIR *opposite*
Better not try to dye it to match head hair – it never looks right.

initially at least, it's probably sensible to make use of the responses you have. If you recognize this kind of reaction, however, don't omit to try the other mode. Mammals seem to vary, according to species, between fight-and-rape-type mating and a version in which the female appears near-indifferent, so there isn't much to be learned from zoology.

The straight, sleepy, non-special intercourse, on your side or in the matrimonial position, is relaxed, but this isn't what we mean. In going for a fully relaxed orgasm, either one partner is totally passive and the other a soloist, or both achieve a state of non-effort in which wholly automatic movements – internal, for the woman – take over. Try both kinds – it is easier initially to work up both modes together.

Probably the easiest initial method is for the less-active partner in ordinary intercourse (this usually but not always means the one underneath) to try stopping all movement just as the orgasmic buildup begins and go completely limp (warn your partner first). Some people do this naturally: if you have had any of the fashionable relaxation training, starting by letting one finger get heavy and so on, use the same technique here. You may find that on the first few occasions the fact of trying produces a different sort of tension, but after a few attempts most easily-stimulated people can learn to let their orgasm happen, and will find that this feels different from the equally pleasant orgasm one produces, either by trying or by struggling and postponing. Don't postpone – don't, in fact, be active at all. Then practice the same kind of relaxation while your partner masturbates or sucks you. The movements he or she makes will be physically the same as for 'slow masturbation' as we've described it, but the operator is looking for quite different feedback – in the 'hard' version, whether the partner is tied or free, you are deliberately holding back or forcing them on, keeping just that much out of step with their reactions. In the 'soft' version you need to be a fraction ahead of those reactions so that they don't need to move or struggle. The difference can't be described, only felt. Practically, it means a quicker, steadier rhythm of stimulation – no slow teasing and no sudden bursts – you are making it and they are letting it happen.

Once you have got this right in intercourse and in other kinds of stimulation, including all the extras we've mentioned, you can go on to complete 'motionless' coitus. It won't of course initially be entirely motionless, but try, after the first round of gentle movement, what happens if you stop thinking. Movements of a sort will continue, but in time and with practice get less and less voluntary, especially if the woman has good vaginal

REAL SEX *opposite*
Permissiveness makes more orgasms, but we miss out on old-style courtship.

muscle control. Ultimately, some people learn to insert and do nothing, but still reach an orgasm in which they totally fuse, giving a sensation of being a single person – not describable, again, and probably not always realizable, but fantastic when it happens. We should stress that this doesn't involve going slow, holding back, or any other voluntary intervention. If you find it not working, switch back to ordinary movements, but without taking too much thought – sometimes you will both sense that the moment has come to shift position and go all out for a big one; complete fusion isn't biddable, and ordinary, athletic sex is fine. If, on the other hand, it does happen you will want to repeat it.

Reliable relaxation, and the almost frightening self-loss that goes with it, are what most sexual yogis have aimed at, except that they usually tried not to ejaculate. Some of these sexual mystics recommend a special relaxed posture (man on his left side, girl on her back at right-angles, knees drawn up, legs bridging his hips, feet flat on the bed). Whether this helps may well depend on your build. What is worth suggesting, even for people who can't totally relax, is that they play through all the techniques we have described, aiming at relaxation instead of maximum tension, and adjusting their feedback accord-

RELAXATION *above*
Essential if you hope to go as far in making love communicate as you are physically and mentally able.

ingly. Similarly people who naturally relax in intercourse should try occasionally to play it for full tension – just as women who like to thrash around should sometimes try being forcibly held still, and vice versa. This sort of experimentation against one's built-in response is better value in widening one's range of lovemaking than mechanical variations of posture or trying out gadgets and stunts. It is one part of lovemaking which requires effort beyond mere curiosity, but it's essential if you hope to go as far in making sex communicate as you are physically and mentally able.

semen

There is no lovemaking without spilling this, on occasions at least. You can get it out of clothing or furnishings either with a stiff brush, when the stain has dried, or with a diluted solution of sodium bicarbonate. If you spill it over each other, massage it gently in – the pollen-odor of fresh semen is itself an aphrodisiac, which is why the smell of fresh grass or thalictrum flowers turns most people on. If you want a very copious ejaculate, he can masturbate nearly, but not quite, to orgasm about an hour beforehand to increase prostate secretion.

size

Preoccupation with the size of their genitals is as built-in biologically to men (it is a 'dominance signal,' like a deer's antlers) as sensitivity about their breasts and figure is to women. That, however, is its only importance. The 'average' penis is about 6 inches overall when erect and about $3\frac{1}{2}$ inches round, but penises come in all sizes – larger ones are spectacular but no more effective except as visual stimuli. Smaller ones work equally well in most positions. Accordingly, excessive preoccupation with size is an irrational anxiety, on which quacks batten – one can't increase it, any more than one can increase stature. Girls should learn not to comment on it except favorably, for fear of creating a lasting hang-up – men should learn not to give it a second thought. The few cases where male genitalia are really infantile go with major gland disturbances and are treatable but rare.

The same applies to vaginal size. No woman is too small – if she is, it is due to inability to relax, or a tough hymen. The normal vagina stretches to accommodate a full-term baby – and a tight woman gives the man extra intense feelings. Nor is any vagina too large – if it seems a loose fit, switch to a posture in which her thighs are pressed together. Genital anatomy probably fixes which postures work best for a given couple, but not more than that. With rare exceptions, men and women are universally adapted.

Non-erect size in the male is equally unimportant – some men before erection show no penile shaft at all, but

extend to full size easily. The same applies to testicle weight – it varies, as does nose or mouth size, but has little to do with function. Small genitals are usually due to active muscles in the under-skin layer – a cold bath will shrink the best-endowed male down to Greek statue proportions. The only practical exception is that with a very big penis and a very small woman she should be careful on top, or she will knock an ovary (which feels as a man feels if you knock a testicle) and he shouldn't thrust too hard until he knows he won't hurt her. As to the size of other structures, such as breasts, these may be individual turn-ons, but every build has its sexual opportunities built-in: use them.

tenderness

This, in fact, is what the whole book is about. It doesn't exclude extremely violent games (though many people neither need nor want these), but it does exclude clumsiness, heavyhandedness, lack of feedback, spitefulness and non-rapport generally. Shown fully in the way you touch each other. What it implies at root is a constant awareness of what your partner is feeling, plus the knowledge of how to heighten that feeling, gently, toughly, slowly or fast, and this only comes from an inner state of mind between you. No really tender person can just turn over and go to sleep. Many if not most inexperienced men, and some women, are just naturally clumsy – either through haste, through anxiety, or through lack of sensing how the other sex feels. Men in general are harder-skinned than women – don't grab breasts, stick fingers into the vagina, handle female skin as if it was your own, or (and this goes for both sexes) misplace bony parts of your anatomy. More girls respond to very light than to very heavy stimulation – just brushing pubic or skin hairs will usually do far more than a whole-hand grab. At the same time don't be frightened – neither of you is made of glass. Women by contrast often fail to use enough pressure, especially in handwork, though the light, light variety is a sensation on its own. Start very gently, making full use of the skin surface, and work up. Stimulus toleration in any case increases with sexual excitement until even hard blows can become excitants (though not for everyone). This loss of pain sense disappears almost instantly with orgasm, so don't go on too long, and be extra gentle as soon as he or she has come.

If we could *teach* tenderness most of this book would be superseded by intuition. If you are really heavy-handed, we agree with a recent book which suggests a little practice with inanimate surfaces, dress fastenings and so on. Male strength is a turn-on in sex, but it isn't expressed in clumsy handwork, bear-hugs and brute force – at least not as starters. If there is a problem here, remember you

TENDERNESS *opposite*
Shown fully in the way you touch each other.

both can talk. Few people want to be in bed on any terms with a person who isn't basically tender, and most people are delighted to be in bed with the right person who is.

The ultimate test is whether you can bear to find the person there when you wake up. If you are actually pleased, then you're onto the right thing.

variety

Plan your menus. Nobody wants a seven-course meal every time. At least seventy-five percent of really reward-ing sex will be your absolutely straight, bedtime or morn-ing, pattern. For longer sessions you need to be rested – weekends, holidays and special occasions on impulse. If you make up your mind that over the course of time you'll try everything and have sex everywhere, the occasions will arise: when you feel one coming on, or know you will have the opportunity, plan together with the book if you like, but don't expect necessarily to keep to what you out-lined. Stick to it sometimes, however, so you don't miss things. Most couples will strike out perhaps a third of our suggestions as not turning them on, and pick up three or four headed 'We must try that,' if they haven't already.

Usually start with vaginal sex, move on to handwork, use mouth-work to get a further erection – maybe have a final orgasm by masturbating together. Prolonged spin-outs involving makebelieve, experiments and so on often go best on waking fresh – so do positions needing a very hard erection. Unlike a man, an untired and responsive woman can afford to take orgasms from any source in any order, unless her pattern is one overwhelming orgasm only – if so, keep it for last. See *Come again*. Varying times of day is well worthwhile but depends on your commitments and how far you can get privacy or clear your mind of other things, but try never to put it off if you both want it, except to 'save up' for something. Planning and thinking about sex to come is part of love. So is lying together in complete luxury afterwards.

virginity

Have a bit of respect for this. The first time doesn't so much 'matter more' to a woman than to a man, but it matters differently. If you find yourself getting into bed with a girl who is a virgin on only a few hours or minutes acquain-tance, you're going too fast for both of you. For a start, she's unlikely to be baby-proof: stay with the non-coital extras until you're both quite sure you know what you are doing. Cutting notches is irresponsible. Whatever you do be gentle and slow, as she's bound to be tense and nervous – even if she doesn't look it.

Girls who are virgins will usually say (you can't tell re-liably by inspection) and a loving man will ask – men don't

VULVA   *opposite*
Lovers should learn early on to watch each other masturbate.

usually advertise the fact. However experienced he seems, the idea should be in the back of the woman's mind that this could be the first time and he may need help: if you're critical or disappointed you could do real mischief. If you're both virgins, you are starting from scratch – don't hurry it.

There's usually no physical problem over first inter-course if you're careful (see *Defloration*) – the commonest is simply male over-eagerness or nervousness (see *Impotence*). If there are problems, get them dealt with at once.

vulva

'The part of you,' as the advertisement says, 'that is most girl,' but also as magic as the penis, and to children, primi-

WOMEN *opposite*
It matters to them who is doing what, far more than it does to most men.

VULVA *below*
As magic as the penis, and to children, primitives and males generally, slightly scarey.

tives and males generally, slightly scarey: it looks like a castrating wound and bleeds regularly, it swallows the penis and regurgitates it limp, it can probably bite and so on. Luckily, few of these biologically programmed anxieties survive closer acquaintance, but they are the origins of most male hangups including homosexuality. Primitives and prudes treat it as if it was radioactive – 'all magic,' said a Papuan wizard, 'radiates from it as fingers do from a hand,' and a lot of female put-downs throughout history grew from this kind of Freudian undergrowth.

Sensitive in all its parts – the phallic-minded male is inclined to make a reassuring rush for the clitoris. Lovers should learn early on to watch one another masturbate – few women enjoy excessive clitorial emphasis at the start. Length of labia, size and tightness of the opening make little difference to performance – position relative to the male pubic bone makes more: some lovers only get really good apposition in one or two postures, though usually the tension produced by movement and pulling on the labia in intercourse more than makes up for this. Normally slightly moist, or women would squeak when they walk, and, of course, wets more or less copiously with sexual excitement. Any staining or offensive discharge indicates infection (usually with trichomonads or yeasts) in the vagina, and needs treating. The normal vulval odor varies greatly between women and between times, but should always be pleasant and sexually exciting.

Whether or not your lover has ever explored a woman's pussy in detail, with fingers, eyes and tongue, make sure he explores yours. Learn to kiss it – you have two mouths to his one.

For care and maintenance see *Bidet, Cassolette, Menstruation*. Don't as a rule douche – wash.

Hide-and-seek with the woman's pubic triangle is one of the oldest human games. See *Clothing, Chastity belt*. Cultivate the cunning use of a really practical g-string.

waking

She says: 'Sleep patterns matter, and it's the man who wakes with an erection. While it's great to be woken with intercourse, this doesn't apply when one has had a ghastly day and has an interview coming up next morning; use some sense. It also doesn't apply in the middle of a dream one has to finish.' Some women take minutes or hours to wake up, and though they enjoy gentle intercourse waking – and it works far better than an alarm clock – don't expect athletics. The trouble is that this is the time when many males are ready for them and expect to be ridden, masturbated, sucked and what have you. Keep these early waking workouts for Sundays and holidays and preferably make coffee first, erection or no erection. Some people are lucky in having roughly the same sleeping hours, but if one were early and the other a night person that too could well give rise to real problems. If you have these, talk about them; some people do use sleep as an excuse for avoiding intercourse, but between lovers who are on different clocks it can be real and doesn't imply rejection.

If you have children, you have to be ready to be woken by them, and restrict yourselves accordingly. Don't lock them out. Rearrange your sex life to get the necessary privacy at other times – if all else fails get a baby-sitter and stay at a motel once a month. The sound and fury of really ongoing sex would give primal scene problems to any small child, so don't take risks; the sort of sex we have, and are talking about here, almost excludes fertility – it's a choice one may have to make, while houses and family-structure are as they are.

women (by her for him)

Women, like men, have direct physical responses, sure, but these *are* different (breasts and skin first, please, not a direct grab at the clitoris) and can't be short-circuited. It matters to them who is doing what, far more than it does to most men. The fact that, unlike you, we can't be visibly turned off and lose erection often confuses men into hurrying things or missing major resources. It isn't true that nudity, erotica, etc., don't excite women – probably the difference is that they aren't overriding things. Is it fair, I wonder, to give a simple instance? You can make orgiastically satisfactory love with a near stranger in half an hour flat. But please don't think for that reason that you can do the same for a woman who loves you personally if at the

end of the half-hour you put her into a taxi with a bunch of roses and go off to a wife. Granted this, however, there are common reactions.

We seem to be less heavily programmed than you for specific turn-ons, but once we see one of these working on a man we care about, we soon program it into our own response, and can be less rigid and more experimental *because* of this ability. Often if women seem underactive it's because they're scared of doing the wrong thing with that particular man, like touching up his penis when in fact he's trying not to ejaculate – *tell* us if you see us at a loss. The penis isn't a 'weapon' for us so much as a shared possession, rather like a child – it's less the size than its personality, unpredictable movements, and moods which make up the turn-on (which is why rubber dummies are so sickening). Another important thing is the tough-tender mixture: obviously strength is a turn-on, but clumsiness (elbows in eyes, twisted fingers, etc.) is the dead opposite. You never get anywhere by clumsy brutality; however brutal good lovemaking sometimes *looks*, the turn-on is strength-skill-control, not large bruises: and the ability to be tender with it. Some people ask 'Tough or tender?' but the mood shifts so fast you've got to be able to sense it. Surely it's possible – because some lovers do it – to read this balance from the feel of the woman. No obsessive views about reciprocity – who comes on top, etc., does in fact even out during the passing of time: there can be long spells when one enjoys and is happy to let him do the work, and others when you need to control everything yourself and take an extra kick from seeing how you make him respond.

Women aren't 'masochistic' any more than men – if they've knuckled under in the past it's only through social pressures. If they're sadistic, they unfortunately don't reify it like a man and act it out in bed by wearing spurs and cracking a whip (any girl who does this is doing it as a male turn-on): they're more likely to express it as no-saying or nagging, which contributes to nobody's orgasm. Men have a real advantage here in the constructive use of play (and can help women to reify). Since we all have some aggressions, good sex can be wildly violent but still never cruel. A little frightening helps some people sometimes. Anyhow the old idea of man as raper and woman as rapee being built-in is contrary to all experience in a world where role-swapping is general.

As to the Women's Lib bit, nobody can possibly be a good lover – or a whole man – if he doesn't regard women as (a) people and (b) equals. That is really all there is to be said.

Our sense of smell is the keener – don't oversaturate early on with masculine odors; just before orgasm is prob-

ably the time for full odor contact. Our own smell excites us as well as yours.

The sort of hand and mouth-work which men like varies enormously. Some like it very rough, some hate it anything but extremely gentle, others in between. There is no way for a woman to tell except by asking and being told – so it's up to the man to say what he likes or he may get the opposite.

Some men are extraordinarily passive, or unimaginative, or inhibited, and – oddly – when they are any of these things, we do not become correspondingly aggressive. We may long to do things and feel thoroughly frustrated, but we won't dare show it in most case . So a woman's love-making will only be good with a good lover and, more important, she will resent any man who is unexciting, not only because it is unexciting but also because she will know she has been unexciting too.

Finally, just as all women are more alike to a man than all men are to a woman, women probably really do differ sexually rather more than men, because of the greater complexity of their sexual apparatus (breasts, skin and so on as well as pussy). Never assume you don't need to relearn for each person. This is true for women with a new man, but perhaps a little less so.

Main
Courses
which everyone needs

bidet

This article of European bathroom furniture is beginning to be trendy in America. It used to be necessary when post-coital douching was the rule, but the Pill has altered that. For washing it can be useful, for example after anal intercourse or cleaning your feet, and less trouble than a shower, though a woman showering looks better than sitting on a bidet like a battery hen. Indiscriminate douching is medically a bad idea in any case – the vagina is self-cleansing and water merely upsets its natural hygiene. Keep the douche, and the bidet, for cleaning-up after menstrual periods.

breasts

'In our maturer years,' wrote Darwin, 'when an object of vision is presented to us which bears any similitude to the form of the female bosom ... we feel a general glow of delight which seems to influence all our senses, and if the object be not too large we experience an attraction to embrace it with our lips as we did in early infancy the bosom of our mothers.' Alfred Perlès greeted a socialite who was seated next him at dinner with the words 'Those aren't bad – fish them out and let's have a look at them!' Breasts are the natural second target, but often the first one we reach. Just how sensitive they are, in men as well as in women, varies enormously – size is unimportant, as with other sexual organs. Some don't answer at all, even in the emphatically non-frigid; some answer to extremely gentle touches, some to very rough handling (but they are sensitive structures – don't let your residual anger at having been weaned get the better of your commonsense).

Round and round the nipple with the tongue tip or the glans, soft kneading with both hands, gentle biting and sucking gently like a baby are the best gambits. She can use these on the man, plus very gentle fingertip friction – men's nipples easily get sore, however. If her breasts are big enough to meet, one can get a surprising degree of mutuality from intermammary intercourse. This is a good expedient on occasions when she is closed to the public. Lay her half flat on pillows, kneel astride (big toe to her clitoris if she needs helping) and your foreskin fully retracted. Either you or she can hold the breasts together – wrap them around the shaft rather than rub the glans with them. It should protrude clear, just below her chin. An orgasm from this position, if she gets one, is 'round' like a full coital orgasm, and she feels it inside. Breast orgasms from licking and handling are 'in between' in feel. Rub the semen well into her breasts when you have finished (see *Semen*).

Breasts, vagina and clitoris all at once make the most concentrated and fastest buildup of sensation once intercourse has begun, for some women at least. Few men can

BREASTS *opposite*
Just how sensitive the breasts are, in men as well as women, varies enormously.

BREASTS *above*
Men still don't understand about breasts – or are in too much hurry to get lower down.

BUTTOCKS *opposite*
Visually, good buttocks are a turn-on almost equally for both sexes.

get a nipple orgasm, but a stiff pair of feathers is worth trying. Many easily-stimulated or well-loved women can get a rather special pleasure from suckling a baby.

She says: 'Men still don't understand about breasts, or are in too much of a hurry to get lower down – unlike a man's nipples, a woman's have a direct hot line to her clitoris. A man who can dial this correctly and will only take the time can do anything. Palm-brushing, eyelid-brushing, licking, and loud sucking like a baby can work wonders; the orgasms one gets from these are mind-blowing, without detracting a jot from intercourse to come after. *Please take time.*'

Intercourse between the breasts is equally good in other positions – head to tail, or with her on top (especially if she has small breasts), or man sitting, woman kneeling: experiment, accordingly.

buttocks

Next in line after breasts, and alternate with them as visual sex stimuli for different cultures and individuals. Actually the original primate focus, being brightly colored in most

apes: apparently equally fancied by the Mousterian culture which produced some of the best Stone Age figurines, while more recent primitives 'made their selection by ranging their women in a line and picking her out who projects furthest *a tergo*' (Darwin). Major erogenous zone in both sexes, less sensitive than breasts because they contain muscle as well as fat, and needing stronger stimulation (holding, kneading, slapping or even harder beating – see *Discipline*). Intercourse from behind is a pleasure in itself but be careful if she has a weak back. In any position the muscular movements of coitus stimulate the buttocks in both sexes, particularly if each holds the partner's rear fairly tightly, one cheek in each hand. These extra sensations are well worth cultivating deliberately. Visually, good buttocks are a turn-on almost equally for both sexes.

cassolette

French for perfume box. The natural perfume of a clean woman: her greatest sexual asset after her beauty (some would say greater than that). It comes from the whole of her – hair, skin, breasts, armpits, genitals, and the clothing she has worn: its note depends on her hair color, but no two women are the same. Men have a natural perfume too, which women are aware of, but while a man can be infatuated with a woman's personal perfume, women on the whole tend to notice if a man smells right or wrong. Wrong means not so much unpleasant as intangibly not for them. Often their awareness of a man includes conditioned extras like tobacco.

Because it is so important, a woman needs to guard her own personal perfume as carefully as her looks and learn to use it in courtship and intercourse as skillfully as she uses the rest of her body. Smoking doesn't help this. It can be a long-range weapon (nothing seduces a man more reliably, and this can happen subliminally without his knowing it) but at the same time a skillful man can read it, if he is an olfactory type, and if he knows her, to tell when she is excited.

Susceptibility and consciousness of human clean perfumes vary in both sexes. Whether these are inborn differences, like inability to smell cyanide, or whether they are due to unconscious blocking-out we don't know. Some children can't understand the point of blind man's buff because they know by smell who is touching them: some women can smell when they are pregnant. Men can't smell some chemicals related to musk unless they have a shot of female sex hormone. There is probably a whole biological signal mechanism here which we are only just starting to unravel. Far more human loves and antipathies are based on smell than our deodorant-and-aftershave culture admits. Many people, especially women, say that

CASSOLETTE *opposite*
Far more human loves and antipathies are based on smell than our soap-and-aftershave culture admits.

when it's a question of bed or not-bed they let their noses lead them.

Women have the keener sense of smell, but men respond to it more as an attractant. In lovemaking, the note changes in regular order, from the totality of skin and *gousset* to her 'excited' note, then to her full genital odor, then, when intercourse has begun, to a different scent. Finally the seminal odor will appear in her breath and trigger the next bout.

Some benighted savages still cut off the clitoris. It's said that women themselves are the most insistent about the necessity of mutilating their daughters. Ours don't go that far, but do still chop off their armpit hair, or did until a new generation started to realize that it was sexy. This might be forgiveable in a hot climate with no plumbing. Now it is simply ignorant vandalism. Some of the nicest of them still do it, and even the wouldbe sexiest are in-educable in the face of fashion. This could be played as an argument for lifeboat whiskers or Sikhism, but men's facial hair doesn't have the day-to-day importance of a woman's little tufts. These are antennae and powderpuffs to introduce herself in a room, or in lovemaking. They are there to brush the man's lips with; he can do the same more circumspectly. Kissing deeply in the armpit leaves a partner's perfume with you. In the genital kiss, start with the lips covered, then brush the closed lips, then open her: when she gives the kiss to a man, she proceeds in the same order. It's the fullest way to become aware of her as a presence, even before you start to touch.

croupade

Any position in which he takes her squarely from behind, i.e. all rear-entry positions except those where she has one leg between his or is half-turned on her side (see *Cuissade*).

cuissade

The half-rear entry positions, where she turns her back to him and he enters with one of her legs between his and the other more or less drawn up: in some versions she lies half-turned on her side for him, still facing away.

earlobes

Underrated erogenous zone, together with the adjacent neck skin – the small area behind the ear has a 'hot line' to the visceral nerves via the vagus – and the nape of the neck. As with all extragenital sites, more effective in women than men. Once established (gentle fingering, sucking, etc., during buildup and before orgasm, to condition the response) earlobes can trigger full climax from manipulation alone. Some women find the noise of heavy breathing excruciating and a definite turn-off, so be careful. Heavy

CROUPADE *opposite*

earrings help, and can actually maintain subliminal erotic excitement, especially if long enough to brush the neck when she turns her head – this is the function of the large oriental and Spanish candelabra-type earrings. The sex difference in response probably accounts for their relative rarity worldwide in male fashions.

Swinging weights as erotic stimuli to condition a particular area aren't confined to the ears. If earrings are the screw-on type, take them off and try them gently on her nipples, labia or clitoris – ask first!

equipment

The Austrian gymnastic professor van Weck Erlen wrote a book in which, along with over 500 postures you draw lots to carry out, he advised a 'sexuarium' complete with gymnastic mat and trapezes. For his sort of sex you'd need

them. The idea of a 'sexuarium' complete with mirrors, red light and black decor turns some people on – there are a good few 1930's palaces in Beverly Hills which have one. On a smaller scale one can fit out the basement. Our preference is for the bedroom, however, and the result needn't be embarrassing.

The bed we've discussed already. The gymnastic-mat idea isn't a bad one at all – a really thick carpet (or carpet piece if you can't afford it wall to wall) is as good, with plenty of room to roll around. Some people favor stools for the bent-over positions, front and back: as one needs a bedroom stool, this can be chosen the right height. A pile of hard square cushions is more suited for diversification. Two of the bed pillows will be hard, for use in bed – the cushions are for floor work. If you like big mirrors these can be inside closet doors, or turn over to show a chaste decoration. The best chair for intercourse is a fully-upholstered one without arms. If you want to tie each other

to it, check for size and convenience – if you only want it for straight intercourse it is best padded all over: or have separate chairs for each. A ceiling mirror is fun, but expensive and obvious if you mind that. You need an adjacent bathroom and shower. The ordinary motel bedroom lay-out is excellent for all these things, except that they don't pick the chairs with an eye to coition.

Naturally it is exciting to set up a fantasy place for fantasy experiences, complete with your own light show, if you have the money and energy. What we don't want to do here is to give the impression that you really need this – you don't, any more than you need a dream kitchen to be a first-class chef. You need the bare minimum – privacy, heating, washing space, a bed, one or two ordinary furniture surfaces, genitalia which work, love and imagination.

If you want extras, these will depend on what you want to do. Acrobatic position-merchants like to have a

CUISSADE *opposite*

EQUIPMENT *above*
You don't need any extras to have superlative sex, given the right person and the right attitude.

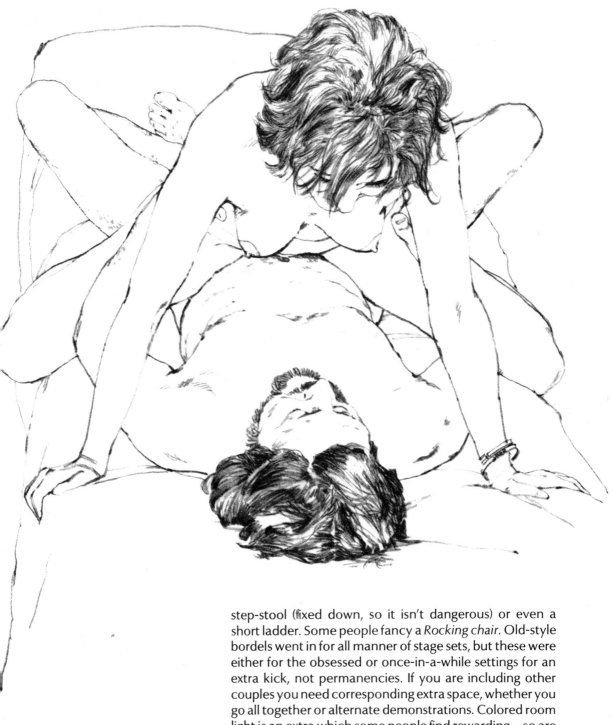

FLANQUETTE *opposite*

FRONTAL *above*
All the face-to-face positions
where one partner has both
thighs between those of the other.

step-stool (fixed down, so it isn't dangerous) or even a short ladder. Some people fancy a *Rocking chair*. Old-style bordels went in for all manner of stage sets, but these were either for the obsessed or once-in-a-while settings for an extra kick, not permanencies. If you are including other couples you need corresponding extra space, whether you go all together or alternate demonstrations. Colored room light is an extra which some people find rewarding – so are a Land camera and a tape-recorder. If you use extras of any sort, from cushions or vibrators to cameras, lubricants, ropes or g-strings, make sure they are at hand and don't have to be fetched. Have a cloth towel ready – paper tissues stick to the skin. But you don't *need* any of these things to have superlative sex, given the right person and

the right attitude.

Probably the only advantage of a really private sex-room is that you can fill it with erotic pictures without erotising 'square' guest-space, and entertain Auntie without her asking what those rings in the wall are for. But a slide projector works fine on any white wall or ceiling, and you'd be surprised how unobservant the uninitiated are.

feet

Very attractive sexually to some people—he can get an orgasm, if wished, between their soles.

Their erotic sensitivity varies a lot. Sometimes, when they're the only part you can reach, they serve as channels of communication, and the big toe is a good penis substitute (see *Big toe*).

Tickling the soles excites some people out of their minds; for others it's agony but increases general arousal. You can try it as a stimulus, or, briefly, for testing bondage. Firm pressure on the sole at the instep, however administered, is erogenic to most people. But so can almost any touch be in a woman who's that way minded – one can get a full orgasm from a foot, a finger, or an earlobe. Men respond less far but equally easily if the handling is skillful.

flanquette

The half-facing group of sexual postures – she lies facing him with one of her legs between his, and consequently one of his legs between hers, the frontal equivalent of the *Cuissades*. These positions give extra clitoral pressure from the man's thigh if he presses hard with it.

food

Dinner is a traditional preface to sex. In old-time France or Austria one booked a restaurant room with no handle on the outside of the door. At the same time there is a French saying that love and digestion went to bed together and the offspring was apoplexy. This isn't quite true. On the other hand, immediately after a heavy meal is not an ideal moment – you can easily make your partner, especially the woman if she's underneath, sick.

A meal can be an erotic experience in itself – for a demonstration of how a woman can excite a man by eating a chicken-leg or a pear 'at' him, cannibal-style, see the lovely burlesque in the film of *Tom Jones*. A meal à *deux* is, quite certainly, a direct lead-in to love play (see *Big toe, Remote control*) but don't overdo the alcohol, and give each other a few minutes after rising from table. Love and food mixed well in Greek and Roman times when you reclined together on a couch, or fed one another (geishas do this still). Some people enjoy food-and-sex games

(custard or icecream on the skin, grapes in the pussy, and so on) which are great for regressive orality but messy for an ordinary domestic setting. Most lovers with privacy like to eat naked together and take it from there according to taste.

History is littered with 'aphrodisiac' foods – these are either magic (eryngo roots, which look like testicles, phallic asparagus and so on), olfactory (fish, tomatoes straight off the plant, which smell sexy) or miscellaneous. One can't prove that onions, eels – phallic and otherwise – ginseng root and so on don't work on some people. The trouble is that any *reputed* aphrodisiac works if you think it will, while many true pharmacological responses can get overriden in particular individuals by other factors. Broad beans are a reputed aphrodisiac – not only do they look like testicles, but they contain dopamine. We both respond so quickly to one another that any effect of this sort is hard to gauge personally. Essential oils which slightly irritate the bladder can excite some girls – try a full dose of green Chartreuse. Hot spices, which induce skin flushing, are another physiologically plausible line of attack. But none of them are lifesavers, or come up to the combined effect of 'the time and the place and the loved one together.' However, experiment by all means. Only very heavy meals and excessive drinking are specific turn-offs.

frontal

All the face-to-face positions where one partner has both thighs between those of the other – he astride both hers or between them. Includes all the varieties of the *Matrimonial* plus most of the more complicated, deep facing positions. Gives more depth (usually) but less clitoral pressure than the *Flanquettes*. To unscramble a complicated posture for purposes of classification, turn the partners round mentally and see if they can finish up face-to-face in a matrimonial without crossing legs. If so, it's frontal. If not, and they finish face-to-face astride one leg, it's a flanquette: square from behind (croupade): or from behind, astride a leg (cuissade). It's as simple as that.

This isn't an intellectual classificatory exercise. Postures are to be used in sequence, and one needs to make as few radical shifts, such as climbing over legs or turning a partner over, as possible – consider, in dancing, the difference between an impetus turn and a natural spin turn. This is important in planning sequences, though once you get used to going through five, ten or twenty postures at a single session you'll do it automatically: at first, whichever partner leads, they need to envisage all the stages in getting where they are going to avoid clumsiness and breaks, other than natural and intended ones.

FRONTAL *overleaf*
Postures are used in sequence and one needs to make as few radical shifts as possible. Avoid clumsiness.

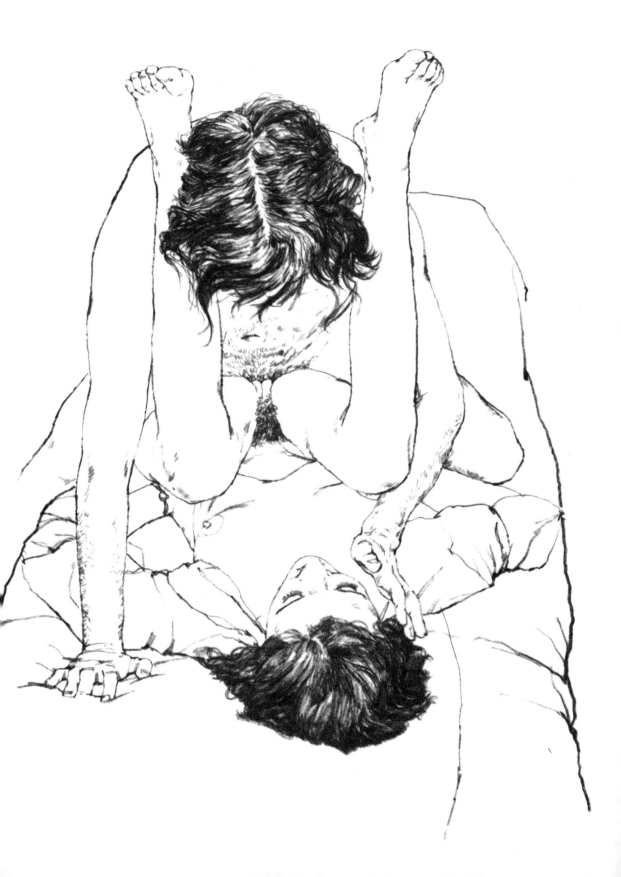

hair

Head hair has a lot of Freudian overtones—in mythology it's a sign of virility, witness Samson or Hercules. Our culture having learned in the last generation to associate long hair with women and short hair with manly conformity is occasionally excited to frenzy when young males now prefer to reject the stereotype and wear their hair, in the words of the seventeenth-century Harvard MS. 'in the manner of ruffians and barbarous Indians'— or of George Washington. Freud thought that long female hair acted as reassurance to the male by being a substitute for the phallus women don't have. Be that as it may, long male hair stirs all kinds of hostility in up-tight people who are upset by anything which looks intersexual in terms of their conventions. This is temporary – in many ages it has been as fashionable as now, and tends to go with a less anxious idea of maleness.

Sex play with long hair is great because of its texture – you can handle it, touch each other with it, and generally use it as one more resource. Some women are turned on by a fair amount of masculine body hair because it looks virile, others turned off by it because it looks animal – this seems to be a matter of attitude. Male face hair is another focus of convention – sometimes everyone has it as a social necessity, at other times it is persecuted, or confined to sailors, pioneers, and exotic people such as artists and chefs. Schopenhauer thought that it covered the parts of the face 'which express the moral feelings,' and disapproved, on the grounds that it was immodest to wear a sex signal in the middle of one's face. Today you can please yourself, or better, your partner.

handwork

Sex for all males and many females begins in the handwork class – both when we start to discover our own bodies and when we start to have access to each other's. For both sexes it is basic training – in mutual sex good handwork is never superseded. A couple who can masturbate each other really skillfully can do anything else they like. Handwork is not a 'substitute' for vaginal intercourse but something quite different, giving a different type of orgasm, and the orgasm one induces oneself is different again from orgasm induced by a partner. In full intercourse it is a preparation – to stiffen the man, or to give the woman one or more preliminary peaks before insertion. After intercourse, it is the natural lead-in to a further round. Moreover most men can get a second orgasm sooner from partner-stimulation than from the vagina, and a third after that if they masturbate themselves.

A woman who has the divine gift of lechery and loves her partner will masturbate him well, and a woman who knows how to masturbate a man – subtly, unhurriedly and

HAIR *opposite*
Sex play with long hair is great because of its texture – you can handle it, touch each other with it and generally use it as one more resource.

mercilessly – will almost always make a superlative partner. She needs intuitive empathy and real enjoyment of a
penis, holding it in just the right place, with just the right
amount of pressure and movement, and timing her action
in bursts to coincide with his feeling – stopping or slowing
to keep him in suspense, speeding up to control his climax.
Some men can't stand really proficient masturbation to
climax unless they are securely tied (see *Bondage*), and
virtually none can hold still for slow masturbation.

The variation can be endless, even if she hasn't the
choice of foreskin back, foreskin not back, which again
yield two quite distinct nuances. If he isn't circumcised
she will probably need to avoid rubbing the glans itself,
except in pursuit of very special effects. Her best grip is
just below the groove, with the skin back as far as it will
go, and using two hands – one pressing hard near the
root, holding the penis steady, or fondling the scrotum,
the other making a thumb-and-first finger ring, or a whole
hand grip. She should vary this, and, in prolonged masturbation, change hands often. For a full orgasm she sits comfortably on his chest or kneels astride him. During every
extended sexual session one orgasm – usually the second
or third – is well worth giving in this way: the French pro-
fessionals who used no other method and called themselves 'les filles de la veuve Poignet' didn't only stay in
business through fear of infection. It is well worth devoting
time to perfecting this technique – it fully expresses love,
and can be domesticated in any bedroom. Rolling the
penis like pastry between the palms of two hands is
another technique, best used for producing an erection.
Firm pressure with one finger at the midpoint between
penis and anus is another. For some occasions she can try
to copy his own favorite method of self-masturbation;
using her own rhythm has a different and sometimes more
startling effect.

He needs to notice how she masturbates herself. Most
men neglect the labia in favor of the clitoris. Clitoral rubbing can be as mind-blowing for her as slow masturbation
is for him, but it can be painful if it is unskillful, repeated too
often or straight after an orgasm achieved in this way. She
says: 'The main difficulty from the man's point of view is
that the ideal pressure point varies from hour to hour·so
he should allow her to guide him to the right place. Most
men think they know automatically, having succeeded
once – they are often wrong.'

For preparation as well as orgasm, the flat of the hand
on the vulva with the middle finger between the lips, and
its tip moving in and out of the vagina, while the ball of the
palm presses hard just above the pubis, is probably the
best method. Steady rhythm is the most important thing,
taking it from her hip movements, and alternating with

gentle lip stretching – then a full attack on the clitoris and its hood with the forefinger or little finger, thumb deeply in the vagina (keep your nails short). For faster response, hold her open with one hand and work gently with all the fingers of the other (in this case she may need to be fixed down). Switch to the tongue occasionally if she becomes dry, because she won't realize until afterwards how sore you have made her.

In mutual masturbation to orgasm you take out your need to move on your partner. It works better than sixty-nine because under these circumstances you can let go without losing your partner or hurting them. Side by side on your backs is probably the best position.

When she masturbates him, she may get extra pleasure from seeing his ejaculation – if you want to avoid spilling semen in a strange bed, use one of the short glans-condoms called American tips (this is their only use – they are dangerous contraceptives, as they come off during intercourse).

However much sex you have, you will still need simple, own-hand masturbation – not only during periods of separation, but simply when you feel like another orgasm. Some women feel left out if they find their partner mastur-

HANDWORK *opposite and above*
In mutual sex good handwork is never superseded.

bating; but if you feel vibrations when he thinks you are asleep and want to get in on the act, tackle him there and then and finish him yourself at full speed – or better, start on him slow-style then stop, tie him, and make him watch you masturbate yourself, slowly and with style, before you put him out of his misery. The unexpected sight of a woman giving herself an orgasm when he cannot move is unbearably exciting for most men. Make sure he can't get loose. Finally, watching each other take the last orgasm separately but together makes a wonderful end to any afternoon in bed.

kisses

These, at one level, don't require teaching, but it's easy to be so set on insertion that one overlooks them. (See *Real sex*). Lip and tongue kisses add immensely to intercourse in all face-to-face positions: breast kisses are essential if the woman isn't to miss a whole range of feeling; genital kisses (see *Mouth music*) are a tender resource on their own. Kisses can be put anywhere on the body, they can be given with lips, tongue, penis, labia or eyelashes – mouth kisses range from a mere touch to the kiss *à la cannibale* which leaves a bruise.

A lot of people maintain mouth contact continuously throughout intercourse, and prefer face-to-face positions for this reason. The deep tongue kiss can either be a second penetration, the man's tongue imitating exactly the rhythm of what is going on elsewhere, or she can give it, penetrating him, to call the rhythm. Even without any penetration, some people favor a tongue-battle which can last minutes or hours, with several orgasms for the girl, a form of non-genital heavy petting called *maraichignage*. If you are in private, move on to breasts, and go from there. Another pleasure is to make her a carpet of flowers, by covering every inch of her body with small, close kisses: then she can reply, using lipstick to mark where she's been. From there it is only a little way to doing the same with a tongue-tip (see *Tongue bath*): moreover, unlike a man, she has two mouths to kiss with, and some women use them beautifully. Eyelids too can be used for nipple, lip, glans and skin kisses.

If you haven't at least kissed her mouth, shoulders, neck, breasts, armpits, fingers, palms, toes, soles, navel, genitals and earlobes, you haven't really kissed her: it is no trouble to fill in the gaps for completeness and makes a touching compliment.

A good mouth kiss should leave its recipient breathless but not asphyxiated (leave an airway open), and nobody likes their nose squashed into their face. Clean your teeth before making love, and if you are having whisky, garlic, etc., both of you have it.

HANDWORK *opposite*
A woman with the divine gift of lechery will almost always make a superlative partner.

KISSES *overleaf*
Make her a carpet of flowers by covering every inch of her body with small, close kisses.

little death

Le petite mort: some women do indeed pass right out, the 'little death' of French poetry. Men occasionally do the same. The experience is not unpleasant, but it can scare an inexperienced partner cold. A friend of ours had this happen with the first girl he ever slept with. On recovery she explained, 'I'm awfully sorry, but I always do that.' By then he had called the police and the ambulance. So there is no cause for alarm, any more than over the yells, convulsions, hysterical laughter or sobbing, or any of the other quite unexpected reactions which go with complete orgasm in some people. By contrast others simply shut their eyes, but enjoy it no less. Sound and fury can be a flattering testimonial to a partner's skills, but a fallacious one, because they don't depend on the intensity of feeling, nor it upon them.

Men don't very often pass right out – that's *her* privilege, though they can give a splendid impersonation of a fit. In any case you'll soon get to know your partner's pattern.

lubrication

The best sexual lubricant is saliva. Except for anal intercourse, most greasy materials such as petroleum jelly are too greasy and being unwettable they leave an unpleasant feel. Jellies tend to cut sensation too much. The normal excited vagina is correctly set for friction; if she is too wet, as may happen on the Pill, dry gently with a handkerchief-wrapped finger (not tissues – you'll never stop finding the bits). To increase friction, try honey – it washes off easily and is harmless.

Interference with friction is the main drawback of contraceptive creams, foams and so on, making them unpopular with some couples.

matrimonial

Every culture has its own fads about best positions, and experiment is essential. If we come back to the good old Adam and Eve missionary position, with him on top, astride or between, and her underneath facing – and we do come back to it – that is because it's uniquely satisfying. Chiefly it's unique in its adaptability to mood; it can be wildly tough or very tender, long or quick, deep or shallow. It is the starting point for nearly every sequence, second only to the side positions, and the most reliably mutual finishing-point for orgasm. If you start in it you can deepen it by raising her legs, move to the clitoris by putting one leg between hers, roll about or right over finishing with her on top, kneel and lie back into the Letter X with each partner lying between the other's legs (see *X position*), move into back, side or standing positions, then come back for the finish. It is also, together with the deeper versions, the ideal

MATRIMONIAL
opposite and overleaf
The good old Adam and Eve missionary position.

quick-orgasm position for both sexes. The only equally quick position for him is from behind if she is very tight, and the only quicker for her is astride on top. In fact, the chief reason for using the other 600 positions is to delay his final orgasm while multiplying hers. Experimentation will show you which suit you best.

Even excluding the leg-raising variants this position has won more medals at international expositions than any other. On the other hand, there is no one surefire sex

position which suits everyone. There are nonfrigid women who never come in this position, or only rarely: whether this is due to unconscious forces or position of the vulva, which can be a problem, doesn't matter a damn – try another position, especially if the man is overweight. The matrimonial and all deep or weightbearing positions are now known to be a bad idea in pregnancy: a few non-pregnant non-responders have had their lives changed by one or two hard pillows under the buttocks. There are non-matrimoniable women who have to be taken sitting, face to face, or from behind, finger to clitoris, or who need to ride. If the man needs her flat to finish, give her several orgasms in her preferred position first, then turn her. A gentleman is defined as one who takes his weight on his hands. There are great advantages anyway in ending in a position where you can settle in each other's arms without exertion.

The tuning adjustments for matrimonials can be highly important – hard enough bed, use of pillows if she is slim or built that way. Bed, cushion and flesh should between them give the consistency of buttocks which would be esthetically a bit too big. Tough or tender, how high you ride, pinned down (fold her arms gently up behind her and hold each of her thumbs in one of your hands) or not pinned down, astride her legs (holding them open by putting a foot under each of her insteps) or between them, spreading her with your legs – all make subtle differences. If your pubis isn't very hard and she needs a touch more clitoris, try a leg-between position or add finger contact. She can for her part hold your foreskin or penile shaft skin forcibly back with her hand (see *Florentine*).

menstruation

Primitives avoid menstrual intercourse because it is bad magic, and many moderns because it is messy. At the same time, the height of a period may be the girl's randiest time. If so, intercourse is harmless unless the male is liable to attacks of urethritis. You can ignore the flow and wash after, or she can douche, put in a cap, and flush afterwards (this is inclined to make her too dry, however). But periods are the natural time to concentrate on learning the full, mutual use of other, replacement techniques. Nature programmed them to encourage your versatility. Shallow, labial penetration is effective with a tampon in place – or you can try having sex under a running shower instead of in bed. The magical hazards can now be discounted, whatever grandmother taught. Try pretending that her g-string is a locked chastity belt and see how many ways, orgasm-wise, you can circumvent it. See *Substitutes*.

missionary position

Name given by amused Polynesians, who preferred squatting intercourse, to the European matrimonial. Libel on one of the most rewarding sex positions.

mons pubis

The decorative fat-pad over the female pubic bone which acts as a buffer in face-to-face intercourse and (more important) serves to transmit sensation to the rest of the area when it moves. Many men are not aware, if they are oversold on direct clitoris stimulation, that most women can be brought to orgasm simply by holding this gently in

MISSIONARY POSITION   *above*

the cupped hand and kneading or shaking it, before, with-out, or as well as putting a finger in the vulva (see *Pubic hair*). You can either grasp it (it exactly fits the palm) or rest the heel of your hand on it while using the fingers on the labia, or you can cup the whole area, mons and closed labia, in your palm and fingers. Practice seeing how much sensation you can produce with your partner lying com-pletely closed.

mouth music

It wasn't many years ago that genital kisses, or rather the taboos on them, were a king pretext for divorce on grounds of perversity, cruelty and so on. We've come some way since then – now there are textbooks, and they figure in movies. Personal preferences and unpreferences apart, most people now know that they are one of the best things in sexual intimacy.

Mutuality is the order of the day, which is why marriage manuals stress soixante-neuf. This is fine, but is has a few practical drawbacks. The chief is that this sort of lovemaking belongs better to the playing-the-instru-ment category than to the completely mutual. It needs attention and care to give your partner your best, and consequently you can't go beserk over it, as you can over a mutual genital orgasm: impending orgasm, especially in the woman, just isn't compatible with careful technique, and the man can even be bitten. Another slight, but in some men, real defect is that in soixante-neuf the woman is the wrong way around for tongue work on the most sensitive surface of the glans (this explains the acrobatics in some Indian temple statues, which aim to get both mutuality and a better approach for the woman). Our own experience is that mutual genital kisses are wonderful, but if you are going to orgasm it's usually better to take turns.

Who goes first is clearly a matter of preference, but one can give the woman dozens of purely preliminary orgasms in this way, as many as she can take, and she will still want to go on from there, so the man had better save himself for later. A few men can't take even the shortest genital kiss before ejaculating – these should save it until they need a new erection, when it is a uniquely effective way of raising the dead.

Some girls do and some don't like the man to go all the way and ejaculate (if they love him very much, that may make all the difference, but not always). Those who don't can easily stop just short of getting him there, shift to another *foyer* (between the breasts, for example) or they can compress with both hands to gain time – this needs alertness and doesn't always work. It's also apt to wreck his orgasm. Others once they are used to it don't

find the experience complete unless their lover does ejaculate. John Hunter wrote, 'The semen would appear both by smell and taste to be a mawkish kind of substance: but when held in the mouth it produced a warmth similar to spices.' If the slight bitterness, rather than the whole idea, is what they dislike, it can easily be avoided by taking him really deeply. With experienced women we guess it is about fifty-fifty, come or not come; in any case you can always ask, and partners soon learn each others' tastes. She says: 'A couple of important points to remember here are the retching is a reflex action if something large is poked down your throat; so if she does retch it may well not be because she hates it but because she can't help herself. A large penis will also stretch the mouth quite a lot and if she is covering her teeth with her lips to protect you, violent movements may lacerate them. Be considerate.'

Normal genital odor is a big part of the genital kiss for both partners, which means that the parties should wash often, but not immediately beforehand: they ought to know each other well enough to say, if it is ever disagreeable, and switch or wait. A few minutes' vigorous intercourse will often put this right, though the woman's odor changes in character. Contraceptives can upset it too. The marketers of intimate deodorants and flavored vaginal douches show evidence only of sexual inexperience – nobody wants peach sauce on, say, scampi. Seaweed odors or musk would be more in key. The woman's *Cassolette* is her secret weapon to an extent that women in America don't seem to realize—French women know better. Some men respond violently to it without realizing the fact; it's also the ideal perfume fixative, and a touch behind the ears at a dance, in advance of, or instead of, bottle perfume can be deadly. His, by contrast, will please her more the longer she loves him. Wash with white soap, and here as everywhere treat deodorants the way a chef would treat deflavorants. How the hippie generation thinks you can live the good sex life without washing defeats explanation.

For some couples the simultaneous, 69-type kiss really does represent the ultimate in sensation. For them, since loss of control will be complete, the woman can't be the beserk type, nor want him to stop short of ejaculating. The woman-on-top position in most books is all right, especially if she combines mouth with handwork, but it gives the man a stiff neck. We favor the no-cushions position, i.e. head to tail on their sides, each with the under thigh drawn up as a cushion for the partner's head. The man can open her widely by slipping his arm in the crook of her upper knee.

The mutual kiss can be long or short; the short is just

in passing – the long can last minutes or hours according to taste and speed. Both fit nicely between rounds of intercourse, as well as acting as hors d'oeuvres or a corpse reviver.

If, on the other hand, they are going alternately, let him start, preferably in this same no-cushions position, while she does very little. Then it can be her turn; or they can go on to intercourse, putting off fellatio until he has had one orgasm and a rest and is due for his next erection. In this way she can abandon herself, and watch her technique when she sucks him. She will probably get the best results with what the Chinese call the 'jade flute' position – an instrument which is self-explanatory, and is played like a recorder, facing him, thumbs underneath, fingers on top. Her technique depends on her man – for instance, on whether or not he is circumcised. Not all men find tongue or lip contact with the glans pleasurable. For some it's ecstasy, while others prefer foreskin movement over the covered glans with the shaft held tight. The various sorts of nibbling, etc., described in sex books come naturally to most people. One finds them out on a basis of learn and teach. For a more active male position and a fast orgasm, she lies back, and he has oral coitus as fully and deeply as she can stand it. She must keep her teeth well open, making him a vagina with her lips and tongue. He needs to keep a little control, to avoid being involuntarily bitten.

The reverse equivalent is when she kneels astride and gives herself, exactly as in a passionate mouth-to-mouth kiss, brushing first, then open and deeply, while he uses long tongue strokes, from the vagina to the clitoris, with an extra twitch to her glans as he reaches it each time.

When it's his initiative, he can do worse than try the cascade position, if she is portable. This is really only 69 standing up, but it gives her the unique sensation of an orgasm head-downward. To get her there he lays her face-up across the bed, head over the edge, stands astride her face, then bends over and picks her up, legs round his neck. She can return his kiss, but near orgasm she had far better slip him between her breasts or into her hand, and abandon herself to full orgasm.

The first genital kiss, to an inexperienced girl, is another 'situation.' Kneeling before her, 'vers le buisson ardent des femmes' looks fine, but one can't reach to do more than nuzzle. We suggest this: with the lady face-up along the bed, sit on the edge half-facing her feet. Kiss her all over; then reach over and pick up her farther leg and kiss her foot. Quickly slip your nearer elbow through her raised knee, open her, and kiss gently on the closed labia until she is ready for deeper and deeper tongue strokes. Fewer and fewer women are now inhibited about

being kissed, though rather more can't get pleasure from kissing the man. A surprising number of girls cannot initially be got there at all *without* prolonged genital kissing, a fact which Indian love books recognize. For a very shy girl (or man), try it in the dark – but certainly try it. In the other direction, good mouth work is perhaps one of the most valued gifts a girl can give to her man, and well worth practicing. A spontaneous genital kiss to a man is one of the most moving gestures in the whole sexual experience.

navel

Fascinating to lovers, like all the details of the human body. It's not only decorative but has a lot of cultivable sexual sensation; it fits the finger, tongue, glans or big toe, and merits careful attention when you kiss or touch. Intercourse in the navel is practicable (there are stories of naive couples who thought that was the usual way, and it's a common childhood fantasy about how sex is conducted). If she is plump she can hold up the skin on each side to make labia. In any case, the finger or tongue tip slip into it naturally in both sexes.

négresse

A la Négresse – from behind. She kneels, hands clasped behind her neck, breasts and face on the bed. He kneels behind – she hooks her legs over his and pulls him to her with them – he puts a hand on each of her shoulder-blades and presses down. Very deep position – apt to pump her full of air which escapes later in a disconcerting manner – otherwise excellent.

postures

Endless. time has been spent throughout history, chiefly by nonplaying coaches, in describing and giving fancy names to upwards of six hundred of these – collecting them is obviously a human classificatory hobby. Most people now know the obvious ones and have learned which make for quick and slow orgasm and how to use them in series. A few people, either for symbolic or anatomical reasons, can only get orgasm in one or two.

We haven't gone into postures here in this kind of detail. Most of the non-freak ones come naturally, and few of the freak postures merit more than a single visit out of curiosity.

The only part we regret is the loss of the fancy names, Arabic, Sanskrit or Chinese, which go with them. Inspection will indicate which fit special situations such as pregnancy, fat male with thin girl, height differences, etc.

NAVEL *opposite*
The finger and the tongue tip slip into it naturally.

POSTURES *overleaf*
Only trial will indicate which work best, or at all.

Only trial will indicate which work best, or at all, orgasm-wise. Couples often start by trying the lot, but nearly inevitably end up with one or two, going back to the book for special occasions. Some of the really wild fantasies in Oriental manuscripts do have a point – the girl astride in Mughal pictures who is balancing lighted lamps on her hands, head and shoulders or shooting at a target with a bow is only showing that she can bring the man off with her vaginal muscles alone while keeping the rest of her still (see *Pompoir*) and so on. Others are mystical or merely gymnastic. All the poses we show are practicable (we've tried them for fit, if not to orgasm) and more or less rewarding.

quickies

Short and sharp has a charm of its own, but it needs a rate of mutual turn-on and physical response in the woman which is learned as a rule *only* in much longer sessions. A really good couple can manage either at will – short and

sweet, or indefinitely prolonged and differently sweet. In
other words you can't fully appreciate the quickie
without mastering the art of prolongation.

Once you've got this, the quickie is the equivalent of
inspiration, and you should let it strike lightning fashion,
any time and almost anywhere, from bed in the middle of
the night to halfway up a spiral stair: anywhere that you're
suddenly alone and the inspiration is bilateral. Not that
one of other won't sometimes specifically ask, but the
inspirational quickie is mutual, and half the fun is that the
preliminary communication is wordless between real
lovers. The rule is never to resist this linkup if it's at all
possible – with quickness, wit and skill it usually is. This
means proficiency in handling sitting, standing and other
postures, and making love without undressing. The ideal
quickie position, the nude matrimonial, will often be out.
This may mean on a chair, against a tree, in a washroom.
If you have to wait and can go straight home, it will
keep up to half an hour. Longer than that and it's a new
occasion. Around the house, try not to block, even if you
are busy.

rear entry

The other human option – for most mammals it's the only
one. Works admirably standing, lying, kneeling, sitting,
or with the woman astride. The lack of face-to-faceness is

QUICKIES *opposite*
You should let it strike lightning
fashion, any time and almost
anywhere, from bed to half way
up a spiral stair.

REAR ENTRY *below*
Works admirably standing, lying,
kneeling, sitting or with the
woman astride.

more than compensated for by extra depth and buttock
stimulation, hand access to breasts and clitoris, and the
sight of a pretty rear view. For the standing positions she
needs something of the right height to support her – in
the head-down kneeling positions you need to be careful

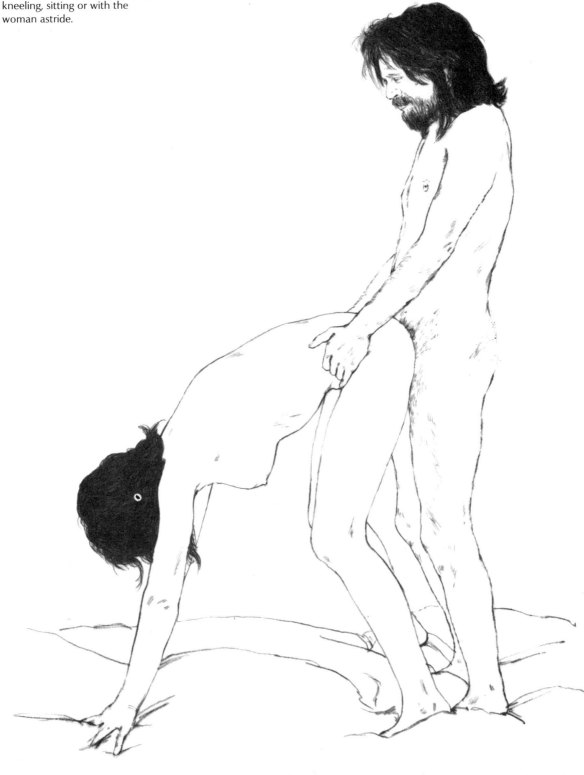

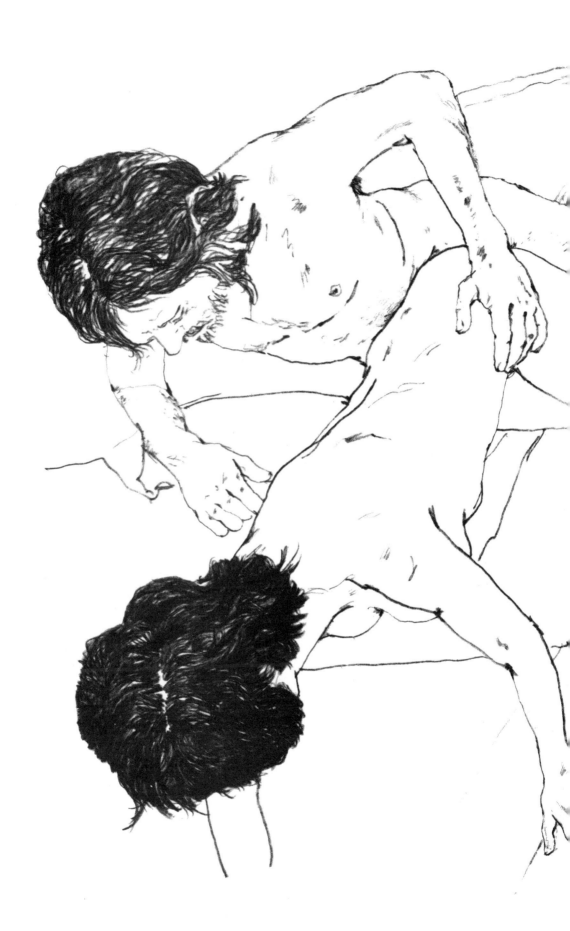

not to push her face into the mattress, and in all of the deep variants you need to avoid going too deep too hard, or you will hit an ovary, which is as painful as hitting a testicle. A few women are put off by the symbolism – 'doing it like animals,' 'not being valued if we aren't face to face' – but the physical payoff is so intense that they shouldn't allow these feelings to make them miss it. They could try it first with the man lying on his back and the girl lying faceup on top of him, or kneeling astride facing away, though these don't give the unique depth and total perineal stimulation of the rear kneeling positions (see *Négresse*). The man can hold her breasts or pubis, or, if she likes to be controlled, grasp her wrists behind her. A pile of hard pillows under her middle will help to prevent the position collapsing if she doesn't like being forcibly held, or she can kneel on the floor with her chest on the bed or a chair-seat. The head-down position is best for depth and total apposition – avoid it if it hurts her, or if she has a weak back, or if she is pregnant. Some women like a finger on the clitoris during intercourse, and this is easy in all rear positions. It's worth trying in any case, as it totally alters the range of sensation. Grasping the whole pussy in one hand gives a different sensation again and doesn't give the excessive sharpness which comes from strong clitoral stimulation. Or you can withdraw briefly and give a few clitoral strokes with the glans, guiding it with your hand.

While the deep kneeling position is, or can be, one of the toughest, from behind on your sides is about the gentlest (à *la paresseuse* – the lazy position) and can even be done in sleep – best if she draws her top thigh up a little and sticks her bottom out. This is one position which, in many women, can be managed with very little or even no erection; it can help to cure partial impotence or nervousness on the male side by restoring morale. It's also excellent if you want it gentle for health reasons, for fat or slightly disabled people, and so on.

It's well worth experimenting with the full range of rear positions at least as fully as with the face-to-face series, because there will be at least one you'll almost certainly use regularly along with the matrimonial and its variants and the woman-astride positions.

scrotum

REAR ENTRY *above*
It's well worth experimenting with the whole range of rear positions.

Basically, a control device to keep the testes at the right temperature for sperm production – moves up when you are cold and down when you are warm. It is also a highly sensitive skin area, but needs careful handling, since pressure on a testis is highly painful to its proprietor. Gentle tongue and finger work or cupping in the hand is about right. You can take it right into your mouth.

showerbath

Natural venue for sexual adventures – wash together, make love together: only convenient overhead point in most apartments or hotel rooms to attach a partner's hands. Don't pull down the fixture, however – it isn't weightbearing. See *Discipline*.

skin

Skin is our chief extragenital sexual organ – grossly underrated by most men, who tend to concentrate on the penis and clitoris; better understood by women.

She says: 'The smell and feel of a man's skin probably has more to do with sexual attraction (or the opposite)

SKIN *opposite*
Our chief extragenital sexual
organ – grossly underrated by
most men.

than any other single feature, even though you may not be conscious of it.'

Skin stimulation is a major component of all sex. Not only its feel when touched, but its coolness, texture and tightness are triggers for a whole range of sex feelings. These can be boosted in some people by emphasis, and by adding other textures, especially fur, rubber, leather or tight clothing. Much underrated part of human sexual response, to be played to the full if it turns you on. See *Clothes, Friction rub, Pattes d'araignée, Tongue bath*. Use these to educate your own and your partner's skin.

standing positions

The traditional 'upright' is a quickie, and apt to produce stiff male muscles unless she is tall. Many women need to stand on two Manhattan phone directories with the yellow pages, or an equivalent. Best undertaken up against a solid object such as a wall or a tree (not a door, whichever way it opens). Alternatively, you can be free standing, legs apart for stability and arms clasped round each other's buttocks – looking down as you move can be really sensual.

There are two kinds of positions – this one, subject to a good match in height, and the Hindu versions where he picks her up: these are tremendous if she is light as an Oriya dancing girl, otherwise they need to be executed in water to make her weightless (see *Bathing*). For a tall girl, try with her arms round your neck, one of her feet on the ground, and the other over your elbow. She can then go legs around waist, both legs over your arms, and even both legs round your neck, lying back, if you are strong enough, into a head-down position. Try this over a bed in case you drop her, but stand on a firm floor, not a mattress. If you are back up to a wall she can swing herself with one foot. Not good orgasm positions – designed rather to spin out coition. Standing positions from behind need no special comment – she needs to lean over or hold onto something rigid. If you have real height problems, try the upright positions on a flight of stairs. The head-down genital kiss is a winner if you are strong enough to hold her up, and she takes a good leg grip.

tongue bath

Going systematically over every square inch of a partner, tied if they like, with long, slow, broad tongue strokes. Start behind, turn them and cover the front surface after, so as to be in position to go on to coition or hand and mouth work. If the woman gives this, she follows it by covering the whole available surface equally systematically with slow strokes of her open vulva. Mini-versions cover particular areas in the same way.

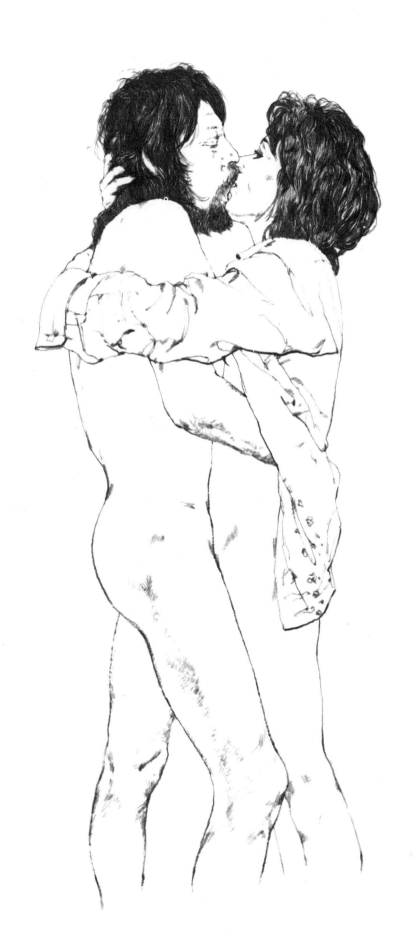

upper hands

If the matrimonial is the king of postures, the queen is her turn on top, 'riding St. George.' Indian erotology is the only ancient tradition devoid of stupid patriarchal hangups about the need for her to be underneath, and unashamed about accepting her fully aggressive role in reciprocal sex. With a woman who has good vaginal muscle control it can be fantastic for the man, but for her it is unique, giving her total freedom to control movement, depth and her partner. She can lean forward for breast or

STANDING POSITIONS
above and opposite
Traditional upright is apt to produce stiff male muscles unless she is tall.

UPPER HANDS *above*
Riding St. George.

X POSITION *opposite*
A winner for prolonged slow
intercourse.

mouth kisses, back to show herself to him, touch her own
clitoris as she moves, delay if she wishes, for emphasis —
the lot. She can also ride him facing or facing away, or turn
from one into the other, once or often. Riding postures
need a stiff erection (or she may bend him painfully with

an over-hurried insertion). This is about the only kind of intercourse in which one or both can be injured by clumsiness or by slipping, so test yourselves gradually. Once in, she can go facing, backing, kneeling, sitting, crosslegged upon him. sideways or round and round, and make movements in three dimensions and circularly with her hips. She can also lie on him (reversed matrimonial), legs astride or between. When she has taken her main orgasm he can either turn her, or she can lie back astride him, head between his feet, without disconnecting, and go on in the letter X or the full matrimonial for his orgasm. Since it needs a stiff erection, and some women prefer to start from foreplay laterally or underneath, this makes a good second-figure of a series. If she wants to bring him to orgasm this way they should try it first, preferably on

waking and when he is fresh, with a hard waking erection. The round-and-round and cinder-sifting motions of the woman's hips – what the French call the Lyons mail-coach (*la diligence de Lyon*) – come easily with practice if you've got the right personality.

x position

A winner for prolonged slow intercourse. Start with her sitting facing astride him, penis fully inserted. She then lies right back until each partner's head and trunk are between the other's wide-open legs, and they clasp hands. Slow, coordinated wriggling movements will keep him erect and her close to orgasm for long periods. To switch back to other positions, either of them can sit up without disconnecting.

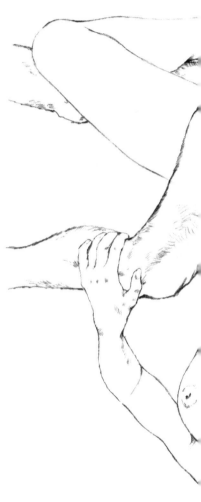

Sauces &
Pickles

for special occasions

anal intercourse

This is something which nearly every couple tries once. A few stay with it, usually because the woman finds that it gives her intenser feelings than the normal route and it is pleasantly tight for the man. In England and in some states of the United States it is actually illegal.

Unlike almost any other common sex practice, this one does have drawbacks. Usually the first try is painful, and while this may go with practice it certainly won't if you have hemorrhoids; it *can* cause injury, as the area wasn't designed for that, and extreme gentleness on the man's part is needed – anal rape, even of a willing victim, is accordingly out. Also, if you use it, don't mix it with straight vaginal intercourse – this leads to troublesome infections in some people with yeasts and other organisms which belong in the gut, not the vagina or the male urethra.

On the other hand, there are lovers who vastly enjoy it, as an occasional, or even as a regular, method, and, as we said, nearly everyone, if honest, would probably be curious to try it once. The technique is quite different from ordinary penetration. With the woman kneeling, head well down, carefully lubricate your glans (this needs oil or vaseline – saliva isn't enough). *Don't*, as in ordinary insertion, make a joyous virile thrust. Put the glans to the spot and press gently and steadily, while she 'bears down' to let you in. At first she will close up tight. Then after a few moments she will begin to open. Go in slowly, never more than glans-deep, and take your friction on the pull rather than the push. Work on her breasts and clitoris meanwhile.

You can use a small vibrator or a greased finger anally during ordinary face-to-face intercourse, in men, women or both (see *Postillionage*) – this, with the little finger, is a great favorite in French sex books. The anus is sensitive in most people, and the sensitivity can be cultivated. Unless you find it very rewarding and are free from the feeling that it's inesthetic, we doubt if it's worth doing more than satisfying curiosity and the occasional impulse this way, however.

armpit

Classical site for kisses. Should on no account be shaved (see *Cassolette*). Can be used instead of the palm to silence your partner at climax – if you use your palm, rub it over your own and your partner's armpit area first.

Axillary intercourse is an occasional variation. Handle it as for intermammary intercourse (see *Breasts*) but with your penis under her right arm – well under, so that friction is on the shaft, not the glans, as in any other unlubricated area. Put her left arm round your neck and hold her right hand behind her with your right hand. She will get her

sensations from the pressure against her breasts, helped by your big toe pressed to her clitoris if she wants it. Not an outstandingly rewarding trick but worth trying if you like the idea.

bathing

Bathing together is a natural concomitant of sex and a splendid overture or tailpiece. Taking an ordinary bath together has a charm of its own, though someone has to lean against the plumbing. Soaping one another all over, and, of course, drying one another, is a 'skin game' which leads on naturally to better things; after intercourse, a bath together is a natural come-back to domesticity or work. There are now large baths and conversation baths, but most of us see them only in expense account hotels.

Actual coitus is possible, and fun, in the shower if your heights match (see *Showerbath*) but no ordinary domestic or hotel bath is big enough for intercourse without punishing your elbows. Beside the novelty there isn't too much point anyway.

Sex while bathing is a different matter. The whole idea of intercourse in water is that it's like weightlessness or flying – the girl who is too big for all those Hindu climbing and standing postures becomes light enough to handle, and one can prop her at angles no acrobat could hold. All this has been rediscovered in the California swimming-

ARMPIT *above*
Classical site for kisses.

pool era; when we get to the design of the future, indoor equivalents will certainly spread among non-millionaires. Meanwhile there is the sea, after dark, when it is warm enough – on a gradually shelving beach one can have enough privacy even by day, and even re-emerge clothed: spectators will take it for callisthenics or life-saving. A pool has extras like steps and handholds, but is usually chlorinated. Water doesn't hinder friction, though its relative chill may mean that it takes some brisk rubbing to get an erection even in a very eager male. It might be a good idea to insert before going in, if possible, or for the girl to wear a diaphragm – we haven't heard of any harm coming from being pumped full of seawater, but chlorinated pool water might just possibly be irritant, as it is to the eyes. You can have excellent straight intercourse lying in the surf if you can get a beach to yourselves, but sand is a problem, and keeps appearing for days afterwards. A floating mattress is effectively a waterbed, but it is hard to stay on it without concentrating. We've heard of people combining coitus with swimming, and even scuba-diving, but they gave no practical details. Underwater coition, if more than a token contact, would use up vast amounts of air because of the overbreathing which goes with orgasm.

big toe

The pad of the male big toe applied to the clitoris or the vulva generally is a magnificent erotic instrument. The famous gentleman in erotic prints who is keeping six women occupied is using tongue, penis, both hands and both big toes. Use the toe in mammary or armpit intercourse or any time you are astride her, or sit facing as she lies or sits. Make sure the nail isn't sharp. In a restaurant, in these days of tights, one can surreptitiously remove a shoe and sock, reach over, and keep her in almost continuous orgasm with all four hands fully in view on the table top and no sign of contact – a party-trick which rates as really advanced sex. She has less scope, but can learn to masturbate him with her two big toes. The toes are definitely erogenic areas, and can be kissed, sucked, tickled, or tied with stimulating results.

bites

Hindu eroticians classified these at huge length. Gentle nibbling (of the penis, breasts, skin, fingers, ears, labia, clitoris, armpit hair) is part of the general excitatory repertoire. Hard bites at the moment of orgasm excite some people, but for most, like other painful stimuli, they are a turn-off. Women tend to bite more often than men, perhaps because they enjoy being bitten more than men do. (Remember that often your partner will do to you what

they really want done to them – being aware of this is the great secret of communicating sex.) Love-bruises, on the neck and elsewhere, which some lovers find act like a constant playback, setting off more lovemaking every time they are seen, aren't made by biting but by strong, continuous suction kisses. Sharp nips to the skin aren't as a rule erotic.

Be careful of biting at or near orgasm – the jaws go into spasm and you can bite really hard – in fact don't have an orgasm deliberately with a breast, penis or finger in your mouth. The need to bite can be taken out on something neutral like cloth or hair. This seems to be a case where the mammalian program of reflexes is over-tough for human enjoyment.

blowing

Not the slang sense (see *Mouth music*) but quite simply making a current of air on the (preferably pre-wetted) skin of any part of the body, either from the lips or from a hair-drier with the heat turned off. The best way to moisten an erogenous area is with the tongue, though for more extensive operations one can obviously use water or lotion. Air on a wet sensitive surface produces a sensation which can drive some people of either sex out of their minds – experiment on a small scale, using your natural equipment (saliva and breath). In the case of earlobes, breathe in, not out, or you'll deafen your partner. Else-where use steady continuous exhalation with the lips about an inch from the skin. The natural sequel to a tongue bath. For a bigger operation, use the hairdrier – the result is far wilder than the conventional routine with feathers, except for palms and soles – try mixing the two by hitching a couple of feathers to the drier nozzle on threads. Never (see *Hazards*) use a strong air source, and never blow into the vagina or any other body orifice (except the mouth – but mouth-to-mouth resuscitation isn't particularly erogenous).

bondage

Bondage, or as the French call it, ligottage, is the gentle art of tying up your sex partner – not to overcome reluctance but to boost orgasm. It's one unscheduled sex technique which a lot of people find extremely exciting but are scared to try, and a venerable human resource for increasing sexual feeling, partly because it's a harmless expression of sexual aggression – something we badly need, our culture being very up-tight about it – and still more because of its physical effects: a slow orgasm when unable to move is a mind-blowing experience for anyone not too frightened of their own aggressive self to try it.

Any restraint upon muscular and emotional activity

BATHING *above*
Taking an ordinary bath together has a charm of its own, though someone has to lean against the plumbing.

generally,' wrote Havelock Ellis, 'tends to heighten the state of sexual excitement.' Men and women have always been excited anyhow by the idea of getting the better of each other, and 'erotic bondage' was always a popular turn-on – every self-respecting folk-heroine and most folk-heroes have to be bound hand and foot periodically so they can be rescued. The best man at a Berber wedding ties up the bride if she struggles, and she is expected to struggle so she can be tied up. Fantasies of the same sort have a big written and pornopicture literature (most of it wildly unpracticable and meant to be seen not felt) which act as a substitute for people who are hung up on aggres-

sion, or need an illusion of rape to be able to lie back and enjoy without guilt. Most of us have traces of these needs, and like to 'dominate' each other symbolically at times, or be dominated (no offence to Women's Lib, because this need is mutual). But bondage games are played by many straight lovers who want kicks, not substitutes, and fill a lot of important spaces. They take a little learning (first efforts are often painful, or come adrift, or waste an erection messing around) but with speed and skill many unlikely people swear by them as an occasional – if only because really professional slow masturbation isn't possible unless the subject is securely tied.

In fact, really skillful bondage works like a bomb, sexually, on most non-timid males, both on the giving and the receiving end (as with any trick which involves both stimulation and symbolism, a well-tied sexual 'prisoner' both looks and feels sexy) – and on a fair proportion of girls once they get the idea; eventual responders of both sexes can require a lot of gentle preparation if they are scared by the aggressive symbolism, but this kind of fantasy only frightens people whose idea of tenderness is over-tender. Some women sense the need to be 'overpowered' sometimes. Others dig the domination symbol and like to be aggressors from the start. The idea is to tie your partner hand and foot, firmly but comfortably, so that they can struggle as hard as they like without getting loose, and then bring them to orgasm. Apart from being a wild sexual sensation, it enables many people who can't otherwise do so to let go to the last degree. They may yell blue murder at the critical moment but love it (one important skill here is to distinguish the noises which mean real distress – kinked wrists, cramp or the like – from the normal protests of ecstasy: the first mean 'Stop at once,' the second 'For God's sake go on and finish me off.')

Games of this sort are an occasional optional extra to all sorts of sex-play and intercourse, since the tied partner can be kissed, masturbated, ridden, or simply teased to orgasm, but they go extra-well in both sexes with the unbearably sharp sensations produced by slow, skillful handwork. 'Restraint' gives the receiving partner something muscular to do while remaining quite helpless to influence the march of events, or the rhythm and speed of stimulation (what Theodor Reik called the 'suspense factor'), and enables the active partner to push the woman, at least, to unbearable lengths (she, when her turn comes, can drive him frantic by spinning things out).

Experienced and unscared lovers will spot at once the context where bondage games fit. They're a natural in the sort of love battle which some boisterous types favor, where she resists as if she meant it: at the end, either he

gets a half-nelson on her, ties her, and carries on from there – or she is still holding out when the oven-timer rings and acquires the right to tie him. Or you can play it less rough and draw lots or take forfeits – in any case you should take turns. The other context, for non-kid's games players, is simply on impulse. One or other asks, or says 'my turn now,' or the active-minded party starts in and realizes their ambitions. He may wake up and find she has turned him over and is just finishing work on his wrists, by which time it's too late to protest (some women can get a lot further than that, with a heavy sleeper). Or he can ambush her when she comes back vulnerable from a shower.

To make this work as a game it obviously needs to be effective but not painful or dangerous. Technique is worth a few words because this is a highly popular sex fantasy, which isn't included in square books, and some skill and care are called for. On any bed with four posts you can stake a partner out, supported by one or more pillows. This is the traditional bordel method, probably because it needs no skill. Extension like this inhibits orgasm in some people – many feel more with the legs open, but the wrists and elbows firmly behind the back, or by being tied to a chair, or upright to a post. The critical areas where compression boosts sex feeling are the wrists, ankles, elbows (don't try to make them meet behind by brute force), soles of the feet, thumbs and big toes (artful women break off halfway to tie these last two with a leather bootlace – if you doubt this, try it). There are divergences of taste over what to use for tying. Leaving aside kinks like straitjackets or boy-scout garters, different couples use leather or rubber straps, ribbons, cloth strips, pajama cords, or thick, soft rope. Straps are easiest for women who aren't very strong, or can't tie reef knots. They need holes at half-inch intervals. Triangular bandages are all right for quick hand-and-foot tying, but don't look very sexy – and it is the neatness and wriggling of the parcel which excite the active party. Old stockings are a favorite resource but murder to untie quickly in an emergency. Chains, handcuffs and so on are quick, but don't give any compression and hurt to lie on. If they lock you can't rely on releasing them quickly. The weird aparatus sold by adult-toy-makers is for the birds unless you only want to pose photographs. If you like it, make your own. For most straight couples a hank of clothesline is fine. Cut it into five or six four-foot and a couple of six-foot lengths, and use a lot of hand-tight turns – don't tie tight enough to bruise.

Some energetic people like to be gagged as well. As one lady put it, 'It keeps the bubbles in the champagne.' Gagging and being gagged turns most men on – most

BONDAGE *opposite*
The gentle art of tying your partner to boost orgasm.

women profess to hate it in prospect, but the expression of erotic astonishment on the face of a well-gagged woman when she finds she can only mew is irresistible to most men's rape instincts. Apart from the symbolism and the 'feeling of helplessness' it enables the subject to yell and bite during orgasm, which helps a total cut-loose, unless you have a rhinoceros hide and live in a soundproof room. It makes prompting impossible, so that your partner's initiatives are outside your control. Most men who are excited by this sort of game like to be silenced thoroughly. Untimid women often come to like it after a few tries if they're the biting kind or like the feeling of helplessness – others hate it and lose their orgasm if they try it. A few like to be blindfolded as well, or instead.

It's actually hard to gag anyone one hundred percent safely, except in movies, where a wisp of silk over the heroine's face enables the hero to walk past without hearing her. This is as well, as the prisoner must *never* be made incapable of signalling if anything is wrong. A long piece of cloth, with several turns well between the teeth, or a small rubber ball fixed in the middle of a one inch strap by a nut and bolt (the 'poire' of French bordel tradition) are quite fierce enough. Adhesive tape will silence someone but is torture to take off. Anything in the mouth must be firm, mustn't block breathing, and must be quick-release in case the subject signals danger – from choking, feeling sick, or any other source of discomfort. This signal (and this goes for *all* bondage games) must be agreed beforehand and never abused or ignored – penalty for illicit use, two further orgasms. A Morse-code grunt, 'shave and a haircut, two bits', is a safe choice. The Federal Safety Code must be observed and displayed in a prominent place on the premises. This is as follows:

1 Nothing may ever be tied round the front of anybody's neck, however loosely, and even if they ask for it.

2 Nothing loose or soft, which can get into the throat, or in general other than we've specified, may be put in anyone's mouth, or over their face, and all gags or knots must be quick-release.

3 Nobody helpless may ever be left alone, even briefly, especially face-down or on a soft surface like a bed. Don't leave a partner tied and go to sleep, especially if you have either of you been drinking. Don't keep anyone tied up for longer than half an hour.

4 Play bondage games only with people you know, not only socially but sexually, never with acquaintances, and avoid group scenes. This goes for couples as well as partners – some people are careless, and others are sadists.

Apart from this, cruelty of any sort, tying someone who is
really scared of the idea, tight cords, stuffing things in
people's mouths, idiot tricks like hanging people up by
any part of their anatomy, and the whole Sadie-Mae
routine, which to straight couples is simply painful and a
turn-off, belong to psychopathology not lovemaking.
Bondage as a pleasurable sex game is never painful or
dangerous. It can, of course, be played simply for the

CHINESE STYLE *opposite*
Wild geese flying on their backs.

symbolic aggression, but at least half the payoff in people (and there are many) who enjoy it is, for the person tied, directly physical, in struggling against restraint and in skin and muscle feeling, plus the release of any surviving childhood blocks which comes from having pleasure 'administered' willy nilly. It also helps get over our cultural taboo on intense extragenital sensations, which belongs in the same package.

Ropemarks usually go in a few hours if you've been gentle. Rope burns and bruises come from clumsy untying – don't saw through the skin, but be quick, so that the man doesn't get stiff through being left tied after orgasm, and the woman comes down to earth lying comfortably in your arms. You can be agreeably, adequately and symbolically fierce, whichever your sex, without being spiteful or clumsy and wrecking things. The right mix here, as in all sex games, is tough plus tender. If you can't sense how tough your partner likes it, ask, then subtract twenty percent to allow for the difference between fact and fantasy. Given these rules, any couple who enjoy violent lovemaking and like the idea could do worse than learn to make each other helpless occasionally – gently, quickly and efficiently. This is neither kinky nor frightening – just human. For the pièce de resistance which goes with bondage, namely *Slow masturbation*, see that section.

boots

Notorious sex turn-on for many people – the longer the better. Complicated symbolism here involving aggression (jackboots and so on), phallicism and the female lower extremity. Used to be the badge of the prostitute – now general wear for straight people: have changed places with corsets, which used to be general wear and are now chiefly a sex kick. Odd how the market in the respectability of sexually symbolic clothing swings over the years. One could learn a lot about human imprinting by plotting the prevalence of such preferences.

Good for dressing-up games if you like them. Not very practical for serious sex unless you keep them for non-horizontal non-bed activities. If your man likes them, try appearing suddenly in long, tight, black, shiny ones.

buttered bun

Woman who has recently had relations with another man: unexpected turn-on for some males. This seems to be a carry-over from a fairly general ape behavior, where sharing a partner is a form of bonding between males. Psychoanalysts have long since suspected that the motive in much wife-swapping (and also the attraction of the gang night out and of the prostitute, who is a 'shared'

woman) was 'homosexual' in character – it's probably more accurate to say that it is an instance of the way in which primate bisexuality is used to cut down overt inter-male aggression. If the woman is your own wife, there is also a component of what psychiatrists have called masochism and biologists call 'stepping-down in the dominance hierarchy.' End of lesson.

chains

The tied-up, tinkling look – fashionable now, and they look well on naked skin. Some women like both the coldness and the symbolism, and some men spend hours locking and unlocking them – you could try them on him too for size. Uncomfortable and only symbolically effective if you want actually to hold a partner still, but they look fierce, and some people find them exciting. Bright tinkling objects turn on magpies as well as people. See *Earlobes*.

chastity belt

A turn-on for some people, they were sold in earnest until recently to 'prevent masturbation.' Like clothes, the real fun is in eventually taking them off. Many commercial ones don't even prevent intercourse. The kind with built-in stimulation, vibrators and so on sound more fun but cost a bomb. The genuine article, as used in the thirteenth century, wasn't meant to lock up the woman, but was worn by her as a deterrent against rape – the woman usually had the key, and some women were buried in them to prevent posthumous violation. The only worth-while chastity-belt game is to try, when she has a period, how many ways you can circumvent a really tight g-string and both get orgasm. Male versions are sold and appeal to some people, presumably as a spinning-out technique. Expensive toys unless you want to make one.

chinese style

In the classical treatises, remarkably like uninhibited European sex, the best thing being the delightful names given to postures: 'Wailing Monkey Clasping a Tree,' 'Wild Geese Flying on their Backs,' for two quite ordinary positions (seated face to face; woman on top facing away). Main elaboration consists in various complicated mixtures of deep and shallow strokes, often in magical numbers – 5 deep 8 shallow, etc. Intercourse naked, on a Chinese bed, in the open air, or on the floor. Woman treated far less as an equal in sex than in Indian erotology. Mystical schools tried to avoid ejaculation (see *Karezza*).

clothed intercourse

Really a heavy-petting technique: she keeps her panties or g-string on, he carries out all the movements of straight intercourse as far as the cloth will allow. Favorite ethnologic variant, chiefly for premarital intercourse – called badana in Turkey, metsha in Xhosa, etc. etc. Odd we have no special word. Not reliable as a contraceptive unless the ejaculation-position is fully interfemoral, i.e. with the glans well clear of the vulva, cloth or no cloth. Some people who used this before marriage like to go back to it either as a starter or during menstrual periods. Inclined to be 'dry' and make the man sore if it goes on too long – many women can get a fair orgasm from it.

corsets

A turn-on for some people – luckily now confined to sex games; they used to be an obligatory article of fashion. Make a woman still more woman-shaped. Firm pressure on the waist and abdomen excites many women. Some men are turned on by being laced into them too. Probably work through tightness and skin pressure, but a lot of symbolisms are involved.

dancing

All ballroom dancing in pairs looks towards intercourse. In this respect the Puritans were dead right. The development of no-contact dances has come about because one doesn't now need a social excuse to embrace a girl, but as an excitant it need not involve contact at all – in fact dances like flamenco or the twist are far more erotic than a clinch because you aren't too close to see one another. At its best this sort of dance is simply intercourse by remote control.

Most good lovers dance well together. They can do it publicly or in private, clothed or naked. Stripping one another while dancing is a sensation on its own. Don't hurry to full intercourse – dance until his erection is unbearable and she is almost coming brought there by rhythm and the sight and perfume of each other alone.

Even then you need not stop. Most couples can insert and continue dancing, either in each other's arms, or limbo-style, linked only by the penis, provided they are the right heights. Unfortunately this means that the woman needs to be at least as tall as the man, while as a rule she's shorter. Otherwise he has to bend his knees, which is tiring. If you can't dance inserted, and if she is small, pick her up into one of the Hindu standing positions, legs round waist, arms round neck, and continue like this. If she is too heavy, turn her and take her stooping from behind, still keeping the dance going.

This is a private game. Stripping at dances is getting commoner in some circles as a preliminary to group sex, but it usually is only a preliminary – after a few dances the floor empties and the couches fill up.

Seduction, or encouragement, while dancing is a natural. In the days of formal dancing one used to wish that the girl had her breasts on her back, where one could reach them, but that would have made it too easy. Gentle pressure, rhythm, sight and scent, and a knowledge of remote-control methods are all that are needed.

Most lovers are against Paul Joneses.

discipline

Codeword for beating each other as a sexual technique.

There is a venerable superstition, starting in English private-school scholars and backed by a vast literature from Meibom's *De Usu Flagrorum*, that beating is a sort of sexual Tabasco, the hottest erotic condiment, and no way-out party and no wide-scope porn is complete without it. Some of this is due to the fact that specialists in this field haven't suffered under the handicaps that affected, say, 69 or straight sex – beating is decent and can even be done in Church; sex isn't.

Beating is a kick which either works or doesn't. It doesn't work on either of us, so here we speak from inexperience. It's a violent skin stimulus, and Freud has been fully into the symbolism of punishment which goes with this – his conclusions go a long way to complicate Skinnerian arguments over what stimuli are 'aversive' and which act as rewards. Quite apart from fantasists and talkers who are far more excited by the idea in prospect and retrospect than the actual performance, some people are wildly turned on by it. For others, who have a real problem here, it may be necessary as a selfstarter. Skin stimulation and the occasional spank at the right moment fit well into most people's repertoire. Most find that anything more is disappointing in proportion to the scale of the performance (and possibly conducive to the thoroughly mischievous idea that women, in particular, enjoy being beaten up).

DANCING *above*
Stripping one another while dancing is a sensation on its own.

As we say, however, the idea of being beaten unquestionably turns some people on, and if it does you could try it. If you are lovers and one of you wants to be on the receiving end, the other need not be scared that they'll let out the beast in themselves by co-operating. If one of you wants to beat the other and he or she doesn't like it, or is turned off by the idea, that's harder – probably the loving answer is to settle for a lot of let's pretend and not much actual beating. This is a clear case where if you can't communicate fantasies, you shouldn't be lovers. Play it through a few times in words during straight intercourse (see *Birdsong at morning*). When you try it in practice, if it's the ritual which is the exciting part, make that big – don't be ashamed to ask for this, or give it: play matters. It can be a naughty-child or a mistress-and-slave routine or whatever – if your partner's fantasy doesn't turn you on naturally, play it as a game and enjoy his or her response. If it's the physical sensation, rhythm and style apparently matter far more than force, plus tantalization and the surprise element when the rhythm is suddenly broken.

Start gently at around one blow in one or two seconds, not more; gradually build up force until it is enough to make your subject want and not want you to stop. For two-way traffic the result, plus struggling, should both look and feel sexy, not cruel. The sauna twig level is nearly enough for most straight couples, but people who really go for beating like it hard enough to mark the skin. You can stick to the buttocks or cover the whole surface – back, belly, breasts, and even penis (careful!) and vulva (put her on her back with her feet attached to the bedposts above her head, legs wide open; start on the buttocks, then give one light switch or two upon her thighs and vulva to finish her off.) Or tie the victim hands over head to the shower nozzle and work over them under running water. For a genuinely decadent European sensation you need real birch twigs. Canoe birch and gray birch, which are the nearest U.S. species, don't grow in the West, so if you live in California and want authenticity you may have to vacation with a chainsaw in the East or in Canada. You cut 2–3 foot straight branches with the twigs before the leaves come out, tie them into a bunch, and wet them before use. If you prefer all the trappings, one can buy ferocious-looking whips and paddles that make a great noise but do no mischief. People who want the physical stimulus usually prefer twigs. Don't use bamboo – it cuts like a knife. Don't play this game with strangers, ever. Lovers have enough feedback not to let the most violent play go sour. And never mix purely erotic beating with real anger or bad-temper–it could be dangerous. A game is a game is a game.

EXERCISES *opposite*
Any new trick you try needs a practice session in anticipation.

exercises

The Viennese Turnergesellschaft professors tried to make sex into a form of physical training. Good general tone certainly helps, but it's equally true that sexual exercise tones you up better than jogging. Adolescent masturbation, if it's guiltless and enjoyed, is one of the best specifically sexual exercises, and the man can use it at any age in learning to slow down his response to a level which gives the girl a chance. She, for her part, can learn to use her vaginal and pelvic muscles (see *Pompoir*) 'by throwing her mind into the part concerned,' says Richard Burton. This superlative knack can be learned, because girls in South India learn it. How exactly they learn has never been written down, unfortunately, and the first person to teach this properly to women who don't have the knack naturally will make a fortune. Whether the commercial device with a rubber cylinder and a pressure-gauge helps we simply don't know, since our female half has the trick naturally. The technique to try would involve having a bulb in the vagina and a light or pressure gauge to enable you to know when you were doing the right thing. Anyone can learn to waggle his ears in any direction in 30 minutes flat if he watches the ear on closed-circuit TV. This makes us think that the commercial gadget is well worth trying. If she 'throws her mind' with him in situ she should master

166
 The Joy of Sex

it, and he can tell her when she is succeeding. Sucking a large, strong Pyrex test-tube into the vulva without hands is another recommended exercise. Once learned it is wholly involuntary and needs no effort.

What we do suggest is that for any new trick you arrange a practice session in anticipation. The time to learn new figures isn't on the ice-rink or dance floor. The most common reason that an elaboration you both wanted disappoints, whether it's a fancy posture or some dodge such as bondage which needs to be quickly and efficiently set up, is the attempt to use it in actual, excited lovemaking 'from cold' – so that you mess about, lose the thread, and wish you hadn't bothered with it or blame whichever suggested it. The usual outcome is never to try again.

Not that rehearsal need be coldblooded or taken out of actual lovemaking. Anticipation being good in itself, you first fantasize about it, sit down together, plan, and rehearse. Then fit the actual trial-for-size into the waiting periods between bouts – when you're both excited enough not to feel silly, but not ready to go completely: try it while waiting for the next erection. Remember even Menuhin has to practice the violin daily, though in love once learned is never forgotten. If it works first time you should get the erection – in that case go where it takes you. This means you can rehearse something new for each special occasion, mastering every movement but quite deliberately holding back and not playing it live until the appointed time. The waiting will help when that arrives.

To practice things you must try in full erection, make the effort, and try the new posture when you have one – either without movement, if you are set on waiting till later, or switching after a few strokes to something else. Of course, if it takes over, as it may, you might as well carry on, and turn practice into performance there and then. For most postures you can try wearing g-strings, so as to get the motions without actual contact, and some people find this exciting in itself.

feathers

Recommended by some for skin stimulation (breasts, body surface generally, rather than the actual genitals, and palms and soles.) Try stiff wiry ones (heron or egret) or an oldfashioned feather mop.

femoral intercourse

Another dodge, like *Clothed intercourse*, to preserve virginity, avoid pregnancy, etc., in cultures which cared about virginity and had no contraceptives. Comes for us

FLORENTINE *below*
Greatly boosts intensity of male
sensation if you get the tension
right.

under the heading of substitutes. Used from before or
behind, or in any other posture where she can press her
thighs together. The penis goes between them, with the
shaft between her labia, but the glans well clear of the
vagina, and she presses hard. Gives the woman a special
set of sensations – sometimes keener than on penetration,

so worth trying. One need not be so rigid about technique as were our forefathers, who had to try to keep sperm out of the vulva at any cost. With care one can do this from behind with the glans actually on the clitoris, with striking results. Good menstrual variant, or for at least a few strokes before you go in as usual.

feuille de rose

Tongue stimulation of the anus and perineum in either sex. Not unesthetic if you wash carefully and happens naturally in a lot of tongue play, but don't do it if you don't like the idea – or be afraid to suggest it if you do.

florentine

Coitus *à la florentine*: intercourse with the woman holding the man's penile skin (and foreskin if he has one) forcibly back with finger and thumb at the root of the penis and keeping it stretched all the time, both in and out. Excellent way of speeding-up ejaculation, and greatly boosts intensity of male sensation if you get the tension right.

foursomes and moresomes

Subject of a whole cult today, of which we aren't members, so we speak from hearsay.

It's becoming socially more easy to arrange, and personal taste apart we see no earthly reason why pairs of friends shouldn't make love together: plenty now do. Whether they also swap partners is a matter of preference. They would need either to be very good friends or total strangers, and we suspect it might go less well in practice than in fantasy – there is high impotence rate in initial tries of this kind, since our inhibitions are often more alive than we realize. Some experienced couples enthuse about exchanges. Others regret them as disruptive or don't try them because they don't want to jeopardize the extraordinary mutuality which grows with real and total sex communication. This wouldn't affect the mere non-swap type of proximity. Since friends already swap hints on sex it seems natural to demonstrate, and one can learn a lot by watching, apart from the turn-on from other people's excitement.

The famous one-way mirror scene is for real non-playing voyeurs or for birdwatchers who don't want to put their subject off. In fact it takes very little intercourse to make most people oblivious of their surroundings, though some might come down with a bump afterwards. Most men could take the social setting; some women are excited by the idea, others turned violently off.

'Orgies,' by contrast, need a hell of a lot of martini-lubrication, which is a point in itself. One can't shed two

millenia of preachments with one's underclothes. They tend to be ruined by liberal intellectuals who invariably end up talking rather than doing – and fall to the ground still talking. Hence we can well believe that the best orgiasts are the prosperous upper middle class, minor jet setters, and showbiz. It would be interesting to see how they manage, but we have a biased suspicion that after a few goes for the hell of it they'd be as dull, or as conscientiously jolly, as the non-sex parties given by the same types: also that we get better fun at home, unless they are *all* experts, which we doubt. If there were a top-grade sex society, it would still either not get over the lack of instinctive feedback between strangers as against real lovers, or end up as a closed circle.

Novelty itself does excite – the key-club, draw-lots game is an occasional in most countries and a religious ritual in India; we suggest this is usually, though not quite always, a secular male enthusiasm. We can't see any prohibitive objection between real friends, if the women, in particular, are adult, well-adjusted and storkproof, and the men not simply trying to prove something. It would be a better bid to organize this only if the women want to draw lots for a man.

Summing up, this isn't in our view a high-grade sex game but connected chiefly with self-reassurance. (All too often the active personnel are those who seem to be unsuccessful in intimate relationships.) That is a worthy aim, but not the point of high-grade sex. There is no reason why sex should not be social if you wish – whether it's also promiscuous is a matter of taste, both partners having equal votes on this, since occasional no-holds-barred orgies are an important anthropological resource for man, there may be a case for them. Usually the woman partner gets shanghaied. There could also be complications and anxieties, but there always can be complications, even at bridge parties. And we don't deny that there are a lot of fabulous party games for such occasions that one could devise. Oddly enough, regular swingers seem to get bored with these after a few tries and go back to at least a temporary couple-relationship. Remember, too, some of your best friends have V.D., and that the Pill makes it easier to catch it. Some groups have been brought to a standstill, not by V.D., but by an increase in minor non-yenereal infections. Try switching to an acid-gel or phenyl-mercuric acetate contraceptive, or using one of these as well, and wash with soap between contacts.

Adjusted people who try bisexual activies in a two-couple setting don't, Errors and Omissions Excepted, run any risk of getting stuck like that, though the bisexual element is an important turn-on in all swapping. We all have a counter-sexual component. Expressed like this,

FOURSOMES AND MORESOMES
overleaf
Since friends already swap hints on sex it seems natural to demonstrate.

without any anxiety, it's if anything helpful. If you feel intuitively that it's better left alone, leave it alone.

friction rub

The original meaning of shampoo, which is gentle kneading massage all over. Much more pleasant if you shed all adult inhibitions and rub each other all over with one of the non-messy scented lotions one can buy now for the purpose – a perfumery gimmick that shows a lot more insight than flavored douches and so on. Sit on something that doesn't matter and rub each other, together or in turns – sunburn oil or soap lather work well if you haven't got a special preparation. This always ends in genital handwork, then intercourse, then bath together. Semen would be the ideal medium, but it is too little and too late – bottled lotion is a substitute for this particular fantasy. She kneads his muscles, with fingers and a vibrator as well if they like; he concentrates on her breasts, buttocks, loins and neck. With practice these sensations are well worth cultivating. The Los Angeles massage parlors may get busted regularly, but they have nothing one can't do at home – apart from the fact that they are male-orientated, not mutual, and lay on a whole troupe of girls for every man. Presumably a devoted woman could call in friends to help – or a devoted man, to make things equal. This could make a good two-couple game, short of wife-swapping, provided the couples like each other.

g-string

Useful sexual accessory – for how to use it, see *Clothes*. For actual use in intercourse, as opposed to dressing up, it is best to make your own. We print a pattern. White or black pure silk are the best materials. When on, it should be absolutely tight and skin smooth, covering only the vulva and pubis. Cotton will do – nylon has the wrong texture. Other materials can be used as turn-ons, for looks, but can't really be kissed through – if you want to use these, wear them over the silk 'leaf.' Open-fronted panties aren't the same thing.

gadgets and gimmicks

The boom in sexual apparatus is quite extraordinary. The great exponents of this sort of hardware previously were the Japanese: in a sex manual one really needs a consumer study of the market, which we have not so far undertaken.

Judging from travellers' tales, most ethnographic sex aids are used by men at the instance of women; they must be unusually keen to please in order to bore through the glans and fit a 'spritsail yard,' like the Kayans, or insert pebbles under the skin of the penis itself like the Sumatrans. In softer cultures such devices are external – chiefly rings

G-STRING *opposite*
White or black pure silk are the best materials. The size should be about 8 by 3 inches – according to the individual.

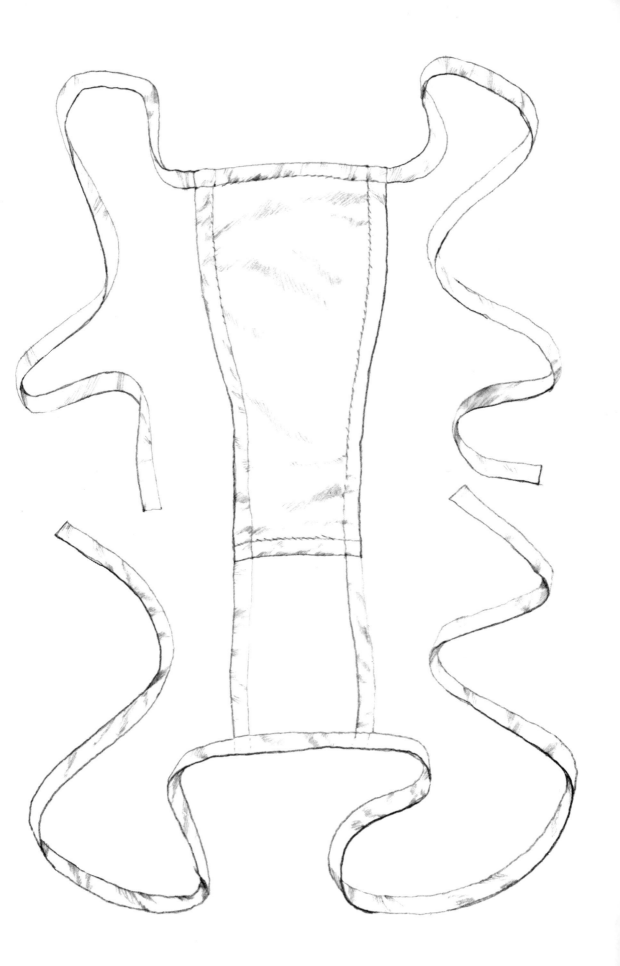

which fit round the coronal groove, made of feathers (palang unus – Malaya), goats' eyelids sewn back to back (Patagonia), or little hair brushes. These things are in museums, or one would wonder if somebody was putting an impertinent ethnographer on. The remarkable thing is that they should stay in place during intercourse. Nearly all are damnably uncomfortable to wear, and either pinch or get caught with hairs.

European equivalents are warty condoms, rings and the like, and dildoes – penis supplements or penis substitutes.

Sheaths are straightforward – they come in all manner of shapes and contours, the aim being to roughen both the penis and the vaginal barrel. Some have knobs or fingers to tickle the cervix. We are at a disadvantage here, in that these are supposed to help the female enjoy, but we've never yet met a woman who liked them. They are not safe contraceptives. Some people who are excited by the idea, if not by the sensation, buy a full set, including all the possible variations of shape. They come complete with a drying frame on which they can be stretched for cleaning, and should then be rolled and powdered with French chalk.

If these appeal to you, they are easily made to your own specification by adding knobs to an ordinary, washable-type or round-ended condom with Copydex or some other latex rubber cement – 'brushes' or larger knobs are cut from foam-rubber and cemented on, and the whole confection well washed with tapwater to remove any irritant chemicals before use. The kind with a thick corona ring strike us as downright painful. They also destroy the direct physical contact which, in communicative sex, matters a lot, but they allow one to experiment and to combine sex with handicrafts – such sexual Easter bonnets at least add novelty if you like the idea. We think they are more likely to precipitate frigidity than cure it, unless novelty is your turn-on. Buying sex gear together from a catalogue helps some people to fantasize and communicate.

Penis extensions, which fit over the real thing, likewise; penis size, it can't be repeated too often, has little to do with sexual feeling, though a big one may be emotionally stimulating in prospect. A large hard extension can do actual damage. The most these do is to boost male morale, though, like a chest wig, one wouldn't like to be found using one.

Rings are another matter. These are basically erection-maintainers; where they work, they can be a real help to better intercourse by stiffening a part-erection after a full orgasm – this is achieved by slightly blocking off the veins of the penis at its root, to keep the hydraulics working. At

GADGETS AND GIMMICKS
above and opposite
Rings are basically erection-maintainers: the finest specimen we've seen is Chinese and made of ivory.

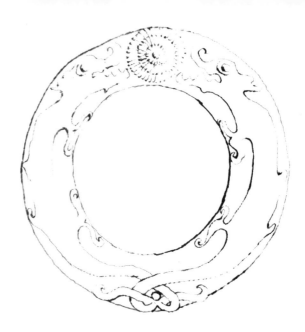

the same time, being worn over the pubis, they can also provide an additional pressure-point for the clitoris. The finest specimen we've seen is Chinese and made of ivory. The two sky-dragons are sporting with a pearl (the semen) – in use, the pearl is a small knob to fit the clitoris, the scales of the dragons open and tickle the labia, and the whole thing is held in place by a long tape passed through the hole, back between the legs, crossing behind the scrotum, up between the buttocks and then round the waist. The Chinese and Japanese also bind thin leather round the whole penis, or its base, and the Japanese favor openwork tubes fitting over the whole thing – in each case, pressure at the base plus roughening of the shaft and pubic area constitute the point. Others are belt-like devices which hold back the foreskin by pulling on the penile root. There are now several up-to-date models in rubber or plastic, which fit round the base of the shaft and have a clitoris tickler to supplement the man's pubic bone. One of the best is hollow and air-filled, so that forward pressure expels air from the penile ring part into the clitoral knob – this is supposed to give a very unusual sensation. It didn't do a thing for either of us.

Quite a few of the clitoral knobs strike us as over-hard to be comfortable, and all rubber rings are apt to pinch one or other partner. We have yet to meet anyone, male or female, who got much out of them. None of these things are surefire erection devices, and most work at all only in the absence of any impotence anxieties. One new arrival, the Blakoe ring, goes round both penis and scrotum-root (it opens and clips shut). This is supposed to stimulate the testes by forming an electric couple, but it may just as well act like other penile rings by pressing on the blood return – it wouldn't be much use in intercourse, but some people swear by it to maintain agreeable erotic sensations, and hence boost morale, during the day. To stiffen erection, a ring needs to go round the roots of both

penis and scrotum – some lovers use a turn of cord. Don't tie too tight or leave on too long.

Dildoes are artificial penises of varying sophistication (some include warmth and ejaculatory capacity, others built-in vibrators). These go back to the most ancient times and presumably have takers – the modern ones have excellent texture. Most women do not naturally masturbate by vaginal insertion, but since the ladies of the Turkish harem 'were not suffered a radish or cucumber to their diet except it be first sliced,' some, with sexual experience, evidently do – and the sight of a woman using one is clearly a turn-on for some males. They can also provide a second penis for simultaneous use. Single dildoes with a harness, or double-ended dildoes, are intended for woman-woman relations.

Merkins are vagina-substitutes – traditionally a warm-water container with a rubber or plastic vagina. Attached to an inflatable plastic doll or not, we doubt their utility – there is no substitute for what they attempt to replace, and, like the traditional hole in a watermelon, the only excuse for using them in two-way sex is if the sight of a merkin in use excites your partner. Vagina substitutes with a pump 'to enlarge the penis,' apart from bolstering the folklore about penile size, are capable of permanently damaging the natural hydraulics and should be avoided.

Chinese bells (now usually Japanese – rin-no-tama) are something else again. These are hollow ivory or plastic spheres, one empty, one containing mercury, and the third a large steel ball and a number of small metal tongues. They can either be inserted (in reverse order) into the vagina or put between the labia. Some are single, egg-shaped devices. Movement, including walking, then produces a quite unique pelvic sensation more intermittent and intimate than a vibrator. Some can be used in actual intercourse, others to maintain a steady stimulation – all day, if you can take it. Follow the manufacturers' instructions.

Skin gloves and skin thimbles have only just appeared on the market, and good ones have yet to be made. These are far better worth trying than any of the foregoing except the last. They consist either of a whole glove, or better a series of finger-cots the size of a thimble, each covered with a bristly cloth ranging in texture from soft fur to hard nylon pile with a tuft of bristles where the nail would be on a finger. They are used for erotic massage of the skin in either sex. With a properly chosen range of bristles and some natural skill, these can produce an effect which ranges from the pleasant to the excruciating. A well-made set would make a fine personal present. See also *Vibrators, Japanese style, Pattes d'araignée.*

Our final judgment is that unless intravaginal gadgets

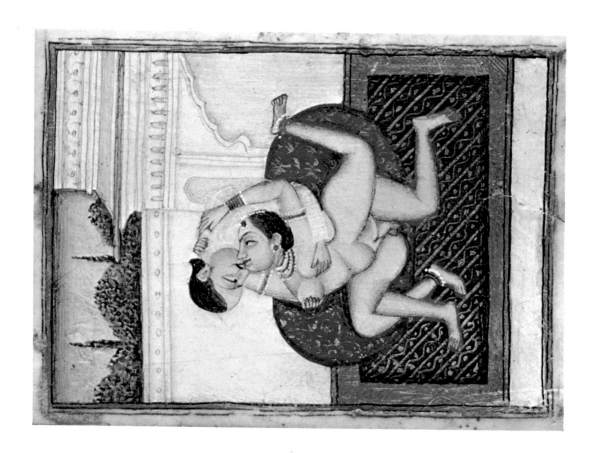

help the sexually handicapped, which we doubt, they're a waste of good money. For most people, they only spoil the intensity of normal feeling. Skin stimulation is another matter. But we may be unusual.

gamahuche

French for extended pussy-kissing. See *Mouth music*.

goldfish

Two naked people tied and put on a mattress together to make love fish-fashion, i.e. no hands. Originally a nineteenth-century bordel joke. It can be done (if you are the victims, try on your sides from behind). Venerable party game, but don't play it with strangers, or leave the players unsupervised, even briefly. There was a nice spoof of this sex stunt in the movie *Soldier Blue*. A good many women can get an orgasm solo in this way simply by struggling, especially if you put them in front of a mirror. Don't both tie yourselves, even if you can manage it – you might not be able to get loose.

grope suit

Diabolically ingenious gadget which has just come on the Scandinavian market to induce continuous female orgasm – unlike most such devices it works, at least on any woman who doesn't shy off it as mechanical. Consists of a very tight rubber g-string with a thick phallic plug which fits in the vagina and a roughened knob over the clitoris. The bra has small toothed recesses in the cups which grip the nipples and is covered all over inside with soft rubber points. Once it is on, every movement touches a sensitive area – the result can be unbearable. Can be worn under day clothes, if you can stand it. When it works, the effects on the wearer rub off on the male spectator. An amusing, and expensive, stunt, but we think it would cut down normal sensitivity if used too often. Its main attraction is novelty – might make an anniversary present. There is no male equivalent.

Less blatant clothing which maintains continuous sexual excitement is an old human expedient, and well worth experimenting with. Most of it is designed for women, not out of male chauvinism but simply because of the difference in physiology: a continuous turn-on enhances the woman's eventual response but would tend to overload the man's and make him unable to perform. The traditional instances are geared to feel sexy for the wearer and look sexy to her partner. Some of them could be of real use in re-learning the proper sexual use of our skin. They range from long heavy earrings to tight straps, corsets and belts, rough textures (hair-shirts, bamboo-ring shirts), ankle-chains, footwear which affects the gait and

presses on the instep, and now, more explicitly, hot pants which fit well into the vulva. See the full history of such devices in Bernard Rudofsky's *The Unfashionable Human Body*.

Most turn women on by their skin and muscle effect and men by their symbolism, but some couples get a special kick by making her wear something wild under ordinary clothes on straight occasions, when one can't go home early. Some commercial ones lock, and you leave the key at home. Could be worth trying for men too, if only in the interest of fair shares. Continuous sexual excitement you can't stop or do anything about would at least make a dull occasion more interesting, and guarantee a good scene when you finally get home. See *Earrings, Clothes, Gadgets and gimmicks, Jokes and follies*.

harness

Quick 'restraint' system for people who can't tie knots, bruise with rope, or like the look of 'apparatus.' Come in all degrees of complication and for all postures – watch out for expensive confections which are really kinky-photo props. Mainstay of way-out Danish sex boutiques. Include some gadgets like the mono-glove which holds the elbows back without cutting into the arms. Give very tight restraint and a lot of skin pressure which some people favor. Some play up the horse-symbolism, or include chastity belts, corsets, etc. The only really useful gadget of this kind is the 'leg stretcher' – a bar of adjustable length with strap collars at the ends to hold the feet apart if you don't have a bed with posts.

horse

The horse is an erotic object (see *Clothes*) and playing at horses, as well as riding them, notoriously turns some people on. One aficionado was Aristotle, who is frequently shown being ridden horseback style by a girl friend. Medieval moralists who took this as an awful warning miss the point. Men also like to dress women up as horses, though they can't usually be ridden in this manner. This seems at least as good a turn-on as disguising them as rabbits. Mentioned here for completeness – it's not our kick – but the game (equus eroticus, pony-girl game) figures in the literature. Either sex can be the steed. Odd how often children's games and grown-up sex games converge. Some people purchase a whole outfit including bit, saddle, etc. See firsthand description in *The Nightclerk*.

horseback

Intercourse like this is attributed to the Tartars, Gauchos and other equestrian peoples. We haven't tried it, lacking the horse and the privacy. He controls the horse, and she

sits astride facing him. If you were really set on this you could – in town – try a large rockinghorse, but whether it is worth the trouble we simple don't know. Quite a few women can get an orgasm when riding (especially bareback) and when jumping.

ice

The last material one would consider sexy – yet with its increased availability we keep hearing of people who use if for its shock-effect on the skin. One sex book suggests that just before orgasm the woman should slap a handful of crushed ice on her husband's back. Other people use an ice cube to go slowly over a partner's skin, including the soles of the feet, put them in each other's navels during sexual games and so on. Some women report

HORSE *above*
Odd how often children's games and grown-up sex games converge.

using them for masturbation, even to the point of freezing an ice 'phallus' in a rubber sheath. Not so strange, when you come to think of it – cold is a strong skin stimulus. We see no objection to experiments if you like the idea – you will hardly catch cold on one ice cube. Don't use super-cooled ice, let alone dry ice; these stick fast to moist surfaces and burn like a redhot iron. Test any ice-cube you use on your tongue, cautiously, otherwise you may be in for a shock.

indian style

Now widely familiar from the *Kama Sutra*, the *Koka Shastra* and so on. Intercourse on a bed or on cushions, fully naked, but with the woman wearing all her ornaments. Many complicated positions, including some derived from yoga which aim to avoid ejaculation (see *Karezza*), standing positions, and woman-on-top positions (purushayita) which are regarded as specially devout, since in Tantric Hinduism she is Energy and he is Immanence. All, if you do it in the original spirit and not for variety only, intimately linked with the Indian love of living at several levels – not only sex, but meditative technique in which one attempts to be subjectively both male and female for mystical purposes, or modified dance in which beside making love one acts out a scene from the hagiography of Vishnu and his Avatars, or the Life of Rama. There is a section on sexual technique in the chief classical dance treatise – dancers were temple maidens or devadasis who gave themselves to the devout as part of a religious exercise. Difficult for us to recapture, in spite of a dawning awareness of the psychoanalytic rightness of much Hindu intuition. Specialities include love-cries (see *Birdsong at morning*), love-blows (struck with fingertips on one another's breast, back, buttocks and genitals), love-bites as tokens of possession, and erotic scratchmarks – much skin stimulation with specially-grown, long fingernails, from mere brushing to a passionate scratch (classically confined to the armpit and the 'girdle path' – pantie region – where marks won't show in Indian day dress). Of all Indian techniques the standing postures are probably the best worth learning, if the girl is light enough. Few women who weren't trained from birth could, for example, stand leaning backwards on feet and hands, limbo-style, then put their arms round their legs and their head between their thighs, so as to take alternate stroke in mouth and vagina – or manage the one-leg-standing, one-leg-around-waist poses cultivated by temple girls. The best Indian accomplishment, the full *pompoir*, comes from the Tamil South, and unfortunately isn't taught in the texts, though the devadasis learned it from their mothers. See *Pompoir, Exercises*.

INDIAN STYLE *opposite*
Specialities include love-cries, love-blows, love-bites as tokens of possession and erotic scratchmarks.

inversion

Not homosexuality, which isn't in our book, but taking him or her head-down. He can sit on a chair or stool and take her astride facing – then she lies back until her head rests on a cushion on the floor. Or she can lie down, raising her hips – he stands between her legs and enters her either from in front or from behind while she rests on her elbows or walks on her hands (the wheelbarrow). He can lie over the edge of the bed, face up, while she sits or stands astride. With orgasm the buildup of pressure in the veins of the face and neck can produce startling sensations. Unless you want a body on your hands, better not try this on a hypertensive executive – remember Attila the Hun's young concubine: but it should be safe enough for youngsters. It is the way to handle those idiotic women who try to persuade a lover to boost their orgasm by throttling them – if you meet one of these, never do anything so damned silly, but teach them this alternative and equally rewarding method. You may save two lives –

hers, and, since most people's grip tightens in orgasm, her next boyfriend's, which could easily be spent in jail for homicide.

Inverted 69 is described elsewhere (see *Mouth music*). This makes a good tryout, always works if you can lift her, and will give her an idea of the quality of sensation involved; not everyone likes it.

japanese style

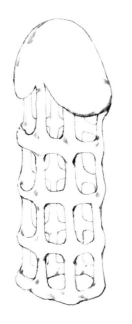

Intercourse on the floor or on cushions, as with most Oriental styles: partial nakedness only, numerous squatting and semi-squatting positions, a lot of bondage, a lot of preoccupation with extras and odd devices. We're talking here about the sexual customs of eighteenth- and early nineteenth-century prints, rather than the modern westernised B-girl version, which is international. What would be hard to copy is the essentially Japanese mixture of violence and formality. Other things are: elaborate finger-stimulation of the woman, thumb in anus, fingers in vagina: and a big range of mechanical devices – a glans-cap of hard material (kabutogata), penile-shaft tubes (do-gata), some of them latticed (yoroi-gata), or with a glans cap as well (yaso-gata): dildoes (engi), often strapped to the woman's heel, while her ankle is held up to a sling round her neck to give a better swing to the movement: thongs to bind tightly round the penile shaft, rendering it both rough and permanently stiff enough for insertion (higozuiki), and merkins to hold in the hand (azuma-gata). Postures cover the whole range, but the lovers of the 'floating world' greatly enjoy the simulation of rape – what George Moore called 'furious fornications' – where the artistic emphasis is on huge parts, copious secretions and so on: sex is played hard in this tradition.

jokes and follies

This, contrary to cultural traditions among squares, is pre-eminently the right place for them. The best of them, too, tend for this reason to be jokes at the expense of the square tradition. The finger-raising quality of lovers vis-à-vis society is as necessary psychologically as their tenderness to each other. That, and not just the spice of danger, is what makes love in odd places and under other people's unperceptive noses so attractive. This is childish, but if you haven't yet learned to be childish in your love-making you should go home and learn, because it's important.

One mustn't let the joke go wrong and sour things: if you can have intercourse in a public restaurant or on Auntie's dining table and bring it off, you can laugh about it after (but if you don't bring it off you'll be lucky if you speak to each other again). Most couples contain, for any

INVERSION *opposite*
The wheelbarrow.

JAPANESE STYLE *above*
Yaso-gata.

given occasion, one dangerlover and one restraining influence, and achieve accordingly a commonsense balance, helped by the angel who watches over such lunatic antics and protects lovers from the consequences. All in all, it would be stupid to recommend them but a pity to have missed them.

The amount of laughter you have in intercourse, pranks apart, is a measure, we think, of how well you are managing to love. It's evidence for, not against, the seriousness of your communication. If you have this, the laughs never fail, because sex is funny. If you haven't, you end with boxed ears or tears or no orgasm all round, through some remark 'destroying the atmosphere.' When it's really going, laughter is part of the atmosphere – even mockery isn't unaffectionate, and there's no joke like love well and mutually completed under unlikely circumstances. It's one of the few contemporary scenes which gets a laugh out of pure joy.

Taking a partner (usually female) around to square occasions nude, or in some kinky gear, under a long coat, is a danger-plus-snook-cocking game which some couples relish.   The danger is there all right – if you must do it, make sure she really enjoys it. The no-panties bit is dangerous enough for most girls unless it's very much their thing.

karezza

The Alice Stockham treatment – going on and on and on while avoiding male orgasm.

This is really an exercise directed against *Hairtrigger trouble* rather than a general coital technique. Long intercourse is great, but the aim will be to ejaculate eventually. Enormously satisfying for the woman: the original Stockham version, where the male didn't ejaculate but allowed his erection to subside inside the vagina has no conceivable advantage over going on equally long *with* orgasm, and is likely to spoil eventual response. Worth knowing about, however, if you read accounts of sex yoga drawn from Oriental sources. The old Tantric-Taoist system held that semen was spiritual gasoline – the man should be careful to conserve it while drawing 'virtue' from the woman. One ejaculation could dissipate this supposed virtue. Accordingly, a great many sexual yogic positions in which movement was difficult were designed specifically for this kind of maneuver – giving the woman several orgasms while the man conserved his semen and performed what was in fact a meditative sexual exercise. Adept yogis also trained themselves to ejaculate internally – an unrewarding technique which deposits the semen in the bladder, whence it is passed with the urine: occasionally the same trick appears spontaneously as a

disability and is difficult to unlearn. This explains the low male satisfaction value of many of the most elaborate Hindu positions. If you intend to use intercourse as a meditative technique, you may well use them, but there seems no rational ground against eventual ejaculation in any case.

Karezza was developed, possibly with similar ideas, by the Oneida community: it also kept conceptions down, albeit not over-reliably, as semen can leak without ejaculation. There was recently an offbeat French priest who canvassed the same idea as an answer to Vatican scruples over birth control, under the title of *continence conjugale*, but he has been put down. The method consists in total control of male movement – allowing the woman internal movements only, and the man sufficient strokes to maintain erection, stopping as soon as tension mounts. Use it solely as a training technique for long intercourse, then switch to full movement and mutual orgasm, for which the woman will be fully ready. See *Pompoir*.

leather

Probably the most popular super-skin turn-on: black hide also looks aggressive or scarey and, being skin, all leather fixes natural sex odors. Unlike rubber you can now wear it fashionably without being thought kinky, which yet another example of the arbitrary social choice of sex turn-ons in clothing. Some men like women encased in it: those who like the ferocious buckled-up look don't go for wet-look, soft leather, and vice-versa. If your partner likes it on you, let him or her do the buying. This is one object turn-on which women respond to as well as men, especially if it feels and smells right – soft leather jock-straps seem to please some people of both sexes. Don't pay racketeer prices, however; most of the elaborate gear in fetishistic toy-shops can be improvized, though if you want an Avengers suit you'll have to pay to have it made. See *Boots, Clothes*. Even if the texture doesn't appeal, try a leather-based (*cuir de Russie*) perfume – it is probably the closest to the normal female attractant odor.

masks

These excite some people: if this seems odd, remember that they are the oldest human device for getting mystical as well as sexual inspiration, by making the wearer menacing, other than themselves, and 'possessed' by the mask, and by altering the body image through partial sensory deprivation. There are inflatable helmets on the market which accentuate this last effect. We find sex better without our head in a bag. Putting the girl's panties over the man's head, an old professional trick, works on quite a different basis (see *Clothes*). Masks, like corsets, were once

a general fashion. Don't fool around with plastic bags – these are dangerous and obstruct breathing.

mirrors

These have always been an important part of sexual furniture in any bedroom not wholly devoted to sleeping. They turn love into a viewing occasion without loss of privacy and help the mise-au-point at a practical level. They also provide a turn-on by letting you see yourselves – he can see his own erection and movements without stopping. She may be turned-on by seeing her own body, watching herself masturbate, seeing herself bound, or any of the other fantasies one can enact, so that both get viewer as well as participant pleasure. Those who don't like them, by contrast, say they spoil the shut-in, non-spectator feeling they need to appreciate sensation to the full, and make the bedroom less like a womb with twins in it and more like Tiffany's. If you have never made love in front of a big mirror, try it. You really need more than one to enable both to see clearly without having to shift around. The exercise is worth it, not only for voyeur effect but to show you how unridiculous you look making love. Sex in cold blood description sounds undignified, but seen as one participates it is natural, attractive and formally beautiful to a morale-boosting extent, even if you aren't beautiful figures. If there does come a time when it's better to feel than look, we haven't reached it yet, in middle-age.

What you have on your premises is your business, but if you want to entertain guests, have the mirrors inside cupboard doors or on a stand. With all the publicity given to the one-way variety some couples are inhibited by anything they can't walk behind.

Old-style bordels went in for rooms of a hundred mirrors. Expense apart, these may or may not work for you; 100 couples acting in unison may be your turn-on, or they may remind you of Red Square on Mayday or an instant Roman orgy rather than lovemaking.

motorcars

These approach our ideal form of locomotion, the 'double bed with an outboard motor.' Big American cars come very close to it (there is room to lie flat, even on the rear seat) – Volkswagens call for neat handling of anything more than breast-and-petting work. The classical postures (she on the back seat, he kneeling between her legs, or both sitting, her legs round his waist) were developed for use by Emma Bovary in hansom cabs. All cars, whether adapted to petting or coition, have greenhouse-like properties unless you live in a climate where the windows quickly mist over. If you rely on condensation it is still a good idea to have a powerful light ready to dazzle cops or

MIRRORS *opposite*
Sex seen as one participates is natural, attractive and formally beautiful to a morale-boosting extent, even if you aren't beautiful figures.

prowlers – a really bright one will give you time to get dressed before sight returns.

For alfresco love the least-screened parking site is the safest, like a French eighteenth-century bower, because you can't be crept up on. If you want to do much of this, buy a small van, or one of those mini-campers known as adultery wagons, which are in effect mobile houses. It takes confidence to strip naked in any of these. For security the best ploy is to make it a foursome, taking it in turns while the other couple drive, or sit stonily in front behaving themselves and providing cover. Mutual masturbation while driving, and trying to score number of orgasms per gallon, are popular fantasies, but against the interest of safe driving. Seatbelts can be worn, or you can tie the non-driving party to his or her seat and work slowly.

motorcycle

Increasingly popular sexual venue, which combines the symbolism of the horse with leather gear, danger and acceleration. Has serious safety drawbacks, calls for the wearing of a hard hat, and you can't rely on the machine to look after itself as a horse can, but if you have access to a private road the hazards are yours. Better not attempted on the public highway. Another limitation comes from the fact that the woman usually sits behind, and you can't, or shouldn't, drive with one on your lap – clothed or not. Probably better as a preliminary to love than a venue for it. Don't let her liking for increased G override your judgment. Nobody looks virile with a broken neck.

open air

Countries with a warm summer have advantages which can't be overstated. In England, to have regular and full love out of doors you need to be frostproof and own a park. In Ireland or Spain, even though it is warm in Spain, you need to be priest-proof as well. Most parts of the U.S. should count their blessings. What is odd is that they don't do more about garden design. The walled or hedged gardens of Europe are nearly all practicable, at least by night.

Outdoor locations in wild areas are often flawed by vermin, ranging from ants and mosquitos to rattlesnakes and officious cops. Surface-wise the best venue is often sand dunes, which give shelter and keep the heat, besides not harboring stinging insects. Lawn grass is fine if well-screened. The safest cover, if you intend to strip right off, is the thicket standing on its own, where you can see out but they can't see in, the 'bower' of Fontainebleau painters. Europeans, who live in crowded landscapes, are adept at quick dressing and using places like Hampstead Heath and the Prater. With so much of America to choose

from, there should be no problem – if you do take risks, however, cultivate the quick getaway and the weather-eye open; danger turns some people on, and others, of both sexes, right off. Enthusiastic larks one gets lost in, like stripping right off or tying each other to trees, call for very remote areas or a walled garden.

What you can do safely in Hyde Park, London, would be asking for gang-rape in Central Park, New York. When traveling, Catholic countries are more up-tight than Protestant, and Stalinist than other-style Marxist such as Jugoslavia, but anyhow you don't want to offend local feeling. A flat roof at night is a standard Oriental venue – you can make love and see the whole city.

Ultimately there will be scheduled areas – we give it another five or six years.

pattes d'araignée

Pattes d'araignée, literally spider's legs, is tickling erotic massage, using the pulps of the fingers, with the *lightest possible* touch, aiming to stimulate not so much the skin as the almost invisible skin-hairs: not on the genitals, but all the next most sensitive places – nipples and around, neck, chest, belly, insides of arms and thighs, armpits, hollow of the back, soles and palms, scrotum, space between it and the anus. Use both hands; keep a steady progression of movement going with one, and make surprise attacks with the other. The whole essence is in the extreme lightness of the touch – more electric than tickling. Feathers, bristlegloves or vibrators give a quite different sensation. If you are agile, don't forget you have toes as well as fingers and hair in various places, including eyelids, to vary the sensation. A set of finger-cots with textures from cardcloth to mink are easy to use; the real and original French style with fingertips is difficult to learn but unforgettable by either sex. It's one of the two general skin stimulants (the other is the *Tongue bath*) which work even on not very skin-conscious males.

pompoir

The most sought-after feminine sexual response of all. 'She must . . . close and constrict the Yoni until it holds the Lingam as with a finger, opening and shutting at her pleasure, and finally acting as the hand of the Gopala-girl who milks the cow. This can be learned only by long practice, and especially by throwing the will into the part affected, even as men endeavor to sharpen their hearing . . . Her husband will then value her above all women, nor would he exchange her for the most beautiful queen in the Three Worlds. . . Among some races the constrictor vaginae muscles are abnormally developed. In Abyssinia, for instance, a woman can so exert them as to cause pain

OPEN AIR *overleaf*
If you do take risks, cultivate the quick getaway and the weather-eye open.

to a man, and, when sitting on his thighs, she can induce orgasm without moving any other part of her person. Such an artist is called by the Arabs Kabbazah, literally, a holder, and it is not surprising that slave dealers pay large sums for her.' Thus Richard Burton. It has nothing to do with 'race' but a lot to do with practice. See *Exercises*.

pornography

Name given to any sexual literature somebody is trying to suppress. Most normal people enjoy looking at sex books and reading sex fantasies, which is why abnormal people have to spend so much time and money suppressing them. The only drawback of the commercial stuff is that because it is based on fantasy, and often inexperienced fantasy at that, it's not much help with sex practice. Depiction of any of the range of sex behaviors we've described helps people to visualize them; porno stories tend to be dull, repetitive, and a strain on credulity: frankly antisocial fantasies about torture and so on worry legislators and others for fear they might induce idiots to imitate them – it's equally possible that by enabling not very bright people to fantasize their unacceptable needs vividly they help to keep them from acting them out, but there is no good evidence one way or another.

Straight couples can use 'pornography' constructively in the exact proportion that it's well done, i.e. it describes feasible, acceptable and pleasurable sex activities they'd enjoy, or fantasies which, though not feasible, turn them on. This is what literature in general does. Many people, male and female, find sex books a real help in raising the level of feeling to bedpoint. Use them as football enthusiasts use books about football – even if the players in the story show superhuman shooting-powers. It isn't true that only men are turned on by sexual literature: it is true that women are most turned on by it if it's written with awareness of other than male feelings.

If you've got literary or artistic ability, use it to express your own fantasies to the full, for private use between you. Most of the squarest writers and artists have done this, even if they didn't publish the results. It's one way of dealing with the things you can't, or wouldn't wish, to do in fact – a kind of accessory to dreams and to play.

The idea of children getting hold of pornography terrifies some people. If it deals simply with normal lovemaking, this fear is probably not justified – young children are likely to be bored: the main objection lies in how badly most of the Mafia stuff is produced – some is enough to put adults off. Some adult fantasy-material, if it's odd or cruel, could be actively frightening, though no more so than non-sex material such as newsreels or religious books. If you do see your children with pornography, remember

far more harm would be caused by any uproar you make about it. For adolescents it's probably innocuous unless they're obviously very disturbed over sex.

postillionage

Putting a finger in or on your partner's anus just before orgasm. Popular in French erotic books, and works on some people. Most prefer firm finger pressure just in front of the anus; in men this can produce an erection used alone. Use a small vibrator rather than a finger if you prefer – don't put it into the vagina afterwards, if you've actually inserted it. Firm pressure with a heel behind the scrotum or between anus and vulva works as well in some postures.

railways

An old and favored site for 'different' sex – now going out, as they won't let you fly united. This means, of course, the oldstyle wagon-lit or roomette. Whether it's the motion and acceleration or the association with love on the run that provides the turn-on isn't clear: it used to be fashionable in the classier Parisian and Viennese bordels to have a compartment fitted up, complete with train effects and noises, and vibrated by a motor and cams. Since it is probably the motion and variable G which score, choose a hard couch and a winding track with numerous intersections and switches. In emergency there is just room for an upright in the washroom.

remote control

It's an old story that you can seduce a complete novice, who has no idea what you mean, by slipping a thumb into a closed fist, or between your lips, and absent mindedly moving it in and out, in and out. We'd like to see this. All of the people we have seen it work on have known very well what it was all about.

This is one version of the pompido telecommando. The lip one works better, nail downwards in the appropriate rhythm – she will feel it where she should. She can do the same 'at' him, for example in eating (see that wild sequence in *Tom Jones*). Once habituated to either of these tele-control devices, most girls and some men can be radio-controlled as to excitement, erection and even orgasm – even by rubbing the lobe of one's ear – from several places down a table, the opposite side of a room, or the opposite box at a theater. The funniest use we've seen of this was when the lady was dancing with someone else, who spotted what was going on in his arms but thought he was the source of the signals – which actually came from her lover, who was sitting out.

The original telecommando is the 'blower' which

connects the restaurant with the kitchen downstairs. Appropriate.

rocking chair

Tried by some as an indoor substitute for that classic piece of sexual gear, the swing. Actually it feels quite different, lacking the sudden bellydropping acceleration which is the source of the swing's effects on women, but more like the sensation of love in a train (see *Railways*).

It works best with an ill-made chair on a very hard, rough floor – better, an erotic rocking chair with a dozen flats or studs on each rocker, hard cushions and no arms. This still needs a hard, preferably stone, floor and is infernally noisy – useless for an apartment if people live under. Normally you sit astride facing, but other positions are possible. We've seen a stool with a powerful vibrator in the top cushion which looks worth a trial, though the feel would be quite different.

rubber

This turns some people on, and is a wholetime fetish with others. Effect seems to depend on its status as super-skin combined with tightness and odor. The odor of latex rubber excites a lot of people if they have come to associate it with using condoms – it also enhances the normal female perfume. Wash anything rubber in soapy water, dry, and keep in french chalk – this includes condoms, ticklers, g-strings and larger items. Black seems to be the preferred sexual color. The livid pink condoms sold in some places don't look as good as the normal translucent variety.

Rubber clothes are one of the few very common turn-ons which for some reason, if you leave out skin-diving and water-skiing, have never got to be fashionable, probably because it's not specially empathic for women (or because it's unbelievably hot).

saxonus

Coitus saxonus – pressing firmly on the male urethra near the root of the penis to prevent ejaculation and (hopefully) conception. No use as a contraceptive, since sperms are around long before he ejaculates – but some women do have the knack, during masturbation, of stopping and restarting ejaculation by urethral pressure so as to spin out the male peak. This is best done by pressing on the shaft near the root with two or three fingers, but you need to press hard (don't bruise). Some people press midway between scrotum and anus. The idea is to allow ejaculation to occur piecemeal. If you stop it altogether, he will eventually ejaculate into the bladder. There's no evidence that this is harmful unless done

ROCKING CHAIR *opposite*
Like the sensation of love in a train.

violently and often, but it's probably better avoided. Interrupting ejaculation is also probably harmless but it is difficult, and won't work on everyone. Women who have this as a party piece say it is appreciated, but that may depend on their partner. You might as well stop just short of ejaculation, then restart the whole business a few minutes later.

shoes

A sex turn-on connected with the foot-pussy equivalence we've mentioned elsewhere (see *Feet*); symbols apart it's interesting that shoe-leather 'fixes' from sweat exactly the same fatty-acids which are present in the vagina and turn on male sex behavior in monkeys and apes. Though these smell rancid rather than sexy, they may still have a subliminal turn-on effect in man. High heels attract some males, chiefly for their effect in increasing the wobble in the female gait, another instance of making the woman more woman-shaped. Probably something of a hide-and-seek effect, too – Chinese women had to hide their feet but could show their genitals. Even for us bare feet are symbolic of nakedness, which is why lady pop-singers shed their shoes.

For most lovemaking you really need bare feet.

slow masturbation

Prostitutes aren't usually much good at advanced sex: this is about the one old-time bordel trick which is worth trying. To make it work, you need to know how to tie your partner (see *Bondage*) and to have a partner who likes struggling against resistance, but it works for a great many people. Traditionally, the woman does it to the man, but it works in either direction. You need good access and a completely helpless partner, though you can try it without if bondage games turn you off, but the result is quite different and you can't get so far. The knack lies in playing on your partner like an instrument, alternately pushing them forward and frustrating them (compare *Relaxation*).

The woman starts by tying the man to her satisfaction, either staked out, or wrists behind and ankles crossed, knees open, naked and on his back. She then 'signs her name' (*le coup de cassolette*). To do this she knees astride him, facing him, and performs a tasteful striptease as far as her panties. Next, holding his hair in her hand, she rubs his mouth firmly over her armpit and breasts, giving him her body perfume. Then she locks her legs carefully round his neck and presses her covered pussy on his mouth. Finally she strips off and gives him the direct genital kiss, (brushing first, then open, taking her time over it), pulls his foreskin well back if he has one, and stands back for a few moments to let him get excited. If she knows her job, he

SLOW MASTURBATION *opposite*
The knack lies in playing on your partner like an instrument, alternately pushing them forward and frustrating them.

will be unable to move, while the kiss ensures that he won't lose the feel of her. Coming back she does the same all over again, stiffens him by hand and mouth if necessary, and starts in real earnest.

She has two focal points to attend to, his mouth and his penis, and the knack, during this warm-up period, consists in keeping both of them occupied continuously, without pauses and without triggering ejaculation. The possibilities are obvious – hand to each, hand to one, mouth or pussy to the other; varied by a touch of her breasts, her armpit, or even her hair. Between the two poles she will work over his most sensitive areas with her fingertips (*les pattes d'araignée*), her tongue, and her pussy – this last with one hand on his penis and her other palm over his mouth, never letting the rhythm slacken. If his erection begins to go down she stops, tightens him up

(this is the moment for thumb-tying if she is strong enough to turn him easily), then re-stiffens him. Then she can begin slow masturbation proper.

This is about the most mind-blowing (and, while it lasts, frustrating) sexual sensation of which most males are capable. (If you still want to know why we include it under bondage games, try it for a few moments with an *un*-bound partner.) Sit well up on his chest, with your buttocks to his chin, and put each of your ankles inside the crook of one of his knees. Hold the root of his penis with one hand and with the other pull the skin back as far as it will go with finger and thumb, thumb towards you. Then start quick, sharp, nervous strokes—each one quick, that is, but timed at one per second, no faster. After about twenty of these, give about ten very quick strokes. Then resume the slow rhythm. And so on. If from the turmoil under you and the general scene you think he is about to ejaculate, drop the speed (you can sense this with practice). Keep it up as long as you think he can stand it. The excitement is his, but is less one-sided than it sounds; the male response is enough to turn most women on, and you can press your open pussy hard on his breastbone, but don't let your attention wander. Ten minutes is about as much as most males can stand. If he goes limp, put him out of his misery, either by quickly masturbating him to climax, or by mouth, or by turning and riding him. When he does come, get him untied as quickly as possible – delay after orgasm will leave him as stiff as if he'd played a hard ball-game.

The domestication of this experience, which veterans will recognize as the Japanese-massage-special-treatment routine, may be the one good thing America gets out of the Vietnam war – the only bar to making it at home, like sukiyaki, is if your are a big girl. The Japanese are artists at making their knots, like their dishes, look really nice, and Japanese masseuses are small enough to sit on a man's chest without killing him. If you are a Brunnhilde, try tying his legs apart and taking your weight on your knees, with your pussy on his mouth: in the story Brunnhilde tied up King Gunther on *his* wedding night, probably for a similar routine – we've given the small woman version. And let him try the same techniques on you.

The man has three points to concentrate on – mouth, breasts and clitoris. A fairly tight couple of turns round the breasts helps (careful!). He can start as she did, with the *coup de cassolette* (armpit and glans) and then rub his hand over *her* cassolette and put it over her mouth, to play back her own perfume. He needs to watch from her sounds and movements how heavy a touch on the clitoris she can stand. He can copy the spinning-out technique and excite her by postponement, but usually he will get better

results by simply pushing her as far and as fast as possible. If she is a responsive subject and not frightened of the whole business the reaction will fully test his skill in securing her. He should kneel astride, but not sit on her, nor hold her down – she should be quite helpless anyway. Finally, and with experienced lovers this will be when she is semi-conscious, he will switch to a few moments of tongue work for lubrication, then vigorous intercourse, and make her scale another, still higher range of peaks taking his own orgasm early on. He should know by the feel of her when to stop – this bears no relation to mewing and struggles, which reach a peak just short of climax. He should then untie her quickly, skillfully and painlessly, so that she comes back to earth lying quietly in his arms.

One unexpected trick is for the lady to tell her partner she's going to give him the time of his life, tie him, and then, when you've made sure he can't get loose or make a sound, make him watch while you masturbate to orgasm. This is more exciting for both of you than it sounds: he, if he's already excited and expecting something else, will go beserk, and his useless struggles will turn her on. Afterwards she can make it up to him – slowly.

south slav style

Well-documented because of the very rich erotic folksong literature of what is now Jugoslavia. Intercourse naked, emphasis on the importance of genital perfume as a stimulus, several reputedly 'national' positions or approaches. Serbian intercourse (Srpski jeb) is mock rape – you throw her down, seize one ankle in each hand and raise them over her head, then enter her with your full weight (do this on something soft – the traditional bare earth is beyond a game). Croatian intercourse (hrvatski jeb) is a woman's ploy – an elaborate tongue bath, with the man free or staked out, followed after leisurely stimulation by riding him astride (reputed by local wise-acres to be 'exhausting'). The Lion position is a male masturbation method – squat down, heels to scrotum, place the penis between your ankles, rest on buttocks and hands, and move legs together. The style is passionate and affectionate as befits a race of bride-stealing warriors whose women were formerly, and still are, natural partisans: tough plus tender.

stockings

Can be a sex turn-on – often the preferred ones aren't the fashionable kind but old-style black stockings which look prossy. Tights are an obstacle unless crutchless, and only erotic, for most males, if worn without panties, and then chiefly visually. It is said that if you can get one stocking off her you're home. Actually in quick undressing or actual

STOCKINGS *above*
Often the preferred ones aren't
the fashionable kind but the
old-fashioned black stockings.

lovemaking modern nylons usually get ruined, but if you
keep your nails and fingers smooth taking them off gently
makes good foreplay, along with mutual undressing
generally. Long gloves turn some people on – they suggest
the old-style great lady. Unless you find shoes sexy,
lovemaking is best with bare feet and toes.

substitutes

Handwork and oral love aren't substitutes for vaginal intercourse but techniques on their own. The listed 'substitutes' are what Europeans formerly used as contraceptive techniques which would ejaculate the male without masturbation and were less taboo than oral sex. The old 'substitutes' have their place – some, like mammary intercourse, can be fully bilateral and all are occasionally fun – during a period, for example, or if she is very pregnant. The *Paradis Charnels* of 1903 gives nine sites: hands (she joins her hands, thumbs crossed, fingers interlaced, and makes him a vagina, wetting her palms first with saliva – an old way of ending straight intercourse without risking pregnancy, though it isn't in fact a safe contraceptive method), mouth, between the thighs (see *Femoral intercourse*), the *Breasts*, the *Armpit*, and also the fold of the elbow and the knee. The other two substitute sites are the hair (long hair or plaits can be rolled into a vagina, or the penis lassooed with a loop of it, though some women may object because it's a bore to wash) and *Anal intercourse*.

swings

These are one erotic extra which emphatically do work. Swinging solo has given many little girls their first orgasm, because the acceleration produces pressure in the pelvis like nothing else. Swings are of two sorts – those mentioned by Eastern writers are simply suspended garden-seat beds, not capable of this kind of acceleration, but giving the agreeable feelings that go with a slightly unstable surface, the proverbial jelly-on-springs. For him, this is like having a woman with infinite buttocks, for her it is a swimmy sensation, devoid of the drawbacks of an over-soft mattress, since the actual surface can be firm.

The real high-velocity swing is the woman's turn-on unless she gets air sick first. The operative thing is the swoop, the falling-elevator sensation of negative G. Swinging with a well-implanted partner is a sensation every girl should have at least once in a lifetime: solo swinging with the Japanese rin-no-tama (see *Gadgets and gimmicks*) is another wild experience of inner movement. A plastic eggshaped saltshaker containing a really large ballbearing will do at a pinch. For intercourse, he sits on the seat, and she astride facing – he works the swing, or a third party pushes (traditionally the maidservant). Ideally one should try the Roller Coaster, but we haven't found a showground which permits that. On a garden swing, watch out for the occasional girl whose orgasm under these conditions is so intense that she blacks out, even if she doesn't do so normally, as she may fall if you don't hold her. Start at rest and penetrated, and use the movements of working up the swing to drive your coitus.

VIBRATORS *overleaf*
Lovers often find them an extra sensation to incorporate into the ritual of skin stimulation.

turkish style

The Sultan of the Ottoman empire, so far from living 'mit Saus und Braus,' was the bottom man of a huge pyramid of functionaries and eunuchs, who lived in fear of his life and was obliged to sign a stud-book at each act of sex. Often he had spent his youth in the company of mistresses known to be sterile, while waiting to know if he would reign or be strangled at the accession of another heir. His innumerable harem were taught the arts of pleasing, but these are not recorded. The chosen lady would enter his bedchamber naked, and in darkness dive under the covers at the bed foot, wriggling her way up alongside him to wait his pleasure. Recalcitrant newcomers were brought in by the Aga Bashi with their thumbs tightly tied behind, and frequently beaten into submission by flogging the soles of their feet. Delinquent concubines were drowned in sacks – silk ones if they were kadins. In spite of the facts, Turkish erotic scenes were a great nineteenth-century fantasy in Christian Europe. They need not be so biased towards the male – she can equally well be Gulbeyaz receiving a chosen Christian stud. Take it in turns.

vibrators

A new standby, which have proved very useful in teaching sexually inexperienced women to stimulate their own responses. There are two main kinds – penis-shaped, which can be used on skin, breasts, clitoris or deeply in the vagina (the small size can be used anally) and larger motor driven kinds as used by masseurs, which strap on the hand like a glove, and can impart wild sensations to almost any part of the body. Vibrators are no substitute for a penis – some women prefer them to a finger for masturbation, or put one in the vagina while working manually on the clitoris. Lovers often find them an extra sensation to incorporate into the ritual of skin stimulation. Vibrating hotel beds, operated by a coin-in-slot timer, are also well spoken of, but are apt to run out at the critical moment, or make you ill. Careful vibratory massage of the whole body surface is a better bet than over-concentration on the penis or clitoris, but it requires skill. Penile gadgets of various kinds for attachment to the standard vibrator base don't seem to have much beyond novelty to commend them.

viennese oyster

Lady who can cross her feet behind her head, lying on her back, of course. When she has done so, you hold her tightly round each instep with your full hand and squeeze, lying on her full-length. Don't try to put an unsupple partner into this position – it can't be achieved by brute force. You can get a very similar sensation – unique

WET LOOK *opposite*
Try showering in a clinging cotton shift: this both feels and looks sexy.

rocking pelvic movement – with less expertise if she crosses her ankles on her tummy, knees to shoulders, and you lie on her crossed ankles with your full weight. Why 'Viennese' we don't know. Tolerable for short periods only but gives tremendous genital pressure for both.

voyeurs

Title to be kept for those who treat sex as a nonplaying, spectator sport. Any active player is likely to be fascinated to watch his game being played, provided the players are worth watching. Real couples are worth watching – the bored, semi-erected participants in blue movies seldom merit the trouble. Real human mating behavior is as interesting as that of birds and far more instructive. If you can watch others, do, unless it violates your sense of privacy. We lose a lot in this society by not being in the habit of making love in company. If we did, fewer books such as this one would need to be written.

wet look

Another super skin releaser which is getting popular – it makes you tight and shiny. Some people like the real thing with real water – try showering in a clinging cotton shift: this both feels and looks sexy. Transparent plastic raincoats worn over the bare skin do something for some wearers and spectators and are a fairly common male turn-on. Ask, try it, or both.

Problems
and what to do about them

age

The only thing age has to do with sex performace is that the longer you love, the more you learn. Young people (and some older ones) are firmly convinced that no-one over fifty makes love, and it would be pretty obscene if they did. Ours isn't the first generation to know otherwise, but probably the first one which hasn't been brainwashed into being ashamed to admit it.

Some couples may be starting on some of our suggestions when they've been through the groundwork and reached the thirties. Since, however, we shall all get older, and superstitions still persist, it is worth giving the facts.

Neither men nor women lose either sexual needs or sexual function with age. In men, the only important changes over the first seven decades are that spontaneous erection occurs less often (accordingly they need more direct penile stimulation from the woman), ejaculation takes longer to happen, which is an advantage, coital frequency tends to fall, but given an attractive and receptive partner, decent general health and an absence of the belief that one ought to run out of steam, active sex lasts as long as life. In later life, the ability and need to ejaculate frequently get less. It's a good idea not to try for it every time, which will give you more mileage and no less mutual pleasure. Women lose their fertility at the menopause, but that in itself often helps rather than spoils their sex life. In fact, there is little if any physical decline in any attribute except frequency up to 75 and beyond. From a quarter to a half of all couples of this age still have regular sex, and that includes all of the people who never had much of a sex life when they were younger. Since continued activity keeps hormone levels up, for couples who make love often it's probably closer to 75 per cent and the other quarter will have stopped because of arthritis or the other ills of age, not impotence or frigidity. 'The things that stop you having sex with age are exactly the same as those that stop you riding a bicycle (bad health, thinking it looks silly, no bicycle).' The difference is that they happen later for sex than for bicycles. Over 50, the important thing is never to drop sex for any long period—keep yourself going solo if you don't for the time being have a partner: if you let it drop you may have trouble restarting (see *Health*).

Women can, of course, be kept menstruating indefinitely with hormones. There's probably little point, unless it boosts morale. A few find they get dry vaginally and need some estrogen, but in fact the results of continued sexual activity and of hormone pills are just about equal.

As with so many things, later life is the time when you've tried everything, and settle down to the things you like most – together.

bisexuality

All people are bisexual – that is to say, they are able to respond sexually to some extent towards people of either sex. Being 'homosexual' isn't a matter of having this kind of response, but usually of having some kind of turn-off towards the opposite sex which makes our same-sex response more evident or predominant. How far people act bisexualy will depend on a great many things, including the society they live in, their opportunities, and how far the same-sex part of their response worries them.

Being actively bisexual makes problems in our society, not least with the other-sex partner on whom, obviously, most of most peoples' most worthwhile sex life depends. We only include it in this book, which is about man-woman sex, because in threesomes and group experiences, which are getting more acceptable socially, 'bisexual' opportunities are inevitable, and a great many straight people worry – either because they find they can respond in this way, or because they are scared afterwards that they will become 'queer.' There is not much risk of this. People with a strong counter-sex bias usually recognize it early (and might be better not to cultivate it, if straight sex has satisfied them so far). Men, both for built-in and cultural reasons, probably bother more about this than women, who seem to relate more easily to same-sex stimulation in a group scene, and women exciting each other are a turn-on for males. Males in most cultures do, or would, play sex games together under some circumstances at ages or under circumstances when there isn't a cultural ban: apes certainly do. If we didn't have this capacity, humans might never have formed male societies, because erotic play between same-sex partners helps to override the rivalry and fighting we see in some other species. At the same time there is a whole biology of human sex identity which isn't fully understood, including the turn-on (releaser) effects of the partner having or not having a penis. Freud highlighted it, and primatologists are trying to fill it out. The point of this discourse is that same-sex play, especially in a two-sex setting, isn't 'unnatural' for man. As with other sorts of sex play, if it worries you or you don't like it, don't do it – but it isn't bad magic, poisonous or odd. Anyhow in a sexual mixup one loses count, unless one is vulnerable to such worries, about what belongs to whom. If you feel you are vulnerable over this, or over group games in general – don't try them. Straight man-woman sex is the real thing for most people – others need something different, but their scope is usually reduced, not widened, by such needs.

children

Children are a natural though not a necessary consequence of having sex. They impose responsibilities – not

least those of being willing to stay together and rear them, and of having to restrict one's immediate sexual spontaneity for several years. For most people, they are well worth these restrictions, but if you aren't prepared to accept the restrictions, don't have them.

Full blooded sex is not exclusive to the childless, but if you want it you must arrange your own privacy. Never involve children in adult sexual activities: militant and exhibitionist liberals who try to acclimatize children to the naturalness of sex by letting them in at any level on their own sex lives probably do at least as much harm as was ever done by the prohibitive sex-is-dirty generation. It is possible for your children to see that love and sex are good from their awareness that your relations outside the bedroom are unanxious (if they are anxiously demonstrative you will transmit the anxiety). What happens in other cultures is no guide here, because our society lacks their other supportive and educative mechanisms.

Most young children are biologically programmed to interpret the sight or sound of adult coition as evidence of a violent assault (they are aware of it earlier than you would expect, so don't keep babies in the bedroom), and the awareness of mother-father sexual relations is on all counts far too explosive a matter to be monkeyed with in the interest of Reichian experiments. Treating their own sexuality (masturbation, interest in the other sex and so on) with acceptance and naturalness is a different matter, but don't push encouragement to the point of incestuous interference with their private lives, either in toddlerhood or in adolescence, or you'll end up trying to use them to enact your own unrealized fantasies and turn them off altogether. Good sex education starts with being unbothered but not exhibitionistic, respecting your children's modesties, answering their questions, and letting them see that you regard this as a topic for pleasurable interest, naturalness – and privacy, not secrecy. Arrange the privacy with an eye to the fact that a normal toddler sees you as a rival, i.e. don't just lock him or her out.

Modern housing makes these counsels of perfection unless you are rich, but if you aren't prepared to make the necessary concessions, stick to having sex and don't have children. Nudity is another matter with which militant liberals can embarrass their children – there is a whole built-in biology of toddler response to adult parental genitals: we would say, 'Don't push it.' Children should see each other and non-parental adults naked, if the parents normally and unanxiously go about naked; but any element of a special educational parade is probably a bad idea. The good thing about family attendance at nudist clubs is that the nudity of people in general lacks the biological and psychological anxiety-overtones of

BISEXUALITY *opposite*
Women seem to relate more easily to same-sex stimulation in a group scene, and women exciting each other are a turn-on for males.

nude parents, but don't push this either, and don't be surprised or discouraging over modesties among your offspring you don't as adults share. Don't forget that father's penis is a dominance signal and mother's vulva an ambivalent object to the normal 3- to 7-year-old boy. If you are being deliberately emancipated you're probably overdoing it.

Preadolescent children should be told about normal sexual phenomena such as menstruation or masturbation before they happen and before more anxious advisers (clergy, teachers and other children) get there first – present them as what they are, part of the process and privilege of growing up: *all* sexual enlightenment, including where babies come from and the nature of intercourse, are best given even before they can be understood, so that the child gows up knowing what is what, and proof against scaremongers.

Egging adolescent children into sex experience is pathological. By that age the test is whether they trust you and are sure enough that you will talk sense to ask your advice, but don't be shocked if they still keep their own counsel. If you are anxious or see trouble, say so frankly and directly, but don't bully. If you've done the job properly and your kids are endowed with reasonably good personalities they will have no less sense, if less experience, than you have. A friend of ours found condoms in his 13-year-old daughter's possession and phoned the parents of her best friend 'to warn them.' Questioned by her father, the best friend said, 'Yes, I know: I bought them for her. She's going with a boy, she wasn't taking precautions, and I didn't want to see her in trouble!'

Parents whose sex life is really unanxious will probably be good parents in this respect, but in our culture they are rarish, and we can't help our anxieties. Not much point in trying to hide these (many of them are built-in to man), and play-acting, whether moralistic or with-it, is bad education and is seen through by children. If you are seen to be honest about your own feelings, that is as good as you are likely to get.

Finally, anyone who deliberately sets out to use a child or a pregnancy to prove something, to 'keep the marriage together,' to boost their ego, or thinks it would be great to bring up a child or children solo, needs to think again. Of course children are ego-boosting and having them is a natural part of being a person, but they are people, not psychiatric procedures. Adoption agencies are on the lookout for those who regard a child as a medicine, a medal or a missile and screen them out. If we could cut out equally motivated natural parenthood it would make for less mental illness, as well as solving the population problem in rich countries.

climacteric

Old name for the menopause, the time at which the woman ceases menstruation. Old John Fothergill the Quaker doctor wrote in the eighteenth century, 'There is a period in the life of Females to which, for the most part, they are taught to look forward with some degree of anxiety: the various and absurd opinions relative to the ceasing of the menstrual discharge, propagated through successive ages, have tended to embitter the hours of many a sensible woman – some practitioners, in other respects able and judicious, if they have not favored these erroneous and terrifying notions, seem not to have endeavored to correct them, with the diligence and humanity which such an object requires.' That about sums it up.

Menopausal changes are complex. The end of ovulation means the end of fertility, and for some women this subtly affects their self-esteem quite apart from any physical effects of a shift in hormone balance. For others it represents a sexual release, when they no longer need worry about contraception. While a few things, like irregular bleeding or hot flushes, are hormonal, personality changes like irritability and depression could be both hormonal and due to the fact that a milestone has been passed and one has stopped being young. Men, who don't have a menopause or any sudden hormone change, often, undergo a 'male climacteric' which coincides with realizing what they haven't done among the fantasies of youth, and that they had better do it now. This can lead to injudicious thrashing about, actual illness, or simply reassessment of their aims and opportunities very like a second adolescence.

Sex life for women doesn't end with the menopause unless they have been convinced that it should or feel they are 'no longer women.' Often it really begins then, if pregnancy has been a worry. Whether the symptoms are physical or mental, such as mood changes, hormones are often worth trying to ease over the readjustment (under medical supervision). The Pill can obscure the menopause by altering or suppressing the cycle: don't stop it until you are sure you are not still ovulating or you may get surprisingly pregnant. After the menopause, a few people need estrogen to combat dryness or soreness – but continued sexual activity seems to work nearly as well as medicine in preserving the function of both sexes far into later life. See *Age*.

defloration

Odd, how this major obsession of past ages has stopped being a problem at all. There was a time when it was a constant preoccupation for the promiscuously-minded male and a real worry to most girls. The change can't be

due to the shortage of virgins (there has to be a first time for everything) nor even to the invention of vaseline – it more probably is due to petting (perhaps) and a change in sexual folklore (certainly). Most girls are now carefully stretched beforehand by considerate boyfriends, and the others don't grow up on the stories of blood, sweat and tears which their great-grandmothers used to tell. In the eighteenth century a girl was disgraced is she didn't bleed like a pig on her wedding night; most modern lovers would reckon not to make her bleed at all unless she asks to be 'deflowered' in the good oldfashioned way. Even then, unusual anatomy apart, it shouldn't hurt her 'more than it hurts a vain young miss to get her ears pierced.'

The first night is a special situation we needn't handle here. Our point is that with the bogy of real defloration exorcized we can revive the eighteenth century play-wise and deflower her again as often as we and she like. The Houris in heaven grow new hymens daily and are perpetually virgin, but so is every woman if she likes to pretend she is. It's not a bad way of celebrating an anniversary. Real enthusiasts can do the whole thing properly, honeymoon hotel and all; the result usually works far, far better than a real first-shot honeymoon. One can even book the same room in advance. Or one can do it oftener, at home, and at shorter notice. All she need do is to say, 'Tonight, I'm a virgin.'

depilation

One way of getting rid of hair you don't want (see *Hair*). Japanese women use a sharpened finger-ring, or you can use chemical pastes (not round the genitals – they often sting) or have hairs taken out individually by electrolysis. This costs several dollars per hair, and is usually only worth it if a girl has a lot of hair on her face.

doctors

There is no special reason why doctors should advise us on sex techniques, but traditionally they often have done so. In fact Avicenna wrote that it was a highly reputable part of their job, because pleasure in sex is 'pertinent to generation.' We'd probably say that it's also pertinent to being a whole person. In view of the clutch of health worries about sexuality which we still inherit, the doctor would be a very good counselor if he knew anything about it. In the past, particularly the Victorian past, medicine collected superconformists with all their age's anxieties and superstitions, plus a line of omniscient homespun moralism which is still with us, occasionally, over things like abortion and the Pill. This isn't the reason, however, that so many people, not only with problems, but simply with straight questions about sexual matters,

draw a blank from their physician and write either to magazines or to total strangers.

The trouble is that normal human sex behavior simply isn't taught and until lately, with researchers like Masters or Kinsey, it couldn't be taught because there was only folklore to teach. When we were medical students thirty years ago, not even birth control was on the syllabus, though at least we were urged to read Havelock Ellis. Also most of what was in the textbooks was tendentious bunk. The sort of folk commonsense which used to figure in ballads and stories had gone, and so had the worldly wisdom of eighteenth-century doctors like John Hunter. Accordingly with the best will in the world, a doctor who wanted to counsel on sex behavior either had to research it first himself, or read it out of one of the books, or go on his own experience – the last of these was fine if the experience was varied, but it could be limited, or eccentric, or absent.

We think this has changed, especially with the younger generation, along with the change in cultural attitudes, though some conscientious office doctors are a little inclined to realize their lack of background and push quite simple matters off onto the psychiatrist, who isn't necessarily any better qualified.

However, sex problems, especially if they involve health, anxiety, or you can't get answers from books, are well worth taking to your doctor. If you are making a choice, a young doctor who talks the language of today or an older man or woman with some personal experience (if you can gauge this) is the best bet. If you have a bad problem and get no joy, persist; if the doctor you consult is hostile or embarrassed, change doctors. Avoid evangelicals – Catholics have hangups over sin, but are often worldly-wise beyond their convictions. Shop around – medicine includes all sorts, and you don't have to put up with a Hippocratic oaf.

It's unfair to your doctor to take the Pill without telling him (if it disagrees with you, he'll have deal with it); to be shy of letting him know, for example, if you have potency problems (they could be due to medicine he ordered, or explain a lot of other symptoms you've been getting); or to be unnecessarily reticent about your sex life generally, any more than you are about your digestion. If you don't trust the man, he can't help you and you ought to change doctors.

excesses

Quantitatively, in sex, these don't exist – nature sees to that; the woman gets sore, the man can't go on. Medical and moral old-wives have spent centuries teaching that sexual overactivity is debilitating – they were never so

admonitory over excessive work or excessive exercise, and rarely over excessive eating, which is our most dangerous hangup at the moment.

Sex is in fact the least tiring physical recreation for the amount of energy expended. If you are flat after it, suspect either your attitude towards it, or (more commonly) secondary loss of sleep. Male lovers forget that women who work or run a home or both aren't as fresh, even though they are as willing, as the idle occupants of the oldstyle Ottoman seraglio. Girls forget that though sex is the perfect tension-relief for both sexes, preoccupation rather than physical fatigue can cause impotence, especially when it goes with a wholehearted wish to perform up to and beyond Olympic standards as a matter of personal pride. Different sleep-needs and sleep-patterns, unrecognized and unaccommodated, can really threaten a sexual partnership. Deal with all these things by speaking out – being really in need of sleep only looks like rejection or sulking to very insecure people who can't communicate with each other.

Sex commonly makes women langorous to the point of sedation. It may make men the same, or boisterously productive – in the second case get up, produce, and let her sleep after a suitable interval of shared quiet and love. At night there is no sleeping pill as good as violent and shared orgasm – active lovers don't need barbiturates.

If ever you do run yourself into the ground, there's no temporary exhaustion a few hours' or days' rest won't cure. Contrary to some belief, plenty of sex makes better and better sex – it damps down overfast orgasm without lowering the peaks: the terrific 'high' after a separation doesn't depend on continence but on reunion. You can both masturbate daily while apart and still get it. Frequent sex also preserves function long into old age – not only is it a habit, but hormone levels depend on it; so, therefore, do looks and vigor.

exhibitionism

Most people from babyhood get a kick (though not in front of adults) out of showing their genitals to the opposite sex – they are, after all, some of the best things we've got, and showing them to a partner is the start of better things. The self-adhesive label gets stuck on people who for a variety of reasons can get their sex in no other way, and show their genitalia to strangers. This would be a harmless but unrewarding activity (these timid characters are by definition not rapists) if people weren't shocked or frightened by it, though it's a disability to the fellow who can't get further than that. Under our extraordinary system, we reward them with public disgrace, imprisonment, etc. No woman need be scared if she meets one.

There was a famous French lady who, when a man exposed himself, remarked 'Monsieur, won't you catch cold?' Exhibitionists don't commonly attack children, and wouldn't frighten them if they were sensibly raised, though adults making themselves look ridiculous, or behaving abnormally in any way, usually upsets them. Children are conservative and easily embarrassed. If your child meets an exhibitionist, tell them the unfortunate chap is stuck at the baby stage, and has so many problems they'd better stay out of his way.

fetish

Something you need instead of, or as well as, a partner in order to reach full sexual response. Less often evident in women than in men, so far as concrete objects or routines are concerned, though women can make fetishes of such things as security, fear and subtler nuances of setting. Can be of all kinds – embryo fetishes are present in almost everyone, and their satisfaction is part of the art as well as the function of love. Many men perform best with a woman who has a particular hair color or length, or big breasts, or looks boyish but are less frank about other turn-on requirements. Particular garments come next – she is more desirable with stockings, or with shoes, or with earrings. Use any of these turn-on circumstances to their fullest extent (see *Clothes*).

A real fetish is any non-sexual circumstance which is obligatory for potency. It becomes a problem if it swamps everything and develops into a consuming anxiety, (shoes only, not even women with shoes) or if it happens to be a fantasy which turns you on and your partner off, or if the performance gets more and more complicated and anxious until a halt has to be called. Normal marital play can meet nearly all demands of this kind if there is real communication, and find them fun, but the partner who is stuck with an anxious ritual can be a big problem which lets-pretend fails to solve.

For a start, a person with a real hangup of this sort, even if fully enacted, can lose interest in anything but his preoccupation. This is a medical problem, however, and time to shout for help. It goes with other personality difficulties of which the loss of interest in love is only a symptom, since most of us at some level have one or more preferred turn-ons, and, if we can't communicate with our partner, tend to get more and more guilty and sensitive about them. Discharged as play, this doesn't happen; but if they can't be discharged in this way, get help. We're talking, remember, about persistent and quite inordinate obsessions which get in the way of the ordinary business of intercourse—refusing to try anything but the missionary position is as much a fetish as only being

FIDELITY *opposite*
What suits a particular couple depends on their needs, situation, anxieties and so on.

potent when wearing a diving helmet. Normal sex involves both fantasy-preferences and variety – variety is the one thing the handicapped ritualist can't enjoy. There's not much wrong with anyone who is willing to try anything once.

It may sound brutal, but don't, repeat don't, take on a partner with a major sex problem such as homosexuality or compulsive ritualism in order to 'cure him by love.' You won't – though if he has your love and comprehension cure by an expert, or at least coming to live with himself, will be much easier. If you have taken on a problem of this kind – and the measure, we repeat, of whether it is a problem is whether it causes anxiety and interferes with sexual joy – work it out between you without fear or recrimination, and go to an expert. It's as much a medical problem as a slipped disc if it interferes with your mutual enjoyment as much as a slipped disc would.

fidelity

Fidelity, infidelity, jealousy and so on. We've deliberately not gone into the ethics of life-style. The facts are that few men and slightly more women in our culture go through life with sexual experience confined to one partner only. What suits a particular couple depends on their needs, situation, anxieties and so on. These needs are a particularly delicate problem in communication: if mutual comprehension is complete and ongoing you can count yourselves lucky. Active deception always hurts a relationship. Complete frankness which is aimed to avoid guilt or as an act of aggression against a partner can do the same. The real problem arises from the fact that sexual relations can be anything, for different people and on different occasions, from a game to a total fusion of identities; the heartaches arise when each partner sees it differently.

There is no sexual relationship which doesn't involve responsibility, because there are two or more people involved: anything which, as it were, militantly excludes a partner is hurtful, yet to be whole people we have at some point to avoid total fusion with each other – 'I am I and you are you, and neither of us is on earth to live up to the other's expectations.' People who communicate sexually have to find their own fidelities. All we can suggest is that you discuss them and at least know where each of you stands.

fighting

The occasional fights, often physical, which all lovers have would have nothing to do with sex if some couples weren't directly excited by them, often without knowing it. That real anger has erotic effects is a matter of true folklore. The

French have a song which goes:
> Hey, mister copper,
> Colin's beating up his mistress:
> Mister Copper, let them get on with it –
> It will end with kisses.

Or, as one woman put it, 'We found the old tenderness routine wasn't enough: he likes to use violence and it excites me to resist him. I find the pain exciting, but he's started to hurt me in other contexts and I'm afraid how far it will go.' The trouble is that, as we've several times remarked, our image of love is up-tight about the very real elements of aggression in normal sexuality – which makes us prone to mix erotic violence with real spite or real anger, and confuse two quite distinct things, the quarrel which lets off steam, or is an appeal for help, and sexual stimulation. We aren't talking here about border-line sadists. There are women who unconsciously want violence (and have timid partners) who needle the man into a fight without knowing why. The mixture is a bad one, and usually goes sour.

To need some degree of violence in sex, rather than the glutinous unphysical kind of love which the tradition propagates, is statistically pretty normal. But the way to meet this need isn't to use rows to fuel it, but rather to learn the purposive uses of play. True, the over-gentle spouse is likely to be blocked about aggression, and non-plussed by a demand 'Now try to rape me.' He's been taught not to treat girls like that – if he's excessively over-gentle, he may be sitting on a strong need to do so. But if these things can once be talked about, you can make him (or her) learn the uses of sexual play – which is why we've included some pretty rough-looking games by Marriage Guidance standards – and this without the need to mix them up with real day-to-day angers and frustra-tions which can get out of hand, especially with the wrong partner. If he's over-gentle, don't needle him, teach him.

In other words, don't be ashamed if you really fight (most people do) but don't treat it as a kick, or a way of turning on a partner's aggression. Use play, and keep it in the sexual situation. Remember too that people are different, and that aggression is now a far more disturbing thing to us than sex – so that a black eye is a sign of caring in one couple and ground for divorce to another. Cultivate pillow talk to unblock fantasies – ask each other just short of orgasm, 'What would you like to do to me, like me to do to you, now?' – 'now' meaning at the fantasy level. See *Birdsong at morning.*

Also, as nearly always with man, symbolisms are generally bigger kicks than over-literal enactments. But some couples get a lot of fun out of extended struggles,

premeditated or impromptu ('love wrestling' in the old Viennese athletic tradition). Enthusiasts go in for elaborate handicaps: time limits, no-biting-or-scratching and so on. Most people find fairly robust but reasonable tussling quite enough, others play elaborate finding-fault-and-spanking games (don't play these over *real* faults). Women who dig an extra sensation of violence and/or helplessness differ whether they feel this more held down or tied up: men can take out quite a lot of the violence component in the actual process of penetration and working for orgasm. Once understood, none of this range of needs is scary, and can be stopped spilling out of sex into cruelty, or the normal resentments felt by any two people who live together. Actually, it tends to discharge these.

Nothing we've said excludes the tenderness of sex. If you haven't learned that sexual violence can be tender and tenderness violent, you haven't begun to play as real lovers, unless you are people (and there are such) whose tenderness is abolutely unalloyed: these needn't worry about the risks of fighting. See *Bondage, Discipline*.

If you do have a real fight, make sure to end it in bed. At least it's the best way to finish.

frigidity

This does not mean failure to enjoy sex when one is dead with fatigue, when children are hammering on the door, in the middle of Union Square, or, generally, with the wrong man, at the wrong time, all of the time every time, or with the wrong vibrations. Males of the vending machine type (put a quarter in and an orgasm comes out) should take note of this. Nor does it mean failure to get a mind-blowing orgasm on every single occasion. If it does mean these things, every woman is frigid. Nor does it really apply to non-response if the man is clumsy, hurried and phallus-struck. We assume you know all this. Real frigidity is when a woman who loves her man and isn't consciously scared of any part of sex still fails to enjoy it when they've both taken trouble to see that she should. This condition, unlike male impotence, which can often be removed by simple reassurance (though not always), isn't easily helped by books. Female sexuality is much less arranged in a straight line than male – where a woman has difficulties of this sort they *have* to be dealt with on an individual basis.

A few cases of non-enjoying are simple; the Pill can produce big swings in libido either way. So can the woman's own internal chemistry, which is cyclical, unlike the man's, and undergoes more sudden changes. If intercourse hurts, that is simple too – see a gynecologist and have it attended to. Pregnancy and having a baby can affect response, physically and psychologically. Assuming

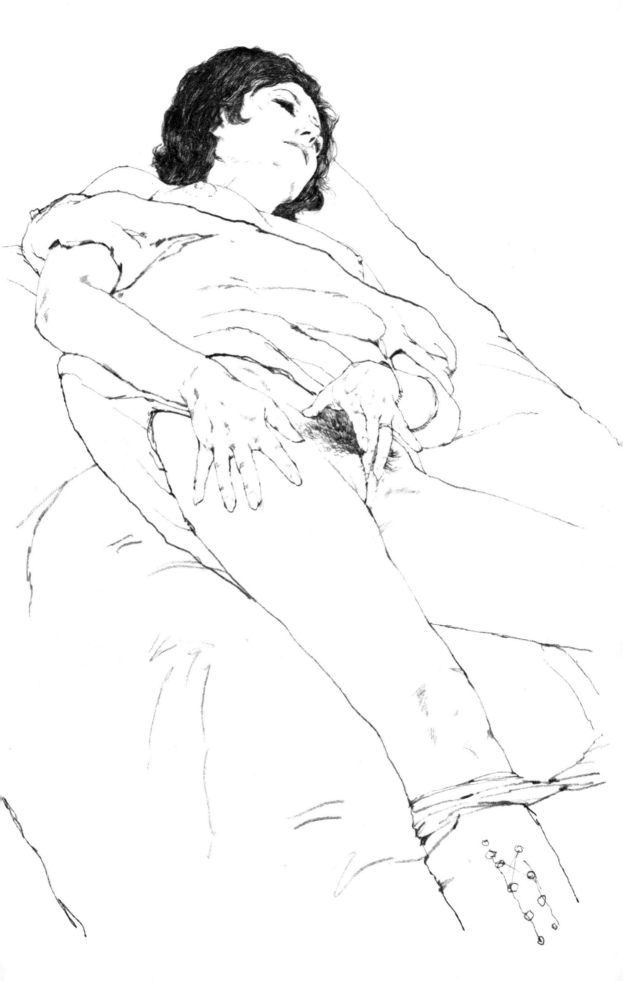

it's none of these, and you have a husband whom you can talk to and fantasize with, and you've eliminated obvious turn-offs like having an overweight lover on top of you, but still nothing really leaves you feeling satisfied, get personal advice. The mix of physical and psychological causes which can produce this kind of dissatisfaction is too complicated to be dealt with in a book.

The only technique worth trying, if you still don't feel, is painstaking self-education through relaxed, gradual and private self-exploration. Masturbation in women is far more a process of continuing self-exploration than it is in man, and many women can and do teach themselves to respond in this way. On widespread testimony the use of a vibrator helps – it can produce some sexual feeling in almost any woman. Once you have found a stimulus which makes you feel at all, whether you discover it solo or with your lover, incorporate it into lovemaking and use it to the full. If you need a finger on the clitoris, or genital kissing, use them fully – the propaganda about 'vaginal orgasm' *is* propaganda, and there is no truth in the value-judgment that unless you are fully satisfied only by deep penetration you aren't a woman; some women are satisfied by it, others aren't. Some women get many orgasms – some so many that they merge and can't be pinpointed as a single event – others get one, like a man. Some women only enjoy breast stimulation, or genital stimulation. Find your pattern. If you haven't experimented with changes of posture, do – by this time we assume you have. And with play and fantasy. If none of these things give you any lead you can develop, you need individual help (or more correctly help as a couple – if you see a counselor, both should go).

For self-training, start by getting really comfortable – naked or not, in front of a mirror or not, just as you prefer. Think and fantasize about anything which stirs any sort of response, then begin gradually to explore your own body, letting your hand go where your body wants it – breasts, the whole skin surface, labia, clitoris. Do the same if you use a vibrator – don't go for orgasm, but set out to discover what you like and what you think you would like. It takes time to learn this if you don't already know. Sometimes, if this doesn't frighten you or turn you off, another woman can help more than a man. That doesn't make you a lesbian. Don't assume that another man will be able to do better than your lover—he may, but it isn't a safe assumption. If you can imagine a situation which would excite you, try to set it up with your lover – as play, if it isn't feasible in earnest – remembering that fantasy-rape isn't real rape or fantasy-cruelty real cruelty. See if any of our suggestions turn you on in prospect. Talk to your man.

FRIGIDITY *opposite*
Doesn't apply to non-response if the man is clumsy, hurried or phallus-struck.

Beyond that, we can't help through the printed page. Female libido is controlled, oddly enough, by the male hormone. See *Impotence*.

hairtrigger trouble

Alias premature ejaculation. Any ejaculation which happens before you both want it to is premature.

Premature coming results from two causes, over-eagerness and anxiety. Over-eagerness may be delightful on occasion, but usually means simply that you are not having enough sex to reach optimal performance. One can ward off this solo by masturbating frequently and using the occasion to develop slow responses, but in the presence of all the stimuli from a real woman this can still break down. Once you get anxious it can become a physiological habit like stammering or impotence. It can rule out top quality sex and most of our suggestions.

There is a set drill for handling this hangup which rarely fails. Tackle it early.

1 Find out, with your partner, just how soon after one ejaculation you can get another erection, either by self-stimulation or with her stimulating you. Use this, holding back deliberately, and aiming not to get an orgasm but to see how long you can stay rigid. Do this often.

2 If the time interval is too long or you lose the second erection quickly, you need specific exercises. Set aside a time for practice and resolve that on the practice occasions you won't have intercourse. Get your partner to stiffen you, if necessary, and begin slow masturbation seated astride. Her aim will be simply to keep you in erection, even if she has to drop her stroke-rate to one in three seconds. If you call 'stop' she must stop. She can tie you if this really gives her better control, but as this itself is an excitant it is better if you deliberately hold still. Don't be worried if on the first occasion you ejaculate at once – try again half an hour later. Do this just as often as you can arrange it, but intersperse with intercourse, however short, so as not to build up an appetite. Either in intercourse or for practice sessions, some people find a local anesthetic jelly a help, and if you find it difficult to get the exercises going, you could try this. In about three weeks of regular practice you should be able to hold at least a second, and probably a first erection, for a full five minutes, and this will get longer and longer. Meanwhile, try and lengthen the straight coitus sessions. Use all the extras to give your partner full orgasm as often as she needs it, but she should be sparing with very stimulating techniques, or indeed any techniques, ahead of penetration. Try holding still inside her for timed minute intervals.

3 If this doesn't work, or you are getting anxious, see an expert. Usually it does work. The important thing is to set up by agreement a definite noncoital session, designed to get you into a state of sexual training. You will both benefit, and she needn't go without meanwhile: learn to use your hands and your tongue and don't forget her breasts. Having times when you specifically set out to satisfy *her* will help you to relax over any virility problems. If the problem remains, take advice before it gets to be a habit. Most men with limited sex experience are overquick to start with, and would benefit from training of the kind we've described.

At the first session with a much-desired partner, at least 50 percent of men either ejaculate too quickly or fail to get an erection. Ensure a whole night, so you can try for a comeback, but don't try too hard. If you go to sleep you will probably wake with a huge erection.

Note for your doctor: Tricyclic antidepressants such as Tryptizol (Rx) or Tofranil (imipramine, Rx) slow down orgasm enormously in some males without blocking erection: minute doses are often enough.

hazards

Contrary to superstition, very few sexual techniques are actually dangerous. Clumsy penetration with the woman on top can injure him or her; violent anal penetration can injure her, and all anal intercourse carries a small risk of urethritis in the man, and vaginitis in the woman if you mix anal with vaginal penetration. Women liable to miscarry need to be gently handled in pregnancy, and women who are very liable to miscarry might do better to avoid orgasm while carrying. Apart from these there are a few tricks which are risky in themselves. None of these are popular, but clearly, since mischief is reported, people occasionally try them.

1 Never throttle anyone, even in play, and especially in orgasm. Many sex 'murders' are accidents overtaking women who treat partial strangulation as a kick: they can get exactly the same sensation safely by intercourse head-down, see *Inversion*. Never block a partner's airway, and be extra careful with bondage games – one can suffocate on a soft surface.

2 Never blow into the vagina. This trick can cause air embolism and has caused sudden death.

3 In spite of writers who talk about the use of household appliances for sex kicks, never fool about sexually with vacuum cleaners or with air-lines. A garage tyre inflator line has ruptured the intestine when squirted 18 inches from someone's anus (this was a practical joke). Vacuum cleaner injuries of the penis are surprisingly common and

very hard to repair satisfactorily. Water at tap-pressure is safe, but direct it at the clitoris, not forcibly into the vagina – anything under pressure can go up the Fallopian tubes and do harm.

4 Cantharides (spanish fly) is not an aphrodisiac but an irritant poison about as powerful as mustard gas. The dose which produces useless, painful erection by inflaming the penis is bigger than the fatal dose for kidney damage. Candy containing it has killed several girls.

5 Nothing you inhale is a safe kick: organic chemicals which produce dizziness also produce death rather easily. Amyl nitrite (used for anginal attacks) produces flushing and other sexy sensations, but is grossly unsafe to fool with. If you want to blow your mind, try loud music through earphones.

Considering the range of human sexual experimentation it is a reflection on conventional fears that only manifestly idiotic sexual experiments are dangerous. Given reasonable gentleness, sex play is by far the safest energetic sport – one can be killed dead by a golf ball.

health

If you're acutely ill you probably won't feel like sex. There are very few longer-lasting medical conditions where a prescription of 'no sex' is justified for more than a shortish time, like getting over a heart attack or a hernia operation, or, of course, if you have an infectious disease such as V.D. or trichomoniasis, or are pregnant and likely to miscarry. Most doctors know this, but a few still give alarmist or thoughtless 'no sex' instructions if their own sex-lives are unimportant.

If the doctor advises the woman to avoid sex, she should find out why. He may only mean that pregnancy would be dangerous. The same applies if there's a heavy genetic risk. In that case a thoughtful male partner would have a *Vasectomy*, to be 100 percent sure. Otherwise the only indications are the ones we've given. If it's the man who gets the red light, discuss it. Even severe heart or kidney illness isn't normally a bar to having gentle sex, nor is hypertension. In these cases it might be sensible to avoid very tense or violent activities. Excitement is greatest, and casualties highest, in extramarital rather than married contexts, and boudoirs and brothels have seen more fatal accidents than the marriage bed. There can be a problem over cancer of the prostate or high blood pressure, because some of the drugs used to treat these can affect potency, and if other types of drug fail to work you may have to make a choice. The important thing is not to take no for an answer unless you've had a full explanation and are sure the doctor knows how much

sex means to you (some doctors still think that sex over fifty is expendable or non-existent – see *Age*). A good doctor will know that stopping sex for any length of time is hard for normal people, and can damage an older man's sexual response when he tries to restart. Really good and informed medical advice, by contrast, may be precisely what could help you to keep going and avoid further illness – you and the doctor should work out the solution together. Some people would feel that if the worst came to the worst, it's the best way to go, and the anxiety and depression engendered by a ban on sex could be more likely to do harm than the very moderate exercise involved in intercourse. See *Doctors*. There is evidence that an improved sex-life can actually lower hypertension where this is due to general anxiety.

impotence

The basis of so much nonsense and anxiety that a few facts are in order.

1 All men are impotent sometimes – usually at a first or a hurried session with someone highly desirable whom they want to impress. The risk is proportional to the buildup. Can also happen domestically, quite without expectation or warning – often from some turn-off one isn't aware of. The only importance of these occasions is not to be thrown by them. The conventional male fantasy of being ready to perform anytime, anywhere is wholly neurotic and impractical.

Only the totally insensitive are all-time fucking machines like a stud-bull, and stud-bulls too have their off-days. Leave yourself a whole night for a first night – you should wake horny.

2 Physical factors which cause impotence do exist – the chief are diabetes, obesity, alcohol, and some drugs prescribed for depression and for high blood pressure.

3 The only other common cause of impotence is psychological – turning oneself off by apprehension about sexual performance. This is the exact analogy to the old man who took thought whether he slept with his beard in or out of the bed and went crazy trying to remember, or the pianist who starts thinking about his fingers.

4 If you can ever get an erection (by masturbation, in sleep, or on waking) there is nothing physical the matter with the hydraulics.

5 Age has absolutely nothing to do with impotence unless it brings illness. Belief that one is aging and must run out of steam has. Normal male potency lasts as long as life. The only change is that spontaneous erection gets rarer, direct skin stimulation is needed, and orgasm takes

longer to come. Impotence in old men is due to turn-offs, lack of health and an attractive partner, attempts to perform too often, or the demands of a younger partner who sets them a proficiency test. These would turn normal people off at any age.

6 Accordingly, persistent impotence means either that you are trying to perform against a specific turn-off – wrong scene, wrong partner, wrong vibrations, record attempts – or that you are turning yourself off by acting as if you were a spectator, not a participant and worrying about how you are doing. This can start if you are badly put out over one of the off-days mentioned in (1) above, and can become a habit. Deal with it exactly as for *Hairtrigger trouble*, except that in this case both of you should use every accessory excitation but with a firm resolve not to have intercourse – full description of the technique in Masters and Johnson which is easily adaptable to do-it-yourself. If this fails, get help from an expert. If everyone knew the facts listed here the task of sex-therapists would at least be lightened by comprehension.

In a few people liable to erection failure male hormone levels are low, but this could be effect, not cause. Taking male hormone turns off your own supply and it can make things worse (though eunuchs stay potent, so huge testicles aren't essential provided you reach puberty safely). Some synthetic hormones avoid the turn-off effect. Testosterone does help significantly in cases of large unexplained swings in libido, particularly after fifty, but needs medical control to avoid trouble: male gonadotropin also helps some cases, but would probably only be available from a research group. There are newer erection turn-on drugs which may eventually have a use; their chief utility would be as morale-boosters – once reassured that you can erect at will, the problem goes.

The Japanese have marketed an electro-erector which it is claimed will work on a near-corpse: we haven't seen this. On no account fool around with home-built electronics or the line supply.

As a final resort, it probably isn't 100 percent true that you can't will an erection. Almost all involuntary body processes can be made controllable by a technique called operant conditioning – one can learn, for example, to slow the heart or alter the brain waves. It ought to be possible to do this with erection, shortcircuiting any psychological hangups – yogis can will instant erection without arousal, so it can be done. But you'd need research-grade help until the technique has been worked out.

Note for the non-sexologist doctor: if you want a short, recent summary of what can and can't be done with hormones in impotence and frigidity, read R. B. Green-

blatt, *Medical Opinion*, September 1971, 7, 22–26. Reading time 5 minutes. Mesterolone is probably the safest and most effective hormone to use.

infertility

A boon if you want it, a curse if you don't. Can be due to the woman not ovulating, the ova not reaching the uterus through tubal blockage, various conditions in the female organs; the man not having any sperms, or enough sperms; and probably also various chemical incompatibilities between partners. These can sometimes be helped by advice including concentration on fertile periods, surgery, or hormones, but need proper medical counseling (both of you must go – if the man has too few sperms there is no point in subjecting the woman to a lot of investigation). Anxiety can sometimes apparently block fertility – overfrequent ejaculation lowers the sperm count, so don't be over-eager. Tight warm clothing around the scrotum can kill off the sperms, which need to develop below body-temperature. Orgasm in the woman doesn't make conception more likely. Infertility can sometimes end suddenly after years, and the treatment or the life situation get the credit. Obstinate lack of sperms in the male is difficult to treat, though you can concentrate the sperms he has and inseminate with them. It has nothing whatever to do with virility judged by sexual performance. Never assume you are infertile unless it has been proved, and be careful stopping the pill around menopause time. For voluntary infertility see *Children, Birth control, Vasectomy.*

obesity

Fatness in our culture is unlovely. We know someone whose pretty, fat daughter can only get Middle Eastern boyfriends because of this norm. Renoir's women, who, when naked, look ideal for sex, would look a little too plump if clothed.

What isn't realized is that in men overweight is a physical cause of impotence. If neither this nor the esthetics of it bother you, you may still have to circumvent it. King Edward VII of Britain ('Tum-Tum'), had a special couch resembling a gynecological table made to enable him to get on target. Most stout men can manage with the woman astride, backing or facing. If this doesn't work, try lying face-up over the edge of the bed, feet on the floor, while she stands astride. An over-heavy man is a bad problem – Cleopatra could say, 'O happy horse, to bear the weight of Anthony,' but he didn't weigh 200 pounds. If you are grossly overweight, set about losing it, whether you value your sex life or only your life. That applies to both sexes. Modern girls, though supple, tend to be

underweight by the sexual standards of the past, especially for rear-entry positions and for making love on a firm surface.

pain

Pain per se isn't a sexual excitant in spite of folklore. What actually happens is that once excitement starts to build, pain-awareness is reduced steadily, until any strongish stimulus, even one which normally would be over-strong, adds to the buildup. This can be true elsewhere – you can lose a tooth in a football game and not notice it until after – but with sex excitement the pain-stimulus can actually be transformed into increased pleasure-feeling provided it isn't too strong. There is a sharp point, however, at which over-stimulation becomes a turn-off, not a turn-on, and if this is overstepped the buildup collapses: tolerance increases the closer you get to orgasm – just before it people can take, for example, quite hard slaps – but the transformation stops as soon as orgasm occurs, so don't continue awkward postures or hard stimuli after this. Some people don't transform at all. If anything you do is perceived as straight untransformed pain it's either too much or too early on, or you've gone on after orgasm. Learning what stimuli are pleasant as buildup and what aren't is an art.

If any part of normal sex actually hurts, due to soreness, internal organs getting knocked, etc., you're being clumsy or something is wrong – in the second case see a doctor if it lasts more than a few days. First coitus can be slightly painful for both parties – if they are excited enough beforehand the transformation-effect will get most girls through the pain-barrier, though if you make her bleed at all give time for abrasions to heal before the next round. If it's more troublesome than this, get advice (see *Defloration*). With gentleness and preliminary stretching it can be quite painless in most women.

Actual craving for pain (mental or physical) as a sex kick isn't uncommon. Usually the idea is exciting in fantasy but a turn-off in practice, unless your partner is skilled enough to keep inside the limits of transformation by excitement, and the fantasy itself isn't too violent. A good many men who have persuaded a not over-intelligent whore to 'beat them hard' because the idea sounded exciting have been choked off a repeat performance. If your partner has such fantasies, keep well inside their powers of stimulus-transformation, subtract a good twenty percent from the fantasy, and watch out for the occasional sick character who really enjoys the idea of being injured. For sane people commonsense, a bit of play-acting, and intelligent use of the transformation effect can more than take care of the normal fantasy-range.

perversion

In books prior to the seventies, this meant, quite simply, any sexual behavior which the writer didn't himself enjoy. More correctly, it means something antisocial which handicapped people use as a substitute for the sexuality from which their hangups debar them. The commonest perversions in our culture are getting hold of some power and using it to kick other people around, money-hunting as a status activity, treating other people, sexually or otherwise, as things to manipulate, and interfering with other people's sex lives to ensure that they are as rigid and as anxious about them as the interferer. Scheduled perversions like digging up corpses or committing lust murder are confined almost wholly to borderline psychotics, and, though obviously serious, are of less social importance than the respectable kinds because they are rare and disapproved of. It's a measure of the prestige of socially approved perversion that most public utterances in legislation, law enforcement and so on genuflect to what are basically perverse attitudes, even when the speakers are privately healthy and don't live by what they say.

Hangups of this sort are extremely difficult to cure, whether they lead to sadistic mutilation, purity crusading, Belsen or Vietnam. However sorry you are for the possessors, they are dangerous people and best avoided as partners or as mentors—you will only be asking for a lot of trouble.

priapism

From Priapus, the Roman garden god with a large stiff wooden penis: erection you don't want and can't get rid of, unaccompanied by any feeling of sexual pleasure or excitement at all.

A painful erection which won't go away is rare, and a sign as a rule of something wrong, and you should see a doctor. What is commoner, though not common, is being woken at night by painful, non-pleasant erections, even when one has had a full ejaculation, so that the patient has to get up and walk around or shower – intercourse or masturbation does not help: the result can be severe loss of sleep. Mentioned here because the sufferers worry themselves gray about it. The cause isn't known – it may be psychological (it often stops away from home). All normal males get repeated erections in sleep, but usually these don't wake them or are accompanied by pleasantly sexy feelings, not pain. There doesn't seem to be a good remedy for this trouble. Drugs which turn it off are apt to turn off potency. Fortunately the symptom usually goes away, and whatever treatment you were having at the time gets the credit. Does not interfere with sex at other times.

prostitution

Prostitutes don't as a rule either practice or enjoy advanced lovemaking. This isn't true in all cultures, but in ours the commonest motive for becoming a regular streetwalking pro is an active dislike of males. Their attraction insofar as it persists is in part mythological, and also due to their un-shocked understanding of unscheduled sex needs, the fact that the man can at least be sure of getting sex from them without social hangups, and a group of feelings connected with sharing a woman with other males. No doubt if we treated the professional as other cultures have done – on all fours with the concert artist who gives up domesticity to an art – the personnel of professional sex would improve and it would lose its present psycho-pathology, and be of help both to bothered clients and the girls themselves, but general sexual freedom is more likely to displace monetary sex altogether, except for those for whom it arises from unconscious needs.

Apart from the attractions we've mentioned, any woman who herself is ready to enjoy and understand sex, and meet her partner's needs as fully as a professional but with love, can outclass anyone hired. She can learn from periods and cultures in which the courtesan was a repository of the art of pleasing, but what we call whores' tricks ought to be called lovers' tricks. A woman who can make love with love and variety needn't fear commercial competition.

If your man goes to a prostitute, it's either because he was away from you, or because he has sex needs you didn't know about, or because of the shared-woman no-responsibility bit (which in the most loving males can still be very strong), or simply because of impulse which he doesn't understand. Even if you are hurt about it, try to find out the reason, because knowing it could help a lot.

rape

Lovers will play rape *games* without end, but the real thing is a frightening turn-off. It may sound unpleasant, but is worth knowing, that the surefire way a woman can resist rape, armed or not, is by suddenly emptying her bowels. Few rapists will persist after that, and it doesn't involve provocative and maybe ineffectual physical assault.

Don't get yourself raped – i.e. don't deliberately excite a man you don't know well, unless you mean to follow through.

smoking

Heavy cigarette smoking considerably shortens life. It can also interfere quite considerably with potency, and can make mouth-to-mouth kissing unpleasant, or at least unrewarding. At the same time the odor of pipe or cigar tobacco registers with some women as part of maleness:

others dislike it. Why we enjoy inhaling smoke isn't biologically obvious – nicotine has some drug action, but quite a few mammals and birds are 'turned on' by smoke. Crows even pick up lighted cigarette butts and pass them over their feathers, while fire, with attendant smoke, was a prehuman social discovery. Sucking, of course, is a universal and lifelong turn-on for man. There's also a whole anthropology of who smokes what connected with sex roles – pipes for women have never caught on fully in our culture.

Luckily, we don't need to spell all this out in order to take a line through it. Cigarettes are better avoided by lovers as by gourmets, both from the danger angle and the slob effect of bad breath and dirty hands: pipes and cigars less so. A lot of nicotine can, in some people, interfere physically with erection. If you aim to stop smoking, do it totally, but make your resolution a day at a time, and use sex as a displacement activity while you are getting over the gap. It's more effective than overeating and better for you.

Pot has complex pharmacological actions, but in our society it acts chiefly as a social irritant, producing a feeling of agreeable defiance in users and a suspension of rational thought in non-users. Its dangers have been deliberately exaggerated as a result of this effect. Doctors who already have to deal with alcohol, pills, aspirin and the like reckon that we need more pharmacological kicks like we need a hole in the head, but there are two views on this. One thing it isn't is an aphrodisiac. Most lovers who really enjoy sex prefer to start straight and let the things they do give them a high – which is what short-cut kicks are a substitute for.

termination

In a well-conducted sex life it shouldn't be necessary. All ethics apart, neither you nor the doctor can be quite sure how a woman – or a couple – will react to it psychologically. The present boom is due less to permissive legislation than to the fact that women who have been scared off the Pill by deliberate alarmism, but have experienced the effects of really reliable troublefree birth control, are simply not willing either to go back to the old makeshifts or to have unwanted children.

At the factual level, early abortion (in the first 3 months) done by a qualified expert in a properly equipped hospital is, physically, a minor and safe operation. Done by an unqualified person, a backroom consultant, or a do-it-yourself method it is dangerous and psychologically searing. Done too late (and some physicians who object to all abortion on principle deliberately try to delay matters until it is too late, and then tell you so with a superior grin)

it involves killing a potentially viable child.

If you plan your sex life properly and take informed and conscientious contraceptive precautions, you shouldn't need to terminate a pregnancy except on exceptional grounds. Odd that the main moral woe-criers on abortion are also the people who have done most to block proper birth control and starve research and education about it of funds.

transvetitism

Many people enjoy dressing in each other's clothes on occasion for the hell of it. That isn't transvestitism. A transvestite is a person who, while staying fully in his or her own sex role, feels an intense compulsion at times to dress the opposite sex role, and an intense release of anxiety (not so much a kick) when they do so. They are not 'homosexual,' and a bisexual person who dresses the opposite sex to please a partner isn't a transvestite. A transexualist is a person, usually male, who actively wants to turn into a person of the other sex, by surgery if necessary, and feels totally miscast as they are. In some simpler societies there are roles or ceremonies which discharge these needs (wizards often cross-dress). In our society they can cause intense anxiety. A transvestite with an informed and unscared wife usually finds that his compulsion, whatever its cause, doesn't spoil his sex-life in the male role (if he has to keep it secret or she thinks he's queer or crazy, which he isn't, he can get really sick from worry); a transexualist needs expert help and may or may not be the happier for a sex-change operation. A lot of unhappiness could be avoided if people knew the facts to the point of not being scared or shocked if they come across them. If you have a partner with any of these problems, help them by comprehension and see they get help from an expert.

vasectomy

This is the one reliable, once-and-for-all male contraceptive method. It consists of closing off, by a small surgical operation, the tubes down which the sperms travel from the testis. The operation is done under local anesthetic. It hurts rather less than having a small cut stitched, and you can go straight home. The long-term result is a completely virile but infertile male. (Repeat, competent vasectomy carries absolutely no risk of physical interference with, erection, ejaculation, sexual feelings, or virility generally – under the name of 'Steinach's operation' it used to be done as a rejuvenation treatment and virility booster.) If you have all the children you-want (which, if you have a sense of responsibility, shouldn't in most cases be more than two) consider it seriously. Certainly consider it rather

than making your woman undergo the much bigger operation needed to sterilize her, or keeping her on the Pill if it doesn't suit her.

There are a few more factual points to consider.

1 Vasectomy doesn't make you sterile at once. Sperms can hang around for months, so you must stick to your previous birth control method until you know you are clear. After that you can both forget about birth control.

2 You can't change your mind. Vasectomy is sometimes reversible, but you mustn't count on that. It's a calculated risk that you might suddenly want to father children later, but not worth hanging back for if otherwise it looks right for you. No decision one takes is one hundred percent safe, but if you wanted more children there are unwanted babies wanting adoption, assuming you are fit people.

3 On the other hand, make sure you know your own feelings – which in any matter connected with sex and reproduction are never wholly reasonable. If the doctor refuses to do the operation 'off the shelf' without discussing your general self-picture of maleness, that only shows that he knows his job. If he refuses on principle or because he doesn't like your life style, consult another doctor.

If you are married, have had two wanted children or don't want children, and have any contraceptive problems, give vasectomy serious thought. If you're spread wider than that and have any sense of responsibility, you should be vasectomized. You can buy a 'vasectomy tie' or pin to advertise the fact. Wearing one when you haven't been operated is a cad's trick – far more so than wearing Guards or Ivy League colors you aren't entitled to. In case of argument, the girl can check the two little scars.

It may be possible eventually to store some of your sperm in the deep-freeze as an insurance, but you won't be able to do this now.

venereal diseases

These have been covertly fostered for several generations by straight Society as God's punishment for sin. On the other hand, they are a real hazard of having intercourse, or heavy petting, with people you don't know. There are two common ones. Syphilis is a killing disease – the first sign is a relatively painless sore where you have been infected (genitals, anus, mouth) followed some time later by a generalized rash, and years later by a great many unpleasant sequels. It can even be transmitted from mother to unborn baby. Gonorrhea ('clap') usually shows up in the male within a week as a painful discharge from the penis. In the woman it can cause discharge and swollen

glands, but may be symptomless and far more easily missed. Both are no trouble to treat if you go at once. *Don't* try to treat them yourselves with antibiotics and whatever the repercussions don't try to cover up, but warn anyone you may have infected. In fact, if it weren't for the aura of magic, either one would be a far preferable choice to having measles. There is another less common 'venereal' disease (lymphogranuloma inguinale), and you can catch crab lice from a dirty partner. People who sleep around, and some who don't, can catch and transmit trichomoniasis – don't assume infidelity if your partner gets this, but both of you, and any third parties, will need treatment to get rid of it.

If you must take risks, washing thoroughly with soap and passing water immediately after intercourse are a fair protection – so is wearing a condom, but remember that syphilis can be spread by kissing. Don't have intercourse with anyone who has a discharge or sores. But one mega-unit or oral penicillin taken within 1–2 hours of contact is practically 100 percent protection, even now, when some germs are relatively resistant. If you know you are taking risks you could take the dose beforehand ('St. Peter's Umbrella' – after the apostle who toiled all night and caught nothing). The moralists are quite right in saying that avoiding partners who are easy is the best prophylactic, but even that isn't 100 percent.

Venereal diseases could be stamped out altogether in our generation if people stopped treating them as a special case, and if nobody had a vested interest in them as a deterrent. Prostitutes aren't the chief source of infection – the big risks are careless and ignorant amateurs. Homosexuals can and do catch them as well as heterosexuals, in fact more frequently. Being on the Pill greatly increases the risk for a woman – not because it affects her morals, but because it knocks out a natural antiseptic mechanism.

Some of your best friends quite likely have V.D.

waterworks

Children are fascinated by watching one another urinate. So are some adults. There is no special reason to be ashamed of this; it's another childhood game, simply.

A few women are embarrassed that intense sex excitement makes them 'spend a penny' involuntarily. This occurs in animals too and can be avoided by emptying the bladder beforehand. Very violent sex for a very long time can bruise the female bladder and produce a good imitation of an attack of cystitis ('honeymoon bladder'). This soon clears with a few days' rest – avoid any positions which set it off. Women liable to repeated attacks of cystitis can sometimes avoid trouble by passing water immedi-

ately after intercourse.

Most males get a stronger erection, and feel more, on a full bladder, but may find some positions painful if it's very full. We never heard of a bladder being ruptured, but older men with prostate trouble might do well not to cultivate the technique. Normally, a male can't urinate with an erection: there is a two-way valve built into the system. In women the mouth of the urethra is nearly as sensitive as the clitoris, but it is a bad idea to put tapers or hairpins into it by way of masturbation – doctors often have to remove these from the bladder.

Index